People and Organisational Development
A New Agenda for Organisational Effectiveness

Helen Francis, Linda Holbeche and Martin Reddington

The Chartered Institute of Personnel and Development is the leading publisher of books and reports for personnel and training professionals, students, and all those concerned with the effective management and development of people at work. For details of all our titles, please contact
the publishing department:
tel: 020 8612 6204
e-mail: publish@cipd.co.uk
The catalogue of all CIPD titles can be viewed on the CIPD website:
www.cipd.co.uk/bookstore

People and Organisational Development

A New Agenda for Organisational Effectiveness

Helen Francis, Linda Holbeche and Martin Reddington

Chartered Institute of Personnel and Development

Published by the Chartered Institute of Personnel and Development,
151, The Broadway, London, SW19 1JQ

This edition first published 2012
© Chartered Institute of Personnel and Development, 2012

Typeset by Fakenham Prepress Solutions, Fakenham, Norfolk NR21 8NN

Printed in Great Britain by Charlesworth Press, Wakefield

British Library Cataloguing in Publication Data
A catalogue of this publication is available from the British Library

ISBN 978 1 84398 269 2

Chartered Institute of Personnel and Development, CIPD House,
151, The Broadway, London, SW19 1JQ

Tel: 020 8612 6200

E-mail: cipd@cipd.co.uk Website: www.cipd.co.uk

Incorporated by Royal Charter. Registered Charity No. 1079797

Contents

List of Figures and Tables

Acknowledgements

We the editors hope that this textbook will provide a timely overview of how Human Resource (HR) professionals can equip organisations to survive and thrive in today's challenging times. In so doing we have identified the need for more fluid disciplinary boundaries between Human Resource Management (HRM) and Organisation Development (OD), that encompass a more strategic and ethical approach to reconciling the inevitable tensions implicit in the employment relationship and HR's role.

We have many people to thank for their kind support.

First, we'd like to congratulate and thank all the chapter authors who have contributed their time, effort, ideas and wisdom to writing this book. They have collectively and flexibly helped shape new thinking about the ways in which HR can and does enable organisational effectiveness. They have truly demonstrated the value of 'changing mental models' (Pfeffer, 2005) by working across disciplinary boundaries to close the 'knowing-doing gap' identified by Pfeffer and Sutton (1999). As a result we believe that the book should aid better practice as much as contribute to theory development.

Then our thanks go to everyone who has generously provided the organisational case studies which appear throughout the book. We'd like to express our appreciation of their willingness to share their ideas and company practices. In particular we wish to thank Deutsche Bank, Essex County Council and Vertex for their comprehensive case studies which are available separately to accompany the book.

In our attempts to formulate a new way of conceiving of organisational effectiveness, we hope we have done justice to the strong foundations laid by others. We have been inspired by the work of many leading thinkers, researchers and practitioners in the fields of strategy, organisational development, organisation studies, HRM and critical HRM. To all of these, too many to mention, we express our gratitude.

We would also like to thank the editorial and production teams at the CIPD for their support, wise counsel and patience, in particular Kirsty Smy, Robert Jones, Heidi Partridge and Georgie Smith.

Above all we are infinitely grateful to our partners and families for their endless support and encouragement.

Pfeffer, J. (2005), 'Changing mental models, HR's most important task', *Human Resource Management,* Vol. 44, No. 2, Summer: 123–8.

Pfeffer, J. and Sutton, R. (1999), *The Knowing–Doing Gap: How smart companies turn knowledge into action,* Cambridge, MA: Harvard Business School Press.

Authors' biographies

Chiara Amati

Chiara Amati is a Chartered Occupational Psychologist who combines academic and practitioner perspectives in her interest in emotion at work. She has over 10 years' consultancy experience primarily in the area of psychological health and well-being at work, and is currently also working as a Lecturer in HRM for Edinburgh Napier Business School. Chiara is currently completing doctoral studies in the topic of emotion in managers and leaders.

Eddie Blass

Dr Eddie Blass is Director of Postgraduate Education in the Faculty of Business and Enterprise at Swinburne University, Melbourne, Australia. She has been researching talent management for a number of years and was the lead researcher at Ashridge for their talent management project with the Chartered Management Institute in 2007.

John Castledine

Dr John Castledine is Director of Learning Solutions at the Institute of Leadership and Management (ILM). ILM partners with over 2,000 approved training providers/employers to raise organisational performance through improved leadership and management. Previously, John was Learning and Organisational Development Director at Pfizer Global Research & Development, managing a team responsible for integrating business-process, personal-effectiveness and change-management training.

Roger Cooper

Roger Cooper is an independent consultant with extensive experience in large, complex projects involving significant organisational change or business transformation. He has undertaken assignments in a wide variety of business sectors and functions and his principal interests are in strategic workforce planning, human capital management, people metrics for business, performance management and the evaluation of learning. He is a Chartered Member of the CIPD and an associate with the Edinburgh Institute of Leadership and Management Practice and the Institute for Local Government Studies at Birmingham University.

Chris Donegan

Dr Chris Donegan has been working in the field of OD and change for the past 25 years. He is a graduate of the University of Edinburgh with a BSc and a PhD in Behavioural Psychology, and is a Chartered Fellow of the Chartered Institute of Personnel and Development (FCIPD). He is currently a consulting partner in The Change Navigators, who are a small team of specialist management consultants dedicated to facilitating culture change in organisations.

Helen Francis

Professor Helen Francis, PhD, is Professor of Business and People Management, and Director of the People Management and Organisational Development Division within the Edinburgh Institute, Edinburgh Napier University. Since her early practitioner experience in personnel management, she has developed a strong profile in the area of HR transformation, organisational change, learning and critical discourse analysis, and has published extensively in these areas. As a Chartered Fellow Member of the CIPD, Helen has developed strong links with the Institute and local business communities and spearheaded the recent creation of a Research Consultancy Framework at Edinburgh Napier.

Adrian Furnham

Professor Adrian Furnham is a Fellow of the British Psychological Society and is among the most productive psychologists in the world, having written over 750 scientific papers and 65 books. He is on the editorial board of a number of international journals and has been a consultant to over 20 major international companies, with particular interests in top team development, management change, performance management systems, psychometric testing and leadership derailment. He is also a newspaper columnist previously at the *Financial Times*, now at the *Sunday Times*. He writes regularly for the *Daily Telegraph* and is a regular contributor to national and international radio and television stations including the BBC, CNN and ITV.

Valerie Garrow

Dr Valerie Garrow is Principal Associate Fellow at the Institute for Employment Studies and an independent OD consultant. She has a degree in French studies, a Master's degree in Organisational Behaviour from Birkbeck College, and a PhD in Management from Kings College London. She has worked for over 16 years in the field of organisational development, specialising in post-merger integration, partnership and alliance working.

Linda Holbeche

Dr Linda Holbeche is co-Director of the Holbeche Partnership; Visiting Professor (HRM and OD) at Cass Business School; Visiting Professor (Leadership Innovation) at Bedfordshire University Business School; Adjunct Professor at Imperial College, London; Visiting Fellow at the UK Commission for Employment and Skills; and Visiting Fellow at the Roffey Park Institute. Her previous roles include Director of Research and Policy for the CIPD, Director of Leadership and Consultancy at the Work Foundation, and Director of Research and Strategy at Roffey Park.

Graeme Martin

Professor Graeme Martin, PhD, is based at the University of Glasgow Business School, where he teaches and researches in the areas of HRM and leadership. He also holds visiting appointments in a number of universities in the UK and overseas. Graeme has authored or edited six books, numerous book chapters and academic articles in the field, and works with a number of organisations in the UK and overseas on consulting projects.

Gillian Maxwell

Dr Gillian Maxwell is a Reader in HRM at in the Business School at Glasgow Caledonian University. She is the author of a number of articles and case studies on both talent management and diversity management.

Carole Parkes

Carole Parkes is Senior Lecturer and Co-Director Social Responsibility and Sustainability at Aston Business School, Birmingham. During 2009 and 2010 Carole took part in the Global Forums for PRME at the UN in New York, the UNPRME Climate Change Conference in Copenhagen, the 10th Anniversary Global Compact Business Leaders Summit and addressed the 2010 Sustainability Conference in the USA. She has also hosted UK universities events at Aston for the UNPRME supported by BAM, ABS and AMBA. Locally, Carole works with a range of community groups. Research interests include CSR, ethics and the role of HRM. Other CIPD publications include: *Strategic HRM: Building research-based practice* (2008).

John Purcell

Professor John Purcell is a Deputy Chairman of the Central Arbitration Committee and an ACAS arbitrator. Between 1995 and 2007 he was Professor of Human Resource Management at the University of Bath and subsequently a research professor at the Industrial Relations Research Unit at Warwick Business, where he is now an Associate Fellow, following retirement.

Allan Ramdhony

Dr Allan Ramdhony is a lecturer in HRM at Edinburgh Napier University. His research interests include critical theory in the tradition of the Frankfurt School, critical HRD, change management and the role of metaphors in organisational analysis. He is currently engaged in writing a set of papers on both the theory and practice of Critical HRD.

Martin Reddington

Dr Martin Reddington blends academic research with consultancy. Formerly Global Programme Director, HR Transformation, at Cable & Wireless, he is a member of the CIPD's national advisory group on technology and HR, and an expert adviser on HR transformation to the Public Sector People Managers' Association (PPMA). He is currently working with a range of public and private organisations on the evaluation and re-architecting of the employment value proposition, using a new and compelling approach developed with **Dr Helen Francis.**

Peter Reilly

Peter Reilly joined the Institute for Employment Studies in 1995 after a 16-year career with Shell where he held a number of HR posts in the UK and abroad. At the Institute he is Director of HR Research and Consultancy. He leads the both consultancy and research work on the HR function. Clients come from all sectors and his involvement ranges from facilitation through expert advice to design and evaluation. He has written various articles and books on the HR function, some of which are listed in the references of Chapter 7.

Douglas Renwick

Dr Douglas Renwick is Lecturer (Assistant Professor) in Human Resource Management at the Management School, University of Sheffield, where he teaches at both undergraduate and postgraduate level. His research interests include involving line managers in HRM, green (environmental) HRM, employee well-being, and HRM in Brazil.

Naomi Stanford

Naomi Stanford is a practising OD consultant and the author of *Organization Design: The collaborative approach* (2004), *Organisation Design: Building adaptable enterprises* (2008) and *Organisation Culture: Getting it right* (2010).

Mark Withers

Mark Withers is a strategic HR and OD consultant and Managing Director of Mightywaters Consulting Limited. He works with a wide range of private and public sector organisations to improve organisational effectiveness through people. He is co-author of *Transforming HR: Delivering value through people* (2005, 2010).

Melanie Wood

Melanie started her career as a graduate trainee for Royal Mail where she led employee relations and performance management for the Midlands. In 2005 Melanie moved to Birmingham City Council where she leads the award winning Workforce Intelligence and Planning team (PPMA and CMI awards in 2010). As a Chartered Fellow of the CIPD, her key achievements to date have been to successfully lead the Excellence in People Management programme, a major transformational programme within Birmingham City Council. She is responsible for setting the strategic direction of workforce planning, people management intelligence and talent development.

Foreword

As employers continue to grapple with the continuing effects of the global financial crisis, there is an urgent need to venture beyond short-term and primarily top-down management initiatives and find more effective and sustainable ways in which to re-build organisations and societies. Unfortunately, in the light of pressing demands to derive greater levels of shareholder value, too many organisations choose the slash-and-burn route to change and in so doing store up greater problems for the future. Far too often these change programmes are driven by a few senior managers who focus on the talented few rather than engaging properly with front-line staff that are essential for the production of high-quality products and/or high levels of customer service.

This book, edited by Helen Francis, Linda Holbeche and Martin Reddington, offers a welcome alternative to this agenda. It looks behind the issues, aims to stretch current thinking, and presents a 'new organisational effectiveness' concept and mindset. This is based around four themes: language and action; paradox and ambiguity; authenticity and mutuality; and leadership and management. I was particularly taken with the focus on mutuality and the search for cultures of engagement and emotion which led us away from simplistic notions of managerial prerogative and omnipotence towards a pluralist and critical realist perspective. This is an underlying message in the book, as is the idea that HR, in its desire to become a business partner, has lost sight of its commitment to other stakeholders.

People and Organisational Development covers a wide range of topics, some of which are found in other publications on HRM – such as voice and engagement, workforce planning, learning and development, and performance management – while others come from different traditions: for example, culture, organisation development, corporate social responsibility, emotion management. The contributors come from diverse backgrounds and approaches, with some predominantly in the academic tradition whereas others are practitioners and consultants. As expected from a book based around pluralist principles, these contributions do not always sit easily with one another, and it is possible to see tensions between the search for underlying meaning on the one hand and prescription and practice on the other. Rather than being a negative, however, this adds to the value of the book.

The pedagogic style of the book follows the broad approach used in my own CIPD book, *Human Resource Management at Work*, now into its fifth edition. This makes it easy to navigate within each chapter given the list of learning outcomes, mini-cases, reflective questions, further reading and extensive follow-up bibliographies. The fact that it challenges current thinking from an evidence-based perspective rather than merely reproducing checklists is welcome. HR and OD students, practitioners and academics who are genuinely interested in sustainable approaches will gain much from reading this book.

Mick Marchington
Emeritus Professor of Human Resource Management, Manchester Business School and Companion of the CIPD
August 2011

Walkthrough of textbook features and online resources

CHAPTER OVERVIEW

This second introductory chapter outlines some of the key context factors which support the argument for a new form of organisational effectiveness, as outlined in the previous chapter. In particular the author highlights how the pursuit of flexibility and cost-effectiveness is driving the installation of new organisational forms, the flexibilisation of labour and changing the nature of the employment relationship for white-collar workers. What this means in terms of HR's strategic contribution and why this requires an OD mindset or 'frame' are considered. The chapter draws on the author's research into the changing nature of workplace relations and her consultancy practice in the development of HR and OD professionals.

CHAPTER OVERVIEW

A brief outline of what is to be covered in the chapter.

LEARNING OBJECTIVES

By the end of this chapter the reader should be able to:

- understand how changes in the business context are shaping the transformation of the HR function – in particular, the need for HR to adopt more proactive change agent roles
- understand key elements of the debate about HRM from 'mainstream' and 'critical' perspectives
- consider some of the complexities of change management, including the HR function's own transformation journey
- explain why HR should embrace an OD perspective and values, and how HR and OD practitioners can work together to produce sustainable change outcomes.

LEARNING OBJECTIVES

At the beginning of each chapter a bulleted set of learning outcomes summarises what you can expect to learn from the chapter, helping you to track your progress.

REFLECTIVE ACTIVITIES

As you read the definitions listed above and the commentary in Table 3.1, consider the following two questions:

- Why are there so many definitions – and what might be inferred from that?
- What do the definitions imply about the relationship between the organisation development practitioner (sometimes called the 'change agent') and the organisational members with whom the practitioner is interacting?

REFLECTIVE ACTIVITIES

These boxes contain interesting questions and activities designed to get you reflecting on what you have just read and to test your understanding of important concepts and issues.

CRESCOM

CRESCOM is an 80-year-old corporate real estate solutions company operating throughout the European Union with headquarters in Nottingham. The company offers clients products and services designed to help them maximise their investments in corporate real estate. It employs 500 staff in the Nottingham office, and across the rest of Europe there are an additional 2,000. It has three major service areas: portfolio management, workplace management, and strategic facility

corporate real estate, evolving working patterns, and competitive pressures converge in a way that continue to make CRESCOM's client organisations look to their real estate to deliver savings, which they tend to resist due to capacity and productivity concerns.

To solve this, CRESCOM must show its clients that it is not just working on space-based savings initiatives. It must demonstrate that new perspectives on corporate real estate can help the

CASE STUDY

CASE STUDIES

A range of case studies illustrate how key ideas and theories are operating in practice, with accompanying questions or activities.

Think about how you, as a 'tiger team' member, would start to tackle this issue. From the start it requires you to have a perspective on the following:

- What you think organisation development is, and how it relates to organisation design and HR. In this instance you are likely to be redesigning the support functions as an organisation design effort and simultaneously developing people's capabilities (and comfort levels) in dealing with this planned radical change. (Look back at the matrix in Table 3.4 and you will see that this is the area of change that people have the most difficulty with.)

- You would then have to make some decisions about whether to tackle the project from a problem-solving perspective or an appreciative inquiry one. With the amount of information you have to hand you would have to do some assessment before you made the choice on this. It seems likely that an appreciative inquiry may be ideal, but you have been given a very short time-scale and typically appreciative inquiry takes time – but again, you'd have to work out the trade-offs, bearing in mind factors such as:

  - cost: Ask yourself how much it will cost to deliver the solution, relative to the cost of your best alternative. Cost estimation may entail both the short term

CASE STUDY COMMENTARY

CASE STUDY COMMENTARY

These boxes draw key thinking points out of the case study and offer critical commentary.

Boonstra, J. (ed.) (2004) *Dynamics of Organizational Change and Learning*. Chichester: John Wiley & Sons. A collection of articles in four parts, the first giving a rounded view of the development of OD, and others discussing change processes, OD in ambiguous contexts, power dynamics, and sustainable change.

Cannon, J. and McGee, R. (2008) *Organisational Development and Change*. London: Chartered Institute of Training and Development. This is a basic, practical toolkit on OD and change. It is useful for HR and OD practitioners looking for inventories, exercises, models and checklists.

Cooperrider, D. L., Whitney, D., Stavros, J. M. and Fry, R. (2008) *Appreciative Inquiry Handbook: For leaders of change*, 2nd edition. Brunswick, OH: Crown Custom Publishing. This is a practical book about AI. There are sections on the background to AI, a detailed explanation of the 4-D cycle, and learning applications with

EXPLORE FURTHER

EXPLORE FURTHER

Explore further boxes contain suggestions for further reading and useful websites, encouraging you to delve further into areas of particular interest.

ONLINE RESOURCES

- Practical tools from CIPD OD toolkits – provides practical guidance on applying the emergent theories of OD and HRM.
- Additional Case Studies – extended case studies applying theory from the textbook to the real world.

For Online resources, please visit **www.cipd.co.uk/orl**

Organisational Effectiveness: A New Agenda for Organisational Development and Human Resource Management

Helen Francis, Linda Holbeche and Martin Reddington

THE PURPOSE OF THIS BOOK

Welcome to *People and Organisational Development: A new agenda for organisational effectiveness*. In this chapter we set the scene for this book, provide a conceptual framework for a new form of organisational effectiveness, and present an overview of the chapters. We illustrate our themes with a couple of short case studies drawn from our consultancy practice.

Our account of this new approach is not just theoretically and methodologically grounded. It is also historically grounded, showing how the original emergence of human resource management (HRM) and organisation development (OD)[1] have been inextricably linked to the changing social and industrialising world of which they are a part.

As HR functions undergo major reorganisations, more focus is being placed on their roles as change agents and business partners within the broader OD agenda. This is creating uneasy alliances between disciplines that have developed separately from each other and are shaped by competing philosophies about whose interests they serve: those of the organisation, of its employees – or perhaps of both.

New and flourishing debates are opening up as practitioners and academics make a more concerted effort to work together in ways that enhance policy and practice development in the field. There remain deep divisions, however, in professional orientations between academics and practitioners about areas of research interest and the ability of academic research to make a positive difference to organisational life. The contribution of this textbook is to provide illustrative examples of emergent theories in HRM and OD and the practicalities associated with their application at different levels of analysis (the individual, team and organisation).

---

[1] Organisation Development (OD) is both the field of applied behavioural science focused on understanding and managing organisational change to increase an organisation's effectiveness and viability, and a field of scientific study and enquiry. US texts refer to this field as 'organization development'. In this textbook we have used the anglicised term 'organisation development'. We have also used the term 'organisational development' relatively interchangeably with 'organisation development' to describe both the field (of practice, and enquiry), and also specific forms of OD intervention.

Our focus is consistent with widespread debate about the need to address the increasing distance of research from its user base and the need for HR practitioners to develop their abilities as 'thinking performers' – a term launched by the Chartered Institute of Personnel and Development (CIPD) in 2002. This book builds on this concept, and the more recent notion of 'insight-driven HR' published in the CIPD's *Next Generation HR* Report (CIPD Report 2011a), encouraging students and practitioners to consider context-sensitive and evidence-based arguments to enhance their own HR practice and develop a better understanding of the relevance and usefulness of research to practitioners. In doing so, it aims at stretching current thinking and practice about the notions of organisational effectiveness and 'added value' typically framing prescriptions about how HR functions might contribute to organisational performance.

The concept of organisational effectiveness is difficult to pin down, not least because there are multiple opposing dimensions underlying thinking about effectiveness, suggested by various studies in the field such as those depicted by Quinn and Rohrbaugh's 'competing values framework', and Evans and colleagues' notion of 'duality-based management' (Quinn and Rohrbaugh, 1983, cited by Ehnert, 2008: 140; Evans *et al*, 2002: 79; see also Chapter 14). Moreover, we argue that these largely derive from unitarist thinking which assumes that what is good for the organisation is good for employees, and vice versa.

While attracted to these various definitions, we believe that today's turbulent social, economic and political context calls for more pluralist definitions of organisational effectiveness. For instance Richard *et al* (2009) define 'organisational effectiveness' as capturing organisational performance that includes usual external business indicators (whether by shareholders, managers or customers), broadening this to a corporate social responsibility. In addition they pay attention to internal performance outcomes normally associated with more efficient or effective operations. We go further, arguing that if these various good outcomes are to be achieved, there must be genuine common cause, benefit and risk shared between organisations and their employees. What we propose is a 'New organisational effectiveness' (New OE) concept and mindset. New OE takes as its desired *end* point sustainable, self-renewing outcomes. This, we argue, requires a *shift in mindset and practice* with respect to organisational change, towards one based on what we describe as *authentic mutuality*, noted in Table 1.4.

We recognise that what we propose challenges established ways of viewing power, status, leadership and management, the nature of employee relations and accountability, as well as the role of HR. We therefore draw on the familiar simile of a 'journey' to describe the movement for change that we hope this book will engender. We recognise that many organisations will be at the first stage of the journey, while others may be much further down the track. Our chapters therefore range in tone from the critical and theoretical to the more practice-based and prescriptive, which sits well with a critical realist lens. In all of them, we have included points of reflection to enable the reader to make sense of the content and to stimulate consideration of the insights contained within the book and the potential application to their own practice.

Evans and colleagues, writing from an international HRM perspective, use the metaphor of 'navigator' to describe an HR specialist able to steer through the tensions created by the paradoxical nature of organisational effectiveness, described in terms of dualities (see Table 1.1). Reflective activities provided throughout the textbook invite the reader to think about these kinds of contradictions and tensions arising within small to medium enterprises in addition to larger multinational enterprises.

We see very little discussion within the practitioner literature of these kinds of contradictory poles or forces which underlie our thinking about effectiveness, and much of the debate is located within scholarly articles cloaked in a jargon that practitioners find hard to relate to. A key aim of this textbook is to enable better problem diagnoses and interventions through the provision of a new lens that supports pragmatic but well-informed strategies for enhancing organisational effectiveness, recognising that

Table 1.1 The paradoxical nature of organisational effectiveness

Short-term	–	Long-term
Competition	–	Collaboration
Decentralisation	–	Centralisation
Entrepreneurship	–	Control/Accountablity
Taking risks	–	Avoiding failures
Flexibility	–	Efficiency
Task orientation	–	People orientation
Planned	–	Opportunist

Source: adapted from Evans, Pucik and Barsoux (2002)

paradoxical tensions are an inevitable and defining feature of organisations (Ehnert, 2008).

Paradoxes are statements which appear incongruous or even unreasonable and include two or more dualities operating simultaneously. Our intention is to help demystify some of the emergent strands of thinking and practice which we believe will be key to sustainable effectiveness over the medium term, and to equip readers with a holistic lens through which to view, and potentially reconcile, seeming paradoxes. We aim to avoid being overly prescriptive and have therefore set out to provide a range of perspectives on some of the key aspects of organisational effectiveness, ranging from the critical realist to the practice-friendly. By interweaving academic with highly practical chapters we believe we have provided genuinely interesting, different ideas and perspectives, put together in an original way.

REFLECTIVE ACTIVITIES

- How do you define 'organisational effectiveness'?
- How would you measure it?

We noted earlier that New OE challenges orthodox views and analytical frameworks about what makes for 'effectiveness' in work and employment practice. In doing so, it combines technologically enhanced methodologies with more standard HR/OD 'tools' and theories. The means and ends with which these are applied are framed by a shift in mindset that consciously seeks to enhance the level of employee involvement, 'agency' and community spirit within the organisation.

Features of this mindset are outlined in the section below entitled *New OE mindset* and summarised in Figure 1.1. We consider the issue of employee agency to be something of a test-bed of our conceptualisation of mutuality of interest between employer/organisation/owner and employee. This argument draws attention to the significance of language, power and politics in strategic decision-making, which tends to be poorly treated in mainstream modelling of HR. It also paints a very different picture of 'leadership' that builds on a more systemic perspective than traditional models, whereby leadership responsibility is dissociated from formal organisational roles, and the action and influence of people *at all levels* is recognised as integral to the overall direction and functioning of the organisation. From this perspective, the key leadership task of executives and senior managers becomes the creation of communities united by a common purpose, a task for which, it might be argued, conventional development approaches do not equip managers well.

Alongside debates about the trajectory of HRM (see Chapter 2), there has been much debate about the future of OD, whether or not the more traditional humanist values are still relevant in the wake of more pragmatic business considerations, and whether it has become overly reliant on tools and techniques, lacking in theoretical rigour. Based on the human relations perspective which stresses collaborative management, conventional OD focuses on values and attitudes as key targets of change in the enhancement of organisational effectiveness and employee well-being (see Chapter 3). Questions have been raised about the legitimacy of trying to alter something as personal as values and beliefs, and the assumption that there is one best way to manage change. A mutation of organisational change management emerged as a subfield of OD and the need for a contingency perspective to change was emphasised by writers such as Dunphy and Stace (1993) who argued that revolutionary change was best managed by top-down coercive strategies for change. These became attractive at a time when the environment facing organisations was becoming increasingly turbulent and culture change programmes were seen to be too time-consuming and costly to implement (Huczynski and Buchanan, 2007; Linstead, Fulop and Lilley, 2009: 644).

Since the 1990s the focus has therefore shifted away from altering employee values to a focus on *outputs and behaviours*, described as 'results-driven' change programmes. These are based on the view that organisations can achieve fundamental change in employee behaviours in the short term through 'hard' structural change strategies that are more 'task-driven'. They are based on the assumption that behaviour change will in the longer term become rooted in social norms and shared values as the changes that 'work' are institutionalised, and links between the new approaches to work organisation and improved performance become clearer (Burnes, 2009; McHugh *et al*, 1999).

This approach sees senior managers acting primarily as facilitators of change, with emphasis placed on a fundamental shift away from central to local control, allowing for the emergence of 'bottom-up' change that is more participative and collaborative. Longer-term sustainability, the editors argue, will require new ways of thinking about leadership and management, and a focus on involving employees in a new form of employment relationship.

Prescriptions for change, however, assume that reaching consensus among different stakeholders regarding the prioritising and nature of quick wins is relatively unproblematic, and there has been considerable debate about the dehumanising effects of what has been described as a ruthless pursuit of efficiency in the form of business reengineering in the 1980s, rationalisation in the 1990s, and aggressive outsourcing in the 2000s (Burnes, 2009). Analysts have called for a 'new narrative' and organising frameworks that combat modern day worker alienation and raised questions about 'sustainable' performance improvements based on meeting individual *and* organisational requirements (Keegan and Francis, 2010).

Within this context, Garrow's (2009) review of OD points to the revival of interest in the UK of social science techniques, framed by concerns about employee engagement, organisational effectiveness and more radical survival techniques – stemming from the combined impact of changes in technology, globalisation, competitive pressures, unpredictable, socio-political and economic factors. As OD evolves and the range of consultancy practices and techniques have flourished, the strong ties between scholarship and practice have considerably loosened, which in part may explain the lack of new technology that has been available for some time being applied within the field (Burke, 2004) – a key theme underpinning Chapters 8 and 17. The 'new' ensemble of OD practices that have emerged since the 1980s are increasingly being placed under the spotlight as organisations seek to gain radical efficiencies, improve performance and engage employees in this endeavour (MacLeod and Clarke, 2009).

NEW MINDSETS AND METAPHORS

Marshak and Grant (2008a, 2008b) argue that 'new' OD practices are based on philosophical assumptions fundamentally different from classical OD (depicted in Table 1.2) but which have been lost in much of the discussion about traditional versus pragmatic views. Examples such as appreciative inquiry (AI) and large group interventions (LGI) continue to be underpinned by humanist and democratic values but challenge many of the key assumptions underpinning 'classical OD' that are firmly rooted in a positivist experimental tradition (see Chapter 3).

Table 1.2 OD in transition

Classical OD	New OD
Based in classical science and modern thought and philosophy	Influenced by new sciences and postmodern thought and philosophy
Truth is transcendent and discoverable; there is a single, objective reality	Truth is immanent and emerges from the situation; there are multiple social constructed realities
Reality can be discovered using rational and analytical processes	Reality is socially negotiated and may involve power and political processes
Collecting and applying valid data using objective problem-solving methods leads to change	Creating new mindsets or social agreements, sometimes through explicit or implicit negotiations, leads to change
Change is episodic and can be created, planned and managed	Change is continuous and can be self-organising
Emphasis on changing behaviour and what one does.	Emphasis on changing mindsets and how one thinks.

THE TREATMENT OF LANGUAGE

Key points of departure between the 'old' and 'new' OD are around the treatment of language and differences in how actors view people and events (see Chapters 5 and 14). OD techniques now typically draw upon constructionist assumptions and methodologies that are better designed to give voice to a greater number of stakeholders, and in doing so acknowledge the central role of language in shaping organisational realities (Marshak and Grant, 2008a, 2008b).

This view challenges conventional wisdom that language simply represents what is going on in organisational life, somehow separate from action and reality (Francis, 2007). Organisational talk is recognised as being far from purely instrumental and value-free, and plays a key role in promoting new meanings and mindsets within the organisation (Mumby, 2004; Butcher and Atkinson, 2001). From this position, a raft of new tools and techniques has emerged, including the application of metaphors as a framework for analysis and a generative tool for creative thinking, and large-group interventions used to surface taken-for-granted values and assumptions, and assess different options and possibilities about work and organisation (Inns, 2009). Here, attention has been placed on shifting mindsets through 'emotionally and contextually driven conversations' (Kakabadse and Kakabadse, 2010; see also Chapter 16) or 'conversations for change' (Ford and Ford, 1995; Francis and Sinclair, 2003).

Organisational change is largely seen as socially constructed and understood in terms of discourse and dialogue, characterised in terms of 'bottom-up' approaches to change, which evoke new sets of metaphors, and that saw increasing use in the 1980s. These treat organisations as living systems, in which managers are like gardeners, seeking to 'nurture' people (Seele, 2003), consistent with models of leadership that emphasise strategic visions and have emotional appeal, rather than operation management and control (Kotter, 1996). OD practices which adopt a discursive or conversational approach place particular emphasis on the treatment of organisations as dialogic or meaning-making systems, thereby focusing on changing frameworks that guide what people say and think, rather than seeking to change behaviour directly (Busche and Marshak, 2011: 355).

Notwithstanding these developments, and the fact that that a large proportion of management time is spent engaged in conversations with various stakeholders in order to get things done, the issue of language is often overlooked by managers in planning for and implementing change. One explanation for this is the presence of ingrained metaphors framing management behaviours, resting on notions of management as 'control' which resist expressions about management as 'shaping' (eg through coaching, interpreting and nurturing).

Discourse theory sheds some light on this process. For example Keegan and Francis' recent discourse analysis of HR work draws attention to the dominant business framing of practitioner talk, leading to an emerging imbalance between people-oriented and business-oriented HR roles. They conclude that any re-ordering of HR discourses will require a significant shift in language use about the championing of employee interests at the workplace (Keegan and Francis, 2010). Their work draws attention to the political relations inherent in language use which is downplayed or ignored in conventional and more contemporary approaches to OD and HRM.

POWER AND POLITICAL STRUCTURES

While contemporary OD techniques have significant potential for generating new possibilities and innovations, they have been criticised by some as naive, failing to take sufficient account of the constraining effects of power and political structures. For instance, Jabri *et al* (2008) explain that even when diverse points of view can be voiced through these 'new OD' interventions, contentious viewpoints are typically 'kept on the margin' because the working models of change upon which they are based tend to remain quite 'monologic' (of a single logic). Change leaders can be so focused on arriving at a consensus that genuine opportunities for surfacing multiple perspectives may be limited, or the opportunities for them to translate new ideas into practice are heavily circumscribed by deeper political and discursive structures, such as those described in Ramdhony's account of action learning sets within a public sector organisation (Chapter 9). Consequently, the potential for real employee agency is reduced.

Critical scholars point to the need for more critical debate about the interdependency between organisational structures and agency and the need for the creation of new structures and systems that support both the emancipatory intent underpinning these OD practices *and* strategic concerns for improved organisational effectiveness and performance (Fleetwood and Hesketh, 2010; see also Chapters 2, 3, 4, 5, 12 and 14).

As editors we share an emancipatory interest as described by Habermas (1986). This is a calling into question, and a deep-seated desire to throw off, relations which repress people without necessity and yet have come to be taken for granted. So, for example, contemporary attempts to understand the nature of employee engagement are unlikely to lead to increased engagement unless they take into account how employee 'disengagement' may be symptomatic of imbalanced power relations, as reflected in top-down instrumental approaches to job design, and so on, which produce a lack of autonomy. As critical analysts we consider the more enlightened way forward is to promote a wider diffusion of power and responsibility within organisations through the democratisation of institutions and practices.

Following this line of argument, we emphasise the potential of technology to create new opportunities for extending the depth and reach of employee involvement and participation, notably through the use of social media technologies such as 'Web 2.0', which have significant potential to change the way people collaborate, work and give voice to their opinions (Martin, Reddington and Kneafsey, 2009).

Our view is that these new social media technologies should be used in the design and implementation of change initiatives, as an accelerant in shaping the language-practice dynamic, a point that is developed further in Chapters 8 and 14. This is an important feature in a dynamically changing context where the senior team is often impatient to achieve some kind of culture change and organisations increasingly expect to see rapid results and returns on their investments in their change initiatives (see also Chapter 5). This dash for results and hard outcomes tends to minimise the importance of the softer side of change management, and HR plays a vital role in intervening to shift such mindsets at senior level about the language of change (see Marshak, 2002) in order to build a high-performing culture informed by humanist and democratic principles. We are mindful of the arguments presented by critical scholars on what has been described as the ethics and practicalities of 'culture control', and this theme is addressed in a number of ways throughout the textbook – see for example Chapters 4, 14, 15 and 16.

This combination of a constructionist outlook and realisation of the more concrete and constraining aspects of organisational life resonates with the 'critical realist' perspective which lies at the heart of New OE (see Chapters 2, 9 and 14). It is based on a social ontology, taken from Fleetwood and Hesketh's 'meta-theoretical toolkit' offered by critical realism (Fleetwood and Hesketh, 2010: 206):

> A social ontology wherein the world is taken to be open, layered, transformational, and consisting not only of human agents but also structures, institutions, mechanisms, resources, rules, conventions, (non-human) powers, as opposed to a 'flat' ontology of events and experiences.

Planned and continuous change models are underpinned by very different images of the organisation and notions of 'managing' (Butcher and Atkinson, 2001). Common themes underpinning a continuous change model centre on the people-focused and relational aspects of leadership that encourage and model a collaborative approach, with different people taking the lead depending upon organisational circumstances (Birkinshaw, 2010).

RECONSIDERING THE LANGUAGE OF CHANGE

A significant paradox is emerging here. While there is a growing body of literature about 'bottom-up' or 'eruptive' models of organisation and change, these models will struggle to take hold in practice because they continue to rely on a vocabulary of change framed by conventional mindsets and approaches (Butcher and Atkinson, 2001; Marshak and Grant, 2008a, 2008b). These portray organisational change and communications in very instrumental terms. The change process is treated as being more or less neat and tidy and the complexities of organisational politics and culture are downplayed or ignored, including the emergent unintended dimensions of change (Burnes, 2009; Francis, 2007).

From this instrumental perspective, changes are seen to result from decisions and directions from senior managers. The language of change is typically framed by 'mechanical' metaphors (Morgan, 1997) as managers are urged to find 'levers' for change, and 'drive' communications to effect change. Consultants have a 'toolkit' used to implement new ways of working (Seele, 2003) or seek to 'build' new 'architectures' for systems change (Watson, 2002) – terms which remain commonplace in everyday talk about organisational change.

Fleetwood and Hesketh (2010) proceed to drop the 'toolkit' analogy, to avoid giving the impression that 'they advocate the mechanistic application of a set of procedures' (p.206). However we have chosen to stick with the analogy of toolkits, recognising the importance of providing practical tools of action for our readership, while remaining faithful to the richness and complexity of New OE (see, for instance, Chapter 14).

These mechanical metaphors emphasise a mode of organising consistent with top-down models of change, and Taylorist control over the efficiency of labour exemplified in the McDonalds case (Morgan, 1997: 24). They draw our attention to the rationale and practicalities associated with planning, organising, prioritising, controlling budgets and work schedules. The content of the language used here is in stark contrast to new mindsets around organisational development and leadership noted earlier. However, the language of top-down models persists, and as a result much of our existing language of change is encumbered with concepts developed in more stable environments, therefore acting to preserve the status quo (Butcher and Atkinson, 2001).

MORPHING MINDSETS

Marshak (2002) talks of the need to create new words that better express continuous whole-system change, described in terms of a *morphing mindset* that could be used as a generative metaphor or analogy to advance our thinking about 'managing change'. The key principles of 'morphing' are outlined below (Marshak, 2002: 283):

- creating limited organisational structures and principles such that there is both enough form and fluidity for rapid, organised action
- creating resource flexibility in terms of both availability and application
- ensuring organisational learning to quickly develop and deploy new competencies
- bridging from the present to the future with clear transition processes while avoiding focusing on the future to the detriment of the present
- having top management mindsets that fully embrace the concepts of continuous change and flexible organisational forms, ie managers with 'morphing mindsets'.

The use of metaphors as a means of giving form and meaning to organisational change has been well documented within the academic literature and popularised by Morgan's seminal work (1997). He explains how everyday conversations are characterised by (mostly unconscious) metaphors, described in terms of embedded metaphors. Analysis of metaphors-in-use is therefore key to the design and implementation of organisational change, especially important in a transformational change programme.

However, there is a dearth of practical guidance for managers seeking to consciously and actively introduce new change metaphors within the organisation, hampered because of the conventional treatment of language within mainstream HRM and OD textbooks and management education. Here, inadequate attention is paid to the creative role (and power effects) of language use and the pivotal role of leaders in this regard, hampered by the dichotomous views of OD and HR (Francis and Reddington, 2010). This is illustrated by images of leadership and management processes outlined in Table 1.3. Our modelling of New OE seeks to avoid such either/or thinking, and in doing so, embraces competing perspectives and metaphors. Although we agree with the need for a new vocabulary for change that promotes employee involvement and continuous open-ended change, we are not advocating wholesale displacement of traditional discourses of change. Rather, we propose the transformation of these in ways which allow for development of practical discourses for managers, enabling them to embrace a 'New OE mindset' and develop sustainable employment relationships.

For instance, in Chapter 14, Francis and Reddington call for a new lexicon of employer branding that allows for a more holistic and discourse-sensitive understanding of the employment deal or employment value proposition (EVP), and the practical implications for doing so. Underlying their approach is the view that discourses are always connected to other discourses produced earlier and in real time, and for new concepts and ideas to 'take' among management practitioners, these must be perceived to be of value in terms of what 'works' within the context in which it is being introduced. For instance, the academic vocabulary around the psychological contract failed to gain much traction within practitioner communities, and has been 're-contextualised' by consultants in the form of an employer branding discourse that allows employers to articulate the employment deal in more actionable terms. However, the language of employer branding relies heavily and, in Francis and Reddington's view, unrealistically upon a unitarist philosophy, and practitioners are encouraged to rethink and refocus EVP on more pluralist grounds consistent with New OE.

The short case study below, based on an interview with a senior manager from the HR function of a global bank, asks the reader to reflect upon how actively connecting a firm's identity with behaviours can facilitate consistent delivery of the firm to all stakeholders.

DEUTSCHE BANK

CASE STUDY

'Deliver Deutsche' is a programme that is part of a larger global cultural transformation at Deutsche Bank, one of the world's largest banks employing in excess of 100,000 people. The main driver behind this programme was recognition of an opportunity to build stronger connections between Deutsche Bank's external brand, its employer brand, and the expected behaviours of employees that link the two. Key outcomes of this programme are to articulate to staff what it takes to deliver on its claim 'passion to perform', and to ensure that the organisational mechanisms are in place to positively reinforce behaviour aligned to the brand identity. This prompted the design of a bank-wide programme by which brand-inspired behaviour becomes part of its DNA, integrated into culture and processes. In this model, the DNA of the external brand (expressed as personality attributes) and the employer brand (expressed as an employment value proposition) are connected together through a Leadership Behaviour Framework.

The programme is introduced via a campaign called The Deutsche Deal and is planned to be embedded globally (called 'hard-wiring') over a two-year period. It presents a range of challenges as it seeks to build on the firm's distinct characteristics across its workforce – qualities to differentiate the bank and produce a responsible high-performance culture.

Questions

How do the terms 'campaign', 'embedding' and 'hard-wiring' reflect the tone and nature of 'Deliver Deutsche'?

1 How might you alter the terms used here, in order to facilitate a more context-sensitive approach to culture change? (See Chapter 5.)

2 If you were going to describe the DNA of your organisation, how would you do it?

3 How would you seek to connect the corporate brand and employer brand of your organisation?

IMAGES OF LEADERSHIP AND MANAGEMENT

We have observed that planned and continuous change models are underpinned by very different images of the organisation and notions of 'managing'. These have led to popular distinctions being made between leadership and management depicted in Figure 1.1 which draws upon Kotter's influential work and recent debate about the complexity of management. Kotter argues that 'successful transformation is 70 to 90 percent leadership and only 10 to 30 percent management'. Management processes are typified as planning, budgeting, organising, and controlling, and distinguished from leadership, associated with setting future direction and vision for change, aligning people with that vision,

Figure 1.1 Leadership and Management

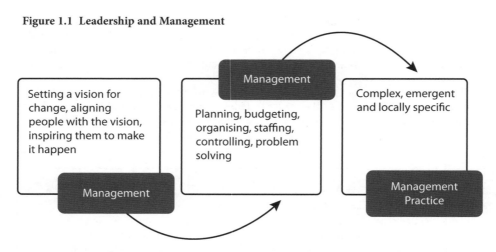

and inspiring them to make it happen (Kotter 1996: 25–26). Bolden (2004) observes the considerable confusion that arises from treating management and leadership as separate processes – particularly the manner in which they are often mapped to different individuals. He notes growing resistance amongst analysts to this popular appeal of leadership at the expense of management, highlighting the importance of good management in maintaining levels of motivation, commitment, trust and psychological well-being, and the need for 'leader-managers', capable of adopting the role in its most holistic form (Bolden, 2004: 7–8; see also Birkinshaw, 2010). Linked with this, we take the view that management practices cannot be easily codified into well-defined 'leadership', or 'management' entities, but are 'inherently complex, emergent and locally specific in impact' (AIM Report, 2004).

Adopting a more holistic view of organisation and moving away from such either/ or thinking about leadership and management is difficult, however, because of the conventional treatment of language and communications within much of the literature about organisational change noted earlier. How managers make sense of these competing logics is recognised as an increasingly important area of study as the gaps between formal HR policy and actual practices are often attributed to limitations of line managers' attitudes and leadership practice (Wong *et al*, 2009). Related to this is the whole question of devolving HR to line managers (see Chapter 10).

Similarly, a fundamental issue for line managers is searching for a balance in the 'What is in it for me?' question by employees and the 'What is in it for the organisation?' question by the employers. Most of the time this is not clearly articulated, and if managers are to become proactive agents in shaping better-balanced HR agendas at the workplace, they will need to understand the diversity of competing perspectives that comprise the field of organisational change and develop new mindsets tuned to embracing paradox and ambiguity (see Chapter 14 for a fuller discussion).

THE SHIFT IN FOCUS FOR HR

We follow Pfeffer's argument that the ability to identify and help others discover their mindsets and mental models, and the capability to change these when necessary, are 'probably among the most critical capabilities an HR professional can have or acquire' (Pfeffer, 2005: 125). Mental models are deeply ingrained assumptions that affect the way individuals think about people, situations and organisations (Senge, 1990, cited by Burnes, 2009: 148.) Having top management mindsets that fully embrace concepts of continuous change is vital here, and a key feature of the 'morphing mindset' that we noted earlier (see also Chapters 4 and 7).

This requires a sensitivity to language, power and politics in shaping processes and outcomes of change efforts. Watson draws on the image of the organisation as a form of 'negotiated order' to describe the nature of this dynamic. He explains that management initiatives typically get mired in competing logics that undermine the desired change, and research points to the need for managers to be better skilled at managing tensions arising from these (Watson, 2002; Watson and Rosborough, 2000). Pivotal to this ability is the persuasive/political dimension of language which is a powerful medium in the hands of top managers in shaping sense-making within the organisation (Tietze *et al*, 2003; Keleman, 2000). We argue that it is important, therefore, that change leaders are 'conversationally responsible' (Ford, 1999) – that is, willing to *take ownership* of the way they speak and listen, and the practical and ethical consequences of this (see Chapters 14 and 15).

BRIDGING THE KNOWING—DOING GAP

Pfeffer (2005) observes the relatively limited diffusion of ideas and business models in contemporary organisations, commenting that this may appear a strange conclusion within a world where there are entire industries set up to spread new concepts and practices such as Six Sigma and Total Quality Management. Nevertheless, in many cases such business models fail to become incorporated into everyday management practice, not least because we fail all too frequently to examine the evidence for, and the assumptions underpinning, beliefs about human behaviour and strategy-making within organisations – a good example is the significant difference in definitions and focus in the analysis of emotion at work (see Chapter 16).

The separation of much HR research from HR practice is often described as the 'knowing—doing gap in HRM', and has attracted growing interest among professional circles in recent years, reflected in the CIPD's Agenda on Shaping the Future of HR (CIPD Report 2011b) and special academic journal issues devoted to the subject (eg *Academy of Management Journal*, 2007; *Human Resource Management Review*, 2007). It encompasses debate from both a practitioner perspective (ie grounding management practice in the evidence-base, eg Rousseau, 2006) as well as academic (eg re-imagining relevance as a necessary condition for rigour: Starkey, Hatchuel and Tempest, 2009). Attention has been drawn to the usefulness of research in terms of creating value for practitioners (eg Lepak *et al*, 2007), or developing *actionable knowledge* that has maximum impact (Antonacopoulou, 2009). Central to the co-construction of new analytical frameworks that talk to academic and practitioner communities is the effective 'conversion' of complex concepts and ideas into the more simple and practical, identified in Harley and Hardy's (2004) analysis of the discursive processes by which academic writing resonates with practitioners – in other words, what types of text 'stick'.

Following this viewpoint we argue for new modes of knowledge transfer based on deep partnerships between academics and practitioners, better able to draw upon multiple perspectives from 'critical' and performance-focused research (as we hope we have illustrated in this book), *and* which engage with the practitioner world in this endeavour. We also call for a shift in mindsets among HR practitioners about what makes for 'good evidence'. With an inbuilt focus on dialogue with internal and external stakeholders, our New OE framework treats the *process* of gathering evidence as important as the evidence itself.

Our focus on process raises the importance of building a reflective approach to the diagnosis of organisational and HR issues – being able to surface and question 'intuitive' understandings of HR issues and test new understandings (Anderson, 2009). If the value of 'research' becomes embedded in the everyday business of HR work, the distinction between HR 'researcher' and HR 'practitioner' becomes a false one and the enquiry process should be treated as a 'routine part of the HR toolkit' (Anderson, 2009: 273). HR professionals must therefore be mindful to focus much more on using insights from current business/HR models and innovations to help themselves, and others when necessary, to change their mental models. This capability is shaped by the *absorptive capacity* of HR and OD functions – the capacity of an 'organisation' to acquire, assimilate and apply knowledge (Cohen and Levinthal, 1990, cited by Edmonstone, 2011; Withers, Williamson and Reddington, 2010).

The short case study below, based on an interview with a senior manager in the HR function at Vertex, a leading business process outsourcing organisation, illustrates the notion of absorptive capacity in relation to building a high-performance culture.

CASE STUDY

HR TRANSFORMATION AT VERTEX

Vertex provides leading services in business process outsourcing (BPO), customer management outsourcing and IT services. It has 15,000 employees and serves over 200 clients worldwide.

A key Vertex corporate goal is to build a high-performance culture through engaging and developing people – part of its Our People, Our Future strategy. For the HR function to play a central role in the delivery of this goal, it inaugurated an HR transformation programme designed to achieve:

- a cost-effective HR back office in line with Vertex's business, scalable, and addressing the needs of the business, including partnering and outsourced services where appropriate – eg immigration services

- deep HR expertise around the critical people issues impacting on or arising from growth and change of the organisation

- a strong HR consulting and HR advisory capability in people management which

enables managers to make better people decisions

- a high-performance culture

- automated self-service HR processes through a developed portal, involving simple content and comprehensive and consistent global data structures, and without the loss of regional input, to ensure a single-conduit means of access for all people data.

- the change to a service culture.

This presented a range of challenges and severely tested the capacity of the HR function to acquire, assimilate and apply knowledge in the pursuit of its transformation vision.

Questions

1 What are the key capabilities required to undertake the HR transformation programme?

2 How can HR acquire those capabilities?

3 How can absorptive capacity be measured?

The current debates about the need for closer academic practitioner partnerships in theory development, and the development of reflective practitioners who are able to draw upon the latest innovations in OEF, are now examined in the form of a New OE mindset.

'NEW OE' MINDSET

New OE blends elements from different (and sometimes competing) contemporary forms of OD and HR, noted earlier. As described here, it can be viewed as a transformational framework which accommodates sensitivity to the four themes: the power of language and action; authenticity and mutuality; paradox and ambiguity; and building leadership and management capabilities. These are shown diagrammatically in Figure 1.2 and explained in more detail in Table 1.3.

Figure 1.2 New OE mindset

Together, these themes challenge current orthodoxies about power and politics that are rarely mentioned within the mainstream management literature. In our conceptualisation of OE we treat language, knowledge and power as being irrevocably connected, to present a more sophisticated notion of human beings as 'agents', and the role of context in shaping their capability to 'take a hand in shaping their lives' (Bandura, 2000: 75; see also Fleetwood and Hesketh, 2010).

We are not arguing that New OE requires HR to be at the heart of OD or vice versa. Instead, we are saying that practitioners in these disciplines need to be more sensitively aware of these themes and infuse them, in a contextually appropriate fashion, into their thinking and practice. Similarly, the idea is not about wholesale application of all OE elements within each of the contributory chapters – some will be more or less relevant depending upon the particular subject area and context of the case(s) presented for study. A range of contemporary issues are explored, framed within broader debates about changing socio-political and economic climates and their effects upon how we view 'sustainability' both for the organisation and the wider society.

The authors do not adhere to any one philosophical view but draw upon a fusion of academic and practitioner insights to challenge current orthodoxies, provide examples of innovations in HR and OD practice, and open up discursive space for the ethos of New OE to flourish.

THE POSITIONING OF OD AND HR

We have chosen not to delve too deeply into the debate about the structural positioning of HR and OD, focusing more on the need for a shift in mindsets – the frame within which HR and OD can play to each other's strengths, operate to ethical and employee-centric values and produce sustainable and self-renewing outcomes for all concerned.

Nevertheless, we need to be mindful of the political and social dynamics inherent in structural designs reflected in Burke's remarks upon the 'languishing' of OD in the US context, which may be rooted in a structural problem, such that most internal OD practitioners are described as being 'buried within the HR function' (Burke, 2004: 423). Five structural models are presented, and a position taken that OD would better serve the organisation being integrated with strategy, consistent with arguments developed in Chapter 5. These models are:

- the *traditional model*: OD as a subfunction of HR
- the *independent model*: freestanding OD, not reporting in to HR but possibly reporting to some senior executive other than HR, such as administration, strategy or operations
- the *decentralised model*: OD practitioners as part of a business or regional unit, reporting either to the HR director of that unit or directly to the unit head

Table 1.3 The four themes of New OE

Language and action	Authenticity and mutuality
Challenges the traditional view of language as simply a tool to describe people and events, and treats it as having an active role to play in shaping change. Francis and Reddington depict this as a 'language-practice' perspective (Chapter 14) to emphasise the interwoven nature of language and action and its effects on processes of change. Language is acknowledged as a powerful medium in the hands of top managers in shaping how realities are construed within the organisation. For instance, the metaphors they use in everyday conversations frame how people think about the world around them, their identity and the nature of the employment relationship. It is important therefore that leaders are 'conversationally responsible' (Ford, 1999) in that they are willing to *take ownership* of the way they speak and listen, and the practical and ethical consequences of this.	Challenges the instrumental view of employees portrayed in mainstream models of HR/OD, where change is largely *driven* by senior management, to one where employees are reconceptualised as more *active players* in constructing their work and organisational environment. Emphasis is placed on achieving greater mutuality of benefits and risks between employer and employee. It requires senior managers to consciously and actively introduce new structures and ways of working that enhance effective sharing of power and control at the workplace. Stimulating progress of this kind rests among other things on building capabilities to surface, diagnose and work with competing structures and perspectives. A key feature of the OE framework is its explicit focus on the potential of social media technologies to facilitate this process.
Paradox and ambiguity	**Leadership and management**
Challenges the highly normative approach to HRM/OD which typically seeks to stifle paradox and ambiguity, the surfacing of which is seen to be too risky or challenging to management control. It is about fostering a caring and pragmatic approach to management which allows for creation of 'constructive tension' (Evans *et al*, 2002) as a source of progressive management and organisational effectiveness. It recognises that managers are often left with little or no support in coping with everyday tensions, such as the need to focus on short-term results and longer-term growth, the need to balance individual and team requirements, and so on. New OE presents an emergent new mindset and tools for action which encourage creative ways to reframe and manage contradictions, and to proactively shape what 'effectiveness' looks like in any given context.	Challenges conventional approaches to leadership and management which do not easily accommodate notions of employee agency and mutuality. We propose that forms of leadership variously described as 'distributed', 'dispersed' and 'shared' are more likely to result in greater innovation and employee well-being by allowing employees to become more active 'producers', not merely 'consumers' of HR policies and practices. Such approaches require of managers an authentic approach to consultation and power-sharing, as described in Chapter 6. Employees, too, must be willing to rise to the challenge of this new form of employee relations. To build new forms of leadership capability, HR itself must exercise leadership, proactively exposing managers at all levels to new ways of understanding the leadership task, and at the same time recognising the need for them not to lose sight of their management responsibilities. This requires HR to work from a strong ethical base, working within OD's humanist value-set while also focusing on organisational performance and commercial outcomes.

- the *integrated model*: OD integrated into all aspects of HR – all HR employees are highly trained in OD skills and competencies, with change as a primary responsibility
- the *strategy model*: OD as an integral part of the strategic planning function reporting to the CEO.

Burke argues that the integrated model, which is the least common within the USA, provides a practical means for strengthening the two disciplines while removing some of the organisational structural problems associated with the other models. Others, writing from a UK context, are more reserved about the potential benefits, suggesting that OD would 'inevitably become part of the establishment' (Garrow, 2009: 14), and that research within the NHS points to the potential 'sanitisation' of OD humanist values in contexts where the function has been 'colonised' by the HRM function (Edmonstone, 2011).

Bunker and Alban, 2006, also highlight a range of possible options among which are: the OD group sits within the Personnel function; OD is an indigenous part of the HR function; OD is part of a matrix function; OD specialists sit within the line organisation; the OD group becomes the corporate organisation development group with unrelated field staff; the OD group becomes the internal consulting team. In the USA, the general tendency is for OD to be part of a corporate centre, reporting directly to the CEO. To a large extent the choice will depend on the size of the organisation, the capabilities of the individuals, their relative power, and the politics of decision-making. Within the UK, IES research Garrow (2009: 14) found close working relationships between HR, internal OD and external consultants but 'considerable confusion' over roles and responsibilities. Garrow argues that OD sits bests at the boundaries of the organisation, rather than part of a functional establishment as part of HR, since this may compromise OD's capacity to challenge.

Clearly, any merger between the two functions will lead to 'uncomfortable tensions' (Peck, 2005), and New OE provides a lens that can be usefully applied to the surfacing of such tensions in ways that can produce fruitful strategies and approaches to people management and organisational change. In Chapter 17 we present our initial research findings from CIPD/NHS surveys. These were conducted between November 2010 and January 2011, and involved 106 respondents comprising HR and OD senior managers from the public and private and voluntary sectors. The survey questions probed the four key themes of New OE, and free text comments were additionally captured verbatim. The surveys show that although the preferred option for a quarter of our respondents is for OD to be a sub-set of HR, this model is *least* likely to adopt bundles of practices associated with New OE (eg associated with 'building agility' and 'sustainable high performance'. In contrast, the integrated approach model was more positively associated with New OE.

THE SCOPE AND STRUCTURE OF THIS BOOK

This section provides a brief overview of the structure and content of the book and additional resource guides available to the reader, explaining how it all reflects the kind of partnership working between academics and practitioners referred to above. It includes the use of the CIPD Toolkits, recommendations for further reading and pointers to available online resources.

The editors have attempted to strike a balance between academic theory and 'real-life' practice. Chapter authors themselves represent an attempt to close the academic/practitioner divide since they include writing teams of practitioners – managers, HR professionals and consultants – and academics drawn from a variety of disciplines. Through the inclusion of case studies and reflective activities, readers have the opportunity to conceptualise the acquisition of new knowledge by the application of theory to practice.

Chapter 2 sets the context for the book as a whole. Linda Holbeche offers a critical realist perspective on the rationale for a new form of organisational effectiveness. She argues that today's turbulent politico-economic context highlights the need for greater organisational flexibility. Organisations will need to be capable of ongoing change while at the same time marshalling and deploying the talents of their diverse workforces effectively. However, change generally undermines 'employee engagement' and potentially damages performance and innovation potential. Conventional approaches to HRM, HRD and OD tend to work within set disciplinary boundaries, thus restricting the potential for a more holistic and sustainable set of solutions. Rising to the challenge of New OE will require new ways of thinking about leadership, employee agency and employee risk.

The author argues that HR should be instrumental in addressing these challenges although HR's role is paradoxical since the function acts both as an agent of managerialism and also as a perceived blocker to managerial intentions. Indeed, in its desire to become a 'business partner', HR may have lost its focus on employees. New OE transcends these limitations by viewing longer-term sustainability and organisational renewal as the *end* of OE, and a disciplinary coalescence as the *means* of New OE.

In **Chapters 3 and 4** we take a practice perspective on organisational development. First, Naomi Stanford provides an overview of the history of organisation development, highlighting key strands of thinking in this diverse field. Naomi discusses the purpose, scope and current status of organisation development, as well as its links to organisational design. The author draws on her consultancy experience to provide a practice perspective on the key phases and methods of process consulting. In Chapter 4, Mark Withers picks up where Naomi Stanford leaves off. He examines organisational development in terms of its implications for HR – in particular, how to develop an OD strategy from an HR perspective. Rich in case studies, the chapter explores the links between business strategy and OD. While highlighting differences in approach, Mark also draws out common themes – contingency thinking, whole system thinking and emergence – which are congruent with constructionist approaches. The author draws attention to the skills and capabilities required to credibly develop and implement an OD strategy.

Of course, any discussion of organisational effectiveness should be informed by an understanding of culture and culture change. In **Chapter 5** Valerie Garrow and Graeme Martin combine practice-based and critical realist perspectives to provide an overview of organisational culture situated within the historical context of OD. The various dynamics of top-down versus more emergent approaches to culture change are discussed, and the authors highlight the particular challenges of cultural integration – for instance, in merger situations. Case studies illustrate some of the dilemmas organisations experience as they attempt to achieve 'cultural agility' in the move towards more diverse and flexible cultures.

Similarly, no consideration of organisational effectiveness, especially in today's turbulent context, is complete without consideration of employee voice. In **Chapter 6** John Purcell charts the changing landscape of UK employment relations (ER) from union dominance to non-union perspectives in the private sector and changing features in the public sector, and draws lessons from the recession and public sector retrenchment. The author considers the implications for employee agency of an authentically collaborative OD approach. Using a case study to highlight the essence of changing agendas, Purcell raises challenging questions related to underlying issues, such as how far should management go in consulting employees on workforce changes and underlying business strategies. The author points to the need to move from defensive behaviours (protecting the management prerogative) to proactive, and sometimes risky, initiatives to 'take the workforce with you'.

In **Chapter 7** Peter Reilly argues that if HR is to successfully support organisational change, HR must transform itself. He looks at what is happening to the HR function and whether it can be seen as a role model of change, particularly in the public sector. The chapter provides useful information about what is happening, and adds to the developing argument about the relationship between HRM and OD. Reilly argues that the requirement to upskill the HR function has been largely ignored, and that New OE would require HR transformation to be approached less from a top-down functionally driven approach and more from a consultative approach to change, involving customers more. Although this may result in greater initial cost, the author argues that such an approach would lead to more sustainable resolution of tensions between the needs for conformity and for flexibility.

In **Chapter 8** Martin Reddington takes a detailed, critical look at the role of technology as an agent of HR transformation. Drawing on a review of the literature and case examples, the author avoids a 'technocratic' discussion about e-enabled HR as he examines the claimed transactional and transformational benefits of significant injections of technology mediation. He highlights the effects on the jobs of line managers when they are progressively required to deal with their own people management issues as a consequence of the introduction of HR technology systems, and the physical separation from HR employees with whom they used to have face-to-face contact. In more recent years the emergence of social media technologies in the form of Web 2.0 and Enterprise 2.0 have introduced new opportunities and challenges, which offer the potential for employers and employees to engage in more meaningful conversations for change. This chapter also looks at the links between ICT adoption and how it is perceived to affect the employment value proposition (see Chapter 14).

The extent to which mutuality of outcomes is achievable depends to a large extent on whether HR processes are 'done to' or 'done with' employees. In **Chapter 9** Allan Ramdhony examines the significance of the newly emerging concept of critical human resource development (CHRD). He provides a brief overview of HRD to chart the rise of strategic HRD (SHRD), which accounts in large measure for mainstream thinking within the field and tends to give primacy to the achievement of performance objectives. Although CHRD remains somewhat abstract and has yet to be fully translated into practice, it provides a powerful counterpoint to SHRD by bringing into focus the possibility of more democratic working conditions and for better addressing employees' learning needs and development. In particular, the author focuses on critical action learning sets as a vehicle for building more employee-centred learning and development activities. Attention is paid to the role of context in shaping the process and outcomes of these.

In similar vein, in **Chapter 10**, John Castledine and Doug Renwick focus on established and emerging practices to learning and development. In particular, the chapter unravels the developments, challenges and questions that surround the increasing involvement of line managers in shaping performance, learning and innovation. Within the emerging field of human capital management (HCM) employees are viewed as being more like investors in their own human capital. Creating a culture and environment in which performance and innovation sit comfortably together is arguably one of the greatest challenges for leaders and managers. Line managers and HR both play vital roles in delivering a 'psychological contract' that creates effective collaboration between employees and the organisation.

In **Chapter 11** the focus switches to the integration of workforce planning with organisation design. Roger Cooper and Melanie Wood draw on their consultancy and corporate experience to present the generic processes involved in strategic workforce planning and organisation design. The chapter includes a detailed case study of Birmingham City Council, an organisation that implemented radical and innovative strategic workforce planning and organisational design solutions within the context of a much broader business transformation programme. The arrival of the global financial crisis in late 2007, and the consequent impacts on public sector finances that followed, added both to the urgency and complexity of the context within which strategic workforce planning and organisation design have been deployed.

The management of performance for individuals, teams and organisations is generally considered central to success since it sits at the heart of the interrelationship between employees, teams and the organisations they work for. In **Chapter 12** Roger Cooper and Adrian Furnham argue that the banking crisis of 2007 and wider subsequent economic problems illustrate the need for the fundamentals of performance management, and the way that this relates to reward, to be re-imagined. In particular, the authors look at performance management from a wider social and organisational psychology perspective and consider the implications of recent economic events for the design and operation of aspects of performance management systems, such as target-setting. They conclude with a discussion of future issues in managing individual performance.

Talent management should provide a pivotal foundation for OD since its essential focus is on the recruitment, development and retention of future leaders and employees in the organisation. In **Chapter 13** Eddie Blass and Gill Maxwell explore the concept of talent management and how it can contribute to the OD/organisational effectiveness agenda contoured in this book. The authors discuss both exclusive approaches to talent management and argue in favour of framing talent management as an inclusive policy, embracing diversity, and illustrate their argument with a variety of case studies. The chapter also discusses the differential roles of HR managers, OD and HRD specialists, line managers and employees in developing a meaningful psychological contract.

Psychological contract theory provides a link to **Chapter 14** in which Helen Francis and Martin Reddington propose a possible way of synthesising the dynamic of the changing employment relationship between the individual and the organisation. These authors seek to reframe the employment value proposition (EVP) or 'deal' as a means of examining the changing employment relationship. They draw on a fusion of practitioner/academic perspectives – OD, HR, branding and critical schools of thought – with the aim of redirecting and reconnecting theory and practice development in this field. They provide a framework (and methodology) designed to encourage practitioners to rethink and refocus the EVP on more pluralist grounds, and which treats employee engagement as an important feature of social exchange within organisations.

The theme of social outcomes is picked up in **Chapter 15** by Carole Parkes, who examines the relationship in theory and practice between strategic HRM on the one hand and the growing interest in business ethics and corporate social responsibility (CSR) on the other. The author calls for the HRM profession to provide inspirational leadership in these areas. She argues that HR's role in establishing codes of practice for what is considered ethical behaviour, communicating these and providing appropriate training and reinforcement mechanisms, is often seen as a starting point. However, the real challenge is one of engaging individuals and groups with the needs of others and broader ethical principles. OD approaches which seek to enhance individual development and organisational performance through surfacing organisational values appear to address this.

The values-based theme of trust within the psychological contract is continued in **Chapter 16**. The last decade has seen a sharp increase in interest in emotion at work, both within research communities and organisations. Emotion is now seen as integral to culture, performance and crucial to success. Chapter authors Chiara Amati and Chris Donegan trace the origins of this interest in emotion, how it has changed over time, and the current trends and implications for practice in organisations. Starting from a critical discussion of the happy-productive worker hypothesis, it presents a picture of emotion in organisations as being the result of a dynamic, complex interplay between the individual and the organisational context.

Finally, we the editors draw conclusions about the future of 'New OE'. We recognise and draw attention to the nature of employee risk, which suggests that the direction of travel articulated in this book is likely to become increasingly core to the way effective organisations and their members function. We take the view that while the treatment of organisations as 'whole systems' usefully encourages us to look at how various structures and social processes relate to each other and to the 'whole', we are attempting to move away from monolithic approaches to OD which rely on prescriptive models of diagnosis. We argue that we need new metaphors and imagery to better understand and address continuous whole-system change (Marshak and Grant, 2008a, 2008b). This shift requires HR professionals to release their existing world views and acquire new mindsets about transformational change and the role of employees in shaping it.

The responses of HR professionals to the editors' survey suggest that many recognise the increasing gap between the effects of strategic HRM and what employees themselves aspire to. HR professionals also appear ready to embrace a new way of thinking about their own potential contribution and a willingness to develop the capability this will require of them. We hope that this book will be helpful to them in their own development journey, as well as aiding the development of an HR profession that can escape perpetual marginality by delivering a new form of organisational effectiveness.

REFERENCES

AIM Report (2004) Delivering the Promise of Management Practices, Advanced Institute of Management Research and Chartered Management Institute: London.

Anderson, V. (2009) *Research Methods in Human Resource Management*, 2nd edition. London: CIPD.

Antonacopoulou, E. A. (2009) 'Impact and scholarship: unlearning and practising to co-create actionable knowledge', *Management Learning*, Vol.40, No.4: 421–30.

Bandura, A. (2000) 'The exercise of human agency through collective efficacy', *Current Directions in Psychological Science*, Vol.9: 75. Available at cdp.sagepub.com from Edinburgh Napier University-LIS [accessed 7 December 2010].

Birkinshaw, J. (2010) *Reinventing Management: Smarter choices for getting work done*. San Francisco: Jossey-Bass.

Bolden, R. (2004) *What is Leadership?* Leadership South West Research Report, University of Exeter.

Bonet, E. and Sauquet, A. (2010) 'Rhetoric in management and in management research', *Journal of Organizational Change Management*, Vol.23, No.2: 120–33.

Bunker, B. and Alban, A. (2006) *The Handbook of Large Group Methods*. San Francisco: Jossey-Bass.

Burke, W. W. (2004) 'Internal organization development practitioners: where do they belong?', *Applied Journal of Behavioral Science*, Vol.40: 423.

Burnes, B. (2009) *Managing Change*, 5th edition. Harlow: Pearson Education.

Busche, G. R. and Marshak, R. (2011) 'Revisioning organization development', *Journal of Applied Behavioural Science*, Vol.45, No.3: 348–68.

Butcher, D. and Atkinson, S. (2001) 'Stealth, secrecy and subversion: the language of change', *Journal of Organizational Change Management*, Vol.14, No.6: 1–11.

CIPD Report (2011a) *Next Generation HR*. London: Chartered Institute of Personnel and Development. Available at http://www.cipd.co.uk/research/_next-gen-hr.

CIPD Report (2011b) *Shaping the Future. Sustainable Organisation Performance. What really makes the difference?* London: Chartered Institute of Personnel and Development. Available at http://www.cipd.co.uk/shapingthefuture.

Cohen, W. and Levinthal, D. (1990) 'Absorptive capacity: a new perspective on learning and innovation', *Administrative Science Quarterly*, Vol.35, No.1: 128–52.

Dunphy, D. and Stace, D. (1993) 'The strategic management of corporate change', *Human Relations*, Vol.46, No.8: 905–23.

Edmonstone, J. (2011) 'Action learning and OD', in Pedler, M. (ed.) *Action Learning in Practice*, 4th edition. London: Sage.

Ehnert, I. (2008) *Sustainable Human Resource Management: A conceptual and exploratory analysis from a paradox perspective*. Heidelberg: Physica-Verlag.

Evans, P., Pucik, V. and Barsoux, J. (2002) *The Global Challenge: Frameworks for international human resource management*. New York: McGraw-Hill/Irwin.

Fayol, H. (1949 [1916]) *General and Industrial Management*. London: Pitman.

Fleetwood S. and Hesketh A. J. (2010) *Explaining the Performance of Human Resource Management*. Cambridge: Cambridge University Press.

Ford, J. (1999) 'Organizational change as shifting conversations', *Journal of Organizational*

Change Management, Vol.12, No.6: 1–14. Available at http:/www.emerald-library.com/brev/12312fb1.htm.

Ford, J. and Ford, L. (1995) 'The role of conversations in producing intentional change in organizations', *Academy of Management Review*, Vol.20, No.3: 541–71.

Francis, H. (2003) 'Teamworking: meanings and contradictions in the management of change', *Human Resource Management Journal*, Vol.13, No.3: 71–90.

Francis, H. (2007) 'Discursive struggle and the ambiguous world of HRD', *Advances in Developing Human Resources*, Vol.9, No.1: 83–96.

Francis, H. and Reddington, M. (2010) 'Redirecting and reconnecting theory: employer branding and the employment "deal"', Paper for the BSA Work, Employment and Society Conference.

Francis, H. and Sinclair, J. (2003) 'A processual analysis of HRM-based change', *Organization*, Vol.10, No.4: 685–706.

Garrow, V. (2009) *OD: Past, present and future*, IES Working Paper WP22. London: Institute of Employment Studies.

Goffee, R. and Jones, G. (2006) *Why Should Anyone be Led by You?: What it takes to be an authentic leader*. Cambridge, MA: Harvard Business School Press.

Habermas, J. (1986) 'Life forms, morality and the task of the philosopher', in Dews, P. (ed.) *Habermas: Autonomy and Solidarity*. London: Verso.

Harley, B. and Hardy, C. (2004) 'Firing blanks? An analysis of discursive struggle in HRM', *Journal of Management Studies*, Vol.41, No.3: 377–400.

Huczynski A. and Buchanan D. (2007) *Organizational Behaviour: An introductory text*, 7th edition. London: Prentice Hall.

Inns, D. (2009) 'Metaphor in the literature of organizational analysis: a preliminary taxonomy and a glimpse at a humanities-based perspective', *Organization*, Vol.9, No.2: 305–30.

Jabri, M., Adrian, A. and Boje, D. (2008) 'Reconsidering the role of conversations in change communication', *Journal of Organizational Change*, Vol.21 No.6: 667–85.

Kakabadse, N. and Kakabadse, A. (2010) 'Leadership and the art of discretion', available online at https://dspace.lib.cranfield.ac.uk/.../Leadership-discretion-Final.pdf [accessed 15 September 2010].

Keegan, A. and Francis, H. (2010) 'Practitioner talk: the changing textscape of HRM and emergence of HR Business Partnership', *International Journal of Human Resource Management*, Vol.21, No.4–6: 873–98.

Keleman, M. (2000) 'Too much or too little ambiguity: the language of Total Quality Management', *Journal of Management Studies*, Vol.37, No.4: 484–97.

Kotter, J. P. (1996) Leading Changes. Boston: Harvard Business School.

Lepak, D. P., Smith, K. G. and Taylor, M. S. (2007) 'Value creation and value capture: a multilevel perspective', *Academy of Management Review*, Vol.32, No.1: 180–94.

Linstead, S., Fulop, L. and Lilley, S. (2009) *Management and Organization, A critical text*, 2nd edition. London: Palgrave.

MacLeod, D. and Clarke, N. (2009) *Engaging for Success: Enhancing performance through engagement*. A Report to Government.

McHugh, M., O'Brien, G. and Ramondt, J. (1999) 'Organizational metamorphosis led by front line staff', *Employee Relations*, Vol.21, No.6: 556–76.

Marshak, R (2002) 'Changing the language of change: how new contexts and concepts are challenging the way we think and talk about organizational change', *Strategic Change*, August: 279–86.

Marshak, R. and Grant, D. (2008a) 'Organizational discourse and new organization development practices', *British Journal of Management*, Vol.19: 7–19.

Marshak, R. and Grant, D. (2008b) 'Transforming talk: the interplay of discourse, power and change', *Organizational Development Journal*, Vol.23, No.3: 33–40.

Martin, G. and Reddington, M. (2009) 'Reconceptualising absorptive capacity to explain the e-enablement of the HR function (e-HR) in organizations', *Employee Relations*, Vol.31, No.5: 515–37.

Martin, G., Reddington, M. and Kneafsey, M. B. (2009) *Web 2.0 and Human Resource Management: 'Groundswell' or hype?* CIPD Report. London: Chartered Institute of Personnel and Development.

Morgan, G. (1997) *Images of Organizations*. London: Sage.

Mumby, D. K. (2004) 'Discourse, power and ideology: unpacking the critical approach', in Grant, D., Hardy, C., Oswick, C. and Putnam, L. (eds) *The Handbook of Organizational Discourse*. London: Sage.

Oswick, C., Keenoy, T., Beverungen, A., Ellis, N., Sabelis, I. and Ybema, S. (2007) 'Discourse, practice, policy and organizing: some opening comments', *International Journal of Sociology and Social Policy*, Vol.27, No.11/12: 429–32.

Peck, E. (2005) *Organizational Development in Healthcare: Approaches, innovations, achievements*. UK: Radcliffe Publishing.

Pfeffer, J. (2005) 'Changing mental models: HR's most important task', *Human Resource Management*, Vol.44, No.2: 123–8.

Quinn R. E. and Rohrbaugh, J. (1983) 'A spatial model of effectiveness criteria: towards a competing values approach to organisational effectiveness', *Management Science*, Vol.29: 363–77.

Reddington, M. and Francis, H. (forthcoming) 'Deployment of Web 2.0 in re-architecting EVP to enhance the employer brand', in Martin, G. and Cooper, C. (eds) *Corporate Reputation: Managing threats and opportunities*. Aldershot: Gower.

Richard, P. J., Devinney, T. M., Yip, T. S. and Johnson, G. (2009) 'Measuring organizational performance: towards methodological best practice', *Journal of Management*, June, Vol.35, No.37: 718–804.

Rousseau, D. M. (2006) 'Is there such a thing as "evidence-based management"?', *Academy of Management Learning and Education*, Vol.6: 84–101.

Schein, E. (2004) *Organizational Culture and Leadership*, 3rd edition. San Francisco: Jossey-Bass.

Seele, R. (2003) 'Story and conversation in organisations: a survey'. Available online at http://www.new-paradigm.co.uk/story_&_conversation.htm .

Senge, P. (1990) *The Fifth Discipline: The art and practice of the learning organization*. London: Century Business.

Starkey, K., Hatchuel, A. and Tempest, S. (2009) 'Management research and the new logics of discovery and engagement', *Journal of Management Studies*, Vol.46, No.3: 547–58.

Tietze, S., Cohen, L. and Musson, G. (2003) *Understanding Organizations Through Language*. London: Sage.

Watson, T., (2002) *Organising and Managing Work*. Harlow: Pearson Education Ltd.

Watson, T. and Rosborough, J. (2000) 'Teamworking and the management of flexibility: local and social-structural tensions in high performance work design initiatives', in Proctor, S. and Mueller, F. (eds) *Teamworking*. London: Macmillan.

Withers, M., Williamson, M. and Reddington, M. (2010) *Transforming HR: Creating value through people*. Oxford: Butterworth-Heinemann.

Wong, W., Albert, A., Huggett, M. and Sullivan, J. (2009) *Quality People Management for Quality Outcomes: The future of HR. Review of evidence on people management*. Work Foundation Report.

CHAPTER 2

The Strategic Context for New OE

Linda Holbeche

CHAPTER OVERVIEW

This second introductory chapter outlines some of the key context factors which support the argument for a new form of organisational effectiveness, as outlined in the previous chapter. In particular the author highlights how the pursuit of flexibility and cost-effectiveness is driving the installation of new organisational forms, the flexibilisation of labour and changing the nature of the employment relationship for white-collar workers. What this means in terms of HR's strategic contribution and why this requires an OD mindset or 'frame' are considered. The chapter draws on the author's research into the changing nature of workplace relations and her consultancy practice in the development of HR and OD professionals.

LEARNING OBJECTIVES

By the end of this chapter the reader should be able to:

- understand how changes in the business context are shaping the transformation of the HR function – in particular, the need for HR to adopt more proactive change agent roles
- understand key elements of the debate about HRM from 'mainstream' and 'critical' perspectives
- consider some of the complexities of change management, including the HR function's own transformation journey
- explain why HR should embrace an OD perspective and values, and how HR and OD practitioners can work together to produce sustainable change outcomes.

INTRODUCTION

Why start with context? In contrast to mainstream academic HRM and human resource development (HRD) theory, the primary focus of which centres on the psychology of the employee and on such factors as individual motivation, discretionary effort and commitment, critical management scholarship (CMS) assumes that the practice of management can only be understood in the context of the wider social–economic, political and cultural factors which shape – if not determine – those practices. As Wong *et al* (2009:3) put it:

Any discourse about people management lacks context without consideration of the changing nature of organisational context, employment models and the employment relationship.

Moreover, CMS has an explicitly political agenda which draws its inspiration from an eclectic mix of Marxian, Weberian, post-structuralist and humanist roots.

Of course, the global business landscape has had a radical shake-up as a result of the financial crisis which began with the 'credit crunch' in 2007 before moving on to full-blown recession in many national economies by 2009. It is evident that some of the old ways of doing business will have to change, although the new 'rules of the game' are only just starting to emerge. There are growing demands for better governance, greater transparency and fairness over executive pay, new forms of leadership, greater accountability. And many of these practices fall directly or indirectly within HR's remit.

Just as some commentators describe the economic events of recent years as a 'crisis' of capitalism (Gamble, 2009; Peston, 2008; Sennett, 2006), it is possible that the HR function's purpose is also at a major watershed, as I shall discuss in later sections of this chapter. As HR professionals will be only too aware, HR is increasingly required to play an active part in organisational change initiatives to help their organisations successfully navigate today's choppy waters. Senior HR professionals are increasingly expected to take a lead in organisation design, culture change, change management and improving the quality of leadership – all of which are key aspects of organisation development. How well equipped they feel to do this is another matter.

As is discussed in the next chapter, the goal of OD is to build healthy and effective organisations. OD is a broad field of knowledge and practice expertise concerned with change management and culture change. Although HR professionals may not themselves be OD specialists, they do need to know how to integrate OD as part of their work, and be able to identify when and how to contract with OD specialists for OD work. Developing organisations involves a shared effort between OD experts, HR and other key players, such as executives and line managers, as well as employees themselves. Together HR and OD specialists can produce some of the key outcomes that matter for sustainable success – ie resilient, flexible, agile and high-performing organisations full of motivated, innovative and productive employees and other workers.

STRATEGIC CONTEXT

Much has changed since OD's beginnings in the 1950s and the development of HRM in the 1980s. In this section we consider how the Anglo-American form of capitalism which has dominated the world economy for the past 30 years has shaped not only aspects of business and work but also what has come to be taken for granted in employment practice and in people's daily lives. As Watson (2010) points out, an understanding of how the employment relationship is structured and regulated, and a concern with how managers manage, ought to be at the heart of HRM. At present, this is not the case: the employment relationship is treated very much as a given, part of the 'background' context; and its complex impact on managerial practice is of marginal concern (Boselie, Brewster and Paauwe, 2009; Keenoy, 2009). So in this chapter we examine some of the context factors which have a bearing on the role of HR and on why OD is of crucial relevance going forward.

ANGLO-AMERICAN CAPITALISM

Of fundamental significance by way of context are the essentially capitalist economic relations which have regulated the global economy for the past three decades. The Anglo-American form of global capitalism, with neo-liberal ideals at its core, was promoted during the 1980s in the UK by Margaret Thatcher and in the USA by Ronald Reagan as President, and subsequently advanced as a political project by the New Right. This aggressive free-market fundamentalism is based on the efficient market hypothesis of which the aim is to maximise individual freedoms through the deregulation of markets thus enabling corporate capitalism to expand free from interference from the state (Marquand, 2008).

During the Thatcher years there was also a political commitment to globalisation and new forms of market – in particular, the financial services industry. Its development was assisted by new information and communication technologies which began to transform traditional manufacturing and distribution systems, and a considerable proportion of traditional manufacturing capability migrated to parts of the developing world. Since the Thatcher era, various UK governments have continued to support regulatory and employment legislation reform to enable flexibility and support economic growth (Peston, 2008).

By the mid-1990s the impact of globalisation, the success of the financial services model and the legacy of Thatcherite economic and fiscal policies on the UK economy were becoming clear. Britain was becoming largely a service and knowledge-intensive economy, with high technology, financial services and travel and tourism as major growth areas. Factors considered to be impeding British success in this global economy were identified and addressed through government policy (Gamble, 2009).

The broader consequences of neo-liberalism on business practices were also becoming increasingly evident during the 1990s. The role of business was conceived as almost exclusively about making wealth for shareholders and investors. Sennett (2006) argues that Anglo-American forms of globalisation, driven by capital, transformed the way businesses themselves were viewed – from being about producing things to being short-term investment vehicles which were themselves bought and sold. Within organisations the combined effect of changes in technology, globalisation, competitive pressures, unpredictable socio-political and economic factors was evident in the ruthless pursuit of flexibility and efficiency, in the form of business re-engineering in the 1980s, rationalisation and de-layering in the 1990s, and aggressive outsourcing in the 2000s (Hutton, 2010).

Within society as a whole from the late 1980s on, the popular ethos came to be about individualism, entrepreneurialism, consumerism, greed and wealth creation. Films like *Wall Street* exemplified the fiercely competitive behaviours and values of extreme forms of capitalism. To some extent this reflected Margaret Thatcher's infamous 1980s dictum 'There is no such thing as society', which in turn echoes the views of neo-liberalism champion Milton Friedman who described the growing demands in the 1970s for US business to have a social conscience as 'pure and unadulterated socialism'. He argued that 'business has a duty to make profit first; anything else will create confusion' (Friedman, 1984:17).

INDUSTRIAL RELATIONS

The development of this form of global capitalism was boosted after the economic crises of the 1970s by the Thatcherite project to transform the essentially adversarial nature of UK industrial relations, since this was thought to impede competitiveness. Labour flexibility is a key element of neo-liberal-inspired policies. In the UK, part of Mrs Thatcher's solution to increase UK competitiveness was to increase labour flexibility (Sennett, 2006). There was therefore a political imperative to reduce employment protections and to break the power of the trade unions. Since then, analysts have argued that the mainly collective industrial relations of the 1980s have been largely replaced by individualised HRM approaches to employee relations, including direct staff communications. Staff councils mostly find themselves impotent to protect 'workers' rights'. 'Partnership' working has been the *modus operandi* of union–management relations over the last decade and it will be interesting to see how well this will work as change looms large, particularly in the UK public sector.

Alongside this, the practice of management was pushed further to the forefront since efficient management was seen as a panacea for a number of economic ills, and the byword of the 1980s was that 'managers have the right to manage'. This led to the development of business schools and the installation of 'managerialism', which refers to the application of private sector management techniques and ideologies within the sphere of the public services and more broadly (Pollitt, 1993; Cutler and Waine, 1994; Clarke *et al*, 1994). High levels of unemployment during the 1990s and their power over hiring and firing decisions allowed managers to further embed managerialism and introduce more flexible structures. This also led to more confrontational styles of management practice across all sectors of the UK economy (Pollitt, 2003).

Since that time managerialism has been endorsed and furthered by the subsequent rise of the 'New Right' and pushed as a form of social domination. For instance, it is reflected in the political attempts under the UK's Labour Government (1997–2010) to achieve a closer functional relationship between the state and a 'modernising' of the public sector, as a result of which public sector institutions have been exposed to market conditions and have had new management structures and targets imposed upon them under the premise that this would lead to greater efficiency and cost-effectiveness within public services.

THE PURSUIT OF FLEXIBILITY

Market disciplines place pressure on organisations to react quickly and flexibly to market changes, and to find more cost-efficient ways of producing and selling goods and services. Since labour is usually considered the main production 'cost', employers will chase cheap labour wherever it is to be found and is not bounded by geography. There were of course alternative economic models to neo-liberal Anglo-American capitalism available to politicians in the 1980s. However, other (Social European) forms of capitalism afford more protection for workers and therefore were perceived to reduce flexibility (Hyman, 2008).

Developments in technology, such as the Internet and call centre technology, have enabled work to be parcelled up into outsource-able chunks of work and 'offshored' to parts of the world where skilled and semi-skilled labour is relatively inexpensive. British workers carrying out routine office work increasingly find their jobs at risk of being made obsolete by technological solutions. In a context where trade unions have little influence and where there are relatively few collective employment protections, British workers have become more vulnerable to redundancy and work intensification than other European workers (Hyman, 2008).

Alongside this managerial drive for flexibility and competitive advantage, new instrumental methodologies – such as total quality, continuous process improvement, and high-performance work practices such as teamworking – were introduced during the 1980s and 1990s to increase productivity gains. Hudson (1989) argues that the use of technology and such methodologies has resulted in employee deskilling and represents just a reworking of modernist production methods.

As the 'knowledge economy', with its new types of post-industrial firms, products and markets, began to take root in the UK during the 1990s, structural forms increasingly reflected aspirations to move beyond the 'modernist' era of large bureaucratic production to smaller, leaner 'post-modern' organisations with responsive and de-layered management structures (Marchington *et al*, 2005). These 'flatter' structures were promoted to workers as more democratic, enabling greater initiative, being freer, more flexible and participative, although the primary reason for de-layering, as many employees perceived it, was to achieve cost savings (Holbeche, 1996). The result of such changes, together with the advent of electronic communications, was that employees found their workloads expanding and managers struggled with ever wider spans of control.

The first decade of the twenty-first century has been described as the era of 'nimble' or 'agile' production (Francis, 2001), as organisations pursue ever greater flexibility and global reach. Technology is facilitating the rise of the virtual world and, thanks to a determination to use technology to replace expensive 'human resources', the nature of work and the workplace continue to be transformed. To service the '24/7' trading environment and the more personalised nature of customer provision, new and more fluid forms of organisation are emerging, with more diverse workforces and ways of working. The terms 'ambidextrous organisation' (Tushman and O'Reilly, 2004), 'high-performance' or 'high-commitment work' systems (Garvin and Klein, 1993; Pfeffer, 1998) and the 'boundaryless company' (Devanna and Tichy, 1990; Hirschhorn and Gilmore, 1992) all refer to the same kind of 'new' organisation, which is seen as being flexible and constantly changing.

Heckscher and Donnellon (1994) describe the ideal features of a post-bureaucratic organisation as follows: decisions are based on dialogue and consensus rather than authority and command; organisation is a network rather than a hierarchy, open at the boundaries. Such features imply that employees will be able to exercise agency since they will have access to the information and other resources required to enable them to exercise their judgement proactively on behalf of the organisation. The nature of management and leadership is more dispersed and democratic than in conventional hierarchies. However, such idealised templates tend to ignore the power politics which characterise human organisations. In this book we consider micro-politics to be an undercurrent flowing throughout, surfacing more explicitly in parts. These idealised templates also tend to ignore contextual factors such as the widening gap in pay ratios between the highest- and lowest-paid in organisations which has, in some cases, increased tenfold over the last three decades. Creating a sense of mutuality and common cause in such situations becomes more problematic (Hutton, 2010).

DESTABILISING THE EMPLOYMENT RELATIONSHIP

The white collar employment 'deal' or 'psychological contract' that was typical of bureaucratic organisations consisted of perceptions – of unwritten mutual expectations, risks and benefits – between employers and employees, such as good work in return for continued employment, and promotion based on seniority. Ongoing restructurings and the pursuit of labour flexibility over the last 30 years have largely undermined these expectations and resulted in a reshaping of the employment relationship. The resulting contract breaches, it is argued (Herriot and Pemberton, 1995), have destabilised the employment relationship since they have shaken the basis of trust and belief in the mutuality of interests between employers and employees.

For employees, flexibility can be a double-edged sword. Whereas many employees have actively sought to work flexibly, others have had flexibility imposed on them. Today's less secure employment arrangements and increased use by employers of flexible forms of labour – such as part-time, temporary, short-term or casual contracts – in response to market fluctuations, are reported to have led to a rise in job insecurity (Heery and Salmon, 2000). With respect to careers, individuals are expected to adapt to changes in work conditions, career structures, pension arrangements, job specifications and job locations. No longer able to rely on a full-time permanent job, workers are increasingly expected to take control of their own training and development needs in order to make themselves 'employable' and place themselves in the best position in the job market. The onus is on the individual to continuously update his or her portfolio of skills and embrace lifelong working. Thus the risks in the employment relationship pass to the employee, which is fine if the person has the skills and capabilities required to meet the changing and seemingly ever-increasing demands of employers, but those employees who cannot maintain the pace face what Sennett (2003: 83) describes as 'the spectre of uselessness'.

THE POWER OF TALENT

On the other hand, in organisations where the link between talent and business success is very visible and direct, some employees are able to exercise considerable influence over their employment relationship or 'deal' with their employer. In industries as diverse as construction, pharmaceuticals, defence and high technology there are serious shortfalls of available global talent, with even greater shortages predicted thanks to demographic trends.

Talent management is a high priority in companies such as Google, Tata and Microsoft, who source talent globally, using intelligence sources to obtain knowledge of where the best talent is to be found (Tansley *et al*, 2007). Many talent management processes are exclusive and focus on a privileged minority of high-potential employees. Employees increasingly want the same kind of individualised attention that customers receive, and skilled workers can and do exercise their options if they are not happy with their lot. In Chapter 13 Eddie Blass and Gill Maxwell explore more inclusive approaches to talent management which embrace a wider diversity of talent.

HR functions usually devise the employment deal or the 'employee value proposition' and, in common with other forms of branding, if the lived reality of the brand is different from the promise, the customer–employee goes elsewhere. In Chapter 14 Helen Francis and Martin Reddington describe a possible basis for delivering an authentic employee value proposition which is true to the brand promise. There is growing evidence that the criteria used by younger workers in particular to select their future employer include the chance for learning and growth, respect for them as individuals and company ethics and values, even more than the pay on offer (Erickson, 2010). In Chapter 15 Carole Parkes considers business ethics in the context of corporate social responsibility and explores the role played by organisational values in enhancing individual and organisational performance.

HRM AND MANAGERIALISM

In recent decades human resource management (HRM) has come to be the preferred international discourse to frame employment management issues. The field of HRM focuses on the study of the employment relationship and is involved in the management of people (Paauwe, 2007: 9). The nature of HRM is contested although there is some consensus that HRM is a business concept reflecting a mainly managerial view of the employment relationship, with theory, policies and practices geared to enabling organisations to achieve competitive advantage and high performance. One definition of HRM is (Price, 2003: 31):

> A philosophy of people management based on the belief that human resources are uniquely important to sustained business success. An organisation gains competitive advantage by using its people effectively, drawing on their expertise and ingenuity to meet clearly defined objectives. HRM is aimed at recruiting capable, flexible and committed people, managing and rewarding their performance and developing key competencies.

In American models of HRM the predominant view is unitarist – ie it assumes that giving primacy to business interests benefits both businesses and their employees. Such a view generally does not challenge economic growth as the purpose of all human endeavours, or the assumptions of functionalist human resource management. Unitarist views represent a legitimising management point of view (see Chapter 5). Critical scholars contend that human resource management (HRM) approaches are a managerial tool for controlling and managing the workforce in ways which entirely meet business needs but which appear less directive than the low-trust command-and-control structures of previous decades.

Similarly, mainstream human resource development (HRD) approaches are largely instrumental, with learning and development approaches designed to align employee skills to the needs of business. In Chapter 9 Alan Ramdhony offers a more critical perspective on HRD and presents the possibility of more employee-centred learning and development approaches. Moreover, HRD activities can be conceived of as tools to instil behavioural compliance with desired cultural norms. For instance, teamworking is one of a combination of HRM practices that broadly corresponds to so-called high-performance work systems. Critics argue that teamworking is 'the work ethic of a flexible political economy' (Sennett, 1998: 136) and a device for achieving compliance since it tends to suppress conflict. Wood (1999) argues that 'high-performance', 'high-involvement' and 'high-commitment' practices such as the development of shared visions, individualised reward and direct employee communications, are just another way for managers to gain control over labour through 'attitudinal restructuring' and the 'manipulation of meaning'.

A critical perspective therefore involves raising ethical concerns about the role played by HRM and HRD in the shaping of a new work culture characterised by flexibility, performativity and potential work intensification, in support of neo-liberal forms of capitalism.

SHIFTING HR DISCOURSE

In conventional terms HR's policies, processes and systems must ensure that people are employed in line with legal and business requirements. And of course HR's mechanisms for achieving this (often referred to as 'levers') – such as management development, reward, performance management, career development, employee communications and employee relations – are intended to ensure that organisations can attract, motivate and retain the talent needed to achieve competitive advantage through people. However, if HR 'levers' are used in a short-termist and instrumentalist way, working exclusively from a unitarist managerial agenda, tensions are likely to ensue – for instance, between productivity and well-being – which become competing goals.

Based on an analysis of large-scale British workplace data, Peccei (2004) questions whether the set of HR practices that are good for management – from the point of view of enhancing productivity, for example – are necessarily also equally good for employees in terms, for instance, of enhancing their well-being. HR practitioners must therefore deal with paradox and complexity on a daily basis and be guided by a philosophy and perspective which helps them deal with potential trade-offs in contemporary organisations between organisational performance and employee well-being.

PERFORMATIVITY

In particular, practices that are grouped in the mainstream human resource management literature under 'performance management' (Beardwell and Holden, 2001) appear to have a strong shaping effect on employee behaviours and, from a critical perspective, form part of an array of managerial domination over work. These include performance targets, appraisal interviews, 360-degree feedback, competence assessments, performance-related pay, peer appraisal, and others (Armstrong and Baron, 1998).

Over the last 20 years, the use of performance management has become normalised, particularly in medium-sized and large organisations (Bach, 2000). Contrary to the views put forward by many mainstream HRM accounts of performance management practices that stress the development of innate qualities of individuals, critical scholars argue that such approaches encourage the discursive shaping of the 'individual project' – ie employees self-regulate their attitudes and behaviours to be consistent with business needs (Townley, 1994, 1998, 2004). In performance appraisal discussions, for example, as employees recount and evaluate their work experiences and ambitions, they do so in a situation where they are observed and judged by others in social (power) relations. As a result, the employee's conception of the employment relationship shifts away from former collectivist ideas, toward a more individualised version, where the primary responsibility for performance lies with the employee and the primary risk in the employment relationship is theirs. In Chapter 12, Roger Cooper and Adrian Furnham explore the fundamentals of these processes and argue that a re-examination of their effects on employee behaviour is called for.

As Ball (2003) points out, there is a paradox in that the apparent move away from 'low-trust' methods of managerial control via high-commitment HRM, in which management responsibilities are delegated and initiative valued, has been simultaneously matched by the installation of very immediate surveillance and self-monitoring in the form of appraisals, etc, making employees subject to greater assessment and control. Smith and Reeves

(2006: 8) suggest that 'the drive to accountability in all corners of organisational life – what Michael Power calls an "audit explosion" – has meant that too many organisations are leaning too heavily on the rule-book to the detriment of professional intuition and ethical behaviour.' Ball (2003: 126) argues that 'the policy technologies of market, management and performativity leave no space for an autonomous or collective ethical self.'

Not only are employees expected to comply with increasing performance demands, they are expected to feel happy to do so. In Chapter 16 Chiara Amati and Chris Donegan consider the increase in interest in emotion in the workplace in recent years and bring a critical perspective to the happy-productive worker hypothesis. They raise questions about the use in practitioner circles of the term 'employee engagement' to describe all those HR initiatives aimed at retaining key employees, targeting key resources at 'talent' and raising performance by encouraging employees to 'engage' with the organisation and 'release their discretionary effort'. Staff surveys and specific employee engagement audits are often used as a means of gauging employees' opinion and management's being seen to listen. This point is examined further by Francis and Reddington in Chapter 14.

HR's role is therefore complex and potentially paradoxical since (Foley *et al*, 1999: 166) it

> reflects implicit issues of performativity, surveillance, information and communication technologies, empowerment, self-actualisation, the demise of hierarchies, individualism and instrumentality as well as aspects of consumerism and consumption-based values.

Many HR professionals are attracted to HR by the thought of working with people and helping them to have satisfying work lives. The HR function is the pivot point between managerial and employee interests. However, in its current state of evolution HR is more obviously an instrument of managerialism and must prioritise business interests. Yet HR is itself often criticised by line managers for not being helpful to the business, for perceived incompetence or for acting as 'company policeman'. For many HR professionals this creates cognitive dissonance since they find that the nature of what they are required to do is sometimes at odds with their personal values and motivations (Francis and Keegan, 2006).

REFLECTIVE ACTIVITIES

- To what extent do your own observations about HR's role align with mainstream or with critical perspectives on HRM/HRD?
- What is the evidence in support of your position? Where is the counter-evidence?

HR'S OWN CHANGE JOURNEY

HR's own change journey illustrates some of the challenges of adapting to changing business-driven requirements.

FROM PERSONNEL TO HR – WHAT'S IN A NAME?

After human resource management theory came to the fore as a subset of management theory from the late 1980s on, the Personnel function itself began a gradual transformation in its purpose, design and terminology. Terms such as 'Personnel' and its various sub-disciplines such as 'Industrial relations', 'Pay and benefits' and 'Training' were gradually replaced by 'Human Resources', 'Employee relations', 'Compensation and benefits', etc. This redesign was driven partly in response to the increasingly strident questioning by businesses of the value of having a specialist people function largely focused on administrative tasks. But this was more than a rebranding exercise. HR was to be fully aligned to the business to ensure that the human resource requirements of the business were met. In its quest to be seen as more business-like, Personnel's old concern for employee welfare largely dropped out of HR's discourse since it was deemed to be 'soft'. High-potential HR managers who were keen to make career progress made their mark by dealing with the 'tough stuff' such as industrial relations, and HR came to be firmly associated with management interests. With the decline of collective industrial relations, HR came to be aligned much more specifically to a unitarist, individualised framing of employee relations.

RE-ENGINEERING HR

The pace of HR's own structural transformation has accelerated over the last decade, due largely to Dave Ulrich's influential thought-leadership. In the light of today's fast-changing context, HR is increasingly urged to become more strategic, proactive, business-driven and specialist. Ulrich's 1997 HR role framework (1997) divided HR contributions along the axes of process–people, strategic–operational. The unitarist framing of the model emphasised the business elements over the 'people' elements. The strategic HR roles are defined as those of business partner and change agent, whereas the operational roles are those of 'employee champion' and infrastructure/administration. My consultancy experience suggests that many HR teams have in practice struggled to develop business partner and change agent roles and in many cases Ulrich's 'employee champion' role remains relatively neglected.

By finding alternative ways of delivering the operational elements of the role, so the theory goes, HR is freed up to make a more strategic contribution. This involves generating new models of service delivery and technical solutions, understanding the possible costs and return on investment of changes in operations. This is not just about streamlining HR to achieve cost-savings but also about understanding where and how to impact on operations in a measurably effective way, such that profitability, share price and price/earnings ratios can be directly improved as a result.

The commonest form of functional structure adopted in large organisations derives from the Ulrich-inspired functional roles framework often referred to as the 'three-legged stool' (ie shared services, business partners, centres of expertise and a small corporate centre concerned with executive pay, top-level succession planning, overall strategy alignment and employee relations). There are various delivery mechanisms – for instance, the shared services element may be outsourced, supported by technology-enabled employee and manager self-service tools, or offshored to an international service centre (see Chapter 8). In the latest iteration of HR transformation, 'business partner' roles are being split out into internal consultants (or junior business partners) who are embedded in the business, and strategic business partners, who often work offline. These may be HR directors or senior generalists responsible for leading a specific major change project, such as a merger integration or relocation exercise.

THE CHALLENGES OF TRANSFORMATION

However, this change journey has not been without its problems and subsequent transformations. One of the common issues relates to the lack of readiness or preparation of line managers to cope with the core aspects of people management now devolved back to them. In Chapter 10 John Castledine and Doug Renwick consider some of the challenges faced by line managers in shaping performance. Another early challenge was the potential for considerable role overlap between business partners and various internal experts, such as learning and development professionals, with ambiguity, for instance, over the question of who 'owns' the internal client. In some cases people have remained confused about what the role of 'business partner' really means. Consequently, despite the new structure, many HR practitioners have found themselves drawn back to their old roles where at least they knew what was expected and where they felt valued. Moreover, since the conventional HR career development path, moving from junior specialist to generalist, has largely disappeared, many professionals are struggling to navigate their way through other career routes which at this stage seem ill-defined (Tamkin *et al*, 2006).

Measurement is a key aspect of HRM and considerable quantities of mainstream research (largely from the UK and USA) have sought evidence on how HR practices:

- contribute to the bottom line, directly or indirectly, through the development and retention of 'human capital' (Huselid, 1995; Armstrong and Baron, 2007; Sparrow *et al*, 2010)
- link with performance (Paauwe, 2004; Purcell and Kinnie, 2006; Guest *et al*, 2003)
- link with sustainable high performance (Holbeche, 2005b)
- link with knowledge management (Evans, 2003).

Because responsibility for some HR processes is devolved back to line managers, the HR function is expected to make a more strategic contribution, including acting as change agent. Ironically, rather than freeing up HR to make that more strategic contribution, the process of HR transformation itself can often prove to be lengthy, expensive, and end up diverting HR teams from making the more strategic contribution their organisations need from them. In some cases, the re-engineering process has been so protracted that HR transformation has come to be seen as the end in itself rather than as a means to making a more strategic contribution. As Martin Reddington argues in Chapter 8, HR teams leading such transformation do not need to fall into these traps and, as Peter Reilly discusses in Chapter 7, if HR is to rise to the challenge of these new roles, HR must itself be up-skilled.

A BUSINESS DISCIPLINE?

More recently the HR profession has sought to become recognised as a business contributor in its own right. HR professional bodies such as the UK and Ireland's CIPD, and the Strategic HRM Society (SHRM) in the USA are keen for HR to step up to the mark and make a positive difference to the future of their organisations. The CIPD construes HR's role as broadening from being about 'people' to 'people and the organisation' and has redesigned its professional standards accordingly.

Ulrich's own thinking about what HR should contribute has moved on since 1997. In his revised model of HR roles (with Wayne Brockbank, 2005), Ulrich argues that HR leaders must grasp and master the concept of value, deliver value-adding services, lead in the development of knowledge capital, have deep functional expertise, be an active advocate for employees, and be a strategic partner (which encompasses the change agent role). Although still heavily unitarist, there is an increasing focus on tailoring services to meet the needs of various stakeholders:

> Value in this light is defined by the receiver more than the giver. HR professionals add value when their work helps someone reach their goals. It is not the design of a program or declaration of policy that matters most, but what recipients gain from these actions. In a world of increasingly scarce resources, activities that fail to add value are not worth pursuing. (Ulrich and Brockbank, 2005: 2)

By implication HR must prioritise its efforts to the needs of those stakeholders which count the most, and the authors argue that in designing HR strategies professionals should work back from the needs of customers and design processes to meet those needs.

A CHANGING AGENDA?

However, we are perhaps at a point of inflexion in the development of the function where the nature, purpose and future contribution of HR needs to be called into question. At one level, HR's core role is to ensure that the organisation has the 'right' people working in the 'right' ways to produce high performance in the short term. Of course, what 'right' means in any given context will be specific to the organisation and the challenges it faces. In light of today's ever more fluid organisational boundaries, diverse employment relationships and the context of ongoing change, talent and culture are intertwined.

But to contribute to a new form of organisational effectiveness HR must look beyond the short term and take into account what is happening beyond organisational boundaries, since, as Caldwell (2005: 111) comments,

> without judgements about the rational intent, or moral purpose of knowledge and the role of agency in organisations, we can rarely have the complacent assurance that our actions are ethical rather than another face of power.

As Carole Parkes observes in Chapter 12, in today's more fluid and turbulent politico-economic environment, organisations are themselves increasingly likely to be held to account for their activities. The consequences of the ongoing economic malaise which began with the banking crisis in 2007 continue to emerge. In many countries public finances are under great strain, and in the UK there are concerns about high levels of unemployment and the increasing difficulties for young people seeking to enter today's tight employment market, with growing fears of an emerging underclass of people who will never enter employment at all. Public sector spending cuts over the next few years are likely to raise unemployment levels further and may lead to growing public protest.

The economic crisis has also brought workplace practice into high profile, such as the morality of rewarding executive failure, or devising reward policies which encourage short-termist behaviour with no thought for any consequences beyond profit. Increasingly, technology is enabling collective protest and those who profit by exploiting others are unlikely to continue to have things their own way. As events of the 'Arab Spring' of 2011 illustrate, collective action is facilitated through the use of social media, and as a number of corporations have already discovered, disgruntled employees use social media to ensure that company brands are also tarnished (Bareto, 2009). These and other risks relating to people are discussed in the last chapter. In such a context, greater transparency is demanded about how organisations operate, about the nature of executive leadership decision-making and rewards. HR is expected to exercise 'stewardship', actively ensuring effective governance and ethical practice (Sears, 2010).

As the professional function with overall responsibility for the people management within organisations, HR's own role must evolve rapidly to address these challenges. Building more equitable and ethical organisational practices, and cultures conducive to high performance and innovation, requires a different level of contribution. HR should use its conventional tools, such as workforce planning and organisational design, to strategically develop more diverse workforces that can proactively address future challenges (see Chapter 11).

If employees are to be able to exercise greater agency, they need to work with the 'right' kinds of management and leadership who can develop change-able, healthy organisations. HR should work to improve the quality of leadership by selecting and developing cadres of progressive managers who can bring the best out of people, including individuals and groups who work on different forms of contract, in different time zones and whom they may have never met. In these days of 'more with less', HR must work out how to stimulate dispersed leadership at all levels. They must enable greater involvement by employees in authentic dialogue, as John Purcell points out in Chapter 6.

People want to be part of something they find meaningful and, as Francis and Reddington point out in Chapter 14, the employer brand can be a powerful source of employee identification or cynicism. Interestingly, in one of his more recent books Dave Ulrich (2010) examines the alienation of employees in today's workplace and their search for more meaning at work. Rather than pursuing potentially trite employee engagement initiatives, HR should perhaps work to unblock the barriers to people's feeling genuine common cause with their employer, and seek to create a more mutual employment relationship. HR practitioners must understand and use political influence constructively to prepare the ground for such shifts in mindset and practice, and model the way forward.

THE JOHN LEWIS PARTNERSHIP

CASE STUDY

One company that appears to be able to maintain employee engagement, even in today's difficult economic climate, is the John Lewis Partnership. In successive polls by retail professions, John Lewis Partnership, or its supermarket chain Waitrose, usually comes at or near the top of 'favourite retailer' categories. The Partnership's 'spirit' is based on four principles:

- ensuring that the happiness of partners is at the centre of everything we do

- building a sustainable business through profit and growth

- serving our customers to the very best of our ability

- caring about our communities and our environment.

John Lewis paid its 70,000 staff their annual bonus in 2009, despite the challenging trading conditions. Staff members ('partners') were delighted to receive

the bonus, despite the bonus pot having decreased by a third, from £180 million in 2007 to £125.5 million in 2008, due to the effects of the recession on profits, which were reported to have fallen by 26% in 2008 to £279.6 million. As they collectively own John Lewis Partnership, all staff receive the same percentage annual bonus (13% in 2009), which is equivalent to just under seven weeks' pay for Waitrose and John Lewis department store employees.

Rewarding employees for their hard work with the bonus is based on the profit-sharing philosophy of John Lewis. Employees celebrated receiving a bonus in the midst of the economic situation. By being true to their principles, John Lewis Partnership is likely to maintain employee trust.

Source: based on 'John Lewis staff delighted with 13% bonus' by Zoe Wood and Graeme Wearden, *The Guardian*, 11 March 2009

While it may be argued that the emphasis on mutuality of risk and reward reflects the ownership structure of the John Lewis Partnership (see the case study), I argue that the characteristic of maintaining faith with employees, and attempting to create a genuinely shared agenda, will assist employee engagement in any organisational context.

THE NEED FOR NEW SKILLS

These new forms of contribution require HR practitioners to expand their repertoire of skills, behaviours and experience – to develop and apply new capabilities with impact and agility to the emerging roles of:

- organisational *prospector* – able to scan and interpret this changing business landscape, anticipate future workforce needs and create employee value propositions which attract and retain skilled employees
- organisational *architect* – designing and enabling organisational agility, 'future-proofing' their organisations by developing flexible structures, supporting behavioural shifts, developing ethical leadership and creating healthy, self-renewing organisation cultures in which employees can experience well-being and exercise agency

- *developer of individual and organisational capability* – growing people's skills, creating working conditions which stimulate people to release their discretionary effort, designing and implementing processes by which their efforts are translated into knowledge capital
- *change agent* – able to initiate and bring about the shifts their organisations need to make. HR practitioners must understand and be able to use political influence constructively to prepare the ground for such shifts in mindset and practice, and model the way forward.

And in today's economic climate this more strategic contribution from HR will be needed more than ever. How well equipped is HR for this role? Here's the rub. For years HR has been criticised for being too reactive and internally focused. Some of the main reported challenges to delivering this strategic agenda include a lack of HR capability, ineffective technology, difficulties in managing the 'push' from the leadership team and the 'pull' from line managers and a lack of ability to manage change within the HR function (Holbeche, 2009). It is in the areas of change management, culture change and organisational design that many senior HR practitioners struggle and where HR's value is most put to the test. This is not surprising in that, because HR's role is evolving rapidly, practitioners' previous career experience and professional development may not have equipped them for these tasks.

THE CHALLENGES OF CHANGE

The economic crisis has served to highlight what we already knew – that change will be an ongoing feature of organisational life from now on. However, over 70% of conventional change efforts are reported to fail. A 2008 study found that companies surveyed in the UK lost £1.7 billion a year from failed change initiatives, while in companies across Western Europe, approximately 10 billion euros per year are being wasted on ineffective business process change projects (Logica Management Consulting and the Economist Intelligence Unit, 2008).

The main causes of change failure usually relate to the way the process of change is understood and managed. More often than not, top-down business change processes drain the very lifeblood from organisations – ie the commitment, discretionary effort and well-being of employees, on which sustainable performance depends. Deep organisational changes have a profound impact on people within organisations. Especially if change results in job losses, the employment relationship between employers and employees can be seriously damaged. The 'survivors' of change are usually beset by the complexities of working life today – the fast pace of change, long working hours, heavy workloads, ambiguities over resources and accountabilities, the common mismatch of employee and organisational needs – which prevent the positive change outcomes from becoming embedded.

Potentially, this kind of culture has important effects on the way in which people look upon their working life. Madeleine Bunting (2004) queries why employees appear to have acquiesced in these working conditions, becoming 'willing slaves' to the demands of employers. She argues that work has taken over our consciousness, creating psychological hardships such as stress and burnout. The consequence, Bunting argues, is that other aspects of our lives suffer, such as family relationships.

Evidence about the impact of organisational change can be found in a CIPD survey of 4,000 UK employees (McCartney and Willmott, 2010). More people (42%) reported excessive pressures at work, compared to six months earlier (38%), and employees were also more likely to say they had seen increases in stress and conflict at work, as well as bullying by line managers. Some 56% of respondents reported that they were anxious about the future. Although people may be hanging on to their jobs in these tough times, how they feel about the way change is managed will affect whether they want to stay or leave when growth returns.

Worse still, failed change efforts may leave behind scar tissue in the form of resentful, cynical and disengaged 'survivor' employees who no longer trust the organisation or its leaders and are unlikely to give of their best to the organisation in future (Holbeche, 2005a). The pursuit of the holy grail of 'employee engagement' by many HR teams in recent years is perhaps symptomatic of a misaligned employment relationship and employee alienation resulting from one-sided change experiences. Perhaps for these reasons, it seems genuinely difficult for many organisations to get onto the 'front foot' and proactively shape the context they are operating in.

If they are to survive and thrive, organisations will need to be 'change-able' – ie agile and capable of ongoing change while also improving performance (Holbeche, 2005a). This change capability requires forward-looking management teams, swift and competent decision-making processes, a happy blend of innovation and risk management and, above all, flexible, resilient and 'engaged' employees.

In the light of the context, people who are able to change organisations to make them more effective and to provide participants in organisations with a higher quality of experience are desperately needed. That's why CEOs are looking to HR to make a more effective contribution to managing change. In particular, they want senior HR professionals' advice, expertise and practical help in change management, culture change, organisation (re)design – all of which requires at least an understanding of, if not deep expertise in, organisation development (Cheung-Judge and Holbeche, 2011).

PARTNERSHIP BETWEEN HR AND OD

But HR practitioners do not have to be the real change experts. In truly change-able organisations there is usually a powerful and effective partnership at work. This consists of strong line leadership (the real OD practitioners), OD and HR experts working together to achieve both the short-term requirements for aligning people and resources with business goals while also working towards the longer-term goal of building future organisational capability.

Why is this partnership so effective? HR and OD bring complementary skills and strengths. Although HR practitioners may not necessarily be change experts, their policies and practices are a key factor in building 'great places to work' which are both affordable to the business and attractive to the 'right' employees. HR systems such as reward are a means of embedding new behaviours. Since even the most talented employee is unlikely to flourish in the wrong context, with its systemic perspective OD can help line managers and their teams to improve working conditions and build high-performance climates. With its reflexive methodologies, OD can help people to make sense of complexity.

OD is a key factor in successful implementation of large-scale organisational changes such as mergers, acquisitions, downsizings, and restructurings – areas in which senior HR professionals are increasingly directly involved and/or expected to take a lead. Conventional approaches to change management tend to neglect the people aspects of change, and a key argument presented by authors in this book is that new approaches to OD are more likely to succeed precisely because they do take employees' needs and personal reactions into account. Even though mainstream OD, like mainstream HRM and HRD, may follow a unitarist agenda, its philosophy and values are democratic and humanist and its methodologies are essentially pluralist. The direction may be set by management but employees are involved in decisions over implementation. 'New' OD is more enabling of 'bottom-up' strategic development as well as implementation – as Naomi Stanford discusses in the next chapter.

In some situations it may be enough for HR to carry out the 'day job' within an OD frame of understanding. In more complex situations it will be useful for HR practitioners to consult with OD specialists and/or work alongside them to deliver the desired outcomes. In major change scenarios, HR may be wise to contract with OD specialists to manage the change process and jointly seek to deliver the change outcomes. In all cases HR needs to work with senior management to help them to become effective commissioners of

OD, ensuring that business leaders also retain a strong commitment to the change effort once it is under way. In Chapter 4 Mark Withers demonstrates how HR and OD feed into organisational strategies and illustrates the practical process and benefits of strategy development with several case study examples.

CHALLENGES OF PARTNERSHIP?

In theory, working together should be easy for HR and OD specialists. For a start they have a number of things in common and, by working together, they can complement the work of the CEO – whose focus in systems thinking terms is typically on the system input – ie the changing market demands and other external environmental factors, and the output, or results. HR and OD work on the throughput: what happens within the organisational system. Their focus is on how this can be improved to make sure that the output matches the input. But there are also real differences between the disciplines which can produce tensions and misunderstandings.

OD's strong humanistic, democratic values and participative methodologies place emphasis upon the need for change not to be something done 'to' people but done 'with' people (Margulies and Raia, 1984). In contrast, HR may perhaps have lost sight of its original values and focus on people's well-being and employee relations somewhere along its functional transformation journey. Indeed, in times of industrial strife or when downsizings are planned, HR is more firmly identified with business interests as reflected in HR discourse. In today's more challenging employee relations climate, people's needs and issues are likely to return to prominence. If positive employee relations are to be sustained through change, HR needs to regain its identity as 'people champion' alongside that of 'organisational champion'.

Similarly, whereas OD is a long-range effort to improve an organisation's problem-solving processes (French and Bell, 1999), HRM's focus is on aligning HR practices and people processes to the requirements of the short-term business agenda. HR's traditional responsibility for ensuring that people are employed in legally compliant ways can sometimes lead to HR's being perceived as 'the function which says no'. In an increasingly complex regulatory and legislative environment, it will be crucial that HR can cope with paradox, both keeping the organisation legal and also ensuring that it can achieve what it needs to do legally, thus moving from 'business preventer' to 'business enabler' status.

The disciplines of OD and HR have followed somewhat different development paths and tend to attract different types of people. As is discussed in Chapter 3, OD specialist expertise is in process, and the role of the OD specialist is that of change agent and catalyst, process expert and helper, applying their skills real-time to group or business-level issues. This may involve challenging senior players, asking difficult questions, using disruptive or large-scale technologies to surface underlying issues, working with clients to diagnose issues and create commitment to solutions. HR in contrast relies more on content expertise which is the function's traditional differential contribution to organisational success. Practitioners tend to play an advisory role, giving direct guidance on employee cases.

As embedded business partner HR may find it difficult to challenge senior management behaviour. OD professionals may or may not be internal to the business. If internal, they need to be able to operate as if from an external consultancy perspective, remaining 'apart' while within the system in order to be able to challenge effectively. For instance, culture change often involves uncovering embedded assumptions, surfacing conflict and working with leaders at all levels to find more constructive ways of working. They need to work closely with the CEO and their credibility and influence must be strong. If HR and OD are working closely together, surfacing and resolving tensions, there is a strong possibility of mutual learning and the real embedding of positive change.

By working closely with OD colleagues, HR professionals can use HR processes more deliberately to create cultures conducive to high performance and employee engagement

– for instance, by rewarding such practices as knowledge creation and sharing and thus creating mutual benefits for employees and organisations (Holbeche, 2005b). OD's participative methods help engage people and shift mindsets. Such active involvement and participation implies mutuality of interest and concern. Rather than passive recipients, employees become active agents of change. That is because they feel well-informed, that their voice is heard and valued and that they have opportunities to grow – classic ingredients of 'employee engagement' and positive psychological contracts.

A MORE MUTUAL EMPLOYMENT RELATIONSHIP

For a sustainable employment relationship, the 'deal' with employees must deliver win/win outcomes. Paauwe (2009) argues that understanding the potentially differing interests of the various stakeholders, and attending to the concerns and well-being of employees, will be crucial to the development of real performance. Such a 'value-laden' pluralistic approach, underpinned by a moral concern for reciprocity, could bring real benefits, even in difficult times.

Purcell *et al's* (2009) study of links between HRM and high performance considers what appears to trigger employees – individually and collectively – to give or withdraw the discretionary effort so crucial to performance. Their AMO (Ability, Motivation and Opportunity) framework has its origins in industrial/organisational psychology and takes various aspects of employee well-being into account. A key factor is job design and how much 'elbow room' employees experience through which they can stretch their limits through multi-skilling, job rotation, career development, training and development.

HR needs to take a leadership stance in crafting this new deal with employees. A positive work environment, the chance for learning and growth, appropriate reward and recognition including work–life balance are important elements (see Chapter 14). Work and learning should be integrated and people should be given opportunities for development through role design and job stretch. For some employees, today's challenges can lead to new career tracks, taking their development in exciting new directions, opening up new networks and opportunities to achieve. Encouragingly, even in a cost-constrained context, many employers remain focused on developing talent since they know that this enables people to give of their best and achieve maximum potential, on which future success depends.

If people have both the tools they need to manage themselves better and good support from the right kinds of management, the transitions of change can be very positive. In return, organisations achieve superior and sustained performance, adaptability and innovative competitive edge.

CONCLUSION

New OE aspires towards sustainable outcomes. And although there may be no universal 'ideal' organisational culture, my own research (Holbeche, 2005a) suggests that sustainable outcomes are more likely in organisations with change-able (ie flexible and resilient), knowledge-rich cultures which are conducive to innovation and performance and employees who are highly committed and engaged. Such organisations are likely to be values-based, great places to work, in which both employee well-being and organisational performance are prized and enabled.

As HR's role becomes increasingly transformational, the adoption of an OD perspective to HR work should assist the development of new forms of organisational effectiveness, characterised by more mutual employment relationships, longer-term perspectives and 'an HR system not only based on added value, but also on moral values' (Paauwe, 2009: 11).

Embracing such an approach will require a shift in the discourse (and therefore priorities and practice) of HR 'business partners'. This will involve reconciling a range of dilemmas and paradoxes such as fulfilling short-term requirements and also meeting longer-term organisational needs, focusing on local activities and also on corporate integration. This both/and strategic tension will require HR practitioners to combine pragmatism and a can-do approach with a more strategic orientation – to both provide excellent short-term delivery and also drive a longer-term agenda informed by a perspective on what will equip the organisation for future success.

That is why it is crucial that HR understands OD, and why collaboration is needed between OD, the change specialists and HR, the expert function on the people aspects of organisations. In other words, as Caldwell (2005: 111) points out,

> Confronted with these dilemmas and their implications, the hybrid and eclectic inter-disciplinary legacy of organisational change theories and change agency practices must affirm the possibility of a positive middle way between competing and increas-ingly fragmented discourses and paradigms for managing change. For without this belief in the mediation of knowledge to inform fragile ideals of 'rational' dialogue, practice and moral action in the face of organisational complexity, risk and uncer-tainty, all our human aspirations for change may lose their vital centre of gravity: *the hope that we can make a difference.*

REFLECTIVE ACTIVITIES

- To what extent do you agree that we have reached a point of inflexion in HR's development? What reasons do you have to explain your point of view?

- How could HR be relabelled, moving away from the resource metaphor?

- What do you consider the main challenges are likely to be in developing a more 'genuinely mutual' employment relationship between employers and employees?

EXPLORE FURTHER

Cheung-Judge, M.-Y. and Holbeche, L. S. (2011) *Organization Development: A practitioner guide.* London: Kogan Page. An overview and primer on the history, nature, processes and value of OD, together with chapters examining HR's growing responsibilities for OD processes of change management, organisation design, culture change and leadership.

Holbeche, L. S. and Matthews, G. (2012) *Engaged: Unleashing your organizations potential through employee engagement.* Chichester: John Wiley & Sons.

Inkson, K. (2008) 'Are humans resources?' *Career Development International,* Vol.13, No.3: 270–9. A good overview of the managerial nature and consequences of the HRM discourse.

Isles, N. (2010) *The Good Work Guide: How to make organizations fairer and more effective.* London: Earthscan. An inspirational introduction to a philosophy of organisation and people management based on principles of voice and equity.

Johnson, J. L. and O'Leary, A. M. (2003) 'The effects of psychological contract breach and organizational cynicism: not all social exchange violations are created equal', *Journal of Organizational Behavior,* Vol.24, Issues, August: 627–47. Outlines the damaging consequences for all concerned of ignoring the impact of change on employees.

To take stock of your organisation's culture, the Cultural Indicators tool (Tool 43) in the CIPD's *Organisational Development and Change* Toolkit can be helpful. This comprises a way of describing an organisation's culture with reference to the current position, to what should continue and be reinforced, and to what should be introduced for the first time or stopped altogether.

REFERENCES

Armstrong, M. and Baron, A. (1998) *Performance Management: The new realities (Developing practice)*. London: Chartered Institute of Personnel and Development (CIPD).

Armstrong, M. and Baron, A. (2007) *Human Capital Management: Achieving added value through people*. London: Kogan Page.

Bach S. (2000) 'Performance management', in Bach S. and Sisson K. (eds) *Personnel Management: A comprehensive guide to theory and practice*. Oxford: Blackwell.

Ball, S. J. (2003) 'The teacher's soul and the terrors of performativity', *Education Policy*, Vol.18, No.2: 215–28.

Bareto, M. (2009) 'Domino's Pizza YouTube video scandal: what to learn from it', *New Media Tips*, LabNotes, 16 April.

Beardwell, I. and Holden, L. (2001) *Human Resource Management: A contemporary approach*, 3rd edition. London: Financial Times.

Boselie, P., Brewster, C. and Paauwe, J. (2009) 'In search of balance: managing the dualities of HRM: an overview of the issues', *Personnel Review*, Vol.38. No.5: 461–71.

Boselie, P., Dietz, G. and Boon, C. (2005) 'Commonalities and contradictions in research on human resource management and performance', *Human Resource Management Journal*, Vol.13, No.3: 67–94.

Bunting, M. (2004) *Willing Slaves: How the overwork culture is ruling our lives*. London: HarperCollins.

Caldwell, R. (2005) 'Things fall apart? Discourses on agency and change in organizations', *Human Relations*, Vol.58, No.1: 83–111.

Clarke, J., Cochrane, A. and McLaughlin, E. (eds) (1994) *Managing Social Policy*. London: Sage.

Conway, E. and Monks, K. (2009) 'Unravelling the complexities of high commitment: an employee level analysis', *Human Resource Management*, Vol.19, No.2: 140–58.

Cutler, T. and Waine, B. (1994) *Managing the Welfare State*. Oxford: Berg.

Devanna, M. and Tichy, N. (1990) 'Creating the competitive organization of the 21st century: The boundaryless corporation', *Human Resource Management*, Vol.29, No.4, Winter: 455–71.

Dunn, S. (1990) 'Root metaphor in the old and new industrial relations', *British Journal of Industrial Relations*, Vol.28: 1–31.

Erickson, T. (2010) *What's Next, Gen X? Keeping up, moving ahead, and getting the career you want*. Boston, MA: Harvard Business Press.

Evans, C. (2003) *Managing for Knowledge: HR's strategic role*. Oxford: Butterworth-Heinemann.

Foley, M., Maxwell, G. and McGillivray, D. (1999) 'The UK context of workplace empowerment: debating HRM and post-modernity', *Participation and Empowerment: an International Journal*, Vol.7, No.6: 163–77.

Francis, D. (2001) 'Managing people in agile organisations', in *Agile Manufacturing: The 21st-century competitive strategy*. Amsterdam: Elsevier Science.

Francis, H. and Keegan, A. (2006) 'The changing face of HR: in search of balance', *Human Resource Management Journal*, Vol.16, No.3: 231–49.

Francis, H. and Sinclair, J. (2003) 'A processual analysis of HRM-based change', *Organization*, Vol.10, No.4: 685–706.

French, W. and Bell, C. (1999) *Organization Development: Behavioral science interventions for organization improvement*, 6th edition. New Jersey: Prentice Hall.

Friedman, M. (1984) 'The social responsibility of business is to increase its profits', *New York Times*, 13 September, p.17.

Gamble, A. (2009) *The Spectre at the Feast: Capitalist crisis and the politics of recession*. London: Palgrave Macmillan.

Garvin, D. A. and Klein, N. (1993) 'A note on high-commitment work systems', *Harvard Business Review*, 1 April.

Guest, D. E. and Conway, N. (2001) *Employer Perceptions of the Psychological Contract*. London: Chartered Institute of Personnel and Development (CIPD).

Guest, D. E., Michie, J., Conway, N. and Sheehan, M. (2003) 'Human resource management and corporate performance in the UK', *British Journal of Industrial Relations*, Vol.41, No.2: 291–314.

Heckscher, C. and Donnellon, A. M. (eds) (1994) *The Post-Bureaucratic Organization*. London: Sage.

Heery, E. and Salmon, J. (2000) 'The insecurity thesis', in Heery, E. and Salmon, J. (eds) *The Insecure Workforce*. London: Routledge.

Herriot, P. and Pemberton, C. (1995) *New Deals: The revolution in managerial careers*. Chichester: Wiley.

Hirschhorn, L. and Gilmore, T. (1992) 'The new boundaries of the "boundaryless company"', *Harvard Business Review*, Vol.70, No.3: 104–15.

Holbeche, L. S. (1996) *Career Development in Flatter Structures*. Horsham: Roffey Park Institute.

Holbeche, L. S. (2005a) *Understanding Change*. Oxford: Butterworth-Heinemann.

Holbeche, L. S. (2005b) *The High Performance Organization: Creating dynamic stability and sustainable success*. Oxford: Butterworth-Heinemann.

Holbeche, L. S. (2009) *HR Leadership*. Oxford: Butterworth-Heinemann.

Hudson, R. (1989) 'Labour market changes and new forms of work in old industrial regions', *Environment and Planning Society and Space*, Vol.7: 5–30.

Huselid, M. (1995) 'The impact of human resource management practices on turnover, productivity, and corporate performance', *Academy of Management Journal*, Vol.38, No.3: 635–72.

Hutton, W. (2010) *Them and Us: Politics, greed and inequality – why we need a fair society*. New York: Little, Brown.

Hyman, J. I., Scholarios, D. and Baldry, C. (2005) 'Getting on, or getting by', *Work, Employment and Society*, Vol.19, No.4, December: 705–25.

Hyman, R. (2008) 'Britain and the European Social Model: capitalism against capitalism', IES Working Paper, WS 19. Brighton: IES.

Keenoy, T. (2009) 'Human resource management', in Alvesson, M., Bridgman, T. and Willmott, H. (eds) *The Oxford Handbook of Critical Management Studies*. Oxford: Oxford University Press.

Kinnie, N., Hutchinson, S., Purcell, J., Rayton, B. and Swart, J. (2005) 'Satisfaction with HR practices and commitment to the organisation: why one size does not fit all', *Human Resource Management Journal*, Vol.15, No.4: 9–29.

Logica Business Consulting and Economist Intelligence Unit (2008): *How to maximise the value of your business process change investments*, Logica Business Consulting.

McCartney, C. and Willmott, B. (2010) *The Employee Outlook*. London: Chartered Institute of Personnel and Development (CIPD).

Marchington, M. P., Grimshaw, D., Rubery, J. and Willmott, H. (2005) *Fragmenting Work: Blurring organizational boundaries and disordering hierarchies*. Oxford: Oxford University Press.

Margulies, M. and Raia, A. P. (1984) 'The politics of organization development', in Hill, R. A. (ed.) *The Best of Organization Development*. Alexandria, VA: American Society for Training and Development.

Marquand, D. (2008) 'Never mind the role of the state', *The Guardian*, 11 December.

Paauwe, J. (2004) *HRM and Performance; Achieving Long-Term Viability*. Oxford. Oxford University Press.

Paauwe, J. (2007) 'HRM and performance: in search of balance'. Inaugural address as Professor of Human Resource Management at the Department of HR Studies at Tilburg University, the Netherlands.

Paauwe, J. (2009) 'HRM and performance: achievements, methodological issues and prospects', *Journal of Management Studies*, Vol.46: 129–42.

Peccei, R. (2004) *Human Resource Management and the Search for the Happy Workplace*. Rotterdam: Erasmus Research Institute of Management.

Peston, R. (2008) *Who Runs Britain?* London: Hodder & Stoughton.

Pfeffer, J. (1998) *The Human Equation: Building profits by putting people first.* Boston, MA: Harvard Business School Press.

Pollitt, C. (1993) *Managerialism and the Public Services: Cuts or cultural change in the 1990s?* Oxford: Blackwell Business.

Pollitt, C. (2003) *Managerialism and the Public Service: The Anglo-American experience*, 2nd edition. Oxford: Blackwell.

Power, M. (2001) *The Audit Society: The rituals of verification.* Oxford: Oxford University Press.

Price, A. (2003) *Human Resource Management in a Business Context.* Harlow: Thomson Learning.

Purcell, J. and Kinnie, N. (2006) 'HRM and business performance', in Boxall, P., Purcell, J. and Wright, P. (eds) *The Oxford Handbook of Human Resource Management.* Oxford: Oxford University Press.

Purcell, J., Kinnie, N., Swart, J., Rayton, B. and Hutchinson, S. (2009) *People Management and Performance.* Abingdon: Routledge.

Sears, L. (2010) *Next Generation HR. Time for a change: towards a next generation for HR.* London: Chartered Institute of Personnel and Development (CIPD).

Sennett, R. (1998) *The Corrosion of Character: Personal consequences of work in the New Capitalism.* New York: W. W. Norton.

Sennett, R. (2003) *Respect, in an Age of Inequality.* New York: W. W. Norton.

Sennett, R. (2006) *The Culture of the New Capitalism.* New Haven, CT: Yale University Press.

Smith, E. and Reeves, R. (2006) *Papering Over the Cracks? Rules, regulation and real trust.* London: Work Foundation.

Sparrow, P., Hird, M., Hesketh, A. and Cooper, C. (2010) *Leading HR.* Basingstoke: Palgrave Macmillan.

Tamkin, P., Reilly, P. A. and Hirsh, W. (2006) *Managing and Developing HR Careers: Emerging trends and issues.* London: Chartered Institute of Personnel and Development (CIPD).

Tansley, C., Turner, P. A., Foster, C., Harris, L. M., Stewart, J., Sempik, A. and Williams, H. (2007) *Talent: Strategy, management, measurement.* London: Chartered Institute of Personnel and Development (CIPD).

Townley, B. (1994) *Reframing Human Resource Management: Power, ethics and the subject at work.* London: Sage.

Townley, B. (1998) 'Beyond good and evil: depth and division in the management of human resources', in McKinlay, A. and Starkey, K. (eds) *Foucault, Management and Organization Theory.* London: Sage.

Townley, B. (2004) 'Managerial technologies, ethics and management', *Journal of Management Studies*, Vol.41, No.3: 425–45.

Tushman, M. L. and O'Reilly, C. A. (2004) 'Ambidextrous organization', *Harvard Business Review*, 1 April.

Ulrich, D. (1997) *Human Resource Champions: The next agenda for adding value and delivering results.* Boston, MA: Harvard Business School Press.

Ulrich, D. and Brockbank, W. (2005) *The HR Value Proposition.* Boston, MA: Harvard Business School Press.

Ulrich, D., Ulrich, W. and Goldsmith, M. (2010) *The Why of Work: How great leaders build abundant organizations that win.* New York/London: McGraw-Hill Professional.

Watson, T. J. (2010) 'Critical social science, pragmatism and the realities of HRM', *International Journal of Human Resource Management*, Vol.26, No.6, May: 915–31.

Wong, W., Sullivan, J., Blazey, L., Tamkin, P. and Pearson, G. (2009) *The Deal in 2020.* London: Work Foundation.

Wood, S. (1999) 'Human resource management and performance', *International Journal of Management Reviews*, Vol.1, No.4: 367–413.

Wright, P. M. and Snell, S. A. (2005) 'Partner or guardian?', *Human Resource Management*, Vol.44, Summer: 177–82.

CHAPTER 3

The Historical and Theoretical Background to Organisational Development

Naomi Stanford

CHAPTER OVERVIEW

This chapter examines the historical and theoretical background to organisation development from the mid-1940s – which marked the advent of the discipline – to the present day. Following this, there is discussion on the scope and nature of OD, and an outline of the typical phases of OD interventions. The author draws on her consultancy experience to present some methods of OD intervention, including process consulting, appreciative inquiry and action research. An explanation of the relationship between organisation development and organisation design clarifies how the two ODs partner each other in sustaining organisational capability.

LEARNING OBJECTIVES

By the end of this chapter the reader should be able to:

- trace the path that organisation development has taken to date, understand why this is the case, and form a view on where it may go in the future
- define organisation development, its scope, sphere of influence and operation
- work with a systematic approach to an OD intervention
- explain the relationship between organisation design and organisation development – to the extent of being able to argue for a combined organisation development and organisation design approach to a proposed change.

INTRODUCTION

New OE takes a cross-disciplinary perspective on people and organisation, requiring practitioners to develop a good understanding of the purpose and scope of organisation development. This chapter outlines some of the core historic/underpinning theories and names the founders of organisation development (OD). It develops a perspective on the definitions of organisation development – why there are so many, what their similarities and differences are, and why these definitions matter. The initial overview of theoretical developments does not include detailed literature references. These follow later in the chapter.

The chapter examines OD's scope and considers the type of questions practitioners are typically asked to address. It also outlines the OD phases and methods of interventions. It first considers the classic consulting sequence, the various levels of intervention – individual, management, group and whole organisation. The discussion then moves to some of the tools and techniques commonly used within each phase, including some specific approaches: action research, appreciative inquiry, storytelling and Future Search conferences.

The chapter provides a perspective on the relationship of organisation development to organisation design. The emphasis is on the complementarities of the 'soft' behaviourally based approaches of organisation development and the 'hard' business systems, processes, structures and measures of organisation design. The discussion highlights how both are necessary to the effective functioning of an organisation, in the same way that learning, nutrition and fitness activity (development) are essential to the full functioning of the body processes and systems (design) of a human being.

THE HISTORY AND UNDERPINNINGS OF OD

THE EARLY PERIOD: 1946 TO 1970

Organisation development has a shorter history than HR, and has its roots in:

- behavioural science – think of the experimental and observational work of Abraham Maslow, B. F. Skinner and Margaret Mead, for example
- psychological concepts derived from psychoanalysts including Carl Jung, Roberto Assagioli and Karen Horney
- social and humanist values related to openness, trust and harmony.

Typically, organisation development practitioners 'intervene' often as process consultants to address an organisational issue, problem or opportunity.

The history of the two disciplines (HR and OD) suggests two very different agendas – personnel management (later becoming HR) originating in a response to worker conditions in the factories of the late nineteenth century concerned with politics, communities, the technicalities of the employment cycle, compliance, legal constraints and getting the right skills in the right place at the right time (see Chapter 8). Some notable and prescient, but sadly under-acknowledged, pioneers in this field were women, including Mary Parker Follett, Mary B. Gilson and Jane Addams – all of whom had, what we now consider, an OD mindset.

However, OD as a discipline made its appearance at the end of World War II, in the mid-1940s, coming out of the felt need to reorganise, rebuild and manage in a new and different world. Its concern was with making and managing organisational behavioural change through the effective mobilisation of employees and other stakeholders.

It was then that researchers in the USA began experimenting with what was called 'laboratory training' – ie unstructured small-group situations and discussions in which organisationally unrelated participants learn from their own interactions and the evolving dynamics of the group and attempt to apply individual changes in behaviour in back-home situations.

Research and experimentation in learning to change through facilitated group dialogue and development, in what were called T-groups, was led by Kurt Lewin, Director of MIT's Research Center for Group Dynamics. Key to the T-group approach was an open-minded appreciation of others and an inclusion of their differences. Lewin's research was instrumental in informing the work of the National Training Laboratories for Group Development, founded in 1947 (now the NTL Institute for Applied Behavior Science), an organisation which has become hugely influential in the field of organisation development.

At this same period in the mid-1940s similar work was going on in the UK. In 1947 the UK's Tavistock Institute of Human Relations was established. Led by the work of Eric Trist, a socio-technical systems theorist, the Institute aimed to find ways to apply both psychoanalytical and open systems concepts to group and organisational life.

In 1948 the Tavistock Institute received grant money to undertake two action research projects. The first focused on internal relations within a single firm (from the board to the shop floor) with the aim of identifying means of improving co-operation between management and labour and also between levels of management. The second focused on organisational innovations that could raise productivity. This latter research took place at a coal mine and demonstrated the value of applying socio-technical approaches to organisational issues, thus proving another powerful influence in the field of organisational development.

From the NTL and the Tavistock Institutes research three threads of organisational development thinking started to emerge, all aimed at developing methods of improving individual, group and organisational performance.

These threads were:

- an interest in the dynamics of individual and group behaviour and in ways of changing these within working teams
- a method of action research by which participants learn new ways of operating through reflecting on their experience and then applying the new ways
- the application of systems thinking – look at Ludwig von Bertalanffy's seminal book *General System Theory: Foundations, development, applications* (first published in 1968) – to organisational life, demonstrating that every intervention does not stand alone but has an impact or ripple effect across the whole organisation.

Over the two decades to the mid-1960s the threads started to weave together to form the underpinnings of organisation development. 1969 saw the publication of Richard Beckhard's book *Organization Development: Strategies and models*. It was at this point that the phrase 'organisation development' entered the mainstream. (There are no book or journal titles with this phrase in it earlier than that date, so it is reasonably safe to assume that 'organisation development' was not recognised as a discipline in its own right before then.) This book was one of a series of six published at the time by Addison-Wesley. The foreword of Beckhard's book notes that

> The series came to be because we felt there was a growing theory and practice of something called 'organisation development', but most students, colleagues, and managers knew relatively little about it.

This philosophical commitment to performance improvement at individual, management, group and whole-organisation levels leads to some interesting organisational tensions when coupled with the deep commitment to humanist values. The work of W. Edwards Deming followed by all the subsequent performance improvement, business process re-engineering, TQM, Six-Sigma and 'lean' techniques related to organisation effectiveness have together always constituted an uneasy marriage. (See Jay Galbraith's chapter 'Organization design' in *Handbook of Organization Development*, edited by Thomas Cummings, for a good story about three consultants each offering a different perspective on the way to address a client's concern.)

However, if there were a 'pure' OD Hall of Fame in the USA you would find there the authors of the six books in the Addison-Wesley series mentioned earlier: Richard Beckhard, Warren Bennis, Robert Blake, Jane Mouton, Paul Lawrence, Jay Lorsch, Douglas

McGregor and Edgar Schein – all among the founding fathers of OD. Other significant US contributors from this period include Chris Arygris, Herbert Shepard, Warner Burke, Larry Greiner, Harry Kolb, the already-mentioned Kurt Lewin, Ronald Lippitt and Ralph White.

Make a note to find out more about these researchers, theorists and practitioners. Much of their early work is still very relevant today, and it is equally interesting to see how some of them have developed their thinking in the field as their work has progressed.

Observe, too, that there are very few names of founding *mothers* of US OD that are instantly recognised by practitioners in the field: Margaret Wheatley is one, Edie Seashore another.

A similar male preponderance of OD 'names' prevails in the UK. If there were a UK OD Hall of Fame, you would discover in it Fred Emery (Australian by birth but a close colleague of Eric Trist), Reg Revans, Eric Trist, Elliott Jaques (a Canadian by birth but he carried out most of his work in the UK) representing the period 1945 to 1969. Significant UK women contributors to the development of the field of OD were Elizabeth Bott Spillius and Isabel Menzies Lyth, both founding members of the Tavistock Institute.

REFLECTIVE ACTIVITIES

- Why do you think it is that so few women, even now, are well known or eminent in the field of organisation development (or, indeed, in the field of management generally)?

- What differences might a more diverse group of theorists and practitioners in the early days of OD have made to the place of women in the workforce today?

DEFINITIONS OF OD 1970 TO 2000

In 1969 Warner Burke established the OD Network and in his 1971 seminal article asked the question 'Organisation development – here to stay?' (Burke, 1971) In the article he points 'to evidence that OD is a popular and growing field. Although [it] has been a part of the language less than fifteen years' (page 170), and forecasts that it is, indeed, here to stay. Perhaps he based that forecast in part on the fact that in 1969 the American Society of Training and Development, obviously thinking along similar lines, had established an OD special interest group which was active in promoting the concepts of organisation development. The OD Network established by Warner Burke is still flourishing today.

Establishment of 'networks' and groups under the label 'organisation development' served to legitimise the notion that OD was a coherent body of work. Thus, in the three decades following 1970 OD evolved into a multifaceted body of knowledge and practice rooted in psychological concepts and social and human values related to openness, trust and harmony. Moreover, during this time OD expanded its focus beyond the social processes that occur mainly among individuals and within groups to include strategies and design components for the total organisation in systems theory terms (Boonstra, 2004).

One way of tracing this expansion of focus is by examining definitions of OD that emerged in this period. Below are 10 of the many available that span the three decades. As you read them, see what similarities and differences there are among them. Look for others from the same time period and see how they compare with these.

1969: Warren Bennis

> OD is a complex educational strategy intended to change the beliefs, attitudes, values, and structure of organisations so that they can better adapt to new technologies, markets, and challenges, and the dizzying rate of change itself. (Page 2)

1969: Richard Beckhard

OD is an effort (1) planned, (2) organisation-wide, and (3) managed from the top, to (4) increase organisational effectiveness and health, through (5) planned interventions in the organisation's 'processes', using behavioural science knowledge. (Page 9)

1970: The NTL Institute

OD is a change effort centred on the human side of the organisation and dealing with such processes as individual motivation, power, perceptions, interpersonal relationships, inter- and intra-group relationships, etc. (Page 342)

1972: Margulies and Raia, referenced in Porras and Berg 1978

OD [is] a body of concepts, tools and techniques used in improving organisational effectiveness and ability to cope with change. (Page 250)

1974: Friedlander and Brown

[OD is a] method for facilitating change and development in people, in technology, in organisational processes, and in technological structures. (Page 314)

1984: French and Bell

OD is … a top-management-supported long-range effort to improve an organisation's problem-solving and renewal processes, particularly through a more effective and collaborative diagnosis and management of organisational culture, with special emphasis on formal work team, temporary team and inter-group culture, with the assistance of a consultant-facilitator and the use of the theory and technology of applied behavioural science, including action research. (Page 17)

1984: Nielsen

Organisation development is the attempt to influence the members of an organisation to expand their candidness with each other about their views of the organisation and their experience in it, and to take greater responsibility for their own actions as organisation members. (Page 2)

1988: Schein (Referenced in Holbeche and Cheung-Judge, 2009)

[OD is] all the activities engaged in by managers, employees and helpers that are directed toward building and maintaining the health of the organisation as a total system. (Page 7)

1990: French and Bell

[OD is] the applied behavioural science discipline that seeks to improve organisations through planned, systematic, long-range efforts focused on the organisation's culture and its human and social processes. (Page xiv)

1997: Cummings and Worley

Organisation development is a system-wide application of behavioural science knowledge to the planned development and reinforcement of organisational strategies, structures, and processes for improving an organisation's effectiveness. (Page 2)

Immediately it is clear that there are both similarities and differences in the definitions quoted. Table 3.1 summarises them.

Table 3.1 Commentary on the definitions of organisation development

Element of definition	Definition it appears in	Comment
Mention of 'change'	Bennis, NTL, Margulies and Raia, Friedlander and Brown	Note that the descriptor attached to the word 'change' is very different in each case. Bennis indicates an intention to change beliefs, values, etc, and the NTL describes a 'change effort' which is similar to Friedlander and Brown's 'method for facilitating change', while Margulies and Raia mention the ability to 'cope with change'. Note too that 'change' is mentioned only in the 1970s definitions. It does not appear in the 1980s or 1990s definitions.
Includes reference to improving 'organisation effectiveness', or other organisational aspect	Beckhard, Margulies and Raia, French and Bell, Cummings and Worley	You'll see that the thread of improving effectiveness runs through the three decades. Bennis does not use the word 'effectiveness', but does say that OD is a strategy that helps organisations 'better adapt to …' French and Bell's two definitions are somewhat different in their focus, the earlier one looking at improving an organisation's problem-solving and renewal processes, and the later one focused on simply improving organisations by focusing on culture, human and social processes. Two definitions (Beckhard's and Schein's) include the word 'health', with the implication that effective organisations are also healthy (although this begs a definition of what is 'healthy').
Suggests a consciously planned approach to change or improvement	Bennis, Beckhard, NTL, Friedlander and Brown, French and Bell, Cummings and Worley	In eight out of the ten definitions there is a stated or implied point made that OD is a consciously planned intervention or 'effort'. Bennis mentions a complex 'educational strategy', Friedlander and Brown a 'method'. Margulies and Raia on the other hand talk more loosely about 'a body of concepts, tools, and techniques', while Schein is even more open, defining OD as 'all the activities …'
Indicates that OD is applied to an organisation's 'processes'	Beckhard, NTL, Friedlander and Brown, French and Bell, Cummings and Worley	Although six of the definitions mention 'processes', a closer look shows that they are not talking about business processes but about social processes. (Friedlander and Brown's 1974 definition may be an exception to this.) Some of the definitions specify which processes, and some mention that they are processes that will benefit from the application of behavioural science knowledge.

Element of definition	Definition it appears in	Comment
Focuses on the 'human side' of the enterprise and/or mentions behavioural science	Bennis, Beckhard, NTL, Friedlander and Brown, French and Bell (1984 and 1990), Nielsen, Schein, Cummings and Worley	Taking a broad interpretation of 'human side', you'll notice that the definitions are focused on this (rather than on the business or operational side of the organisation). Bennis mentions the beliefs, attitudes and values. The NTL is explicit about motivation, power, perceptions and relationships in general. Similarly French and Bell's 1984 definition is clear that OD is directed at work teams. Friedlander and Brown talk about 'development in people'.
Views the organisation as a system	Schein, Cummings and Worley	Only two of the definitions explicitly use the word 'system'. Cummings and Worley talk about a 'system-wide application', and Schein the 'total system'. Beckhard may imply a system when he mentions 'organisation-wide'. Others, by calling out specific organisational elements – for example, the 'structure, … technologies, markets, challenges' (Bennis), or the 'technological structures' (Friedlander and Brown), or the 'strategies, structures, and processes' (Cummings and Worley) – also imply that OD is viewing the organisation as a system and not as a set of discrete elements.

REFLECTIVE ACTIVITIES

As you read the definitions listed above and the commentary in Table 3.1, consider the following two questions:

- Why are there so many definitions – and what might be inferred from that?
- What do the definitions imply about the relationship between the organisation development practitioner (sometimes called the 'change agent') and the organisational members with whom the practitioner is interacting?

As the 1990s drew to a close, some interesting papers appeared to start to answer the questions posed in the Activity. On the first question, 'Why are there so many definitions – and what might be inferred from that?', the response came that OD as a discipline was very fragmented. Several perspectives on OD were current during these decades. They included, for example, OD from the socio-technical perspective, OD from the planned change management perspective, OD from the human relations group processes perspective, and OD from the general systems theory perspective. (See von Bertalanffy, *General Systems Theory*, 1968.)

Andrew Pettigrew, a UK academic, made the point that there were almost as many definitions of OD as there were OD practitioners. His research at the time showed that OD as described in the literature was significantly different from OD as practised. He scorchingly viewed the latter as often involving the application of an incoherent set of conceptual frameworks of unproven scientific validity, with limited empirical evidence of its efficacy (Cooke, 1998).

The second question, 'What do these definitions imply about the relationship between the organisation development practitioner and the organisational members with whom the practitioner is interacting?' raises ethical questions. Nielsen's (1984) definition, for example, is explicit in its statement that OD 'is the attempt to influence the members of an organisation', while Bennis (1969, page 2) states that OD 'is a complex educational strategy intended to change the beliefs, attitudes, values and structures of organisations'.

Researchers started to remark on the wielding of power and control that planned OD efforts involved – despite the ostensibly espoused 'humanist values' of OD practitioners. Marie McKendall, a US Professor of Management, felt that organisational development practices, through the creation of uncertainty, induced compliance and conformity in organisational members and increased the power of management. Her view was that practitioners and theorists, instead of examining these consequences, engaged in self-deception since they were unwilling to acknowledge that planned organisational change is a political and value-laden process that changes people's working lives and identities, often against their will.

So the closing of the 1990s showed OD in a state of fragmentation, if not dysfunction, perhaps reflecting an imperfect weaving together of the three threads evident at the end of the 1960s.

OD FROM 2000 ONWARDS

As OD moved into the new century, organisations were starting to look very different from the way they had looked in the 1970s, 1980s and early 1990s. First, they were now operating in a world of fast and complex change (see Chapter 2). There were the continuing and massive technological advances, particularly in the communications and social media sphere, the increasing global presence of emerging market organisations, economic and financial downturns, a developing concern about climate change and sustainability, and in many areas ageing workforces.

Second, and partly in response to the changing operating conditions, what comprises an 'organisation' is now up for grabs as boundaries blur, markets shift, 'virtual' is as ubiquitous as 'real', and stakeholders of all types start to have a greater say and a stronger influence on the way organisations operate.

So, for example, at any point an organisation might comprise a number of companies that operate differently one from another, that might be simultaneously competing and collaborating with each other, and that might all continuously have to predict and respond in a chameleon-like way to this changing business environment.

The result of the changing context is that organisation development is moving away from the themes noticeable in the definitions shown earlier, since what we understand about changing organisations is being increasingly informed by new insights and research in biology, physics and other natural sciences – all bundled under complexity theory as evidenced in the work of Ralph Stacey, Brenda Zimmerman, David K. Hurst, John H. Holland, and more popularly in the work of such people as Dan Ariely, Nicolas Taleb, Daniel Kahneman, Richard Thaler and Daniel Pink. To put it bluntly, how the world works is changing and what we *know* about how the world works has shifted radically in the last 20 years.

Table 3.2 illustrates the shift. What this means is that rather than becoming a more coherent field, organisation development is becoming less coherent as it moves away from the three original threads of:

- the dynamics of individual and group behaviour and ways of changing these within working teams
- action research by which participants learn new ways of operating through reflecting on their experience and then applying the new ways
- the application of systems thinking to organisational life.

Table 3.2 The shift in the understanding of definitional elements

Element inherent in definitions (see Table 3.1) Moving from	Moving to
Change in relatively stable contexts	Continuous change in very unstable contexts
Improving effectiveness	Creating continuous adaptability while improving organisational effectiveness (which is evaluated and measured). Note, however, that 'health' is a term that is beginning to supplant 'effectiveness'
Planned approach to a forecast/desired 'new state'	Flexible approach to various types of change (planned radical, planned incremental, unplanned radical, unplanned incremental)
Human processes	Human and business processes, structures, technologies
Behavioural social/science	Ethnography, anthropology, neuro-economics, positive psychology, etc
Systems theory	Complexity theory, chaos theory, quantum theory

To say that OD is becoming less coherent is not a negative statement. Rather, it reflects the fact that, as the OD Network says,

> [OD] draws from multiple disciplines that inform an understanding of human systems, including applied behavioural and physical sciences. (Retrieved from: http://www.odnetwork.org/?page=PrinciplesOfODPracti)

The fact that OD derives from 'multiple disciplines' means that a unifying theory may not be possible, and it also means that OD can be perceived, as critics of OD have suggested, as a bundle of tools and techniques that might give an impression of fragmentation or trend-following lack of rigour.

In the light of this situation it is worth addressing the questions, 'Does it matter that during the early 2000s

- there is no standard definition of OD?
- there is no unified underpinning theory of it?
- there is no method of evaluating its effectiveness?'

Not necessarily. The fact that there is no standard definition of OD can be explained by the point that Thomas Cummings (2004:39) makes in the book *Dynamics of Organizational Change and Learning*:

> Because OD is an action science, it will continue to grow and evolve as it helps organisations change and improve. As organisations face new challenges, OD will create new methods and applications. It will draw on new concepts and approaches to guide future practice. OD's success will depend largely on how well those ideas and innovations account for the fact that organisation change is essentially a social process requiring human beings to change their behaviour. Continued attention to the psychological foundations of OD can help this occur.

Notwithstanding any ethical or power implications of 'requiring human beings to change their behaviour', which could be at odds with the humanist values that OD practitioners generally espouse, OD could be likened to the field of medical science. Beyond the mainstream medical doctors there are a range of 'alternative' treatments with practitioners qualified in their own fields of acupuncture, hypnosis, Bach flower remedies, homeopathy, Chinese medicine, Ayurvedic medicine, and so on, each of which is underpinned by its own theory.

Taking this view starts to explain why there is no unified, underpinning theory of OD. Instead, there is a range of organisational 'healing treatments' each having skilled, and sometimes certified, practitioners. The difference between medical and OD practice is that arguably there are no mainstream OD practitioners. The cohering forces – which do not amount to a unifying theory – among the practitioners are that they:

- support managers/organisations in managing change
- subscribe to 'humanist values' such as respect, inclusion, collaboration, authenticity, self-awareness and empowerment
- are committed to improving organisational health, effectiveness and performance (with some issues on how this would be measured in relation to the practitioner's intervention)
- take a holistic view of the organisation.

This perspective of OD's being grounded on a mindset, rather than arising from a rigorously tested theory, is reflected in the OD Network 2010 definition of OD, which reads:

> Organisation development is a dynamic values-based approach to systems change in organisations and communities; it strives to build the capacity to achieve and sustain a new desired state that benefits the organisation or community and the world around them. (Retrieved from: http://www.odnetwork.org/?page=PrinciplesOfODPracti)

So what are the 'treatments' or capacity-building techniques that OD practitioners use as they work with organisational members, in a way that helps the members change their behaviours and/or respond effectively to change, and through this enhance the organisation's performance?

Looking at the services practitioners offer under the umbrella term 'OD' reveals a long list, including:

- action learning
- action research
- business process redesign
- change management
- conflict management
- culture analysis
- executive coaching and development
- group problem-solving
- large group intervention – eg Future Search, World Café, Open Space, IBM-style 'jams'
- meeting design and facilitation
- organisation assessments
- organisation (re)design
- organisation dynamics
- talent management
- team development
- team-building.

Note that these are not all new OD techniques, but they are being applied in new contexts and in new ways. Note, too, some overlap with what might be considered HR spheres of operation.

Now think about the question of evaluation. If you were trying to decide whether an organisational culture assessment or a business process redesign would be a better approach to developing your organisation's performance, how would you do that, and how would you compare the two? Both services are considered OD interventions, and both may or may not work. Doing nothing may also work. An interesting report of a medical trial in which patients were told they were getting a placebo nevertheless had the effect of relieving their symptoms and improving their scores on a range of measures of disease control (see http://www.npr.org/blogs/health/2010/12/23/ 132281484/fake-pills-can-work-even-if-patients-know-it?ps=rs). It is possible that any change intended to make a positive difference at an individual or organisational level makes it so, as both proponents and critics of the Hawthorne studies – which were conducted in the late 1920s and which had a strong influence on the development of OD – would profess.

Suffice it to say that the decades from the 1970s onwards have not seen much progress in the field of OD evaluation, as a 2009 report from the Roffey Park Institute highlights (Finney and Jefkins, 2009). Whether this matters to the person paying for the OD services, or the OD practitioner, is up for debate.

With these points about definition, theories and the evaluation of OD in mind, let us now consider the scope of OD.

THE SCOPE OF OD

As you will see from the list in the previous section, the 'service lines' of OD work are broad – perhaps necessarily so, because the questions OD practitioners address are equally broad. A typical list might include:

- What are the right skills to drive my organisation forward?
- How do you engage the people you need to deliver success?
- How do you speed up processes?
- How will tomorrow's leaders need to be different from today's leaders?
- How do you create collective leadership?
- How does customer focus become embedded in the organisation's DNA?
- How do you create a culture of performance and innovation?
- How can you create and transmit values that bind the organisation together?
- How can we manage change effectively and not 'throw the baby out with the bathwater'?
- How do you maintain trust and keep people motivated through change?
- How can we merge two business units as we acquire another company?
- Are we organised to compete in a new market?

But as you look at these questions, remember that for the most part OD consultants take a holistic view of an organisation – their work is grounded in 'humanist values', they take a systems view of the organisation, and they are addressing all these questions from the 'people' perspective, not from (say) a technology perspective.

It is not enough to have expertise in organisation behaviour or social sciences to play a role in helping managers answer the types of questions listed above. Because OD is carried out at a whole-systems level, and to have success in developing workforce performance, you need to really understand the business and operation of the organisation you are working in. Among the aspects you need to be clear about are:

- the business model and strategy
- the business systems
- the structures, policies and procedures
- the business processes
- how organisational performance is managed and measured
- the styles and methods of leadership and management of the organisation.

Only with this information in hand can you start to design an intervention that is appropriate for the specific organisation, or part of it, that you are working in.

Now note that in much of the English-speaking 'Western' world there is a mindset that satisfied workers lead to satisfied customers – a concept commonly called the 'service–profit chain'. This was well described in the *Harvard Business Review* article 'Putting the service profit chain to work' in 1994. Its authors, James L. Heskett *et al*, state that:

> profit and growth are stimulated by customer loyalty; loyalty is a direct result of customer satisfaction; satisfaction is largely influenced by the value of services provided to customers; value is created by satisfied, loyal, and productive employees; and employee satisfaction, in turn, results from high-quality support services and policies that enable employees to deliver results to customers. (Page 164)

Rightly or wrongly, this concept of satisfied employees is the business rationale that drives the work of organisation development consultants. In organisations calibrated to traditional Western management styles, OD practitioners are hired to help managers address issues, problems and opportunities related to people, their social systems and their interactions. All this with the expectation that if they can help employees be more 'engaged', 'satisfied', 'included' or 'happy', then the organisation will be more 'effective' – ie more profitable, more high-performing or more productive – depending on the type of organisation and how its success is measured.

It is debatable whether organisation development as discussed and practised in the 'Western world' is appropriate or even replicable in non-Western cultures. It will be interesting to see how the influence of emerging market organisations, new business models and new technologies converge to change the landscape of organisational operations.

If you take another look at the questions above and think about the way OD practitioners work, you'll see that answering them requires more than a quick-fix, off-the-top-of-the-head formulaic response. When the questions are first posed, you do not know enough about the issues to present a solution to these types of complex questions, even if you think you do. Indeed, a golden rule for OD consultants is to keep an open mind, and a curious, non-judgemental stance from the start. Moreover, in order to get a robust and successful outcome, you need to deploy a systematic approach – and the next section outlines this.

THE METHODS AND PHASES OF OD INTERVENTIONS

Think about the question listed above: 'What are the right skills to drive my organisation forward?' Now think about how you might find out the answer to it. (See also Chapter 10.) You can't simply say you need more innovative skills, a higher level of collaborative skills, or whatever. At a minimum, you need to know more about the context, more about the future strategy, and more about the type of organisation and workforce. Then you need to find out whether answering the question is the end of the assignment or if there's a plan to develop those skills in the organisation, and if so, whether it is your role to do that – or at least to advise on it. If it does go down that road, you would need to work out how you will help the organisation develop those skills, then how you will actually start developing the skills, and finally you would need to find out if your methods are working effectively.

Additionally, you would need to determine whether you are intervening at the individual level – in which case you might look at one-to-one coaching; at the management level – which might require something like team-building activities; at the group level – for which you could use facilitated workshops on particular topics (for instance, conflict management); or the whole-organisation level – where you could look at Future Search conferences or World Café approaches.

Regardless of the level at which you are intervening, you need to be systematic in your approach. There are a number of methodologies you can apply that will help you to address the question systematically. These can be applied equally effectively at every level. Below are some to consider. As you read down the list, ask yourself which ones you need to find out more about.

- process consulting, with a five-phase methodology:
  - establishing relationships with key personnel in the organisation (often called 'entry' and 'contracting' with the organisation)
  - assessing the organisation to understand dysfunctions, opportunities and/or goals of the systems in the organisation ('diagnosing' the systems in the organisation)
  - identifying approaches (or 'interventions') to improve the effectiveness of the organisation and its people
  - applying approaches to improve effectiveness
  - evaluating the ongoing effectiveness of the approaches and their results.
- application of a systems model. There are many to choose from, including the McKinsey 7-S model, Galbraith's 5-star model, Burke and Litwin's model, Nadler and Tushman's Congruence Model(s) – original and updated versions, Kilmann's model and Stanford's model
- appreciative inquiry – this has a four-phase approach:
  - *discover*: People identify the actions and areas that have worked well in the past. Asking such questions as 'What did we do when we solved a similar problem before?'
  - *dream*: In this phase people envisage possibilities and future states. Asking such questions as 'What is the best possible outcome we could get in solving this problem?'
  - *design*: This is the phase for charting a course of action and developing an implementation plan. Asking such questions at this stage as 'Where's the best place to start?' and 'What will it take to succeed?'
  - *deliver*: The plan moves into implementation. Questions here include 'What's helping keep us on track?', 'Where are things working well?' and 'What are we learning as we go along?'
- the seven-step change management approach presented in the CIPD Toolkit *Approaches to Change: Building capability and confidence*.

Generally, good OD consultants are well grounded in process consulting and use this skill in their application of the other approaches and methodologies. Be aware that the underpinning assumption of process consulting is that there is some kind of 'problem' that needs 'fixing'. The client may not know what the problem is exactly, but knows that something is not right. The consultant's role is to help the client both identify the problem and then to fix it.

Peter Block's (2011) book, *Flawless Consulting*, 3rd edition, is very good on the first four phases but rather misses an opportunity to discuss the evaluation and measurement of success. Equally Edgar Schein's (1998) book *Process Consultation Revisited* is a classic on the methodology – indeed, anything he has written on the topic is well worth reading.

Appreciative inquiry (AI) takes almost the opposite approach to process consulting. Rather than looking for what is broken and fixing it, as process consultants tend to do, AI searches for solutions that already exist – ie what is working well in the organisation – and then builds on these.

For example, process consultants are likely to start tackling the question 'What are the right skills to drive my organisation forward?' by discussing with the potential client the context in which this question has arisen, and getting a feel for the situation. With this in hand, the next step would be to assess, through various methods, the skills the organisation is forecast to need in the future – mapping what it already has, and then devising ways to bridge the gap.

AI practitioners, on the other hand, might begin by *discovering* where in the organisation people are taking things forward and/or demonstrating leading-edge skills. Then they would *dream* of what could be and what will be if these skills were amplified across the organisation. Essentially, the process builds on the known to take people into the unknown – what these skills are, what the conditions are that make them thrive. And then they would *design* a method of amplifying these across the organisation.

As you consider these different perspectives, think which is better for you and your organisation to use in addressing organisational questions and issues. Both approaches are systematic, and skilled practitioners go through all phases where possible. Sometimes it is not possible and you have to begin in the middle, as it were. Either way, buying time to get a good grasp of the context is worth arguing for, since getting things wrong for lack of information is resource-costly.

Being systematic in an OD project is the best way to keep it on track and get a successful outcome. Using a structured project management approach in tandem with the OD methodology provides the disciplined framework often lacking in the messy and unpredictable world of OD.

In each of the phases of the intervention you will usually deploy 'tools'. These may be inventories, surveys, assessments, exercises, models, games, and so on. (See the CIPD's range of toolkits.) Skilled OD practitioners usually have a personal toolkit at their disposal. In many cases both the methodologies and the tools that you use in organisation development projects are the same as those used in organisation design projects.

So what is the difference between organisation design and organisation development, and are they linked? The next section tackles these questions.

THE RELATIONSHIP BETWEEN ORGANISATION DEVELOPMENT AND ORGANISATION DESIGN

The roots of organisation design are embedded in the ways people think about organisation structures – ie the organisation chart. Table 3.3 summarises the history of organisation design as structure. Indeed, a very large proportion of organisation design theory is based on research around the best form of structure for organisational performance. Structure types frequently discussed are functional, process, matrix and network, and all of these have their pros and cons, which should be consciously examined in relation to the business strategies and objectives.

Equating organisation design with organisation structure is a recipe for disaster (as anyone who has taken part in a 'restructuring' that only tackles moving people from one box on the chart to another will testify). This blinkered approach fails to recognise that organisations are complex adaptive systems and that each part is interdependent on other parts. But it does start to beg the question that if 'structure' is not 'design', then what *is* 'design', and what is its relationship to 'development'?

Briefly, an organisation design includes all the elements of an organisation that are explicit (both visible and virtual) in a systems model. 'Drilling down' into each of these explicit elements – for example, the 'strategy' element in the 5-Star and 7-S models – reveals more explicit 'stuff' that can be either written down or explained: the business model, a strategic plan, the strategic planning cycle, governance documents, balanced scorecards, etc. Think of organisation design as focusing on aligning the non-people (hard) parts of the organisation.

Organisation development, on the other hand, relates – as we have seen – to elements of the organisation that are implicit and cannot be so easily codified or explained: culture, behaviours, relationships, interactions, the way a written process operates in practice, and so on. Think of organisation development as the people (soft) parts of the organisation.

Clearly, the distinction is not absolute – for example, training and development programmes are explicit but they are not usually included in the 'bucket' called organisation design; rather, they are put with organisation development because people taking the programmes contribute to the development of the organisation.

But with the hard and soft organisational aspects in mind, a useful way of thinking about organisation design in relation to organisation development is to begin by thinking about four types of change. The matrix in Table 3.4 illustrates these.

Table 3.3 Organisation design history from the 1920s to the 2000s

	1920–1955	1955–1965	1965–1975	1975–1985	1985–2000	2000 on
Model traits	*'Mechanistic' (ie mechanical)*	*'Mechanistic' – human relations*	*Open systems – product and geography structure*	*Matrix and shared services*	*Entrepreneurial and self-managed work teams*	*Organic*
Structure/ work organisation	Strict hierarchy of control, authority and rules Tasks are highly defined and specialised Few teams	Emphasis on the employee Beginning of lateral career progression Strict hierarchy of control	Combination of external focus and flexible structure Transformation of inputs to outputs (output is the final product)	Dual hierarchy: vertical and horizontal Flexible sharing of employees across product and organisational lines	Emphasis on teams Share of tasks Network of interaction[1] Encourages learning environment	Flat hierarchy, flexible rules Shared tasks, empowerment Highly flexible and adaptable work environment Customer-centric culture[2]
Management/ power and control	Management knows best, tells employees what to do, low worker trust Centralised decision-making, highly regimented	Preoccupation with the human side of the individual Centralised decision-making Limited employee empowerment	Project management Breakdown of silos Management controls information Organisation has to innovate	Project and product teams created across department lines Management is the decision-maker Moderate centralisation	Employee empowerment Strong horizontal collaboration and co-operation Senior management gives teams free range guided by the parameters and values they have set[3]	Decentralised decision-making Self-managed teams Authority shared with employees, high trust, collaboration and partnership
Communication	Vertical, top-down, controlled	Concern for human and social needs Vertical, top-down	Vertical and lateral mixed	Vertical mixed with horizontal Specialised to project Cumbersome, including all partners	Information freely shared throughout the organisation Cross-fertilisation of ideas Teams and customers work together	Horizontal and vertical communication Open access to information and communication technologies at all levels
Driving forces	Stable external environment Bureaucracy viewed as ideal structure to ensure organisational efficiency[4]	Post-World War II	John F. Kennedy as President, ideas of innovation	High inflation Slow growth in economy Environment generating new problems and concerns	Corporate downsizing and global competition Era of turbulence and change US dependence on international investors Technology advances global trade[5]	Development of 'global economy' idea Understanding of an era of multiple cultures Individual perceives that hierarchy of authority has limitations

	1920–1955	1955–1965	1965–1975	1975–1985	1985–2000	2000 on
Pros	Efficient for one or a few products Allows economies of scale within specialised units In-depth, highly specialised skill development	Employee considered as an individual, emphasis on motivation techniques	History of the organisation considered important (causation) Multiple goals can be achieved by a lot of paths (diversification)	Opportunity for product and functional skill development Meets multiple customer demands Responsive to specific markets and products[6]	Emphasises team-building Encourages innovation Creates a sense of self-achievement Teams discuss conflicts and propose resolution to problems Requires changes in culture, management practices and reward systems	Highly creative and adaptive to the global marketplace Everyone has a broader view of organisational goals Employees empowered to share responsibility, make decisions and be accountable for outcomes
Cons	Slow response to environmental changes Inefficient Poor co-ordination across departments	No consideration for the effect on production efficiency	Management focused on growth Consideration only for current stage of the organisation	Dual authority confusing for the employee[7] Great effort required to balance vertical relationships Conflicting goals between vertical and horizontal lines of authority	Start-up may be time-consuming Shared decision-making seen as time-consuming Traditional bureaucratic culture not compatible with self-managed work team	Significant training required for employees and managers Total systems and culture redesign required[8]

[1] Morgan, G. (1989) *Creative Organizational Theory: A resource book.* Newbury Park, CA: Sage Publications

[2] Galbraith, J. R. (2005) *Designing the Customer-Centric Organization – A guide to strategy, structure, and process.* San Francisco: Jossey-Bass

[3] Morgan (1989)

[4] Wren, D. A. (2005) *The History of Management Thought,* fifth edition. New York: John Wiley & Sons

[5] Wren (2005)

[6] Morgan (1989)

[7] Morgan (1989)

[8] Galbraith (2005)

Source: Beakey, D., Webster, K. W. and Rubin, J. (2007) http://gbr.pepperdine.edu/wp-content/uploads/2010/08/Organizational-Chart.pdf

In the matrix (Table 3.4), the two left-hand boxes (continuous and intermittent incremental change) both involve much more organisation development than organisation design, and the two right-hand boxes (continuous and intermittent radical change) both involve organisation development with fairly significant organisation design. Situations categorised as intermittent radical change are likely to need very high levels of both organisation development and organisation design support. This becomes obvious if you think of something like a merger where you are aligning all the hard (explicit) elements of both organisations, and also the soft (implicit) elements.

Table 3.4 Four types of change

Continuous incremental change	Continuous radical change
eg adjustments to people leaving and joining a team	*eg 15% downsize year on year*
People can cope well	People find this hard
May need some organisation development support but not much change in terms of design	Likely to need lots of organisation development support and a fair amount of organisation design support as structures or processes are changed
Intermittent incremental change	**Intermittent radical change**
eg a new software release	*eg a merger with another company*
People find this fairly hard, but not as hard as radical change	People find this very hard
May need lots of organisation development support and a little organisation design support	Likely to need high levels of both organisation development and organisation design support

There are many systems models of organisations. Three commonly used ones – mentioned earlier – are the Galbraith 5-star model, the McKinsey 7-S model and the Burke–Litwin model all of which conceptualise an organisation in terms of core elements. The basic premise of organisation design work is that it seeks to align the core elements in a way that when they operate together effectively, the business strategy is delivered efficiently and is characterised by high performance, productivity and profitability (or any proxies for profitability that a non-profit or government body adopts).

All organisation design work then assumes a level of organisation development activity. Look at Table 3.5 and you'll see why. The design elements of, for example, reward systems must mesh with the development aspects of how these are implemented. Many organisations have designed reward systems that appear fair and equitable on paper but are experienced by the workforce as subject to the preferences and vagaries of individual managers. There is little alignment. To get a workable alignment you would most likely have to develop manager awareness and skills in rewarding people, involve people in designing a fair reward system and ensure that the reward system design supported the delivery of the business strategy (and other organisational elements).

Table 3.5 Aligning organisational development and organisational design elements

	Organisation development (implicit)	Organisation design (explicit)
People	How people interact with each other The values people exhibit The behaviours that are encouraged/discouraged How people feel about working for the organisation The experiences people participate in The expectations people have The way expectations are met	Human capital management system Workforce planning Competencies Leadership profiles Training and development Performance management Reward systems

	Organisation development (implicit)	Organisation design (explicit)
Process	How decisions get made How supply chains work What the budgeting process is like How marketing and selling happens What style of tracking performance is adopted – risk-based, outcome based, etc	Activities and tasks Sequence Rules Targets and outputs Structure that organises process (aka organisation chart)
Technology	The choices made around software The freedom of people to access data The transparency of data	Data Applications Technology Infrastructure Performance management
Physical infrastructure (space)	The choices around space allocation The visible emblems and symbols The types of furniture choices made	Locations Facilities at a given location Workplace environment Space and utilisation targets

A fruitful question to ask when faced with an organisational issue or opportunity is not 'Is it organisation design or organisation development?' but 'What degree of organisation design and organisation development is required by this particular situation?'

What you're deciding is where the emphasis should lie and how to deliver the project in a way that both develops the organisation and aligns the design of it effectively and efficiently to the strategic intent.

The case study below illustrates this relationship.

CRESCOM

CRESCOM is an 80-year-old corporate real estate solutions company operating throughout the European Union with headquarters in Nottingham. The company offers clients products and services designed to help them maximise their investments in corporate real estate. It employs 500 staff in the Nottingham office, and across the rest of Europe there are an additional 2,000. It has three major service areas: portfolio management, workplace management, and strategic facility management.

The corporate real estate market is driven by economic upturns and downturns which are unpredictable in their scope and range. Combined with this, technology,

cost of corporate real estate, evolving working patterns and competitive pressures converge in a way that continues to make CRESCOM's client organisations look to their real estate to deliver savings, which they tend to resist due to capacity and productivity concerns.

To solve this, CRESCOM must show its clients that it is not just working on space-based savings initiatives. It must demonstrate that new perspectives on corporate real estate can help the client's businesses think about how work needs to be done in the future to avoid big productivity risks, while capturing productivity gains, and yes, driving savings. This requires corporate real estate thinking to be more deeply integrated with the business, particularly when it comes to planning around future work-related changes. The paradox is that to do this successfully CRESCOM needs to act as a 'living lab' – a showcase for its clients ... and it has not been good at this.

CRESCOM corporate services are organised functionally (IT, HR, Finance, Corporate Real Estate, etc) with HR staff at the headquarters function and, within each of the countries, more or less autonomous HR functions. There is very little internal organisation development capability. Traditionally, when there has been a 'change management' or organisation development need, it has been bought in from external consultancies. The new CEO of CRESCOM – who came from an organisation that had a very small HR function with many of the services outsourced, but with high levels of organisation development skill deployed from a consulting pool reporting to the CEO – was very concerned that CRESCOM

was not 'walking the talk' when it came to future-of-work planning: that is, how the core elements of 'work' – staff, process, technology and space – collectively evolve to drive productivity in the future.

She wanted HR to realise that what CRESCOM needed to focus on going forward was how to work more closely (ie deepen integration) with the business and the other support areas to help drive better future-of-work planning, and to do this in a way that not only benefited CRESCOM itself but also showed clients the way to do it. Additionally, she noted that CRESCOM had its own challenges related to the costs of both corporate real estate and of running duplicative, inconsistent and very traditional support functions.

To address these issues the CEO established a 'tiger team' with a very clear mandate to examine four of CRESCOM's support functions (HR, IT, Finance and Corporate Real Estate) in relation to the four aspects of future of work planning:

	Examine
People	Trajectory of employee engagement Evolving demographic patterns Changing work–life balance preferences
Technology	Advances in communication potential (via social media, video, etc) Changes to mobility opportunities Relative cost of new technology Methods of reducing environmental footprint
Space	Space type and space combination trends Successes as tool for advancing employee engagement Use as a driver of brand and cultural awareness
Process	Openness to process enhancement Awareness of changing process patterns across the industry Trends towards sustainability (which she described as as 'all activities and actions of an organisation that are designed to create value for itself and society, refrain from overly consuming and negatively impacting natural resources, and enhance the life of people and their communities').

From this assessment the CEO wanted the team to come up with a new model for operating these support services that could be scalable and replicable across the other support functions. In the back of her mind

she had an idea that she would like to see an organisation development capability emerge that acted as a connector between the support functions and the operational areas. She did not have a view on how this would be structured or integrated into CRESCOM's operation, although she knew that, in most organisations, the OD capability is associated with HR services. The purpose of organisation development would be to ensure that CRESCOM was well equipped to meet a continuously emerging set of demands across the future of work planning areas, and in doing this, to be able to offer learning, best practice and tested experience to share internally and with clients. The mantra 'We are a living lab' recurred in her discussions with staff.

Because CRESCOM operates in a very competitive and volatile marketplace the CEO set an aggressive schedule for completing this assessment work. The team was to come up with options for offering support services in a cost-effective, streamlined, very different way that included a specific organisational development role while recognising the local regulatory frameworks, cultures and levels of expertise in the different European Union countries that CRESCOM operated in.

Think about how you, as a 'tiger team' member, would start to tackle this issue. From the start it requires you to have a perspective on the following:

- What you think organisation development is, and how it relates to organisation design and HR. In this instance you are likely to be redesigning the support functions as an organisation design effort and simultaneously developing people's capabilities (and comfort levels) in dealing with this planned radical change. (Look back at the matrix in Table 3.4 and you will see that this is the area of change that people have the most difficulty with.)

- You would then have to make some decisions about whether to tackle the project from a problem-solving perspective or an appreciative inquiry one. With the amount of information you have to hand you would have to do some assessment before you made the choice on this. It seems likely that an appreciative inquiry may be ideal, but you have been given a very short time-scale and typically appreciative inquiry takes time – but again, you'd have to work out the trade-offs, bearing in mind factors such as:

  - cost: Ask yourself how much it will cost to deliver the solution, relative to the cost of your best alternative. Cost estimation may entail both the short term and the long term. This involves working out which of your options is the most affordable.

  - feasibility: Which option is the most feasible? Which one can you realistically apply over all the rest of your available options?

  - impact: Which of your options will have the most immediate positive influence on your current state of affairs?

  - consequences: What do you think or estimate will happen as you consider each option as a possible solution?

- Your own role in this project. Often organisation development consultants are part of the situation in which they are being asked to act or intervene. You need to have a strong sense of self and how you present, what your assumptions are and whether you have the objectivity needed to effectively carry out this piece of work.

- Part of this case requires you to gauge how crucial it is for support function people (including HR) to have a strong sense of the business in their response to customers. It appears at this point that they do not have this sense. And without this, how would they be able to recommend 'future of work' strategies that have a positive impact on business performance? Part of your work therefore will be to make some recommendations, or at least put forward actionable ideas – from your assessment phase work – on how will they get this strong sense of the business. This could be both a design and a development response.

- One of the aspects the CEO does not specifically mention – but you would need to be aware of – is the difficulty of designing and using metrics that show a return on investment (ROI) on organisation development and design work. In this instance someone could argue that there is no point in having an organisation development capability if it is not possible to link its efforts to improvements in business performance. Again, as you started to tackle the project you would have to think this through and come up with an approach to addressing it.

- A model, or models, for thinking about the HR/OD/line relationship. You may not need this at the start of the assessment but you will need to develop it as the project progresses.

- Similarly, you will need to have a view on the skill sets required by HR and OD practitioners – their similarities and differences. Having this will help you recommend where and how the service offerings should be positioned in relation to each other.

- How to professionalise OD: people know what HR 'does', but will employees know what OD 'does'? How would you get the business interested and engaged in supporting and using OD expertise?

- The barriers and drivers to thinking about OD and HR in a new way: are you limited by your own perspectives and assumptions? What tactics could you employ to generate creative and different ways of offering effective OD and HR services?

CONCLUSION

This chapter has summarised the history and progress of organisation development, described some of the approaches to it, its scope and its relationship to organisation design. As you will have gathered, this is a contested field reflecting the variety of backgrounds and experiences of researchers and practitioners in it. Nonetheless, a unifying element is OD's humanist values. A key principle underpinning New OE is that work can, and should, be purposeful, enjoyable and productive. For many employees that is currently not the case. The challenge for organisation development practitioners is thus to build the business case for their work, to help organisational members and the business to be sustainably successful, and then to be able to demonstrate the return on investment in OD. Rather than constituting disciplinary 'blinkers', OD's diversity makes it a field rich in possibilities for achieving a more balanced and ethical blend of organisational outcomes.

EXPLORE FURTHER

Boonstra, J. (ed.) (2004) *Dynamics of Organizational Change and Learning*. Chichester: John Wiley & Sons. A collection of articles in four parts, the first giving a rounded view of the development of OD, and others discussing change processes, OD in ambiguous contexts, power dynamics and sustainable change.

Cannon, J. and McGee, R. (2008) *Organisational Development and Change*. London: Chartered Institute of Training and Development. This is a basic, practical toolkit on OD and change. It is useful for HR and OD practitioners looking for inventories, exercises, models and checklists.

Cooperrider, D. L., Whitney, D., Stavros, J. M. and Fry, R. (2008) *Appreciative Inquiry Handbook: For leaders of change*, 2nd edition. Brunswick, OH: Crown Custom Publishing. This is a practical book about AI. There are sections on the background to AI, a detailed explanation of the 4-D cycle, and learning applications with resources for practitioners.

Jones, B. B. and Brazzel, M. (eds) (2006) *The NTL Handbook of Organization Development and Change*. San Francisco: Pfeiffer. This is a comprehensive guide presenting the NTL perspective on the field and profession of OD. The many contributors are all well-known OD theorists, educators or practitioners.

Sorensen, P. F., Head, T. C., Yaeger, T. and Cooperrider, D. (eds) (2004) *Global and International Organization Development*, 4th edition. Champaign, IL: Stipes. This book contains many fascinating articles on the applications of OD methods in different national cultures. There is also a detailed three-part chronological OD bibliography.

Stanford, N. (2004) *Organization Design: The collaborative approach*. London: Elsevier. This book offers HR and OD practitioners a practical step-by-step framework for organisation design together with tools, cases and models for immediate application.

Stanford, N. (2007) *The Economist Guide to Organisation Design*. London: Profile Books. This book is for executives and managers who want to change the design and structure of their organisation or part of it. It provides comprehensive guidance on the approaches and methods of design.

Van Assen, M. (2009) *Key Management Models*, 2nd edition. Harlow: Pearson Education. A reference guide to 61 management models. For each model there is a brief overview plus a description of when and how to use it.

Wheatley, M., Griffin, P., Quade, K. and the National OD Network (2003) *Organization Development at Work: Conversations on the values, applications, and future of OD*. San Francisco: Pfeiffer. A thought-provoking series of conversations among experienced professionals in the OD field. It picks up on the concepts of 'humanist values', and provides useful tools, tips and stories.

Websites
Human Resources at MIT http://web.mit.edu/hr/oed/od.html. Helpful site on OD consulting with tools for downloading.

Organization Development Network (US) http://www.odnetwork.org. A US-based membership organisation for OD practitioners; publishes three journals, holds conferences and events.

Organization Design Forum (US) http://www.organizationdesignforum.org.

A membership organisation with the mission to build and advance the community, practice and leadership of the field of organisation design through partnership, education and research.

Visit this book's Tutor Support Site for free access to the following tools taken from the CIPD's OD toolkits:

Tool no 16 Appreciative inquiry

Tool no 17 Appreciative inquiry as a method of change

Tool no 56 The OD practitioner as consultant.

NTL Institute http://www.ntl.org/inner.asp?id=263&category=2. Established over 60 years ago, the NTL Institute is active in the field of applied behavioural science, providing training and learning in organisation development and effectiveness for individuals and organisations.

Tavistock Insitute of Human Relations http://www.tavinstitute.org/ was registered as a charity in 1947. Today it offers a range of products and services focused on developing individuals in the social sciences.

REFERENCES

Afuah, A. (2001) 'Dynamic boundaries of the firm: are firms better off being vertically integrated in the face of a technological change?', *Academy of Management Journal*, Vol.44, No.6: 1211–28.

Anand, N. and Daft, R. L. (2007) 'What is the right organization design?', *Organizational Dynamics*, Vol.36, No.4: 329–44.

Ansoff, H. I. and Brandenburg, R. G. (1971) 'A language for organization design': Parts I & II, *Management Science*, Vol.17: 705–31.

Beakey, D., Webster, K. W. and Rubin, J. (2007) 'Organizational design and implementation', *Graziadio Business Review*, Vol.10, No.4.

Beckhard, R. (1969) *Organization Development: Strategies and models*. London: Addison-Wesley.

Beckhard, R. (1989) 'What is organization development?', in French, W. L. (ed.) *Organization Development: Theory, practice and research*, 3rd edition. Homewood, IL: BPI Irwin.

Bennis, W. G. (1969) *Organization Development: Its nature, origins, and prospects*. Reading, MA: Addison-Wesley.

Bertalanffy, L. von (1968) *General Systems Theory*. New York: George Braziller.

Block, P. (2011) *Flawless Consulting*, 3rd edition. San Francisco: Jossey-Bass.

Boonstra, J. J. (ed.) (2004) *Dynamics of Organizational Change and Learning*. Chichester: John Wiley & Sons.

Brodbeck, P. W. (2001) 'Complexity theory and organization procedure design', *Business Process Management Journal*, Vol.8, No.4.

Buchanan, D., Claydon, T. and Doyle, M. (1999) 'Organization development and change: the legacy of the nineties', *Human Resource Management Journal*, Vol.9, No.2.

Burke, W. W. (1971) 'Organizational development. Here to stay?', *Academy of Management Proceedings*, 1971: 170–7.

Burke, W. W. and Litwin, G. H. (1992) 'A causal model of organizational performance and change', *Journal of Management*, Vol.18, No.3: 523–45.

Cooke, B. (1998) 'Participation, "process" and management', *Journal of International Development*, Vol.10: 35–54.

Cooperrider, D. L. and Whitney, D. (2005) *Appreciative Inquiry: A positive revolution*. San Francisco: Berrett-Koehler.

Cummings, T. (2004) 'Organisation development and change: foundations and applications', in Boonstra, J. J. (ed.) *Dynamics of Organizational Change and Learning*. (pp.25–42) San Francisco: John Wiley & Sons.

Cummings, T. G. and Worley, C. G. (1997) *Organizational Development and Change*, 6th edition. Cincinnati, OH: South Western.

Daft, R. (2000) *Organizational Theory and Design*. New York: South Western College.

Dive, B. (2005) 'Why organization design is critical to global leadership development', *Executive Action*, April: 144.

Ensign, P. C. (1998) 'Interdependence, coordination and structure in complex organisations: implications for organization design', *Mid-Atlantic Journal of Business*, Vol.34, March: 1.

Finney, L. and Jefkins, C. (2009) *Best Practice in OD Evaluation*. Roffey Park Institute.

French, W. L. and Bell, C. H. (1971) 'A definition and history of organization development: some comments', *Academy of Management Proceedings*, 1971: 146–53.

French, W. L. and Bell, C. H. (1978) *Organization Development: Behavioral science interventions for organization improvement*. Englewood Cliffs, NJ: Prentice Hall.

French, W. L. and Bell, C. H. (1984) *Organization Development: Behavioral science interventions for organization improvement*, 3rd edition. Englewood Cliffs, NJ: Prentice Hall.

French, W. L. and Bell, C. H. (1990) *Organization Development: Behavioral science interventions for organizational improvement*, 4th edition. Englewood Cliffs, NJ: Prentice Hall.

French, W. L., Bell, C. H. and Zawacki, R. A. (1989) *Organization Development: Theory, practice and research*, 3rd edition. Homewood, IL: BPI Irwin.

Friedlander, F. and Brown, L. (1974) 'Organizational development', *Annual Review of Psychology*. Annual Reviews, California.

Galbraith, J. (2008) 'Organization design', in Cummings, T. (ed.) *Handbook of Organization Development*. Thousand Oaks, CA: Sage.

Golembiewski, R. T. (2004) 'Twenty questions for our future: challenges facing OD and ODers, or whatever it is labeled', *Organization Development Journal*, Vol.22, No.2: 6–20.

Goold, M. and Campbell. A. (2002) 'Do you have a well designed organization?', *Harvard Business Review*, March.

Graham, P. (ed.) (2003) *Mary Parker Follett – Prophet of Management*. Knoxville, IL: Beard Books.

Greiner, L. E. and Schein, V. E. (1988) *Power and Organisation Development: Mobilizing power to implement change*. London: Financial Times.

Grieves, J. (2000) 'Introduction: the origins of organizational development', *Journal of Management Development*, Vol.19, No.5: 345–447.

Harris, M. and Raviv, A. (2002) 'Organization design', *Management Science*, Vol.48, No.7, July: 852.

Heskett, J. L., Jones, T. L., Loveman, G. W., Sasser, W. E. Jr and Schlesinger, L. A. (1994) 'Putting the service profit chain to work', *Harvard Business Review*, March–April: 164–74.

Holbeche, L. (2009) 'Organisation Development: what's in a name?' *Impact, CIPD*, Issue 26, February.

Hurst, D. K. (1984) 'Of boxes, bubbles and effective management', *Harvard Business Review*, May–June: 78–88.

Irving, R. I. (1978) *The History of Psychology and the Behavioral Sciences: A bibliographic guide*. New York: Springer.

Karakas, F. (2009) 'New paradigms in organization development: positivity, spirituality, and complexity', *Organisation Development Journal*, Vol.27, No.1: 11–25.

Kates, A. and Galbraith, J. (2007) *Designing Your Organization: Using the STAR model to solve five critical design challenges*. San Francisco: Jossey-Bass.

Katzenbach, J. R. and Khan, Z. (2010) *Leading Outside the Lines: How to mobilize the informal organization, energize your team, and get better results*. San Francisco: Jossey-Bass.

Kilmann, R. (1983) 'A typology of organization typologies: toward parsimony and integration in the organizational sciences', *Human Relations*, Vol.36: 523–48.

Kotter. J. (1978) *Organizational Dynamics: Diagnosis and intervention*. London: Financial Times.

Laise, D., Migliarese, P. and Verteramo, S. (2005) 'Knowledge organization design: a diagnostic tool', *Human Systems Management*, Vol.24, Issue 2: 121–31.

Lawler, E. (2006) *Built to Change: How to achieve sustained organizational effectiveness*. San Francisco: John Wiley.

McKendall, M. (1993) 'The tyranny of change: organizational development revisited', *Journal of Business Ethics*, Vol.12: 93–104.

Margulies, N. (1972) 'The myth and magic in organization development', *Business Horizons*, Vol.15, No.4: 77–82.

Margulies, N. and Raia, A. P. (1972) *Organization Development: Values, process and technology*. New York: McGraw-Hill.

Marshak, R. J. (2006) 'Organizational development as a profession and a field', in Jones, B. B. and Brazzel, M. (eds) *The NTL Handbook of Organization Development and Change*. San Francisco: Pfieffer/Jossey-Bass.

Mintzberg. H. (1981) 'Organization design: fashion or fit?', *Harvard Business Review*, Jan–Feb.

Morgan. G. (2006) *Images of Organization*. Thousand Oaks, CA: Sage.

Nadler, D. and Tushman, L. (1982) 'A model for diagnosing organizational behavior: applying a congruence perspective', in Nadler, D., Tushman, L. and Hatvany, N. *Managing Organizations: Readings and cases*. Boston/Toronto: Little, Brown.

Nielsen, H. (1984) *Becoming an OD Practitioner*. Englewood Cliffs, NJ: Prentice Hall.

NTL Institute for Applied Behavioral Science (1970 and later editions) *Reading Book for Human Relations Training*. Washington, DC: NTL Institute.

Olson, E. M., Slater, S. F. and Hult, T. M. (2005) 'The importance of structure and process to strategy implementation', *Business Horizons*, Vol.48: 47–54.

Organization Development Network, *Principles of OD Practice*. ODN website. http://www.odnetwork.org/?page=PrinciplesOfODPracti [accessed October 2011]

Porras, J. I. and Berg, P. O. (1978) 'The impact of organization development', *Academy of Management Review*, 3: 249–66

Powell, W. W. (1987) 'Hybrid organizational arrangements: new form or transitional development?', *California Management Review*, Vol.30: 67–87.

Quijano Ramos, C. V. (2008) 'The current state of organization development: organisational perspectives from Western Europe', *Organization Development Journal*, Vol.26, No.4: 67–80.

Reason, P. and Bradbury-Huang, H. (2008) *The Sage Handbook of Action Research: Participative inquiry and practice*. London: Sage.

Roberts, J. (2004) *The Modem Firm: Organizational design for performance and growth*. Oxford: Oxford University Press.

Ropohl, G. (1999) 'Philosophy of socio-technical systems', *Phil & Tech*, Vol.4, Spring: 3.

Rothwell, W. J. and Sullivan, R. (eds) (2005) *Practicing Organization Development: A guide for consultants*. San Francisco: Pfeiffer.

Santos, F. M. and Eisenhardt, K. M. (2005) 'Organizational boundaries and theories of organization', *Organization Science*, Vol.16, No.5, Sep–Oct: 491–508.

Schein, E. (1988) *Process Consultation, Volume 1: Its role in organization development*. New York/London: Addison-Wesley.

Schein, E. (1998) *Process Consultation Revisited*. New York/London: Addison-Wesley/Longman.

Stacey, R. D., Griffin, D. and Shaw, P. (2000) *Complexity and Management – Fad or radical challenge to systems thinking?* New York: Routledge.

Tichy, N. M. and Ulrich, D. O. (1984) *The Challenge of Revitalization*. Working paper 397. University of Michigan. Retrievable from http://quod.lib.umich.edu/b/busadwp/images/b/1/4/b1407892.0001.001.pdf

Warner, M. (2007) 'Kafka, Weber and organization theory', *Human Relations*, Vol.60, No.7, July.

Waterman, R., Peters, T. and Phillips, J. R. (1980) 'Structure is not organization', *Business Horizons*, Vol.23, No.3: 14–26.

Weick, K. (1999) 'Theory construction as disciplined reflexivity: tradeoffs in the 90s', *Academy of Management Review*, Vol.24, No.4: 797–806.

Wheatley, M. (2003) *Organization Development at Work: Conversations on the values, applications, and future of OD*. San Francisco: John Wiley & Sons.

Wheatley, M., Tannenbaum, R., Griffin, P. Y. and Quade, K. (2003) *Organization Development at Work: Conversations on the values, applications and future of OD*. San Francisco: Pfeiffer.

Worley, C. and Feyerherm, A. (2003) 'Reflections on the future of OD', *Journal of Applied Behavioral Science*, Vol.39: 97–115.

Wrege, C. D. and Greenwood, R. G. (1978) *Mary B. Gilson: A historical study of the neglected accomplishments of a woman who pioneered in personnel management*. Rutgers University and University of Wisconsin-La Crosse.

CHAPTER 4

Developing an Organisational Development Strategy from an HR Perspective

Mark Withers

CHAPTER OVERVIEW

This chapter will help you think through the strategic role of OD and how an OD strategy can be shaped from an HR perspective. The chapter also considers the different players who are involved in shaping OD strategy and points to the skills and capabilities needed in HR professionals to support effective OD.

LEARNING OBJECTIVES

By the end of this chapter the reader should be able to:

- explain how an OD approach can help organisations with the process of strategy development
- show how aspects of OD need to be reflected in the content of business strategy
- demonstrate the importance of OD in the implementation of business strategy
- identify the new/different skills and capabilities required of HR professionals, line managers and OD professionals in developing an OD strategy from an HR perspective.

INTRODUCTION

Creating and sustaining organisational high performance requires effective responses to ongoing changes in the external environment, as discussed in Chapter 2. This interface between the external environment and the internal organisation is the point at which strategy is formulated. How strategy is formulated and executed is the primary focus of this chapter, which addresses five areas:

- business strategy
- expressing an OD strategy
- the relationship between OD and business strategy
- developing an OD strategy from an HR perspective
- skills and capabilities.

BUSINESS STRATEGY

How organisations create and execute strategy has changed dramatically over recent decades. The days of large strategic planning departments are long gone. As far back as 1994 Mintzberg argued in his work *The Rise and Fall of Strategic Planning* that strategic planning is an oxymoron because planning is about analysis (requiring facts, operations and budgets) and strategy is about synthesis (requiring creative thinking about mission and values and how to gain competitive advantage). Most compellingly, Mintzberg notes the difficulty in predicting the future in an increasingly turbulent world and points to a more dynamic way of developing strategy.

James Collins and Jerry Porras (1994) in *Built to Last* present evidence to show that companies with a strong sense of mission, values and culture outperform their competitors in virtually every instance. Gary Hamel and C. K. Prahalad (1989) in their *Harvard Review* article 'Strategic intent' and in their later work *Competing for the Future* emphasise the need for a shared understanding of the future and the importance of expressing strategic intent – an animating dream or stretch goal – that energises the organisation. This focus on strategic intent builds on the thinking of Michael Porter (1980) in stressing the importance of understanding what competitors are likely to do, how to get the most out of supplier relationships, and how to enter or create new markets.

Edward E. Lawler (2006: 545) writes, 'An effective strategy provides the formula an organisation needs in order to win. It should state the organisation's purpose, direction, goals and objectives and in most cases specify the tasks it must accomplish to succeed.' Lawler goes on to argue that mission, core competencies, organisational capabilities and the environment need to align (he expresses this through what he terms 'the Diamond Model'), and he therefore makes a clear link between responses to the external environment and changes in the internal organisation. In developing his thinking around alignment Lawler defines *core competencies* as technology and production skills (an example would be Sony's core competency of miniaturising technology or, more recently, Apple's ability to blend leading-edge design with technology shifts such as the i-phone) and organisational capabilities as work systems, culture, knowledge and organisational structure (an example being ABB's ability to work both locally and globally simultaneously).

There is, therefore, no one single approach to strategy development – Mintzberg *et al*'s work *Strategy Safari* (1998) presents ten distinct schools of strategic thinking. Against this backdrop we can draw out three core concepts of strategic thinking that are particularly relevant to this chapter:

- competitive potitioning
- the resource-based view
- business model thinking.

Competitive positioning is an 'outside-in' approach by which analysis of the external environment (industry, markets, customers, suppliers) enables the organisation to analyse its value chain in order to identify how best to secure competitive advantage. Decisions can then be taken on internal organisation and alignment (Porter, 1980).

The resource-based view is an 'inside-out' approach by which organisational performance and profitability lies in an understanding of an organisation's resources. These resources can be tangible (such as physical, financial or human) or intangible (such as intellectual know-how, creativity, speed or technological innovation). Such resources have value only when they are marshalled together to create a competitive advantage. Flexibility and agility in the configuration of these resources in ways that create competitive advantage is critical. As Sparrow *et al* point out (2010: 8):

A central tenet of the resource-based view is that the value that is embedded in any strategy increases when the bundle of resources and capabilities that the strategy comprises becomes more difficult to imitate, less transferable and more complementary.

Business model thinking: Sparrow *et al* (2010: 13) describe how new thinking that emerged from 'Internet revolution', particularly with regard to the creation of vistual organisations and networks, changed value propositions. They argue that organisations found ways to exploit information flows along the value chain and took opportunities to improve parts of the organisation that added value, such as

> the purpose of the business, its service offerings, how organisational structure helps focus on key activities, the way infrastructure is managed, and important business processes or policies on which performance is crucially dependent.

This business model approach challenges us to think differently about organisation and how to create value through more effective working across organisational boundaries.

Although each of these approaches to strategic thinking places different emphases, there are some common characteristics:

- *Contingency thinking* – Strategy needs to reflect the unique set of circumstances faced by the organisation. There is no 'one size fits all' and organisational strategies cannot be copied.
- *Whole-system thinking* – Strategy needs to take account of the whole organisational system including suppliers, partners and other organisational entities that may enable the organisation to create and sustain high performance.
- *Emergence* – Strategy formulation is not static. What we intend as strategy may not be what transpires, and the assumptions we make in formulating our thinking may not be correct. New circumstances emerge, and dealing with this 'emergent strategy' calls for an ongoing dialogue to enable the organisation to make sense of the new realities.

Although senior management are primarily responsible in leading strategy development, they cannot do so in isolation – they need to involve others in the organisation, as was discussed in Chapter 3. As organisations seek to exploit points in the value chain to create added value, there are growing calls for a more inclusive approach to strategy development and to hear the employee voice.

Employees have distinctive interests. In both framing and implementing strategy there is increasing recognition that high performance will only be fully realised if employees are engaged with and motivated to deliver the organisation's vision. This balance between employer and employee-driven interests and motivations is often termed 'duality' (Francis, 2007). Exploring ways to bring the employee voice into strategic conversations has been addressed by Keegan and Francis (2010) who have focused on employee-centred discourses and stressed the agency role employees play in shaping HR practice and the organisational experience. Weick and Quinn (1999) explore the use of whole-system organisational learning through large group interventions and approaches such as *appreciative inquiry*. Marshak and Grant (2008) challenge us to embrace contentious viewpoints so that we rethink change in terms of change dialogues, allowing more space for upward influence in shaping vision and the adoption of a more positive frame in dealing with negative reactions to change. Employee agency – where employees are active players in shaping their organisational work – is a feature of New OE (see Chapter 1).

This rapid tour of the main concepts in strategic thinking highlights three key facets:

- *strategic content*: the content of the organisational strategy itself, which focuses on both the external environment and internal organisation
- *strategy process*: the process of strategy formulation, which requires engagement of critical voices in shaping strategic content
- *strategy implementation*: the implementation of strategy, which involves the development of sub-strategies and the alignment and mobilisation of organisational resources.

A final comment on business strategy is to state the obvious – that not all strategies will be the same. Scale and complexity of change will vary enormously, and we will consider the implications of this on the chosen OD strategy later in this chapter.

EXPRESSING AN OD STRATEGY

Perhaps the most surprising feature of a chapter that examines OD strategy and its relationship to HR is that few organisations have anything they would describe as a written OD strategy and there is little explicit mention of OD strategy development in OD or related academic and business books or articles.

In researching this chapter I posted the question: 'Do you have an OD strategy?' One practitioner replied that he wasn't sure what an OD strategy was and whether he ought to worry because his organisation didn't have one.

Although there is little explicit reference to OD strategy, practitioners are clear that in their organisations an OD strategy exists and is generally 'nested' within the broader organisational strategy. Instead of the term 'OD strategy' there is often reference to the 'OD agenda' and, to all intents and purposes, these terms are interchangeable.

In Chapter 3 of this book Naomi Stanford sets out the historical and theoretical background to OD. Many OD interventions aimed at improving organisational health and performance have now become mainstream. OD has had a profound influence in shaping the way we think about how organisations work and has therefore become less distinguishable from approaches adopted by HR and other management theory. Edgar Schein (in Gallos, 2006: 18) points out that

> many elements of OD have evolved into organisational routines that are nowadays taken for granted: better communications, team-building, management of inter-group relationships, change management, survey research, meeting designs, feedback and learning loops, organisational design, effective group processes, conflict resolution … to name but a few.

Additionally, we can highlight the following features of OD that are critical to its role in shaping and implementing strategy:

- OD takes a whole-system view and is therefore multi-layered, diagnosing and intervening at organisational, inter-group, group and individual levels
- OD is concerned with understanding the present reality (both positive and negative forces, known and emergent circumstances) faced by each organisation as the starting point to explore future possibilities
- OD brings tools, methods and approaches which enable organisations to deal with its particular issues in order to shape and implement strategy effectively
- OD addresses the perennial organisational dilemma – how to meet individual needs and aspirations while simultaneously meeting the performance, survival and growth needs of the organisation
- OD is not bound by formal organisational structures but works with whatever parts of the system are relevant in achieving the target outcomes.

Figure 4.1 considers the three facets of strategic thinking mentioned at the end of the previous section on business strategy, and shows how OD plays a part in each.

An OD approach is also founded on a specific set of values and beliefs about organisations and the people who work in them. Robbins and Judge (2009: 663) outline the values underpinning most OD efforts:

- *Respect* – Individuals are perceived as being responsible, conscientious and caring. They should be treated with dignity and respect.
- *Trust* – Effective and healthy organisations are characterised by trust, authenticity, openness and a supportive climate.

Figure 4.1 The strategic context for OD

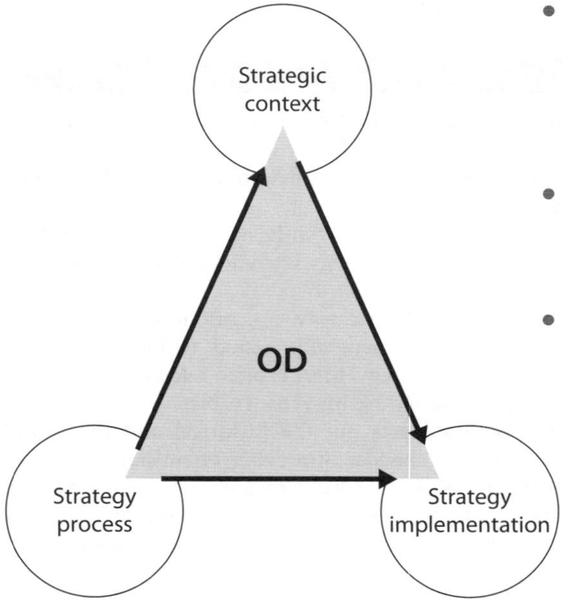
Strategic context
OD
Strategy process
Strategy implementation
• OD contributes to strategic **content** not so much in determining what business we are in but in thinking through the organisational implications of strategic choices
• OD shapes the **process** of strategic thinking: through bringing tools, methods and people together to enable them to think strategically
• OD has a strong role in strategy **implementation**, enabling the organisation to identify not only *what* needs to be done to deliver the strategy but *how* change is implemented (including dealing with resistance and 'politics').

- *Power equalisation* – Effective organisations de-emphasise hierarchical authority and control.
- *Confrontation* – Problems should not be swept under the rug. They should be openly confronted.
- *Participation* – Involving people affected by a change and the decisions surrounding that change will result in greater commitment to those decisions.

OD is therefore closely allied to strategy but will look and feel different in different contexts. Garrow *et al* (2009: 53) state that

> While the OD agenda is essentially driven by business needs, it is shaped and honed by a number of factors including the organisational purpose, the organisational strategy and the personalities and preferences of the most senior people.

Garrow *et al* go on to explain that

> the OD agenda is often driven from the top of the organisation by an enlightened CEO or managing director. However, it can also gain ground through other senior leaders who appreciate the value that OD can add, are in a position to support it and are able to influence their peers. In many cases, however, it is OD practitioners themselves who are connecting with the business and obtaining organisational data to inform the development of the OD agenda. (p.52)

This research underlines that OD is not the sole domain of OD professionals, and that OD strategy is shaped through a combination of senior executives, other business leaders and OD and HR professionals.

THE RELATIONSHIP BETWEEN OD AND BUSINESS STRATEGY

Jeffrey Pfeffer (2005) argues that strategic insight often fails to materialise because of limitations in the mental models of strategic leaders:

- the organisation proves incapable of implementing what they consider important based on evidence or insight (the knowing–doing problem)
- they do not act on the basis of good evidence (the doing–knowing problem).

He goes on to say that 'mental models affect organisational performance and ... are a high leverage place for human resources to focus its organisational interventions' (2005: 123–8).

The aim of an OD strategy is therefore to deploy 'strategies that mobilise the involvement, contributions and commitment of people throughout the organisation' (Gallos, 2006). OD therefore seeks to address head-on the limitations noted by Pfeffer through providing ways to enable business leaders to:

- hold the right conversations about strategy
- test the impact of strategic options and assess the readiness of the organisation to deliver them
- support the implementation of the chosen strategy.

If we return to our three facets of strategic thinking, we can summarise the scope of an OD strategy as shown in Table 4.1.

Table 4.1 The scope of an OD strategy

Strategic content	
OD is less concerned with the external-facing decisions concerning markets, customers, products and services, and financials. OD strategy does address how to create the organisational capability and core competencies needed to deliver the strategic intent.	*OD addresses such areas as organisation design, culture, organisational capability, business impact and change-readiness, cross-organisation and intra-organisational working.*
Strategy implementation	
OD strategy addresses how to best implement and embed strategic content within the context and realities faced by the organisation.	*OD approaches would be multi-level, examples of which include change leadership, organisational values, employee engagement, coaching/mentoring, organisational restructuring, intra-group working, team-building, change management, supporting individual transitions.*
Strategy process	
OD strategy addresses how best to involve the right people in the right conversations to shape and implement strategic content.	*OD tools would include action research, process consultation, large group interventions, board and senior-level facilitation, transition support, conflict resolution, diagnostics and data, engagement, creating the right conversations, focus groups and workshops.*

A further distinction to be drawn is that for both strategic content and strategy implementation there will be *substantive interventions* in addition to *enabling interventions*:

- Substantive interventions are the core actions associated with the business strategy. For example, strategic content may include goals concerning acquisitions or territorial expansion, whereas strategy implementation may include actions addressing organisational design.

- Enabling interventions are actions that may have to be taken in order to deliver the substantive actions. For example, although a goal may be to secure acquisitions, the organisation may need to develop capability in acquisition integration if that is not currently a core capability. Similarly, organisational redesign may require more sophisticated ways of working with external partners/alliances, and this may have to be addressed if it is not a core capability.

ORGANISATIONAL EXAMPLES

In this section we provide organisational examples to illustrate the relationship between OD and business strategy.

A MENTAL HEALTH FOUNDATION TRUST

CASE STUDY

This large mental health Foundation Trust provides a range of mental health services for adults and young people.

The current Director of Organisation and Workforce Development recalls that before she was recruited into her current role, the Trust board was aware that they were facing some deep-seated organisational issues. They believed that these issues were cultural and behavioural, but didn't really know exactly what the issues were or how to tackle them. An early task for the OD Director was, therefore, to understand the problem more clearly and develop a strategy to address what she had discovered.

Her approach to working on the problem deployed solid OD techniques:

- Research – using existing Trust publications and internal documents to extrapolate from them strategic intents. This enabled her to develop a picture of the 'end state' – what the Trust was aiming to become.

- Involvement – holding conversations with a range of people in the Trust to validate whether this 'end state' was an accurate picture of what the Trust ought to become and, if so, to discuss what needed to change to deliver this 'end state'.

Through research and involvement of key people, the organisation was able to understand its strategic direction more

clearly (which focused on de-layering and upskilling front-line managers) and the changes that were required to take place to enable the board to execute this strategy effectively.

As the Trust moved to strategy implementation, de-layering was underpinned by a range of OD interventions – *substantive OD interventions*.

Without an OD approach, the board might have taken a narrow approach to restructuring, focusing primarily on structure. *With* an OD approach structural issues were addressed, along with a number of other important areas such as:

- assessing the impact of change on the whole organisation and not just the parts directly affected

- defining the capabilities required in new roles – so that assessment of fit between individual and role could be made

- thinking through the capability shift expected of people in new managerial roles – so that appropriate support and development could be put in place

- involving key people in shaping implementation – to ensure business ownership of the changes

- ensuring that the rationale for change held together – so that communications were tailored to different audiences and that the language used conveyed both fact and a human element.

The first case study also highlights an overlap between OD and HR. A typical HR approach would have been to focus on the legal compliance of what was being done, on the clarity of factual message and process. An OD approach took this HR thinking further so that implementation also addressed how people would experience change, creating a positive experience where this was possible or mitigating any negative impacts associated with organisational restructuring.

A helpful distinction can also be drawn between intellectual and emotional buy-in to an OD approach – the fundamental difference between understanding that something needs to happen and knowing that you personally need to make this something happen. Equipping people to play their part in strategy delivery requires *enabling OD interventions*. In this example enabling actions included:

- helping the leadership team to work more effectively together as change leaders
- providing individual directors with support by means of coaching, drafting communications and helping them think through the likely impact of change on their organisation
- dealing with the composition of the leadership team itself.

CASE STUDY

A CIVIL SERVICE GOVERNMENT DEPARTMENT

The second organisational example is taken from a large UK Civil Service Government Department and starts with a board meeting held in November 2009 that focused on how best to respond to the deteriorating economic situation and unprecedented fiscal deficit. Specifically, the board decided that the organisation needed to be proactive in identifying options, in the expectation that there would be a requirement post the 2010 UK General Election to reduce costs dramatically. The outcome of this discussion was to appoint two board members to co-sponsor work to develop alternative organisation design options. Key requirements for this work were that it was organisation-wide and that those options and associated business cases must be developed by April 2010, a period of around four months.

With the HR Director General as co-sponsor, the Organisation Design and Development (OD&D) team, part of the Department's HR function, were asked to develop a high-level plan that would enable these requirements to be met. The OD&D team created a process of engagement, which became known as ODR (Organisation Design Review). Within two weeks of the initial board discussion a proposal had been developed and approval given to proceed.

The proposed approach embraced a number of core organisation development approaches:

- application of an organisation design methodology and programme management
- the use of research/diagnostics to work on the problem
- collaboration between internal OD/HR expertise, business leads and an external consulting partner
- ownership for the solutions by the business with OD&D creating a process to create options and innovative solutions
- leadership and architecture coming from within the organisation, not externally
- an understanding and use of the role of emotion in organisation design (not just lots of PowerPoint presentations, analytical tools and methods)
- a whole-system approach.

The scale and complexity of this work cannot be understated, but the business need was for urgency. The team also were required to deliver this work in an organisation where:

- there was a limited grasp of organisational data, even if the data was abundant
- in-house capability to deliver a project of this pace, scale and complexity was constrained, and it was felt that external challenge and benchmarks would add value
- the reconciliation of many different stakeholder perspectives on future organisation design would be challenging.

To address these immediate hurdles, actions were taken to:

- rapidly form a small internal multi-disciplinary core project team, comprised of OD professionals, strategy and policy, HR policy, workforce planning, employee relations, IT and finance, initially to lead data-gathering and subsequently to support the organisation design process and creation of associated business cases
- appoint 'business leads' in each area of the business so that business ownership was created from the beginning and a much broader virtual project team was established
- align HR Directors and HR Business Partners to advise and support business leads
- appoint an external consulting partner to bring additional capability, extra capacity to drive pace and ensure world-class analysis.

The development of organisation design options was systemic, requiring interaction and collaboration between each of the programme strands (such as corporate functions and executive agencies). Options were only considered if they could evidence input from stakeholders across the other programme strands. Although this was clearly an approach that added logistical complexity at a time when speed was needed, it ensured that, as far as possible, the views of key stakeholders across the organisation were being captured to guarantee that the whole system was being addressed and not just its parts.

An important event in crystallising thinking on options was a two-day work-through of the data and the generation of an initial set of options. This event involved around 60 leaders from across the Department who were given the authority to generate whatever options they felt were appropriate. Participants included around half the board, all the virtual team, other senior directors in the business, the OD&D team and other senior players in HR. The event was designed so that it was engaging, enabled contribution from everyone and created ownership of the outcomes. Other critical events were a series of workshops held with the Department's executive team, chaired by the Permanent Secretary and facilitated by the OD&D team. These created regular opportunities for the senior leadership of the Department to debate the options and provide their input throughout. A steering committee comprising members of the Executive Committee created additional opportunities for the OD&D team to test the process and to generate key decisions along the way.

Options were then evaluated against a set of organisation design principles and a business case was developed for viable options. At this stage there was considerable testing and challenge of options across the organisation.

The project delivered its remit, enabling the board to understand what organisation design options it had and what each would deliver in terms of the business case. Ownership of the project and its implementation was then transferred to the business leadership. HR Business Partners and the OD&D team adapted their roles to ones of support to the business. The process of organisation design and transformation was essentially catalysed by this project. However, the process was not complete as a result of the project. There were several challenges associated both with making decisions about the future design of the organisation and with implementing the decisions made. The OD&D team continued to facilitate and support that process, primarily using a 'process consultation' type of approach. It is also important to note that this project was part of a much broader organisation development agenda that included the improvement of engagement outcomes within the Department. The OD&D team is linking the engagement strategy very closely to organisation design and aims to strongly align these activities as the Department's strategic change process progresses.

These two case studies illustrate well how OD and HR work together as disciplines to steer a process that enables the development of strategic content. As examples they also illustrate:

- that strategic direction is often unclear and that an OD approach creates a process to enable key stakeholders to make strategic choices
- that the process of generating strategic options has to be owned and driven by senior business leaders (which could include senior OD/HR leaders)
- that strong stakeholder engagement throughout is key in building commitment and ownership.

DEVELOPING AN OD STRATEGY FROM AN HR PERSPECTIVE

There are those who would argue that the HR function has little part to play in the development of strategy and that HR's greatest value is to stick to its core functions: the effective delivery of operations, processes and practices that impact on people. Withers, Williamson and Reddington (2010) point to several research sources which underline that although many senior executives consider people issues very or highly significant to strategic decision-making, few turn to their HR functions to help them address such issues.

Garrow *et al* (2009: 29–31) posit that OD has a much broader remit than HR: 'Some people see HR as having tightly defined boundaries whereas with OD the feeling is that nowhere is off-limits.' Their research finds that practitioners see a clear link between OD and strategic HR but that there is a strong disconnect between operational HR and OD – even suggesting that they pull in opposite directions, as was discussed in Chapter 2. Additionally, their research notes that an increasing number of HR professionals have 'OD' included in their job titles and that in-house OD teams are located within HR functions as *centres of expertise*, and that these developments are adding to the confusion about the relationship between the two disciplines. To many, OD and HR are not natural bedfellows.

As someone whose professional roots are within HR and whose career has taken me firmly into the world of OD and strategic HR, I see much common ground and mutual interest. In particular, the ongoing debate within the HR profession about its strategic role (stretching back way before Ulrich and others appeared on the scene) suggests that there is a real desire to shift HR's contribution in organisations. As Withers *et al* (2010) have argued, HR working strategically requires an ability both to deliver within the traditional areas of HR capability (such as resourcing and talent planning, learning and talent development, performance and reward, employee engagement, employee relations and service delivery and information) and also to apply new capabilities such as strategic thinking, business acumer, change management, client relationship and project management skills, which overlap extensively with an OD mindset and approach. In the new Chartered Institute of Personnel and Development professional map, these new capability areas are recognised in the core professional areas of 'strategy insights and solutions', 'organisation development' and 'organisation design'. We therefore need to accept that how HR contributes in organisations is still in a process of transition – an observation well reflected in the CIPD's recent report *Next Generation HR* (Sears, 2010). There is clearly a distinction between operational and strategic HR requiring differing skills and contributions, but this is no different from the range of skill-sets required of other functions, such as finance, that also have distinctive operational and strategic roles.

Using the framework set out in Figure 4.1 presented earlier in this chapter, it is clear that HR's primary strategic focus is in strategy implementation – working with senior business leaders to identify the people and structural implications of the strategic intent – although the most effective of HR leaders will be playing a key role in working with colleagues to shape strategic content and strategy process. As Holbeche (2009: 26) writes: 'A business strategy only has value when it is implemented, and HR has a key role to play in enabling strategy implementation and business success.' Organisations that can quickly turn strategy into action, involve and engage employees and create the conditions where changes can be implemented effectively will be those organisations that succeed. Holbeche goes on to argue that

> For this to happen, HR managers and their teams must understand how their business strategy can be effective in the competitive and fluid environment in which today's business operate. This is not necessarily about analysis and planning, but about how strategy operates both as a way of thinking and acting so HR strategies and policies ensure that employees can deliver value to their customers and organisations can enjoy competitive advantage.

We noted earlier that many OD approaches have become mainstream. At a strategic level the boundaries between HR and OD have overlapped. This fusion at a strategic level is partly about mindset and partly about how the people agenda is addressed and taken forward.

For HR professionals seeking to work more strategically, Withers *et al* (2010) propose three mindsets, positioned within the context of contingent thinking:

- *Systems mindset* – thinking about the organisation from a whole-system perspective, both the external environment and the internal organisation (broad and big thinking). This way of thinking includes understanding the business: what success means and how it secures competitive advantage. This way of thinking also involves anticipation – being on the front foot and future-focused.
- *Process consulting mindset* – working through a set of dilemmas, in partnership with business colleagues, in order to find a solution. At a strategic level, this way of thinking and working has a strong focus on change, ensuring that the right stakeholder voices are included. It also underlines the importance of relationships (intentional and intuitive) in order to influence, broker and reach agreement.
- *Project mindset* – structuring work so that there is transparency about what is being done and dealing with practical strategy implementation issues such as clarity on priorities, deliverables, time-scales, dependencies, risks and resources.

With regard to the concrete aspects of the people strategy, Table 4.2 contrasts operational and strategic HR and points to how HR can support the development of an OD strategy.

What is also striking about Table 4.2 is that all eight of the areas in which OD and HR overlap are also areas in which HR and management overlap, and arguably, in all eight of these areas, it is line management that leads and HR/OD who support.

Areas in which an HR/OD perspective can be particularly beneficial to managers are employee engagement and change management, particularly in ensuring that the employee voice is brought into strategy content and implementation (see Chapter 6). However good the strategy, if organisations are to build a committed and engaged workforce (and realise the performance gains that flow from that), employees have to feel that their personal hopes and desires are aligned with those of the organisation. As Lynda Gratton writes (2000),

Table 4.2 The HR–OD strategic interface

Operational HR	OD strategy from an HR perspective
Areas in which Operational HR needs to excel: • Administration • Record-keeping • Compliance • Case work • Process management and improvement • Policy administration and advice • Running surveys • Interviewing • Counselling • Job evaluation • 'Help desk' • Training • Management information	Areas in which HR and OD overlap: 1 *Understanding the business and strategic drivers of the organisation:* identifying the impact of strategy on the internal organisation; aligning HR policies, practices and processes to support delivery of business goals and organisational values 2 *Attracting and retaining key talent:* understanding the kind of people needed to deliver the strategy; workforce planning; creating a compelling employer brand with strong corporate reputation; working through the psychological contract; strengthening the talent pipeline 3 *Aligning organisation design with strategy:* understanding core organisational competencies; helping the organisation to work more effectively with outsourcers, partners and alliances; enabling the organisation to collaborate more effectively through inter-team working and teamworking; designing roles 4 *Developing organisational capability:* supporting organisational learning; developing skills and capabilities at all organisational levels; creating change leadership capability; ensuring good people management practices; equipping managers to perform in ways that build competitive advantage/high performance 5 *Building high-performance cultures:* supporting the definition of core organisational values and behaviours, fit-for-purpose cultures (high-performance, agile, innovative, etc) 6 *Engaging employees:* working with managers to create a motivated and committed workforce; ensuring that the employee voice is heard; creating positive employee relations environments that help both organisation and individual to thrive 7 *Change management:* applying effective change management tools and techniques to support strategy implementation; applying process consulting skills to develop and implement strategy; supporting individuals through change and transition 8 *Business insights:* being involved in key conversations; providing information that gives business leaders insight into critical issues.

HRM needs to pay more attention to employees. Seeing people primarily as resources emphasises their commodity nature. Although a step in the right direction is to see people as a resource *to invest in* rather than a cost to minimise, Gratton stresses that HRM must not fail to take account of the distinctive interests of employees. This is particularly important in reframing resistance and workplace conflict with the more constructive terms of engagement and dialogue.

AN HR-LED OD STRATEGY

Two more examples from different sectors illustrate points addressed in this chapter.

CASE STUDY

VIRGIN ACTIVE

A good example of how OD/HR work in partnership with managers and how the employee voice is brought into the heart of strategic thinking can be seen at Virgin Active.

Virgin Active was launched in 1999 as part of one of the world's most recognised and respected global brands. Virgin Active is a growing health club business and currently has nearly over 70 clubs and around 5,000 employees in the UK. Dominic Boon, Head of People and executive team member, stresses that Virgin Active is a people business and highlights a number of key characteristics of the way the business is run:

- a very integrated executive team – CEO, Sales and Marketing, Operations, Finance and People – and this team works very collaboratively to address business problems

- a strong entrepreneurial culture, which is reflected in a strong action orientation

- a focus on shaping the right culture and employing the right people to drive this culture

- little protection of 'turf' – Boon recalls that the people agenda is driven as much by business colleagues as by the People function.

In Virgin Active, organisational development strategy is therefore driven by the executive team with the People function playing a key role in shaping and implementing OD strategy.

Boon highlights four critical areas that focus the integration of the People, OD and business agenda:

- *Capability* – developing people with the right skills and capabilities across the business through a branded, centralised approach to development and a focus on core skills. Member feedback is used

to identify and prioritise training needs. Many decisions are taken locally by club managers and their teams, so helping them to make the right decisions for members and the business is critical.

- *Awareness* – a strong emphasis is placed on communication and ensuring that the employee voice is heard. Boon himself uses social media (such as Twitter, LinkedIn, YouTube) to both engage with and recognise employees. Because the clubs are dispersed, much emphasis is placed on formal and informal senior-level visibility – including regular senior team use of club facilities.

- *Role modelling* – the senior team are very aware that how they act has a huge impact on the organisation. So the senior team are accessible and talk a lot to employees about the business context, the competition and how Virgin Active creates a different member experience.

- *Reinforcing* – through putting in place people policies that reinforce the desired culture. For example, policies endeavour to ensure that new employees are 'Virgin people' with a strong alignment to the culture, and that excellence in customer service is recognised. Member feedback and use of measures such as 'net promoter score' are used to extensively to guide the people agenda.

To illustrate how this integrated approach is brought to life in practice, Boon recalls that there has always been a strong business focus on locating clubs in the most convenient areas and offering innovative fitness products. However, there was also a need to remind everyone that what really had to be at the forefront of everyone's mind was the member experience. Starting from a position that employees in clubs were best placed to know what members wanted, a 'bottom-up' approach to change was initiated that got employees directly involved in formulating a new service strategy and the five service behaviours.

Additionally, Boon led a review of the relationship between Head Office and clubs (primarily because Boon is from a non-traditional HR background, having spent some years working in a large consultancy). The approach used was a classic OD approach involving a range of diagnostic tools to work on the problem and build ownership of the solutions. One of the areas addressed was Head Office communication, which was largely focused on sales and revenue figures. As part of the change to a more customer-centric culture the senior team deliberately changed the focus of their first questions from sales to the member experience – 'What are members saying about their workouts?' and 'Can I meet some of the staff who have recently been praised by our members?'

 ## ZENEUS PHARMA

CASE STUDY

Another example of how HR, using an OD approach, has taken a proactive role in helping leaders shape organisational strategy was at Zeneus Pharma.

Zeneus Pharma was a new company created through the acquisition of an existing commercial pharmaceutical business from a larger pharma company. It was funded through venture capital and, for HR, there was effectively a clean sheet. There were around 250 employees, and a new Head of HR was brought in to create and manage the HR function. Although the Head of HR was a member of the senior management team, there was little understanding in the business of how HR could contribute at a strategic level. This is a good example of how, by using organisational insights and framing the right questions, HR can add significant value.

The Head of HR (Jacqui Cookson) noticed that people in the organisation were drifting – there was no real excitement and no knowledge or understanding of the business vision. She therefore proposed to help the organisation to think about its mission, vision and values. Despite initial scepticism from some of the senior executives, this work was given approval and, through using a consultative OD approach to explore and diagnose the issues and invite contributions, a mission, vision and values statement was agreed. HR then worked with the other business leaders to establish the new internal brand and engage all employees in the vision and values. The values were fully integrated and became central to the way the business operated. The level of buy-in and engagement was extremely high and the initiative drove a significant culture change. Zeneus was acquired by a larger business within two years of start-up, for a value three times that of the initial investment, providing the investors with a significant return. The engagement of the employees and the passion they exhibited was identified by the acquiring company as one of the most attractive features of Zeneus.

In both these organisational case studies the strategic contribution came from within HR, not a specialist OD function. The key in both cases was a strong business-centric approach – tuning in to what is important for their business to succeed and working closely with business colleagues to shape strategic direction. The demonstration of the three mindsets mentioned earlier is evident, as is a strong focus on the areas of OD/HR overlap set out in Table 4.2.

SKILLS AND CAPABILITIES

In the previous section I noted the shift in capabilities required of senior HR professionals if a more strategic OD approach to HR is to be taken. I have also noted throughout this chapter that the process of strategy formulation and implementation is business-led and supported by HR/OD professionals. Similarly, OD strategy involves multiple stakeholders and has to be rooted in, and owned by, the business as a whole.

In this concluding section I consider:

- the extent to which HR professionals already have the capability to work strategically in delivering an HR/OD strategy
- the role of HR directors in particular in leading the OD agenda
- the role of managers in shaping an OD agenda
- the role of OD professionals in supporting strategy development and implementation.

HR PROFESSIONALS

Withers *et al* (2010) cite recent research in the UK and USA that suggests that despite the proliferation in job titles containing the words 'business partner' and 'OD', there is still a significant skills gap to be bridged between operational and strategic HR capabilities. Although the areas of strategic impact set out in Table 4.2 are understood and are 'on the radar screen', too few HR professionals (whether generalist or specialist) have the skills to operate effectively at a strategic HR/OD level. Withers *et al* go on to propose an approach to capability development that embeds an OD approach within the senior-level HR skill-set. What is clear is that candidates from non-traditional HR backgrounds are increasingly being placed in senior, strategic HR/OD roles. (This is also a point noted by Linda Holbeche in her book *HR Leadership*, 2010: 26). Of those senior HR practitioners who have contributed case study material to this chapter, only one has built a career solely in HR. Others have a blend of OD, line management and consulting experience. That OD is now placed firmly within the CIPD professional framework is a welcome development, but it remains to be seen whether the profession is able to either develop existing practitioners or attract people of sufficient calibre to work strategically.

THE ROLE OF HR DIRECTORS

Sparrow *et al* (2010) argue that it is critical to bring HR into strategy development. The question of strategic capability turns on how HR helps organisations understand the implementation of strategy from a people perspective, without insisting that HR is the common denominator in all things strategic. Sparrow *et al* go on to argue that HR directors must understand how the organisation strategises and must become skilled at boardroom engagement: 'More than ever HR directors must engage in and use the language of strategy in order to demonstrate the value of their function' (p.9). Throughout the case studies presented in this chapter the role of the HR director (or HR lead) has been instrumental in the strategy process, the development of strategic content and strategy delivery. For HR directors it is not a question of being invited to the top table. HR directors are at the top table – it is how they choose to place limits on their role that will determine how effective they are in working strategically with colleagues.

THE ROLE OF MANAGERS

It has already been noted that an OD strategy has to be fully integrated with business strategy and that its development and execution is shared between HR/OD professionals and business managers and leaders. How we develop and prepare our managers and business leaders to think with an OD mindset is not so clear. Many OD approaches are now embraced within capability development programmes that may fall under the umbrella of 'leadership', 'change management' and 'business management'. In these capability development programmes a strong emphasis tends to be placed on the 'what' – OD tasks and tools – and less on the 'how' – relational, emotional skills that inspire and enlist people to follow. A number of our case studies illustrate this point well, and this suggests that there is still a capability gap to be bridged in equipping managers and business leaders to apply OD tools and techniques to support effective strategy formulation and execution.

THE ROLE OF OD PROFESSIONALS

Not many organisations have the luxury of having in-house OD professionals. Often OD expertise is sourced externally to work either with in-house HR professionals and/or senior business leaders. Where OD expertise is used it is important to focus it in the most effective way. A framework (see Figures 4.2 and 4.3) developed by Frances Allcock and Peter Ainley-Walker when they worked together in OD roles at BT, and later developed further by Frances Allcock as Director of OD for the BBC, provides a helpful guide to understanding the contribution of OD professionals and how best to deploy OD expertise.

Figure 4.2 The contribution of OD professionals

With grateful acknowledgement to Frances Allcock and Peter Ainley-Walker

We can see how the practical application of the framework in Figure 4.3 works through the experience of a large financial services business. Let's say that a large and diverse financial services business had grown through multiple mergers and acquisitions. The Head of OD identified that although there was significant value to be added by operating at the top level (agenda-setting), there was no track record of OD thinking when agenda-setting. In order to establish the credibility and 'pull' for more strategic OD the team also needed to work at the lower delivery and consultancy levels. The matrix shown in Figure 4.3 was used to categorise and determine the projects with the biggest return on investment (ROI) on OD support. As a result the OD strategy was built around three points of focus:

Figure 4.3 Deploying OD expertise: the OD centre of expertise focus

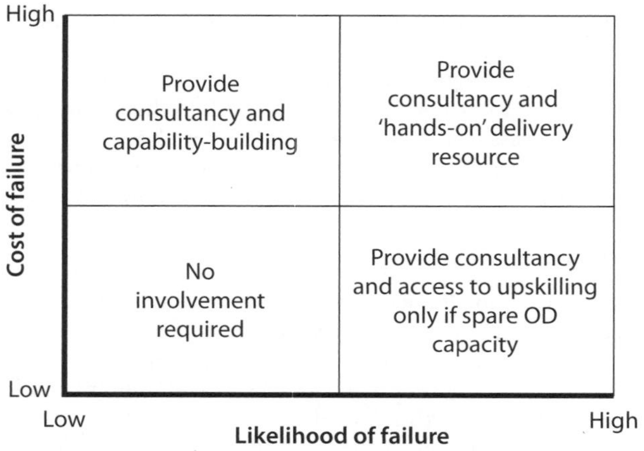

Level 1 – Dedicated
Projects where likelihood of failure and cost of failure is high. Usually large, complex change projects with significant behavioural, process or geographical change.

Level 2 – Diagnose and recommend
Projects where cost of failure is high but likelihood of failure is low. OD support may include scoping change management/OD requirements and agreeing level of OD support either directly or skilling senior HR professionals in a number of change tools and approaches.

Level 3 – DIY+
Projects where risk of failure is high but cost of failure is low – potentially a good environment for people to acquire and practise OD skills. OD support involves exploratory conversation with HR and business to establish risk/cost status with commitment to coach senior HR professionals if resource is available.

1 *Supporting the delivery of critical business projects*: demonstrating the value of OD while addressing critical business needs (eg organisation design, culture and leadership capability change)

2 *Building OD awareness and capability*: educating HR and business managers on the strategic importance and value of effective OD, largely through hands-on involvement of OD specialists

3 *Preparing for the future*: building on the delivery track record of **1** and **2**, which involved taking a slightly opportunistic approach to identifying and helping to resolve emergent strategic issues.

By demonstrating the business value of OD and the ability to deliver, this strategy built credibility and positioned OD to operate at the strategic agenda-setting level going forward.

ANOTHER EXAMPLE

The following case study illustrates how an HR-led OD approach can help an organisation to develop a people strategy while the organisational strategy is being formed. It is presented here:

● to help you think through how HR can work strategically in the absence of an organisational strategy

- to illustrate the dynamics between strategic content, strategy process and strategy implementation
- to identify the different people involved in delivering an OD strategy.

THE CIVIL AVIATION AUTHORITY (CAA)

CASE STUDY

The CAA is the UK's civil aviation regulator with responsibilities for economic, consumer and airspace regulation along with safety. The CAA employs around 1,000 people in mainly professional or administrative roles. In August 2009 the CAA appointed its first CEO along with a new Chair. A small internal HR function provided primarily advisory and administrative support for the business.

The CAA's core regulatory functions are funded by the aviation industry, and the CAA therefore faced a number of external challenges that impacted on the way it operated: pressure to demonstrate value for money in the face of economic downturn and fiscal tightening; the implementation of better regulation principles; stakeholder feedback on the CAA's approach to regulation; and a more joined-up approach internally. To respond effectively to these external pressures required internal change of which a significant part was the people agenda.

At the start of this journey the small HR team was largely focused on operational and transactional HR. The Head of HR and her Capability Development manager were engaged early on in the process to work with the CEO and executive team to help shape the people strategy.

An early decision was to engage an external consultant whose role was to bring OD and HR expertise to support the shaping and delivery of the people strategy and to develop the capability of the HR team. An OD approach was used to engage the organisation. Through using questionnaire research and workshops, employee feedback was gathered on a range of topics – communication, management capability, performance and culture/values. Additionally, feedback was

also obtained from external stakeholders. This enabled the executive team to engage directly with feedback from employees and stakeholders and identify common themes. The research found a number of key areas that required to be addressed internally and enabled the executive team and board to accelerate work on the people strategy ahead of work on the overall strategic plan.

This approach was not quite 'textbook' but illustrates that if the strategic direction is known, you don't need a finalised business strategy before you can take action to address known people and organisational issues – which were primarily enabling interventions. The people strategy had eight areas of focus:

- to define and embed new CAA values and behaviours
- to develop leadership capability
- to manage for high performance
- to achieve higher levels of colleague engagement
- to define the future workforce profile
- to review terms and conditions
- to articulate a clear CAA employment brand
- to improve communications with colleagues.

There were high levels of colleague involvement in developing this people strategy and the new CAA values – an approach to involvement, which was in itself new to the CAA. Within each of these eight areas there was a strong HR element (new policies, procedures, processes) and a strong OD element (organisational climate, future-focused, emotional engagement).

Questions

1 In the absence of an agreed strategic plan, was it right to initiate work to develop a people strategy before the overarching strategic plan was in place?

2 Because the HR function was quite traditional and operational in its focus, how would you have shifted the capability of the HR team to enable them to take a lead in shaping and implementing the strategy?

3 Although the process used to develop the people strategy was collaborative and drew on core OD approaches, what specific OD approaches might you have used, and why?

4 Who drove the OD approach, and what was significant about this?

5 What strategy implementation challenges were likely to surface, and how could an HR-led OD approach help to address these challenges?

CASE STUDY COMMENTARY

This case study highlights the positive role an OD approach can have in helping the organisation to shape its strategic thinking. The process used enabled the executive team to understand better the direction the organisation was required to take and to agree the critical enablers that had to be put in place in order to support the anticipated change in strategic direction. A particular insight that emerged from the diagnostic work was to highlight the importance in reorienting the culture of the organisation – for example, taking a different approach to regulation; moving from its Civil Service 'rights and entitlements' heritage to one focused on value and outcomes; introducing behaviours as a measure of performance.

What we can note from a process point of view is that:

● A change in organisational leadership (new CEO/Chair) provided the impetus for the strategy review and the introduction of an OD approach.

● Early HR engagement in leading the process and framing the discussion on culture/people agenda was key in helping the organisation to address what 'different' could look like.

● There was early engagement with the executive team, who needed to rethink their role as part of this process.

● Recruitment of a small group of experienced external consultants was undertaken to provide additional expertise for projects and support in developing the capability of the internal teams.

CONCLUSION

OD strategies are not typically written as separate documents but interwoven into business strategies. Many OD approaches have become mainstream and therefore may not be labelled as OD. The process of strategy formulation is not always clear. An OD approach can therefore help organisations shape strategic content and strategy implementation.

Although many people do not see HR and OD as natural bedfellows, the strategic end of HR has clear overlaps with OD, and an OD mindset is crucial if HR professionals are to work strategically. The development of OD strategy is not the sole prerogative of OD or HR professionals but something that is shaped and delivered by multiple stakeholders in organisations.

EXPLORE FURTHER

Gallos, J. V. (2006) (ed.) *Organisational Development: A reader*. San Francisco: John Wiley & Sons. This reader contains chapters from some of the best OD thinkers and is a must for those wanting to sustain organisational effectiveness.

Garrow, V., Varney, S. and Lloyd, C. (2009) *Fish or Bird? Perspectives on Organisational Development (OD)*. Institute of Employment Studies, Report 463. This excellent research paper explores how OD can add value in delivering organisational strategy.

Holbeche, L. (2009) *Aligning Human Resources and Business Strategy*. Oxford: Butterworth-Heinemann/Elsevier. This practical book draws on sound academic research and case study examples to show how HR can better align its work with business strategy and add value.

Mintzberg, H., Ahlstrand, B. and Lampel, J. (1998) *Strategy Safari*. Harlow: Prentice Hall. This excellent book sets out different schools for strategic thinking.

Withers, M., Williamson, M. and Reddington, M. (2010) *Transforming HR: Creating value through people*. Oxford: Elsevier. This book explores the process of transformation from envisioning and business alignment through implementation and sets out thinking on the new capabilities HR professionals need to acquire to work as strategic partners.

REFERENCES

Collins, J. C. and Porras, J. I. (1994) *Built to Last*. New York: HarperCollins.

Francis, H. (2007) *Discursive Struggle and the Ambiguous World of HRD, Advances in Developing Human Resources* Vol.9, No.1 83–96

Gallos, J. V. (ed.) (2006) *Organisational Development: A reader*. San Francisco: John Wiley & Sons.

Garrow, V., Varney, S. and Lloyd, C. (2009) *Fish or Bird? Perspectives on Organisational Development (OD)*. Institute of Employment Studies, Report 463: 42–3.

Gratton, L. (2000) *Living Strategy: Putting people at the heart of corporate purpose*. Harlow: Pearson Educational.

Hamel, G. and Prahalad, C. K. (1989) 'Strategic intent'. Boston, MA: *Harvard Business Review*.

Holbeche, L. (2009) *Aligning Human Resources and Business Strategy*. Oxford: Butterworth-Heinemann/Elsevier.

Holbeche, L. (2010) *HR Leadership*. Oxford: Butterworth-Heinemann.

Hyczynski, A. A. and Buchanan, D. A. (2007) *Organisational Behaviour*. Harlow: Pearson Educational.

Keegan, A. and Francis, H. (2010) 'Practitioner talk: the changing textscape of HRM and emergence of HR business partnership', *International Journal of Human Resource Management*, Vol.21, No.4–6: 873–98.

Marshak, R. and Grant, D. (2008) 'Organisational discourse and new organisational development practices', *British Journal of Management*, Vol.19: 7–19.

Mintzberg, H. (1994) *The Rise and Fall of Strategic Planning*. New York: Free Press.

Mintzberg, H., Ahlstrand, B. and Lampel, J. (1998) *Strategy Safari*. Harlow: Prentice Hall.

Pfeffer, J. (2005) 'Changing mental models: HR's most important task', *Human Resources Management*, Vol.44, No.2: 123–8.

Porter, M. E. (1980) *Competitive Strategy: Techniques for analyzing industries and competitors*. New York: Free Press.

Robbins, S. and Judge, T. (2009) *Organizational Behavior,* 13th edition. Pearson International Upper Saddle River, NO:??. Pearson/Prentice Hall.

Sears, L. (2010) *Next Generation HR: Time for change – towards a next generation for HR.* CIPD report.

Sparrow, P., Hird, M., Hesketh, A. and Cooper, C. (2010) *Leading HR.* Basingstoke: Palgrave Macmillan.

Weick, K. and Quinn, R. (1999) 'Organisational change and development', *Annual Review of Psychology,* Vol.30: 361–86.

Withers, M., Williamson, M. and Reddington, M. (2010) *Transforming HR: Creating value through people.* Oxford: Butterworth-Heinemann/Elsevier.

CHAPTER 5

Organisational Culture and Cultural Integration

Valerie Garrow and Graeme Martin

CHAPTER OVERVIEW

This chapter explores the concept of organisational culture, why it is important, how we can begin to understand its influence, and the role it plays in a major change programme such as a merger, acquisition or alliance. Through a blend of academic theory and practical examples it considers how we can best understand culture. Although OD has traditionally drawn on the behavioural sciences to understand organisational phenomena, it increasingly looks to the new sciences – and this chapter introduces concepts from complexity theory to add a new perspective on traditional unitary approaches to culture change. The chapter also uses case studies from original research conducted by the lead author to illustrate the key learning points and provides an extensive reference list for readers who wish to explore the concept further. Finally, it makes explicit links to the model of New OE that provides the organising framework for the book.

LEARNING OBJECTIVES

By the end of this chapter the reader should be able to:

- understand what organisational culture means and why it is important
- perceive how new concepts from complexity theory can shed light on our appreciation of organisational culture
- reflect upon frameworks used to measure or assess organisational culture
- participate in current debates about the manageability of organisational culture.

INTRODUCTION

This chapter explores the fascinating concept of organisational culture, why it is important, how we can begin to understand its influence, and the role it plays in a major change programme such as a merger, acquisition or alliance.

As OD emerged in the 1950s with a humanist response to the scientific management principles of the war years, early practitioners started to expose the myth that organisations behaved in a controlled, rational and logical way like simple machines (Garrow *et al*, 2009). Whereas early OD focused on personal effectiveness and small group dynamics, by the 1980s there was intense interest in Japan's manufacturing success, which seemed to be based on strong cultural traditions of family, loyalty and *kaizen*, a discipline of continuous improvement and total quality. The Western industrial tradition, which had relied on creating value through structure and technology, began to suspect that organisational culture was in some way contributing to high performance and could therefore be a source of competitive advantage (Martin, 2006).

Peters and Waterman (1982) in their book *In Search of Excellence* championed the case for 'strong' cultures, many of which, however, were so inflexible that they were unable to adapt to a changing economic environment and struggled to survive. Nevertheless, by this time it was widely recognised that culture has a strong influence on behaviour and can either inhibit or enable change, and culture-clash emerged as one of the chief causes of failure in mergers and acquisitions. It started to become common practice to approach organisational change through what Jack Welch, the GE CEO, called the 'hardware' of an organisation – that is, its structures and processes – as well as its 'software' – that is, its norms and culture (www.welchway.com).

Innappropriate organisational cultures are still regularly blamed in the press and by academics for organisational and institutional failure and poor performance, as for instance BP's 'performance-driven culture' for the 2009 Gulf of Mexico disaster; a 'bonus culture' in the banks for the 2008 'credit crunch'; a 'culture of waste' in MOD procurement at the time of the strategic defence review in 2010; a 'target culture' in the NHS preventing a focus on quality and patient experience; and a 'claiming culture' at Westminster during the MP expenses scandal (see, for example, Davis, 2009).

UNDERSTANDING CULTURE

A key question, however, is whether organisational culture actually exists in a form that can be engineered and harnessed to support organisational goals and strategic change. And to answer that question we need to understand the controversy among academics and consultants about organisation culture, because it can be defined and understood in quite different ways, all of which have distinctive practical implications.

There are at least four such views worth contrasting (Martin, 2006), which relate back to some of the ideas introduced in Chapter 1 on New OE's dimensions of mutuality, paradoxes and tensions, the power of language and the need for more ethical and reflective leadership:

- the unitary view and mono-cultures
- the anthropological view and the importance of subcultures
- the conflict view and 'brandwashing'
- the fragmented view and paradoxes and tensions.

THE UNITARY VIEW

Culture has long been recognised in the fields of anthropology and sociology as playing a significant role in the formation of beliefs, attitudes, values and behaviours, and in making social meaning.

(Schein, 1992: 9) suggests that cultures are patterns of

> basic assumptions invented, discovered or developed by a given group as it learns to cope with its problems of external adaptation and internal integration.

When new members are inducted into an organisation they begin to understand how to behave in that environment through recognising which behaviours are valued and rewarded or discouraged. A 'long hours' culture, for example, means that although formal working hours might be 9am to 5pm, people would feel uncomfortable leaving before 8pm. Such behaviour is a norm which is reinforced by peer pressure and individual desire to conform.

The idea of culture as a lilypad illustrates how culture operates on three different levels (Schein, 1992). On the surface the blossom is the visible manifestation of culture or 'artefacts' that are seen in the way people dress, the language used, the rituals performed and the stories told. Still visible below the waterline, the stems represent the values that form the basis for making decisions or choices and solving problems based on 'what ought to be'. Over time these may become basic assumptions which are the invisible roots of the lily. These are the taken-for-granted truths that are not consciously known or debated and are very difficult to change, often going back to the values of the owner or founder of the enterprise. French and Bell's (1979) iceberg is a similar above and below the waterline analogy emphasising the importance of the informal system hidden from immediate view.

These are essentially unitary views of organisations resting on the assumption that organisations, under normal circumstances, are best characterised by consensus among different stakeholders. For example, it is assumed that employees and managers are broadly in agreement about the aims of the organisation and the rights of managers to be able to set the direction of the organisation and control the work of employees without outside interference from bodies that represent staff such as trade unions or professional associations. When conflict does surface, it is seen as a pathology – a disease to be cured – attributed variously one or more of three causes: (a) to poor managers who lack supervisory skills and emotional intelligence, (b) to a failure of employees to understand the 'realities' of business life, or (c) as the result of self-interested and disruptive employees, trade unions and professional associations who are opposed to 'progress' or who wish to pursue their sectional interests at the expense of the common good. Thus, from this perspective an organisation is assumed to possess a unified culture under normal circumstances, which can be measured, usually through culture audit surveys (see next section on metrics), and managed in much the same way as you would measure and control employee performance or other key organisational 'variables'. This is a view widely held by many managers and HR staff, who believe in the power of good leaders and communications and stories to create and change cultures in organisations (see discussion about language and 'New OE' in Chapter 1).

Critics argue that such unitary assumptions and analysis may have a degree of validity in certain organisations and contexts, but in others are likely to provide a naive and highly misleading view of organisational cultures. For example, the aims of the NHS in the UK to provide a high-quality and free service for all commands near-universal agreement, but the means of achieving this aim are often highly contested. As a consequence, organisational cultures, particularly in the acute sector of the NHS, are rarely depicted in unitary terms by researchers, managers or clinicians – indeed, a strongly held view among many doctors is that managers lack the education, ability and authority to exercise control over clinical work and thus have no right to impose what they see as a managerial culture on the NHS (MacIntosh, Beech and Martin, 2011).

THE ANTHROPOLOGICAL VIEW

This is a quite different perspective on culture from the unitary view, and has much less to do with managerial control than with understanding the fundamental nature of organisations. Rather than being treated as something an organisation possesses, which is thus open to manipulation, cultural values and norms are seen as the very *essence* of the organisation. In other words, culture is something an organisation *is* rather than *has*. And usually this means characterising organisations as a multiplicity of sometimes conflicting subcultures – business units, departments, functions and professional groups, all of which have their own 'ways of doing things around here'. The previous example of the NHS typifies this perspective very well. For instance, Blackler's (2006) study of successful chief executives in the NHS in England painted a picture of leaders who, by their own admission, were very much the meat in the sandwich between the powerful clinical professions who sought to safeguard clinical practice and politicians who sought to change it, although both claimed to being doing so in the interests of patients. Blackler concluded that these leaders were leaders in name only, with little or no scope to change the cultures of their respective organisations despite intense political pressures on them to do so.

Another implication of this anthropological view is that it is difficult for people who are part of a culture, and who create and recreate it every day through their enactment of reality, to be able to distance themselves enough to understand why they act as they do and change the culture. One of the most important features of culture is that often we cannot see it, especially if we are steeped in an organisation's history and way of thinking. In such a situation, we require outsiders (researchers or consultants) to 'help us see ourselves as others see us'.

THE CONFLICT VIEW

A third view, widely held among critical organisational theorists, some union officials and employees, is to see strong organisational cultures as a form of socially engineered discourse of domination, in which leaders attempt to manipulate organisations for their own ends, often through the selection and development process, corporate communications exercises, and major 'vision and values' programmes. This approach questions the efficacy and ethics of such attempts to create strong organisational or corporate cultures, seeing them as little more than unsustainable exercises in brainwashing and creating organisation men and women. Joel Balkin's (2004) book *The Corporation* is a good example of this conflict perspective on organisational culture, which argues that the attempts to 'brandwash' employees into accepting the views of a business culture are detrimental to their long-term interests and those of society as a whole, so neglecting employee agency, which is a key feature of New OE. Strong organisational cultures are thus seen in a negative light because they discourage diversity, which is sometimes evidenced by the lack of women and racial minorities in senior leadership positions, and marginalise employees who do not adhere to the corporate vision and values. As a result, strong cultures often result in a lack of innovation and so fail in the long run.

THE FRAGMENTED VIEW

The fragmented view is associated with the school of thinking called postmodernism. We do not have time and space to go into the ideas of postmodernism in any depth, but it is sufficient to point to one of its key contributions to management thinking. This is to question the notion of a single and permanent reality such as an organisational culture. For example, Joanna Martin's (2002) account of culture highlights the fragmentary, contradictory and paradoxical aspects of organisational culture (see Chapter 1), especially the gaps that often exist between official leadership language or rhetoric and the actual behaviour of leaders (see New OE framework and the power of language). Thus, we sometimes find organisations espousing an official language of 'resourceful humans' and employers of choice while treating employees as 'human resources' to be cut or controlled like any other resource.

However, it is not only leaders that hold fragmented views of culture. Ordinary employees also make contradictory comments and take up inconsistent positions, making the notion of organisational culture as a robust analytical tool a difficult one to believe in. One famous example of this was a study of workers at a car plant in the south-east of England, who were asked to state their degree of agreement with the statement 'A firm is like a football team with workers and managers on the same side and kicking into the same goal for most of the time.' This statement is often used to assess the nature and strength of organisational culture in such studies. In this case, 75% of the workers agreed with the statement – but three months later they were seen to be marching through the factory, singing the well-known communist anthem *The Red Flag* and threatening to hang the industrial relations manager (Goldthorpe *et al*, 1968). We therefore have to question whether most employees – or managers, for that matter – hold a coherent worldview of their organisations as a unified culture. Obviously, as OD and HR managers we need to look for generalisations about organisational life, especially about cultures, otherwise we couldn't do our jobs. However, this should not blind us to the potential for differences of interests and values among groups in organisations, sometimes quite fundamental ones: 'What we see depends on where we stand.'

It is clear that this fragmented view sees organisation cultures as consistent and inconsistent, contradictory and confused, all at the same time, thus illustrating the paradox and ambiguity theme of New OE. Postmodern academics argue that there is no such thing as strong and endurable corporate or subgroup culture, and that culture is better described as a jungle, in a permanent state of flux and transformation. Understanding this view of organisations prevents us from placing too much faith in culture management techniques and programmes of culture change, because organisations are always in a state of becoming something else – summed up by the aphorism 'The only constant is change.' Your views on understanding whether or not they can be managed thus depend very much on your definition and perspective of culture.

MEASURING CULTURE

There are many tools on the market today that purport to help diagnose or measure culture. Each targets different dimensions of culture, such as organisational energy (Stanton Marris); achievement, support, power and role (Harrison and Stokes, 1992); satisfaction styles, people/security styles, task/security styles (OCI); managerial behaviour, risk-taking, feedback (Deal and Kennedy, 1982); sociability and solidarity (Goffee and Jones, 1998); business styles such as attitudes to risk, power and control (Davis, 1968); mission, adaptability, involvement and consistency (the Denison model).

Hofstede (1980) further introduced the international dimension of culture in his study of the values of people working for IBM in over 50 countries worldwide. According to Hofstede (2010: 6), culture is the 'collective programming of the mind' that differentiates groups of people. He identified four main dimensions that distinguish national cultures: a *power distance index* (the degree to which members of an organisation or society expect and agree that power should be unequally shared, suggesting that a society's level of inequality is endorsed by the followers as much as by the leaders); an *individualism-collectivism index* (the degree to which individuals are integrated into groups which protect them in return for loyalty, as opposed to loose societal ties where individuals take responsibility for themselves and their immediate dependants); an *uncertainty avoidance index* (which deals with a society's tolerance for uncertainty and ambiguity and the extent to which members feel comfortable in unstructured or novel situations); and a *masculinity-femininity index* (relating to the distribution of roles between the genders and the dominance of male and female values). A fifth dimension relating to *long-term versus short-term orientation* was added following a study by Chinese scholars. These dimensions have been influential in increasing cultural understanding in international mergers and partnerships, which for many global organisations has become a core competency.

From a unitary perspective, culture tools and measures, then, can be used to benchmark against other organisations in the same sector, track progress in culture change programmes over time, provide a focus for subsequent OD interventions, assess compatibility with a potential partner organisation or simply raise cultural awareness so that employees become open to change. They are also valuable in providing the senior team with evidence of the need for change in a format that is concise, visual and persuasive.

THE LIMITATIONS OF METRICS

Although culture diagnostics provide a good springboard for action, they can often lead to a false sense of security by reducing complex phenomena to relatively simple scores. As our discussion of the different views of culture has shown, even ostensibly similar cultures prove challenging to integrate.

Complexity theory, which is loaded with notions of paradox and ambiguity consistent with a New OE mindset, suggests that small differences in the initial state of a system become extremely important over time. Lorenz (1972) uses the metaphor of a butterfly flapping its wings to explain how minute differences can have large-scale effects in weather patterns, making them difficult to predict precisely. Similarly, in human systems and organisations the number of potential contextual variables is so great that, coupled with the fact that there is no common agreement about which of them should be included, measurement can at best only be a crude indication of how people perceive their work environment and culture. Survey results are influenced by any number of short- and long-term factors, and no two organisational contexts will ever be the same. This variation in initial conditions explains why best practice is so hard to spread, and a change programme that has worked well in one organisation does not work in another even where the culture might appear quite similar in a number of dimensions.

RAISING CULTURAL AWARENESS

Although data from culture surveys can help to start new conversations in an organisation, there are many other techniques used to surface hidden assumptions and values, such as drawings, drama, story-telling and metaphor. For example, we might ask people to describe what the organisation would be if it were an animal or a mode of transport, and as people share the stories behind their drawings, they engage with each other in making meaning and finding common understanding. Metaphors are widely used in management, and enable us to conceive of one thing in terms of another (Lakoff and Johnson, 1980; Morgan, 1986) and offer a sense of safe distance, freeing people up to speak about issues they would not normally confront. They offer a means of exploring the future by changing the metaphor. In one example, people described their current organisation as a classic car or a Spitfire, while they imagined the future as a Ferrari or a Concorde. The metaphors revealed to them that although they were passionate and valued the present, they realised that it was time to move on.

A further route into culture is through the psychological contract, which represents the perceptions of mutual expectations and obligations between the employer and employee. The psychological contract has a similar function to culture in increasing predictability in organisational life. According to McFarlane Shore and Tetrick (1994) it does this by:

- reducing insecurity by establishing agreed-upon conditions of employment
- shaping employee behaviour based on the belief it will lead to future reward
- giving the employee a feeling of influence in the organisation in that they are party to an agreement.

Like culture, although psychological contracts are subject to natural evolution through normal feedback mechanisms, once they reach a level of completeness they have a durable nature which resists radical change (Rousseau, 2001).

An important question remains, therefore, whether culture is ever accessible enough to manipulate and work with at a practical level.

HOW CAN WE WORK WITH CULTURE?

BUILDING CULTURAL SKILLS

During a study into how senior OD directors had built their skills and expertise (Garrow and Varney, 2011), cultural understanding featured as a key aspect of their experience. One of the directors describes the challenge in a global organisation involving 50 separate companies all with their own products and brands, to understand the culture of these different companies and find enough common elements to link them, while at the same time valuing diversity and difference. This paradox between managing and respecting diversity and difference while building a corporate culture was a common theme for practitioners in the study.

Another ethical dilemma for OD practitioners is that deep cultural change should not be undertaken lightly. One director warned (Garrow and Varney, 2011) that

> if you start an ambitious process of real culture change at a behavioural level and don't see it through, it can leave people in a very difficult place as expectations are raised but not met

OD practitioners are constantly working with these tensions and develop a kind of cultural agility.

Cultural agility is also required by alliance workers who work between parent cultures. Garrow *et al* (2000: 60) describe it as, 'sensitivity to other people's behaviour and ability to modify one's own behaviour patterns where appropriate'. With the increase in strategic and global alliances they also identified a 'new alliance culture' where certain patterns of behaviour formed 'a cultural repertoire' that alliance workers used in different situations and modified according to who they were working with.

CHANGING A CULTURE?

What happens when there is a clear requirement for an organisation to change its culture to meet the challenge of a new business environment? A typical traditional, linear approach to culture change from a unitary perspective would be to:

- describe the current culture
- set out a desired future culture
- examine the gaps between the current and future state
- identify likely areas of agreement and conflict
- consider barriers to achieving these goals
- plan how to overcome barriers
- measure movement towards the overall goal.

It is not uncommon in a large change programme to see a separate 'culture' workstream while other teams independently focus on reward, structure, leadership, communication and other business aspects of change.

New OE considers culture more as a way of being and becoming (Tsoukas and Chia, 2002) than as a discrete variable. Culture influences but also emerges as a direct result of the ways in which these other workstreams make their decisions about what is valued, rewarded and communicated.

WORKING WITH THE PSYCHOLOGICAL CONTRACT

Any change in culture is ultimately reflected in the psychological contract, but Garrow (2003) found that one post-merger organisation was able to shift the predominant cultural values from a very paternal pre-merger culture to one more in line with its new status as a listed company on an international stock exchange by renegotiating the psychological contract. A new MD decided to bring about a deliberate shift from the relational psychological contracts of employees, suppliers and customers in order to meet the new international challenges of the business. It was done principally by articulating new expectations and obligations in discussions with middle managers who, in turn, had similar discussions with their staff. The result was to push responsibility down the line, liberating senior managers from constant fire-fighting and empowering staff to find their own solutions and take more accountability.

These links between the psychological contract and culture are important because they highlight the importance of the informal, unwritten perceptions of expectations and obligations and the need for different conversations to bring about change. In Chapter 14 Francis and Reddington present a 'conversational approach' to the construction of employee value propositions which illustrates the active role of language in shaping perceptions about the psychological contract.

YOU CAN'T PAINT THE CULTURE ON AFTERWARDS

As the conflict and fragmented views of culture highlight, and as our extensive research into mergers and acquisitions (Devine *et al*, 1998) has shown, employees get the feel for organisational culture through their experience of how change and transitions are managed. Seeing people treated well and with dignity (including outgoing senior managers) sets the tone for the values and codes of behaviour throughout the organisation. Examples of poor decisions and badly managed transitions become the symbolic myths and horror stories of change that are remembered long after the event. As one interviewee said, 'You can't paint the culture on afterwards!'

Values become even more important during tough times and periods of major change when they are tested as to whether they are really meaningful. When people and particularly senior managers do not 'walk the talk', it can lead to cynicism and future resistance to change. But if you can't paint the culture on afterwards, can you design it in advance? Clearly, this is the position taken by many HR and OD practitioners, who adopt a unitary perspective.

Our first case study (see below) tried to do exactly that and design a culture for a joint venture company. Although it was a new organisation, the move to set up Infineum involved a substantial culture change for staff as well as for the top team arriving from two large, well-known oil companies. The design was initially a 'top-down' initiative, largely because the senior team was in place before the joint venture went live and had time to think about and plan the kind of organisation that would best serve the market they were in.

CASE STUDY

CULTURE BY DESIGN AT INFINEUM

This case study was first carried out in 2000 (Garrow et al, 2000) and has been updated for this publication.

Infineum was formed in 1999 as a joint venture between Shell and Exxon to enable both organisations to rationalise their petroleum additives businesses in a mature market. At the time of set-up the venture had around 2,000 employees globally and 350 staff on one site in the UK. Although both organisations held equal shares, Exxon staff outnumbered those from Shell, and this was an initial concern for Shell employees. No staff would have a career route back into the shareholder organisation once they joined Infineum.

The senior team for the joint venture had been in place for some time while awaiting regulatory clearance, and this provided a valuable period during which to consider and plan the shape and feel of the integrated organisation. They were keen to establish a new and distinctive culture rather than simply allow one of the existing organisations to dominate. At the same time, they felt it would be appropriate to move away from the 'big oil company' culture to a more agile high-performing organisation that could respond quickly to customer needs.

In order to bring the issue of culture to life in a creative way, the top team set out their vision for the organisation in a hypothetical 'Benchmarking report' which described organisational life three years hence.

The name 'Benchmark report' came from the idea that the report had been written by outsiders 'benchmarking' Infineum and how it operated three years after start-up.

The report aimed to help people visualise what it would be like to work for Infineum based on the core values and mission statement articulated by the senior team. These core values were:

- being customer-driven and market-focused
- integrity and openness
- respect for the individual
- shared commitment to success.

The Benchmark report painted a vivid picture of a potential future, and covered organisational structure, accountabilities and decision processes, work location and physical appearance, the employee/company work relationship, the multicultural environment, employee morale/attitudes, career concept and personal/professional development, life–work balance, recognition and rewards, quality and customer service, relationships with shareholders, and the senior leadership team.

This vision was supported and brought to life by a central OD post of 'worldwide change manager' and a network of 20 volunteers who ran events and workshops to help employees understand the journey towards a new culture. A 360-degree feedback measurement tool was used to assess leadership behaviour, and it was acknowledged from the start that management behaviour was vital to fostering the new culture.

Early challenges were around moving to a new business philosophy. For example, Exxon was traditionally more operationally excellent in its approach, whereas Shell was traditionally more marketing-oriented. Six months in, there were challenges of developing and embedding business strategies and processes in line with the new culture that had been set out so clearly.

Over 10 years later Infineum believe that the early work on culture laid the foundations for the company as it is today, and created a separate Infineum identity. However, the 'aspired to' culture was not achieved in its totality within the original three years time-frame. Some aspects took longer to achieve, such as the desired level of customer performance, and

some, such as risk-taking, are still being worked on. The Benchmark report was subsequently built on by other initiatives, such as Organisational Excellence, which was launched in 2007 and was aimed at unleashing the full capabilities of all employees. The underlying principle – that it is the leaders, what they do and how they behave – that shapes the organisational culture has remained constant. In employee attitude surveys Infineum has consistently achieved scores indicating enviable levels of employee engagement, which it feels underpins its very respectable business performance, even in difficult economic conditions.

Key features of this approach:

- a clearly articulated picture of what the future would look like, taking a whole-system approach

- unity and commitment of the new top team to a set of values and to role-model the desired behaviours

- the new culture by design aligning with organisational strategy and the business environment

- measures in place to track progress, including 360-degree feedback.

Questions

1 Identify the three levels of culture identified by Schein (the lilypad approach): what are the visible aspects (blossom), what are the underpinning values (stems below the surface), and what are the roots (fundamental assumptions)?

2 Most joint ventures do not have the luxury of such a lengthy set-up period. How might the vision have been communicated without the Benchmark report?

CULTURAL INTEGRATION IN MERGERS, ACQUISITIONS AND ALLIANCES

Perhaps nowhere is organisational culture more important than when organisations try to work together, whether on a permanent or temporary basis. Geert Hofstede suggests on the front page of his website (www.geert-hofstede.com) that

Culture is more often a source of conflict than of synergy. Cultural differences are a nuisance at best, and often a disaster.

We consider firstly the challenges of merging two or more cultures into one, and then the more ambiguous context of strategic alliances.

MERGERS AND ACQUISITIONS

Bearing in mind the learning from complexity theory about sensitivity to initial conditions, we know that no matter how similar cultures may appear prior to a merger or acquisition, subtle differences will emerge which often grow out of all proportion. Choosing a partner on cultural fit may lead to a false sense of security, and cultural 'due diligence' is still unsophisticated. Furthermore, Cartwright and McCarthy (2005) suggest that a good cultural fit between merger partners is an insufficient guarantee of wealth creation without good integration planning.

Buono *et al* (1985) describe the dynamics of the merger process as an attempt to combine different organisational cultures. This fusion of cultures produced by a merger or acquisition has been referred to as *acculturation* (Nahavandi and Malekzadeh, 1994), a concept again derived from anthropology. Elsass and Veiga (1994) see the acculturation process as the function of two opposing forces: *cultural differentiation*, or the desire to maintain cultural identity, and the need for *integration*. When these forces are weak, they suggest, *deculturation* occurs, allowing the organisation to embrace tolerance and diversity. Another possibility is that the integration force is stronger than the differentiation force resulting in *assimilation*, where one culture is absorbed by the other. Yet another outcome is that opposite forces produce *separation* where cultural identities are preserved. Their final option is where both forces are strong, resulting in *acculturative tension* where people experience high levels of stress and emotion.

'Mergers of equals' often fall into this latter category, where both organisations seek to maintain an equal presence in the post-merger organisation, involving parallel senior appointments and an equal legacy of practices and processes. Such cultural battles are often characterised by the 'them' and 'us' climate, in which opposing sides keep a watchful eye on symbolic victories and defeats, such as who gets promotions or larger offices (Devine *et al*, 1998).

Our second case study highlights the challenge of integrating cultures that were on opposite sides of the historical divide in South Africa, and where 'equality' had a particular significance. There was no partner selection involved other than their geographical location on adjacent sites.

THE DURBAN INSTITUTE OF TECHNOLOGY (DIT) LIBRARIES MERGER

CASE STUDY

The DIT case study was originally a longitudinal case study developed during 2001 and 2002 (Garrow, 2003) and was updated in 2010 for this publication.

The National Plan for Higher Education, February 2001, marked the beginning of the end of apartheid in South African education and the start of the transformation of the sector. Technikon Natal (TN) and ML Sultan (ML), on adjacent sites in Durban, were the first institutions to voluntarily undertake a merger and to overcome the historical divide between them. In 2002 they became the Durban Institute of Technology, and later the Durban University of Technology. This illustration focuses on the smaller but well-executed merger of their two libraries.

The cultural challenge of integration was extremely complex. As well as organisational differences and the inevitable duplication of roles, the merger reflected the ongoing process of racial integration. TN and ML had traditionally been perceived as uneasy neighbours, representing 'historically advantaged' and 'historically disadvantaged' institutions. The libraries, based on several sites, were determined to take control of their own future within the larger organisational merger.

ML's culture reflected a long historical and social struggle as well as a different educational philosophy. It originally served the Indian community and prided itself on managing creatively with few resources. Because of staff shortages, junior staff at ML often took on much broader roles than their TN counterparts, although the latter were better paid. The management style was paternal and caring but could also be seen as somewhat autocratic and centralised, and staff tended to lack confidence in making their opinions heard.

At TN the cultural legacy was seen as one of freedom and autonomy, and staff were used to taking part in decision-making. TN had experienced few financial constraints but was found to be in deep financial trouble at the time of the merger.

The key to the success of this merger was the commitment and outstanding leadership of the two library directors who started to formulate their approach during a development programme funded by the EU higher education libraries programme. Together they explored the challenges of bringing their organisations together and agreed some integration principles and a code of conduct for themselves as leaders. They agreed, for example, that although they were both in competition for one director's job, they would continue to work as 'first among equals'. This meant that they would not air disagreements publicly and they would ensure that they communicated the same messages to staff, sharing cross-organisation management to avoid a feeling of 'us and them'.

Secondly, there was a general recognition that redress and equity were to be central principles in the merger, and that each individual had a part to play. Staff from all sites were able to get together to make connections and establish relationships. Some became known as 'trailblazers' and went to work with counterparts on the other library sites.

Thirdly, all staff were allocated to facilitated work groups which were given the task of establishing joint practices and procedures for their own areas of the new library structure. For some this proved challenging because they had little experience of negotiation or debate, and they were supported, where necessary, by assertiveness or negotiation training. The group facilitators who were themselves staff members also had to develop new skills quickly, and all were given project management training.

Because of the historical divide, language was used very sensitively. Staff tended to select vocabulary cautiously, aware that some of their fears regarding the merger might be perceived as racism. As they got to know each other better, however, they found common ground, and before the following summer break they celebrated by making a giant fruit salad. This activity was also based on the principle that everyone would contribute, and became highly symbolic of cultural integration. It was recognised that the culture would become more participative as staff took responsibility for their own areas of work.

One of the directors summed up the experience:

Against this difficult background are the small day-to-day relationships and networks made successful by individuals that have worked in project teams, attended training courses and sustained the vision of a new DIT library. The experience of the merger has been a huge learning curve. Finding the confidence to speak out in meetings, influence others and work through difficult issues has provided a major development challenge for all concerned.

Some time later, the learning and skills from this early experience of integration were again important during a further process where DIT became Durban University of Technology (DUT).

The challenge that faced the staff of both institutions was a microcosm of the challenges the country faced at large. Several years later, like the country, the institution is far more settled: it has a common identity and a common purpose. While some may reminisce on the past, the majority have accepted DUT as their institution, with its own culture and systems of operation.

Key features of this approach include:

- It was based on new South African societal values which were seen as vital for the next generation of post-apartheid students.

- There was a strong leadership alliance committed to a self-imposed code of conduct and to role-modelling new behaviours across the divide.

- There was compulsory involvement of all staff even though it was not welcomed by all and some people found it extremely uncomfortable.

- Staff were supported by training and development to enable them to have a full voice in the integration process.

- There were strong symbols of unity such as the 'trailblazers' and the fruit salad.

Questions

1 Identify the multiple layers of cultural complexity in this case study.

2 Using Elsass and Veiga's definition of acculturation, what do you think DIT achieved in the integration process: deculturation, assimilation, separation or acculturative tension? What did they do to achieve this?

CASE STUDY COMMENTARY

We recognise that this case study has attempted to make sense of what was an extremely complex situation and by doing so we have identified what seemed to be important in terms of symbolism at the expense of myriad interactions between multiple players each bringing to the table their own personal history of 'struggle' (ie their experience during apartheid). It is important, therefore, to stress that the library staff were engaged in co-creating both their own organisation's future and also that of the wider society, carefully exploring a language that would help them work together across a difficult divide.

The researcher role often seemed to stray into that of therapist as people found it a cathartic experience to talk about the merger to an outsider and sometimes asked for further meetings to continue their reflection. Many said that it was the first time they had taken time to talk through their feelings and that the unstructured interviews and focus groups provided an important opportunity for sense-making and telling their own stories. This sense-making process meant that the stories sometimes changed, evolved or took on new significance as people had good and bad days, positive and negative experiences and encounters. A year later, during the second phase of interviewing, it was also clear that reading the first phase of the case study had contributed to a shared understanding of that early period.

In order to bring all of these stories together the case study gives the impression of providing a coherent whole, a clear pathway through which a new culture emerged. This is far from the true situation, and we are conscious that we have only highlighted a few of the landmarks along the way. The key tool of validation is that participants recognised, valued and enjoyed reading an account of their journey.

STRATEGIC ALLIANCES

Strategic alliances are more fluid and complex than mergers, operating on the basis of shared ownership and governance. They vary in the amount of organisational integration and interdependence required and therefore each alliance relationship is unique. They are usually temporary and have more fragile arrangements than mergers, often also involving complex lines of control and accountabilities (Garrow et al, 2000). Alliances tend to require more personal commitment to establishing 'rules of engagement' and 'values' that lead to a new culture which Spekman et al (1996) describe as the 'spirit' of the alliance. Interpersonal relationships and trust become strong determinants of alliance success, and attention to partner selection features strongly in the literature.

Rather than select culturally similar partners, however, alliances are often set up to exploit new avenues and create innovative tensions between diverse cultures. A case study of UKTV (Garrow et al, 2000) showed how BBC Worldwide and Flextech established a hugely successful joint venture, which created new commercial opportunities for the BBC's archive material. While working at UKTV, BBC employees were exposed to more commercial practices and values brought to the venture by Flextech, which was a young company created through aggressive acquisition. UKTV was at that time a 'very results-driven culture' in which the two parent bodies put 'different emphasis on the measures of success in terms of revenue and share of the market'. The then chief executive played an important role in ensuring that difficult decisions were seen as learning opportunities to avoid a 'blame culture' developing. Alliances are good places to learn new ways of working cross-culturally, and in many ways demonstrate the properties of self-organising systems – which we consider next.

CHANGING CULTURE IN SELF-ORGANISING SYSTEMS

We have already drawn on complexity theory to highlight the importance of being sensitive to 'initial conditions' and context and to the unpredictable and emergent nature of cultural change. We now borrow a further concept of 'self-organisation'. Organisations are collections of individuals who shape their environment as well as being shaped by it. Weick (1979) described the way reality is shaped and structured as a process of *enactment* where individuals play a proactive role. In self-organising systems individuals act as 'adaptive agents' who, with different motivations, respond to their environment in unique ways forming networks and alliances. Feedback from inside and outside the system continually modifies behaviour, but although feedback can amplify and accelerate change, it can also serve to reinforce the status quo much like a thermostat.

Westley et al (2006) argue that self-organisation is critical to achieving change. This might occur, as in our Health and Safety Executive (HSE) case study below, through a few change agents who disrupt the underpinning behavioural patterns so that new behaviours are introduced and role-modelled. In the HSE the aim of the change agents was to encourage networking and knowledge-sharing, but in order to achieve genuine culture change, new behaviours and values had to spread from the few to the many. Social movement theory has attracted the interest of public sector organisations offering insights into the rapid spread of ideas and mass mobilisation.

PUSH AND PULL TECHNIQUES

Motivational and engagement theories have long recognised that it is easier to 'pull' or draw people towards change rather than 'push' them into new ways of working. Learning from some of the large social movements such as civil rights and environmental movements suggests that widespread and rapid change can be brought about by 'framing' a message that resonates with individuals' own deeply held values and harnessing their energy for change. 'Framing' has been described as the single most important aspect of social movement theory (Bibby *et al*, 2009). As more people engage with the message and pass it on, the speed of change accelerates exponentially until a 'tipping point' is reached where the new assumptions become a cultural norm. For example, consider how attitudes have changed over time to recycling, corporate social responsibility and equal rights for minorities. In some cases, however, support can wane as quickly as it builds, when people see no beneficial outcomes or the movement has no structure or poor leadership. The result then is widespread cynicism which makes future change more difficult to achieve.

BE THE CHANGE YOU WANT TO SEE

Our final case study is a good illustration of a small group of 'agents' within a system who 'nudge' the culture towards the strategic goal of creating a more networked, knowledge-sharing organisation. Sensitive to the initial conditions, they recognised that large change programmes had not previously been successful in the HSE and there was a degree of cynicism about the organisation's ability to change.

Better ... together was therefore not badged as a culture change programme but gradually people began to see a change in the kinds of conversations they had and the ways in which they communicated and shared information.

CASE STUDY

BETTER ... TOGETHER: SUPPORTING CULTURE CHANGE AT THE HSE

This case study is taken from a study commissioned by the HSE (Garrow, 2010).

Better ... together is the story of a small internal team who championed the people and cultural aspects of change during and after the HSE's move from a split headquarters in London and Bootle to a single HQ in Bootle.

Although the HSE was very good at responding to a major incident and was well organised vertically, it was less successful in sharing learning across the organisation. There had also been an influx of some 200 new recruits from other parts of the Civil Service and the private sector, and it was clear that the new knowledge-sharing culture, identified in the strategy for a single HQ, was not going to emerge simply by putting everyone into the same building.

In October 2007 a workstream set out to identify some cultural enablers that would help to foster a more positive working climate. The aim was to involve staff in generating ideas, translating those ideas into action, keeping senior managers updated and acting as champions, collecting evidence for evaluation and maintaining a strong focus on delivery.

By the time *Better ... together* was branded as a work programme at the end of 2008, it had already completed some of the preparatory work and had data to show the gaps between future aspirations and current perceptions and some idea of the task ahead. The name itself was chosen through a small competition, and *Better ... together* started to be used to badge events and establish its own identity on the intranet site where people could find priority areas, feedback from various sessions and event details.

One of the advantages of having a small team is that it has had to work through others to get things done, and *Better ... together* was highly successful in mobilising support across the organisation. The five team members were well-networked and knew who to contact to make things happen and how to challenge barriers and blockers. One of the principles was always to transfer ownership, and for some things the team simply acted as a catalyst to inspire new ways of working.

The *Better ... together* 'brand' comprised a multi-faceted range of activities and initiatives in two phases, generated by listening to staff. These ranged from the physical use of the building and helping people find their way around more easily, to social events, fund-raising, learning events, a conference for Band 1 managers, a new staff suggestion scheme and an ambitious large-scale event, HSE Live.

The first phase of *Better . . . together*, 'making the connection', was about encouraging people to get to know other colleagues in the building, starting to share knowledge and making connections between areas of work. A lot of the early work was about improving communications, and the new *Better . . . together* intranet site enouraged people to keep abreast of developments, widen participation to the regions and engage with the events and activities.

Phase 2, 'collaborate and innovate', was officially launched in June 2010 to maintain momentum generated in the first phase. The second phase was about embedding the new behaviours that had started to emerge and actually doing things differently. For the team it also meant planning an exit strategy before the baton was eventually handed over to the Communications Directorate, HR and general line management in 2011.

Better . . . together evolved using regular temperature checks through surveys and informal feedback. The results of the HSE-wide People Survey provided further data to work with and develop a work plan using the results.

The team were keen to emphasise that *Better . . . together* was not a 'culture change' programme as such – it didn't re-examine corporate values, for example – but it was 'a good time to look at identity'

and played an important role in highlighting the importance of organisational culture at a time when the HSE was undergoing a significant period of change. It was built around staff concerns and suggestions, and used 'pull' techniques rather than 'push', recognising that where there is no energy or enthusiasm, change is less likely to be sustainable.

Key features of this approach were:

- It was led by a small, committed and well-networked team with strong senior management support.

- It was driven by continuous employee feedback and evaluation, always listening and using ideas from staff in order to move forward.

- The team worked through others and knew who to involve to get things done.

- They continually transferred ownership back to the organisation.

- The team role-modelled the new behaviours in the way they themselves worked.

- The team constantly challenged basic assumptions about why things could not be done.

Questions

1 Why was the *Better . . . together* programme appropriate in the context of the HSE?

2 In what ways could the *Better . . . together* programme be described as a culture change programme even though it was not badged as such? What links do you see with New OE?

CONCLUSION

Our journey across different case studies, examples and theories does not fully resolve the issue of what culture is. Instead, it leaves us with a series of paradoxes which the change practitioner must learn to navigate.

PEOPLE BOTH SHAPE AND ARE SHAPED BY CULTURE

Change leaders frequently approach organisational culture as though it is a variable that can be changed, controlled and measured, and leaders strive for a culture score that will support their strategy and give them a competitive advantage. From another perspective we can approach culture as socially constructed reality that rests on a shared system of meaning developed through an infinite number of daily conversations and interactions. In complex adaptive systems agents influence culture but do not control it.

There may be structural and political barriers such as organisational charts and reporting lines which dictate who is allowed to talk to whom. Below the surface of these formal structures is the informal life of the organisation in which people discuss what is really happening with their networks and colleagues. Metaphors and stories offer ways of sense-making and of changing the types of conversations that take place in organisations.

CULTURE CHANGE IS BOTH TOP-DOWN AND BOTTOM-UP

A new culture demands a whole-system change so that systems, processes, structures all support new behaviours.

The Burke–Litwin model of organisational change (1992) highlights leadership, culture and mission and strategy as the transformational variables in an organisation. Visible top-level commitment, active support for change agents and role-modelling of values have been important aspects in all of our three case studies. The DIT leadership 'code of conduct' sent a particularly strong message to staff about promoting a new participative culture and bridging the divide.

Culture change cannot, however, simply be handed down by management decree, and one of the biggest challenges is to frame the vision and the message in a way that will create a groundswell of support that spreads throughout the organisation. The vision of life in the new joint venture at Infineum, for example, was framed in a very visual and engaging way.

It then requires a degree of 'letting go' – a period of self-organising to allow new cultural norms to emerge in line with the vision and strategy. The HSE chief executive's support for *Better … together* was such that he refused to hijack it for management ends even during the recession. He believed strongly that this was a staff-led movement for change and not a management tool to achieve higher performance or cost-cutting.

At DIT we also saw some 'push' techniques and stronger top-down direction in ensuring staff involvement in the integration process, but they were supported by receiving the training and development required to allow them to participate fully. This ensured that they would design their own new ways of working and thereby be more committed to them. Even so, it was a difficult process, and some felt that the workgroups achieved the lowest rather than the highest common denominator in terms of outcomes. The process, however, took precedence over the task outcomes in establishing a culture of full equality and participation.

CULTURE CHANGE IS BOTH PLANNED AND EMERGENT

We see from the case studies that although there is a degree of direction and often a strong vision, culture emerges in the way individuals relate to each other and form relationships in organisations. Individuals and groups of 'adaptive agents' with strong agendas can start to create new trends and greatly impede or accelerate change. Complexity theory encourages us to see change in a less linear and less predictable way so that while a large change programme might have minimal impact, some seemingly minor events or interventions create ripples of change that swell into a genuine movement for change. The HSE case study is a good example of a small group of individuals having a far greater impact than a previous major change programme.

ORGANISATIONS SEEK BOTH A COMMON CULTURE AND TO VALUE DIFFERENCE AND DIVERSITY

We saw that a common dilemma in global organisations is how to provide sufficient commonality to bind an organisation together while at the same time enjoying the creative tension that diversity and difference bring. OD practitioners constantly wrestle with this issue so that 'valuing difference' itself often becomes part of the organisational culture through its stated values.

FEEDBACK PRODUCES BOTH CHANGE AND RESISTANCE

Culture fulfils the role of reducing ambiguity in organisations so that people know what to expect and how to behave. It therefore has a durable quality, for it would be very unsettling to work out the rules of the game on a daily basis. As an organisation responds to its environment, the competition, financial constraints and other challenges, it gradually changes and adapts but it will still be recognisable. When major change occurs, perhaps through a merger, the organisation can feel very resistant to change as people try to protect their old ways of doing things (sometimes described as 'the good old days' syndrome).

When times are tough, leaders and their people often revert to type and culture programmes start to unravel. 'Blame' cultures, command-and-control styles of leadership and greater centralisation start to re-emerge at a time when organisations need to be learning, networking, listening to feedback and empowering staff to meet the challenges they face.

HSE employees expressed concern that the changes they had seen as a result of the *Better … together* programme might not last when the team disbanded in 2011, particularly in the face of public sector cuts. Infineum and DIT found that constant reinforcement and role-modelling of values, particularly by leaders, was vital. The idea of culture change implies a sense of enduring change so that new values and ways of working become second nature to people.

Finally, not all change, of course, necessarily involves a change of 'culture'. Many organisations now focus on developing a culture that enables them to respond flexibly to ongoing change and market turbulence. 'Cultural agility' with high tolerance of ambiguity and a willingness to challenge assumptions and existing ways of doing things is perceived as essential in maintaining creativity and innovation. As organisations strive to develop a 'high-performing culture', the successful management of change is already built in to the underlying assumptions and values.

EXPLORE FURTHER

Martin, J. (2002) *Organisational Culture: Mapping the terrain*. Foundations for Organisational Science series. Newbury Park, CA: Sage. Her work is the classic analysis of different perspectives on organisational cultures.

Morgan, G. (1986) *Images of Organisation*. Thousand Oaks, CA: Sage. This book explores various metaphors as a way of thinking about organisations, and provides insights into the complexity of culture and organisational life.

Sackmann, A. (2006) *Success Factor: Corporate culture*. Gutersloh: Bertelsmann. This book examines six European case studies to understand how culture contributes to organisational success.

Stahl, G. K. and Mendenhall, M. E. (eds) (2005) *Mergers and Acquisitions: Managing culture and human resources*. Palo Alto, CA: Stanford University Press. This book integrates international theory and practice on the cultural and human resources processes associated with mergers and acquisitions.

REFERENCES

Balkin, J. (2004) *The Corporation: The pathological pursuit of profit and power*. New York: Free Press.

Bibby, J., Bevan, H., Carter, E., Bate, P. and Robert G. (2009) *The Power of One, the Power of Many*. London: NHS Institute for Innovation and Improvement.

Blackler, F. H. M. (2006) 'Chief executives and the modernisation of the English National Health Service', *Leadership*, Vol.2, No.1: 5–30.

Bridges, W. (1992) *The Character of Organisations: Using Jungian type in organisational development*. Palo Alto, CA: Consulting Psychologists Press.

Buono, A., Bowditch, J. and Lewis, J. W. (1985) 'When cultures collide: the anatomy of a merger', *Human Relations*, Vol.38, No.5: 477–500.

Cartwright, S. and McCarthy, S. (2005) 'Developing a framework for cultural due diligence in mergers and acquisitions: issues and ideas', in Stahl, G. K. and Mendenhall, M. E. (eds) *Mergers and Acquisitions: Managing culture and human resources*. Stanford, CA: Stanford Business.

Davis, G. F. (2009) *Managed by the Markets: How finance re-shaped America*. New York: Oxford University Press.

Davis, R. (1968) 'Compatibility in corporate marriages', *Harvard Business Review*, Vol.46: 86–93.

Deal, T. E. and Kennedy, A. A. (1982) *Corporate Cultures*. Reading, MA: Addison-Wesley.

Devine, M., Hirsh, W., Garrow, V., Holbeche, L. and Lake, C. (1998) *Mergers and Acquisitions: Getting the people bit right*. Horsham: Roffey Park Institute.

Elsass, P. M. and Veiga, J. F. (1994) 'Acculturation in acquired organisations: a force-field perspective', *Human Relations*, Vol.47, No.4: 431–53.

French, W. L. and Bell, C. H. (1979) *Organization Development: Behavioral science interventions for organisation improvement*. Upper Saddle River, NJ: Prentice Hall.

Garrow, V. (2003) *Managing on the Edge: Psychological contracts in transition*. Horsham: Roffey Park Institute.

Garrow, V. (2010) *Better ... Together*. London: Health and Safety Executive.

Garrow, V. and Varney, S. (2011) *Learning to Swim, Learning to Fly: A career in organisational development*. London/Brighton: Institute for Employment Studies.

Garrow, V., Varney, S. and Lloyd, C. (2009) *Fish or Bird? Perspectives on Organisational Development*. London/Brighton: Institute for Employment Studies.

Garrow, V., Devine, M., Hirsh, W. and Holbeche, L. (2000) *Strategic Alliances: Getting the people bit right*. Horsham: Roffey Park Institute.

Goffee, R. and Jones, G. (1998) *What Holds the Modern Company Together?* London: HarperCollins.

Goldthorpe, J., Lockwood, D., Bechhofer, F. and Platt, J. (1968) *The Affluent Worker: Industrial attitudes and behaviour*. Cambridge: Cambridge University Press.

Harrison, R. and Stokes, H. (1992) *Diagnosing Organisational Culture*. San Francisco: Jossey-Bass/Pfeiffer.

Hofstede, G. (1980) *Culture's Consequences: International differences in work-related values*. Beverly Hills, CA: Sage.

Hofstede, G. (2010) *Cultures and Organizations: Software for the mind*, 3rd edition. New York/London: McGraw-Hill.

Lakoff, G. and Johnson, M. (1980) *Metaphors We Live By*. London: University of Chicago Press.

Lorenz, E. (1972) 'Predictability: does the flap of a butterfly's wings in Brazil set off a tornado in Texas?' Paper presented to the American Association for the Advancement of Science, Washington, DC.

McFarlane Shore, L. and Tetrick, L. E. (1994) 'The psychological contract as an explanatory framework in the employment relationship', in Cooper, C. and Rousseau, D. M. (eds) *Trends in Organisational Behaviour*, Vol.1. Chichester/New York: John Wiley & Sons.

MacIntosh, R., Beech, N. and Martin, G. (2011) 'Dialogues and dialectics: limits to clinician–manager interaction in healthcare organisations', *Social Science and Medicine*, available online at doi:10.1016/j.socscimed.2011.03.014.

Martin, J. (2002) *Organisational Culture: Mapping the terrain*. Foundations for Organisational Science series. Newsbury Park, CA: Sage.

Martin, G. (2006) *Managing People and Organisations in Changing Contexts*. Oxford: Butterworth-Heinemann.

Morgan, G. (1986) *Images of Organisation*. Thousand Oaks, CA: Sage.

Nahavandi, A. and Malekzadeh, A. R. (1994) 'Successful mergers through acculturation', in VonKrogh, G., Sinatra, A. and Singh, H. (eds) *Managing Corporate Acquisitions. A European and American Perspective*. New York: Macmillan.

Peters, T. and Waterman, R. (1982) *In Search of Excellence*. New York: Harper & Row.

Rousseau, D. M. (2001) 'Schema, promise and mutuality: the building blocks of the psychological contract', *Journal of Occupational and Organisational Psychology*, Vol.74, No.4, November: 511.

Schein, E. H. (1992), *Organizational Culture and Leadership: A dynamic view*, 2nd ed. San Francisco: Dossey-Bass.

Spekman, R., Isabella, L., MacAvoy, T. and Forbes, T. (1996) 'Creating strategic alliances which endure', *Long-Range Planning*, Vol.29, No.3: 346–57.

Tsoukas, H. and Chia, R. (2002) 'On organizational becoming: rethinking organizational change', *Organization Science*, Vol.13, Sep–Oct: 567–82.

Weick, K. E. (1979) *The Social Psychology of Organizing*. Reading, MA: Addison-Wesley.

Westley, F., Zimmerman, B. and Patton, M. (2006) *Getting to Maybe: How the world is changed*. Toronto: Random House Canada.

CHAPTER 6

An ER Perspective on Organisational Effectiveness

John Purcell

CHAPTER OVERVIEW

This chapter argues that if organisational effectiveness is to be achieved, the HRM approach to employee relations must widen beyond the individual. It looks at the importance of managing employees as a collective whole, whether or not they are members of a trade union. It considers how the topics covered by collective bargaining have shifted from the traditional areas and sets out an approach to employee voice in the more ambiguous and complex area of change. The author's thought leadership combines insights from extensive research and practice in the fields of industrial and employee relations and human resource management.

LEARNING OBJECTIVES

By the end of this chapter the reader should be able to:

- appreciate the importance of managing employees as a collective whole and not just as individuals, and to see the importance of new forms of work organisation based on teams, devolved responsibility and line manager leadership
- make judgements on the social legitimacy of management decisions and behaviour, especially in managing change
- sum up the legal requirements to engage in consultation with employee representatives, and know the building blocks for effective consultation
- understand the complexities in handling and consulting over redundancies while ensuring employee engagement.

INTRODUCTION

It is strange that discussion of employment relations is often overlooked in analyses of organisational development and organisational effectiveness. Employment relations is the process of managing both the individual and the group in terms of contracts, regulations and collective behaviour – the way staff are dealt with across the firm in terms of management style and the 'voice' employees have in company decisions. It is commonly assumed that individualism is the dominant characteristic of the employment relationship in the early twenty-first century. This is to be perceived in contemporary interest in employee engagement, talent management, motivation and reward systems (see Chapters 13 and 14) and the management of change. These and other policy areas are sensible features of sophisticated human resource management linked to organisational strategies to achieve and improve effectiveness. The argument in this chapter is that this focus on the individual and the immediate work group is necessary but not sufficient in a proper understanding of the routes to organisational effectiveness. A wider perspective is needed, looking at the relationship between senior managers and employees collectively, including the influence that each has in determining the quality of the employment relationship.

One reason for this neglect of employment relations is the decline in collectivism, especially if this means trade unions and their preferred method of regulation, collective bargaining. The first section of the chapter looks at this in some detail, making distinctions between the public and private sectors and between large and smaller employers. This reveals that predictions of the 'death of collectivism' are premature. The second section places the focus firmly on the management of change since the topics covered by collective bargaining have shifted from contract-setting in pay and conditions, the traditional area, to the more ambiguous and complex area of change, especially big changes associated with mergers and acquisitions and restructuring with consequential threats to employment and work organisation. This affects all employers whether they recognise trade unions or are non-union. One reason for this had been the impact of legal regulation, much emanating from the European Union (EU), requiring consultation on change.

The third section explores this in some detail. The underlying point is that regulations require employers to consult with their staff on proposed changes and their consequences. Of course, some firms wriggle out of this obligation, which raises questions about the social legitimacy of what they are doing or, more probably, not doing. The penultimate section provides a case study of employment relations in action in change management, followed by a reflective commentary. The challenge is 'what would you have done?' in the circumstances described in the case. There is always a management dilemma in building and sustaining high-performance organisations when tough decisions have to be made. How far should, and can, management go in taking staff with them? Does this imply a risk of sharing of power and control which challenges the management prerogative? These are questions to be returned to in the conclusion.

THE END OF COLLECTIVISM?

In the second half of the twentieth century the dominant idea in employment relations – then referred to as industrial relations – was that trade unions represented the interests of employees and did so largely through the medium of collective bargaining. This was never quite an accurate picture because there always remained a sizable minority not in membership and outside the scope of collective bargaining. It was certainly the central assumption that trade unions were the only organisations capable of representing employees – what was called the 'single channel' of representation. Trade union membership grew steadily and, by its peak in 1979, 55% of employees were members: some 13.2 million workers. In 1980 half of all workplaces with 25 or more employees in the private sector had pay and conditions fixed by collective bargaining, either at the workplace or higher up in the company or in multi-employer bargaining covering whole sectors. Where there were joint consultative committees, they were most likely to be union-only bodies from the workers' side.

By 2004 the position had changed hugely. By then, according to the authoritative Workplace Employment Relations Survey (WERS), which has been conducted regularly since 1980, collective bargaining in the private sector covered only just over one in five workplaces (22%) and around three-quarters of employees had their pay fixed by management either where they worked or higher up in large multi-site firms. In 'construction, distribution and hospitality, and banking and finance, the retreat [from collective bargaining] has been steady and sustained over the whole period since 1980' (Brown, Bryson and Forth, 2009: 24–5). Union-only consultative committees were found in only 6% of workplaces in 2004 (Gomez, Bryson and Willman, 2010: 388). Union membership had halved by 2009 to 6.7 million workers, with only 15% of private sector employees in membership. Around 70% of private sector workplaces were union-'free' in the sense that a trade union was not reported to have any presence there. Only 18% of private sector workers had their pay influenced by collective bargaining (Achur, 2010). And just to confirm the massive changes, in 1980 there were 1,338 strikes starting that year involving nearly 12 million workers. In 2009 there were just 455 strikes, or 'stoppages' as the official statistics put it, involving only 209,000 workers (Hale, 2010: Table 2). These strike data cover both the public and the private sectors. This is not the place to explore why there has been such a collapse in the private sector (see Arrowsmith, 2010) but to note that the consequence was a major paradigm shift from managing the collective to motivating, and some would say manipulating, the individual.

The importance of these trends is summed up by Brown *et al* (2009: 47):

> This has been the story of the decline of the principal means of protecting labour standards in Britain. Collective bargaining developed over the twentieth century as a result of employers being able to compromise with organised labour. They could do this so long as the markets in which they traded were sufficiently imperfect in their competition. … Tougher competition has undermined this tacit settlement between employers and their employees' trade unions. Labour standards have become more vulnerable as a result.

There are two substantial caveats to this picture in the private sector. First, even within the sector, a much higher proportion of big employers recognise trade unions and set pay for a large part of their workforce by collective bargaining. For example, in private sector workplaces with 500 or more employees, half set pay and conditions by collective bargaining covering 49% of the employees (Kersley *et al*, 2006: Table 7.2). 'The character of the employment relationship for most employees is determined by practice in large workplaces' (*ibid*: 15). In light of their size and market dominance it can often be that the way these large firms cope with employment relations issues sets a marker for other firms. Their symbolic importance can be greater than their actual size. One example would be British Airways in the protracted way in which it had to deal with the strike action by cabin crew, especially at Heathrow in the period 2010/11. Another might be the action taken by some of the large vehicle manufacturers to deal with the market collapse in 2008/9 in discussion with their trade unions.

The second exception comes from the public sector. Some 35% of those in employment in the UK in 2006 worked in this large and diverse sector (Bach, 2010: 153). Well over half belong to trade unions. Not surprisingly, there is a union presence in virtually all (86%) of workplaces in the sector and over two-thirds are covered by collective bargaining. Industrial relations in the public sector has potential to be an area of major conflict as the government pursues policies to reduce the budget deficit and reorganise health (1.5 million employees), education (1.4 million) and central administration (1.2 million) (*ibid*: 160). The management of change can be complex and inevitably must include some form of dialogue and discussion with trade unions at national, sub-sectoral and workplace levels. Anyone writing, researching or practising OD cannot avoid the need for collective discussions, consultation and negotiation via trade unions in the public sector. In the private sector, or parts of it, some appear to believe that the whole issue of collective relationships can be avoided, but it cannot. The UK is going through a period of turbulent change, and gaining workforce co-operation and commitment will be a challenge yet remains critical. The need for a new ER, not based only on trade unions, is more evident now than it has been for many years.

EMPLOYEE RELATIONS AND THE MANAGEMENT OF CHANGE

A seminar was announced by UKWON recently. The speaker was Edwin van Vlierberghe, the CEO of Tower Automotive, Belgium, who was described as 'an inspiring leader'. The interest is in the bare bones of the story he had to tell since it encapsulates many of the key issues in employment relations and its links with organisational efficiency and development. He instigated a change process within his organisation designed to create high-trust working practices based on autonomous teamwork and participation. Some 30 different nationalities work within the organisation which has developed innovative approaches to communication and participation involving employees and union representatives. When the Tower organisation hit a crisis, management worked hard to avoid redundancies and liaised closely with union delegates in order to identify new activities and other companies which would provide temporary employment until such time as they could return to their jobs (UKWON, 2011).

Unpacking this, at least four dimensions of what might be called 'the new employment relations' can be identified. The first is leadership. This is to imagine what is possible and what is right or appropriate not just in financial terms but for reasons of social legitimacy – one of the goals of human resource management and ER (Boxall and Purcell, 2011: 19–22). Leadership also means having access to power and authority to make things happen. But this is never just power since individuals always have the capacity to resist, so with power comes the need for consent.

The second dimension is changes made to the organisation of work seen here in teamworking and participation. This is part of what is increasingly known as high-involvement work systems (HIWS) (*ibid*: 125–40), which require both on-the-job and off-the-job participation seen in team briefing systems, problem-solving groups, an emphasis on communication, and autonomous, or more often semi-autonomous, teamworking. Some would call all this 'employee involvement', or EI for short. There is very clear evidence that the use of EI has increased markedly in the last 20 years. In 1984 team briefings were used in a third of workplaces, but by 2004 their use had extended to just under four out of five (Millward, Bryson and Forth, 2000: Table 4.12; Kersley *et al*, 2006: 135). The importance of HIWS is the contrast with what came before in rigid factory work, low-discretion jobs, and clear separations of authority as prescribed by F. W. Taylor way back in the early twentieth century. As one observant Japanese businessman put it, 'Your firms are built on the Taylor model: even worse, so are your heads. With your bosses doing the thinking while the workers wield the screwdrivers, you are convinced deep-down that this is a right way to run a business' (cited in Boxall and Purcell, 2011: 134).

The change to HIWS involves delegation of authority direct to employees and new, more facilitative and leadership roles for front-line managers. While the powerful role of the chief executive is paramount in bringing in these changes, the critical need is for line managers to take responsibility for introducing the 'high-trust working practices based on autonomous teamworking and participation' at Tower Automotive. It cannot be done without them. 'Some elements of decision-making and problem-solving always remain with management and advanced specialists, but high-involvement work practices grant greater autonomy to … workers and enhance their responsibilities, thereby necessitating a greater investment in employee development' (*ibid*: 136). This is discussed further in Chapter 10. The move to HIWS is not restricted to manufacturing work. There has been a concomitant growth in employee responsibility for customer service in the service sector, confirmed in survey evidence that higher levels of employee satisfaction with aspects of their job are associated with high levels of customer satisfaction (Purcell and Kinnie, 2007).

The third dimension in the Tower Automotive story is hinted at but never made explicit. This is the forging of the company into a community, made more difficult, no doubt, because there were 30 nationalities among the staff. Organisations are social entities. Frequent reference is made to corporate or organisational culture, implying that there are distinctive characteristics in each workplace, but describing them, like capturing national culture in a sentence, is hard. People fall back on the cliché, 'the way we work around here', and those who move from one employer to another will note how different 'work' is (see Chapter 5). A community implies a sense of 'we' as well as 'me'. One of the leading survey agencies in employee engagement, Gallup, always uses a question in its survey about 'having a best friend at work'. This is one of the 12 areas or 'elements' that Gallup claim, with some justification, make for employee engagement where positive. Other elements which tap into a sense of community include 'co-workers committed to doing quality work', 'someone at work who cares about me as a person' and 'someone at work encourages my development' (Wagner and Harter, 2006).

Communities have rules and norms which can be negative by being oppressive, punitive or exclusive. The aim in employment relations is the creation of inclusive communities with high levels of trust and mutual support. Here there would be positive psychological contracts with an emphasis on longer-term relational, as opposed to transactional, market contracts (Rousseau, 1995). In redundancies there is a well-known phenomenon of a 'survivor syndrome', in which remaining employees feel a sense of guilt that they escaped the fate of their dismissed colleagues (Baruch and Hind, 2000). This vividly illustrates the group dynamics in a community that are always present but come to the fore in traumatic circumstances. Employees judge management not so much by the decision to make people redundant but by the 'fairness' and 'justice' of the decision-making process (Dietz and Fortin, 2007: 1168; Folger and Cropanzano, 1998). This means that people judge justice and fairness by how it applies not just to them individually but to the group they belong to, as well.

The fourth dimension evident in Tower Automotive is the involvement of the union delegates in high-level discussion and consultation both in the design of new ways of working and, when tough times came, in working with senior management to find ways of preserving jobs. The use of works councils is widespread in continental Europe in countries like Germany, the Netherlands, France and Belgium and others but is less well developed in Britain. It is a form of 'indirect participation' by which employee representatives, who may be directly elected or appointed employees or trade union delegates, have the great advantage over 'direct participation' in team briefing sessions, in that they meet senior managers. In the most effective consultative committees these meetings take place to discuss proposed strategic decisions such as redundancy, technical change and restructuring and their implications for jobs and work arrangements. Particular attention is usually given to how a decision is to be implemented. The legal basis for this is discussed in the next section.

An illustration comes from the overall winner of the CIPD People Management Awards in 2010: Nampak Plastics Europe. This company also won the category for employee engagement. A wide range of initiatives were adopted much as described here but included the involvement (Evans, 2010: 24) of its employees much more in strategy. Goals and the future direction of the business are regularly discussed by a team comprising the board of directors and ten nominated employees from around the business, who are entrusted with highly confidential information to enable them to make the right decisions for the organisation.

Boxall and Purcell (2011: 178–82) summarise the evidence on the impact of participation. This is especially positive in increasing employees' organisational commitment where such indirect schemes, seen in consultative committees, are combined with direct forms of EI at the workplace. Underlying all this is a participative style of management. Research in five Anglo-American countries on what workers want at work concluded that 'all the studies underline the message that workers want more co-operative styles of engagement with management' (Boxall, Haynes and Freeman, 2007: 216). Positive ER is all about tapping into this latent need for co-operative relationships between management and employees. The outcomes are higher levels of satisfaction and engagement and better organisational efficiency.

CONSULTING ON CHANGE: THE LEGAL BASIS OF GOOD PRACTICE

The management of employment relations always has to take account of the law and ensure at least minimal compliance. There are now over 60 individual rights in employment law covering all aspects of the employment relationship. Collective labour law is less pervasive but still important, especially if trade unions are recognised. Often, questions of law only rarely impact on employment practice in the sense of a claim or case being taken to an employment tribunal. In fact only around 5% of firms experience such an unwelcome event in any one year. The influence of law is on the design of policies and procedures and the training of line managers. There is one area of law, however, which directly impinges on aspects of change management and potentially on the way employers in 'undertakings' (the legal term used) with 50 or more employees consult and communicate with staff. This relates to the practice of consultation usually through employee representatives whether union or non-union.

Consultation has a long, and not very distinguished, history in British employment relations. Some employers, even back in the nineteenth century, created consultative committees but these were rare and it usually reflected the owners' ethical and religious background. There was a big boost to the establishment of consultative committees in the two World Wars of the twentieth century, especially in World War II. With the strong backing of the coalition government, joint production committees (JPCs) were set up in many war factories. The idea was to improve productivity and efficiency by tapping into employees' ideas and gaining consent to proposed changes. The employers did not like it and only went along with JPCs when the government threatened to use legislation to force compliance (Dukes, 2008). Trade unions have always been ambivalent since they prefer collective bargaining and fear that some employers would use consultative committees as substitutes for unions – in other words, union avoidance strategies. There are plenty of examples of employers doing just that. In some periods after the war there appeared to be a renaissance in consultation, only for it to fall back again as employers lost interest and unions did not push for it.

The latest picture we have is from the 2004 Workplace Employment Relations Survey (WERS). This showed that in workplaces with ten or more employees, 14% had a consultative committee on site, and a further 25% had one higher up in the company. A bank, for example, may have a consultative committee at regional levels or just nationally, but would be unlikely to have one in each branch. This low figure of just 14% is a bit misleading since consultative committees in very small workplaces would not fit in well. However, as the size of the workplace increases, so does the probability of having a consultative body. Once there are 50 employees or more, over half of workplaces have a consultative committee. Where there are 200 to 499 employees, three out five establishments have a committee on site and a further 13% have one at headquarters. In the largest category of 500 or more employees the incidence rises to three-quarters (73%) with a further 9% at a higher level (Kersley *et al*, 2007: Table 5.6). What is particularly interesting is that two-thirds of these consultative committees were non-union and only 11% organised exclusively by the recognised union. Around one in five (22%) had a mixture of union and non-union representatives working alongside each other. These are generally called 'hybrids' (Hall *et al*, 2010). It was very common (over 75%) for these consultative bodies to discuss work organisation, future plans, health and safety, training, employment issues and welfare services and facilities. Two-thirds discussed financial issues like profits and turnover.

Consultation is based on co-operation so it may be surprising to find that disagreements and differences of opinion are a common feature of the consultative process. In fact, it is the sign of a healthy consultative body since people will have different views on issues which affect jobs and work organisation. A passive body of 'nodding heads' would not be in anyone's interest. Consultation is about 'the exchange of views and the establishment of dialogue' (this is the EU definition). 'When participation works well, disagreements are resolved smoothly' (Heller *et al*, 1998: 147) and 'conflicts facilitate innovation and consensus' (*ibid*: 46). Consultation is not negotiation, and it is management who have the last say on what is to be done, when and how. The CIPD (2004: 9) says that 'consultation involves managers taking into account employees' views before making a decision'. This is important since it places the onus on management to bring ideas and options to the consultative body before the final decision is made, thus allowing for employees, through their representatives, to have some influence.

An interesting picture emerges from the WERS research on how consultation is practised (Kersley *et al*, 2007: 130). The management respondents in the survey were given three statements about how consultation took place and were asked which best described their own practice. Just over two in five (43%) said that their usual approach was to look to the committee to provide solutions to problems (what is known as 'option-based consultation'). Just under half (45%) said that they usually sought feedback from the committee on a range of options put forward by management. One in ten (11%) only provided the committee with management's preferred option, implying that there could be little or no discussion of alternatives. Interestingly, managers who engaged in option-based consultation were much more likely to say that the committee had a substantive influence over managerial decision-making, a quarter of them saying that the committee was 'very influential'. In the other direction, a quarter of managers with committees where there was little discussion, not surprisingly, said their consultative committee was 'not very influential'. Three-quarters of consultative committees met at least four times a year (*ibid*: 128).

This was in 2004, but in 2005 the Information and Consultation of Employees Regulations (ICE for short) came into force for undertakings with 150 or more employees, and by 2008 this size threshold had been reduced to 50. This means that there is a presumed obligation on employers to consult with their staff. The EU sees the provision of information and the practice of consultation as a 'fundamental right' in the same way as there is a fundamental right not to suffer from discrimination in employment. A right is indivisible. The way the regulations are drawn up gives considerable freedom to choose the form and frequency of consultation. The need to take steps to set up a consultative body is only 'triggered' when 10% or more of the employees ask for one. What evidence we have suggests that very few employees have organised themselves to exercise this right. Consultative committees come with a wide variety of titles such as 'joint consultative committee', 'works council' and 'voice forum'. The term used here is 'staff council'.

There is nothing to stop an employer from setting up a staff council without an employee request. There is technical advantage in doing so, from the employer's perspective, in that the subsequent council is established as a 'pre-existing agreement' (PEA), provided a majority of employees in a ballot have backed it, or all employee representatives have endorsed it. A PEA is not legally enforceable unless or until 40% of employees say they want to overturn it. This is highly unlikely. Some companies have responded to the regulations by setting up a staff council, but many have not and the 'do nothing' option is clearly available in law. This is a pity since an effective council can contribute hugely to the management of change by getting acceptance of management proposals, sometimes modified, and often improving the implementation plans. This is a question of ethics or social legitimacy as well as good business sense. Why are so many senior managers opposed to consultation?

Even those who oppose it cannot escape completely. There are two particular circumstances where consultation must be carried out and there can be quite tough financial penalties for not doing so. The first is the Transfer of Undertaking and Protection of Employees Regulations 2006, which apply when business ownership changes hands. The second concerns redundancies when 20 or more dismissals are envisaged within a 90-day period. Where a trade union is recognised, the consultation must be with the union. But where there is no union a special representative body of employees must be created especially for the purpose, unless employees say they do not want it. The law requires that employees affected by the redundancy or the business transfer be invited to elect representatives 'long enough' before the changes to be provided with information about the changes and to consult. It is no good doing this after the announcement. The employer must decide how long the representatives will be needed to enable the consultation to be completed, and there must be enough representatives to ensure that everyone's interests are represented (Deakin and Morris, 2009: 802–6, 818). It is clear from case law that:

- consultation must begin when proposals are still in a formative stage, or being contemplated
- adequate information must be provided in sufficient detail to allow employee representatives to formulate a response
- adequate time must be allowed for the representatives to respond, and
- a conscientious consideration must be made by management of the representatives' response.

The purpose of consultation is to explore ways of avoiding the dismissals, to reduce the number affected and to mitigate the consequences. This would include consideration of alternatives such as redeployment, reducing overtime and offering more flexible hours such as job-share (Ranieri, 2010: 3). Ranieri provides some examples of good and bad practice. In one case, employee representatives considered the consultation process had been a sham. In this firm management had allowed the representatives to go back and speak to their constituents and gather their views over a three- or four-day period. Once the representatives presented feedback on the management proposals, management took less than an hour to respond. The view was that no serious consideration was being given to alternatives put forward and representatives were being railroaded (*ibid*: 7). A much better example comes from a food manufacturer going through a restructuring process.

Initially the employer proposed making 140 employees redundant. The consultation process was approached by the company in a structured and sensible way. It was a 90-day process and meetings were scheduled in both the company's northern and southern sites every three weeks to allow enough time for feedback to be gathered and for representatives to take back proposals to employees. The agenda for each meeting was determined jointly with some aspects led by the representatives. For example, the company had wanted to hold back on discussing voluntary redundancy packages in the early stage but the representatives indicated that this was a high-priority item for the employees. Management agreed with the request. Despite initial predictions of 140 redundancies, the consultation process was very successful, particularly regarding alternatives to compulsory redundancy such as voluntary redundancies, job-sharing and part-time arrangements by agreement. This resulted in only having to make 50 people redundant, a little over a third of the company's original proposal (*ibid*).

The WERS survey asked management respondents who had had redundancies why they were necessary. The most common reason in over one-third of cases (37%) was because of a 'reorganisation of working methods', followed by 'lack of demand for products and services' (28%), 'improving competitiveness/efficiency/cost reduction' (19%) and 'reduction in budget' (16%). It is probable now that, from the onset of the recession in 2008, the reason for redundancies, in the main, will be economic. Even in these types of redundancies, unless a whole plant or company is closing, but certainly in redundancy for reorganisation of working methods, the effect of the cuts is to require a careful reorganisation of work and jobs for many people. This can require very high levels of co-operation at a time when the atmosphere is tense. We know that when there was a high level of pre-existing trust between management and employees and their representatives, even though the psychological contract had been breached or even violated – a typical outcome in redundancy – the damage is much less and management are less likely to be blamed (Robinson and Rousseau, 1994). The finger is pointed at outside events, such as bankers these days. The more the possibility of externalising blame, the greater the internal unity and common purpose in rebuilding. Consultation can provide a very helpful means of doing this.

Trust is central to effective consultation but it is not easy to build, and very simple to destroy. Trust has to be mutual. Only saints trust people who do not reciprocate. To trust is to take a risk and make you vulnerable: 'How do I know you won't tell the press about these confidential plans or put them on FaceBook?' Trusting behaviour is about co-operation and sharing, and this can go against the grain for managers, and some companies. Sometimes people look for ulterior motives: 'Why is he telling us this?' And the sharing of information can be a burden to some employee representatives: 'Ignorance is bliss; it is folly to be wise.' Consultation is not an easy option.

The management dilemma often faced, especially where employee representatives are non-union and so have no access to external advice and training, is how to create an effective representative body. If management want to consult seriously, it must have an authoritative body to talk with – one that can carry the workforce with them and know how and what to communicate. An added problem is that if consultation is on proposed or contemplated plans, the information will have to be given in confidence. This requires the members of the staff forum to be 'representatives' rather than 'delegates'. A delegate always reports back and takes advice from constituents. A representative has to be able to act independently and take the consequences at the next election, and has to be able to keep confidential information under wraps until an agreed time later.

For active consultation to take place, representatives need to be organised. This will mean being trained after having been elected, and it helps if line managers share in this training too (see the ACAS booklet *Non-Union Representation in the Workplace*). In some companies this training is followed up by 'development days' on which better ways of working are examined. There is a need for representatives to have a pre-meeting to work out their response to items raised by management in advance of the forum meeting. In one large IT company the pre-meeting of 24 representatives lasts the whole day immediately before the council convenes. They also use this to decide which items they want to raise and filter out some of the trivial items best dealt with elsewhere. This avoids the forum degenerating into just a 'tea and toilets' gripe session. Representatives need agreed time off from their job not just to attend meetings but to communicate with their constituents and with each other. In the IT company there is a one-hour conference call every Friday afternoon.

One feature of effective consultation is that management will devote considerable effort in 'selling' it to employees, using all communication means possible to promote the staff council and report on the work it is doing. This is a visible proof that there is a participative style of management in place, and this in turn influences line managers' behaviour, taking a cue from the top management team. In other words, consultation helps reflect and reinforce the organisational culture, sense of community and distributive leadership. But in particular it helps the successful management of change where management are prepared to discuss proposals in advance of taking a decision, where information and time is given for plans to be scrutinised by employee representatives and where their questions, ideas and suggestions for modification are given proper consideration. The outcomes are an 'increase in organisational performance and harmony, serving employees' interests by improving terms and conditions of work and satisfaction with the job and the company in a relatively non-adversarial manner' (Kaufman and Taras, 2010: 277).

The law plays an important part in getting such good practice embedded. As Gollan (2010: 221) has observed, 'Regulatory rules and laws encourage or force certain behaviours that otherwise would not have taken place.' While the ICE regulations have so far been a bit of a 'damp squib' (Hall, 2006) the equivalent regulations covering multinational companies in Europe creating European Works Councils (EWC) will be strengthened in 2011. This will now give legal rights to EWC members to obtain the financial and material resources needed to carry out their duties, to undertake training, call special meetings, hold pre-meetings and seek external advice (Hall *et al*, 2010: 64). Consultation is most deeply embedded in Germany through works councils and has been supported by law since 1952. This includes provision for worker-directors, something which has proved to be a step too far for Britain. In a careful comparative study of work reorganisation in US and German call centres, Doellgast (2010: 390) concluded that in Germany 'unions and works councils use their stronger participation rights to encourage management to adopt a high-involvement approach to work organisation and performance management'.

BLOOD ON THE CARPET AT VALLEYCO

CASE STUDY

Valleyco employs – or employed, when this story begins – 450 workers in its plant in the Welsh valleys, making quite complex medical equipment. There is a 'hybrid' joint works council (JWC) for the unionised manual workers and non-union staff. The JWC works well. 'Management are always upfront with us.'

In January the site manager gave 90 days' notice that major redundancies were planned. Seventy per cent of the work would be transferred to Turkey and Poland, entailing the loss of around two-thirds of the jobs. The union response was that 'They were not having it,' while the staff representatives wanted to explore alternatives. During the 90-day period corporate managers came to meet JWC representatives but it proved impossible to come up with viable alternatives to save the £9 million needed.

A day after the consultation period expired it was announced that 185 jobs 'will be phased out over the next 14 months, with a further 27 positions still under review'. A further period of consultation was begun 'to discuss how best to achieve the necessary redundancies'. The company promised that 'a range of support services will be available for affected employees, including outplacement assistance, financial advice and training for alternative careers'. No compulsory redundancies would happen before September. The union and the staff representatives decided that they had to work with management to try to save the plant. They objected to the use of compulsory redundancies, but because of the paucity of volunteers and the scale of the cutbacks, redundancies were inevitable.

Management had three challenges. How would the rump of the factory be organised to preserve future work? How could they 'keep the wheels on the wagon' to ensure that existing customers continued to be supplied? How could they keep employees engaged while transferring production to Turkey and Poland and while reducing head-count?

The new organisation

The design of the new organisation was centred on the introduction of lean manufacturing principles involving significant flexibility. New production teams were created, with employees required to be flexible both within and between teams. This affected most people. A substantial training programme aimed to get people to the standard of 'a fully effective operator'. Maintenance fitters now had to be team members, so some operators lost their jobs to make room for these more skilled workers. The JWC officers worked intensively with each supervisor to manage the transfers, getting agreement on a person-by-person basis.

The most difficult decision concerned shiftwork flexibility. A five-shift pattern existed, but under the new arrangement management wanted to be able, at short notice, to run only four shifts when orders were low. An early proposal was for the fifth shift to be manned by agency workers. This was rejected by the union, which wanted all jobs for Valleyco staff. It was eventually agreed that when the fifth shift did not run, the workers would lose shift pay, and this could happen for up to 38 weeks in a year.

Keeping the wheels on the wagon

The redundancies had to be phased to keep production going until the new factories in Poland and Turkey were ready and trained. An incentive scheme was introduced, payable for continuing employment over a specified period. Initially, this was paid to all employees for three months and then only to those on the redundancy list. Some people still left. What was hard was introducing the new organisation at the same time. This required moving some operators into training before reassignment, introducing fitters on the line, and matching positions which became vacant to existing team members. Overtime was banned.

Managing the transition

It was necessary to transfer knowledge to Polish and Turkish operatives, some of whom came to Valleyco before the machinery was moved. This was not popular. Agreement was reached that there would be advance notice of any visitors on site and the JWC informed. After the compulsory redundancies, co-operation with visitors was withdrawn for a while. It was decided to send volunteer Valleyco workers to Turkey instead.

Previously, redundancy selection was on the 'first in, last out' basis, but this now broke age discrimination rules. A new points system was designed by the JWC after long discussion. This gave points for competence (requiring a new appraisal system), sickness record, time-keeping and discipline, and length of service.

The process of consultation in redundancy and restructuring

The JWC was too formal to cope with the intense discussion required. A sub-committee was formed and no minutes were taken. Weekly, often day-long meetings in the nearby Owen Hotel evolved. It was here that the key discussions took place. One manager recalls that there was a lot of table-thumping while the union chairman said 'There was blood on the carpet – the usual stuff – ours as well as theirs.' Those present recall that there was often no set agenda, with the usual ritual of management making a detailed proposal and it being knocked back by the union. Rather, 'Agreement came around the table. We [management] did not have a definitive plan entering the discussions.' 'We were jointly designing a survival operation for the plant,' said the branch chairman. The redundancy selection procedure emerged in this way.

The eventual package of measures was taken to a branch meeting for a vote on a Saturday morning. It was rejected.

Management had to do something to rescue the deal. They met each employee with a job in the new organisation, asking, 'Do you want to work here under the new arrangements?' Each was given 48 hours to decide. Virtually everyone did sign. This was unilateral action by management. The union chairman praised management for 'doing the drastic thing and not backing off – hats off to them'.

Now, around 110 people work at Valleyco. There is a thriving sports and social club for everyone, including those who left in the redundancies.

Senior management took the 90-day consultative period seriously. They would have known that the chances of the union and the staff representatives coming up with a viable alternative which would save £9 million were remote. The JWC employee members asked to meet senior managers from the UK office and the US head office. Why did the senior managers bother to come? One answer is that this was their corporate style, which they felt they had to live by. Another is that they knew they needed the co-operation of the workforce during the massive changes which would follow the announcement of the redundancies. If consultation is not meaningful, it can destroy the last vestige of trust.

Once every option had been explored in the 90-day period, the union and the staff representatives decided they would work to make the plant viable. They could have chosen not to and devoted all their energies to getting the maximum redundancy terms and left management to get on with the downsizing. But remember: this is a big employer in a Welsh valley with a strong sense of community and everyone knowing everyone else, and many managers lived locally too. To walk away would have been a dereliction of what they thought was their duty, but it also meant they had to make very difficult choices which some would rather have avoided. This is leadership in action.

● Would you have taken such a big step?

To focus on the redundancies is to miss the point. The problem faced by the top managers at Valleyco was not just how to choose who was to go but how to keep the plant going in the rundown, how to get Polish and Turkish workers trained, and how to build a whole new way of working to improve efficiency. In redundancies the management of change is much wider than downsizing. Quite a few managements don't realise this and think that cutting numbers is enough.

● How would you have approached this?

The new organisation became the focus of much of the discussions in the JWC and in the Owen Hotel meetings. This was sensible, since one feature of good change management is to focus on 'the future perfect' rather than dwell on current problems. Management also recognised that to get the new work organisation up and running would require investment, especially in training. This gives a sense of hope as well as practical benefits. Difficult choices had to be made, such as making some operatives redundant even from sections which were untouched by the movement of machinery to Poland and Turkey. This known as 'bumping', where one worker has to make way for another more skilled or valuable person. The union had a big dilemma, too. It would have been easier to accept agency workers on the fifth shift since, when that was cancelled, the agency workers would not be needed, while Valleyco employees would have stable jobs and fixed incomes from the other four shifts. But the union chose to protect as many jobs as possible and refused to have agency workers on site. The cost was that for up to 38 weeks in a year workers were in danger of losing shift pay. This may have contributed to the union members turning down the final agreement in the branch meeting.

● Did the union do the right thing in refusing agency working?

'Keeping the wheels on the wagon' meant ensuring that workers who knew that they were to be made redundant would keep on working until the last moment when their work ceased.

● How would you have done that?

It is a hard problem managing redundancies. Often, as in Valleyco, volunteers are asked for, but it often happens that it is the best workers who volunteer since they find it easiest to get another job, while less able people stay on. And in this case, at the same time as trying to keep workers, other changes were having to be introduced.

It was a tough call to get employees in Valleyco to help train the very people from Poland and Turkey who were to take their jobs.

● Would you have done that, and if so, how?

There were limits to how far the union felt it could go with this, and co-operation was withdrawn for a period when the compulsory redundancies were made, but for much of the period there was co-operation. The key feature was the high level of trust between management and the representatives and the fact that they were also working on building the future, and that this was a transitional cost which would not last long.

It used to be that redundancy selection was straightforward on the principle of 'first in, last out'. This protected older workers and was seen to be fair. It was the union, following legal advice, which concluded that this was no longer possible since it was open to challenge in an employment tribunal on grounds of age discrimination. But what should go in its place? It means, usually, opting for selection criteria not based on clear objective 'facts' but on subjective judgement like 'competence', and this is not something that can be defended so easily.

● What criteria would you use? But, before you answer this, just imagine that you are the manager who has to tell Meg and Mark why they have been chosen for redundancy.

The key point here is that the criteria which were adopted were agreed after long and painful discussion around the table at the Owen Hotel. This made choices defensible and seen to be 'fair', especially as everyone had been offered training to become the 'fully competent operator' which was the chief criterion for selection.

The way discussions were handled, especially in the Owen Hotel, was critical to their success. Normally, collective bargaining is adversarial, with the 'parties' in opposing camps edging close to agreement in a process of 'haggling'. This encourages exaggeration, especially in initial positions. Here management deliberately adopted a 'round-table' approach by specifying the problem – say, redundancy selection – and not proposing a solution but allowing it to be explored jointly. This does not mean that management did not have a clear idea of their preferences. It was the process that was important – a better way to seek agreement – but it was tough. 'There was 'blood on the carpet.' Mature negotiators know that there can be conflict and disagreement – 'the usual stuff', as the union put it – but this 'inter-party conflict' is never confused with 'inter-personal conflict'. Never get 'personal' in consultations and negotiations.

● Do you think management were taking too big a risk in not presenting plans at the Owen Hotel meetings?

It all nearly went wrong when the branch rejected the proposed agreement.

● What would you have done then?

It was felt that there was no room for renegotiations. In the end, talking to each employee on a one-to-one basis was felt to be the only option. And it worked.

An employee satisfaction survey was conducted two years before these massive changes, and again afterwards. The results are startling: 'How good are management here at seeking employees' views?' Up from 41 to 79%. 'How good

are managers here at keeping their promises?' Up from 37 to 77%. 'How fair
are managers?' Up from 50 to 76%. And the crucial question on organisational
commitment up from 70 to 90%. One respondent wrote in the survey form:

The past 14 months have been a huge challenge to [Valleyco] and its employees. Levels of consultation and communication reached unprecedented levels following the announced closure of two-thirds of manufacturing operations. Workplace consultation has delivered an amazing result considering the scale of job cuts. Levels of quality, productivity, safety and attendance all exceeded the average run-rate for the previous two years.

CONCLUSION

Employment relations (ER) are about the management of groups, at the level of teams, of sections and departments and of the organisation as a whole. Organisational efficiency and development cannot be achieved without reference to group dynamics. This, of course, is not to downplay the importance of the individual, and in contemporary ER both the wider group and individual variances are recognised. In practical terms this is seen in debates on work organisation and especially in how much 'voice' employees have at work.

Voice is especially important and valuable in the relationship with line managers – for example, in the types and ranges of communication between line managers and their team members. Communication has to be two-way to be effective. This means, for instance, time being devoted in briefing sessions for team members to have an opportunity to say what they want and to ask questions. It also means tapping into employees' views in satisfaction or engagement surveys. More meaningful, however, are arrangements to cede some responsibility to teams for organising their work, monitoring quality and taking corrective action. It can also mean taking part in problem-solving groups so that participation is both on the job and off the job.

The generic term used for these types of work organisational arrangements is 'high-involvement work systems'. It is increasingly common to find these types of HIWS in advanced manufacturing where there is a greater reliance on employee skill and knowledge and job discretion. This is also the case in the service sector where staff are increasingly responsible for gaining customer satisfaction through the quality of service. HR has to be involved in the project, but they have to rely on line managers for leadership. And nothing can be achieved without the consent of team members and the wider group of employees.

Increasingly managers are looking for 'engaged' employees – that is, staff with positive attitudes towards the company, their manager, co-workers and customers, and action-oriented behaviours. This is sometimes described, wrongly, as 'going the extra mile'. It does not mean doing more but doing things better. The key point, which some managers forget, is that employees cannot be forced to be 'engaged'; commitment to the organisation cannot be ordered. It has to be earned. Incentives may help get compliance, but this is not the same as engagement. Here we fall back on words common in ER: trust, respect, fairness, justice, co-operation. At its heart, the employment relationship is about mutuality.

So far so good, perhaps, but there is more to ER than HIWS and the search for employee engagement. The extra dimension is how employees collectively can express their views and gain some participation in strategic decisions taken by senior managers, few of whom still have a role in managing employees on the shop floor or in the office, school or hospital, on a daily basis. Historically, this collective voice has been provided by trade unions in collective bargaining on terms and conditions of employment. The decline in union membership in the private sector and in the coverage of collective bargaining has sometimes meant that this aspect of ER is now discounted as a historical legacy. It is a mistake, as shown in the chapter, to write off collective relationships since unions are still to be found in many large companies and are certainly embedded in the public sector.

The focus on collective bargaining over pay, hours and holidays, while still much in evidence in the public sector, is now much less important and influential than collective discussions on major strategic change such as restructuring, redundancy, changes in ownership and relocations. This is where ER meets business strategy (see Chapter 2) and shapes the strategic role of HR (see Chapter 7). This is recognised in labour law, emanating from the EU. Companies are required to consult, either with their recognised trade union or with a specially created consultative body, on large-scale redundancies and company mergers or acquisitions. Consultation has to be meaningful in the sense of giving information about planned or contemplated changes before a decision has been taken, with time, and often resources, provided for employee representatives to formulate questions and make suggestions, and for these to be treated seriously by management. Successful consultation is inevitably a form of power-sharing albeit with management having 'the last say'.

The provision of timely information and consultation on management proposal is asserted to be a 'fundamental right' in the EU Social Chapter. It extends to the operation of multinational companies in Europe in the European Works Council and now applies to all enterprises in the UK, and the rest of Europe, with 50 or more employees. The justification for this can be seen in stakeholder analysis: the right for employees to have their interests taken into account alongside shareholders and the avoidance of excessive short-termism. Another justification is how it contributes to the successful management of major change by giving employees a voice in the process. There is plenty of evidence to support the positive effect collective, or indirect, participation has on employees' commitment to their organisation when operating alongside direct employee involvement in team briefings and problem-solving. This, in turn, feeds through to efficiency.

This new face of collectivism, or new employment relations, is, as yet, under-developed in the UK, certainly in comparison with mature continental European systems in the Netherlands, Germany, Demark and France, for example. The majority of staff councils are non-union, so it is not something that has to wait until a trade union comes knocking, although union support is most often a positive benefit. Management are always the lead player in ER generally and consultation specifically. Now that the law is in place, there is a new opportunity for British managers to embrace consultation as a form of partnership and co-operation in the effective management of change and building robust systems to maximise organisational efficiency.

EXPLORE FURTHER

It is always sensible to follow up cited references on particular topics. The books recommended below provide a comprehensive coverage of ER and strategic HRM.

Boxall, P. and Purcell, J. (2011) *Strategy and Human Resource Management*, 3rd edition. Basingstoke: Palgrave Macmillan. Make sure you have the 3rd edition because it provides the most up-to-date and authoritative examination of key issues in strategic human resource management including participation and 'voice'.

Brown, W., Bryson, A., Forth, J. and Whitfield, K. (eds) (2009) *The Evolution of the Modern Workplace*. Cambridge: Cambridge University Press. This collection of essays is the most authoritative analysis of trends in ER using the WERS database. It is written by the leading scholars in ER in the UK.

Colling, T. and Terry, M. (eds) (2010) *Industrial Relations: Theory and Practice*. Chichester: John Wiley. Based in the main on contributions from academics at the

Industrial Relations Research Unit at Warwick Business School, this collection of original essays unpacks the complexities and contradictions in contemporary ER.

Wilkinson, A., Gollan, P., Marchington, M. and Lewin, D. (eds) (2010) *The Oxford Handbook of Participation in Organisations*. Oxford: Oxford University Press. This is a handbook with 25 topic areas on all aspects of participation and consultation, written by leading authorities in the field.

Learning signpost: Relevant overviews of practical activities can be found in the CIPD's *Organisation Development and Change* Toolkit – eg Tools number 27 (Communication and consultation) and 28 (Checklist of methods of communication).

REFERENCES

Achur, J. (2010) *Trade Union Membership 2009*. A National Statistical Office Publication. London: Department for Business, Innovation and Skills.

Arrowsmith, J. (2010) 'Industrial relations in the private sector', in Colling, T. and Terry, M. (eds) *Industrial Relations: Theory and practice*. Chichester: John Wiley.

Bach, S. (2010) 'Public sector industrial relations: the challenge of modernisation', in Colling, T. and Terry, M. (eds) *Industrial Relations: Theory and practice*. Chichester: John Wiley.

Baruch, Y. and Hind, P. (2000) 'Survivor syndrome – a management myth?', *Journal of Managerial Psychology*, Vol.15, No.1: 29–45.

Boxall, P. and Purcell, J. (2011) *Strategy and Human Resource Management*, 3rd edition. Basingstoke: Palgrave Macmillan.

Boxall, P., Haynes, P. and Freeman, R. (2007) 'Conclusion: what workers say in the Anglo-American world', in Freeman, R., Boxall, P. and Haynes, P. (eds) *What Workers Say: Employee voice in the Anglo-American workplace*. Ithaca, NY: ILR Press.

Brown, W., Bryson, A. and Forth, J. (2009) 'Competition and the retreat from collective bargaining', in Brown, W., Bryson, A., Forth, J. and Whitfield, K. (eds) *The Evolution of the Modern Workplace*. Cambridge: Cambridge University Press.

CIPD (2004) *Information and Consultation: A Guide*. London: CIPD.

Deakin, S. and Morris, G. (2009) *Labour Law*, 5th edition. Oxford: Hart.

Dietz, G. and Fortin, M. (2007) 'Trust and justice in the formation of joint consultative committees', *International Journal of Human Resource Management*, Vol.18, No.7: 1159–81.

Doellgast, V. (2010) 'Collective voice under decentralised bargaining: a comparative study of work reorganisation in US and German call centres', *British Journal of Industrial Relations*, Vol.48, No.2: 375–99.

Dukes, R. (2008) 'Voluntarism and the single channel: the development of single-channel worker representation in the UK', *The International Journal of Comparative Labour Law and Industrial Relations*, Vol.24, No.1: 87–121.

Evans, R. (2010) 'The whole package: CIPD People Management Awards', *People Management*, 25 November: 23–4.

Folger, R. and Cropanzano, R. (1998) *Organizational Justice and Human Resource Management*. Thousand Oaks, CA: Sage.

Gollan, P. J. (2010) 'Employer strategies towards non-union collective voice' in Wilkinson, A., Gollan, P. J., Marchington, M. and Lewin, D. (eds) *The Oxford Handbook of Participation in Organisations*. Oxford, Oxford University Press.

Gomez, R., Bryson, A. and Willman, P. (2010) '"Voice in the wilderness"? The shift from union to non-union voice in Britain', in Wilkinson, A., Gollan, P. J., Marchington, M. and Lewin, D. (eds) *The Oxford Handbook of Participation in Organisations*. Oxford: Oxford University Press.

Hale, D. (2010) 'Labour disputes in 2009', *Economic & Labour Market Review*, Vol.4, No.6: 47–59.

Hall, M. (2006) 'A cool response to the ICE Regulations? Employer and trade union approaches to the new legal framework for information and consultation', *Industrial Relations Journal*, Vol.37, No.5: 456–72.

Hall, M., Hutchinson, S., Purcell, J., Terry, M. and Parker, J. (2010) *Information and Consultation under the ICE Regulations: Evidence from longitudinal case studies*. Employment Relations Research Series No 117. London: Department of Business, Innovation and Skills. Available online at http://www.bis.gov.uk/assets/biscore/employment-matters/docs/i/10-1380-information-consultation-ice-regulations.

Heller, F., Pusic, E., Strauss, G. and Wilpert, B. (1998) *Organization Participation: Myth and reality*. Oxford: Oxford University Press.

Kaufman, B. and Taras, D. (2010) 'Employee participation through non-union forms of employee representation', in Wilkinson, A., Gollan, P. J., Marchington, M. and Lewin, D. (eds) *The Oxford Handbook of Participation in Organisations*. Oxford: Oxford University Press.

Kersley, B., Alpin, C., Forth, J., Bryson, A., Bewley, H., Dix, G. and Oxenbridge, S. (2006) *Inside the Workplace: Findings from the 2004 Workplace Employment Relations Survey*. London: Routledge.

Millward, N., Bryson, A. and Forth, J. (2000) *All Change at Work? British employment relations 1980–1998, as portrayed by the Workplace Industrial Relations Survey series*. London: Routledge.

Purcell, J. and Kinnie, N. (2007) 'HRM and business performance' in Boxall, P., Purcell, J. and Wright, P. (eds) *The Oxford Handbook of Human Resource Management*. Oxford: Oxford University Press.

Ranieri, N. (2010) *Collective Consultation on Redundancies*. ACAS Policy Discussion Paper. London: ACAS.

Robinson, S. and Rousseau, D. (1994) 'Violating the psychological contract: not the exception but the norm', *Journal of Organizational Behaviour*, Vol.15: 245–59.

Rousseau, D. (1995) *Psychological Contracts in Organizations*. Thousand Oaks, CA: Sage.

UKWON (2011) 'Employee engagement in volatile times'. Seminar paper, produced in association with the Institute for Business Ethics. 24 March. Available online at http://www.ukwon.net [accessed 22 March 2011].

Wagner, R. and Harter, J. (2006) *Twelve Elements of Great Managing*. New York: Gallup Press.

CHAPTER 7

Transforming HR to Support Strategic Change

Peter Reilly

CHAPTER OVERVIEW

This chapter will help you think through the opportunities and challenges in transforming HR to enable it to support strategic change in other parts of the organisation. The chapter draws upon evidence from research on how HR transformation has been managed to date, and proposes that the function should learn to effect change using the methodologies described elsewhere in this book. It is also illustrated with case study examples which seek to combine theoretical and practical perspectives.

LEARNING OBJECTIVES

By the end of this chapter the reader should be able to:

- understand the reasons for and the nature of HR transformation
- produce a critique of HR transformation to date
- articulate the issues associated with HR modelling a change approach usable by the rest of the organisation
- appreciate how the Lloyds Banking Group addressed these issues in its merger/acquisition of HBOS.

INTRODUCTION

For organisational change to be successful, HR must be in a position to support it effectively. The argument of this chapter is that HR must transform itself if this is to happen. Moreover, HR has to demonstrate that the way it changes itself is by adopting the same approach that it commends for wider organisational change. We are critical of how HR transformation has been managed because, in our view, it has taken too narrow a view of the organisational benefits to be obtained and conducted the process in too introverted a manner. This insight, and others in this chapter, are less referenced by academic research and more by interviews and discussions with HR practitioners, and described in IES's three reports for the CIPD (Tamkin *et al*, 2006; Reilly *et al*, 2006; Reilly *et al*, 2007) and the three books co-written with Tony Williams at Royal Bank of Scotland (Reilly and Williams, 2003, 2006, forthcoming). The style is deliberately intended to challenge, precisely because we believe there is room for improvement in managing a functional, let alone organisational, transformation.

Some organisations might believe that their HR transformation is complete. Others argue that transformation is a continuous journey rather than an event (Reilly and Williams, forthcoming). The latter contention appears to be more plausible. Change is an organisational constant, as structures alter, products and services arrive or cease, technology innovates and the socio-economic landscape shifts. The private sector has had to respond to a severe recession and the public sector is now going through the same pain of another round of cuts. Furthermore, many companies are frequently grappling with globalisation either as a player or as an affected bystander, or having to react to a merger or acquisition, new strategic partnership or joint venture. As a result, HR is always having to adjust to fit its environment, and follow the business model.

However, if the broad aim of the HR function is that it should become better regarded, more efficient and able to make a more effective contribution to organisational performance, then it can be said that only a certain number of organisations have met those transformational goals. Of course, they can still make improvements, but the value-adding challenge has not been sufficiently met.

Such a claim can only be made by some organisations. Many organisations are still too expensive in terms of HR resources consumed. Customer surveys (if undertaken) reveal serious shortcomings in service delivery. HR has neither positional authority through a seat on key decision-making bodies, nor great influence over the decisions that are made in these forums. Its lack of reputation means that the function is not seen as a contributor to organisational success; rather, it is an administrative activity that is necessary but not important. These impressions have been borne out in, for example, Roffey Park's *Management Agenda* report for 2011, which showed a decline in the proportion of managers, to only just over half, who acknowledged HR's influence on the business and valuing-adding to the organisation.

Probably many more organisations are still on the transformational journey. According to a 2007 CIPD survey, 81% of respondents had restructured the HR function (Reilly *et al*, 2007). The big question is: how successful and thoroughgoing has that been? A case can be made that HR transformation, as opposed to change, has too rarely happened because too often the concentration has been solely on structural and processual reform. This is because the focus has been on cost reduction more than service enhancement. The interests of customers, especially line managers and employees, have been subordinated to the imperative of bettering the HR ratio. In addition, the necessity of tackling the improvement of people management as a whole has received insufficient attention or even been ignored. This has been reinforced by excluding managers in the process of change. Moreover, the requirement to upskill the function itself has played second fiddle. Without the right capability HR cannot deliver the promise of higher value-added, let alone strategic, participation.

From the perspective of this book, HR is not going to be an effective partner in organisational change if it does not address its substantive weaknesses and does so in a truly good-OD-practice manner. Approaching HR transformation in this way would mean taking a less top-down functionally driven approach and instead taking a more consultative approach to change involving customer perspectives more. This would likely lead to more choice for business units in the service delivery model and more support for managers in operational HR. It might be a more costly outcome for organisations, but it is likely to be a more sustainable resolution of the tensions between conformity and flexibility.

Attention would also be given, not just to selecting and training business partners, but also to their role specification so that they can successfully deliver both what customers say they want and what the organisation, in a corporate sense, needs.

With a more effective HR function, organisational change can be supported in such a way that people visions are created, ways of achieving performance through people articulated, and cultural reconfiguration managed within the context of organisational effectiveness, as described in other chapters of this book.

COMPONENTS OF HR TRANSFORMATION

Before we look at how HR has managed its own change, we will review the content of that change.

There have been two strands to HR transformation, not always well linked, and a third which has been left behind. The first strand concerns structural, processual and technological change to make the function more efficient and to a lesser extent more effective. The second strand involves changing the relationship between HR and line management, often focusing on devolving activities from HR to managers. The neglected element, certainly more in the initial stages of change than later, is the building of capability within HR to deliver on the promise to be a more strategic and higher value-adding function.

STRUCTURAL CHANGE TO HR

The structural components of HR change have of necessity varied with the organisational context. Large, complex and widely dispersed organisations have been drawn to the so-called 'Ulrich' or 'three-legged stool' model (Robinson, 2006). But this has not been the preferred route for smaller, single-site organisations. The reason for this divergence is that 'Ulrich'-style service delivery models have been primarily adopted to obtain economies of scale through the creation especially of shared service centres (to aggregate HR administration), but also centres of expertise and, in fewer cases, consultancy pools. Smaller organisations do not benefit from these economies of scale.

The idea behind shared services is that activities performed locally by business units are re-engineered and streamlined and then combined so that the business units 'share' the service delivery solution. So there is a common provision of services with (in theory) the nature of the services determined primarily by the customer. 'The user is the chooser', to employ Ulrich's graphic expression (1995: 14). Unlike centralised services, in which services are corporately determined, in this model they are transferred from operating units to the shared services centre, but pooled for general use. They are shared for common provision with the customer exercising choice.

This option has become popular because of the cost-reduction opportunities it offers through the lower staffing numbers obtainable in shared service and call centres, common procurement opportunities and cheaper accommodation.

However, it is also true that HR directors also claim to seek quality enhancement from shared services. A Hewitt survey in 2007 found that 78% of respondents wanted to 'improve end user satisfaction', compared with 70% that sought cost reduction. Moreover, in a CIPD study in the UK (Reilly et al, 2007), 86% of those who had introduced HR shared services reported better service quality, against 73% who had seen cost savings. The quality enhancements may come as much from the fact that structural change has facilitated modernisation of processes and a higher use of technology (partly funded through service delivery savings) as from the creation of a shared services entity itself. Standardised, corporately assured services are cheaper to support, but also bind the organisation more together and reduce the risk that maverick policies or practices will threaten organisational integrity.

Centres of expertise build on the importance of specialist knowledge – something that has become even more important as people management becomes more complex. The idea is that you group together those knowledgeable in specific spheres into an expertise hub. Centres of expertise are typically found in training and development, employee relations, reward, resourcing and OD. The role they perform varies: the combination of tasks ranges from being the next or final tier on a problem-escalation ladder of referrals from a call centre, to support for business partners' in-depth know-how of a particular HR area and in the development of corporate policy.

Sometimes associated with centres of expertise or with shared services is the idea of having a project or consultancy pool of advisers that can tackle longer-term problems and be available as an extra, more flexible, resource. They can be cheaper than external consultants, if fully deployed, and they can build up both organisational know-how and subject-matter expertise. They can be accessed by business partners or they can be deployed to support policy projects run by the centres of expertise. The key point is that they are a cross-organisation group, wherever they are located – in other words, another consolidated resource.

The objective of launching centres of expertise is the wish to deepen the level of HR expertise and make it available across the organisation. Moreover, centres of expertise can also be the agents of standardisation. They can design policies and processes that should apply to the whole organisation and can also monitor adherence to these 'binding standards', ensuring compliance with them.

The introduction of HR business partners is the clearest evidence of repositioning the HR function. Indeed, three-quarters of the organisations in the 2007 CIPD survey (Reilly et al, 2007) reported that business partners had helped HR become a more strategic contributor, and two-thirds thought they had increased business focus. It is now commonplace in the bigger organisations to have an HR person in a customer-facing role, frequently described now as a business partner. Although usually embedded with their clients, business partners may either report to a line manager or to a senior HR manager, mostly separate from the shared services organisation. This individual, or in some cases small business partnering team, is expected to support line clients in terms of strategic development, organisational design and change management. It is described by some as offering 'transformational' activities, to be contrasted with transactional services delivered by the shared services centre. The business partner may act as a broker between line customers and the shared services operation or be accountable for the services without being responsible for their delivery.

STANDARDISATION

Standardisation is the second of the means to achieve change goals towards efficiency. It applies to some or all of an organisation's philosophy, policies, processes and systems. It means having, say, a common variable pay policy, performance management process or HR Information System (HRIS). This can reduce the number of people in HR because there is less of a requirement for local adjustment. Some of the cost and quality benefits come from having just *one* of something. It is particularly true of IT systems – lowering purchase and maintenance costs. As with the 'Ulrich'-style service delivery model, it is only really relevant for organisations with dispersed operations to worry about standardisation. If the different parts of the organisation have, for example, different performance appraisal processes, there is a cost to permitting variation in supporting HR systems (people and technology). Supporters of standardisation believe that HR colleagues fiddle too much with policies and processes in the unjustified belief that that they need to be adapted to specific business units, countries or cultures. Standardisers think that most HR work is the same, irrespective of setting. The only allowable exception is a legal requirement to do things in a particular way.

Bringing HR practices together in a common format makes their delivery more efficient, but there is also the contention that standardisation drives up quality, because it allows corporate HR to set out a best-practice approach and then apply it everywhere. Moreover, a standard model protects the organisation from deviant behaviour. The business brand can be damaged by locations or business units pursuing divergent practices – think of management bonuses or recruitment selection methods. So having corporately assured programmes is a way of managing risk.

The business context may be a factor in driving organisations towards standardisation. Recession-hit businesses or cash-strapped public sector bodies may want to take out money now. A common approach facilitates the prioritisation of resources. Reputation-hit firms want to find out what went wrong and want to stop it from happening again. Those engaged in post-merger or -acquisition integration see standardisation as a helpful vehicle. It permits easier integration if systems, policies and processes are aligned. The same applies to those wishing to reduce the power of divisional baronies and assert the corporate view.

AUTOMATION

The impact of technology on HR transformation is felt in a number of ways (see also Chapter 8). It offers cheaper and faster service delivery through reducing the manual handling of paper – appraisal forms, bonus recommendations, training bookings and application forms. Processing may be more accurate because there is less chance of error and out-of-range mistakes are highlighted. It offers higher-quality management information, vital for more informed decision-making. It gives more responsibility to managers and staff to ensure that their own data is correct. It helps communicate HR policies and procedures more effectively, ensuring, almost literally, that everyone is on the same page. This means it is easier for HR to operate standardised policies and practices, and control management behaviour through electronic sign-off rules or pre-set limits. Shared service centres rely on these standardised and automated processes to be able to deal with high volumes of data entries. Electronic external representation of the organisation can offer brand harmonisation – consistent positioning in the labour market.

Technological investment takes a number of forms: integrated HRIS, combined HRIS and payroll, manager/employee self-service, the use of intranets as information repositories and e-enabled processes like learning, recruitment, performance management, reward, etc.

DEVOLUTION

Over many years, HR has tried to shift some of its activities on to managers (see also Chapter 10). The aim has been to make line managers more self-sufficient, less reliant on HR, while simultaneously allowing HR to withdraw from these tasks on cost or philosophical grounds so that the focus of the HR function moves away from routine transactional work to more strategic matters.

'Devolution' is the term used to describe this process, but it has not been without its critics. One view is that 'devolution' is a misnomer, because HR does not have anything to devolve. People management responsibility rightly belongs to the line. The other objection, related indirectly to the first, is that we are confusing three sets of activities: people management administration (completing overtime, absence, leave forms, etc), manager involvement in people management policy-making, and the exercise of their people management responsibilities vis-à-vis their own staff (eg giving feedback, coaching and objective-setting).

The response from managers has been largely to focus on the first of these activities and complain that they are being 'dumped upon' in having these administrative tasks transferred from HR for them to do. They feel they have neither the time nor the knowledge to carry out this sort of administration in what they see as a poor use of an expensive resource.

There has been less debate about management participation in policy-making despite the academic view (McGuire *et al*, 2008) that this could lead to a more positive relationship between management and HR, as well as a positive improvement in people management performance, replacing the complaints about HR's controlling and policing methods.

The third element – the people management skills of managers – should not be a matter of debate, and certainly not in the context of devolution. This seems to be the main message of the retail company case study. It was more pithily put by the recently retired HR director of RBS, Neil Roden, that if managers do not regard people management responsibilities as being part of their role, they should be prepared to forgo a proportion of their pay (Reilly and Williams, 2006)!

The anonymised case study below illustrates the above points. The notion of partnership between HR and the line with different levels of responsibility/involvement by subject matter came through in two CIPD surveys (2003, and Reilly *et al*, 2007). The case study raises the interesting question, not in our view sufficiently considered, of what definition of organisational value/cost should determine the correct allocation of tasks between HR and line management.

CASE STUDY

DEVOLUTION IN A HIGH STREET RETAIL COMPANY

In interviews with a high street retail company HR staff there was uncertainty about what devolution meant. If it meant giving managers more people management responsibility for policies, they challenged this logic because the company needed standardised policies and processes since with a large workforce it did not make commercial or practical sense to have individuals making different policy and procedure decisions, constantly 'reinventing the wheel'. If devolution meant encouraging managers to manage their staff, this had long been part of the company culture. Responsibility was devolved to the lowest possible level in the organisation. Its business ethos was for managers regularly to consult, inform and involve their staff and be ready to be challenged in a two-way drive for performance improvement. In a service environment, managers are all the time talking to employees to ensure that each team delivers good customer service and to 'nip in the bud' any problems with attitudes/behaviours.

The company's HR staff also questioned the rationale for the devolution concept: they did not consider devolution was necessary for HR to be 'more strategic'. Line managers, in their view, should be freed of HR and other administrative burdens to manage staff, sell goods or provide excellent customer service, not have extra HR administration devolved to them to perform. HR could be strategic through other means.

The relationship between HR and the line was really one of partnership. The division of labour reflected different interests and skills. So the line would lead on work organisation, whereas on reward HR would have the greater say. But in each case, the other party was involved to the extent necessary for good management.

SKILL DEVELOPMENT

In order to support HR transformation, the function needs capable people. As Ulrich emphasised (1997), excellence is required in all fields of activity, from administrative to strategic. However, if part of the point of HR transformation is to shift the emphasis away from transactional work to more business-attuned, higher value-added contribution, then it is at the strategic end of the spectrum that the capability development should concentrate. The need for improvement comes through in various surveys. An ADP/HROA report (2008) put the skills of HR staff as the greatest hurdle to HR transformation, while a Mercer's survey of HR executives (2007) placed the skills within the function as the second biggest barrier (after the people management skills of line managers). The CIPD 2007 survey (Reilly *et al*, 2007) found that it was influencing/political skills and strategic thinking that were the principal challenges in skill development – precisely the areas that relate to the higher value-added work.

In researching their 2006 book, Reilly and Williams felt that organisations had neglected the skills issues when making structural change, assuming either that there would be a straightforward match between people and roles, or that any issues would sort themselves out naturally. This sense is reinforced by looking at the CIPD research both on careers (Tamkin *et al*, 2006) and the survey on HR transformation (Reilly *et al*, 2007). The latter suggests that senior HR leaders believe that structural change has made little difference to career paths, whereas the employee focus groups of both studies clearly report real concerns over their development. The 2007 survey also suggests that skill gaps are being tackled mostly through formal courses and that experiential learning (very important in skill development) is relatively underused.

The frequently reported problems in obtaining good-quality business partners (the critical role in growing a strategic input) and in certain expertise areas (eg reward and OD) reinforces the need to give attention to capability-building.

MODELLING THE CHANGE PROCESS

One could summarise this account of HR transformation by saying that there is a lot of logic in HR's attempts at structural, technological and processual reform, but its relationship with line management has not been sufficiently explored. Moreover, the HR leadership has not always got to grips with the people issues of its own change programme, particularly the skills required for success.

This provides a convenient *segue* into consideration of whether the fashion in which HR has effected its own change process can act as a model for the rest of the organisation. If HR has any hope of having its change management credentials accepted by management colleagues, it has to be seen to demonstrate its capabilities in the way it transforms itself. This means following its own precepts in how to deliver change effectively.

For reasons of space we will concentrate on the nature of the change goals, the extent to which stakeholders have been engaged, whether HR has had control of the process and leadership has been demonstrated, and whether HR has properly monitored, measured and evaluated the change. The long case study from the Lloyds Banking Group (towards the end of this chapter) illustrates some of the challenges in meeting the desirable process aims.

So that the reader can see the thrust of the argument we make, it is summarised here. We believe there has been a lack of clarity in goal-setting, a frequent failure to consult and engage customers in the nature of that change largely because HR was solving its own problems more than those of its customers. The function has at times been in charge of its own destiny, but really where it already has substantial credibility, and the same is true of its leadership of change – except that we believe HR directors and heads must involve themselves in the detail of what is proposed. Process monitoring has improved, but there has been too little attempt to understand whether the strategic elements of change have been achieved.

CLARITY

All good change programmes need clear objectives. This enables the organisation to monitor progress during the change and to assess the successful delivery against objectives after the change. HR transformation in this regard suffers from two distinct types of problem. Firstly, its change objectives are too woolly – 'becoming more strategic', 'adding greater value'. These things can be described, but too often there is an implicit sense of where HR wants to be rather than an explicit definition. This makes post-change assessment extremely difficult.

The second issue is that HR may speak with forked tongue. It may claim that HR transformation is all about improving HR services when actually the main driver is cost reduction. This is not to say that there are not advantages to consolidation, standardisation, automation and devolution, in terms of speed and efficiency, but there are disadvantages as well. Managers may benefit from the funds saved by transferring HR administration to remote shared service centres and/or call centres, but they may also miss the personalised service they got from their friendly neighbourhood HR colleague.

Although HR directors might claim a quality focus, we are more persuaded by the evidence of the Deloitte survey (2005), which suggested that cost considerations dominated the early adopters of the 'Ulrich model', and that other private sector and certainly public sector organisations have followed suit for the same reasons. Service quality might improve in some areas, but that is a helpful by-product, not driver, of the change. The same applies to the other aspects of HR transformation.

If the 'forked tongue' metaphor is too strong, then there is the risk that hope will triumph over experience. It is extremely difficult to pull off the trick of reducing costs and simultaneously improving services. In theory, the use of self-service can do it, but managers may not be as enthusiastic as HR project managers, frustrated by what is often still immature technology. Call centres can offer more accessible HR support than previously in widely distributed companies (think of high street banks and shops) so long as the centres work to problem-solve rather than repeat pre-scripted answers to the irritation of managers (Reilly et al, 2006). Good HR business partners can really put people issues on the map and change management thinking, but as we have suggested, there is a challenge in getting/developing these 'good' practitioners. If a full cost/benefit analysis was done (Tool number 8 in the CIPD's OD toolkit), taking account of management time as well as HR resources, the advantages of some structural and processual reconfiguration might be not so clear.

Thirdly, HR has taken too narrow a view of the necessary improvement in people management. Managers rightly focus on the transfer of administrative tasks aspect of devolution because this has been HR's focus too in changing its relationship with the line. Even if HR claims that it is seeking managerial empowerment or self-reliance, concerned with reducing cost and HR numbers, and using the benefits of manager self-service, HR is perceived as really only seizing this opportunity to get managers to do more. A fair criticism of this approach is that the other two aspects of the line manager role (direct people management and contribution to HR policy) have not been remodelled or even debated, resulting in a rather sterile argument about who completes an overtime form! The underlying tensions between HR and line management have not been surfaced but ignored, as we suggested in our earlier case study description.

If this analysis is correct, HR must think through its change objectives more carefully and communicate them more honestly. For example, Hugh Mitchell, HR Director of Shell, did not dissemble when presenting plans for a much-reduced HR function and saying, 'It is the best function we can afford' (Reilly and Williams, forthcoming).

INCLUSION

Overlapping the last point, there has been an absence of customer consultation by HR on both the overall proposition of HR transformation and its different aspects. As other chapters in this book indicate, it is vital for the change process to include stakeholders (in this case customers and HR staff themselves) in shaping outcomes if the changes are to be successfully embedded (see Tool 14). Regarding HR transformation, part of the problem may indeed stem from a lack of clarity as to the message or a reluctance to engage customers because of a fear of their response. This was evident in some organisations choosing not to conduct customer surveys (Carter et al, 2011). They might want to retain services, keep HR colleagues by their side or object to process change. HR may not accept these requests because they do not deliver the requisite savings. The change is to be on HR's, not customers', terms. Although decisions on financial investment will have been signed off at board or senior executive level, the detail of what has been delivered has frequently been determined exclusively within HR. Boards are less interested in the detail of the implementation (so long as their own cost-saving imperatives are met).

Take automation: the drive towards the e-enablement of processes such as recruitment, training and performance management has been done to meet HR objectives in terms of reducing functional numbers and speeding up processes. There may be benefits to managers especially, in terms of lower cross-charges, quicker and more consistent delivery, and better management information. Users of e-recruitment and e-training tools may have enhanced the opportunity to connect remotely and obtain faster and quality-assured services. The same can be said of manager self-service (not so much employee self-service) where tasks once performed by HR are switched to the line (see also Chapter 10). The e-enablement of these processes should have made this transfer acceptable to the recipients. Unfortunately, too often (and certainly in the early stages) the technology has been 'clunky', to say the least, or not very 'intuitive'. The descriptions may well be covering up the fact that managers are spending more time completing absence, overtime or performance appraisal forms than they did before. No wonder they feel 'dumped on'.

As for standardisation, HR has – again – chosen the terms of what to standardise and how, with frequently limited customer engagement or debate on the merits of having no deviation from the defined and centrally determined processes. Customers have not always been asked whether they believe it is in the organisation's best interests to have the same performance appraisal system across the global company or whether it would be better to adjust it by geography or business unit. There are advantages to customers: managers moving between Bogota (or Bournemouth) and Algiers (or Aberdeen) are working to the same model – but does this advantage outweigh the downside that the contexts and cultures may be very different, requiring different policies or even processes?

Structural change offers a similar message. Shared services are not necessarily loved by those who were used to their HR adviser along the corridor, but for the HR director the economies of scale benefits are decisive whatever managers, let alone employees, might say. As for the creation of business partners, the overnight mushrooming of the job title has not been accompanied enough by a proper discussion inside organisations on what the role might look like. At one organisation that tried to do this (non-published research), it was evident that managers had widely different views of what the role offered or could offer, paralleled by a disparity in what the business partners themselves thought they were expected to do.

Most surprising of all has been the lack of debate in many organisations about the relative roles of HR and the line in people management. This has been missing both at the philosophical level – What does the line's responsibility for the staff consist of? Is HR's duty always to assist managers, or is it ever legitimate to challenge? – and at the practical level – What value does HR offer to the recruitment process? What help does the line need regarding learning and development? As we remarked earlier, the CIPD research (CIPD, 2003; Reilly et al, 2007) demonstrated that partnership is the order of the day on many subjects, but that this is often an unspoken arrangement. It should be acknowledged that there may well be benefits in having a creative tension in the relationship – that 'who does what' is constantly renegotiated according to changing circumstances. Nevertheless, this suggests that an open dialogue is even more desirable than operating from fixed positions without mutual agreement.

If readers say that it is unreasonable to expect HR to consult where there is a cost-saving imperative, then the leadership of the function has to show whether it has consulted on the 'how' if not the 'what' of change. So has HR worked through with managers how e-enabled processes will work, the nature of access to a shared service centre or what role business partners will play? At the level of who to contact and which number to call, HR may have informed customers. But we are talking about working through the 'nitty-gritty' of handling a complex disciplinary case, how a business partner contributes to talent management, how exceptions to HR policies are determined, etc. If HR really wants transformation, not just change, it needs to get into this detail.

AGENCY

Change is more effective if it is owned by those involved. In the case of HR transformation, there are two issues we will pick out: how much is HR in charge of its own destiny, and how much does the HR community feel part of the change process?

With respect to the first question, it was evident 10 years ago that some of the early movers – at least as far as the creation of shared services was concerned – divided into those, like RBS, where it was HR driving the functional change against its analysis of requirements and priorities, and those where HR was subject to a corporate injunction to restructure on the lines it determined – eg to fit into a cross-functional shared service centre, like Powergen (Reilly, 1999).

Many practitioners would agree with Wilfried Meyer of Siemens that it is critical to a successful change process that HR is doing it to themselves, not being driven by external forces. One advantage, as he said, is that at least if things go wrong, there is nobody to blame but yourself. It also helps shape the objective-setting and communication process if HR is determining its own destiny (Reilly and Williams, forthcoming).

To be in this position, HR has to seize the initiative: it has to act before the CEO or finance director decides that change is necessary. This comes back to HR analysing properly its current condition (customer perception, benchmarked performance and resource levels, insight into competitor behaviour, awareness of academic thinking, etc) and setting out a convincing route for the future. Herein, however, is the difficulty of the chicken and the egg. Looking at, say, the research on HR's role in mergers and acquisitions (Antila and Kakkonen, 2008), HR is a full participant when it already has high credibility, but how does it gain that credibility in the first place? The answer is, of course, by delivering business-centred solutions and well-managed change, as was evident in the Centrica case reported in the CIPD research (Tamkin *et al*, 2006) where an HR director's status rose after contributing to one change programme to such an extent that he was asked to lead a major business reconfiguration. The same message emerges from the Roffey Park study referred to earlier. Where HR has handled redundancies and similar change well, it has been seen as more influential and value-adding.

An alternative scenario is that customer dissatisfaction or unacceptable costs cause the organisational leadership to impose their vision of change. The more likely setting is that HR has to fit in with a CEO-inspired view of the organisational structure, in which HR's role is often diminished. At the time of writing this is happening in local government, where HR executive directors are downgraded to accommodate corporate service roles as part of de-layering, and parts of the function are hived off into strategic partnerships without the HR leadership having much of a say.

Turning to whether the wider HR community is engaged in the change process: again, what evidence there is suggests that the HR leadership struggles with its participation. Data from the 2007 CIPD survey (Reilly *et al*, 2007) suggests that HR colleagues are one of the major obstacles to the change process, especially shared services where in a third of organisations existing HR staff objected to service centre structures. Part of the reason is that, with the inevitable job cuts, 'turkeys' are indeed unlikely to 'vote for Christmas'. It goes beyond this to objections to the model – its depersonalistion ('My HR representative is not a person, it's a floppy disk'), de-skilling (You are 'no longer required to think: just *do*'), demeaning of administrative work ('Just get rid of it'), etc – and to a lack of cost/commercial awareness or customer sensitivity in a rule-bound, procedural approach to tasks. In other words, HR transformation challenges the existing functional culture and tries to move it to another place. However, it should be noted that winning hearts and minds is not helped by the sort of terminology used in the quotes above. Evidence from the early days of shared services suggested that transfers to call centres (now rebranded contact centres) were handicapped by their poor reputation – the jobs lacked 'kudos' (Reilly, 1999). The cost imperative will mean a continuing threat to administrative jobs that still need to be excellently performed, so greater care with language is essential.

What would HR advise other functions to do in this situation? Would they suggest steamrollering the objections, changing the workforce to obtain more commercial-/customer-centric people or putting up with the griping and sniping because there is no better alternative? All of these 'solutions' are to be found in examples of HR transformation, along with much better engagement of the HR workforce that accepts the challenge and tries to respond constructively to it (see Tool number 74). Missing from many organisations is a serious attempt to conduct cultural mapping (see Tool number 42) of where the HR community is in terms of attitudes and behaviours, where it needs to be, and how to get from one point to the other.

The advantage of such an approach is that it surfaces tensions, anxieties, misconceptions and suchlike rather than leave them buried (see also Chapter 14). This is especially important when considering the 'Ulrich model'. One of its strengths is one of its weaknesses: the segmentation of the transformational from the transactional can lead to fragmentation as the HR service delivery model is chopped into at least three bits. In these circumstances one of the risks is that at best there is strained communication across the team boundaries and at worst a beggar-thy-neighbour approach. Negative attitudes get entrenched – 'As a business partner I could do my job properly but for the shared service failures.'

LEADERSHIP

Against this background we require HR leadership to shape the direction of change and to deliver against its goals. We need a coherent vision of where the function is headed, rooted in an analysis of its current strengths and weaknesses, aligned with the business model and cognisant of customer preferences. The vision must balance cost and quality, and give due attention to the capability to deliver against this promise. Besides the vision, though, we need leadership to successfully transform the function. As we have suggested above, this requires a lot of skill, navigating between the different interest groups and squaring the efficiency-versus-effectiveness circle. It also has to get into the 'weeds' of new structures, roles, reporting lines, job descriptions, etc. It means building 'workable arrangements' between HR and its customers (see also Chapter 14), which again requires a detailed understanding of tasks and their execution.

This suggests – as would be true of all good change programmes – that leadership is not just at the top of the organisational tree, it has to be found throughout the function. So leaders at all levels must carry the vision with them and implement it with drive and sensitivity.

How does HR appear to be meeting these requirements? There are obviously many examples of real leadership from HR directors or within the function. If one was being critical, however, the challenges in this area seem to come from:

- HR directors looking to manage the relationships more with their senior colleagues than involving themselves in functional matters
- leaders not giving enough attention to delivery, content merely to have done the design
- a lack of engagement of the middle layer of HR managers who feel more 'done unto' than 'doing' the change. This is especially true of situations where external consultants are hired
- relying too much on the said consultants for the design of the new model such that the leadership insufficiently understands what it has bought. Again this is particularly true when design is a standard product not adapted to the specific organisation's needs
- not appreciating technological opportunities or risks, over-reliant on the views of those who may have a vested interest
- not trying to win the hearts and minds of the whole function. This may be because leaders, especially the HR directors, are too remote from colleagues, insufficiently aware of their hopes and fears. They may make too little attempt to work through the issues with them – What will their job be like in future? How will they relate to customers and other colleagues? Alternatively, the leadership may not be working hard enough

to convince colleagues of the new vision, not explaining the reasons for it. This may be made worse if the middle-level managers have not been brought on board.

None of these challenges is insurmountable. As this book confirms, change is not easy, but these sorts of obstacles can be overcome by clarity, persistence and engagement. Change will not be successful if attention to these key processes is missing. The leadership must step forward to make change happen, devoting time and energy to seeing it through, as well as appreciating how their own behaviour in modelling the sort of intended process will be judged. (See Tool number 113.)

EVALUATION

If CIPD authors (2003) thought a weakness in implementation was HR's Achilles' heel, a case can be made that the failure to evaluate HR initiatives is another candidate for this dubious description. Research in the specific area of reward (Armstrong *et al*, 2010) revealed that organisations too infrequently consider how effective reward change had been. The same charge could be made about HR transformation.

The first problem is the frequent failure to undertake a current status assessment before the change begins – eg by conducting a customer survey or an activity analysis of how HR colleagues are spending their time. Without a baseline, how do you judge what progress has been made? Although one would hope all aspects of its performance, relating to both effectiveness and efficiency, would be considered, even the easier bits of measurement are missed. As an example, you need base data to see whether the proportion of time/resource spent on transactional work has gone down and that on strategic work has gone up.

Secondly, have success criteria been established against which to judge whether HR transformation is achieving its aims? The absence of such criteria may stem from a failure to define the change vision in sufficient detail.

Thirdly, there are problems with measurement. The measurement of the HR function's performance has improved enormously, partly due to advances in what technology can offer. Monitoring service delivery is well executed in many organisations, but the metrics used are process ones (relating to speed or accuracy). What organisations find harder to judge is how well centres of expertise and business partners are doing beyond customer satisfaction. What might adding more value look like? How do you describe increased influence? What is the nature of strategic contribution? There is a tendency to measure inputs/outputs and the cost of the service, not the value of the outcome. Partly, this is attributable to the absence of good-quality data or the difficulty of assessing qualitative information, but a lot of the problem comes again from a failure to define the elements of success. If, say, we want a world-class HR function, on what basis do we determine whether we have achieved it – cost, ratios of HR to workforce, customer satisfaction? Or, if we want to demonstrate greater organisational performance through people, where can HR claim some credit? Is it through policies, culture, line manager facilitation or advice? The attribution of value deserves frequent further thought. For example, HR commonly has the reduction of absence or an increase in employee retention as two of its main metrics. Yet the extent to which HR (as opposed to line management) directly affects these issues is questionable. Few organisations appear to be using more sophisticated measures of HR value-adding to business performance.

Fourthly, as a consequence, the measurement of success may be very narrow, simply relating to cost. You could argue that if reducing expenditure on HR is the goal, it is right to focus on just this aspect. However, presumably the organisation still requires services from HR and wants some sort of contribution from it. This has to be of a certain standard, and the HR director needs to check that the optimum balance has been achieved between cost and quality. So, are pre-change customer satisfaction levels the same or different compared with post-change? Are turnaround times in important areas like recruitment better or worse?

Finally, evaluation can be challenging because it might not give the right answer after HR has 'declared victory'. The project team may have disbanded so there is no ownership any more of the change programme. The pressure is to get on with it, not wallow in unproductive reflection, and certainly not divert resources – money for an external evaluation or people for an internal review.

The obvious risk is that HR continues to repeat the same mistakes over and over again. This is most clearly evident in structural change. The response to perceived failure is often to reorganise again, but without knowing which part of the previous structure 'failed' or indeed whether the structure is the problem rather than people's attitudes or skills, the role descriptions or the fit with their incumbents. To take an analogy from the NHS, there have been '15 major reorganisations of the NHS in 30 years' and 'few were properly studied' (Goldacre, 2011). Where there have been evaluations, the evidence is mixed or absent (Walshe, 2010). The National Audit Office (2010) found similar problems with central government restructuring with little attempt to establish the costs of change (high) versus benefits (low).

Surely a high-performing HR function would build in evaluation into any change programme so that the learning can be taken forward into other areas and so that time and money are not wasted on unnecessary exercises. This process can be modelled by HR and applied to the rest of the organisation. (See Tools 114 and 115.)

Picking up a number of these themes, the case study below is based on an interview with a senior manager in the HR function at Lloyds Banking Group.

LLOYDS BANKING GROUP

CASE STUDY

The deal between Lloyds TSB and HBOS was as great a change challenge as HR is likely to get both in business and functional terms. This has much to do with the context in which the deal was struck – the trading conditions and political involvement. What it shows is how clear-headed leadership can drive the function forward, but also the complexities of effecting functional change alongside organisational, serve as an antidote to overly simplistic change management injunctions.

The acquisition of HBOS by LloydsTSB to form the Lloyds Banking Group is well known. The challenge it presented HR was that the function was vital in supporting the company-wide integration as well as needing to create a 'one HR' entity itself. The HR leadership team understandably chose to concentrate on helping the business achieve its demanding goals while not losing sight of the need to form its own cost-effective team.

The focus of this case study is on change within the function, and this was assisted by the fact the two HR structures followed the same 'Ulrich model'. There were some differences – for example, LloydsTSB had an outsourced payroll whereas HBOS delivered

this in-house – however, they were not significant issues. The other important factor was that the Executive Committee of the new Group made the decision to adopt the LloydsTSB way of doing things unless there was a sound business reason for doing otherwise, and this added pace and clarity to the change programme.

Against that background, the HR leadership team prioritised the appointment of business-facing HR colleagues to their new posts. This enabled HR to provide support in the creation of new management teams who would drive the company forward and also assist in the delivery of suitable policies and practices to help deliver business integration. In addition, the change-critical centres of expertise, like Employee Relations and Organisational Effectiveness that had a key part to play in the integration journey, were also a priority to reorganise. Those parts of the HR function that, although important, were not directly supporting the business leaders with integration (eg Training and Recruitment) were tackled later.

Once finalised, the Executive Committee signed off the new HR function model and, although it acknowledged the change in HR roles and structures, was much more interested in how selection criteria and performance management would operate in the new Group.

As far as line managers were concerned, the change for them in terms of the HR service delivery model was minimal except in one important respect. In addition to a telephony-based contact centre, HBOS had a centralised but geographically based field team to assist managers in dealing with complex casework, whereas such support in LloydsTSB was provided by divisional HR teams. It was decided that the future model would follow the HBOS approach to ensure that a flexible and specialist service was provided, and this meant realigning resources from the divisional HR teams to a central team. It was carried out in a progressive manner, demonstrating through evidence to divisional managers (and HR leads) the effectiveness of the centralised field approach. In addition, the HBOS model supported both colleagues and line managers via a centralised telephony model rather than the line manager-only approach within LloydsTSB. It was agreed that the HBOS model was the preferred route.

The approach taken to managing HR colleagues through the change process has to be understood against the environment of the time – ie the crisis in financial services of closure, job losses, squeezed operating margins, etc. HR people realised that bringing two organisations together would mean fewer and changed roles. Given the size of the function (1,900 people at the outset) and the speed of change, it was unrealistic to envisage deep consultation. What was required, however, was clarity of message, frequent and open communication, and difficult messages being communicated by the decision-makers and not by their subordinates. In areas where there was less urgency – eg with future payroll arrangements – there was greater consultation at least to team leadership level. Successful delivery of functional change and active communication (via emails, face-to-face and teleconferencing) went a long way in rebuilding any initial lost faith in the leadership.

The delivery of 'one HR' was carefully monitored using a balanced scorecard approach that allowed the HR leadership team and executive management not just to see cost savings but also to check that performance standards were being met. There was no formal attempt to test whether cultural integration had been achieved, although there was an unspoken sense that it had and performance against service standards bore this out. Employee engagement in the HR team was, however, closely tracked. Interestingly, customer surveys were eschewed for the time being on the basis that as HR was seeking to control and standardise more processes, negative feedback could be a sign that HR was being effective if somewhat unloved. Equally, this might be an indicator that HR was failing to deliver. However, if that was the case, the HR leadership team believe it would have appeared clearly enough in the performance monitoring.

One of the characteristics of the acquisition was the significant investment in colleague development. Several functional academies were set up, including one for HR. Nominations were also put forward for HR colleagues to participate in other Executive Development Programmes – for example, in Operational Management. There was also a great deal of attention given to on-the-job training so colleagues could learn to use new technology and processes or to operate in new roles.

Questions

1 If you had to transform an HR function to support wider organisational change, what aspects would you consider to be most important, and why?

2 Are the lessons learned from the acquisition of HBOS by LloydsTSB generally applicable to activities of this type, or highly context-sensitive?

3 How would you manage the resourcing implications of supporting organisational change while simultaneously reforming HR itself?

A key learning point from this acquisition is that the attempt to separate business as usual from integration activity is misconceived, not just because there may be content overlap (eg performance pay) but even more because there is a need to plan workload, resourcing and tasks. This requires a combined and very detailed picture with thousands of milestones, but which allows a genuine 'heads-up' for the whole function to allow informed planning to take place where necessary. Effective project delivery was also greatly assisted by having in the team a blend of skills from HR and the business, each able to bring specific expertise to bear and close working relationships with other functions heavily involved in integration. For the future, in the company's view, having a standing 'fourth pillar' in programme and project management would make sense for large and complex organisations.

CONCLUSION

As the Lloyds Banking Group case study illustrates, change management can be very tough for HR. Not only is the function to be involved in wider organisational change, but usually the pressures that drive that reconfiguration (financial savings, new business model, changed product mix, etc) also require HR to restructure itself. At a time when HR needs extra resources to contribute to the wider change programme, from specifying objectives to implementing plans, it is under severe resource constraints. The better regarded the function, the greater the role it has in all aspects of change management, putting the most pressure on its capacity.

In this context, the criticisms levelled against HR may seem unfair and the demands placed on the function unreasonable. However, our rejoinder would be of two kinds. Firstly, as a matter of principle, HR should be the exemplar for change management practice. If it claims to be the custodian of the OD toolkit (we will avoid here the debate about the relationship between the different people management functions), it should demonstrate competence in its use. Secondly, if HR change is to become transformation – ie profound rather than superficial, long-lasting not short-term, broad instead of narrow in its purposes and effects – then it has to be done properly – ie in accordance with HR's own definition of the precepts of good change management. These mean much greater clarity and, in particular, detail in relation to its change objectives. Too often there is the rather glib 'becoming more strategic' goal that has more to do with keeping up with the Joneses than with a true understanding of what strategic HR looks like. The failure to consult the key line manager players and involve them in the HR transformation debate is not just a missed opportunity but reveals a lack of understanding of holistic people management. Where not bringing all the function with the change process occurs, one accepts that this may well be partly a consequence of the negative employment impact it has on many of the existing team, but it also demonstrates the failure of the HR leadership to get out there and win hearts and minds.

There are reasons why change evaluation does not take place, but they are not good enough to justify the failure to learn from mistakes or to celebrate genuine successes. We have to accept that organisational politics might suggest that we cannot always be honest with ourselves, but that is not a good basis upon which to run an organisation – and HR should clearly say so.

Thus, to support organisational transformation, yes, HR must transform itself, but also it must do so in a manner that other functions/business units would want to follow.

EXPLORE FURTHER

The appropriate change management literature is referenced in other chapters in this book.

The nature of HR transformation is described in the CIPD research, referenced below, but also in publications from the various management consultancies active in this field – eg Aon Hewitt, Mercer, Booz Allen and Deloitte.

Other HR function change case studies are well represented in the pages of *People Management*, although of necessity these are not full evaluations of the change process within these organisations.

Academic research often offers a different perspective and is often better looking at specific change issues, like:

- the devolution of work to managers: Renwick, D. (2003) 'Line manager involvement in HRM: an inside view', *Employee Relations*, Vol.25, No.3.
- evaluation of the HR function: Cabrera, A. and Cabrera, E. F. (2003) 'Strategic human resource evaluation', *HR Resource Planning*, Vol.26, No.1, March: 41–50.
- strategic formulation: Purcell, J. (2001) 'The meaning of strategy in human resource management', in Storey, J. (ed.) *Human Resource Management: A critical text*. London: Thomson Learning.
- change management: Whittington, R. and Molloy, E. (2005) *HR's Role in Organising: Shaping change*. Research report. London: CIPD.

Visit this book's Tutor website for free access to the following tools taken from the CIPD's OD Toolkit:

Tool 8: Cost-benefit analysis
Tool 14: Stakeholder analysis
Tool 42: Measuring cultural differences
Tool 74: Dealing with resistance to change
Tool 113: Checklist of principles for successful change implementation
Tool 114: Checklist of criteria for judging your method of evaluation
Tool 115: Pre- and post-evaluation checklist

REFERENCES

ADP and HROA (2008) 'Global HR transformation report'.

Antila, E. M. and Kakkonen, A. (2008) 'Factors affecting the role of HR managers in international mergers and acquisitions', *Personnel Review*, Vol.37, No.3.

Armstrong, M., Brown, D. and Reilly, P. (2010) *Evidence-Based Reward Management: Creating measurable business impact from your pay and reward practices*. London: Kogan Page.

Carter, A., Hirsh, W., Mercer, M. and Reilly, P. (2011) *Obtaining Customer Feedback on HR: finding out what managers and employees think of HR services and the HR function*. Institute for Employment Studies Report 479. Brighton: IES.

CIPD (2003) *Where We Are, Where We're Heading*. HR survey. London: CIPD.

Deloitte Consulting (2005) *Global HR Transformation*. Survey report. London/New York: Deloitte.

Goldacre, B. (2011) 'Evidence supporting your NHS reforms? What evidence, Mr Lansley?', *The Guardian*, 5 February. Viewed on 28 September 2011 at: http://www.guardian.co.uk/commentisfree/2011/feb/05/lansley-use-word-evidence

Hewitt (2007) *HR Shared Service Centres: Into the next generation*. Report. London/Chicago: AonHewitt.

McGuire, D., Stoner, L. and Mylona, S. (2008) 'The role of line managers as human resource agents in fostering organisational change in public sector services', *Journal of Change Management*, Vol.8, No.1: 73–84.

Mercer (2007) *HR Transformation in Europe*. Report. London: Mercer.

National Audit Office (2010) *Reorganising Central Government*. London: The Stationery Office.

Reilly, P. (1999) *Back Office or Shared Service and the Re-alignment of HR*. Institute for Employment Studies, Report 368. Brighton: IES.

Reilly, P. and Williams, T. (2003) *How to Get Best Value from HR: The shared services option*. Aldershot: Gower.

Reilly, P. and Williams, T. (2006) *Strategic HR: Building the capability to deliver*. Aldershot: Gower.

Reilly, P. and Williams, T. (forthcoming) *Global HR: Challenges Facing the Function*. Aldershot: Gower.

Reilly, P., Tamkin, P. and Broughton, A. (2007) *The Changing HR Function: Transforming HR?* Research into Practice. London: CIPD.

Reilly, P., Tamkin, P. and Strebler, M. (2006) *The Changing HR Function: The key questions*. London: CIPD.

Robinson, V. (2006) 'Three legs good?', *People Management*, 26 October.

Roffey Park Institute (2011) *Management Agenda*. Report. Horsham: RPI.

Tamkin, P., Reilly, P. and Hirsh, W. (2006) *Managing HR Careers: Emerging trends and issues*. London: CIPD.

Ulrich, D. (1995) 'Shared services: from vogue to value', *Human Resource Planning*, Vol.18, No.3.

Ulrich, D. (1997) *Human Resource Champions: The next agenda for adding value and delivering results*. Boston, MA: Harvard Business Press.

Walshe, K. (2010) 'Reorganisation of the NHS in England', *British Medical Journal*, No.341: c3843.

CHAPTER 8

Technology as an Agent of Transformation

Martin Reddington

CHAPTER OVERVIEW

This chapter builds upon the wider arguments surrounding the people and technology debate and provides more focused coverage in terms of technologies, including social media, which have an impact on HR's role and people management more generally. A blended approach combining academic and practitioner insights, and informed by the author's own experience in this field, illustrates touch points with the model of New OE framing the book.

LEARNING OBJECTIVES

By the end of this chapter the reader should be able to:

- list the concepts that inform the people and technology debate
- describe the factors that shape HR technology strategy and architectures
- outline the emergence of social media technologies
- critically examine the potential for social media technologies to add strategic value.

INTRODUCTION

This chapter examines the use of technology within the context of New OE – in particular, how it is at the centre of a 'practice shift' in the enablement of high-involvement work systems (HIWS) and the shaping of the employer brand. Although reference is made to the factors that shape HR technology strategy and architectures, the primary focus of this chapter is on the potential for the emerging social media technologies to be an agent for transformation, both for HR and for the wider organisation.

FACTORS INFORMING THE PEOPLE AND TECHNOLOGY DEBATE

Typically, the arguments that apply to the more critical literature concerning technology, knowledge and skills, whether from a labour process or socio-technical perspective, tend to focus on the dialectics of technological change or a perspective that highlights the co-existence of domination and liberation. These themes are set out diagrammatically in Figure 8.1, which is based on the work of Martin (2005). In broad terms, the appearance or promise of liberation, empowerment and decentralisation is shown with its contrast of control, domination and centralisation, leading to a key question (Martin, 2005: 2):

> To what extent is there a choice between using technologies as a dominating and centralising force, perhaps leading to a deskilling of employees, or as a potentially liberating and empowering force, enhancing the role of employees and HR managers and in re-skilling work?

Different forms of technology and technological change have been at the heart of many of the issues concerning the management of people and the work of HR professionals for a good number of years. In more recent times, however, these issues have emanated from the role of newer technologies in transforming societies, transforming economic progress and in how we work in such societies. Excellent overviews on different aspects of the role of information and communication technologies (ICT), the 'new' economy and work can be found in the work of Castells (1996), Coyle and Quah (2004), Slevin (2000) and Taylor (2004). This has resulted in a renewed interest in the relationship between these new technologies and the management of people (see, for example, Malone, 2004; Nathan *et al*, 2003; Maravelias, 2008).

These more macro and intellectual concerns have been accompanied by the actual influence of technologies on the practice of HRM. For example, Sparrow, Brewster and Harris (2004) singled out technology as a transforming force, especially in the e-enablement of HRM (e-HRM) and its impact on the creation and transfer of knowledge.

The introduction to this book explained that the old paradigm of top-down control and hierarchical organisation appears to have exhausted its capacity to generate innovative responses to turbulent business conditions and intensifying global competition. The fundamentally 'Newtonian paradigm' of organisations as machines and strategy by numbers is problematic in environments where the emphasis has shifted from physical inputs and outputs to less intangible ones such as knowledge, learning, creativity and initiative. In this context there is growing recognition of employee agency as a prerequisite of sustained performance and the need for a new language of change that can accommodate this (Francis and Reddington, 2010).

Figure 8.1 The contrasting impacts of technology

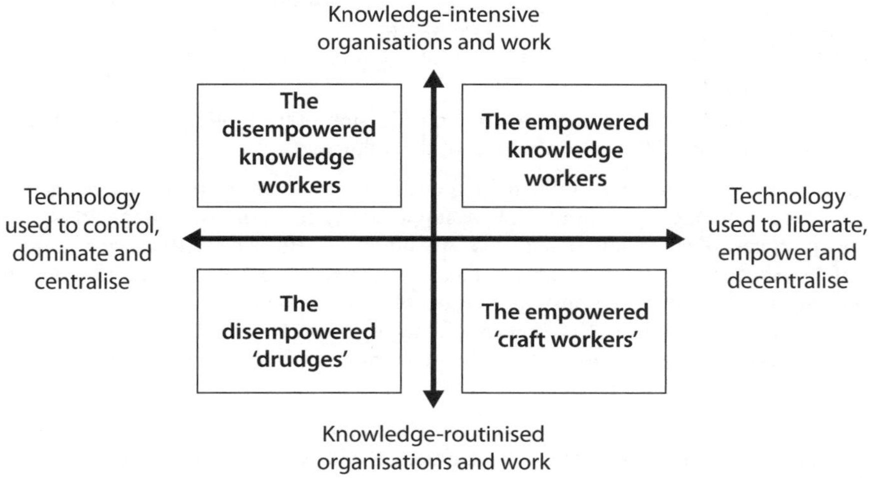

Source: Martin (2005)

The preliminary analysis of the literature – old and new – helps to inform the debate about the impact of, and relationship between, new technologies and people management. It suggests that these technologies are a moving target, which is likely to pose new problems and new contexts for organisations, especially as they move into newer stages of technological development (Malone, 2004; Martin, Reddington and Kneifsey, 2009).

With the new knowledge-based technologies advancing at a rapid pace, people management becomes an important mechanism for challenging the 'forces of conservatism', whether found in management or the workforce, and thus enabling organisations to more rapidly translate investments into better performance. This implies that in a knowledge-based economy, organisations certainly need to invest more in research and development, technology and capital equipment and skills, but these are not sufficient in themselves to make a step change in performance. In order to work, they therefore need to be knit together in a truly people-centred business model, working as a system to learn and improve the offering to customers.

From an HR perspective, organisations typically respond to the competing pressures with a mix of reorganisation of the HR function itself and adoption of new ICT architectures (Marin, Reddington and Alexander, 2008). The reorganisation of the HR function involves new HR service delivery approaches, often based on a tripartite model of shared services, centres of excellence and strategic or business partnering along the lines recommended by Ulrich and Brockbank (2005) with *outsourcing* and, in some cases, *offshoring* of key services, especially shared service centres (see Chapter 7 for a much fuller explanation of shared services). The introduction of ICT, often in combination with new HR delivery models, can then rationalise or transform HR's internal operations (Reddington *et al*, 2005; Withers *et al*, 2010).

It should be emphasised at the outset that these organisational, process re-engineering and ICT approaches are interdependent. Without progressively sophisticated ICT, new HR delivery models would not be as effective. Indeed, it is the increased reach and richness of technology-enabled information and organisational learning that have facilitated simultaneous centralisation and delegation of decision-making in HR, cited by academics, observers and practitioners as the single most important claimed distinctive capability of new HR delivery models (Cairncross, 2003; Evans and Wurster, 1999; Ulrich and Brockbank, 2005; Withers *et al*, 2010).

One of the logical consequences of these developments is the potential 'virtualisation' – or at least the significant 'leaning' – of HR which results from simultaneously reducing the numbers of specialists required to deliver HR services internally while improving the quality of these same services and developing new HR business models. Research into the social and political implications of this trend is underdeveloped. From a CHRM perspective, analysts have called for practitioners to reflect more carefully upon the shrinking 'human face' of HR from its customer base, and the implications for HR professionals themselves in terms of career opportunities and the development of new capabilities (eg Keegan and Francis, 2010; CIPD, 2007).

Taking account of these arguments, the introduction of technology therefore offers the potential to transform HR's role in respect of the following:

- increasing the HR function's influence as consultants focus on the needs of managers and employees (moving from administrative support to value-adding consultancy)
- enabling new flexible and responsive methods of delivering HR services, such as self-service via the Internet or intranet (reducing process costs and enabling line managers to take more responsibility for people management)
- expanding HR's reach as the experts of the organisation's people processes and the developers of value propositions for different employee groups (becoming more involved in shaping the employer brand).

Thus, the 'bandwagon' of technology-enabled HR solutions seems to be growing at a rapid rate driven by some evidence of promising practices and positive evaluations of technology and outsourcing projects. However, this bandwagon in support of technology adoption is also fuelled by some 'dangerous half-truths' or 'total nonsense' (Pfeffer and Sutton, 2006), and influenced by the persuasive powers of the growing number of consulting firms selling web-based HR as part of a package of 'enterprise resource planning' (ERP) solutions (Lengnick-Hall and Lengnick-Hall, 2006).

Both of the largest HR professional bodies in the world – the CIPD and the US-based Society of Human Resource Management (SHRM) – have made this issue one of their key areas for research and for educating members. HR and information systems academics have also begun to see the application of ICT to HR as a key area of interest and the subject of specialist conferences in Europe (eg the European Academic Conferences on e-HRM held in October 2006 and May 2008) and tracks in the Academy of Management.

Notwithstanding this groundswell of opinion among the HR community in support of e-HRM, re-engineering the HR function and outsourcing, progress in the form of the more transformational benefits and payoff in terms of cost reductions seems to have been more piecemeal and problematic. For example, concerns were illustrated in a CIPD report (2007), which highlighted 'ineffective technology' and 'resistance to technology' as two of the top six challenges facing the transformation of HR practices.

From an academic perspective, Bondarouk and Ruël (2010) provide a useful reflective account of the different streams of theoretical studies which have characterised e-HRM, and conclude (2010: iv) that:

> e-HRM research is in a transformational stage and is now moving towards crystal-lising its theoretical backgrounds, broadening its methodologies and meeting the needs of real-life e-HRM projects

– by which they signal a move towards new research probing e-HRM as an agent of transformation rather than looking in more purist terms at the technocratic arguments surrounding ICT adoption and associated HR processes *per se*.

FACTORS SHAPING HR STRATEGY AND TECHNOLOGY ARCHITECTURES

As mentioned previously, it is not proposed here to provide a detailed coverage of the factors involved in technology design, implementation and acceptance. There are a range of excellent academic and practitioner publications which cover these topics comprehensively (eg Reddington, Martin and Bondarouk, 2011; Withers *et al*, 2010; Martin and Reddington, 2010; Shrivastava and Shaw, 2004; Florkowski and Olivas-Luján, 2006; Fisher and Howell, 2004). The purpose of this section is to signpost ways in which technology can act as a transformation agent, a perspective which is then elaborated through the examination of emerging technologies – Web 2.0 and Enterprise 2.0.

Suffice to say that HR technology strategy both shapes and is shaped by what are called *transactional* and *transformational* goals (Snell, Stueber and Lepak, 2001). The former focus on reducing the costs of HR services or improving their productivity, and improving service delivery to managers and employees; the latter focus on freeing up time for HR staff to address more strategic issues than basic administration, and transforming the contributions that HR can provide the organisation with. The transformational goals involve extending HR's reach to more remote parts of the organisation to create a sense of 'corporateness' or internal integration in extended enterprises (eg through HR portals); enabling more sophisticated recruitment searches (eg through widely available social media to uncover people not actively seeking jobs) and (self-)selection through online tools; creating new forms of organisational community and methods of communications through new applications of Web 2.0 (eg interactive employee engagement surveys, virtual communities of practice, 'blogging' and 'wikis') (Martin, Reddington and Kneafsey, 2009).

Some organisations may already have advanced technology-based applications or tools in place, whereas other organisations may be engaging with these more advanced technologies for the first time, as HR seeks to move from being a traditional support function to being a more strategic partner.

The technology architecture will also be influenced by the *absorptive capacity* of HR (Martin and Reddington, 2009) to seek out knowledge and exploit these architectures to the full. Absorptive capacity in this context can be defined as the potential for the HR function to seek out and assimilate knowledge about HR technologies and incorporate such knowledge into their vision for a changed HR function (Jansen *et al*, 2005). It can also be defined in terms of the capacity of the HR function to realise potential by good implementation practices and ongoing support. This realisation phase is also marked by the ability of the HR function to combine face-to-face and technology-mediated HR approaches to produce a new business model for HR – that is, HR's ability to transform what it can currently do with available knowledge and technology into a more strategically oriented function that addresses the key strategic drivers of the organisation (Huselid *et al*, 2005). There is a clear tension here between people and process: from the perspective of New OE, absorptive capacity would involve attempts at creating a 'constructive tension' between these competing logics.

The concept of absorptive capacity also resonates very strongly with the attention afforded to rigour and relevance associated with evidence-based decision-making in New OE (see Chapter 1). In this instance, HR functions with high absorptive capacity would assimilate knowledge about HR technologies from multiple sources – eg practitioner and academic publications, published research, internal and external stakeholders – to design and implement the most appropriate solution.

Research conducted by the editors in the build-up to the CIPD National Conference in 2010 captured the views of 69 delegates (representing HR and OD functions in a broad range of private and public organisations) in a survey about New OE, and the results relating to the use of different forms of evidence when designing and implementing strategies for change are set out in Table 8.1. It should be noted that these results are not specific to

Table 8.1 OE survey responses relating to the use of different forms of evidence

Evidence type	Designing (%) n = 69	Implementing (%) n = 69
Practitioner bases (eg consultancy reports, trade journals, professional media)	64	58
Academic bases (eg peer-reviewed journals, articles, reports)	49	37
Dialogue with external stakeholders	64	66
Documentary sources (eg internal surveys, reports, intranet, business data)	75	73
Dialogue with colleagues, internal specialists, employees, front-line managers, trade unions or other employee groups, executive group	91	92
My own practitioner judgement	82	89

Note: Percentages represent an amalgamation of 'strongly agree'/'agree' responses to the statements:

a) In my role, I rely mostly on the following sources of evidence when *designing strategies* for change

b) In my role, I rely mostly on the following sources of evidence when *implementing strategies* for change

technology change but they signal an intention of organisations willing to assemble a broad evidence base as part of their design and implementation processes. Conspicuously, perhaps, the reliance on evidence from academic sources is rated as the lowest.

Understandably, the organisation and resourcing of the HR function also has an important bearing on technology architecture, and refers to the different configurations of organisational structures used by organisations to deliver their human resources strategy, including decisions on the centralisation of decisions, outsourcing and specialisation among HR professionals (see also Chapters 4, 5 and 7).

The CIPD survey referred to in Table 8.1 also captured views in relation to the use of social media technologies, and the results are rather striking, signalling concerns about the absorptive capacity and resourcing of HR functions to exploit these technologies – see Table 8.2. The reported usage is very low compared with more conventional self-service applications and suggests that for now at least, the transformative potential of these technologies is not being exploited by HR professionals (see also Chapter 17).

Table 8.2 OE survey responses relating to the use of different forms of technology

Survey statement	Response (%) n = 69
Social media technologies are used as a means of encouraging employees to have a voice in decision-making	27
Social media technologies enable effective two-way channels for communication between managers and employees	34
Providing technology-enabled HR self-service (eg online leave booking, payslips)	61
Extensive use is made of social media technologies when *designing* strategies for change	21
Extensive use is made of social media technologies when *implementing* strategies for change	28
My organisation is willing to experiment with social media technologies	52
Concerns about reputational damage (eg outspoken comments on Twitter or employee blogs) inhibit the use of social media technologies	60

Note: Percentages represent an amalgamation of 'strongly agree'/'agree' responses to the statements cited

There is some evidence to suggest that HR functions are becoming more willing to experiment with these technologies, but the risk of reputational damage is clearly a concern.

The next section takes a more in-depth look at these newer technologies and examines their potential and associated risks as agents of transformation.

THE EMERGENCE OF SOCIAL MEDIA TECHNOLOGIES

The previous sections of this chapter have been predominantly concerned with technology systems that support interactions with a variety of user types, such as HR experts, managers and employees, and modern systems allow these interactions to be performed through web browser software. These systems, however, mostly operate on pre-defined processes, controlled by the organisation. The most recent developments in web-based technology represent a move away from prescriptive, organisation-centred systems to collaborative web-based applications, collectively called social media technologies or Web 2.0.

This section draws heavily on a CIPD report by Martin, Reddington and Kneafsey (2009). It describes the key elements of these new technologies and how they are being used to support strategic HR initiatives.

The term Web 2.0 is now freely used in the popular press and has been the subject of recent articles in HR professional publications such as *People Management*. However, the available evidence on the use of these social media technologies in HRM and people management (eg Birkinshaw and Pass, 2008) suggests that HR professionals have little understanding of the nature and potential of these technologies, although they are aware of the risks of allowing employees access to social networking sites at work and of employee 'misbehaviour' on blogs and social networking.

According to e-HR experts, these media have enormous potential to change the way people collaborate, communicate, organise their work, and give voice to their opinions and expectations, especially when they are physically dispersed across time and space. Equally importantly, they help organisations communicate with and learn from a new generation of employees who have grown up with such technologies – the so-called V(irtual) Generation. Because of these features, Web 2.0 offers HR professionals an opportunity to transform its 'business model' – new ways of adding value to internal stakeholders and a more contemporary organisational architecture – to make a greater contribution to their organisation's strategic and reputational aims (Martin and Hetrick, 2006; Martin, Reddington and Alexander, 2008).

Analysts writing from a contrasting CHRM perspective have drawn attention to the 'tyrannical dimension' of new technology, such as its role in enabling people to work longer hours and intensify their work – Martin (2005) – and in driving employees to engage in intranet discussion forums because they are afraid of being 'unseen and left behind' – Maravelias, 2008: 350. Indeed, Maravelias' study of technology-enabled 'professional communities' within a large insurance company points to the unintended effects of employees' feelings of a constant lack of trust rooted in a desire to 'make their presence known as trusted employees' (Maravelias, 2008: 362).

WHAT DO WE MEAN BY WEB 2.0?

Although such work is still at an early stage, a family of powerful web-based technologies are being adopted by some organisations to:

- encourage greater collaboration among employees, customers, suppliers and partners
- give customers, business partners and employees greater opportunity for more authentic forms of 'voice' on issues that matter to them
- help organisations, employees and potential employees learn about each other, and share their knowledge and experiences to create organisational learning.

These 'social and sociable' media technologies have come to be known as Web 2.0, following the introduction of the term in 2004 by Tim O'Reilly, a media guru. The most highly publicised of these technologies among HR professionals are blogs, social networking sites such as Facebook, Twitter and LinkedIn, and virtual worlds such as Second Life.

The Martin, Reddington and Kneifsey (2009) research report showed that it is important to be clear on our use of terms and our understanding of the key features of Web 2.0, why it is different from earlier, web-based applications and what its potential is forecast to be. A working definition is provided below, culled from a number of sources:

- Web 2.0 is different from the earlier web 1.0, which focused on the one-way generation and publication of online content. Web 2.0 is a 'read–write' web providing a democratic architecture for participation, encouraging people to share ideas, promoting discussion and fostering a greater sense of community. In this sense it is a 'people-focused' web, embracing core elements of the philosophy and practice of modern human resource and people management – conversations, interpersonal networking, personalisation, authentic voice and individualism.

The important points to take away from this definition are the differences with earlier non-interactive, web-based technologies and the people-centred, rather than organisation-centred, nature of these new technologies. To elaborate a little, some of the identified characteristics of Web 2.0 that resonate with the central tenets of New OE and which have enormous importance for HR are described below:

- Web 2.0 is driven by increased *participation and collaboration* among users, most obviously apparent in social networking, social bookmarking, blogging, wikis and multimedia online gaming. Indeed, it is these so-called 'network effects' that define Web 2.0 and make it so valuable – as illustrated with examples later.
- Web 2.0 has come about because of a spirit of *openness* as developers and companies increasingly provide open access to their content and applications. Good examples include the emergence of open-source course material, online encyclopaedias such as Wikipedia and web browsers such as Firefox and Google's Chrome. For some writers, it is this open-source element that is the most important feature of Web 2.0, differentiating it from in-company attempts to deploy social media behind their firewalls – which go under the term Enterprise 2.0 (see the definition of Enterprise 2.0 later)
- Web 2.0 features *user control*: users control the content they create, the data captured about their web activities, and even their identities – they can choose to be anonymous, create virtual identities or present their real selves. In the case of the latter, David Cameron, the British Prime Minister and Barack Obama, the President of the USA, have done broadcasts on YouTube which have been viewed around the world.
- Web 2.0 is also a *decentralised* architecture – relying on distributed content, applications and computers – rather than a centralised system controlled by managers or IT departments. Although decentralisation is necessary for wider participation, openness and positive network effects, it is also the most worrying aspect of Web 2.0 for many HR professionals because of the potentially damaging effects to brands through the organisational misbehaviour of 'ranting' bloggers (Richards, 2007) and because they are not able to control corporate messaging.

HOW DOES THIS AFFECT HR?

There are undoubtedly challenges and degrees of risk associated with the adoption, diffusion and exploitation of Web 2.0. So despite the fact that most of the evidence on Web 2.0 diffusion shows a rapid take-up among Internet users (McKinsey, 2008; Madden and Jones, 2008), recent reports have noted some dissatisfaction among existing users of Web 2.0 and conventional networking tools. And from the survey evidence (including Table 8.2) it seems that HR continues to be reluctant innovators and to be more worried about employee misbehaviour, their lack of control over these technologies, and the uses to which they are sometimes put (see the case study below).

CASE STUDY

EMPLOYEE MISBEHAVIOUR ON FACEBOOK

On 24 July 2010 the BBC website covered a story in which an employee of the Yorkshire Ambulance Service spoke out about other colleagues. The employee reportedly said that the NHS employed 'too many who are lazy, unproductive, obstinate, militant [and] aggressive at every turn'. He went on to claim that some employees 'couldn't secure a job anywhere outside the bloated public sector where mediocrity is too often shielded by weak and unprincipled HR policies'.

The BBC reported the following statement from the service's NHS Trust: 'These are the opinions of an individual and in no way reflect the sentiment of the organisation.' A spokesman for the Trust added:

We hold our dedicated and professional staff in extremely high regard and work alongside them, in partnership with our trade unions, to provide a high-quality ambulance service for the people of Yorkshire. Yorkshire Ambulance Service has dealt with this matter under normal trust procedures and would now like to draw a line under this for all concerned.

Question

How might you have handled this employee misbehaviour situation – including any changes to HR policy?

But perhaps far exceeding the potency of the case described in the case study is the way in which social media has been linked to the exposure of celebrities previously protected by legal 'super-injunctions'.

Although the term is used more generally to refer to a range of gagging orders, a super-injunction specifically refers to a UK court order that not only prevents journalists from reporting the details of a court case but also prevents them from mentioning the fact even that the injunction has been taken out.

In the case of a Premiership footballer who wanted to suppress all aspects of alleged indiscretions in respect of his off-the-field conduct, his identity was revealed via Twitter on May 2011, in direct contravention to the super-injunction. This prompted some analysts to predict that Twitter could undermine the justice system and brought into focus the potential legal ramifications for those tweeters who were publicly sharing information in defiance of legal restrictions (*Business Insider*, 23 May 2011).

This particular aspect was at the centre of a landmark case (*BBC Online News*, 28 May 2011) in which representatives of an English local authority launched a legal action against Twitter in an attempt to unmask an anonymous whistle-blower who had levelled allegations via tweets against councillors ranging from ballot-rigging and fiddling expenses to drug-taking.

In pursuing the court action, they alleged that the defendant had unlawfully posted false and defamatory statements about the Council representatives, and were able to obtain a subpoena ordering Twitter to release the name, address, email address, telephone number and geographical location of the alleged whistle-blower. In defending their actions, the Council claimed it had a duty of care to protect its employees and was justified in pursuing legal action on the basis of the damaging claims being made.

This case and other similar reported cases provide an important, if negative, justification for HR professionals to understand the challenges presented by Web 2.0 and to develop realistic HR policies and programmes of education to prevent problems like this from recurring. While such problems continue to dominate media headlines, the core argument from the perspective of New OE is that HR professionals need also to take advantage of the genuine opportunities created by Web 2.0 to enhance collaboration, learning, employer branding and employee voice. If they fail to do so, they are likely to be left behind in a groundswell that is forecast to take root among new generations of employees (Li and Bernoff, 2008; Schuen, 2008).

Leaving aside for the moment the genuine problems posed for organisations in relation to the NHS and English local authority cases, support for a more optimistic and strategic view comes from evidence produced by academics, consultants and application providers. The weight of this evidence is that Web 2.0 is emerging as a major force in altering how organisations function and in the business models they employ. One such example comes from John Chambers, CEO of Cisco, who recently claimed that Web 2.0 is 'the future', causing him to change the direction of his company. As he pointed out (Martin *et al*, 2009: 11):

> We are moving our company as fast as we can to collaboration and Web 2.0 because of its potential for significant impacts on productivity and product design.

In another example, the administration of the US President, Barack Obama, arranged for the first Twitter 'town hall' meeting, at which the President answered questions posed by users of the micro-blogging website. Mr Obama used a live webcast to answer questions, submitted via tweets containing the hashtag #AskObama, on issues from jobs to the economy. Described as a 'Tweet Up', it was held at the White House, streamed live on Twitter and moderated by Twitter's co-founder, Jack Dorsey. A panel of users re-tweeted questions to choose those to be asked.

Macon Phillips, the White House director of digital strategy, said in a statement (reported in *BBC Online News*, 6 July 2011) that the purpose of the Twitter town hall is to 'try to find new opportunities to connect with Americans around the country'.

These examples appear to support the views of Don Tapscott and Anthony Williams (2008), authors of the bestselling book *Wikinomics*, that Web 2.0 social media are 'the biggest change in the organisation of the corporation in a century …'

So if HR professionals are to be judged by these prophecies and the sheer volume of current articles, books, blogs and discussion in media and technology publications, they could be forgiven for thinking they are in danger of being left behind in the race to become virtually connected to everyone and anyone in their social and work-related networks.

Sifting through a significant body of evidence which includes apparent 'hyperventilation' from technology gurus and the more sanguine evidence from various surveys, the Martin, Reddington and Kneifsey (2009) report draws attention to developments which offer significant value-adding opportunities to organisations and to the HR function. The first of these is the 'generational driver' encapsulated by Adam Sarner – see the short case study below. This is evidenced by various claims made for a distinctive V-Generation of 'digital natives' or 'networked employees' (Madden and Jones, 2008; Prensky, 2001; Sarner, 2008) which has grown up working, learning and communicating with social media, more prosaically illustrated by the rapid growth of social and professional networking sites such as Facebook, Twitter and Xing (*Economist*, 27 September 2008).

THE V(IRTUAL) GENERATION

CASE STUDY

Among the most recent attempts to set out a new group of online users is one by Gartner, a leading firm of technology consultants, which coined the term 'Generation V'. This expression encapsulates multiple age groups which make social connections online. As Adam Sarner – one of Gartner's principal consultants – writes (Sarner, 2008):

Unlike previous generations, Generation Virtual (also known as Generation V) is not defined by age — or gender, social demographic or geography — but is based on demonstrated achievement, accomplishments and an increasing preference for the use of digital media channels to discover information, build knowledge and share insights. Generation V is the recognition that general behaviour, attitudes and interests are starting to blend together in an online environment.

The second development relates to the need for organisations to *collaborate* to add value in modern economies. Collaboration is essential for knowledge creation and innovation among organisations. However, collaboration costs money, especially in large-scale geographically distributed organisations. Yet one of the promises of Web 2.0 is that it can substantially reduce the costs of such collaboration, especially when these forms of virtual communication become standard in organisations. Such apparently economic networking effects rely not only on cost reduction claims but also on better-quality decision-making and knowledge creation. The 'wisdom of crowds' thesis, which underpins applications such as Wikipedia (Tapscott and Williams, 2008), states that collective intelligence by groups often results in better decision-making than could be made by any individual.

THE POTENTIAL FOR SOCIAL MEDIA TECHNOLOGIES TO ADD STRATEGIC VALUE

The argument therefore follows that the use of these social media technologies in organisations helps to substantially improve business performance in five important ways (Li and Bernoff, 2008), as set out in Table 8.3. It should be noted that these opportunities for adding strategic value also have touch points with New OE in the way that they incorporate the active role of language, employee agency, employer branding and engagement (see also Chapter 14).

These aspects illuminate the potential for using social media technologies in priming 'conversations for change' and the development of employer branding strategies – see Chapter 14 for more information. It is clear that HR professionals need to keep abreast of these developments and gain the knowledge and confidence to help shape the approach to Web 2.0 adoption.

Table 8.3 Adding strategic value: applications to HR and people management

Strategies for adding value through Web 2.0 to HR and people management	Applications to key functions in HR and people management
More effective listening to understand employees and other internal stakeholders through richer social media research	*Employee engagement* Promoting the use of employee blogs and online discussion forums to raise issues which are important to employees, so surfacing authentic employee voice rather than responses to attitude surveys. Good examples are the use of employee blogging in Microsoft (Walker Rettberg, 2008), in some of the research on the positive application of employee blogs by Richards (2007) and the use of discussion forums.
Talking to employees and others by increasing the reach and richness of messages and learning using Web 2.0	*Learning* Using corporate blogs and RSS feeds to help people learn about important and up-to-date knowledge of matters that are relevant to them. IBM is a good example, but unions too are beginning to use blogs in interesting ways to open communications with members (see Richards, 2007). *Employee communications* Using corporate blogs and social networking sites to keep employees and partner organisations up to date with key areas of company business.

Strategies for adding value through Web 2.0 to HR and people management	Applications to key functions in HR and people management
Motivating and energising employees and others by building on the enthusiasm of key influencers and using the power of word of mouth to spread the message/ medium	*Employee motivation and managing psychological contracts* Tapping into and engaging with enthusiastic employee bloggers and contributors to media-sharing sites about your organisations to demonstrate that you are listening and acting on what is being discussed 'on the street' about the organisation. *Recruitment* Using the power of these online opinion-formers to 'virally' market positive messages about the organisation for recruitment purposes. Research shows that the opinions of users of products and services in the consumer field are the most trusted source of knowledge among potential consumers. Bloggers and comments on blogs are also trusted as a source of information. Social networking has become an important media for both of these activities. *Impacting on employer brands* Participating in and encouraging online communities which discuss your employer brand.
Supporting employees and others by using Web 2.0 tools to help them support each other	*Knowledge creation and knowledge-sharing* Knowledge creation and learning are two of the most important ways in which social media can be used, especially where employees and partner organisations are geographically dispersed. The use of wikis, which draws on the 'wisdom of crowds' (Surowiecki, 2004; Tapscott and Williams, 2008) is an extremely important example of how social media can be used to great effect to create collective knowledge and help contributors and readers learn at the same time. *Promoting work–life balance* Just as some organisations (such as Dell) have set up online self-help to support users through technical problems, others are beginning to use discussion forums to help support employees in managing their careers and work–life balance.
Reaching out to employees and other stakeholders to participate in innovation in people management and HR policy and process design	*Employer branding and value creation* One of the key issues in developing corporate values and employer brands is authenticity. Currently, most organisations take a top-down approach to this, sometimes consulting employees about decisions that have already been taken but that often lack authenticity with employees, particularly those remote from head office locations. Some organisations have begun to use discussion forums to surface the values, attitudes and opinions that 'really matter to staff' before taking such decisions. *Designing rewards systems and benefits* Increasingly, organisations are incorporating customers into the design of new products using Web 2.0 tools.

Source: based on Li and Bernoff (2008)

Indeed, notwithstanding the earlier cases involving the misuse of Twitter and Facebook, HR professionals can assist transformation at work by helping implement these social media technologies to provide the basis for more effective collaboration and knowledge-sharing, more effective two-way communication with employees, and by giving employees interesting and authentic alternatives to the traditional ways of expressing their opinions and ideas – improved employee voice (Birkinshaw and Pass, 2008; Martin *et al*, 2009). This is seen to be an increasingly important way of creating a participative culture, in which employees across the organisation can help shape appropriate workable arrangements to respond to the competing challenges faced by their organisations (see Chapter 14).

In recognition of the associated reputational risks of creating uncontrolled 'conversational arenas', more organisations are attempting to regain some measure of control by developing the technologies of Web 2.0 inside their firewalls and encouraging or facilitating employees to make use of them. According to Andrew McAfee from Harvard University, who is usually credited with coining the term 'Enterprise 2.0' in 2006, this route is probably the most promising way forward for organisations seeking the benefits of Web 2.0 but wishing to minimise the downside.

McAfee defines Enterprise 2.0 as 'the use of emergent social software platforms within companies and their partners or customers'. He uses the term 'social software' to describe how 'people meet, connect and collaborate through computer-mediated communication and form online communities'. Platforms are defined as 'digital environments in which contributions and interactions are widely visible and persistent over time'. 'Emergent' means that the software is freeform, in the sense that people can choose to use it or not, is egalitarian and can accept different forms of data. He rules out (a) open web-based platforms, such as Wikipedia, YouTube, Flickr and Facebook, because they are widely available to individuals, (b) corporate intranets because they are not emergent, and (c) traditional email and SMS because they are not persistent.

MOBILE APPS

A good example of emergent media is to be found in the growing area of mobile 'apps' – self-contained programs or pieces of software (*applications*) designed to fulfil a particular purpose, especially as downloaded by a user to a mobile device. Apple's online apps store is probably the best known of its kind. As an indication of how fast this channel to market is growing, Apple proclaimed that in just three years it has served up 15 billion apps through its online store (*BBC Online News*, 12 July 2011).

This technological innovation allows organisations to extend the reach of their own technical systems to employees or prospective candidates on the move, through smart mobile devices such as the Apple iPhone and iPad and Google Android devices. Some human resource information system (HRIS) and payroll providers provide apps that allow users to access their tasks, book holidays and check their payslips on the move. In October 2010, Adidas Group UK, the sportswear manufacturer, launched an iPhone app designed to reinvigorate the company's graduate recruitment process. According to Jennifer Cunningham, recruitment manager at Adidas Group UK (*People Management*, 11 February 2011):

> The app does truly represent our brand in terms of the look and feel of it, and it will hopefully put us on the map in terms of being innovative and forward-thinking in our approach to recruitment, and position us as an employer of choice [and endorsing the view that] in general, mobile recruitment technology is going to become very high up on the agenda, along with Web 2.0.

REFLECTIVE ACTIVITIES

- If you were asked to design a social media technology strategy, what are the most important characteristics and contextual factors that would shape your thinking?

- In the light of the current evidence in relation to the claimed benefits and problems associated with social media technologies from the perspective of New OE, what are the factors likely to affect their adoption in the future?

The case study below captures the nature and extent of the use of technologies described thus far in this chapter as an agent of organisational transformation. Based on an interview with the Head of HR Operations at FinTechCo, it is intended to give the reader an idea of the possibilities associated with a well-thought-out technology strategy.

CASE STUDY

FINTECHCO

FinTechCo is a leading financial technology company with a global footprint across Europe and Asia, employing about 1,500 people and with an income in excess of £600 million per annum.

The company's investment in technology was designed to modernise and transform the HR function and to alter the nature of the services from a reactive 'personnel' style to a strategic partner within the business. At the outset, the specific objectives linked to the design and delivery of the investment in technology were:

- supporting the transition to a business partner model by:
  - increasing the range and quality of services
  - reducing the overall cost of HR to the business
  - allowing more HR professionals to engage in value-adding work
  - better allocating HR resources

- creating the tools for managers and employees to take responsibility for HR-related employment life-cycle events

- developing commercially focused management information

- developing an international model for HR involvements in corporate acquisitions.

This led to the development of a common HR portal, through which all online services

could be accessed. The intention of this portal was also to help HR to create a greater sense of corporate identity among employees in the extended enterprise using an internal employer branding strategy (Martin and Hetrick, 2006).

Supporting the business partner model

Traditionally, the Personnel function at FinTechCo was largely a paper-based administrative support function, ensuring that basic personnel processes were carried out in accordance with the business requirements. Activities such as recruitment, management of company employee relations policies, training administration and payroll services were the core responsibility of the function. These involved both the 'hand-holding' of the managers and employees as well as the administration of what was a lengthy paper-based bureaucracy.

The aim of the Business Partner Model was to move the now renamed HR department into a place that would be able to give strategic input into business decisions while offering a higher value of HR service to the business. At the same time, this had to be achieved with a very watchful and disciplined stance on HR costs and overall headcount.

Over a period of four years the investment in HR technology as an agent of transformation produced a profound change in perception about the way that HR activities were managed and their value-adding contribution, primarily by shifting the emphasis away from traditional services and administration to a far greater self-help culture.

Thus, the technology transformation was built along three key lines:

- *Understanding the end game* – allowing the development of robust system foundations that could 'future'-proof development and leverage the interdependencies between the various HR services

- *Demonstrating value to the business* – transforming HR services over time to the wider business that delivered a measurable increase in quality and speed or significantly reduced cost

- *High quality and intuitive services* – ensuring that any service delivered via the technology transformation was high-quality, instantly recognised as the HR brand, and was easy to use. It was an important rule of thumb that if a new service required training (other than super-users/administrators), it would not be launched.

As an example, one particular service – recruitment – encompassed all of these attributes. By implementing an automated process and revaluating the requirements, a recruitment service was developed that allowed HR to fully integrate recruitment administration with both agencies and websites in order to source, administer and select new talent via one system and process. This reduced the number of staff working on administration, reduced overall dependencies on agencies, and brought candidates straight to the managers' desktop, saving time and cost and increasing speed and quality of applications.

Progressively, the HR function had to tackle three main challenges in order to achieve the transformation:

- the technology challenge – the level of technology-related skills and capabilities required to determine the optimum technical architecture

- the process challenge – the level of HR process re-engineering skills and capabilities required to break down every service from a process perspective, looking at possible enhancements and mapping interdependencies

- the transformation challenge – understanding the scope of change management activities in the wider organisation and designing and implementing an approach to create a favourable environment for the new technology-enabled solutions among the users.

These challenges were confronted with a combination of in-house expertise and external consultancy, leading to the establishment of a 'road map' for transforming the HR services over time. The following key features were incorporated into its design and implementation:

- a recognisable 'HR brand'

- intuitive services that did not require training

- 'drip feeding' the functionality over a period of time (no 'big bang')

- focusing on key groups that would drive particular benefits

- listening to clients and continually evaluating the services provided

- showing how the interdependencies added value (such as reporting)

- clear communications and support from HR staff to line managers.

The latest technical innovations currently being considered involve mobile apps – for things such as the ability to view payslips on the move – and virtual links to a variety of HR tools within an online development forum. There is also the possibility of 'relocating' the core HR data system to a private 'cloud' – a proprietary network or a data centre that supplies hosted services via a secure Internet connection.

Questions

1 If you were made responsible for a project to design and implement a new range of technology-enabled HR services, how would you go about it?

2 In your view, what are the main interdependencies among the three main

challenges – technology, process and transformation – identified in the case study?

3 In the future, to what extent do you think technology-enabled HR services will act as an agent of transformation in organisations?

CASE STUDY COMMENTARY

- The potential opportunities and challenges illustrated in the case study resonate well with the literature (see *Explore further*) and my own personal experience in running a global technology-enabled HR transformation programme. It is arguable that the technologies available now and in the foreseeable future have the potential to deliver services which are bounded only by time, budget and imagination. However, it is important to understand that technology is essentially an 'enabler', which depends on the skills of HR professionals and users across the wider organisation to convert technology-enabled processes into perceived value.

- Indeed, the process challenge is in some ways the most complex. Breaking down every service, mapping the interdependencies, looking at the possible enhancements and then pulling this together into an understandable plan takes time and involves bringing together people with the appropriate capabilities and experience.

- The transformation challenge almost invariably involves changes to the structure and roles of HR (see Chapter 7) and securing the buy-in (and budget) of both HR and the wider business.

- New OE provides an excellent organising framework for stakeholders to use as a way of surfacing tensions that inevitably arise and to stimulate innovative thinking in response to the challenges described.

CONCLUSION

There is a growing and substantial body of literature available to academics and practitioners to provide a basis for new theory development and to inform practice in respect of the agency potential of HR technology to transform organisations.

On the question of new theory development, Bondarouk, Ruël and Looise (2011: Intro) question whether e-HRM research is 'a new and substantial research area or at the "crossroads" of other academic domains, such as innovation management, IT implementation and/or HRM'. They also argue that 'this lack of clarity … deepens the divisions between the various academic domains' – a call to the academic community to address this, recognising its practical consequences for technology projects and their management.

Elaborating the position of Bondarouk *et al*, and in the spirit of New OE, there are many opportunities for academics and practitioners to collaborate on finding out how different organisations innovate and exploit new HR technology effectively. In collaborating in this way we would find out more about the treatment of tensions – such as the promise of liberation in the form of a Web-2.0-inspired 'democratic architecture' as a channel for authentic employee voice versus the intensity of 'always-on' technology, and the vulnerabilities associated with the progressive replacement of face-to-face social contact with technology-mediated ones.

Such collaboration could potentially lead to the development of practical tools and techniques designed to assist technology acceptance and diffusion of e-HRM and Web 2.0, and to providing the basis for creating a more effective shared language through scenario-planning and communities of practice.

EXPLORE FURTHER

Bondarouk, T. V., Ruël, H. J. M. and Looise, J. C. (2011) *Electronic HRM in Theory and Practice*. Bingley, UK: Emerald Group. This book is aimed at helping researchers and HR practitioners understand the academic and corporate agenda for research and practice in the emerging field of electronic human resource management (e-HRM).

Martin, G., Reddington, M. and Kneafsey, M. B. (2009) *Web 2.0 and Human Resource Management: Groundswell or hype?* Research Report. London: CIPD. This report aims to inform HR professionals about some of the latest thinking in the field as it applies to people management and HR, and to help them develop appropriate strategies for Web 2.0.

Reddington, M. (2011) 'Managing technology and process – an expert guide'. Paper written for the Public Sector People Managers' Association. This paper was written very much as an informative hands-on guide for HR practitioners undertaking technology-enabled change.

Withers, M., Williamson, M. and Reddington, M. (2010) *Transforming HR: Creating value through people*, 2nd edition. Oxford: Butterworth-Heinemann. Written by three reflective practitioners, this book provides a combination of their own HR research, knowledge of the relevant literature and experience in HR management and consultancy, all blended in with the critical insights of senior contributing practitioners.

REFERENCES

Birkinshaw, J. and Pass, S. (2008) *Innovations in the Workplace: How are organisations responding to Generation Y employees and Web 2.0 technologies?* London: Chartered Institute of Personnel and Development.

Bondarouk, T. and Ruël, H. (2010) 'The intersection of IT and workforce management: a maturing field', *International Journal of Technology and Human Interaction*, Vol.6, No3: i–v.

Bondarouk, T., Ruël, H. J. M. and Looise, J. K. (eds) (2011) *Electronic HRM in Theory and Practice*. Bingley, UK: Emerald Group.

Cairncross, F. (2003) *The Company of the Future: Meeting the management challenges of the communications revolution*. London: Profile Books.

Castells, M. (1996) 'The rise of the network society', in *The Information Age: Vol. 1 – Economy, Society and Culture*. Oxford: Blackwell.

CIPD (2007) *The Changing HR Function*. Report. London: Chartered Institute of Personnel and Development.

Coyle, D. and Quah, D. (2004) *Getting the Measure of the New Economy*. London: The Work

Foundation. Available online at: http://www.theworkfoundation.com/research/ isociety/ new_economy.jsp.

Evans, P. and Wurster, D. (1999) *Blown to Bits: How the new economics of information transforms strategy*. Cambridge, MA: Harvard Business Press.

Fisher, S. L. and Howell, A. W. (2004) 'Beyond user acceptance: an examination of employee reactions to information technology systems', *Human Resource Management*, Vol.43: 243–58.

Florkowski, G. W. and Olivas-Luján, H. R. (2006) 'The diffusion of human resource information technology innovations in US and non-US firms', *Personnel Review*, Vol.35, No.6: 684–710.

Francis, H. and Reddington, M. (2010) 'Redirecting and reconnecting theory – employer branding and the employment "deal"'. Paper presented to the BSA Work, Employment and Society Conference, September 2010.

Huselid, M. A., Becker, B. E. and Beatty, R. W. (2005) *The Workforce Scorecard: Managing human capital to execute strategy*. Boston, MA: Harvard Business School Press.

Jansen, J. J. P., Van Den Bosch, F. A. J. and Volberda, H. W. (2005) 'Managing potential and realized absorptive capacity: how do organizational antecedents matter?', *Academy of Management Review*, Vol.48: 999–1015.

Keegan, A. and Francis, H. (2010) 'Practitioner talk: the changing textscape of HRM and emergence of HR business partnership', *International Journal of Human Resource Management*, Vol.21, No.4–6: 873–98.

Lengnick-Hall, C. A. and Lengnick-Hall, M. L. (2006) 'HR, ERP and knowledge for competitive advantage', *Human Resource Management*, Vol.45, No.2, Summer: 179–94.

Li, C. and Bernoff, J. (2008) *Groundswell: Winning in a world transformed by social technologies*. Boston, MA: Harvard Business Press.

McKinsey (2008) 'Building the Web 2.0 enterprise: a McKinsey global survey', *McKinsey Quarterly Survey*. Available online at: http://www.mckinseyquarterly.com/ PDFDownload.aspx?L2=16&L3=16&ar=1913 [accessed 22 February 2010].

Madden, M. and Jones, S. (2008) 'Networked workers'. Pew Internet and American Life Project. Available online at: http://pewinternet.org/pdfs/PIP_Networked_ Workers_ FINAL.pdf [accessed 22 February 2010].

Malone, T. W. (2004) *The Future of Work: How the new order of business will shape your organization, your management style and your life*. Boston, MA: Harvard Business School Press.

Maravelias, C. (2008) 'Make your presence known! Post-bureaucracy, HRM and the fear of being unseen' *Personnel Review,* Vol.38, No.4: 349–65.

Martin, G. (2005) *Technology and People Management: The opportunity and the challenge*. Research Report. London: Chartered Institute of Personnel and Development.

Martin, G. and Hetrick, S. (2006) *Corporate Reputations, Branding and Managing People: A strategic approach to HR*. Oxford: Butterworth-Heinemann.

Martin, G. and Reddington, M. (2009) 'Reconceptualising absorptive capacity to explain the e-enablement of the HR function (e-HR) in organizations', *Employee Relations*, Vol.31, No.5: 515–37.

Martin, G. and Reddington, M. (2010) 'Theorizing the links between e-HR and strategic HRM: a model, case illustration and reflections', *International Journal of Human Resource Management*, Vol.21, No.10: 1553–74.

Martin, G., Reddington, M. and Alexander, H. (2008) *Technology, Outsourcing and Transforming HR*. Oxford: Elsevier.

Martin, G., Reddington, M. and Kneafsey, M. B. (2009) *Web 2.0 and Human Resource Management: Groundswell or hype?* Research Report. London: Chartered Institute of Personnel and Development.

Martin, G., Reddington, M., Kneafsey, M. and Sloman, M. (2009) 'Scenarios and strategies for Web 2.0', *Education and Training*, Vol.51, No.5/6: 370–80.

Nathan, M., Carpenter, G., Roberts, S., with Ferguson, L. and Knox, H. (2003) *Getting By, Not Getting On: Technology in UK workplaces*. London: Work Foundation.

Pfeffer, J. and Sutton, R. I. (2006) *Hard Facts, Dangerous Half-Truths and Total Nonsense: Profiting from evidence-based management*. Boston, MA: Harvard Business School Press.

Prensky, M. (2001) 'Digital natives, digital immigrants', *On the Horizon*, Vol.9, No.5: 1–6.

Reddington, M., Martin, G. and Bondarouk, T. (2011) 'Linking HR strategy, E-HR goals, architectures and outcomes: a model and case study evidence', in Bondarouk, T., Ruël, H. J. M. and Looise, J. K. (eds) *Electronic HRM in Theory and Practice*. Oxford: Elsevier.

Reddington, M., Williamson, M. and Withers, M. (2005) *Transforming HR: Creating value through people*. Oxford: Butterworth-Heinemann/Elsevier.

Richards, J. (2007) 'Unmediated workplace images from the internet: an investigation of work blogging'. Paper presented to the 29th Annual Labour Process Conference, University of Amsterdam, 2–4 April.

Sarner, A. (2008) *The business impact of social computing and 'Generation Virtual'*. Special Report. Gartner Consulting, ID Number: G00161081.

Schuen, A. (2008) *Web 2.0: A strategy guide*. Sebastopol, CA: O'Reilly.

Shrivastava, S. and Shaw, J. B. (2004) 'Liberating HR through technology', *Human Resource Management*, Vol.42: 201–22.

Singapore Institute of Management (2009) *How Types of Organisational Cultures Contribute in Shaping Learning Organisations*. Research Report. Singapore.

Slevin, J. M. (2000) *The Internet and Society*. Cambridge: Polity Press.

Snell, S. A., Steuber, D. and Lepak, D. P. (2001) 'Virtual HR departments: getting out of the middle', in Henan, R. L. and Greenberger, D. B. (eds) *Human Resource Management in Virtual Organizations*. Greenwich, CT: Information Age Publishing.

Sparrow, P. R., Brewster, C. and Harris, H. (2004) *Globalizing Human Resource Management*. London: Routledge.

Surowiecki, J. (2004) *The Wisdom of Crowds*. London: Little Brown Publishing.

Tapscott, D. and Williams, A. (2008) *Wikinomics: How mass collaboration changes everything*, 2nd edition. London: Atlantic Books.

Taylor, R. (2004) 'Skills and innovation in modern Britain'. ESRC Future of Work Programme Seminar Series. Available online at: http://www.leeds.ac.uk/ esrcfutureofwork/downloads/fow_publication_6.pdf

Ulrich, D. and Brockbank, W. (2005) *The HR Value Proposition*. Boston, MA: Harvard Business School Press.

Walker Rettberg, J. (2008) *Blogging*. Cambridge: Polity Press.

Withers, M., Williamson, M. and Reddington, M. (2010) *Transforming HR: Creating value through people*, 2nd edition. Oxford: Butterworth-Heinemann.

CHAPTER 9

Critical HRD and Organisational Effectiveness

Allan Ramdhony

CHAPTER OVERVIEW

This chapter sets out to expand and link the emerging concept of Critical HRD (CHRD) to the notion of New OE. In doing so, it identifies ten defining characteristics of CHRD which not only serve to reinforce the current conceptualisation of CHRD but also offer fresh insights into its nature and that of its relationship with New OE. Putting CHRD in context, attention is drawn to the potential pitfalls of CHRD practice and to the merits of micro-emancipatory projects, which can become a powerful platform for such practice. A case study focusing on action learning sets in a healthcare organisation is used to highlight the tensions and dilemmas facing OD/HRD specialists responsible for delivering CHRD strategies and to consider the conditions for sustainable CHRD practice.

LEARNING OBJECTIVES

By the end of this chapter the reader should be able to:

- understand the context and significance of the newly emerging concept of Critical HRD (CHRD)
- explain the defining characteristics of CHRD and link them to the notion of 'New Organisational Effectiveness'
- critically examine the potential pitfalls of CHRD practice and the merits of micro-emancipation as a powerful platform for such practice
- appreciate the tensions and dilemmas faced by OD/HRD specialists responsible for delivering CHRD strategies and consider the conditions for the possibility of sustainable CHRD practice.

INTRODUCTION

Although HRD is now seen as a distinctive field of research and practice, which is growing in maturity and accommodating of a wide range of perspectives (McGoldrick *et al*, 2001), the critical paradigm was not, until recently, one of these perspectives. As reminded by

Fenwick (2005), it is only at the beginning of this century that the concept of CHRD has emerged within the HRD field, when a 'critical turn in HRD' was included as a stream of a Critical Management Studies (CMS) conference in 2002.

The chapter begins by putting CHRD 'in context', with a brief overview of the key developments that led to an engagement of HRD with the critical paradigm. It then identifies ten defining characteristics of CHRD with reference to the pioneering works of leading authors in the subject area before establishing the links between these characteristics and the notion of organisational effectiveness. In so doing, the chapter not only reviews the current conceptualisation of CHRD in extant literature but also, in line with the constructionist epistemology that permeates it, offers fresh insights into the nature of CHRD and that of its relationship with the notion of New Organisational Effectiveness explained in Chapter 1 ('New OE').

The chapter proceeds to critically examine the potential pitfalls of CHRD practice and consider the merits of micro-emancipation (experimentation with small, localised emancipatory projects), which, it is argued, can become a powerful platform for such practice. A case study derived from doctoral research focusing on the potential of action learning sets as a medium for CHRD practice in a healthcare organisation (given the name of HealthServ for the purposes of confidentiality and anonymity) is used to highlight the tensions and dilemmas facing OD/HRD specialists tasked with the responsibility for delivering CHRD strategies and to consider the necessary conditions for the possibility of sustainable CHRD practice.

A CRITICAL TURN IN THE HRD FIELD

This section charts the emergence of CHRD. It includes a cursory analysis of HRD history and a critical review of some of the key tensions within the field, leading to what has been referred to as *the critical turn in HRD* (Rigg *et al*, 2007; Sambrook, 2004).

A DISORDERLY HISTORY

It has been suggested that the HRD field has not been too successful in chronicling its own history, which remains somewhat 'disorderly' (Gold *et al*, 2003: 451). Although the origin of HRD has been traced back to ancient Greek and Roman societies and even to the dawn of human civilisation, it is, for the sake of brevity, more important here to mention some of the more recent influences which have shaped HRD as a 'predominantly Western concept' and field of research and practice (Lee and Stead, 1998: 297).

In the USA these influences include the formation of the Training Within Industry (TWI) agency in the early 1940s, a wartime initiative that sought to address the shortage of skilled labour across industries by injecting apprentice-training programmes with humanist principles and a commitment to continuous performance improvement (Ruona and Swanson, 1998); the development, in the same period, of the 'instructional systems design' (ISD) model, which promoted a systematic approach to training design, development, implementation and evaluation in order to enhance the overall effectiveness of training interventions (McGuire and Cseh, 2006); and the creation of National Training Laboratories (NTLs) in the mid-1940s in which training groups (more widely known as T-Groups), operating under the OD principles of diversity and inclusion, were perceived as a critical success factor for organisational change and effectiveness (Grieves and Redman, 1999).

Lee and Stead (1998) see the end of World War II as a major turning point in the history of HRD and draw on Maslow's hierarchy of needs to consider key post-war developments in HRD in the UK. According to them, little attention was paid to the developmental aspect of HRD immediately after the war and the focus tended to be on national safety and security needs. During the 1950s and 1960s, this focus shifted to Maslow's social needs, more attention being given to employee needs for self-expression and self-development. The 1970s and 1980s witnessed another shift in focus to esteem needs, where HRD was driven by the development of strategies geared towards both individual and organisational success in the context of the rise of free-market entrepreneurialism. Finally, the 1990s onwards saw the emergence of strategic HRD but also of HRD as a field of integrity committed to learning and performance in line with 'the vision of a caring, sharing and prosperous society' and the needs of individuals for self-actualisation (Lee and Stead, 1998: 306).

With the recognition of the 'imprint' of the USA and the UK on HRD history, it has been argued that it is now time for a less ethnocentric approach to the development of HRD (Wang and McLean, 2007). In the age of globalisation, in which HRD is becoming increasingly cross-national and being shaped to meet context-specific needs around the world, efforts have been made to explore the meaning of International HRD (IHRD) as a nascent area of study (McLean and McLean, 2001).

Although one would struggle to plot a neat and linear history of HRD, the above accounts are indicative of its critical milestones. Commenting on the current status of HRD, Stewart (2005: 90) described HRD as a healthy area of research and practice which is 'growing in diversity and maturity'. As it sinks deeper into the fabric of organisational life, HRD seems poised for a leadership role in 'changing the nature of organisation, management and work' (*ibid*) within twenty-first-century organisations, with a firm intent on broadening the scope of its activities to include nearly all of the key areas of the HR function (McLagan and Suhadolnik, 1989).

TENSION AND CONTENTION

The rather rosy historical account of HRD provided above belies the fact that its journey has been far from straightforward and has been filled with tension and contention (Gold *et al*, 2003). The tension and contention have been mostly around two key issues which have sustained animated debates about the nature of HRD for the past two decades. The first issue concerns the question of whether HRD should be defined or not, and whether or not its theoretical identity should be clearly established (eg Kuchinke, 2001; Lee, 2003). The other issue has to do with whether the primary goal of HRD should be performance or learning (eg Barrie and Pace, 1998, 1999; Kuchinke, 2000).

Regarding the first issue, a robust case has been made for achieving a greater definition of HRD in order to reduce the 'fog factor' in the field if it is not to remain ambiguous and run the risk of losing its credibility (Megginson *et al*, 1993). On the other hand, there is an equally robust case for not defining HRD and trying to pin down its conceptual boundaries. For example, Lee (2001) argues that to define HRD would be to 'fix' its meaning while denying others the opportunity to attach their own meanings to it depending on the specificity of their organisational context. The constructionist outlook that underpins Lee's argument ascribes a more creative role to human agency in shaping HRD as an organisational phenomenon – a view which, as will become clearer in the following sections, bears a strong resonance with CHRD.

The second key issue of contention – the performance versus learning debate – has even greater relevance to CHRD and deserves particular attention here. Leading authors who favour the performance paradigm (eg Kuchinke, 1998; Swanson, 1994) ascribe a more instrumental role to HRD as responsible for training and developing employees as a means of achieving strategic objectives and maximising performance, productivity and profitability – which, it has to be underlined, remains the predominant view within the field and acts almost subliminally on the way HRD is conceptualised and played out. However, HRD academics who resist the primacy given to the performance paradigm (eg Barrie and Pace, 1998; Watkins, 1991) argue that such a view is severely limited in that it obscures the higher calling of HRD, which is to support the learning and development of employees, and condemns HRD to the soulless role of promoting the mercantile interests of profit-centred organisations. Therefore, for those authors who resist an undue emphasis on performance, learning represents an advanced paradigm, which ensures the commitment and valued contribution of employees to the achievement of organisational goals and can thus be considered a necessary precondition for sustained performance.

A CRITICAL TIME FOR A CRITICAL TURN

The contentious nature of the HRD field has raised some concerns that the unending debates over the same old issues may only serve to reduce dialogue, congeal polarised views and perpetuate a dichotomous mode of thinking within the field (Callahan and de Dávila, 2004). Following Sambrook (2007), now is perhaps a critical time for a critical turn in the HRD field. CHRD could cut a timely swathe through the persistent (and some might argue pointless) debates about the nature and purpose of HRD to challenge academics and practitioners alike to think about HRD in more critical terms and help the field achieve a more complex and complete understanding of itself.

The pressing questions at this point are:

● What are the key reasons for advocating a critical turn in the HRD field?

and

● What is the primary purpose of CHRD?

In considering the key reasons for advocating a critical turn in HRD, one has to revisit the now ubiquitous statement from Elliott and Turnbull, who organised the first critical session at an AHRD Conference in 2002 and explained the rationale behind it (Elliott and Turnbull, 2002: 971):

> We are concerned that the methodological traditions that guide the majority of HRD research do not allow researchers to engage in studies that challenge the predominantly performative ... focus of the HRD field ... We seek to unpick the assumptions behind the performative orientation that dominates much HRD research ... We therefore perceived the need to open up HRD theory to a broader range of methodological and theoretical perspectives.

Following Elliott and Turnbull's statement, a key reason for embracing a critical turn in HRD is to equip HRD theorists and researchers with an analytical lens enriched by a range of critical perspectives that can effectively challenge the prevalent mode of thinking and taken-for-granted assumptions within the field that serve to legitimate an almost exclusive focus on performance and the achievement of strategic objectives – all too often to the detriment of the well-being and developmental needs of employees. The above concerns are echoed and developed in Rigg et al's four main reasons for advocating a critical turn in the HRD field (Rigg et al, 2007: 3–8):

● the predominance of 'performative values', characterised by a preoccupation with improving individual and/or organisational performance, which are consistently described in economic terms
● 'an unbalanced reliance on humanist assumptions' that perpetuates an instrumental view of individuals
● an 'impoverished' HRD research hinged on quantitative research that represents organisational structures as immutable and independent of human agency
● an HRD curriculum and pedagogical methods which pay 'minimal attention to issues of power and emotion' and remain impotent when it comes to challenging and transforming existing social orders.

In light of the above, the primary purpose of CHRD is therefore to challenge mainstream thinking and taken-for-granted assumptions within the HRD field that serve to legitimate a one-sided focus on performance and an instrumental view of employees which can be potentially exploitive and oppressive. This 'negative' dimension of CHRD is balanced by a more 'positive' one: an emancipatory agenda that aims to promote a more humanistic approach to HRD and frame change efforts towards more democratic and enabling working conditions in which a fundamental symmetry can be achieved between performance and learning, strategic and moral imperatives, and organisational and employee needs (Fenwick,

2005). It is now appropriate to engage with the concept of CHRD at a deeper level by considering its defining characteristics and exploring its links with the notion of 'New OE'.

REFLECTIVE ACTIVITIES

- What are the key reasons behind the recent emergence of CHRD?
- Explain in your own words the primary purpose of CHRD.

CHRD AND NEW OE

This section examines ten key defining characteristics of CHRD and explores their links with the notion of New OE. An overview of these linkages is provided in Table 9.1, followed by more detailed discussion.

Table 9.1 Defining characteristics of CHRD and links to New OE

Defining characteristics	Summary explanation	Links to New OE
1 *A non-exclusive focus on performance*	Resists an exclusive focus on performance, productivity and profit to call for a fundamental symmetry between individual and organisational needs and interests.	Is aligned with the central theme of *authenticity and mutuality* in New OE, which warrants a rebalancing of interests between organisation and employee as a prerequisite for long-term employee engagement and organisational performance.
2 *A concern for denaturalisation*	Refers to a responsibility to 'de-normalise' and treat as 'unnatural' ideological strongholds, knowledge and power relations and other organisational arrangements that are potentially oppressive and exploitative.	Centres on New OE's notion of *language and action* – by which language is used as a creative tool to expose oppressive/exploitative power structures and to frame change towards more empowering working practices.
3 *A commitment to critical reflection*	Denotes a faculty of the mind that penetrates the deeper layers of organisational reality in order to uncover and remove deep-seated sources of domination in the workplace that frustrate the possibility for radical change.	Resonates with New OE's challenge to change agents to develop their abilities as *thinking performers* and 'clear the path' for high employee engagement and organisational performance.
4 *A non-conformist posture*	Aims to institutionalise a tradition of non-conformity that can firmly stand against any order of discourse and action that impedes critical reflection, suppresses opposition and deprives individuals of their rights.	Strikes a chord with the central theme of *paradox and ambiguity*, which emphasises the need to effectively manage contradictions and dissent as a source of 'creative tension'.

Defining characteristics	Summary explanation	Links to New OE
5 *An emancipatory intent*	Upholds a special qualitative kind of employee freedom to self-develop, to experience a sense of well-being and to maximise their potential resulting from a deliberate removal of unwanted and unnecessary barriers that stand in the way.	Endorses New OE's explicit *emancipatory interest* involving a 'deep-seated desire' to rid organisations of power structures and relations that needlessly repress human beings and to champion employee needs and interests.
6 *A radical mindset*	Seeks to produce a type of change that, even if gradual or tempered, is nothing less than thoroughgoing and emancipatory. Favours, to this effect, essentially qualitative modes of inquiry.	Is in synch with the notion of a *morphing mindset*, which promotes a particular frame of mind that is 'change-ready' and embraces continuous, system-wide change conducive to employee engagement and sustainable employment relationships.
7 *An ethical stance*	Aims, in view of the broader principles of social justice and equity, to resist the unfair treatment of employees and involve them in the moral validation of proposed ends and courses of action.	Shares New OE's ethical concerns based on an *ethos of partnership and mutuality* to enable greater employee participation in moral validation of proposed ends and courses of action.
8 *A facilitator of participatory dialogue*	Seeks to create opportunities for greater dialogue brought under the guiding principle of free discourse as a means to 'denaturalise' a purely performative approach to HRD and reconcile organisational and individual needs and interests.	Echoes New OE's call for a more *dialogical approach* to change through which greater mutuality of gains between employer and employee can be achieved.
9 *A critical realist outlook*	Displays affinities with critical realism, which shares a commitment to human emancipation and ontological assumptions that promote emancipatory change.	Is aligned with New OE's critical realist perspective on organisational life, which lies at its very core and carries similar ontological assumptions geared towards emancipatory change.
10 *An agent of workplace democracy*	Forces a shift from a performative/ instrumental approach to human beings and work to a form of participatory and deliberative democracy to enable a fundamental symmetry between performance and learning objectives, strategic and moral imperatives, and system and social integration.	Locks on to the central theme of *leadership and management*, which also emphasises the need for a move away from conventional approaches to leading change in favour of a more democratic, distributed and diffused type of leadership that can allow for greater employee agency and mutuality.

1 A non-exclusive focus on performance

CHRD resists a one-sided focus on performance, productivity and profit, which are all too often achieved at the expense of the well-being and 'true' learning needs and interests of employees (Elliott and Turnbull, 2005). Although recognising that performance objectives are vital to the survival of the organisation and can thus never be ignored, CHRD calls for a synthesis in which both performance and learning are on an equal footing, where learning is seen as a necessary precondition for sustained performance and vice versa – ie where both paradigms are seen as interdependent, mutually reinforcing and warranting a fundamental symmetry between individual and organisational needs and interests, which ought to be reflected in the HRD agenda.

CHRD's non-exclusive focus on performance bears a strong resonance with one of the central themes of New OE, *authenticity and mutuality* (see Chapter 1). In line with OD's humanist principles, the theme of authenticity and mutuality opposes an instrumental view of human beings and calls for a rebalancing of interests and gains between organisation and employee as a prerequisite for long-term employee engagement and organisational performance, which are also regarded as self-renewing and mutually reinforcing outcomes (again see Chapter 1).

2 A concern for denaturalisation

CHRD's concern for denaturalisation stems from another key theme in the CMS literature. The term 'denaturalisation' refers to an attempt to 'de-normalise' and treat as 'unnatural' (and irrational) ideological strongholds, unequal knowledge and power relations, and other organisational arrangements that are potentially oppressive and exploitative yet well entrenched and hard to displace since these are usually portrayed by dominant groups as 'natural and inevitable' and thus beyond challenge (Fenwick, 2004: 202).

'Denaturalising traits' in New OE centre on issues of *language and action* – where language is seen not just as a means to describe existing organisational orders but also as a creative tool that can be used to effectively expose and explain the alienating effects of oppressive/exploitative relationships and power structures that are usually embedded (and normalised) in mainstream HR models and, importantly, to frame change efforts towards more empowering and life-enriching working practices.

3 A commitment to critical reflection

CHRD's commitment to critical reflection is yet another characteristic which it inherits from CMS, although it is also a common theme in Critical Pedagogy (CP). Critical reflection denotes a faculty of the mind that goes beyond surface understandings and mere appearances to penetrate the deeper layers of organisational reality – the aim being to uncover and remove deep-seated sources of domination in the workplace that frustrate the possibility for radical, emancipatory change. (This is explained in more detail in the following subsections.)

In similar vein, New OE aims to bring into the mainstream a preferred approach to organisational change that invites change agents and business partners to keep on the mantle of the *thinking performer* and develop their ability to deal with the complex and dynamic nature of their operating context (both internal and external) so that they can 'clear the path' for high employee engagement and organisational performance and intended change outcomes.

4 A non-conformist posture

This particular characteristic reinforces and qualifies CHRD's commitment to critical reflection. As explained by Sambrook (2009: 64), CHRD, as the critical paradigm, is pitted against mainstream HRD, the 'apparently uncritical paradigm' which conforms to prevalent modes of thinking and behaviour and fails to challenge organisational arrangements and practices that serve, in unitarist fashion, to legitimate a performative approach to HRD. As opposed to mainstream HRD, CHRD aims to institutionalise a tradition of non-conformity that can stand firmly against any order of discourse and action that impedes critical reflection, suppresses opposition and deprives individuals of their right to well-being and self-development.

The central theme in OE, *paradox and ambiguity*, displays some affinity with CHRD in that it warns against a unitarist and 'consensus-oriented approach to HRM/OD' (see Chapter 1) that prevents management and change agents from effectively coping with paradox and ambiguity and even more with diversity and dissent, which can pose a serious threat to their power bases. New OE therefore recognises the need to effectively manage contradictions and dissent – which can eventually become the source of the constructive tension needed to build powerful coalitions around change projects geared towards enhanced organisational effectiveness (Evans *et al*, 2002).

5 An emancipatory intent

What sets CHRD apart is its commitment to *employee emancipation*. While the term 'employee emancipation' is yet to be more widely adopted by academics and practitioners alike, it entails 'a special qualitative kind' of employee freedom to self-develop, to experience a sense of well-being and to maximise their potential resulting from a deliberate and conscious change effort to remove the 'unwanted and unnecessary' barriers that stand in the way (Bhaskar, 1986: 171). The onus is therefore on CHRD to find ways to remove such barriers and bring about working conditions in which employee emancipation can become a real possibility.

New OE shares CHRD's commitment to employee emancipation and, drawing from Habermas (1987b), articulates in no uncertain terms the emancipatory interest that drives it. This emancipatory interest involves a 'deep-seated desire' to rid organisations of power structures and relations that needlessly repress human beings in order to champion employee needs and interests, which are seen as interlocked in a virtuous cycle with enhanced organisational performance.

6 A radical mindset

CHRD is inherently radical in that it seeks to produce a type of change that, even if gradual or tempered, is nothing less than thoroughgoing and emancipatory – where the endpoint is a qualitative change in working conditions and a decisive step towards the establishment of a social order in which employee emancipation can become a real possibility. To this effect CHRD favours essentially qualitative modes of inquiry that are not hinged on quantitative measures (Valentin, 2006) but allow for context-sensitive, meaning-rich investigations through which the existing social order can be intelligibly probed with a view to bringing about emancipatory change.

CHRD's radical mindset is in synch with New OE's endorsement of a *morphing mindset* (Marshak, 2002) – a generative metaphor which is used to explain a particular frame of mind that is 'change-ready' and embraces continuous, system-wide change whereby organisations can be transformed into a workplace environment conducive to employee engagement and sustainable employment relationships.

7 An ethical stance

One of the main objectives of CHRD is to reinstate ethics 'as a category of [organisational] life' (Habermas, 1971: 112) through an attempt to preserve a harmony between the organisation's moral norms and values and the principles of social justice and equity prevailing within its wider operating context (Fenwick, 2005). Although a more in-depth discussion of CHRD's ethical stance is beyond the scope of this chapter, it is important here to point out that, as guardian of workplace ethics, CHRD's primary responsibility is to resist the unfair treatment of employees as 'mere means to an end' (which is the callous pursuit of capital and profit) and to find ways to involve them more in the moral validation of proposed ends or courses of action, which are all too often predetermined and imposed upon them by dominant groups.

New OE entertains CHRD's ethical concerns in that it also resists the unfair treatment of employees as soulless factors of production and is driven by an *ethos of partnership and mutuality* that 'consciously seeks to enhance the level of employee involvement, agency and community within the organisation' (Francis *et al*, 2012) – which undeniably opens up the opportunity for greater employee participation in the moral validation of proposed ends or courses of action. This point is reinforced in the following subsection.

8 A facilitator of participatory dialogue

CHRD is called to take a leading role in creating opportunities for greater dialogue as a means to 'denaturalise' a purely performative approach to HRD and to find ways to translate its emancipatory intent into practice (Sambrook, 2009). This can involve the facilitation of HRD initiatives such as micro-emancipatory projects (described in more detail in the following section) brought under the binding force of free discourse – psychologically safe learning environments in which unconstrained interaction between participants-in-communication 'counts as the genuine and irreplaceable medium' for reaching understanding' (Habermas, 1984: 342) and co-ordinating action around what can be collectively regarded as fair and morally right with a view to reconciling employees' emancipatory needs and the organisation's performance objectives.

In its constructionist treatment of language, New OE fully recognises the power of talk in framing action and shaping organisational realities (Marshak and Grant, 2008) and calls for a more *discursive or dialogical approach* to managing change – leading to more inclusive and positive 'background conversations of change' (Ford *et al*, 2002) that can not only minimise resistance to change but more importantly achieve greater mutuality of gains between employer and employee which, as previously explained, is a central theme in New OE.

9 A critical realist outlook

A case is made here for a rapprochement between CHRD and critical realism, which can effectively clear the path for CHRD research and practice. For the sake of brevity, the following points should suffice to support this case:

- Critical realism shares with CHRD a firm commitment to the project of human emancipation and an unswerving belief in the power of scientific inquiry and critical reasoning to fulfil such a project.
- Critical realism upholds a transformational model of social activity which accommodates a view of pre-existing organisational structures as only 'relatively enduring' and therefore subject to change towards more emancipatory working conditions via the agency of committed CHRD practitioners.
- Critical realism promotes a 'depth ontology' in which organisational reality is viewed as complex, multidimensional and multilayered – offering the possibility for in-depth explanatory investigations into the causal powers and mechanisms that can either frustrate or support CHRD practice.
- Critical realism alerts CHRD to the importance of addressing both the discursive (cognitive) and material (non-cognitive) dimensions of employee emancipation if its emancipatory strategy is not to remain impotent and inevitably followed by dissonance and despair (refer for example to Bhaskar, 1986, 1989; Collier, 1994; Sayer, 2000).

As underlined by Francis *et al* in Chapter 1, the primarily constructionist outlook that underwrites New OE has to be combined with the 'more concrete and constraining aspects of organisational life' to locate a critical realist perspective on organisational life at its very core. In this way, New OE embraces a social ontology that accounts for the complexity and multilayered nature of organisational reality and, importantly, recognises the need to pay attention to both the discursive and material dimensions of change projects if its intended outcomes in the form of self-renewing and sustainable employee engagement and organisational performance are to be achieved.

10 An agent of workplace democracy

As can be readily inferred from its other defining characteristics explained above, CHRD, as an agent of workplace democracy, attempts to force a shift from a performative and instrumental approach to human beings and work to a form of participatory and deliberative democracy rooted in free discourse – whereby a fundamental symmetry between performance and learning objectives, strategic and moral imperatives, and system and social integration can be achieved (Habermas, 1984, 1987a).

The central theme in New OE, building *leadership* capability, also emphasises the need for a move away from conventional approaches to leading change in favour of a more democratic, distributed and diffused type of leadership that can allow for greater employee agency and mutuality and that is more likely to result in the fundamental symmetry described above.

REFLECTIVE ACTIVITIES

- Review your personal understanding of the defining characteristics of CHRD and their links to the notion of New OE.

- Think about how a CHRD lens can help you understand a particular problem you may have observed at work or experienced following the implementation of a particular change project.

THE PRACTICE OF CHRD

Because the concept of CHRD is still in an early stage of development, it is understandable why there is a dearth of empirical evidence on the practice of CHRD 'in context' and a disjuncture at this point in time between CHRD theory and practice. It is, however, timely to critically examine the potential pitfalls of what can be considered CHRD practice before considering the channels through which it can be effectively delivered.

POTENTIAL PITFALLS OF CHRD PRACTICE

As remarked by Rigg *et al* (2007: 11) CHRD is 'not so easy to expedite in practice as to articulate in theory'. The process of translating CHRD ideals into practice can prove problematic and is not without its potential pitfalls. For example, Sambrook (2009: 70) warns against the dangers of practising CHRD by drawing attention to the personal and organisational barriers that stand in its way and to its unintended 'negative consequences' (eg 'dogma, fear, misunderstanding, and perceived threat of loss').

It is useful to revisit the work of Reynolds (1999a, 1999b) who examines in more detail some of the pitfalls of critical reflection and critical pedagogy which equally apply to CHRD. The first pitfall is *resistance* by both dominant and subordinate groups. Resistance by dominant groups is hardly surprising, since one would not expect them to be too inviting of a critique of taken-for-granted assumptions and of the oppressive working practices that pose a threat to their power bases and status. Resistance by subordinate groups can result from the fear of being marginalised, victimised or even summarily dismissed, but also, and perhaps more importantly, from the 'natural fear of freedom' in the oppressed who often doubt their own ability to exercise the freedom they crave and/or are unable to trust those leading the way to that freedom (Freire, 1970: 150) – aspects of resistance which are often naïvely overlooked by change agents.

A second pitfall is that of *presentation*. Critical theories have been severely criticised for being no more than 'esoteric intellectual speculations' and 'grand Utopian utterances' that come across as self-righteous and disconnected from the practicalities of everyday life while remaining inaccessible to a larger audience (Reynolds, 1999b: 177; also Alvesson and Willmott, 1996; Grey, 1996). This points to the need to rearticulate critical theories in more accessible language and relocate them within the 'concrete reality' of organisational actors in order to release their emancipatory potential.

Another pitfall is that of *assimilation*. There is always the danger that critical reflection will be stripped of its 'socio-political element' and emancipatory potential to be readily assimilated into the mainstream and become yet another tool in the managerial toolkit – serving the sectional interests of those in power while 'leaving the superficial impression that a more critical approach has been applied' (Reynolds, 1999b: 178) when what in fact has been achieved is 'little more than thoughtful problem-solving' (Reynolds, 1999a: 549).

A final pitfall is that of *dissonance,* which Brookfield (1994) refers to as the 'dark side' or disruptive consequences of critical reflection. Dissonance occurs when increasing awareness of oppressive ideologies and practices achieved through critical reflection is not followed by a change in the social conditions that sustain them – that is, when the growing realisation of oppressive social realities is not followed by transformative praxis. Dissonance can result in a (false) sense of 'impostorship' (doubting one's capacity to challenge prevailing views and taken-for-granteds), 'loss of innocence' (a feeling of disenchantment and despair in the face of unchanged oppressive social realities), 'cultural suicide' (facing the threat of reprisal because of one's critical stance) and the risk of being 'excluded from the cultures that have defined and sustained [one] up to that point in [one's life]' (Brookfield, 1994: 205, 208).

As shown above, the potential pitfalls of being critical are real and arise from the concrete and harsh realities of organisational life. Translating CHRD into practice thus remains a tall order and, to borrow from Reynolds (1999b: 182), there are 'nettles to be grasped' and caveats to be posited if CHRD is to have any significant bearing on HRD practices and, by extension, on organisational life without being 'swept away as irrationality' or dismissed as pure heresy (Alvesson and Willmott, 1996: 174).

THE MERITS OF MICRO-EMANCIPATORY PROJECTS

The question then remains: 'How can one steer clear of the pitfalls of being critical and effectively translate CHRD theory into practice?' It would be ill-advised to follow a 'doctrinaire blueprint' for practising CHRD – which would otherwise make it guilty of creating an orthodoxy of its own, leading to its degeneration into a hollow prescriptive model and an alienating 'reactionary blah' (Freire, 1970: 19). There is a need to contextualise CHRD practice while retaining the emancipatory ideals of the critical perspectives that inform it.

To this end, Alvesson and Wilmott (1992, 1996) have proposed a form of intervention, which they have termed *micro-emancipation* and which can provide a way forward for CHRD practice. Micro-emancipation involves experimentation with small, localised emancipatory projects that can effectively 'combine pragmatic action with critical analysis' to 'target specific oppressive practices' at the micro level and frame action towards more democratic and empowering working practices within the realm of the day-to-day experiences of organisational actors (Fenwick, 2004: 203–4).

Micro-emancipatory projects therefore enable a more tempered yet radical approach to change which, when successful, can secure valuable 'small wins' or incremental gains for CHRD practice while reducing the risk of full-blown opposition from dominant groups (Meyerson and Kolb, 2000). Moreover, they can effectively clinch the connection between micro- and macro-level organisational processes and serve as a catalyst for organisation-wide radical change that can precipitate the conditions for more democratic and emancipatory working practices (Alvesson and Willmott, 1996).

Micro-emancipatory projects can take the form of feminist projects, learning communities, critical thinking episodes, critical action learning sets, and appreciative inquiries (Fenwick, 2005; Rigg *et al*, 2007) – all of which, it is argued, can deliver in varying degrees the emancipatory ideals embedded in the ten CHRD characteristics detailed above and effectively contribute to a wider emancipatory thrust that is necessary for an organisation-wide model of CHRD practice.

The HealthServ case study below focuses on action learning sets as a platform for CHRD practice and, importantly, brings to the fore the tensions and dilemmas facing OD/HRD specialists responsible for delivering CHRD strategies while considering the necessary conditions for the possibility for sustainable CHRD practice and organisational effectiveness.

HEALTHSERV: IN PURSUIT OF SUSTAINABLE ORGANISATIONAL EFFECTIVENESS

CASE STUDY

HealthServ is one of the largest health boards in the UK and provides a comprehensive range of healthcare services to a diverse population both across the UK and abroad. Since its establishment in 2001, change has been the only constant for HealthServ, which has undergone a major redesign and subsequent restructuring efforts to modernise its services and ensure sustainable organisational effectiveness in the longer term. The key drivers of the change process at HealthServ include:

- the need to realign the organisation with the Government Health Directorate, which aims to tackle health inequality and improve the quality of healthcare in the UK

- an intent on establishing 'The HealthServ Way' – a cultural value system aligned with the democratic principles of social justice and inclusion and based on an ethos of person-centredness, partnership and integrity, which are seen by top management as key to sustainable organisational effectiveness, and form the building blocks of the dominant order of discourse driving change

- the need to devolve decision-making powers and set up new management structures to ensure the effective and efficient delivery of healthcare services within the strategic framework set nationally and at board level

- the need to embark on a whole-system improvement programme based on lean principles to integrate and streamline processes in order to eliminate waste, reduce waiting times and add value to service delivery.

A lever for strategic change

Since the beginning of the change process, HealthServ Learning (HSL), the organisation's HRD function, has expanded its role as change agent, and its overriding concern is to be perceived as a lever for strategic change. To this effect HSL has developed, in partnership with external training providers, a Learning Plan that aims to address the developmental needs of a wide stakeholder base and deliver learning solutions on a continuum from pre-employment through induction and clinical training to management and leadership development. HSL has also increased its capacity for blended learning approaches to support e-learning, continuous professional development, and career progression – so that staff can be 'fit for purpose' and effectively contribute to change efforts, especially when it comes to the successful delivery of lean projects.

Action learning sets and a glimpse of CHRD practice

HSL has also been entrusted with the responsibility to provide visible leadership in establishing The HealthServ Way across the organisation. This entails embedding the moral values and democratic principles underpinning The HealthServ Way in the HRD curriculum and acting as a catalyst in the creation of a workplace environment in which such values and principles can become a living reality. HSL has been experimenting with action learning sets with a 'critical edge' that seem to be particularly conducive to the establishment of The HealthServ Way and offer a glimpse of the possibility for CHRD practice across the organisation.

According to the HRD specialist leading the project, action learning has been quite successful and is often referred to as an 'island of good practice'. The primary purpose of HSL's action learning sets is to provide a facilitation service for employees to help them cope with workplace problems that might be the cause of ongoing emotional turmoil and poor performance and find solutions that effectively address their specific learning needs. In terms of content, facilitators have recourse to investigative, counselling and modelling techniques to promote self-reflective learning and a collaborative approach to problem-solving. In terms of process, no effort is spared to translate into practice the fundamental principles of The HealthServ Way. Facilitators endeavour to create a safe environment devoid of power inequalities and based on inclusion, mutual respect and free speech whereby members can help and challenge each other to better understand their situations and make the best of the learning opportunities offered to them.

A reversal of fortune

Although it seemed that all was going well with the delivery of action learning sets, facilitators have recently met with a reversal of fortune. Following the economic downturn and mounting pressures for cost-reduction measures, top management announced that action learning sets would have to be 'frozen' and resources 'rechannelled' to more pressing projects such as e-learning and lean. This came as both a shock and a disappointment to all those involved, as expressed by the lead facilitator:

Nobody was consulted. It's happened because we apparently don't have the resources any more ... but I think that there are certain people in senior positions who would not support it and criticise it at the first opportunity and have now found a way to get rid of it ... I've now been asked to help out with lean.

The lead facilitator's retrospective assessment of top management's decision to freeze action learning sets contains a thinly veiled scepticism over the 'official reason' behind it. There is a shared view among members of action learning sets that the 'real' reason is that management never really supported the project and have now found a way to suppress it.

Questions

In line with one of the defining characteristics of CHRD established in this chapter, the case analysis that follows is underpinned by a critical realist outlook and, in typical critical realist fashion, attempts to answer the following 'explanatory' questions:

1 What led to the 'freezing' of HSL's action learning sets?

2 What are the conditions for the possibility of CHRD practice within HealthServ?

In addressing Question 1, it is not possible here, because of the space constraints, to provide a thorough account of the complex, contingent and countervailing causal influences that led to the freezing of HSL's action learning sets. What follows is a partial and simplified explanation of the entities at play within HealthServ (these can include human beings, relationships, intentions, structures, interventions, etc) and of their causal influences that combined into a mechanism (or in this case a 'tipping point') that brought about the main event described in the case study, which was the 'freezing' of HSL's action learning sets. The diagram below illustrates this process.

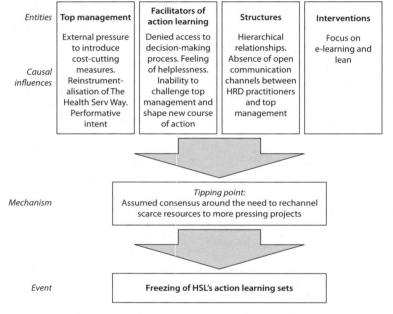

As top management at HealthServ came under increasing pressure from government officials to introduce cost-reduction measures following the economic downturn, they unilaterally and almost instantly decided to withdraw commitment to action learning sets and redirect 'scarce' resources to more pressing projects in the form of e-learning and lean. Triangulated evidence from doctoral research suggests that top management never really subscribed to the democratic principles and moral values underpinning The HealthServ Way, which was re-instrumentalised into a means to an end – ie as a motivational tool for enhanced performance and the precipitation of strategic objectives. The decision to focus change efforts on e-learning (as a 'cheaper' means to cater to the learning needs of a wide stakeholder base) and lean (to maximise efficiency) tends to confirm top management's performative intent and concern *to do more with less*.

Facilitators of action learning sets were denied access to the decision-making process because of the highly hierarchical relationships prevailing within HealthServ and an absence of open channels of communication with top management. This resulted in a feeling of helplessness operating at both intra-personal and inter-personal domains (Houston, 2001), which left facilitators unable to challenge top management, force them to make good on the democratic principles underpinning the dominant order of discourse and shape the new course of action.

The combined effects of the causal influences explained above led to a generative mechanism in the form of a *tipping point*: an assumed consensus around the need to focus on more pressing projects, which inevitably brought about the 'freezing' of action learning sets – a 'luxury' that had to be dispensed with in times of financial austerity. Facilitators of action learning sets were in the process effectively robbed of their emancipatory role and assimilated into the 'technocratic apparatus' of efficiency and performance maximisation – and were left with nothing but scepticism for the real motives of top management.

In addressing Question 2 and examining the conditions for the possibility for CHRD practice within HealthServ, it is important to begin by drawing attention to the tensions and dilemmas faced by HSL's specialists tasked with the responsibility for delivering strategies containing elements of such practice.

First, HSL's facilitators of action learning sets were confronted with a paradox with which they were unable to cope: the fact that the emancipatory ideals underpinning the organisation's cultural value system are at source *instrumental* – ie they exist by virtue of the need to achieve the performance and strategic objectives of the organisation, the very thing that CHRD aims to challenge.

Second, they were taken aback by the sequence of events leading to the freezing of action learning sets. Although adept at critical reflection and problem-solving because of the very nature of their work, they were unable in this particular situation to exercise these skills and challenge top management's sudden and arbitrary decision to freeze action learning and come to a solution that could meet with the approval of all.

Third, facilitators of action learning sets were not particularly aware of how the dominant discourse underpinning The HealthServ Way was in effect 'colonised' and weakened by the economic imperatives of powerful external agents, which served to exacerbate the performative intent of top management and legitimate the withdrawal of both political and resource commitments to action learning (Habermas, 1984, 1987).

The 'difficulties' faced by the facilitators of action learning sets elicit thinking about what needs to be done for CHRD practice to become a real possibility within HealthServ. First, OD/HRD specialists leading emancipatory projects will have to develop an ability to manage paradox and *stretch* their reflective and problem-solving skills (even in the most undesirable and potentially threatening circumstances) not only to address workplace events as they are 'experienced' but also to identify the underlying causes that must be effectively addressed if a greater balance is to be achieved between organisational and employee needs – all of which harks back to the central themes of *authenticity and mutuality* and *paradox and ambiguity* in New OE.

Second, the HRD function as a whole must take a leading role in the development of an effective communication strategy, which can open up channels of communication with top management and provide a psychologically safe platform, devoid of power inequalities and brought under the binding force of free discourse (Habermas, 1984) – where HRD practitioners can have the opportunity, in collaboration with top management, to validate and co-ordinate courses of action that have a direct impact on the HRD process, especially those that can frustrate or simply annul the possibility for employee emancipation.

Third, there is need for a greater awareness of how the prevailing order of discourse, however democratic and well-intentioned, is never rigid or secure but always at risk of being 'colonised' and corroded through interaction with powerful key players or change agents (Fairclough, 2001). It is therefore important for HRD practitioners to increase their political influence and develop the capacity to shape the dominant order of discourse in favour of their emancipatory agenda and to frame action towards the realisation of such agenda. In this case, HRD practitioners will have to 'stretch' their vocabulary as a means to reframe action learning as a 'strategic imperative' and convince top management of the urgent need to reinstate it as a key determinant of long-term organisational effectiveness.

Last, attention has to be paid to both the discursive and material dimensions of employee emancipation and to secure both political and resource commitments to emancipatory projects for a solid move towards workplace conditions in which sustainable CHRD practice can become a real possibility (eg refer to Bhaskar, 1986).

REFLECTIVE ACTIVITIES

- How appropriate would action learning sets of the type described in the HealthServ case study be for your organisation?
- What challenges might be faced by HRD practitioners responsible for their delivery?

CONCLUSION

CHRD has recently emerged to challenge the predominantly performative intent of mainstream HRD and promote an approach to HRD rooted in humanist values and democratic principles. This chapter has served to reinforce and expand the current conceptualisation of CHRD by identifying ten defining characteristics that foreground its most salient features and key concerns. These ten characteristics were then linked to the central themes and issues revolving around the notion of New OE as construed by the editors of this textbook.

What arises from the intersection of CHRD and New OE is a robust emancipatory agenda that warrants a fundamental symmetry between performance and learning objectives, strategic and moral imperatives, and system and social integration – whereby the needs and interests of both organisation and employees can be reconciled and a greater mutuality of gains can be achieved.

Recognising the difficulty of enacting CHRD's emancipatory ideals, due consideration was given to the practice of CHRD to draw attention to its potential pitfalls with reference to those identified in CP – in the form of resistance, presentation, assimilation and dissonance – which, it is argued, equally apply to CHRD practice. An argument was also made in favour of micro-emancipatory projects, which can secure valuable incremental gains for CHRD practice and serve as a catalyst for organisation-wide emancipatory change.

Importantly, a case analysis underpinned by a critical realist perspective was carried out to illustrate the tensions and challenges facing OD/HRD specialists responsible for delivering CHRD strategies – enabling the identification of causal influences that combined to put out of play an emancipatory project in the form of action learning sets with a 'critical edge'. In the same breath, OD/HRD specialists were provided with a set of measures challenging them to stretch their reflective and problem-solving skills while increasing their political influence in order to effectively manage these tensions and dilemmas and bring about working conditions in which sustainable CHRD practice and New OE can become a real possibility.

It is hoped that this chapter has further clarified the meaning and purpose of CHRD, and that it provides some food for thought about what should be done to move it to the centre of organisations, where it can have a more agentive role and serve as a key determinant of sustainable effectiveness.

EXPLORE FURTHER

Rigg, C., Stewart, J. and Trehan, K. (eds) (2007) *Critical Human Resource Development: Beyond orthodoxy*. Harlow: Pearson Education, FT/Prentice Hall. This collection of essays by pioneering authors in the subject area engages with the key theories and debates underpinning CHRD, while providing useful insights into the benefits and pitfalls of practising CHRD.

Sambrook, S. (2009) 'Critical HRD: a concept analysis', *Personnel Review*, Vol.38, No.1: 61–73. This paper provides the first ever concept analysis of CHRD and identifies its attributes, antecedents and intended outcomes. Its aim is to provide useful guidance for the practice, teaching and researching of CHRD.

Trehan, K. and Rigg, C. (2011) 'Theorising critical HRD: a paradox of intricacy and discrepancy', *Journal of European Industrial Training*, Vol.35, No.3: 276–90. This article provides a useful update on the concept of CHRD to elicit thinking about the internal contradictions and practical significance of CHRD theory.

Trehan, K., Rigg, C. and Stewart, J. (2004) (eds) Special issue on Critical Human Resource Development, *Journal of European Industrial Training*, Vol.28, Nos8/9. This important collection of articles represents an early articulation of the key themes and theoretical issues revolving around the concept of CHRD.

REFERENCES

Alvesson, M. and Willmott, H. S. (1992) 'On the idea of emancipation in management and organisation studies', *Academy of Management Review*, Vol.17, No.3: 432–64.

Alvesson, M. and Willmott, H. S. (1996) *Making Sense of Management: A critical introduction*. London: Sage.

Barrie, J. and Pace, R. W. (1998) 'Learning for organizational effectiveness: philosophy of education and human resource development', *Human Resource Development Quarterly*, Vol.9, No.1: 39–54.

Barrie, J. and Pace, R. W. (1999) 'Learning and performance: just the end of the beginning – a rejoinder to Kuchinke', *Human Resource Development Quarterly*, Vol.10, No.3: 293–6.

Bhaskar, R. (1986) *Scientific Realism and Human Emancipation*. London: Verso.

Bhaskar, R. (1989) *The Possibility of Naturalism*, 2nd edition. Hemel Hempstead: Harvester Wheatsheaf.

Brookfield, S. (1994) 'Tales from the dark side: a phenomenography of adult critical reflection', *International Journal of Lifelong Education*, Vol.13, No.3: 203–16.

Callahan, J. L. and Dunne de Dávila, T. (2004) 'An impressionistic framework for theorizing about human resource development', *Human Resource Development Review*, Vol.3, No.1, March: 75–95.

Collier, A. (1994) *Critical Realism: An introduction to Roy Bhaskar's philosophy*. London: Verso.

Elliott, C. and Turnbull, S. (2002) 'Critical thinking in HRD: a panel-led discussion', *Proceedings of the Annual AHRD Conference, Academy of Human Resource Development*, Honolulu, Hawaii: 971–3.

Elliott, C. and Turnbull, S. (eds) (2005) *Critical Thinking in Human Resource Development*. New York: Routledge.

Evans, P., Pucik, V. and Barsoux, J. (2002) *The Global Challenge: Frameworks for international human resource management*. New York: McGraw-Hill/Irwin.

Fairclough, N. (2001) 'Critical discourse analysis as a method on social scientific research', in Wodak, R. and Meyer, M. *Methods of Critical Discourse Analysis*. London: Sage.

Fenwick, T. (2004) 'Toward a critical HRD: in theory and practice', *Adult Education Quarterly*, Vol.54, No.3, May: 193–209.

Fenwick, T. (2005) 'Conceptions of critical HRD: dilemmas for theory and practice', *Human Resource Development International*, Vol.8, No.2, June: 225–38.

Ford, J. D., Ford, L. and McNamara, R. T. (2002) 'Resistance and the background conversations of change', *Journal of Organizational Change Management*, Vol.15, No.2: 105–21.

Freire, P. (1970) *Pedagogy of the Oppressed*. Harmondsworth: Penguin.

Gold, J., Rodgers, H. and Smith, V. (2003) 'What is the future for the human resource development professional? A UK perspective', *Human Resource Development International*, Vol.6, No.4: 437–56.

Grey, C. (1996) 'Critique and renewal in management education', *Management Learning*, Vol.26, No.1: 5–20.

Grieves, J. and Redman, T. (1999) 'Living in the shadow of OD: HRD and the search for identity', *Human Resource Development International*, Vol.2, No.2: 81–102.

Habermas, J. (1971) *Toward a Rational Society*. London: Heinemann.

Habermas, J. (1984) *The Theory of Communicative Action: Reason and the rationalization of society*, Vol.1. Cambridge: Polity Press.

Habermas, J. (1987a) *The Theory of Communicative Action: The critique of functionalist reason*, Vol.2. Cambridge: Polity Press.

Habermas, J. (1987b) *Knowledge and Human Interests*. Cambridge: Polity Press.

Houston, S. (2001) 'Beyond social constructionism: critical realism and social work', *British Journal of Social Work*, Vol.31: 845–61.

Kuchinke, P. (1998) 'Moving beyond the dualism of performance versus learning: a response to Barrie and Pace', *Human Resource Development Quarterly*, Vol.9, No.4: 377–85.

Kuchinke, K. P. (2000) 'Debates over the nature of HRD: an institutional theory perspective', *Human Resource Development International*, Vol.3, No.3: 279–83.

Kuchinke, K. P. (2001) 'Why HRD is not an academic discipline', *Human Resource Development International*, Vol.4, No.3: 291–4.

Lee, M. (2001) 'A refusal to define HRD', *Human Resource Development International*, Vol.4, No.3: 327–41.

Lee, M. (2003) *Human Resource Development in a Complex World*. London: Routledge.

Lee, M. and Stead, V. (1998) 'Human resource development in the United Kingdom', *Human Resource Development Quarterly*, Vol.9, No.3, Fall: 296–308.

McGoldrick, J., Stewart, J. and Watson, S. (2001) 'Theorizing human resource development', *Human Resource Development International*, Vol.4, No.3: 343–56.

McGuire, D. and Cseh, M. (2006) 'The development of the field of HRD: a Delphi study', *Journal of European Industrial Training*, Vol.30, No.8: 653–67.

McLagan, P. A. and Suhadolnik, D. (1989) *Models for HRD Practice: The research report*. Alexandria, VA: American Society for Training and Development.

McLean, G. N. and McLean, L. (2001) 'If we can't define HRD in one country, how can we define it in an international context?', *Human Resource Development International*, Vol.4, No.3: 313–26.

Marshak, R. (2002) 'Changing the language of change: how new contexts and concepts are challenging the way we think and talk about organizational change', *Strategic Change*, August: 279–86.

Marshak, R. and Grant, D. (2008) 'Organizational discourse and new organization development practices', *British Journal of Management*, Vol.19: 7–19.

Megginson, D., Matthews, J. and Banfield, P. (1993) *Human Resource Development*, London: Kogan Page.

Meyerson, D. and Kolb, D. M. (2000) 'Moving out of the armchair: developing a framework to bridge the gap between feminist theory and practice', *Organization*, Vol.7: 553–71.

Reynolds, M. (1999a) 'Critical reflection and management education: rehabilitating less hierarchical approaches', *Journal of Management Education*, Vol.23, No.5, October: 537–53.

Reynolds, M. (1999b) 'Grasping the nettle: possibilities and pitfalls of a critical management pedagogy', *British Journal of Management*, Vol.9: 171–84.

Rigg, C., Stewart, J. and Trehan, K. (eds) (2007) *Critical Human Resource Development: Beyond orthodoxy*. Harlow: Pearson Education, FT/Prentice Hall.

Ruona, W. E. A. and Swanson, R. A. (1998) 'Foundations of human resource development', in Stewart, B. R. and Halls, H. G. (eds) *Beyond Tradition: Preparing HRD educators for tomorrow's workforce*. Columbia, MO: UCWHRE.

Sambrook, S. (2004) 'A "critical" time for HRD?', *Journal of European Industrial Training*, Vol.28, Nos8/9: 611–24.

Sambrook, S. (2007) 'Exploring the notion of "time" and "critical" HRD', in Rigg, C., Stewart, J. and Trehan, K. (eds) *Critical Human Resource Development*. Harlow: Pearson Education, FT/Prentice Hall.

Sambrook, S. (2009) 'Critical HRD: a concept analysis', *Personnel Review*, Vol.38, No.1: 61–73.

Sayer, A. (2000) *Realism and Social Science*. London: Sage.

Stewart, J. (2005) 'The current state and status of HRD research', *The Learning Organization*, Vol.12, No.1: 90–5.

Swanson, R.A. (1994) *Analysis for Improving Performance: Tools for diagnosing organizations and documenting workplace expertise*. San Francisco: Jossey-Bass.

Valentin, C. (2006) 'Researching human resource development: emergence of a critical approach to HRD enquiry', *International Journal of Training and Development*, Vol.10, No.1: 17–29.

Wang, X. and McLean, G. (2007) 'The dilemma of defining international human resource development', *Human Resource Development Review*, Vol.6, No.1: 96–108.

Watkins, K. E. (1991) 'Many voices: defining human resources from different disciplines', *Adult Education Quarterly*, Vol.4, No.4: 241–55.

CHAPTER 10

The Role of Line Managers in HRM, Learning and Innovation

John Castledine and Douglas W. S. Renwick

CHAPTER OVERVIEW

This chapter focuses on shaping organisational development through established and emerging approaches to learning and innovation. It introduces the reader to the increasing devolution of people management practices to line managers more generally, and then moves on to explore the area of learning and innovation as an emerging field of study. In doing so, the chapter blends academic and practitioner insights, including our own experience and research.

LEARNING OBJECTIVES

By the end of this chapter the reader should be able to:

- understand the benefits and challenges associated with the devolution of human resource management to line managers
- critically appraise the concepts and approaches associated with the role of line managers in managing learning and innovation
- understand the impact of HRM policies and practices on organisational learning and innovation
- articulate the emergent features and case study application of a learning and innovation strategy.

INTRODUCTION

Involving line managers in human resource management (HRM) work appears to be such a common practice in work organisations today that it may be viewed as a core element of an HRM approach to the employment relationship itself. The logic of why line managers are used in HRM seems simple: they are closest to customers and employees, and occupy a key role in motivating, communicating, developing, rewarding, disciplining and releasing people at work. Assignment of HRM to line managers could potentially free HR specialists to engage in more complex, strategic HRM work. But research on involving managers in HRM also reveals a number of issues in doing so – questioning their assumed usefulness in HRM *per se*.

Involving line managers in HRM is not a totally new development – for example, in the UK it has always been recognised that line managers have been both accountable and responsible for managing people (Guest, 1987). But it is the seemingly greater extent of manager involvement in HRM, and the attendant greater publicity and transparency associated with it, which appears to make the headlines in practitioner circles. In short, it is 'in vogue'.

Line managers can be defined as front-line (also termed 'first-line'), middle and/or general managers – eg departmental heads – as opposed to being functional specialists – eg HR managers. Crucially, the responsibility shared by all line managers is that they are tasked with achieving organisational outcomes through the actions of other employees. This role is common to first-line managers and an organisation's CEO.

Despite this shared objective, it is to be expected that differences exist in terms of how such line managers participate in HRM – for example, as managers being 'assigned' HR work or being responsible/accountable for it (Brewster, 2009).

HRM must balance the near-term needs with ensuring that the organisation can access the skills to compete effectively in the future. Managing performance in the near term may be viewed as a combination of skilfully aggregating the collective efforts of employees and amplifying individual effort through creating high levels of engagement in completing the required tasks (Hamel, 2007).

Moreover, in knowledge-driven service-led economies such as that of the UK, organisations increasingly refer to their staff as their greatest asset. However, there is recognition that this metaphor can be misleading. Within the emerging field of human capital management (HCM) employees are viewed as being more like investors of their own human capital (Ingham, 2007). Thus organisations may be seen as renting rather than owning these assets. Line managers and HR both play vital roles in delivering a 'psychological contract' (see Chapter 14) that creates an effective collaboration between employees and the organisation.

Technological advances, social and environmental factors are rapidly changing the skills required in many industry sectors. For this reason an organisation's talent needs at each stage in the pipeline are also constantly changing. These challenges place greater emphasis on innovative approaches to learning. Managing innovation creates additional challenges: typically, innovation requires processes of trial-and-error, enabled through sponsorship and the resources provided by line management. However, performance management places an emphasis on success and eliminating errors. Creating an organisational culture and environment in which performance and innovation sit comfortably together is arguably one of the biggest challenges for leaders and managers.

Throughout this chapter, the touch points with other chapters are signposted so that the reader can obtain a better appreciation, for example, of the interconnectedness of learning and innovation, performance management and the employment value proposition.

THE DEVOLUTION OF HUMAN RESOURCE MANAGEMENT

Purcell and Hutchinson (2007: 5, 7) have previously identified three interlocking debates on the role of line managers in HRM:

- the return of HRM to line managers
- clear evidence that first-line management roles have been broadened
- distinctions between 'espoused' and 'enacted' HR practices.

The common driver behind these debates is organisational performance. Their own empirical survey of 608 employees in 12 'excellent' UK-based firms found employee commitment towards both the employer and the job being influenced by the quality of leadership behaviour and satisfaction with HR practices, which 'both have a strong effect on employee attitudes'. Their results show leadership behaviour and HR practices explaining

34.6% of the variance in perceived employee commitment (Purcell and Hutchinson, 2007: 3, 9, 11).

Moreover, the Gallup Organisation (Buckingham and Coffman, 2001; Wagner and Harter, 2007) has clearly mapped the links between employee opinion and business unit performance, identifying 12 statements that get to the heart of the matter. The 12 statements as listed (Buckingham and Coffman, 2001) are:

- I know what is expected of me at work.
- I have the materials and equipment I need to do my work right.
- At work, I have the opportunity to do what I do best every day.
- In the last seven days, I have received recognition or praise for doing good work.
- My supervisor, or someone at work, seems to care about me as a person.
- There is someone at work who encourages my development.
- At work, my opinions seem to count.
- The mission or purpose of my company makes me feel my job is important.
- My associates or fellow employees are committed to doing quality work.
- I have a best friend at work.
- In the last six months, someone at work has talked to me about my progress.
- This last year I have had opportunities at work to learn and grow.

From their analysis, employees who responded that they 'strongly agreed' with the 12 statements were 50% more likely to work in business units with lower employee turnover, 38% more likely to work in business units that were more productive, and 56% more likely to work in business units with high customer loyalty. The authors also reinforce the widely held view that 'People leave managers, not companies.' (See Chapter 14 for further insights into the factors impacting on the affinity of employees with their organisations.)

Returning to the themes identified by Purcell and Hutchinson, the wider literature provides further insights to help inform HRM.

Mesner-Andolsek and Stebe's (2005: 311) study of changes of the HRM function in 20 European and five non-European countries found a shift of HRM tasks from HRM departments to line managers. They argue that HR devolution to line managers has developed in all areas but occurs less in large organisations that have highly developed HRM teams. In other words, it is important to bear in mind that a large percentage of organisations are SMEs (small and medium-sized enterprises) unable to support highly differentiated and specialised job roles. Within this working environment the debate is not about HR–line management devolution and/or assignments in HRM, but rather about the priority given to HRM.

THE ROLE OF LINE MANAGERS IN HRM WITHIN AN SME

CASE STUDY

North Services Group (NSG) is an SME organisation, consisting of two operating companies – Cook Services and Dickens Services – who enjoy an equal partnership while continuing to retain their separate identities and operating locations. They provide residents of local communities in the north of England with personal services.

The organisational culture of NSG, according to the chief executive and financial director, is 'open'. Managers and

staff are given their responsibilities and objectives, and then trusted to get on with their jobs. Cook Services has twice been awarded Charter Mark status and Investors in People recognition.

HR policies and procedures tend to be designed by the directors of NSG, because there is no specialist professional HR presence on-site. Cook Services makes use of a number of consultancies to assist with policy development in HRM as and when required – eg in health and safety, appraisal, and recruitment. Occasionally, line managers have been involved in developing such HR policies and procedures.

A survey of NSG line managers indicated that the majority viewed HRM as 'very important', with recruitment, training and personal development reviews the HRM activities most line managers were involved in undertaking.

Written HRM policies are acknowledged as an important part of how line managers learn to manage people. Equally, instead of using formal written policies and procedures in making decisions, they rely mostly on guidance from peers, their line manager and personal role models.

A much fuller version of this case study can be found in the paper 'Involving British line managers in HRM in a small non-profit work organisation', Hunter and Renwick (2009).

For more work on the role of HRM in SMEs, readers are directed to Marlow et al (2010).

Questions

1 If you had responsibility as a CEO for some line managers in an SME where you know there is either a very small or non-existent HR function, how would you advise, guide and support them on a practical level in HRM?

2 If you were a line manager at this SME case organisation, what changes would you like to see to help you to deliver your role in HRM?

3 What lessons do you think can be learned from the involvement of line managers in HRM in SME environments? Are such lessons applicable to SMEs only, or can we see trends and patterns across many different work organisations here, regardless of their size?

CASE STUDY COMMENTARY

Key learning points from this case study include the need to understand that not all work organisations, and SMEs in particular, have a large, or indeed, any HR department to guide, advise and support line managers in HR work. Many work organisations in Britain, for example, and some across the globe too, are of this SME type, in which no such HR presence always exists. It may therefore be up to line managers themselves in such organisations to 'take ownership' of the HR duties allocated to them, or which are included in their job roles. Issues for line managers arising are whether they, as managers, have the attitude, motivation or opportunity to complete such HR-related duties effectively, efficiently and consistently. The focus of this case study (and the larger, more detailed description of it in the journal article it originates from) is to illustrate such points.

Within Europe, Larsen and Brewster's (2003) Cranet study of 22 countries – and over 4,000 respondents – found that the assignment of HRM to line managers in the UK and the Republic of Ireland was low compared to other European Union (EU) states. (It is far more frequent in, for example, Denmark and Finland.) Also, the extent of manager autonomy in

HRM tends to vary by subject. The authors argue that the most frequent pattern in the EU is one of shared responsibilities between HR and line managers in HRM (including training), and that many organisations are still very centralised in a lot of aspects of HRM. However, they also detail anecdotal evidence which could imply that both HR and line managers are unhappy about such HR assignments being allocated to them.

Other empirical work on the devolution of specific HR tasks to line managers has seen difficulties arising. For example, Lynch (2003) noted a department manager in the retail sector stating that employee development is difficult to complete because they do not have time to do it, and Whittaker and Marchington (2003) discovered that senior managers still wanted specialist HR help because they found doing HR work difficult when other business pressures took priority.

As reported by Brandl *et al* (2009), previous research has identified a number of aspects that influence line managers' ability to embrace HRM effectively (Lowe, 1992; Hyman and Cunningham, 1995; McGovern *et al*, 1997). The literature reveals that HR duties are often low on the list of priorities of line managers. It suggests that personal motivation for conducting HR duties – ie believing in the importance of involvement in HR – is a primary factor behind the successful involvement of line managers in HRM.

Based on a survey of 1,500 Danish managers, Brandl *et al* (2009) found that 'motivating others' is considered the most important HR duty, whereas 'team-building', 'handling conflicts' and 'coaching' are considered the least important HR duties. Female top managers in the public sector exhibited the greatest interest in HR, whereas men at lower managerial levels in the private sector gave lowest priority to HR work.

Not only is there apparent reluctance by line managers to accept responsibilities previously viewed as the domain of HR. The literature also suggests that senior line managers may question the value in 'freeing up' HR to move away from operational work. For example, in the People's Republic of China, Mitsuhashi *et al* (2000: 197) examined the differences in perceptions of an expatriate (survey) sample of top HR and line executives on the importance and effectiveness of HR practices in 25 multinational Chinese firms. They found that line executives perceive HR performance effectiveness as 'significantly less' than HR executives do in terms of strategic (non-administrative) HRM – ie communications, measurements, and responsibilities. They argue that such results match those of other previous studies in Chinese HRM (with the exception of those involving compensation), and conclude that some line managers in China do not feel that HR are presently performing well enough to become a 'strategic partner' (Mitsuhashi *et al*, 2000: 209, 211–12). This raises the question of how to provide internal and/or external HR support for line managers who are undertaking HR duties, and give them good advice in HRM.

Marchington and Wilkinson (2002) (quoting Currie and Procter, 2001) detail how HR managers can provide middle managers with support:

- HR strategies should be composed of broad themes that can then be contextualised by middle managers at an operational level.
- Middle managers should be encouraged to contribute towards an elaboration of these broad themes.
- Opportunities should be provided for middle managers to span boundaries within the organisation through membership of project groups.
- The HR function should be organised to allow HR professionals to work closely with middle managers at the point of delivery.
- The development of middle managers is directed towards their contribution to strategic change.

In a 2004 CIPD publication (*Bringing Policies to Life: The vital role of frontline managers in people management*), Hutchinson and Purcell focused on the support required by front-line managers (FLMs). The study confirmed the accountability typically placed on FLMs to implement HRM policies and bring these policies to life within their organisation. The policies that were identified as most supportive to line managers were based upon:

- ensuring good working relationships with their managers
- providing career opportunities
- working to support their work–life balance
- allowing them to participate and feel involved in decisions
- having an open organisational culture that allows them to raise grievances or discuss matters of personal concern
- giving them a sense of job security.

In a similar summary, Ulrich and Brockbank (2005) suggest four ways for HR to help line managers build organisational capability:

- Resolve misconceptions of HR.
- Build relationships of trust.
- Focus on the 'deliverables'.
- Prioritise capabilities and create an action plan for delivering them.

They also advocate (2005: 72) that:

> To make HR practices work, line managers must model what they want others to accomplish – and HR leaders need to ensure that line managers stay aware of and accountable for HR work.

However, from the literature it is unclear if HR managers show the commitment, preparation and support for line managers in HRM (Brewster and Larsen, 2000: 208), and if a 'simple, seamless transfer of responsibility' between HR and the line is achievable since HR want to keep an operational role in HRM (Currie and Procter, 2001: 54).

If involving line managers in HRM is successful, there may seem to be little need for work organisations to employ HR managers. So a challenge for HR managers is how to increase the involvement of line managers in HRM (to spread responsibility and accountability in HRM overall) without sowing the seeds of their own (HR) redundancy (ie the erosion of HR functions/departments or an increase in HR outsourcing). Studies from the European and Chinese literature (above) could be thought to imply that HR also need to assess the challenge of how devolution in HRM helps the success of their work organisations (Mesner-Andolsek and Stebe, 2005), and to what extent such devolution supports a case from HR to become a strategic partner (Mitsuhashi et al, 2000).

As previously stated, involving line managers in HRM is not a new development. Moreover, the logic for their involvement as those closest to customers and employees is long-standing. The variability in current approaches, espoused and enacted, thus suggests that this can be leveraged as a source of competitive advantage if expertly managed.

It can be postulated that the pace of technological change and the increasing focus on a knowledge-driven service-led economy are underlying forces that should drive greater devolution of HRM (or at least greater competitive advantage for those who build effective real-time collaborations between HR and line managers). This is particularly the case for the role of HRM in learning and innovation, as 'just in case' training is replaced by 'just in time' learning, and as the psychological contract (see Chapter 14 on the employment value proposition) moves from 'job for life' to a focus on employability.

Equally, Gibb's (2003) analysis and review of the idea of 'managers as developers' found that line managers still need specialist HR advice in a knowledge management era because there is a need to realign work, organisation and management together.

CASE STUDY

ENGAGING THE LINE MANAGER IN IMPROVING BUSINESS PERFORMANCE THROUGH PEOPLE

Atkins Ltd is a FTSE-250 company, the largest engineering consultancy in the UK and the second largest multidisciplinary engineering firm in Europe. The organisation employs 18,000 staff, of which 10,000 are UK-based, and has an annual turnover of £1.4 billion.

As part of a strategy to drive an improvement in HR service delivery flexibility and efficiency, Atkins elected to adopt the 'Ulrich model' of shared services, operational HR, centres of expertise and HR business partners.

A key challenge was the engagement of line managers, because their positive acceptance of the new model was regarded as crucial to success. When defining the qualities and skills for the role of HR business partner there was a 'light-bulb moment' when it was realised that the talent pool for HR business partners should include line manager applicants as well as those from the HR function. Line managers could bring a depth of business knowledge and their established peer networks to positively impact on the role.

The HR leadership team therefore engaged the organisation's senior management on the importance of explicitly recruiting

from two pools: the HR applicants, and business-line applicants. High-potential line managers were directly approached and encouraged to apply.

Ultimately, this led to the HR business partners team being formed from a mix of both HR and line managers. All selected candidates attended an assessment centre, which was specifically designed to test a range of skills and capabilities in addition to undergoing a structured interview process. Both HR and business-line candidates did well, and it became clear that a team consisting of members from both HR and the business line would be beneficial. Multiple benefits have been derived from this approach. The HR business partner team has a collective expertise that brings together the required knowledge and skills to realise the initial objective of the HR service delivery model. As a team they have learned from each other. The greatest impact, however, has been that line managers now see the overlap in their role and skill set with that of the HR business partners, their former peers acting as role models for improving business performance through people.

MANAGING LEARNING

Change is inevitable within the workplace. Employees retiring from organisations create career 'pipelines'. Typically, these individuals have a wealth of experience that has been recognised through evolving job roles of increasing complexity and seniority. Replacing this talent requires a strategy of either building internal capabilities (by investing in learning) and/or buying the talent (through recruitment). As mentioned above, technological advances, social and environmental factors are also significantly changing the skills required in many industry sectors. An organisation's talent needs at each stage in the pipeline are thus also constantly changing. (For more information on talent management, see Chapter 13.)

As previously stated, the shift from 'job for life' to one of ongoing employability and career progression is increasingly recognised by employees, and there is consequently a growing expectation that organisations will provide the learning opportunities to support this.

In 2005, the CIPD published a report, *Who Learns at Work? Employees' experiences of training and development*. This was based on a survey of 750 employees across different sectors. Just under half of the respondents said that it was their line manager who initiated their most recent training activity, compared with a third who nominated the HR/training department. Where this training was evaluated, it was the line manager who led the discussion on the effectiveness of the training in more than half the cases.

The report concluded (2005: 15) that:

> The role of the line manager is critical to training and development in organisations. Line managers initiate a high percentage of the training that takes place. They are also responsible for over half of the discussions with employees on the effectiveness of training that takes place. Ensuring that line managers have the skills for, and are committed to support, learning and development is essential.

However, despite a compelling business case for manager-led development, many managers score poorly in activities related to employee development, some managers lacking the skills and/or resources required to develop employees successfully.

In his book *The Changing World of the Trainer* (2007), Martyn Sloman reports on nine propositions developed by an expert panel of HRM practitioners assembled by the CIPD. Subsequently, CIPD members involved in training and development were invited in a poll between November 2005 and May 2006 to indicate the extent to which they agreed or disagreed with the statements.

Four propositions received significantly more support than the others. These were:

- Effective individual learning is critical if employees are to acquire the knowledge and skills needed to support the organisation's business objectives and delivery targets.
- Those in senior management need to be aware of the implications of the shift from training to learning and give their full support to the new processes and practices that must be implemented in the organisation.
- The delivery of effective people development practices requires a considerable increase in commitment and enhanced skills from all managers, particularly first-line managers.
- A review of training and development interventions must ensure that learning achieved is aligned with business activity.

This was explored further in the report *Learning and the Line: The role of line managers in training, learning and development*, written by Hutchinson and Purcell (2007), which reinforced the earlier findings and provided additional guidance for HRM. Their research describes the role of line managers as 'critical conduits' of learning. Particular emphasis is placed on the processes of induction, giving access to challenging work, providing performance feedback and day-to-day coaching/mentoring.

The authors explore the implications that front-line managers are understandably interested primarily in short-term deliverables. This can result in a lack of consideration of the longer-term career development of their staff. Consequently, organisations demonstrating best practice provide both encouragement and active support of line managers in their learning and development activities, while planning for future talent needs through the provision of more forward-looking learning and development.

The authors also recognise that organisations face dilemmas concerning the trade-off between formal systems and informal processes. Consequently, many learning activities within an organisation may be 'out of sight' of HR, not captured in learning management systems, staff development plans, etc.

Five themes are presented in the report by Hutchinson and Purcell (2007) summarising the significance for HRM:

- Organisations need to encourage line managers' buy-in and commitment to learning and development by clarifying their responsibilities through job descriptions, performance appraisal and communicating the importance and value of development-related activities.

- All managers need time to carry out their learning and development activities. Often the 'softer' people management areas of responsibility get driven out by other, more traditional, management duties.
- Line managers need training courses and development programmes. But they must be given support, both in terms of time to access them and through feedback.
- Senior management commitment is essential, and leaders must be encouraged to act as role models.
- It is important to select line managers carefully, paying particular attention to behavioural competencies that facilitate learning and development in themselves and others.

In conclusion, 'managing learning' within an organisational context may be more comprehensively expressed as 'enhancing the capability to realise business results from the investment in learning'. Success is a combination of the learning generated and the application of these skills, knowledge and abilities. Consequently, HRM actions relating to learning and development cannot ignore the central role of line managers in realising the business benefits.

CASE STUDY

DEVELOPING THE COACHING SKILLS OF LINE MANAGERS

Arla Foods Limited, with an annual turnover of £1.5 billion, is home to some of the UK's leading dairy brands including Cravendale, Lurpak and Anchor. Processing approximately two billion litres of milk a year, Arla continues to be one of the UK's leading dairy companies and a supplier of fresh liquid milk, cream and a wide range of high-quality dairy products to the top seven retailers. Behind this leading business is a team of around 2,800 people across the UK located at the dairies, distribution centres and head office.

In 2007, the company was going through a significant amount of change following the full acquisition that year of the UK business by Arla Amba. To support its growth ambitions, Arla launched 'ONE' – its new vision, strategy and values – and sought to fully engage its colleagues in delivering high performance to meet its five-year strategic goals. The HR director, Max Morgan, recognised the importance of developing the leadership skills of the first-line leader population, and the HR team worked in partnership with Alison Williams of Organisational Development Ltd to develop a programme 'for the people, designed by the people'.

The key aim of the programme was to develop the leadership, people management and coaching skills of their first-line leaders. This was a strategic decision by HR to devolve the people management skills to the front line – and to date 79 first-line managers have achieved their ILM Level 3 Certificate in First-Line Management.

To further support the HR strategy, and to ensure that all managers understood their role in helping to embed the learning, Worth Consulting Ltd provided coaching and mentoring skills training for the managers of all the first-line managers attending the programme and a further 60 middle managers. The senior managers have been trained in the OSCAR coaching model, and in turn act as coaches and mentors to the first-line leaders and middle managers, thus ensuring that the ethos of informal development is embedded across the organisation.

The First-Line Leader Programme has proved to be a huge success and is now in its third year. The benefits and results include:

- 90% of the leaders who have been through the Programme said that their behaviour had changed for the better, with improvement in confidence, a greater self-awareness and improved skills of coaching and giving feedback.

- Over 60% of their line managers had also seen a visible shift in behaviour.

- The leaders involved with all of the development programmes are also used as champions/role models in the business that support facilitation on various programmes in the business and additionally act as coaches and mentors to others.

- Those who have had experience of the programmes now see HR as business partners and work together to solve issues in a more consultative way, which

has in turn freed them up to focus on more strategic issues.

- 11% of the candidates have been promoted.

All of Arla Food's management development programmes support the goal of HR to devolve the people management skills to the front line and have a strong link to the role of leadership and empowerment of leadership accountability. The company is well on track to establishing a true coaching and learning culture.

MANAGING INNOVATION

Double-loop learning (Argyris and Schön, 1978) is a well-recognised concept for organisational development. It involves questioning the underlying processes and norms rather than just seeking to take corrective action to address performance gaps. This highlights the interlinked nature of learning and innovation.

Research undertaken by Shipton *et al* (2005) indicates that well-designed HRM systems can provide support for organisational innovation through creating a climate for learning. They present longitudinal data from 35 UK manufacturing organisations to suggest that effective HRM systems – incorporating sophisticated approaches to recruitment and selection, induction, appraisal and training – predict organisational innovation in products and production technology. They further show that organisational innovation is enhanced where there is a supportive learning climate, and inhibited (for innovation in production processes) where there is a link between appraisal and remuneration.

Global competition, rapid technological change and an increased focus on environmental impact is placing a premium on creativity within the workplace. Managing innovation creates additional challenges for the organisation. Typically, innovation requires processes of trial and error to address complex, ill-defined problems, enabled through sponsorship and resources provided by line management. However, performance management places an emphasis on success and eliminating errors. (For more information on performance management see Chapter 12.) As stated previously, creating an organisational culture and environment where performance and innovation sit comfortably together is arguably one of the biggest challenges for line managers.

Although many variables influence creativity and innovation in organisational settings, leaders and their behaviour represent a particularly powerful influence (see also Chapter 2). Mumford *et al* (2002) argue that the leadership of creative people requires expertise. Moreover, the successful leader must employ a number of direct and indirect influence tactics – tactics consistent with the needs of creative people working in an organisational environment.

A key finding from Mumford *et al* (2002) is that the leaders' technical skill is found to be the best predictor of creativity and innovation on the part of group members. They postulate that:

> Given the strong professional identity of creative people, it may prove difficult for leaders lacking technical expertise and creative problem-solving skills to (a) adequately represent the group, (b) communicate effectively with group members,

(c) appraise the needs and concerns of followers, (d) develop and mentor junior staff, and (e) assess the implications of group members' interactions.

This suggests particular implications for HRM talent management practices (see also Chapter 13). Whereas it might be expected that line managers of creative teams would need substantial social 'soft' skills to influence stakeholders, secure resources and manage expectations on risk-taking, the data also highlights possible limitations in being able to successfully deploy leaders between different functional disciplines.

Mumford *et al* (2002) also demonstrate that there is widespread evidence in the literature for the importance of providing organisational support for creative endeavours (see also Chapter 14). Because creative work typically focuses on complex, ill-defined problems, the imposition of structure is a key component of the innovation process. Three types of support involved in the leadership of creative ideas are identified: *idea support, work support* and *social support*. From their review of the literature Mumford *et al* conclude (Proposition 20, page 274) that:

> Resources supporting work activities, tangible manifestations of support, are likely to have a particularly powerful impact during idea development and implementation, while idea support and social support are likely to prove more important in initial idea generation.

A US study by George and Zhou in 2007 examined the ways in which supervisors can provide such a supportive context towards employee creativity. It was undertaken via a survey of 161 (matched) supervisors and employees in an oilfield services company. Their results indicate that line managers can provide a supportive context towards employee creativity

- by giving employees developmental feedback
- in displays of inter-actional justice to such staff
- through being trustworthy in their general dealings with employees overall.

They also noted that where such a supportive context exists, it is likely that both positive and negative moods contribute to creativity (George and Zhou, 2007: 605, 610).

Later studies examining the relationship between leadership practices and team members' trust in their leaders during periods of change have concluded that trust in leaders is strongly associated with team effectiveness. Research from the Institute of Leadership and Management (2009) has created unique insights relating to the understanding of trustworthiness of line managers and leaders. Trust can be characterised by six drivers: ability, understanding, fairness, integrity, openness and consistency. In general, line managers are more trusted than CEOs by employees. This partly relates to a combination of proximity (and thus visibility) to staff as well as time in post. In other words, organisations with frequent changes in reporting structures erode trust and damage the ability of line managers to build employee engagement (see also Chapter 14) and drive innovation.

Moreover, despite the evidence that HRM systems can have a positive impact on innovation, the wider picture is less positive. From a survey of selected UK FTSE-500 companies employing over 100 staff, Searle and Ball (2003) found that although they attached importance to innovation at a conceptual level, organisations failed to consistently translate and support it in HR policy. Furthermore, the authors observed that the application of HR policies to encourage innovative behaviour is generally targeted at specific groups of employees, typically at lower organisational levels. So although organisations encouraged their non-managerial employees to innovate, there was a lack of attention paid to using HRM practices to support the management of innovation.

In summary, leaders seeking to promote a climate for innovation must balance the social support that fosters risk-taking in idea-generation with performance management to drive application and business results. In the words of Birkinshaw and Gibson (2004) (cited in Dotlich *et al*, 2009), too much emphasis on social support leads to a 'country club' atmosphere; too much emphasis on performance management leads to a burnt-out and rigid workforce.

Consequently, Dotlich *et al* (2009) have developed a helpful six-step model to help both line managers and HRM practitioners understand the requirements for building an organisational climate that encourages innovation (see also Chapter 5). These dimensions are:

- clarity of purpose
- an outside-in perspective
- innovation discipline
- idea generation
- idea support
- idea recognition.

The first three dimensions broadly align with providing performance management, and the latter three with providing social support.

Line managers both need, and need to cascade, clarity in the purpose of making innovation a business priority. They also need to encourage ideas from a wide range of stakeholders and feed them into a disciplined process that allows ideas to 'fail fast and fail cheaply'.

Idea generation involves risk-taking. Dotlich *et al* (2009: 65) report that:

> One of the most difficult insights for leaders is how much impact they have on their subordinates. Most leaders feel they are open and understanding, full of empathy and concern for their people. They cannot understand why anyone would fear them or be hesitant to tell them what they are thinking.

Consequently, line managers may underestimate the extent to which risk-taking is inhibited by a fear of the potential negative consequences. Similarly, line managers are typically the 'gate-keepers' of the resources required to support the implementation of new ideas, and the recognition with which individuals and teams are rewarded.

An understanding of these six dimensions may help translate the conceptual importance of innovation into HRM policies, and thus go some way to address the concerns identified by Searle and Ball (2003).

ENGAGING INNOVATION AT CITY & GUILDS

CASE STUDY

City & Guilds is the UK's leading vocational awarding organisation, employing over 1,000 people and focused on creating relevant qualifications that help learners gain the skills employers' value.

Founded in 1878 to establish a national system of technical education, the City & Guilds Group now offers over 500 qualifications in 28 industry areas, awarding over 1.9 million certificates every year. Its vocational qualifications are delivered by international and UK-based colleges, training providers and employers, all focused on enabling learners to acquire the skills they need to advance their careers.

Evolving beyond this proud heritage, City & Guilds is now dedicated to creating a stronger UK economy through vocational education by bringing together learners, training centres and employers to ensure that the Group drives economic growth.

With this strategy in place and set within the context of a fluid and dynamic market environment, the Group board – and specifically the Director General, Chris Jones – sought an approach which would engage individual employees to provide ideas for and solutions to the range of emerging challenges facing the Group.

To achieve his aim, Chris approached the board's HR Director Sharon Saxton in late 2009 with his request. What quickly emerged was an ideal launch opportunity in the form of the annual Managers' Conference scheduled for January 2010. Already under design by Group L&D led by Mark Hammond, the theme for the Conference was 'Shift Happens', highlighting innovation and providing an opportunity for Chris to introduce four board-level commitments on innovation to the 150-strong management population.

The design of the Conference was critical to engagement around innovation and therefore aimed to set a different tone from the outset. Chris addressed this in his opening comments to managers, which focused on exploring the opportunities and challenges for the business. He talked about key shifts in demographics, technology and flexible working, and how these will challenge businesses over the next decade and impact on skills development in the future.

In addition to the opening remarks ensuring a clear alignment with strategy and defining the need to change, the morning schedule provided further opportunities for managers to understand the business case for innovation through presentations from commercial customers and a professor from one of the UK's leading academic institutions, detailing his consultancy work on innovation in leading multinationals.

Putting innovation into action was a challenge, and the Conference addressed this by asking delegates to get 'comfortable with being uncomfortable'. The group was then introduced to a blues band that collaborated with cross-functional teams, tasking 10 groups to write a song identifying group discontinuities and orthodoxies that were required to shift in order to address the business challenges. All delegate groups then had to step up on stage and sing their song with the band to the entire audience. What immediately became apparent was the shift the majority of delegates experienced personally, in their teams and as the management group. The entire Conference, and in particular the afternoon's experiential activities, achieved

the Conference objectives of introducing the business case for innovation and initiating a cultural shift driving new ways of working.

Beyond the Conference, internal communications created a sustained campaign across multiple communication channels ensuring that the stories, experiences and business case for innovation as well as new ways of working permeated through the organisation. In addition, the lyrics from each team appeared throughout the offices in the form of posters providing a link to team briefings and further invigorating the story-telling that infused the Group, which helped to redefine its culture.

The four board commitments around innovation were driven initially by HRD and senior managers across various directorates. This group designed a scheme to encourage innovation and recruited a team to lead the scheme. Team members were asked to demonstrate how they approached innovation in their role as part of this process. The scheme was branded the 'iFactor', and was introduced across the organisation prior to an organisation-wide launch event.

At the same time and as part of the drive for new ways of working and innovation, Group L&D, in collaboration with business teams, developed the Market Place Event. This all-staff event was designed to increase employees' knowledge of the business and customer base, ensuring interaction with City & Guilds learners. Scheduled for June 2010 at Battersea Power Station, it was also the launch event for the new innovation scheme 'iFactor'.

Over the two days of the Market Place Event, iFactor was launched, ensuring that the model underpinning the initiative was explained as well as how ideas progressed through three stages up to a review by the board. In addition, the idea of mentoring support was introduced and the individual benefits explained to all. Over the two days 150 ideas were submitted, each receiving a one-off incentive payment in the form of a £50 voucher to drive take-up.

Since then, three ideas have progressed to board level and are currently being assessed. To complement the cultural change, the development of the scheme has centred on individual ownership and accountability to deliver the ideas, significant cross-functional working, and a sustained focus on commercial and financial aspects required by the scheme of successful ideas. Following the launch, the organisation has seen greater evidence of improved collaboration and empowerment of both the individuals involved in running the scheme and those who have submitted ideas.

The scheme is now evolving further as it focuses on innovations that specifically drive costs savings or revenue and efficiency gains. There is also a direct link to the Group's new values leadership, integrity and imagination; and a wider group of people have been recruited to be involved in the mentoring support for new innovators.

Innovation is still a key theme at City & Guilds, and will be for the foreseeable future. The employee opinion survey 2010, issued prior to the iFactor launch, from the outset showed an increase in the number of people who felt motivated to develop new ideas.

Questions

1 If you had to devise a strategy to help your organisation better engage individual employees to contribute innovative solutions, what would be the key activities you would require from the line managers?

2 In your view, how important is it that there is individual ownership and accountability to deliver new ideas within an organisation?

CASE STUDY COMMENTARY

- A key learning point from this case study is the importance of engaging staff when organisations are seeking to evolve their culture. To bridge the distance between the board and individual employees, line managers should be positioned as advocates, reinforcing the sponsorship provided by the executive team.

- Creating relevant and challenging experiences, shared across the peer group of line managers, provided the foundation for City & Guilds to start to cascade the board's commitments around innovation. This was subsequently supported through multiple communication channels.

- It was also important to link the drive for innovation with learning interventions that were designed to increase business acumen at all levels within the organisation. This ensured that the commercial and financial aspects were not overlooked when individuals were empowered to deliver new initiatives.

CONCLUSION

Although line managers have always been involved in managing human resources, it is within human resource management (HRM) that their involvement has been placed centre-stage as a core element of an HR approach. Significant organisational benefits and costs exist from involving the line in HR work (Renwick, 2003, 2009).

Understanding the role that line managers can perform to influence learning and innovation is thus of critical importance for HRM. Line managers provide the channel for both establishing organisational needs and building/mobilising talent to deliver organisational performance. Where line managers are engaged and supported in these roles, HR has the opportunity to operate effectively as a strategic partner in shaping organisational development.

Some chief executives appear to be quite positive about increasing the involvement of line managers in HRM because they see it as 'good people management' (Guest and King, 2001: 25), meaning that whether line managers are keen on doing more HR work or not, their role in HRM is with us for now (as their senior leaders exercise the strategic choice of using them in this way). A number of cases in the literature reinforce this view, for line management involvement in HRM has increased in some leading-edge firms (eg Hutchinson and Purcell, 2003; Larsen and Brewster, 2003; Purcell *et al*, 2003; Purcell and Hutchinson, 2007).

However, a question still arises as to whether involving line managers more in HRM is a positive development. This is because the contingencies of different work contexts seem to account for a lot of variance in such outcomes. For example, many of the studies (just mentioned) that are positive about involving line managers in HRM tend to come from 'excellent' firms where we might perhaps expect good outcomes to occur (because they invest resources to support and develop line managers in HRM). But in other work organisations employees may be managed poorly by line managers because these organisations may have neither the resources to fund such support and development, nor an HR presence on-site to 'police' line management practices in HRM – eg small to medium-sized enterprises (SMEs).

The data that does exist on assessing the usefulness of involving line managers in HRM (especially in the UK, but also now beginning to emerge from the People's Republic of China, New Zealand and the USA) arguably requires us to be cautious when doing so.

One challenge for line managers in HRM lies in developing employees to help deliver organisational outcomes while attending to employee concerns regarding their well-being. But in delivering both organisational development/performance and employee needs/wishes, line managers may feel that they are 'the filling in the HR sandwich' (McConville and Holden, 1999) or that they are stuck between a rock and a hard place. This is because managers need to balance requests and the increasing expectations of their employer (and potentially other stakeholders) to deliver against relevant performance criteria for which they are accountable, with the need to develop people at work in a wider sense as resourceful humans (ie to ensure that employees are motivated, and have job satisfaction). This is the (arguably classic) challenge of reconciling the 'soft' and 'hard' elements of HRM in practice (Legge, 1995), or in Huy's (2002) terms, of line managers' needing to engage in 'emotional balancing' (see also Chapter 16).

Involving line managers in HRM thus requires such managers to work in environments that are characterised by meeting the performance demands of a series of internal and external stakeholders, and managing in contexts of high levels of change and uncertainty. They have to reconcile the search for cost control and higher creativity in HRM with demands of higher levels of responsibility for people and financial management, and to make choices on how they manage people at work. Coping with such expectations and demands places great pressure on line managers. But line managers must practise HRM in a more consistent and professional way, as their expediency in it has long been understood.

So we now face a series of questions:

- How do we want line managers to manage people at work?
- What roles should non-specialists and HR specialists take in HRM?
- Is involving line managers in HRM a positive development for all of the stakeholders in HRM today?

Obtaining answers to these questions may help us understand if the greater involvement of line managers in HRM is a development that employers are pursuing to add value for all stakeholders in HRM, part of a cost-cutting exercise by them, a mixture of both, or something different altogether.

EXPLORE FURTHER

Visit the CIPD's OD Toolkit website for free access to the following tools:

Tools for creativity and innovation Overview 225
Tool no. 44 Establishing a creative culture 229
Tool no. 45 The use of metaphor and story-telling 235
Tool no. 46 Structured problem-solving 237
Tool no. 47 Brainstorming 240
Tool no. 48 Morphology strips 244
Tool no. 49 Visualisation 246
Tool no. 50 Other creative methods 249
Tool no. 51 Leadership questionnaire 254
Tool no. 52 The 'pebble in the shoe' 260

REFERENCES

Argyris, C. and Schön, D (1978) *Organizational Learning: A theory of action perspective.* Reading, MA: Addison-Wesley.

Birkinshaw, J. and Gibson, C. (2004) 'Building ambidexterity into an organization', *Sloan Management Review*, Vol.45, No. 4: 47–55.

Brandl, J., Madsen, M. T. and Madsen, H. (2009) 'The perceived importance of HR duties to Danish line managers', *Human Resource Management Journal*, Vol.19, Issue 2: 194–210.

Brewster, C. (2009) 'Changing roles in HRM', in Muller-Camen, M., Croucher, R. and Leigh, S. (eds) *Human Resource Management: A case study approach*, London: Chartered Institute of Personnel and Development.

Brewster, C. and Larsen, H. H. (eds) (2000). *Human Resource Management in Northern Europe: Trends, Dilemmas and Strategy.* Oxford: Blackwell.

Buckingham, M. and Coffman, C. (2001) *First, Break All the Rules.* New York: Simon & Schuster.

CIPD (2005) *Who Learns at Work? Employees' experiences of training and development.* Survey Report. London: Chartered Institute of Personnel and Development.

Currie, G. and Procter, S. (2001) 'Exploring the relationship between HR and middle managers', *Human Resource Management Journal*, Vol.11, No.1: 53–69.

Dotlich, D., Cairo, P. and Rhinesmith, S. (2009) *Leading in Times of Crisis.* San Francisco: Jossey-Bass.

George, J. M. and Zhou, J. (2007) 'Dual tuning in a supportive context: joint contributions of positive mood, negative mood, and supervisory behaviours to employee creativity', *Academy of Management Journal*, Vol.50, No.3: 605–22.

Gibb, S. (2003) 'Line manager involvement in learning and development: small beer or big deal?', *Employee Relations*, Vol.25, No.3: 281–93.

Guest, D. (1987) 'Human resource management and industrial relations', *Journal of Management Studies*, Vol.24, September: 503–22.

Guest, D. and King, Z. (2001) 'HR and the bottom line', *People Management*, 27 September.

Hamel, G. (2007) *The Future of Management.* Boston, MA: Harvard Business School Press.

Hunter, W. and Renwick, D. (2009) 'Involving British line managers in HRM in a small non-profit work organisation', *Employee Relations*, Vol.31, Issue 4: 398–411.

Hutchinson, S. and Purcell, J. (2003) *Bringing Policies to Life: The vital role of front-line managers in people management*. London: Chartered Institute of Personnel and Development.

Hutchinson, S. and Purcell, J. (2007) *Learning and the Line: The role of line managers in training, learning and development*. Survey Report. London: Chartered Institute of Personnel and Development.

Huy, Q. N. (2002) 'Emotional balancing or organizational continuity and radical change: the contribution of middle managers', *Administrative Science Quarterly*, Vol.47, No.1, March: 31–69.

Hyman, J. and Cunningham, I. (1995) 'Transforming the HRM vision into reality. The role of line managers and supervisors in implementing change', *Employee Relations*, Vol.17: 8, 15–20.

Ingham, J. (2007) *Strategic Human Capital Management*. London: Butterworth-Heinemann.

Institute of Leadership and Management (2009) *Index of Leadership Trust*. Research Report. London: Institute of Leadership and Management.

Larsen, H. and Brewster, C. (2003) 'Line management responsibility for HRM: what's happening in Europe?', *Employee Relations*, Vol.25, No.3: 228–44.

Legge, K. (1995) *Human Resource Management: Rhetorics and realities*, Basingstoke: Macmillan.

Lowe, J. (1992) *Reassessing Human Resource Management*. London: Sage.

Lynch, S. (2003) 'Devolution and the management of human resources: evidence from the retail industry'. Paper presented to the Professional Standards Conference, Chartered Institute of Personnel and Development, University of Keele.

McConville, T. and Holden, L. (1999) 'The filling in the sandwich: HRM and middle managers in the health sector', *Personnel Review*, Vol.28, No.5–6: 406–24.

McGovern, P., Gratton, L., Hope-Hailey, V., Stiles, P. and Truss, C. (1997) 'Human resource management on the line?', *Human Resource Management Journal*, Vol.7, No.4: 12–29.

Marchington, M. and Wilkinson, A. J. (2002) *People Management and Development: Human resource management at work*, 2nd edition. London: Chartered Institute of Personnel and Development.

Marlow, S., Taylor, S. and Thompson, A. (2010) 'Informality and formality in medium-sized companies: contestation and synchronization', *British Journal of Management*, Vol.1, No.4, December: 954–66.

Mesner-Andolsek, D. A., and Stebe, J. (2005) 'Devolution or (de)centralisation of HRM function in European organizations', *International Journal of Human Resource Management*, Vol.16, No.3, March: 311–29.

Mitsuhashi, H., Park, H. J., Wright, P. M. and Chua, R. (2000) 'Line and HR executives' perceptions of HR effectiveness in the People's Republic of China', *International Journal of Human Resource Management*, Vol.11, No.2: 197–216.

Mumford, M. D., Scott, G. M., Gaddis, B. and Strange, J. M. (2002) 'Leading creative people: orchestrating expertise and relationships', *The Leadership Quarterly*, Vol.13: 705–50.

Purcell, J. and Hutchinson, S. (2007) 'Front-line managers as agents in the HRM–performance causal chain: theory, analysis and evidence', *Human Resource Management Journal*, Vol.17, No.1: 3–20.

Purcell, J., Kinnie, N., Hutchinson, S., Rayton, B. and Swart, J. (2003) *Understanding the People and Performance Link: Unlocking the black box*. London: Chartered Institute of Personnel and Development.

Renwick, D. (2003) 'Line manager involvement in HRM: an inside view', *Employee Relations*, Vol.25, No.3: 262–80.

Renwick, D. (2009) 'Line managers and HRM´, in Redman, T. and Wilkinson, A. (eds) *Contemporary HRM*, 3rd edition. London: Pearson Education.

Searle, R. H. and Ball, K. S. (2003) 'Supporting innovation through HR policy: evidence from the UK', *Creativity and Innovation Management*, Vol.12, Issue 1, March: 50–62.

Shipton, H., Fay, D., West, M., Patterson, M. and Birdi, K. (2005) 'Managing people to promote innovation', *Creativity and Innovation Management*, Vol.14, Issue 2, June: 118–28.

Sloman, M. (2007) *The Changing World of the Trainer*. London: Butterworth-Heinemann.

Ulrich, D. and Brockbank, W. (2005) *The HR Value Proposition*. Boston, MA: Harvard Business School Press.

Wagner, R. and Harter, J. (2007) *Twelve Elements of Great Managing*. London: Gallup Press.

Whittaker, S. and Marchington, M. (2003) 'Devolving HR responsibility to the line: threat, opportunity or partnership?', *Employee Relations*, Vol.25, No.3: 245–61.

CHAPTER 11

Strategic Workforce Capability – Planning For a New Era

Roger Cooper and Melanie Wood

CHAPTER OVERVIEW

In this chapter we draw upon recent academic thinking about strategy and change to assess conventional workforce planning techniques, recognising the importance of language and context in shaping them. Calling for a more strategic approach to workforce planning, we consider the interrelationships between strategic workforce planning, business strategy and organisation design, illustrating our argument for a more fluid form of planning with a case study of a major British local government body.

LEARNING OBJECTIVES

By the end of this chapter the reader should be able to:

- understand the theoretical context in which strategic workforce planning takes place
- describe the key aspects of strategic workforce planning in organisations and be able to critically appraise how well the arrangements work
- compare and contrast academic and 'real-world' practitioner accounts of strategic workforce planning
- describe the way that strategic workforce planning affects, and is affected by, the culture and the agenda for change within different types of organisation.

INTRODUCTION: THE CONTEXT OF WORKFORCE PLANNING

In this section you will learn about the theoretical context of strategic workforce planning (the first learning objective listed above).

Workforce planning is dead! Long live strategic workforce planning ...

The old stereotype of workforce planning as a regimented, numerical process based on unrealistic and often over-optimistic assumptions is, in our opinion, being consigned to history, and with it, the idea that the workforce can be in some way controlled by ever more complex and scientific modelling frameworks – a point first made by Reilly (1996). The literature is replete with examples of the search for the philosopher's stone of workforce planning that somehow turns increasing quantities of numerical data into workable plans that meet the needs of organisations. Recent examples include Narahari and Murthy (2009), Größler and Zock (2010) and Jackobson (2010).

At its simplest, strategic workforce planning is about making informed decisions about changes in the workforce, guided by the strategic direction of the organisation. We argue that workforce planning is concerned with an organisation managing its capability through its people. We acknowledge, however, the importance of the way that we describe these processes, the language we use to describe strategy and change, and the importance of taking a pluralist view of change. One of the reasons that we believe the traditional view of workforce planning is so unhelpful in gauging the future needs of an organisation is the assumption of 'command and control' – the view that it is possible for one part of the organisation (planners, leaders, managers) to have a single, 'right' view of all of the problems and all of the solutions.

In our exploration of the subject we establish links with the core themes of this book, looking at how this new approach to Organisational Effectiveness (OE) is transforming the way organisations think about and practise strategic workforce planning. This new approach to OE holds that there is no single reality, no single problem, and therefore no single answer. As we shall see, the way that change within the workforce is motivated, led, managed and transacted, the way that potential and hidden talent is recognised and developed in organisations, and the resulting changes in organisational performance are far more the currency of contemporary strategic workforce planning than the simplistic notions of having a 'grand plan' which is rigidly adhered to.

Our treatment of the subject in this chapter is unapologetically practical – for two reasons:

- We have seen evidence in practice to support the view that if strategic workforce planning is to be effective, it should be introduced in a way that is engaging for practitioners – and in our view, this equally applies to students.
- The body of peer-reviewed academic literature on strategic workforce planning is not extensive, particularly in the way that it relates to the themes of the New OE. We therefore do not dwell on theory for its own sake, although we obviously take theory into account, especially where practice appears to be leading theory development.

THE WORKFORCE PLANNING PROCESS

In this section you will learn about the key aspects of strategic workforce planning, building the ability to critically appraise how well the arrangements work in practice (the second learning objective listed).

At its most effective, strategic workforce planning is iterative and dynamic, taking account of the:

- strategic needs of the organisation
- level of change being managed
- extent to which the process and practice of strategic workforce planning is embedded in the organisation as a whole
- degree to which employees feel engaged with the organisation
- quality and content of workforce information and intelligence.

Where there is significant organisational uncertainty, strategic planning is at its most valuable. A more formal process is often required to enable a critical review of potential business scenarios, emergent strategy, and to foster effective organisational engagement.

Figure 11.1 Strategic workforce planning: process landscape

We consider this part of our treatment of strategic workforce planning to be the minimum methodology necessary.

INTELLIGENCE

We have found through experience that intelligence is the beating heart of strategic workforce planning: it provides validation, direction and insight into the workforce planning process. By the term 'intelligence' we mean obtaining hard facts from inside and outside the organisation that could affect the future capability of the workforce, and the interpretation of those facts into themes that are of strategic relevance; then distilling these into planning assumptions and recommendations. But we argue that 'intelligence' also means *insight* into how the organisation actually works – its cultures and the attitudes, beliefs and language of its members. A recurrent theme of New OE is the way that Organisation Development has influenced human resource management, and this is no more evident than in the intelligence aspects of strategic workforce planning. The way that hard facts are interpreted by an organisation in the pursuit of strategic workforce planning is as much determined by organisational values, beliefs and attitudes as it is by operational imperatives.

The process of building intelligence involves selecting, gathering, preparing and analysing information to provide insight into the factors affecting the supply, demand and management of the workforce so as to inform key decisions on workforce strategy (see Chapter 4). This approach has been developed partly through the experience and practice of the authors (see the Birmingham City Council case study below) but has also been influenced by Reilly (1996) and Sinclair and Robinson (2003).

1 Strategy

The strategy aspect of strategic workforce planning explores organisational capability and considers how best to configure the workforce in the light of:

- purpose and vision of the organisation – whether, and if so how, these have changed
- strategic business drivers with most significance for the workforce
- buying and selling markets in which the organisation operates
- strategic implications for the organisation's products, services and value chain
- key assumptions underlying business strategy

- workforce impacts of planned changes in strategy or its execution
- current and potential workforce issues – e.g. talent management.

One of the objectives of strategic workforce planning is to manage the gap between the demands placed on the workforce and the capacity ('supply') of the workforce. Stages 2 and 3 explore these factors. Both demand and supply are continuously and independently variable. As Lynch (1997) points out, success is not measured by the quality of analysis or by the sophistication of the plan, but by the extent to which the organisation is able to take best advantage of the conditions in which it finds itself. By implication this means change within the organisation as it reacts to the conditions. The success of strategic workforce planning is therefore inextricably linked to the successful leadership and delivery of business change. This point is expanded in Figure 11.2. It also illustrates neatly one of the aspirations of strategic workforce planning, which is to be one of the means by which organisations increase their flexibility and agility in reacting to market conditions. This flexible capability is a key element of the New OE, and strategic workforce planning as discussed here appears in stark contrast to the historic view of workforce planning as a mechanism by which an organisation is controlled in order to maintain a 'status quo' of capacity in relation to demand.

2 Service needs analysis

The 'traditional' approach to workforce planning focuses most attention on stages 2 and 3, and indeed any contemporary analysis and intelligence relating to the dynamics of the

Figure 11.2 Leadership within the context of workforce planning

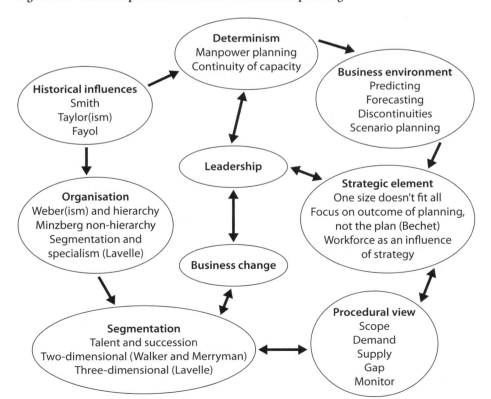

workforce contains some elements of quantitative data analysis on which potential future scenarios are modelled. This typically addresses the following:

- current and future volumes of work expected
- workforce implications of planned developments in product or service delivery
- potential external impacts on product, service or workforce – this will normally involve intelligence produced by PESTLE analysis
- what is envisaged in the future planning landscape.

PESTLE analysis in turn involves the investigation of six types of factors:

- **Political**
- **Economic**
- **Social**
- **Technological**
- **Legal**
- **Environmental**.

3 Service and workforce analysis

Here the workforce supply capacity is addressed. Critical success factors include the ability to produce complete, accurate and timely analysis of workforce size, availability and dynamics. The most effective strategy includes both 'lagging' and 'leading' indicators of the workforce profile. Lagging indicators are fact-based measures and may include long-term seasonal trends – eg the percentage of workforce capacity lost to sickness absence during the year. Leading indicators are projections of future assumptions – eg a projection of sickness absence percentage loss based on assumptions about seasonality and on long-term historic trends.

It is a common misconception that headcount, starters, leavers and absences provide a good enough foundation to build workforce capacity. Good practice is to understand how the organisation treats its high-potential and high-performing talent to ensure that talented individuals are deployed most effectively, taking into account current and future business needs. The ideal outcome is to build an environment that creates strong multilateral psychological links through formal and informal 'contracting' between individuals and the organisation (see Chapter 14).

A complete picture of workforce supply will include an analysis of the way that roles are designed individually and how they are organised into structures. For this reason, some organisations consider organisation design to be an almost indistinguishable part of the planning continuum that also contains strategic workforce planning (see Chapter 3). This theme is also developed in the concluding section of this chapter where the evolving and converging relationship between Organisation Development and HR is considered.

A robust workforce supply analysis typically includes:

- the current workforce, including segmentation by diversity characteristics such as grade, age, gender, ethnicity and disability
- trends affecting capacity, such as starters, leavers and absences
- skills and capability
- performance
- key factors affecting capacity using correlations and establishing causal links wherever possible.

Although some of this may be included in regular monthly management information reporting, analysis, projections and forecasts, this form of analysis is considerably more complex and requires a much greater level of business understanding and insight.

To summarise: knowledge of existing workforce resources gives organisations the ability to analyse the impacts of business strategy on workforce requirements. A good grasp of workforce supply helps to reveal how best to utilise workforce skills, talent and succession abilities to meet these needs. Insights from planning assumptions and future service requirements can be used to build a workforce plan that meets the current and future needs of the organisation.

4 Action planning, and 5 monitoring and review

This part of the process is iterative and dynamic. Action planning is concerned with addressing the gaps between demand and supply with the objective of maintaining the minimum possible gap in the short, medium and longer term. A strategic workforce action plan typically includes:

- the conditions in which to explore workforce 'capability'. This is about understanding the business drivers and strategic vision and ensuring that workforce knowledge, skills and capacity are responsive to meet any forecasted or emergent needs
- an analysis of the gaps between demand and supply required to achieve an agreed strategic outcome, and an investigation of the underlying causes of the gaps
- a list of planned actions to address the underlying causes for the gaps
- plans for monitoring and reviewing how the planned actions are progressing and the extent to which the planned strategic outcomes are being achieved. This should include returns on workforce investments, which can be expressed financially or socially. An exploration of these terms is beyond the scope of this book; for further reading, see Kearns (2010), Cascio and Boudreau (2011) and EQUAL Social Economy Scotland Development Partnership (2007).

A CRITIQUE OF WORKFORCE PLANNING PRACTICE AND THEORY

Next you will have the opportunity to consider some of the limitations of workforce planning practice and to learn about the relationships between workforce planning and organisation design (the second learning objective).

Figure 11.2 features a 'road map' of key subjects and influential writers on this subject, all of which are referenced in the *Explore further* and/or *References* sections at the end of the chapter.

As a concept, workforce planning has been used in organisations for centuries. The notion of planning the size and characteristics of the workforce was central to the needs of large-scale industrialised manufacturing that emerged in the Industrial Revolution at the end of the eighteenth century. Formalised workforce planning in a way that would be recognised in the contemporary world emerged in the 'modernist' approach to manufacturing in the US motor industry in the early part of the twentieth century, under the influence of Taylor (1911) and his 'scientific management', Fayol (1916) on the functions and principles of management, and Weber (1909) on bureaucratisation.

Although this framework worked well in the high-volume mechanised manufacturing industry and in the fixed structures of public administration, it has a number of limitations as a discipline with relevance to organisations in the early part of the twenty-first century. Potential limitations include:

- flexibility – the ability of such an approach to react to changes in the internal and external business environment and to the development of people's skills and talents
- agility – the ability of such an approach to enable organisations to move quickly to exploit opportunities and challenges presented by the external environment
- applicability – the extent to which the approach could be applied in organisations without fixed 'Weberian' hierarchical structures or mechanised high-volume manufacturing
- over-reliance – the risk that a simple model of workforce planning would provide the answers to all workforce problems.

Legge (2005, p223) describes these techniques as 'hard human resource planning'.

The reappraisal of the role of strategic workforce planning in recent years has been brought about by a series of factors that make the employment market more volatile and more complex, and which underline the importance of effective workforce strategies (see Chapter 2). They include:

- the globalisation of business
- the 'war for talent'
- the increasing international mobility of key workers
- differential economic growth, particularly in neighbouring geographic areas (for example, Eastern Europe versus Western Europe in the early years of the twenty-first century)
- the emergence of regional trading blocs (eg the European Union and ASEAN) with reductions in the regulations restricting internal mobility
- increasing interlinking of financial systems, the result of which is the greater and faster global impact of economic events, as evidenced by the banking crisis of 2007 followed quickly by the continuing poor global economic conditions since early 2008
- a fundamental sociological change in the way that people feel about work and its balance with personal life. This is seen in the differing perceptions of demographic groups towards employment and the 'psychological contract' between individuals and their employers.

PRACTICE PERSPECTIVES

From a practitioner perspective, people's understanding, perceptions and views about workforce planning vary considerably from organisation to organisation. A sample of practitioner definitions of workforce planning is given below:

- Planning the numbers of staff needed to meet a short-term service need, such as a staff rota.
- A way to review the workforce profile, such as numbers of staff by pay bands or by characteristics of diversity; or in more numeric ways giving the precise amount of workforce capability needed to perform a role, resulting in a prescriptive approach.
- In more advanced practice, a way to forecast and review the effects of external labour market flows; a strategic tool to model different business scenarios and assess the impact in terms of human capital returns on workforce investment.

Sullivan (2002) provides further examples.

The fundamental shift in economic conditions has changed organisational requirements for workforce planning and management. Public, private and third sector organisations all face common issues – for instance, in attracting and retaining high-performing and highly skilled workers.

It is within the public sector that the most significant shifts are taking place, that provide the greatest challenge, and where there is the greatest drive for change in strategic workforce planning practice. Within Europe there has been an ideological shift among politicians and the public in general about the role of government – a fundamental change in the way this is seen, moving away from the notions of control and provision towards notions of facilitation and commission. Within this emerging environment, civil servants and public sector leaders continue to digest the impact for national and local government and relationships with other public bodies. The implications for the workforce involved in the delivery of public sector services include:

- a change of allegiance away from employers and towards physical location and service
- a drive for high levels of flexibility and agility in the workforce
- pooled budgets, shared facilities and resources, merging services and a focus on income generation.

For public sector managers, a clear understanding of this fundamental change and a thorough analysis of the stocks and flows of the workforce are critical to successful strategic workforce planning. Having a clear planning platform gives greater confidence and the ability to assess impacts and create organisation design alternatives. It also helps to identify the workforce skills required to achieve a successful transition to a new model of working.

For the private sector, the need for strategic workforce planning is just as great, although different from the public sector. As organisations plan for emergence from recession or acceleration of economic growth, it will be their ability to recognise the sectors in which growth is most likely to take place, to maximise their talent base and to make the necessary changes early enough that will have the most significant effect on shareholder value.

Evolving practice in both public and private sectors forms a sharp contrast to the large-scale prescriptive, and often over-complex approaches to strategic workforce planning that developed from the notions of 'scientific management' at the beginning of the twentieth century.

REFLECTIVE ACTIVITIES

- What are the potential risks of poor workforce planning practice and its symptoms?

- How would you know that workforce planning had gone wrong or was absent?

You may wish to consider these two key questions in relation to organisations with which you are familiar.

ACADEMIC PERSPECTIVES

Sinclair and Robinson (2003: 4) note that 'It appears that the renewed interest amongst practitioners is yet to be matched by academics.' Within this context there is an argument for the critical appraisal of the body of knowledge.

So why should strategic workforce planning re-emerge at this time as a high priority for organisations? The easy answer to this question would be to cite the economic conditions prevailing at the end of the first decade in the twenty-first century within the West – the idea that without strategic workforce planning it would not be possible to navigate a survival route through the credit crisis and subsequent economic recession. However, this would be to ignore emergent practice and academic interest in the subject in the years immediately prior to the financial crisis of late 2007 in which private and public sector organisations recognised the need for strategic workforce planning. Baron, Clark, Pass and Turner (2010) cite case studies from six diverse private and public sector organisations, the preparation for which clearly preceded the financial crisis.

There is an implication in much of the literature in our *References* section – with the exception of Bechet (2000) – that some level of corporate control over strategic workforce planning is both necessary and desirable.

There is little within the literature regarding the way that strategic workforce planning should take account of sociological changes affecting the workforce. Much has been written about the potential effects of 'baby boomers' exiting the workforce – Lavelle (2007) providing one example – but relatively little about the expectations and attitudes of Generation Y and beyond (ie workers born after 1981). As is evident from readily available UK population statistics, the potential labour market is certainly not homogeneous with regard to age.

So what does this tell us about strategic workforce planning in the context of the continuing convergence between HR and Organisation Development? We offer the following as a set of requirements for workforce planning to be truly strategic:

- The process should be supported by the best people management intelligence available and to a time-scale that is driven by that intelligence, not solely by the demands of the business planning cycle.
- Internal and external environmental scanning should be undertaken by specialists to ensure that timely information is collected and analysed to assure its relevance. It is necessary that the analysis of impacts on and implications for business strategy are owned by the organisation, because this forms part of the core purpose of the organisation.
- Intelligence and insight are achieved by answering exploratory questions arising from environmental analysis – e.g. what can the organisation learn from high levels of turnover with regard to its talent management strategy?
- A thorough, shared understanding of market intelligence is required to allow planning for future business opportunities. This will include analysis of competitors, product and service value in the market place, competitiveness of features and pricing. Workforce implications must be fully analysed. For example, does the organisation have the optimum workforce size and the right skills to help to develop its market proposition? What are the potential requirements for reskilling, redesigning roles or redesigning structures? How will the workforce respond to changes? How flexibly can it transition into future roles?

THE EVOLVING PRACTICE OF BUILDING CAPABILITY

In this section you will have the opportunity to contrast academic and 'real-world' accounts of strategic workforce planning (the third learning objective listed).

Effective strategic workforce planning is partly determined by the process by which it is undertaken – partly by the resulting organisational interventions, partly by the cultural norms of the organisation, and partly by the capability of the organisation to adapt to and exploit changes in the internal and external operating environment. Turning now to the actual practice of strategic workforce planning, there have been a number of significant developments in recent years that not only show the development of strategic workforce planning as a subject but also address some of the criticisms outlined previously in this chapter.

WORKFORCE SEGMENTATION

Sullivan (2002) argues that 'failure to prioritise' and being over-ambitious in scoping are two of the most common reasons that workforce planning initiatives fail. Attempting to create a single 'master plan' for the entire workforce can become a fruitless ambition that is bound to fail. It is therefore necessary to segment, to subdivide, the workforce of an organisation into smaller parts as a way to help to identify and manage the most significant workforce planning issues.

We noted in the introduction to this chapter that early approaches to workforce planning and organisation design were based on fixed hierarchical organisation structures as the 'currency' of workforce planning. Sociological changes since the early 1990s have fundamentally changed the psychological contract between individuals and organisations (see Chapter 14). At the same time, the ways that organisations do business – and in particular the ways that they communicate with customers and service users – have been revolutionised by technology and social attitudes (see Chapter 2). Under these circumstances, assumptions of a 'Weberian' hierarchy are no longer fit for purpose in either describing or planning organisations. But what are the alternatives?

Workforce segmentation is a powerful way to think about this question. The work of Mintzberg (1979) has been influential in this area. In his 'organizational configuration model', Mintzberg used the terms 'strategic apex', 'middle line', 'operating core', 'technostructure' and 'support staff'. This model is useful for our purposes because it segments the workforce both by seniority and by types of skills and personal attributes necessary to perform each role, and yet it is not a rigidly hierarchical model. Influential as this idea has been, there are alternative approaches to workforce segmentation.

Lavelle (2007) argues that many workforce planning interventions become embroiled in analysing and managing the gap between demand and supply, that there is a need to extend the theoretical framework of strategic workforce planning to release such organisations from gap analysis, and that effectively segmenting the workforce from a planning perspective is one way of doing this.

Walker and Merryman (2005) propose a two-dimensional model of segmentation: see Figure 11.3.

Lavelle (2007: 376) extends this view of workforce segmentation with the addition of a third dimension that relates to the optimal employment relationship/employer value proposition required to retain skills: see Figure 11.4.

In considering the question of the optimum employment relationship, and acknowledging the influence of Capelli (1999), Lavelle proposes an employment life-cycle with specific characteristics – see Figure 11.5.

The contribution of Capelli (1999), Lavelle (2007) and Walker and Merryman (2005) to contemporary strategic workforce planning practice includes:

- the recognition that 'gap management' can become embroiled in data analysis
- the notion that segmenting the workforce is a valuable tool in identifying which roles to focus the most effort on in order to achieve the greatest effect, thus addressing one of the key points identified by Bechet (2000) to 'focus on particular positions, not all positions'
- the notion that the workforce can be segmented along three dimensions, helping to address the question 'So what should we do about this?' that often arises from strategic workforce planning practice.

Now consider the series of questions below as a way to help thinking through the wider strategic workforce planning agenda that is likely to emerge in the medium- to long-term future:

1 What does it mean 'to work for' an organisation?

2 How does an organisation imbue its extended workforce with the same values, beliefs and attitudes as the core organisation personnel?

Figure 11.3 Walker and Merryman's model: business impact versus talent scarcity analysis

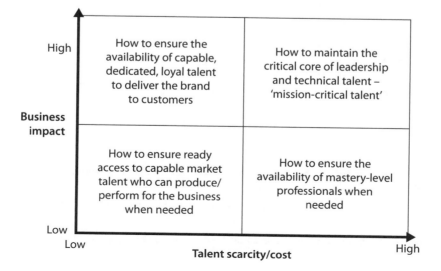

Figure 11.4 Lavelle's dimensions: impact versus scarcity versus the optimum employment relationship

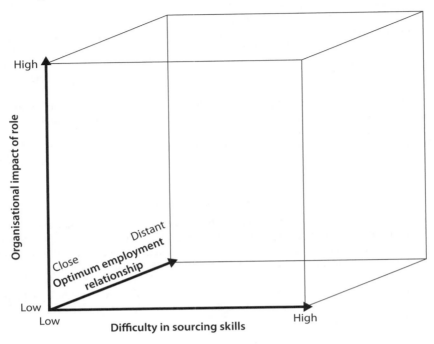

Figure 11.5 Lavelle's stages in the employment life-cycle

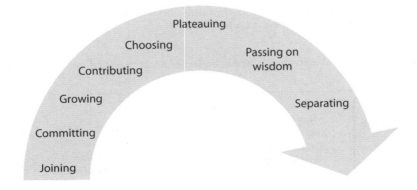

3 What does 'allegiance'/'loyalty' to an organisation mean?

4 How does this affect the conversations between individuals within the extended workforce?

5 What does this mean in terms of the management of performance of individuals and groups?

6 What are the implications for people that are increasingly likely to fall into more than one segment?

WORKFORCE CAPABILITY

The purpose of strategic workforce planning is to match the capability of its workforce to an organisation's needs. We have established previously in this chapter that for us, capability includes knowledge, skills, capacity, flexibility and agility. That said, the dynamics and the content of the capabilities needed by different organisations vary widely. Compare, for example, a firm of corporate lawyers with a firm developing smart phone applications. The 'selling point' core capabilities of lawyers include a deep subject knowledge, long-term relationships, continuous professional development and experience of complex cases. In contrast, the 'selling point' capabilities of a smart phone application development firm

Figure 11.6 The changing landscape of local government

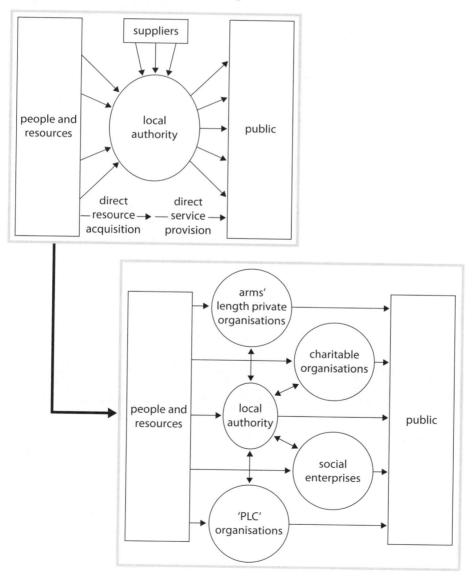

include innovation, speed to market, very specific and current technical capability and cost. The workforce strategy for the law firm would involve long-term planning and long investment–return cycles, whereas for the smart phone development firm, short-term opportunist planning and short investment–return cycles would be more typical.

A more complex example that helps to develop an understanding of this idea is that of UK local authorities. Two fundamental factors are currently driving the biggest change in local authority structure and service provision for a generation. The first is a substantial reduction in funding, arising from the financial crisis of 2007/8 (and the subsequent surge in public borrowing, and the need to reduce public debt (see Chapter 2). The second is a political/philosophical shift to reduce the size of central government and to encourage localism and the provision of services through the voluntary sector, social enterprises and the private sector. Figure 11.6 summarises how this is affecting the role of local government and the wider, and much more complex, workforce implications.

Clearly, strategic workforce planning is operating in a much more complex environment. Under these circumstances the implementation of workforce plans is far more concerned with influence and outcome than the 'command and control' of the past.

Whereas previously the key functions of local government were the direct provision, regulation and control of service, the future role of local government is concerned with commissioning, market shaping, purchasing and devolving. These attributes demand an entirely different set of workforce capabilities. Workforce planning therefore feeds into a much more strategic influencing role for local government, and is less about a controlling management process. The workforce planning for this future is shaped by the general transition to much smaller organisations (driven partly by financial constraints, partly by emerging management practice), requiring different roles in different numbers, more specialisms for some, more flexibility for others, and more agility for all.

MANAGING TALENT

In their chapter (Chapter 13) on inclusive talent management and diversity, Eddie Blass and Gillian Maxwell argue that, for talent management to be effective, it must be open, transparent and inclusive. Their treatment of the subject covers the selection, development and management of talent, and one of their conclusions is that talent is topical – it relates to the needs of the organisation, the environment and the time. As discussed in the introductory chapter, one of the implied criticisms of a unitarist approach to people management is that it may fail to recognise that 'talent' also relates to the needs and capabilities of individuals.

Our purpose for including talent management in the context of strategic workforce planning is as a vehicle through which the demand for talent can be established in relation to supply and planning can take place as a way to close the gaps that emerge.

REFLECTIVE ACTIVITIES

As is often the case, it is helpful to think about questions as a way to explore the role of strategic workforce planning in the management of talent:

- To what extent does/should the term 'talent' relate to individuals whose capabilities match a specific organisational need?
- What capability does the organisation need, and how is this articulated in terms of individuals with exceptional talent?
- Where are the measures and indicators of success/failure in a talent management process?

By considering these points you should be able to conclude that 'talent' is one of the ways of segmenting the workforce from a strategic planning perspective.

Emergent practice in managing talent includes role design, a focus on developing the 'vital few' and the management of challenging individuals. It is increasingly recognised that by combining insights from strategic workforce planning with organisation design, it is possible to consider developing alternative role designs as a way to develop the potential in talented individuals. This contrasts with the traditional approach of drawing on talent pools to find the best person to succeed for a specific role.

One of the difficulties of managing talent is that talented people are not necessarily liked in an organisation, and to single them out may represent a particular risk for senior managers and leaders. Any group of talented individuals identified as being necessary for the organisation in five years' time is likely to be influential. They will be expecting to make fundamental changes which the incumbent management team is likely to resist. At an extreme, there is a risk that the 'talented' will make themselves unpopular with the established leadership and management. Planning for the continual but effective integration of new talent into leadership and management teams is therefore a non-trivial task.

LEVELS OF ANALYSIS AND PLANNING

Two of the questions frequently encountered by strategic workforce planning practitioners are: 'At what level in the organisation does workforce planning become strategic?' and 'What is the difference between resource planning and strategic workforce planning?'

If the workforce segment being considered has strategic implications, or if successful deployment of strategy is dependent upon one particular element of the workforce, then workforce planning is of strategic importance. To illustrate the point, a continuum is suggested as a way to illustrate the fact that the size of a workforce segment is not an accurate indicator of its strategic importance. At one end of such a continuum would be the entire workforce of a large organisation which is undergoing a significant shift in strategy or operating environment. At the other end might be a small part of the organisation operating in a highly constrained supply market, where the ability to attract and retain a small number of people with specific skills is a potential threat to the entire business.

HUMAN CAPITAL MANAGEMENT (HCM)

One of the concepts that have emerged during the early years of the twenty-first century is that of human capital management. Human capital is defined as 'the knowledge, skills, abilities and capacity to develop and innovate possessed by people in an organisation' (Baron and Armstrong, 2007: 6). If the value of businesses is becoming increasingly dependent on the skills, abilities and capacity of the workforce, then planning and managing the workforce is itself becoming an increasingly important driver of shareholder value. Human capital management is therefore an increasingly important aspect of strategic workforce planning. Effective integration of the principles of HCM into strategic workforce planning has the following implications:

- analytics – the measurement of those aspects of knowledge, skills and abilities that are of strategic value to the organisation, and identifying which of these have the most significant effect on the purpose of the organisation (note here the influence of HRM–performance thinking)
- measuring people value – identifying where the value is added within an organisation (that is, value perceived by customers, service users and owners/governing stakeholders) and ascertaining which people management practices enhance value most cost-effectively
- modelling and forecasting factors affecting the supply of, and the demands on, those parts of the workforce which create value
- influencing the business planning process to ensure that human capital gaps are given appropriate priority within the overall management of the workforce.

LEADERSHIP AND MANAGING CHANGE

An alternative way to think about the processes and implementation of strategic workforce planning is in the context of managing change. It can be argued that as an agent for change, strategic workforce planning is influenced at least as much by the philosophies of Organisation Development as those of human resource management. There is no single view of change management. Indeed, Helen Francis, Linda Holbeche and Martin Reddington argue in Chapter 1 that change is more effectively managed as a continuous process in a 'living system' approach than when managed according to the 'classic' change-management thinkers writing as recently as the 1990s, of whom Kotter (1996) is a much-quoted example.

This is important for our study because strategic workforce planning is a change-management challenge on three levels:

- Its introduction into an organisation represents a significant change to a number of key stakeholder groups. The management of the predictable resistance to change, particularly in well-organised groups such as professionals and trade unions, is one of the critical success factors in introducing strategic workforce planning.
- Strategic workforce planning acts as an influence on business change. In our opinion, using intelligence and developing an understanding of the future workforce requirements is likely to give rise to significant change.
- The successful implementation of strategic workforce planning as a business change depends upon committed and inspirational leadership.

WORKFORCE PLANNING AS AN INFLUENCE ON STRATEGY

Here you will learn about the way that strategic workforce planning affects and is affected by the culture and the agenda for change within different types of organisation (the fourth learning objective listed).

We have explored the idea of intelligence being the 'engine' that drives the strategic workforce planning process and how it helps shape organisation design. Here we develop the idea that intelligence derived from strategic workforce planning is a key component of business strategy and can even act as a driver of strategy (see Chapter 4). For further reading on the various ways in which organisations develop strategy, see Lynch (1997) in *Explore further* at the end of this chapter.

CULTURE

We argue that the way that strategic workforce planning integrates with the wider approach to strategy planning is influenced by the cultural norms of an organisation. For those organisations in which strategy is the outcome of an open and consultative approach and where employees are multilaterally engaged in the process, it is more likely that workforce planning will be integrated into business strategy. By contrast, where strategic planning is restricted to a small number of powerful individuals, workforce planning is less likely to be integrated and more likely to be reactive to predetermined business plans. The disadvantage of the latter example is that the workforce is much less likely to be recognised as a potential influence on business strategy.

THE IMPACT OF CHANGE ON WORKFORCE STRATEGY

An emerging area of focus in the analysis of workforce strategy is understanding the impact of change, and this is particularly the case in the UK public sector. Today's organisations are operating in a context of potentially extreme change, yet management attitudes towards risk tend to be reflective of an organisation's culture. This can be expressed as a continuum: at one end is high tolerance of the risk, which tends to support initiatives for service reform; at the other is low tolerance of risk, which tends towards 'service retrenchment', withdrawing resource and service quality in incremental slices. Experience has shown that the impact of change analysis has proved effective in challenging the way that leaders think about planning changes in:

- funding
- scope of services delivered
- service design
- service performance
- size of the workforce
- roles in the workforce
- citizen engagement
- staff engagement.

SCENARIO-PLANNING

It is obvious that forecasting cannot be a precise science and that it relies on a set of assumptions about how the world currently is, and how it is likely to change. All forecasting activity involves producing a model to predict the future based on what is known about the present and the past. Whereas this may be a valid approach most of the time, it is clear from history that the business world can be taken completely by surprise by what can best be described as 'environmental discontinuities' (Faircloth *et al*, 2006). Such discontinuities may be:

- local – for example, the earthquake and tsunami in Japan in 2011
- regional – for example, the banking crisis in the Eurozone in 2010
- global – for example, the oil crisis of 1973.

Scenario-planning offers managers a way of thinking about the future in a way that is not necessarily influenced by what they know of the present or the recent past. This process helps with contingency planning, since it entails analysing 'what ifs' and also considering possibilities that would not otherwise suggest themselves. Shell has used scenario-planning as part of its strategic analysis since the early 1970s and continues to do so (see Shell, *Looking Ahead: Scenarios* in *Explore further* at the end of this chapter for more details).

For strategic workforce planners, scenario-planning can be a powerful strategic tool. It is useful in promoting a more lateral approach to thinking about workforce strategy and as a way to identify radical alternative outcomes. It can also show commonalities between alternative scenarios and give indications of issues that in periods of great uncertainty must be addressed regardless of the chosen scenario.

THE WORKFORCE AS A DRIVER OF BUSINESS STRATEGY

The workforce may act as a driver of business strategy where an organisation is operating in workforce markets that are highly supply-constrained. The strategic implications can be seen as either limiting, suggesting exit from a particular market, or offering potential opportunities, leading towards competitive advantage.

The example of the British Gas maintenance and repair business illustrates this idea. The company operates in a highly regulated and constrained labour market for qualified gas engineers. It takes two to three years to fully train a gas engineer, and demand for them outstrips supply, particularly during the autumn and winter. The labour market is active, highly competitive and staff turnover rates are high. The performance of the business is strongly influenced by its ability to maintain and grow this part of the workforce.

In 2002, the company announced a programme to recruit an additional 5,000 engineers. To manage the task, they established the British Gas Engineering Academy, combining training and recruitment into a single team. The Academy provides instruction for trainees at five locations across the UK and has been successful in delivering apprentice programmes that supply newly qualified engineers. As well as supporting business growth, the Academy has provided mandatory five-yearly competency training and assessments for existing, experienced engineers.

In this example it is clear that the company not only recognised the supply issue relating to domestic gas engineers but also recognised it as a long-term structural weakness in the education and training system in the UK. Perceiving this as an opportunity, the company took a strategic decision to invest in the Academy and now attracts significant government funding to train domestic gas engineers.

THE BIRMINGHAM CITY COUNCIL CASE STUDY

In this section you will learn about practical approaches to developing workforce planning strategies (the second, third and fourth learning objectives listed).

Birmingham City Council has taken a fresh perspective in its approach to workforce planning, abandoning the traditional scientific approaches in favour of a more holistic approach to managing the capability of the workforce to meet the future needs that it identified through a thorough analysis of its internal and external operating environments. For those involved, this required them to have the courage of their convictions, flying in the face of more conventional, less innovative wisdom.

The objectives of workforce intelligence and planning are to:

- increase Council efficiency through intelligence-led reorganisations
- increase the proportion of management positions filled through internal promotion
- improve the planning and management processes
- embed talent management and succession planning
- target a sustainable reduction in workforce costs
- reduce reliance on agency and temporary staff.

CASE STUDY

BIRMINGHAM CITY COUNCIL

Creative design and implementation

The Council's Workforce Intelligence and Planning team (WIP) was designed to provide more than a standardised approach to workforce management – it was to provide a bespoke combination of workforce planning, talent management, business intelligence and information. The team uses a planning logic, which may be represented diagrammatically thus:

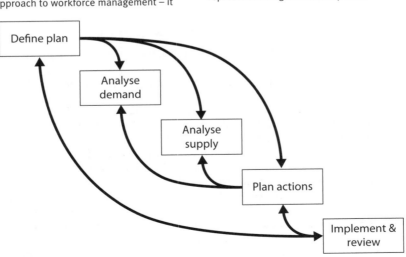

Early analysis of workforce data showed that the Council had had a static headcount for a decade. This was seen as a problem for a number of reasons:

- Management reporting of workforce characteristics had previously been limited in its scope, timeliness and accuracy.

- Whereas there had been a perception among senior stakeholders that the workforce was highly dynamic and that its management was reactive to changing business conditions, modelling and projections conducted by the WIP team indicated that without specific intervention, the size and composition of the workforce would remain unchanged. Understanding the future needs of the workforce must be looked at holistically, which is why planning, design and development are integrally linked. Because the workforce represents the biggest single category of cost to the authority, any attempt to manage or reduce costs would inevitably be influenced by the size of the workforce.

Collaborating with the service management leadership team, the WIP group developed a new resource management strategy, enabling the authority to predict and plan its workforce needs on a three-year basis using business tools, helping to generate a clearer insight into how the budgetary pressures could be met.

The use of a structured approach to workforce intelligence provided objective, analysis-based, accurate workforce information; it also took into account continuous scanning of the internal and external operating environment to identify the key PESTLE factors (which might represent risks or requirement for change coming from environmental scanning). The external environmental scanning service was provided partly by local universities (Aston Business School at Aston University and the Institute of Local Government Studies at the University of Birmingham). The interpretation of the full business environment and workforce recommendations for managers and planners (on how and when to react to the issues identified) were included in the design of the workforce intelligence function.

Organisation Design (OD)

Using the market intelligence and planning logic, the Council has been able to harness its capability to model and understand the impact of a variety of longer-term business scenarios and strategies. OD builds on these scenarios and strategies and provides a methodology that supports service redesigns, the process from conception to implementation typically taking from three to nine months.

The impact on the organisation

Starting from a low baseline, these approaches have developed the capability to take a strategic view towards the workforce. The Council now has reliable workforce intelligence enabling it to take a longer-term, less reactive approach to the management of its workforce.

As a result the Council can now predict and plan its workforce needs on a three-year basis using business tools, which will help to generate a clearer insight into how the financial budgetary pressures can be met. There are now clear links between business strategy and workforce outcomes and a planning framework that manages the workforce cost base effectively. Management decisions about the workforce can now be made based on hard intelligence.

The future

For the WIP team, the challenge for the future is to continually support the Council in achieving redesigned services within tightening budgetary constraints. Having an active HR capability to help steer at both strategic and local level, change is critical. Delivering what is required to enable the Council to fulfil its mandate will test even the most advanced HR functions. Being aware of the impact of the stocks and flows in the labour market, understanding the external operating conditions, and developing radically different business models are all necessary ingredients for organisational survival in a newly reconfigured public sector environment. In this context, the Council has to be able to work with multiple stakeholders and providers within Birmingham in order to continue to deliver the most necessary of services to the vulnerable in society, and to maintain a city that has a global reputation. For Birmingham, the returns on its investment are starting to pay dividends during one the most difficult periods in local government history.

Questions

1 How would you set about making the business case to implement a new function such as the Birmingham City Council Workforce Intelligence and Planning team? What would be the key elements of cost and benefit in such a business case?

2 The Birmingham City Council Workforce Intelligence and Planning project was initiated in mid-2007, before the financial crisis and consequent implications for public sector funding. In what ways would this change in the external environment influence your approach to setting up and running the WIP team on an ongoing basis?

3 In its organisational design for HR, the Council chose a structure in which the new Organisational Design team was separately managed from Workforce Intelligence and Planning. In your opinion, what would be the key arguments for and against this approach?

4 How could Birmingham City Council leverage workforce planning tools in the light of significant and fluctuating political and economic agendas?

5 In what ways could Birmingham City Council get the most out of workforce intelligence and planning and organisation design?

CASE STUDY COMMENTARY

The case study from Birmingham City Council highlights a number of themes that run through this book. Of particular note is the notion that the workforce is treated as a business system and that workforce planning and its implementation is one of the ways in which change is managed within the organisation. This is a very Organisation Development-influenced view of strategic workforce planning. At the same time, the Workforce Intelligence and Planning function is seen as one of the centres of expertise within the HR operating model. In making this point we are not arguing that the function should be given one categorisation rather than another – we are instead noting that strategic workforce planning really is at the convergence of the two disciplines. Other points of reflection are:

● Because strategic workforce planning sits at the convergence of OD and HR, it is difficult to find, attract and retain staff with the required blend of skills and experience.

● The nature of strategic workforce planning is non-deterministic: it does not drive the organisation towards one particular outcome. The business strategy of a large local authority is by definition huge and diverse, and it would be silly to expect workforce planning to be any less diverse. But because workforce intelligence, heavily influenced by the external environment, is a key driver of workforce strategy, there is always an element of the unexpected in good workforce plans. To set up such a function in which outcomes on the workforce could never be fully predicted took a significant leap of faith on the part of the Council, in terms of both its political leadership and its management agenda.

● During the time in which the Workforce Intelligence and Planning team was conceived, designed and delivered, the external business environment changed almost beyond all recognition, driven by the unfolding financial and economic crisis of 2007/8. The fact that the team was able to fully support the Council as its business objectives changed so much adds weight to our argument that a broad base of intelligence, workforce planning, talent and succession management capability is of far more relevance to business needs than the detailed design of individual workforce planning tools or approaches.

SUMMARY AND CONCLUSION

By way of summary and conclusion, we would like to leave you with some final thoughts on strategic workforce planning.

The ability to plan and to analyse levels of risks is a good thing, regardless of whether the economic cycle is characterised by growth or by recession. Understanding the capacity, capability and requirements of both the current and future workforce is a crucially important part of strategy planning and implementation.

It is not, and never has been, possible to predict everything, and for this reason scenario planning has an important role to play in the strategic workforce planning toolkit. Part of its value is that it encourages strategists to think about possible outcomes and contingency plans that are not necessarily obvious. This is equally true for business strategy and workforce strategy.

It is important to bear in mind that business strategy does not necessarily have to precede workforce strategy – indeed, it is sometimes right that workforce capacity and capability should drive business strategy. Effective strategic workforce planning is iterative. Expect, therefore, to revisit strategy and issues of demand and supply on the basis of new intelligence.

One of the advantages of strategic workforce planning is that it helps to build organisations that are flexible, agile and sustainable. Experience has shown that a good understanding of the dynamics and potential of the workforce provides managers with the ability to create higher returns on the investment in the workforce than would otherwise be the case – a point supported by Cascio and Boudreau (2011).

The academic world has yet to fully analyse and document the evolving practice of strategic workforce planning.

Since 2007 there has been a fundamental shift in the operating environment which has escalated strategic workforce planning up the business agenda for many organisations. We argue that this should not be carried out in an overly procedural way. The new era is one in which existing economic models have been challenged to breaking point. Brave leaders are needed who are prepared to make bold decisions without necessarily knowing all of the answers or even all of the questions. However, this does not give leaders *carte blanche* to rely on pure guesswork. The strategic workforce planning described here supports strategic decision-making by providing leaders and managers with a lens through which to focus on the key workforce issues.

Returning to this book's key theme of Organisational Effectiveness, the strategic workforce planning we describe above is a multi-faceted subject that combines the more traditional objective notions of performance-driven HRM with more emergent critical HRM theory. Strategic workforce planning is rapidly being adopted by practitioners as a way not only to address the needs of organisations; but also increasingly to take into account the behaviours and preferences of people.

Our view of strategic workforce planning is that, for it to be effective, it should strike a balance between the sometimes conflicting needs of the organisation and the ways in which people interact and relate to each other and the organisations for which they work. We believe that wisdom in strategic workforce planning is in knowing where the optimum balance can be struck – a quest that is at the heart of the new agenda for Organisation Development and human resource management.

EXPLORE FURTHER

Baron, A., Clarke, R., Pass, S. and Turner, P. (2010) *Workforce Planning: Right people, right time, right skills.* London: Chartered Institute of Personnel and Development. A practical guide based on research by the CIPD, including UK-based case studies from the private sector, public sector and NHS, and a short literature review.

Cascio, W. and Boudreau, J. (2011) *Investing in People*, 2nd edition. Upper Saddle River, NJ: Pearson Education. A review of the various numerical approaches to measuring the value of investments that organisations make in people.

EQUAL (2008) *Investing in Impact: Developing social return on investment.* Scotland: EQUAL Social Economy Scotland Development Partnership. A practical guide to the subject of social return on investment from the perspective of UK public sector organisations.

Kearns, P. (2010) *HR Strategy: Creating business strategy with human capital*, 2nd edition. London: Elsevier. A review of the way that people strategy, HR strategy and business strategy are developed, and the interdependencies between them.

Lynch, R. (1997) *Corporate Strategy.* London: Pitman. An exploration of the different ways that corporate strategy is developed in organisations.

Shell, *Looking Ahead: Scenarios.* http://www.shell.com/home/content/aboutshell/ our_strategy/shell_global_scenarios/. Background on scenario planning and an analysis of two potential future scenarios.

Sinclair, A. and Robinson, D. (2003) *Workforce Planning – The wider context. A literature review.* London: Employers Organisation for local government/Institute for Employment Studies). http://www.improvementservice.org.uk/library/download-document/2327-guide-to-workforce-planning-in-local-authorities/. This provides a review and bibliography of many of the influences of workforce planning, particularly from the perspective of UK local authorities.

REFERENCES

Armstong, M. (2000) *Strategic Human Resource Management: A guide to action.* London: Kogan Page.

Baron, A. and Armstrong, M., (2007) *Human Capital Management: Achieving added value through people.* London and Philadelphia: Kogan Page

Baron, A., Clarke, R., Pass, S. and Turner, P. (2010) *Workforce Planning: Right people, right time, right skills.* London: Chartered Institute of Personnel and Development.

Bechet, T. B. (2000) *Developing Staffing Strategies That Work: Implementing pragmatic non-traditional approaches.* Available online at: http://unpan1.un.org/ intradoc/groups/public/documents/UN/UNPAN021815.pdf [accessed 15 February 2011].

Capelli, P. (1999) *The New Deal at Work: Managing the market driven workforce.* Boston, MA: Harvard Business School Press.

Employers Organisation for local government/Institute for Employment Studies. (2003) *Guide to Workforce Planning in Local Authorities*. http://www.improvementservice. org.uk/library/download-document/2327-guide-to-workforce-planning-in-local-authorities/ [accessed 15 February 2011].

Ethics Resource Center (2010) *Millennials, Generation X and baby boomers: who's working at your company and what do they think about ethics?* Arlington, VA: Ethics Resource Center. http://www.ethics.org/files/u5/Gen-Diff.pdf [accessed 23 May 2011].

Faircloth, J. B., Valentine, S. R. and Bronson, J. W. (2006) 'Environmental discontinuity impacts on small business strategic marketing adaptation', *Journal of Applied Management and Entrepreneurship*, Vol.11, January: 58–73.

Fayol, H. (1967) [1916] *General and Industrial Management*. London: Pitman.

Größler, A. and Zock, A. (2010), 'Supporting long-term workforce planning with a dynamic aging chain model: A case study from the service industry', *Human Resource Management*, Vol.49, Issue 5, Sep/Oct: 829–48.

Jacobson, W. S. (2010), 'Preparing for Tomorrow: A Case Study of Workforce Planning in North Carolina Municipal Governments', *Public Pesonnel Management*, Vol.39, No.4 Winter 2010.

Kotter, J. P. (1996) *Leading Change*. Boston, MA: Harvard Business School Press.

Lavelle, J. (2007) 'On workforce architecture, employment relationships and lifecycles: expanding the purview of workforce planning and management', *Public Personnel Management*, Vol.36, No.4: 374–85.

Legge, K. (2005) *Human Resource Management: Rhetorics and realities*. Basingstoke: Macmillan.

Lynch, R. (1997) *Corporate Strategy*. London: Pitman.

Mintzberg, H. (1979) *The Structuring of Organizations*. Englewood Cliffs, NJ: Prentice Hall.

Narahari, N. S. and Narasimha Murthy, H. N. (2009) 'System dynamic modelling of human resource planning for a typical IT organization', *CURIE Journal*, Vol.2, Issue 3: 33–45.

Reilly, P. (1996) *Human Resource Planning: An introduction*. Brighton: Institute for Employment Studies.

Sinclair, A. and Robinson, D. (2003), *Workforce Planning – The wider context. A literature review*. Employers' Organisation for local government and the Institute for Employment Studies. http://www.employment-studies.co.uk/pdflibrary/2605eowfp.pdf [accessed 4 October 2011].

Smith, A. (1776) *An Inquiry into the Nature and Causes of the Wealth of Nations*. Available online at: http://www.econlib.org/library/Smith/smWN.html [accessed 16 February 2011].

Sullivan, J. (2002) *Before You Try It, Understand Why Workforce Planning Fails*. Available online at: http://www.ere.net/2002/08/12/before-you-try-it-understand-why-workforce-planning-fails [accessed 22 May 2011].

Taylor, F. W. (1911) *The Principles of Scientific Management*. Available online at: http://www. maine.gov/dhhs/btc/articles/taylor-principles-scientific-management.pdf [accessed 14 February 2011].

Ulrich, D. (1997) *Human Resource Champions*. Boston, MA: Harvard Business School Press.

Wack, P. (1985) 'Scenarios: uncharted waters ahead', *Harvard Business Review*, September–October.

Walker, J. and Merryman, J. (2005) *Workforce Architecture: Aligning talent with strategy through segmentation*. Available online at: http://walkergroup.com/ council/WF_ ARCHITECTURE_FINAL.doc [accessed 15 February 2011].

Weber, M. [1909], cited in Grusky, O. and Miller, G. A. (eds) (1970) *The Sociology of Organisations*. London: Free Press.

CHAPTER 12

Performance Management and Reward

Roger Cooper and Adrian Furnham

CHAPTER OVERVIEW

In this chapter we critically examine academic theory and the real-world practice of performance management and the way that it relates to reward. Exploring the mechanics of performance and reward management, we look at some of the wider impacts of performance and reward and use a case study of a multinational energy company based in the UK to illustrate some of the practical aspects of the subject. We go on to argue the case for re-imagining performance and reward, influenced by increasingly complex relationships between people and the organisations for which they do work and the idea that both Human Resource Management and Organisational Development have a part to play in this re-imagination.

LEARNING OBJECTIVES

By the end of this chapter the reader should be able to:

- explore the infusions of academic and 'real-world' practice and take both perspectives into account in obtaining a clear understanding of the theoretical context in which performance management and reward management take place
- describe, critically examine and appraise the key aspects of performance management and reward management arrangements in organisations, and how well the arrangements work, being cognisant of different types of evidence available
- clearly understand the distinctions and links between the processes involved in managing performance in relation to reward
- describe and evaluate the process by which reward is managed within different types of organisations.

INTRODUCTION: WHY MANAGE PERFORMANCE?

The management of performance for individuals, teams and organisations is arguably the single most important driver of success for increasingly complex organisations (Furnham, 2005). There has never been a better time to re-evaluate the fundamentals of performance management, and in doing so, we make the case for re-imagining the relationship between employees, the teams and organisations they work for and the best ways to manage the performance of all three.

We start with the most fundamental question (although one that is all too rarely asked): 'Why should we manage performance?'

At the core of the question is the perfectly reasonable worry that if we don't manage performance, it may not be as good as we may hope. Philosophically, if we don't manage our performance, there would be the danger that our competitors would, and in doing so, outperform us. This could affect us in any number of ways: our market share, our access to funding or our ability to attract and retain the best talent (see also Chapter 13). At the heart of our need to manage performance is the need to compete, whether we like it or not.

Taking this simple argument a step further, there are a small number of key assumptions on which the management of performance and its links to reward are based. It would be helpful to bear these in mind as we explore the subject:

- Although individuals and groups have upper limits to their capability and level of performance, they certainly have a capacity to improve performance. This implies the need to manage performance.
- For any individual, incentives form part of the approach to managing performance and can have a material effect on the level of performance achieved and the rate at which its improvement takes place. This does not imply anything in particular about the nature or size of incentives.
- From the perspective of the employer, there is an optimum balance between the costs of employing people and the value created by the performance of their work. If individuals are not managed appropriately, there is the risk of not achieving the best balance of cost and value. This implies that there is a law of diminishing returns in the management of performance (Furnham, 2008).

Put simply, if we are able to strike the right balance between the needs of the employee, the needs of the employer and what we are prepared to put into the management of both, we can potentially outperform our competitors.

If only it were that simple!

The extent of this over-simplification is revealed by analysing what we mean by the term 'management', because this raises questions about the complexity of the subject. What would 'right' look like? What would 'wrong' look like? By thinking about these questions we start to recognise that that there are no universal 'rights' or 'wrongs'. Evidence suggests (and this can be seen from the case study) that what is 'right' in one set of circumstances might be completely wrong in another – this even may even occur within the same organisation at the same time. Clearly, to explain the 'why' of performance management we need a more sophisticated understanding of the theory and practice and the links with reward.

There is a significant body of knowledge on performance management, part of which concentrates very specifically on performance appraisal (Bernardin and Beatty, 1984; Murphy and Cleveland, 1995). Early papers set out a conceptual framework for studying performance management (Broadbent and Laughlin, 2009; Ferreira and Otley, 2009; McKenna, Richardson and Manroop, 2011; Otley, 1999) while others have concentrated on such things as managers' reactions to these systems (Taylor *et al*, 1998) as well as more recent ideas around strength-based performance (Bouskila-Yam and Kluger, 2011). Some papers are very practical, such as that by De Waal (2003) who considers the behavioural factors important for the successful implementation of systems, or that of Waldman (1994) who looked at performance management systems and total quality implementation.

Some researchers have looked at performance management in unionised settings (Brown and Warren, 2011) or their role in global organisations (Busco, Giovannoni and Scapens, 2008) or their effect on employee engagement (Gruman and Saks, 2011). Many attempt to help those introducing new systems (Amaratunga and Baldry, 2002; Flapper *et al*, 1996).

There appear to be two basic philosophic underpinnings to performance management systems: equity and feedback.

EQUITY

Equity theory is based on ideas from Brockner *et al* (1986) and Parnell and Sullivan (1992), and is fairly straightforward:

- Individuals evaluate their 'deal' at work by comparing their inputs (what they do and how much they do) with outputs (their total 'benefit package').
- Individuals compare their input/output package with others' in the workplace (superiors, colleagues/peers, subordinates).
- If the ratios for peers are perceived to be unequal, a deep sense of inequity exists.
- This could be over-rewarded or benefited inequitably, leading to guilt; or under-rewarded or benefited inequitably, leading to anger.
- The greater the inequity, the greater is the stress and the greater the motive to restore equity.
- Equity can be restored psychologically (cognitively by re-evaluating the circumstances *or* by changing the comparison *or* by terminating the relationship).

Put simply, people at work compare themselves with others all the time. Satisfaction with pay and other benefits is almost always a function not of absolute benefit but of (peer) comparison benefit. It is not how much you are paid, but how much *compared to other peers*.

Equity is different from equality. Being paid equally means you are paid for the job you do, not for how you perform on the job. Equity suggests that you have to measure performance and then pay people according to their inputs (ie performance).

Although there are various theoretical problems with the equity concept (such as how to evaluate negative inputs), one really important issue is *equity sensitivity*. This concerns an individual difference in how people perceive and react to equity issues at work. That is, some people seem to make these comparisons more frequently than others. Further, some seem more upset by even small perceived inequity than others. Such sensitivity may be a function of both personality and values. People who believe in the Protestant work ethic are accordingly more likely to favour equity over equality – that is, they believe that people should be individually rewarded for their hard work. On the other hand, those with strong communitarian values who believe in equality, brotherhood, etc, may be less unhappy about inequity. For some, the ethic of selflessness, service-above-self, the importance of the greater goal, are all-important.

FEEDBACK

The second theoretical issue refers to the importance of feedback (London and Smither, 2002). People cannot learn and develop without clear and accurate feedback on their performance. People need to know:

- how they are doing
- what they need to do differently to be better
- what their boss thinks about their work style and outcomes.

It is essential to the learning process. There are all sorts of issues here, such as whether feedback is best given in words or in figures (Brutus, 2010).

You can get feedback from people (subjective) or from recordings/records of behaviour (objective). Ideally, you get both. That feedback can be:

- general or specific
- positive or negative
- spoken or written
- immediate or delayed.

Feedback increases our self-awareness, offers options and encourages personal development, so it can be important to learn to both give it and to receive it effectively. Feedback does not mean only positive feedback or feedback we want to hear. Negative feedback (framed as improvement suggestions), when given skilfully, can be very important and useful. Feedback given in an emotive, punishing and unskilful manner can leave the recipient feeling bad with seemingly nothing constructive on which to build, or pointers for learning.

One of the core themes of this book is to explore where and how the disciplines of Organisation Development (OD) and Human Resource Management (HRM) have the potential to converge and how this affects practitioners. At a broad level, the discipline of Organisation Development adopts a whole-systems view of an organisation, taking into account its cultural values, its business strategy and the ways that it behaves as a complex group of people – a point made by Broadbent and Laughlin (2009). At the same level, Human Resources is concerned with building and maintaining a workforce that has the right skills in the right places at the right time, deployed in the right activity. Traditionally, the 'process' and the 'procedure' of performance management and the links to reward are 'owned' by Human Resources. Practitioners report that effective performance management is reliant on:

- processes that are fit for purpose – 'good enough'
- an organisation that is ready, willing and able to undertake the necessary processes, that has a clear shared understanding of who does what, when
- clear and shared expectations for each stage of the processes and its outcomes
- clarity in the minds of employees – how they are expected to perform, the behaviours that are both encouraged and discouraged, what to expect if they perform well … and what to expect if they do not.

To think of performance management simply as a process would give only a partial understanding of the subject: processes of themselves rarely create commitment, nor do they change behaviours. The notion of performance management simply as a behavioural framework to support strategy and employee development would be similarly incomplete. Effective performance management relies on multilateral engagement, commitment, good communications and management, and this is further evidence of convergence between the disciplines of OD and HRM. This point is illustrated by Rich, Lepine and Crawford (2010); see also Chapters 1 and 17.

In our exploration of the subject we start with the perspective of process.

THE PROCESS OF PERFORMANCE MANAGEMENT AND REWARD

At a broad level, the process by which performance management is undertaken in organisations and the way that it relates to reward are generic. Practically, there are few variants, although that is not to say that there is only one way to think about the process.

Starting with a simple linear view of the process (as in Figure 12.1), the generic elements follow a sequence of setting performance objectives for a period, the management of development activities (to support the objectives), monitoring and managing performance throughout the period, assessing performance, and using this as an influence on reward. The linear process normally provides an input into the objective planning for the following period, and this is shown as the 'feedback loop' in Figure 12.1. There are numerous examples

Figure 12.1 Performance management and reward as a linear process

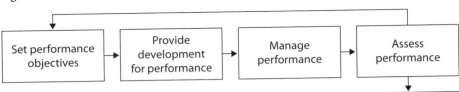

in the literature that illustrate this point – Helm, Holladay and Tortorella (2007) providing one example from the public sector, and Hope and Fraser (2003) providing a more robust academic review and private sector examples.

This loop implies a cyclical process, and indeed, in many organisations, performance management takes the form of a yearly 'performance cycle'. In the linear view, there is a point in the process at which performance is assessed against some form of ratings framework, and it is at this point that performance data is 'locked' before being moved into the reward process. Here it is used to influence the way that salary, bonus and other rewards are calculated and paid to employees. During this part of the process it is quite normal for the performance management process for the following period to run in parallel with the reward process for the previous period.

The linear representation gives a limited view of performance and reward management, however. Many organisations think and communicate about performance management and reward using circular representations, and the one that is included here as Figure 12.2 shows reward at the heart of the process, affecting and affected by each stage of the performance management process.

Figure 12.2 Performance management and reward as an iterative process

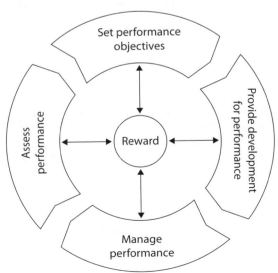

This is deliberate, because the whole organisational system by which performance is managed is iterative and bi-directional. Reward policy, for example, can influence the way that performance is managed, and the process of managing performance influences the policy and practice of reward. The fact that performance and reward are considered to be parts of a wider system within an organisation, and the way that this influences the development of the organisation, reflects the basic premise of OD set out in this book. The Centrica case study later in this chapter illustrates this point.

The performance management process is now examined in more detail and provides a foundation on which to develop a critical framework to analyse the effectiveness of performance management and reward.

SETTING PERFORMANCE OBJECTIVES

The purpose here is for managers to agree with employees a set of activities to be undertaken during the performance period that can be assessed to evaluate performance. Although this appears to be relatively simple, it is important to bear in mind the different perspectives. From the employee's perspective, the purpose of objectives is to have a clear idea of what is expected both in terms of what needs to be achieved, and what kind of behaviours are acceptable and unacceptable, but also how performance will be assessed. From a manager's perspective, it is important for the employees for whom they are responsible to have performance objectives that support the objectives for the group. From an organisational perspective, it is important for objectives to support the overall objectives of the organisation. From the perspective of leaders and stakeholders, it is important that the organisation's objectives strike a balance between short-, medium- and long-term needs and plans – in other words, that the objectives support the organisational strategy.

Let us look at the sometimes complementary and sometimes conflicting relationship between scholars writing from a Critical HRM (CHRM) perspective, such as Valentin (2006) and Townley (2004) and scholars of mainstream Human Resource Management-Performance (HRM-P), which is well covered in the literature and illustrated, for example, by Guest (2011) and Guest and Conway (2011). CHRM scholars tend to argue that management practices such as performance management form part of an array of management domination at work (see also Chapter 2). In contrast, mainstream HRM scholars focus on how such practices work (eg Purcell and Hutchinson, 2007), and this is the stance we adopt in this chapter. HRM-P researchers in particular seek to establish causal links between various HR practices and measurable aspects of organisational and business performance.

At the core of HRM-P is the notion of measurement as an important factor in managing a process, and for our study this is highly influential in the way that performance management systems have evolved. Its influence is never stronger than in the area of objective-setting. The argument goes that if performance is to be managed, objectives must be measurable. This has given rise to the SMART mnemonic as a way to help managers to set objectives in an 'objective' way – to ensure that objectives are appropriate and aligned to the needs of the business.

SMART objectives are:

- *Specific* – clear in scope and business context. The scope can include business area, geography, organisation, processes, people involved, and what is not involved in the objective. Getting the specific right is really about answering the question 'How will we know whether or not the objective has been achieved?'
- *Measurable* – implying the extent to which the objective should be achieved. It relates to the business outcomes of performance: what in the business will have changed, and by how much, as a result of achieving the objective
- *Achievable* – suggesting the practicability of the objective, the extent to which it is possible to achieve it. Often this means what is agreed as being achievable between a

manager and an employee, and implies an element of risk and some form of performance contract (either formally or informally)

- *Realistic/Relevant* – denoting the relevance of the objective in the business context, and the extent to which it is realistic to complete the objective in the light of other constraints, such as time and opportunity
- *Timely* – referring to precisely when the objective is to be completed. For a manager, the sequence in which performance objectives are tackled and completed may be important in relation to the objectives of other team members and the team as a whole.

Many organisations emphasise the importance of linking the individual's objectives to the overall business strategy of the organisation. The basis of this argument is that successful deployment of strategy is the sum total of the successful achievement of all of the objectives of the employees, although it is fair to say that this is not universally accepted. Guest and Conway (2011) argue in favour. Vittorio Chiesa *et al* (2009) argue, for example, that different organisations involved in R&D measure different aspects of performance for different purposes, and that co-ordination and communications are as much key factors in organisational performance as the objectives and performance of individuals.

Whether or not we accept the view that strategy could ever be completely deployed through the completion of individual objectives, there is soundness to the logic of objectives that support strategy, and this is sometimes described as a 'golden thread' (Micheli and Neely, 2010). The process by which objectives of senior executives are transmitted down the organisation is sometimes described as 'cascading objectives'. Common as it is, the practice of cascading objectives has its limitations:

- Cascading relies on an articulation of business strategy that is clear enough and complete enough from which to form SMART objectives.
- The accuracy and consistency of translation within the cascade influences the extent to which individuals' objectives support the strategic direction of an organisation. This is linked to the idea described by Golden (2011) as 'strategic grip'.
- Cascading implies a sequence with which objectives can be set and therefore requires careful or even prescriptive management.
- Top-to-bottom cascading limits the extent to which ideas from within the organisation can feed through into strategy through the performance management system.
- There is an assumption that strategic planning aligns with the timing of the performance management cycle – the timing of strategic planning, however, is more likely to be aligned with the needs of the organisation and its stakeholders.

DEVELOPMENT FOR PERFORMANCE

It is common practice to link the management of performance to the management of the training and development of employees. Indeed, the process by which objectives are set and performance is reviewed is sometimes referred to as the 'performance and development review' (PDR). The rationale here is that employees need development in order to achieve performance objectives, and as they undergo it, they not only increase their capability but also 'engage' better with the organisation (Gruman and Saks, 2011) – see also Chapter 14. In the case study featured in this chapter, Centrica chose to make performance and development separate but connected parts of their talent management framework as a way to ensure that both are given the right priority by managers.

MANAGING PERFORMANCE

There are a number of risks in the management of performance, one of which is the way that employees behave as a result of agreeing incentivised objectives. It has become common practice for organisations to encapsulate their cultural beliefs in statements of values and for these statements to form the basis of behavioural frameworks. This is described to a certain degree by Collins and Porras (1994) and in *The Whys and Hows of Corporate Values* (2009) published by the UK organisation Business In The Community.

The way that employees behave pursuing their objectives can be taken into account either formally or informally in the assessment of performance.

Due consideration has to be given to the way in which performance management discussions are conducted, specifically around the types of conversations that take place between individuals and managers within an organisation. This is recognised both in the theoretical world – an example of which is the 'EVP conversational model' (Francis and Reddington, 2010) – and within practice, as illustrated by the priority given to 'honest conversations' in the Centrica case study.

ASSESSING PERFORMANCE

The performance management process concludes with the measurement and assessment of progress towards objectives, how the performance of employees changed, and the way that the behaviours of the individuals affected their own performance and that of other people around them. These are two separate things: measurement of *performance* and *assessment*. We return to this later in considering the statistics of performance management.

A process of 'levelling' or 'calibration' takes place in most organisations at the point where performance management links to reward. The purpose is to bring together performance ratings for many or all parts of the organisation and to compare the ratings with each other and to overall business performance, and in doing so:

- to identify and address any large differences between different groups
- to check for fairness and the absence of discrimination within the combined data set. This is to manage potential legal, regulatory or employee relations risks that may arise from conscious or unconscious systemic discrimination between different groups
- to correlate individual performance ratings against group and organisational performance
- to assess the impact on remuneration costs resulting from performance-related pay
- to check actual performance rating distributions against expected or target distributions (there is more on this in the section on the statistics of performance later in the chapter).

This part of the process is normally facilitated by HR but may or may not be completely owned by HR. Experience shows that there is always some form of governance attached to this process, especially in the case of senior staff within the private sector where a remuneration committee (including independent non-executive directors) typically has the ultimate accountability.

CRITICAL ANALYSIS OF PROCESS

Part of our purpose in this book is to encourage you to think through some of the wider issues of HRM at a deeper level, and in analysing the process of performance management we suggest the following points for consideration.

Setting objectives

The process of setting objectives needs careful consideration and agreement. The outcome of this stage of the process is sometimes called a 'performance contract', and may be formally recorded or informally agreed, but the point of challenge is that it is deceptively easy to set and agree objectives that do not contribute to the management, or more importantly, the improvement of performance.

From the perspective of HRM-P, the purpose of SMART or any other framework providing guidance for objective-setting is to provide managers with tools to help to produce a well-thought-through and rounded set of objectives.

There is always some form of risk built into the performance management process. It should never be the case that all objectives can be met without some form of personal challenge for employees, and it is this that gives rise to risk. The management of the full portfolio of personal objectives in performance management has some of the characteristics of the management of a portfolio of risks. The more thoroughly the objectives are set, the better the management of risk. Within this discipline the key point is to establish links between the factors that enable, or indeed inhibit, performance and to manage them. This is based on the philosophy that all elements of performance are measurable and controllable to some degree, and that having a conceptual model of the enablers and inhibiters is not only possible but desirable – this is a key part of HRM-P thinking.

An alternative way of thinking about the objective-setting process is to approach it from the perspective of CHRM. This is where the process for setting, managing and monitoring improvements in performance is considered to be the context in which rich conversations take place within an organisation. In this view, the prime purpose of the process is to provide a shared understanding, a shared context in which conversations can take place and in which negotiated outcomes can be agreed and managed. This approach addresses the factors that engage and motivate employees rather more than consisting of the pure fact of measurement and monitoring.

REFLECTIVE ACTIVITIES

- To what extent do theoretical frameworks affect the practice of performance management?
- How much of the academic debate is about the way that practice is observed and interpreted?
- To what extent should academic debate influence the way that performance management evolves?
- How do the different world views of HRM help us to interpret the strengths and weaknesses of 'real-world' performance management practice?

Feedback

Although we have described the psychological theory of feedback in performance management in the opening section of this chapter, it is worth spending a little time on thinking about where the term originated. Feedback is a term that has its origins in engineering (Black, 1934) and is used extensively in control systems as a way to assess the way the actual output of a system is performing in relation to the required output. Feedback loops in control systems are designed very carefully to make sure that the right amount of feedback of the right accuracy is fed back at the right time. Inaccurate feedback causes permanent errors between the actual and required states. Too much feedback, too quickly, can cause an over-reaction; the output overshoots the required state and can never hit the target before it changes. Too little, too late, causes the system to be too sluggish to ever reach the required state or to keep up with environmental changes. This has direct relevance to the way that feedback is used in human performance management systems.

Objectivity

The diverse nature of performance information for the full range of roles and performance objectives within an organisation means that it is never possible to be truly objective about either measurement or assessment, and this has impacts on the way that employees perceive the fairness and consistency of the process. It is sometimes tempting, particularly when statistical terms are used, to think of assessment and consolidation of ratings as being a completely fact-based process and that all data is numerically evidenced and completely objective. Nothing is further from the truth, however: performance ratings are subjective judgements – and this is no bad thing. Ultimately, performance management is a human process in which emotions and opinions have an important part to play in the way that humans work, are motivated and ultimately perform. Purcell *et al* (2003) note the impact of a series of factors on discretionary effort as a proxy for performance. We pick this point up again in our exploration of the statistics of performance management.

REFLECTIVE ACTIVITIES

- Where should an organisation be on the continuum between striving for perfection in assessing performance and promoting open dialogue about the limitations?

- What are the factors that determine where any particular organisation should sit on the continuum?

Complexity versus transparency

The process of performance management, and in particular the measurement and assessment of performance, can be complex – and we explore this in more detail later in this chapter. Some of the tools used in the measurement and comparisons between different groups rely on statistical analysis, and this can cause the system to appear to be opaque. There is a trade-off between the statistical complexity that can be built into performance management processes and the needs of employees to understand and to work with the system as a whole. The particular details of this trade-off are different for every organisation and are determined as much by the cultural norms as by the design of the process or the IT systems that support it.

THE KEY CHALLENGE TO PERFORMANCE HRM

From what we have seen about the process of performance management, the key challenge for HRM-Performance is that there has to be either a specific set of measures for all employees within the scope of performance management or generic sets that exist for many groups of employees. The downside of the former is that the process within the entire organisation is very complex and costly; the downside of the latter is that it is not necessarily easy to show the impact on a generic measure of an individual or a small group. Establishing causal links between practically measurable outcomes and the performance of individuals and measurable business outcomes is not only the most difficult aspect of HRM-P but is also the cause of some of its severest criticism.

THE STATISTICS OF PERFORMANCE MEASUREMENT AND RATING

The 'hard' edge of performance management and reward centres on the use of statistics in the analysis and utilisation of performance management and reward data.

There is an argument that the use of the language of statistics to describe performance causes undue faith to be placed in the approach by those of a less mathematical persuasion. Without going into complex theory, we look at the underlying principles and how they are applied, as a way to help you to build an understanding of the strengths and limitations of statistics.

In this exploration, we assume that a performance management framework exists and that the process of managing performance is embedded within the organisation. There are a variety of reasons for using a statistical approach to performance management, unsurprisingly influenced by HRM-P thinking:

- In order to calculate performance-related remuneration, it is necessary to express performance numerically.
- From the perspective of HRM-P, it is necessary to correlate performance with other variables as a way to understand the factors that either improve or diminish performance, and this links with the concepts of human capital management. Baron and Armstrong (2007) among others describe this in more detail.
- Practitioners stress that performance and particularly reward should be demonstrably fair, and the only way in which this can be done is objectively, and therefore numerically.
- There are potential legal and regulatory risks within performance management, but particularly reward that can be evaluated and therefore managed more effectively using statistical techniques.

MEASUREMENT

How is performance measured? What is the statistical basis for the setting and management of performance ratings?

To answer these questions, we refer to our description of SMART objectives earlier in this chapter where we made reference to objectives being 'measurable'. Practitioners report that a good measure is one in which continuously variable data is used to show the extent to which an objective has been met.

Continuously variable performance measures have the advantage that it is possible to compare actual performance levels with targets, and so assess merit. It is possible to 'normalise' performance data so that performance towards each objective is measured on the same basis, such as expressing it as a percentage.

Although it is common to see objectives measured using attribute data (such as 'achieved' or 'not achieved'), this is less useful for managing performance because it conveys very little about the extent to which an objective was achieved or otherwise. Meeting performance objectives is determined by ability, capability, discretionary effort and 'growth' of the individual. Setting objectives with a simple achieved/not achieved measurement provides little scope for conversations about personal development. The *extent* to which an objective has been met provides rich conversational material about the capability development of individuals and groups.

There is an important statistical distinction between assessment and rating of performance. Assessment takes into account performance against objectives using factual data. Rating of performance also takes account of behavioural factors involving matters of *opinion* rather than fact, and as a practical observation this distinction can be overlooked in the analysis of performance ratings. Because they contain some element of subjectivity, performance ratings are typically articulated using descriptive labels rather than numerical values – eg 'met performance targets', 'exceeded expectations'.

There are a number of ways that performance rating data is analysed and utilised, but typically, organisations start by levelling or calibrating performance data. In this process, performance data is analysed by numbers of ratings against each performance rating category, forming a distribution of performance rankings most commonly articulated in the form of tabular data and histograms – see Table 12.1 and Figure 12.3.

Calibration involves reviewing data from different subsets of the organisation, looking for consistency but also any apparent anomalies. This may be comparing distributions between business units or geographic locations but can also include comparison of different aspects of diversity that have legal or regulatory significance – eg comparing the distribution of performance ratings between the genders or between different ethnic groups. Typically (and this is illustrated in the Centrica case study), such reviews also take into account business performance information relating to business units and the organisation as a whole and

Table 12.1 Performance distribution in the form of tabular data

Category	Number of employees
Below expectations	67
Meeting expectations	408
Above expectations	473
Outstanding	52

Figure 12.3 Performance distribution in the form of a histogram

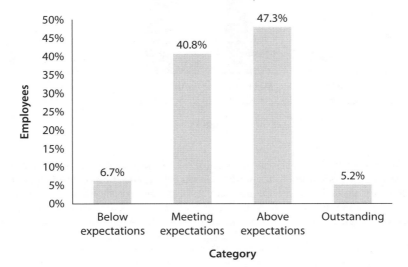

seek to correlate performance distributions and business performance at a business unit level.

One of the more controversial aspects of performance management and its links with reward management is the notion of statistical distributions of performance ratings in general but specifically the management of employees whose ratings fall in the extremes of the distribution. This is where the notions of 'forced distribution' and 'forced distribution ranking system' (FDRS) appear.

Forced distribution is where a predetermined distribution of performance is used for calibration and any anomalies are required to be re-evaluated and amended until the actual performance distribution curve fits the forced distribution – see Figure 12.4.

The shape of the distribution histogram is of more than passing interest. It is not untypical for organisations to use an approximation to a 'normal' distribution curve, although the evidence to support this notion, from the perspective of organisational dynamics and from a statistical perspective, is sparse. Billikopf (2003) provides an illustration of this point.

FDRS has always been the subject of some controversy, particularly in the media. We argue that the principal weakness of forced distribution is its inability to address statistical aberrations in small populations and the measurement and weighting of objectives. We develop this argument in the paragraph below.

Figure 12.4 An example of forced distribution

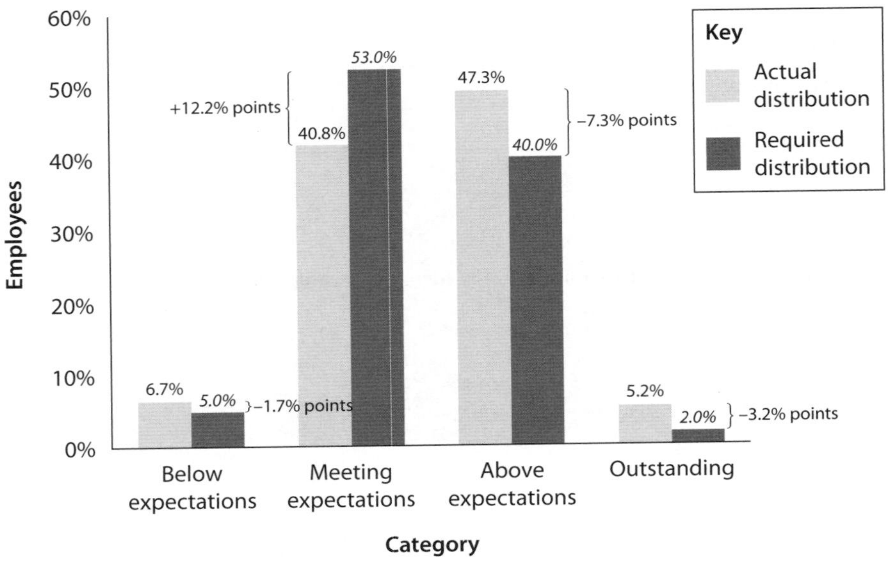

The accuracy with which statistically significant conclusions can be drawn is dependent on the size of the population in the statistical test. For organisations comprising thousands of people, it is possible to estimate the number of people that should fit within any given performance rating interval with a good degree of accuracy, and it is therefore statistically justified (although that is not the same as business justification) – for example, it would be possible to make a statement such as 'We expect between 250 and 270 people to fall into the "failing to meet objectives" category.' The margin of error (20) in relation to the size of a large organisation is a very small percentage. Practitioners have reported examples of organisations citing business rules for forced distributions for small populations – a project team of tens of people, for instance. For small populations, the margin for error becomes much higher; it may only be possible to make a statement such as 'We expect between five and 25 people to fall into the "outstanding performance" category.' In a small organisation, the margin of error (20) may represent a significant percentage of the workforce. This is a point of some statistical subtlety that may not be fully appreciated by all policy-makers in performance management. Another point often overlooked is that performance data frequently does not follow a statistically 'normal' distribution, and many of the assumptions around categorisation and expected distributions are based on that type of distribution. For this reason, the number and nature of statistical tests that are available for non-normally distributed categorical data are limited – see 'The goodness of fit tests' in Anderson, Sweeney and Williams (2002), listed in *Explore further.*

THE MEASUREMENT AND WEIGHTING OF OBJECTIVES

One of the key criticisms of performance management as a subject and HRM-P in general is that data on performance against objectives has to be grouped and compared. Because of the variation in the types of objectives and the methods by which progress and performance is measured, the categorisation of performance is left to managers as a subjective judgement. Not all objectives have the same performance value. The value of objectives may be *weighted* equally for the purpose of consolidation, but this represents an assumption in the process calculation and should not be treated as a matter of fact.

This can have an effect on the credibility of the end result, in terms of both performance management and its links to reward, and can be an influence on perceptions of equity (as established in the introduction to this chapter).

In forced distribution ranking, the performance of employees is ranked and a lower limit is set in the ranking order below which all employees may be dismissed for poor performance – see Figure 12.5.

FDRS is attributed to the General Electric Corporation and specifically to the influence of the CEO John ('Jack') Welch in the 1990s, who said:

> A company that bets its future on its people must remove that lower 10% and keep removing it every year – always raising the bar of performance and increasing the quality of its leadership.

The arguments in favour of FDRS are that:

- the same employees tend to continually occupy the lowest-ranking positions, and that removing them from an organisation raises the overall performance of the organisation
- fear of dismissal through poor performance acts as a motivator towards good performance
- ranking all employees in a fair way allows more equitable reward
- for higher-ranked employees, FDRS gives the opportunity to invest in their development in the reasonable expectation of a good return.

Opponents of FDRS argue that:

- fear of failure does not necessarily result in motivation to succeed
- the performance of employees placed in the lowest performance categories may not necessary be unacceptable or without value to an organisation
- dismissing those employees in the lowest performance categories arbitrarily increases costs of staff turnover with no guarantee of improving performance
- the risks of litigation for claims of unfair treatment outweigh any potential benefit.

These arguments are explored in more detail by Johnson (2004).

Figure 12.5 Forced ranking

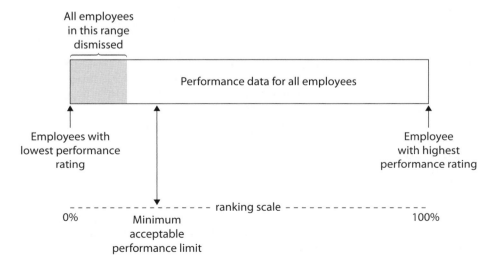

REFLECTIVE ACTIVITIES

You are encouraged to think through your own opinions with regard to forced distribution and forced ranking. The following questions may be helpful as a guide to your thinking:

- Would the benefits outweigh the disadvantages in the organisation(s) with which you are familiar?
- How would these approaches sit with the values, beliefs and attitudes of the organisation?
- How would behavioural frameworks influence the implementation of forced distribution and/ or FDRS?
- Is it possible to separate the measurement of performance from assessment of performance? What is the difference, and why is it important?

By way of a summary, the statistics of performance management has a wide impact on the practice and perceptions surrounding performance management and reward. Waldman (1994) echoes the experience of practitioners in declaring that there are no universal rights or wrongs but that the approach taken by any particular organisation is a compromise – a balance between:

- the business needs of the organisation and the process
- the cultural norms of the organisation (values, beliefs and attitudes) and the need to manage performance
- accuracy of information and usability of the process as a whole
- fairness and transparency – it is not possible to be both all of the time
- the needs of the organisation, the needs of the individuals, and the rights of both.

LINKING PAY TO PERFORMANCE

At the start of the chapter we established the importance of the psychological relationship between employees and organisations, and the general role of incentives within those relationships. We have looked at the processes of performance management and reward and, briefly, at the way that statistics are used within the management of both processes. We now expand this to look at the ways in which reward is linked to performance and how this affects the interrelationships of individuals and others in the organisation.

Starting with first principles, the reason for linking reward to performance is in support of the notion that incentives (financial and non-financial) are an important element of performance management – employees are more likely to improve performance if they feel that they have something to gain in the process. The extent to which reward is financial, and the ratio of performance-related reward in relation to 'regular' reward is dependent on a number of factors, including:

- the organisational business context (eg private sector, voluntary sector)
- the prevailing business conditions
- the actual business performance
- the organisational culture and remuneration policy
- external regulation.

There is a wide range of practice in this area, ranging from the highly leveraged incentive packages in financial services to the wholly non-financial incentives present in the voluntary sector, and any notion of absolute right or wrong in any individual case is a subject of considerable debate, particularly as played out in the media since the global financial crisis of 2007/8.

The key elements linking reward to performance, however, are the effect that reward has on the individual and the relationships between individuals and organisations – points made in more detail by Brockner *et al* (1986) and Parnell and Sullivan (1992).

It is too simplistic to say that merely by increasing the potential reward, performance will continue to improve, either at an individual level or at an organisational level. The reason for highlighting this point relates to stakeholder value and return on investment. It is notoriously difficult to measure the leverage factor of reward on performance as a causal link, if only because there are so many dependent variables that can affect the outcome – it is never possible to isolate the effect of reward from all of the other factors. Although this would be the ultimate prize for HRM-P, it is unlikely ever to be achieved, and for this reason HRM-P thinking can never provide an accurate enough predictive tool by which to manage the process of performance management: see Figure 12.6.

This means that there will always be an optimal return on investment for performance-related reward below which potential performance improvements have not been realised for want of improved incentives and above which the cost of incentives is not justified by the achieved improvements in performance. In the absence of reliable measurement, modelling and forecasting, the design of performance-related pay can only ever be a matter of judgement, interpretation of conditions and management of risk.

But what of non-financial, intrinsic reward and its effects on performance, and vice versa?

The terms 'non-financial' and 'intrinsic' reward cover a broad range of concepts, but for our purposes we include:

- recognition of others for discretionary effort or improvement in performance
- interest in the type of work on offer
- constructive feedback from others
- job design – how well the content of a job is matched to the interests and capabilities of the individual
- access to development or training
- access to, or opportunity to act as, a mentor.

Figure 12.6 Diminishing returns from increasing reward

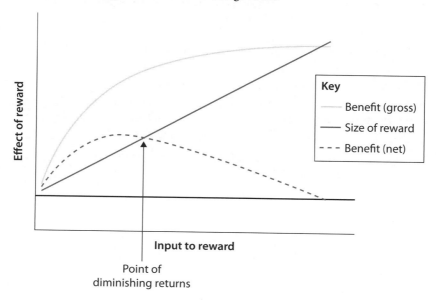

It is worth pointing out from a practical perspective that non-financial and intrinsic reward are not necessarily totally free of cost either to the organisation or the individual. At a minimum they all involve an investment in time. It is also helpful to consider the balance of intrinsic and non-financial rewards in relation to the management of performance and the cultural norms for the organisation. Returning to the purpose of reward in this context, the objective is to use reward as an incentive to performance improvement. The ideal situation for the design of any performance-related reward is to maximise the return (in performance) for the (total) investment in reward.

Thinking now about the debate between CHRM and HRM-P, we accept the absolute necessity for measures of performance and that they have a vitally important contribution to make in terms of the quality of conversations and the language used to describe good performance and how it will be recognised. This point emerges clearly from the Centrica case study below. Although the process is well established and mature, the company increasingly recognises the critical importance of the type and quality of conversations in the context of performance management. There is a role to play for CHRM in the way that performance is set up and measured.

For proponents of HRM-P, there is the recognition that although performance has an objective and numerical dimension, there is a need to accept that the way that it is managed is not just about the links between incentives, behaviours and performance. If it were that easy, everybody would be doing it! The way that performance is managed has just as much influence on the outcomes and behaviours as the hard facts and metrics that are used in setting objectives and measuring success in completing them.

It is clear that neither CHRM nor HRM-P has all of the answers in successfully managing performance. There is a healthy debate between the two opposing views, and the balance of influence between the two in any organisation is a determinant of how successful the system will be. This point is really about Organisation Development – thinking about the organisation from a systems perspective (see Chapters 1 and 4).

REFLECTIVE ACTIVITIES

To conclude this section, you may wish to reflect on non-financial and intrinsic reward in the context of the organisation(s) with which you are familiar – and in doing so, the following questions may be helpful:

- What would be the effects of removing performance-related reward?
- What quantitative (ie numerical) methods are used/could be used to show the overall effectiveness of reward as an incentive to performance improvement?
- What qualitative (ie factually informed-opinion) methods are used/could be used to show the overall effectiveness of reward as an incentive to performance improvement?
- What are the key cultural factors that determine the links between reward and performance?
- How would you construct the business case for designing job roles around the intrinsic rewards perceived by employees?

CENTRICA

Centrica is a multinational energy business headquartered in the UK, with a group turnover of nearly £22 billion and employing 34,000 people. 'Upstream' operations include oil and gas extraction and storage, power generation and energy trading. 'Downstream' activities include consumer energy supply and domestic installation and servicing.

At the core of its approach to performance management is the belief that the quality of conversations is key, and that effective performance management and reward make a real contribution to the deployment of business strategy. Over the last few years, the company has re-evaluated the approach, the process and the supporting IT systems.

Employees on personal contracts (around 20% of the workforce) participate in the annual performance cycle, a common process across all business units comprising objective-setting, development, monitoring, half-year and full-year reviews, assessment and reward.

The general approach is that employees agree around six strategically linked performance objectives with their line manager at the start of the year, forming an individual performance contract (IPC). Progress is monitored, managed and ultimately assessed in terms of performance and behaviours – performance being tracked against objectives, and behaviours against the company's Leadership Behaviour Framework:

- being one team
- creating a positive environment
- putting our customers first
- seizing responsibility
- seeing beyond our own goals.

As part of the company's investment in supporting infrastructure, the process is enabled by an online performance management system accessible by both managers and employees.

For Centrica, however, the process and supporting infrastructure are only half of the story, recognising that managing performance is really about human interactions – about honest, open and focused conversations, about responding to good leadership, and ultimately about effective feedback. This 'softer' aspect of performance as a whole system is another area in which the company has invested. The business has prioritised clear and consistent communication and has provided development to support effective conversations between managers and employees. There is a shared view that performance management has a key role to play in personal development, and for this reason a clear distinction is drawn between conversations about *performance* and *development*.

At the end of the year, managers formally review objectives and behaviours, making an overall assessment of performance that is used as feedback for planning the following year's objectives and as input to the reward process. Performance is rated as one of four possible categories:

- below expectations
- achieving expectations
- exceeding expectations
- outstanding.

Before ratings are finalised, they are subject to 'calibration' in which they are reviewed and compared across groups and business units to ensure consistency across the business. Although HR is responsible for providing guidance, senior managers are accountable for agreeing calibrated ratings for their business units. And although there is a desired distribution of performance ratings which is used for guidance, there is flexibility for business units to manage this locally, aligned to business performance.

The end-of-year reward process starts when the finalised ratings are released into the annual reward review tool (ARRT), after which performance ratings are 'locked'.

ARRT is used by managers to model and implement changes in basic pay and bonus payments. Target bonus levels are set by level within the organisation, expressed as a percentage of salary, and comprise business and individual performance metrics. This places upper limits on performance-related pay at an organisational level. The actual bonus paid is determined by the business results and the manager's assessment of the individual performance. A 'below expectations' rating would receive 0% of the personal element, working through to an 'outstanding' rating which could receive as much as 200% of the personal element. As part of the ARRT process, managers are provided with guidance and where possible market data to help them make informed reward decisions. All bonus and pay proposals are subject to sign-off by a more senior manager. This is managed through electronic 'workflow' in the ARRT that routes approval requests to approving senior managers. Although there is no corporate cap on the individual element of bonus, expenditure is managed through adherence to the performance curve. Managers are accountable for keeping within the agreed operating budget for salary increases.

Thus far, the description of performance-related pay has focused on short-term incentives. Centrica also recognise the importance of long-term incentives for a number of reasons:

- the desire to maintain the right management balance between short-term business needs and long-term business strategy

- the recognition that reward is one of the factors that supports retention of key individuals

- the belief that reward for senior individuals should be linked to long-term shareholder value

- the number of long-term elements of reward: for more senior executives, longer-term incentives are more complex and are more tailored to individual circumstances

- the nature of the business: there are relatively few roles for which the reward is subject to external regulation, although it is recognised that this may change in the future. The governance of remuneration and reward within the organisation is managed by the remuneration committee, and this is appointed by the board of directors.

In addition to its bonus and long-term incentive schemes, the company operates a variety of cash and non-cash recognition schemes, the objectives of which are to recognise good performance and extraordinary short-term discretionary effort.

Questions

1　What factors should influence the balance between short-, medium- and long-term incentives arising from performance management?

2　To what extent does sentiment in the equity markets towards an organisation influence the organisation's policy towards performance management and reward?

3　Starting in 2005, Centrica re-evaluated its approach to performance management and reward. Thinking of an organisation with which you are familiar, identify the factors that would suggest the need (or otherwise) for a similar re-evaluation.

4　In what ways has business strategy shaped the performance management process?

5　Which aspects of performance management and reward would you expect to be common to the energy industry?

6　To what extent does performance and reward influence the competitive position of an organisation (this could include competition for talent and is therefore equally applicable to public sector and third sector organisations)?

CASE STUDY COMMENTARY

Centrica has recognised that managing performance has a significant impact on its ability to deliver its business strategy. By focusing its performance management activities on those 20% of employees that have personalised contracts, the company has identified the segments in its workforce that have the most influence on shareholder value. By taking this approach, Centrica seeks to receive the highest return on its investment in performance management and reward. However, although the company has invested in the process and the infrastructure, it has not ignored the importance of communications, relationships and people interactions in the management of performance.

The study illustrates the difference in approach between performance measurement and rating and forced distribution ranking. Although expected distributions of performance are established and used for comparisons, the final performance outturn and its impact on reward are not predetermined. This is more than a procedural difference, however. The approach used by Centrica reflects the culture of the organisation and its beliefs in how performance management and reward are part of a much wider organisational system in which people, relationships, honest conversations and language play an important part in the management of shareholder value.

The performance management and reward systems are designed to provide a healthy balance between short-term targets and longer-term strategic aims. In doing this, the company has taken into account the behaviours that it seeks to espouse and has recognised the part that performance management and reward has to play in achieving these behaviours. This point reflects both the internal culture of the organisation and the way that the company wishes to position itself externally, with investors, regulators and its wider stakeholder community.

CONCLUSION

In our description and analysis of performance management and its links to reward, we have looked at the overall business rationale, the generic processes, the statistics and some of the cultural aspects of the subject. Our purpose has not been to produce the definitive 'How to' reference or to produce an academic literature review. We have looked at the evidence of how the disciplines of OD and HRM are converging and what this means for incentivised performance management in the future. For HR, we have compared, from a practitioner's perspective, views of HRM-P and CHRM and concluded that for performance management there are some similarities – but also significant differences.

Our overall conclusion is that there is no single view that adequately describes the approach, frameworks and rationale for incentivised performance management. It is a complex, many-faceted subject in which soft skills and human interrelationships have as important a part to play as hard-edged data and process. To think of managing the performance of people in a way that is somehow divorced from the performance of the organisation is irrational as is the notion that incentives, both financial and otherwise, do not affect the attitudes of employees. Clearly, the interrelationships between organisation, people, process and systems of performance form a key component of a complex system, and to ignore any part is to run the risk of not fully understanding the management of the organisation. We have seen the influence of behavioural frameworks as a way to encapsulate cultural norms of an organisation into the management of performance – as a way to influence the types of behaviours that the organisation values, believes in and espouses. But at the heart of this there is the anomaly that performance management is currently seen as a one-way process, in which employees are encouraged to address corporate goals as a 'given' – a unilateral process. Evolving theory (particularly New OE) and practice in the way that people relate to their work and the balance with their personal lives suggests that more performance value can be achieved by acknowledging and building on the much richer human relationships that exist in reality.

Part of the rationale for this argument is the fundamental sociological shifts that are taking place in the workforce, evidence of which is seen in Chapter 11 on strategic workforce planning and organisational design. As 'baby boomers' start to retire from the workforce, they are being replaced by Generation Y and 'the noughties' – generations of highly educated digital natives that have never known life without the Internet or work life without social networking and Web 2.0 technologies (Martin, Reddington and Kneafsey, 2009). For these generations, competition is fierce – and in some economies, employment opportunities are scarce. Current expectation of reaching the highest levels in organisations is low, and in our opinion this is more likely to drive allegiances towards the team/project rather than towards the wider organisation.

In this environment the nature of contracting between individuals and organisations is becoming much more complex. This is seen in the increasingly diverse formal and informal agreements made between employees, managers, other individuals and groups (examples include employment contracts, performance contracts, financial reward, assignment to projects, commitments to deadlines, personal work arrangements and intrinsic reward). Complexity is also seen in the increasingly diverse needs of organisations and in the way that they contract with the people that work for them (examples include full-time employment, fixed-term and temporary contracts, casual work, advisers and consultants, the use of shared services and outsourcing, commissioning and partnership service provision).

Taking into account the increasingly complex relationships between organisations and the people that work for them, the idea that performance management and reward is exclusively a process conducted between a line manager and a full-time employee, based around an organisational strategy and a behavioural framework, is increasingly anachronistic. This is not to argue that incentivised performance management is no longer appropriate in the contemporary business world. It is to argue, however, that a single-dimensional unilateral approach to incentivised performance management will not meet the needs of organisations in the future. The potential offered by social networking and Web 2.0 technologies in the workplace (see Chapter 8) offers opportunities to the organisations that are able most quickly to embrace them and in doing so outperform the organisations that don't – and that, as we established at the start of this chapter, is the whole point for managing performance.

EXPLORE FURTHER

Anderson, R., Sweeney, D. J. and Williams, T. A. (2002) *Statistics for Business and Economics*, 8th edition. Cincinatti, OH: South-Western/Thomson Learning. This is an introduction to the way that statistics are used within a business context. As we have argued, the statistical capabilities of HR professionals are not always strong enough to allow them to make an informed, critical analysis of the processes with which they are often confronted in the area of performance management and reward.

REFERENCES

Amaratunga, D. and Baldry, D. (2002) 'Moving from performance measurement to performance management', *Facilities*, Vol.20: 217–23.

Baron, A. and Armstrong, M. (2007) *Human Capital Management: Achieving added value through people*. London: Kogan Page.

Bernardin, H. and Beatty, R. (1984) *Performance Appraisal: Assessing human behaviour at work*. Kent HRM Series. Boston: MA: PWS.

Billikopf, G. (2003) *Performance Appraisal (Negotiated Approach)*. Berkeley, CA: University of California. Available online at: http://www.cnr.berkeley.edu/ucce50/ag-labor/7labor/06. htm [accessed 4 June 2011].

Black, H. S. (1934) 'Stabilized feed-back amplifiers', *Transactions of the American Institute of Electrical Engineers*, Vol.53, January: 114–20.

Bouskila-Yam, O. and Kluger, A. N. (2011) 'Strength-based performance appraisal and goal-setting', *Human Resource Management Review*, Vol.21: 137–47.

Broadbent, J. and Laughlin, R. (2009) 'Performance management systems: a conceptual model', *Management Accounting Research*, Vol.20: 283–95.

Brockner, J., Greenberg, J., Brockner, A., Bortz, J., Davy, J. and Carter, C. (1986) 'Layoffs, equity theory, and work performance: further evidence of the impact of survivor guilt', *Academy of Management Journal*, Vol.29: 373–84.

Brown, T. C. and Warren, A. M. (2011) 'Performance management in unionized settings', *Human Resource Management Review*, Vol.21: 96–106.

Brutus, S. (2010) 'Words versus numbers: a theoretical exploration of giving and receiving narrative comments in performance appraisal', *Human Resource Management Review*, Vol.20: 144–57.

Busco, C., Giovannoni, E. and Scapens, R. W. (2008) 'Managing the tensions in integrating global organizations: the role of performance management systems', *Management Accounting Research*, Vol.19: 103–25.

Business In the Community (2009) *The Whys and Hows of Corporate Values*. Available online at: http://www.bitc.org.uk/resources/publications/corporate_values.html [accessed 3 June 2011].

Collins, J. C. and Porras, J. I. (1994) *Built to Last: Successful habits of visionary companies*. New York: HarperBusiness,

De Waal, A. A. (2003) 'Behavioural factors important for the successful implementation and use of performance management systems', *Management Decision*, Vol.41: 688–97.

Ferreira, A. and Otley, D. (2009) 'The design and use of performance management systems: an extended framework for analysis', *Management Accounting Research*, Vol.20: 263–82.

Flapper, S. D., Fortuin, L. and Stoop, P. P. (1996) 'Towards consistent performance management systems', *International Journal of Operations and Production Management*, Vol.16: 27–37.

Francis, H. and Reddington, M. (2010) 'Redirecting and Reconnecting Theory – Employer branding and the employment deal'. Paper for the BSA Work, Employment and Society Conference 2010: Managing Uncertainty: A new deal? Brighton, September.

Furnham, A. (2005) *The Psychology of Behaviour at Work*. Hove: Psychology Press.

Furnham, A. (2008) *Management Intelligence*. Basingstoke: Palgrave Macmillan.

Golden, M. (2011) 'The nature, implementation and impact of Human Resource practices in London borough councils'. Unpublished PhD thesis, Kings College, London.

Gruman, J. A. and Saks, A. M. (2011) 'Performance management and employee engagement', *Human Resource Management Review*, Vol.21: 123–36.

Guest, D. (2011) 'Human resource management and performance: still searching for some answers', *Human Resource Management Journal*, Vol.21, Issue 1: 3–13.

Guest, D. and Conway, N. (2011) 'The impact of HR practices, HR effectiveness and a "strong HR system" on organisational outcomes: a stakeholder perspective', *International Journal of Human Resource Management*, Vol.22, Issue 8, April: 1686–1702.

Helm, C., Holladay, C. and Tortorella, F. (2007) 'The performance management system: applying and evaluating a pay-for-performance initiative', *Journal of Healthcare Management*, Vol.52, Issue 1, Jan–Feb: 49–62.

Hope, J. and Fraser, R. (2003), 'New ways of setting rewards: The beyond budgeting model', *California Management Review*, Vol.45, Issue 4, Summer, 104–19.

Ilgen, D. and Pulakos, E. (eds) (1999) *The Changing Nature of Performance: Implications for staffing motivation and development*. San Francisco: Jossey-Bass.

Johnson, G. (2004) 'The good, the bad, and the alternative', *Training*, Vol.41, Issue 5, May: 24–34.

London, M. and Smither, J. W. (2002) 'Feedback orientation, feedback culture, and the longitudinal performance management process', *Human Resource Management Review*, Vol.12: 81–100.

McKenna, S., Richardson, J. and Manroop, L. (2011) 'Alternative paradigms and the study and practice of performance management and evaluation', *Human Resource Management Review*, Vol.21: 148–57.

Martin, G., Reddington, M. and Kneafsey, M. B. (2009) *Web 2.0 and Human Resources Management: Groundswell or hype?* Research Report. London: CIPD.

Micheli, P. and Neely, A. (2010) 'Performance measurement in the public sector in England: searching for the golden thread', *Public Administration Review*, Vol.70, Issue 4, July–Aug: 591–600.

Murphy, K. and Cleveland, J. (1995) *Understanding Performance Appraisal: Social, organisational and goal-based perspectives.* London: Sage.

Otley, D. (1999) 'Performance management: a framework for management control systems research', *Management Accounting Research*, Vol.10: 363–82.

Parnell, J. A. and Sullivan, S. E. (1992) 'When money isn't enough: the effect of equity sensitivity on performance-based pay systems', *Human Resource Management Review*, Vol.2: 143–55.

Purcell, J. and Hutchinson, S. (2007) 'Front-line managers as agents in the HRM-performance causal chain: theory, analysis and evidence', *Human Resource Management Journal*, Vol.17, Issue 1: 3–20.

Purcell, J., Kinnie, K., Swart, J., Rayton, B. and Hutchinson, S. (2003) *People and Performance: How people management impacts on organisational performance.* London: CIPD.

Rich, B. L., Lepine, J. A. and Crawford, E. R. (2010) 'Job engagement: antecedents and effects on job performance', *Academy of Management Journal*, Vol.53, Issue 3, June: 617–35.

Taylor, M. S., Renard, M. K. and Tracy, K. B. (1998) 'Manager's reactions to procedurally just performance management systems', *Academy of Management Journal*, Vol.41: 568–79.

Townley, B, 2004, 'Managerial technologies, ethics and managing', *Journal of Management Studies*, Vol.41, No. 3, May.

Valentin, C. (2006) 'Researching human resource development: emergence of a critical approach to HRD enquiry', *International Journal of Training and Development*, Vol.10, Issue 1, March: 17–29.

Vittorio Chiesa, V., Frattini, F., Lazzarotti, V. and Manzini, R. (2009) 'Performance measurement in R&D – exploring the interplay between measurement objectives, dimensions of performance and contextual factors', *R&D Management*, Vol.39, Issue 5, Nov: 487–519.

Waldman, D. A. (1994) 'Designing performance management systems for total quality implementation', *Journal of Organisational Change Management*, Vol.7: 31–44.

CHAPTER 13

Inclusive Talent Management and Diversity

Eddie Blass and Gillian Maxwell

CHAPTER OVERVIEW

This chapter explores the concept of talent management and how inclusive talent management contributes in a practical way to the OD agenda. Talent management can act as a pivotal foundation point for OD activity because essentially it is about the recruitment, development and retention of the future leaders and employees in the organisation. The chapter looks at the early development of talent management as a means of creating an exclusive cadre of 'HiPos' (high-performance high-potential employees) within the organisation, and more recent examples of organisations that are actively using talent management to increase diversity and inclusion. The chapter demonstrates how talent management can be used as a driver of change and can embed OD activity within the business, bringing HR and line managers together to work as business partners. The short case study material within the chapter has been developed from a talent management research project carried out by Ashridge and the Chartered Management Institute. The longer case study – of the BBC – in this chapter has been developed through empirical work especially for the chapter.

LEARNING OBJECTIVES

By the end of this chapter the reader should be able to:

- appreciate the nature of, and differences between, talent management as an exclusive policy and as an inclusive policy in organisations
- understand the role of diversity in talent management and note the alignment of talent management with OD strategy
- analyse the differential roles of HR managers, HRD specialists and line managers in the implementation of talent management
- describe the contribution of talent management and diversity policy and practice to the achievement of New OE.

INTRODUCTION: DEFINING TALENT MANAGEMENT

The McKinsey Consultancy organisation published a paper in 1998 which declared 'the war for talent' (Chambers *et al*, 1998), and since that time the concept of talent management has become commonplace in organisations. That is not to say that organisations did not undertake activities that might be construed as talent management prior to 1998 – they simply were not labelled as such at the time. Some claim that every talent management process in use today was developed half a century ago (Cappelli, 2008) and so there is nothing new in the idea – which may be the case – but it is the bringing together of the activities and processes with a specific focus that may not have been around for so long, and it is this combining of practices with intent that distinguishes talent management from other practices within OD. Chapter 11 discusses how workforce planning can be applied across the whole of the organisation, whereas talent management is applied to a specific segment of the workforce at a particular point in time, which is why it is less widespread in application.

Talent management can be perceived as including a number of activities. Lewis and Heckman (2006) reviewed the available literature base at that time and identified three different strands:

- a collection of typical HR department practices and functions such as recruitment, development, etc
- activity focused around the concept of talent pools, which consist of people identified for a particular purpose – usually the future leadership of the organisation
- a wider, more generic approach to managing talent throughout the whole organisation.

It does not really matter which strand an organisation falls within – the point is that they are doing something different for a group of people at a particular point in time that they are recognising as 'talent', however that may be defined. This is an important point to note. The definition of who is and who is not 'talent' can and should change, as the organisation develops and as the markets in which it operates change. Talent should not therefore be a permanent label in an organisation but something that everyone has the opportunity to be considered for at an appropriate time in both their career and the organisation's development.

Defining talent in such a way ensures that neither the organisation nor the individual holds the balance of power in the relationship between them. Most of the anecdotal literature on 'how to do' talent management describes it as a process that is *done to* employees, ignoring any issues around employee agency (see, for example, Branham, 2005, or Friedman, 2006). In reality, early adopters of talent management programmes have found the opposite to be true: the individuals who are identified as 'talent' develop an invincibility about them and believe that they irreplaceable (Mellahi and Collings, 2010). If individuals were to believe that once they were talent they would always be talent, and the future of the organisation depended on them, then they would be dominating the psychological contract. And if the organisation believed that the talent would never leave the organisation because no other organisation could offer them as bright a future, then it would be paying no attention to the employee value proposition (see Chapter 12). It is creating the right balance between organisational structures and individual agency that underpins talent management's contribution to developing organisational effectiveness, rather than talent management becoming an exclusive activity for an elite cadre only.

EARLY HISTORY: TALENT MANAGEMENT AS AN EXCLUSIVE ACTIVITY

The idea behind 'the war for talent' was that organisational success in the future would be dependent on the calibre of the top leadership team, and that there was not and would not be enough good leadership potential about in the labour market to go round.

Organisations would thus need to literally 'fight' to both attract and to keep hold of their talented employees (Cappelli, 2000). There is a logic to this argument. The Western world has a shrinking population, and the growth of the so called 'knowledge economy' means that more and more people are employed to do white-collar, intellectually challenging jobs rather than traditional blue-collar manual jobs. So it is easy to conclude that there are not going to be enough 'good' people to go round (Frank and Taylor, 2004).

The difficulty with this argument is that it is based on the assumption that only some people are 'good' people. If you believe in the exclusive approach to talent, you believe that some people are 'talent' and the rest are not. This makes the concept of talent management very divisive in organisations because the implication is that you either 'have talent' or 'are talentless'.

Needless to say, lots of organisations could then undertake their talent management activities secretly because they were worried that people would leave if they found out that they were not being considered to be 'talent'. The number one problem that most organisations were dealing with was whether or not to tell people they were considered to be in the talent pool. Many early talent management processes arguably lacked transparency, and organisations therefore struggled to see the benefit of engaging in the process. It was very difficult to prove any contribution to the bottom line or any return on investment when you could not get information from people because they did not know they were being counted.

MILLS & REEVE, LAWYERS

CASE STUDY

One organisation to buck this trend was a large legal firm based in Cambridge. They decided that they would be honest with their employees who were hoping to be made partners of the firm. Achieving partnership depended on a number of factors including an ability to bring in new business and the expansion of their specialist element of the firm (or the death of another partner). The partners decided that it was only fair to let those people know who were hanging around hoping for partnership status whether or not they were likely to get it. The risk was that those people who they said 'no' to would leave. They decided that this was only fair because those people should have the opportunity of trying to obtain a partnership elsewhere – so they took the risk. In actuality, there was no immediate surge of departures. When they told some of their excellent, senior lawyers that they would not be considered for partnership, they were on the whole relieved. They said that they could now stop trying to succeed in the areas they were not good at – such as bringing in new business – and just be very good lawyers. Their stress was reduced, their work–life balance improved, and they remained with the firm as highly committed members of staff.

THE ISSUE OF TRANSPARENCY

Mills & Reeve were an early adopter of a transparent approach to talent management, even though they were applying it in an exclusive manner. They were giving people feedback on whether they were considered to be 'talent' when talent was being defined in a very exclusive manner – that of the top echelon of the organisation, the partnership. What their case shows is that even if you are adopting an exclusive approach, it still pays to be honest with people and transparent.

Organisations that still struggle with transparency are doing so because they are not being honest with their staff. There is absolutely no point at all in operating a talent management system without being transparent about it. The whole purpose of the process is to attract and retain good people for your organisation. If you do not tell people that you consider them to be good, how are they going to know? If you're trying desperately hard to keep certain people in the organisation but do not tell them that that is the case, they will more than likely leave you. Equally, if someone really wants to be considered 'talent' and you do not think they are, they should be given the opportunity to go somewhere else where they may be considered talent. If you are that worried about losing them, perhaps they are talent after all.

Permanency undermines transparency

The principal reason that transparency is ever an issue is if the people who are driving the talent management process consider the label of 'talent' to be permanent. When talent management was first promoted by McKinsey's, the idea was that there was not enough talent to go round, so organisations had to compete to find and keep talent within them (Chambers *et al*, 1998). (Chapter 2 discusses wider organisational contexts.) This implies that talent resides permanently within certain individuals and only they are worth concentrating on. It implies that talent is innate – or born – and not constructed or developed, and goes against the principles of development and education that underpin a civilised society. It is almost, in a metaphorical sense, monarchic in its approach: one is born a prince/princess and will become a monarch. Although this may be the case to some extent in that people with, say, predisposed leadership ability may become CEOs, it is not necessarily the case for all or for people with different predisposed abilities.

REFLECTIVE ACTIVITIES

If work-related talent is more innate than developed, an individual's future in the workplace may be largely predetermined.

- To what extent do you agree with this assertion?
- How much power does an individual have over influencing how talented they are and their future in work?
- Reflect on the issues raised in Chapter 9, and on where power lies in both organisations and society.

By suggesting that talent is limited to a few privileged people, organisations found that they were developing a small pool of individuals who could be elitist and arrogant. After all, when people are put on a pedestal, there is possibly only one way to go – and that is down. By identifying people as 'talent' early in their career and then assuming that label would remain with them throughout the rest of their career, organisations ensured that those who were presumed less able *became* less able, by not affording them the same development opportunities that the supposed talents received (Morton, Ashton and Bellis, 2005).

Moving away from an exclusive approach is going to be difficult for some organisations because it has sustained a top management team in a certain image for a very long period of time, propped up by an HR system designed to support this tradition. Even the public sector is struggling with this, for example, in its Teach First initiative (Smart *et al*, 2009). Some organisations undertake their annual graduate recruitment process by holding recruitment fairs at the Russell Group universities (the older universities in the UK that are considered to be the best by many and that tend to take the top places in the university rankings). They tend to recruit first-class and upper-second-class honours degree students from these universities, on the premise that academic achievement is a predictor of job performance. These students are disproportionately likely to be white, middle-class students who may have had private school education, as compared to the average student across the whole university sector (Harrington, 2010). But is this a sound way to detect talent? It is certainly likely to be an indicator of above-average intelligence, although it is questionable that this alone constitutes talent. Such students are less likely to have experienced failure in their lives, significant injustice, or personal sacrifice. They have probably had the sort of childhood that most of us would want our children to have – but does this place them in good stead to be talent in today's global organisations? It raises questions about what is driving these individuals to succeed other than greed and comfort, and if those are the drivers and life experiences wanted at the top of global organisations in the future. It also arguably calls for a wider interpretation of 'talent' away from being a permanent fixture for individuals.

Removing permanency from the definition

Most organisations have some sort of talent identification process which is based around current performance and perceived potential for the future. Many utilise what is known as a nine-box matrix, with performance on one axis and potential on the other (Coyne, 2008): see Figure 13.1. The bottom left of the matrix shows poor performance and low potential, and the top right-hand box shows high performance and high potential – from which is derived the abbreviated term HiPo.

Graduate recruitment schemes generally tend to seek out those people that the organisation thinks will be in the top right-hand box at the beginning of their career. They come in on a 'fast-track' scheme and are offered opportunities and promoted in a manner exclusive to those who entered the organisation on this basis.

Other organisations link their talent identification process with their performance management process and complete the nine-box matrix as part of the annual performance review cycle. How well the matrix works for the organisation depends on how the organisation defines 'potential' and 'performance'.

Figure 13.1 A typical nine-box talent identification matrix

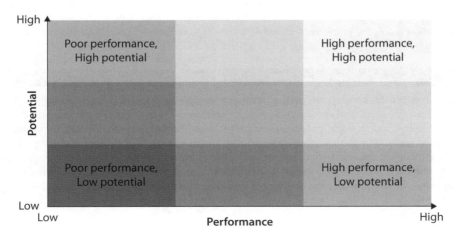

A GERMAN PHARMACEUTICAL ORGANISATION

In the pharmaceutical industry, most staff are highly skilled and highly educated when they join a company, having a minimum of a science degree; many also have postgraduate and doctoral qualifications. On paper, they all have tremendous potential to excel in their job areas and to take the German organisation forward in a number of ways. Considerable effort is therefore spent by the organisation in assessing their performance and potential. The first consideration is that their performance must be reasonably good – they must satisfactorily perform their role at least to an expected level, preferably beyond expectations, and perhaps even far exceeding expectations (corresponding to the three boxes left to right along the bottom of the matrix in Figure 13.1).

As for potential, the company's requirements are that employees must show the potential to progress in their current role, must exhibit a readiness to be promoted up one level, or at best, display qualities that suggest promotion up by two levels.

If senior management feel that someone is exceeding all expectations in current performance and could cope with a job two levels up from where they are, they then make it to the HiPo (top right-hand) corner of the matrix grid. What happens after that? They are given additional training and opportunities and are generally promoted during the next year. At their next performance review it would be regarded as exceedingly unlikely, however, that they would after such promotion remain in the top right-hand corner. Individuals thus enter and leave the HiPo box as part of the annual cycle, and there is no shame attached in not remaining in the top right-hand corner – indeed, it is expected that no one will remain there for long.

Once any notion of permanency is removed from the talent management process, the issue of transparency becomes resolved as the fear of not being labelled 'talent' is not a permanent one and can be addressed through development plans and discussions with HR and line managers. In a context of genuine transparency talent is no longer an exclusive domain and a more inclusive approach can begin to be adopted. This can start to redress any power imbalances that may arise if an employee feels that he or she is too talented for the organisation to lose, or if the organisation feels it does not have to address individual issues for employees on how they are feeling both in and about their work (see Chapter 16).

AN INCLUSIVE APPROACH TO TALENT MANAGEMENT

The fundamental assumption behind an inclusive approach to talent management is that talent is developed, and so everyone in the organisation has the potential to be included in the talent pool at some point in their career should they meet the specific talent needs of the organisation at that point in time. Time becomes much more of a defining factor in an inclusive approach than in an exclusive approach. With an exclusive approach, someone is born 'talent' and remains 'talent' for the whole of their career. With an inclusive approach, different people are considered to be 'talent' at different points in time according to the needs of the organisation. The inclusive approach recognises that the needs of the organisation will change over time, and therefore the definition of talent will also change over time.

An inclusive approach to talent management additionally allows for multiple talent pools to be considered simultaneously, rather than all the focus going on HiPos as future leaders.

This enables the organisation to develop pools of specialist expertise at different levels and within different job roles, and can specifically contribute to strategic workforce planning and organisational design (see Chapter 10).

B&Q RETAIL PROVISION

CASE STUDY

Retail providers operate numerous talent pools at different levels in the organisation. They also need to differentiate between in-store talent pools and head-office talent pools. One of the issues they all struggle with is the transition between the stores and head office. In their stores, B&Q offer an inclusive approach to talent management allowing everyone to put themselves forward to be considered for their talent pool. Once accepted into the pool, the employees are moved around stores and promoted into 'acting' roles to ensure that they can succeed and perform at the higher level required in a store that is not the one they normally work in. If they are successful, they receive a permanent promotion. If not, they can return to their previous job role in their original store without any loss of status. This provides a safe environment in which people can push themselves outside of their comfort zone, knowing that there is a safety net if they find they don't like the additional responsibility in their new role.

In order to facilitate an inclusive approach, the organisation's culture (see Chapter 5) must be supportive of people moving into new job roles. Colleagues must endeavour to support new members of staff rather than leaving them to perform well or otherwise through their own efforts. Such a workplace culture would be one in which people look out for one another and help each other – for example, in avoiding mistakes by offering information and knowledge or being responsive to questions, rather than watching people struggle or fail without positive intervention.

DIVERSITY IN TALENT MANAGEMENT

However talent management is defined or approached, it is about selection – so potentially, at least, it is also about discrimination. Even an inclusive approach is about discriminating within a group of people because the aim is to find and develop the best talent for the organisation's needs at that point in time and affording the talent an additional opportunity not open to others. But this does not mean that it has to be negative discrimination, for a number of reasons, as set out below.

Firstly, an inclusive approach to talent management is founded on principles of equality of opportunity that are particularly notable in Western countries. It may be that not everyone should be considered 'talent', but everyone should have the same opportunity to be considered for inclusion in the talent pool (Ng and Burke, 2005). By assuming that talent is nurtured rather than a result of nature, everyone should be considered from an equal base point, and it is then ambition, experience, a specifically developed expertise and so forth that will determine whether someone is included in the talent pool at any particular point in time. When someone is not included, they should be given feedback and support to develop to a position in which they may be reconsidered the next time.

Secondly, many organisations are engaging in talent management to ensure their competitiveness and to address any talent shortfalls (Cooke, 2011). In the increasingly global market that organisations find themselves operating in, there is an even greater need for diverse representation at the top decision-making levels than there ever has been before.

Although we may not know what the future board of directors will be facing, we can be pretty sure that it is not going to be the same in 10 years' time as it is now. Many boards of directors currently comprise white middle-aged, middle-class men – not the profile necessary for a globally successful organisation. The promotion of a diverse talent pool should thus be a key priority for organisations (Tucker *et al*, 2005).

Thirdly, some organisations are using their talent management process as a means to manage change and thereby address a lack of diversity through positive discrimination. Internationalisation, for example, can bring about a greater need for internal diversity and organisational change (McKenna and Beech, 2008). By targeting specific groups within the workforce on the basis of gender, ethnicity, disability or some other categorisation, the organisation can furnish additional support and opportunity to this talent pool to redress imbalances that may have arisen through historical organisational practice.

THE PROBATION SERVICE

The Probation Service is part of the Ministry of Justice and employs approximately 21,000 people. It offers a positive action programme to encourage the progress of disabled and ethnic minority staff into senior management positions because they are grossly under-represented at this level. The programme is called Accelerate and lasts two years; entry on to the programme is by assessment centre. The programme offers a range of skills and competency training, but above all creates a supportive network within which the participants can share their stories and experiences. As a result, the participants have developed a new, positive language in the workplace which shifts them away from being 'victims' within the organisation to being drivers of change.

The case studies thus far have specifically highlighted individual elements of the talent management process and how these interact with HR or OD practice. In the BBC case study below we show how BBC Scotland has adopted an organisation-wide talent management approach that is meeting the needs of the organisation for the future while increasing diversity within the organisation as a whole. A number of questions and tasks are posed after the case study to engage you with the subject and to help you reflect and develop your own learning and practice by considering the issues that arise from it.

TALENT MANAGEMENT AND DIVERSITY AT THE BBC

The BBC – the British Broadcasting Corporation – is a UK-based worldwide broadcasting organisation of high standing. The talent of all employees is essential to organisational effectiveness across the entire organisation. The inclusivity of talent is reflected on its website. In 2009/10 they report, for example, on the total amount spent on 'talent', on their executive producer policy of commissioning talent, and on their numerous talent schemes and awards. The central role of developing people's talent in order to develop the Corporation itself is clearly expressed in the *BBC People Strategic Goals, 2010–2016* (BBC People Strategy presentation, 2010):

● We will develop our people so that they continue to be at the forefront of media excellence and [so that] the BBC is an exemplar of value in public service.

CASE STUDY

- We will encourage, challenge, and support our people to reach their potential, stretch their performance and deliver outstanding results for our audiences.

Developing performance and potential (DPP) is a formal talent strategy and annual appraisal process in the BBC. Performance is rated in nine well-defined categories ranging from 'unsatisfactory performer' to 'star performer'. A star performer, for example, consistently exceeds expectations in delivering results and leadership behaviour. Similarly, potential is well defined. It centres on characteristics around capability, adaptability and motivation, which make it likely that an individual can take on a more senior or more complex role with a high degree of predictable success.

Opportunities for developing performance and potential within the formal DPP strategy and process at an individual level are 'well resourced', explains an HR business partner at BBC Scotland. For instance, people are encouraged to take responsibility for their own development, which is an expression of the importance of self-initiated development. The Head of Radio Sport at BBC Scotland did this recently through his own initiative in shadowing a senior national sports coach, as part of his personal development. This positive experience has resulted in his initiating an approach to talent management of 'working on the basis that each person has a level of responsibility – we develop their skills and decision-making ability in order to produce better programme output'.

Other development opportunities are initiated by the BBC. The Corporation is very much aware that black, ethnic minority, and disabled staff are currently under-represented at senior management and higher grades. As a result, the Mentoring and Development Programme (MDP) aims to increase diversity at senior management level across the BBC, as does its engagement in the Diversity 2010 programme run in conjunction with Channel 4. More than half of the places on the scheme are reserved for black, ethnic

minority, and disabled staff. Successful applicants are appointed a senior mentor, one of whom could be the Director-General of the BBC.

Located in an iconic new building in Glasgow, BBC Scotland is one of many divisions of the Corporation. Sitting on the executive board in BBC Scotland, alongside the Heads of News and Current Affairs, Programmes, Radio, Strategy, and Human Resources is the Head of Talent and Operations. As noted by the Head of Talent and Operations, 'the importance of talent management is much more in everyone's vocabulary now, although it's been a phrase that's been about for the last 10 years'. He sets out a clear rationale for the corporation 'committing' to talent management:

Our products – whether online, television or radio – are only as good as our production and craft people making them, so my job is to ensure that we have the best people across a range of projects ensuring that we deliver value for the licence fee which is paid for by the public. My role and that of the talent management team is to take a holistic view of the totality of our people and, fundamentally, exploit their talent as effectively as possible.

With nine talent managers across different genres like news or drama being responsible for around 600 people, the focus and scale of the responsibility for developing and delivering high-quality performance products is clear. The talent managers are all experienced in programme making, so they are in effect line managers who proactively contribute to the BBC's organisational effectiveness. The Head of Talent and Operations sums up his responsibility as 'getting the right people, with the right skills, in the right project at the right time and at the right cost, with equality of opportunity, fairness in selection, and parity in reward'. A broad view of talent and diversity is reflected in this summary. Expanding on the link between talent, equality, and diversity, for example, a reporter who joined BBC Scotland under a disability scheme before securing a permanent contract states that 'good talent managers understand talent *and* diversity'. For this employee, a hallmark of success in talent and diversity management, building on the evident progress to date, would be the BBC's output portraying people with a greater range of diversity factors than at present.

Despite its progress in embedding talent management into the strategy, structure, processes, and programme-making at the BBC, further improvements can be made in response to four main current challenges recognised by an HR business partner. One is 'driving the quality of managers' feedback conversations' in formal appraisals and informal discussions with their staff so that they receive the feedback they seek on their performance. Another is achieving more active management of talent in encouraging managers to 'always be thinking about questions such as "Am I getting the best from X?" and "Who could succeed Y in their job?"' A third is achieving more transparency in 'calibrating' assessments of individuals across the various managers they may work for and in getting managers to let their staff know their overall rating in the nine performance categories that they record in their formal appraisals. Last is the challenge of removing some permanency around specific appointments and, consequently, permanency in performance ratings. Having less permanency would lead to more movement across roles, so a 'star performer' in one role may for example become a 'rising star' in another.

For the reporter, a key challenge – indeed, a priority – in further improving diversity in the BBC is changing the attitude of some middle managers towards greater support for diversity. This could be achieved by their recognition of the full potential of people who can do the job, or of people who could be developed to do the job, including people with a disability.

In rising to these challenges, organisational effectiveness may be further enhanced through talent management and diversity. Essentially, employee creativity is at the heart of the BBC's competitive advantage. Continuously developing talent management, in concert with increasing diversity in recruiting and developing people with different backgrounds, experiences and characteristics, is a significant contribution to creativity.

Questions

1 The BBC People Strategy presentation 2010 does not specifically mention talent management. How is talent management implied within the strategy?

2 Is the BBC adopting an inclusive or exclusive approach to talent management? Find examples within the case study to support your answer.

3 How can individual employees contribute to the development of their talent in the BBC?

4 The BBC is working with Channel 4 in the Diversity 2010 initiative. Why is it appropriate for organisations to work with others for OD purposes?

Group tasks

1 The BBC uses capability, adaptability and motivation to assess potential. How would you assess/measure these three characteristics?

2 Why does the BBC want to increase diversity among its management team? (Try to discuss several reasons.) Why might the team have developed with a narrow representation of the population? (Try to discuss several reasons.)

Hopefully these questions and tasks demonstrate to you that there is no single right answer to questions around talent management and diversity. Every organisation is unique and the process it designs must meet its specific needs. Evaluating the process, however, is vitally important – otherwise, you will never know if talent management is succeeding or not. Measures of success do not need to be return-on-investment measures against the bottom line: they may include increased employee engagement and satisfaction, increased innovation and creativity, or other factors that impact indirectly on the bottom line.

Talent management is implied in the people strategy through the commitment to support the BBC's people to reach their potential and stretch their performance. This is typical talent management language in that it is referring to developing people to their limit. The BBC takes an inclusive approach because its strategy does not differentiate between any groups of employees and implies that the process is open to everyone. This is evidenced by the people strategy, the use of DPP at the annual appraisal cycle, the importance of the role of Head of Talent and Operations within the organisation, and the specific addressing of diversity issues to ensure that they are not perpetuated but genuinely addressed within the organisation.

Individual employees can contribute to their own talent management development by being proactive in their discussions with their talent manager. Using feedback from their annual appraisals, they can also use their initiative to seek new opportunities to develop their performance and potential. The Head of Radio Sport illustration in the case study is one example of this initiative.

When organisations work with other organisations in OD, it can increase the rate of learning and enhance the quality of learning, thus building OD effectively. More, it can lend internal and external credibility to initiatives, setting new forms and standards of leading practice. Sharing initiatives on diversity can provide useful examples across many organisations, encouraging a greater uptake of diversity initiatives.

Assessing and measuring potential is very often difficult. Capability could be a measure of current performance, or a measure of competence in certain key skills, or successful experience in a number of job roles or functions. Adaptability is an individual's ability to cope with different roles, contexts and opportunities, while motivation is an individual's desire to do so. Other indicators of potential might include learning agility to consider how quickly an individual employee can learn in a new context or job role.

The BBC senior management team may have developed across a relatively narrow stratum of the workforce population because of the history of the organisation, the fact that it is located in Glasgow, the culture of the organisation, and the previous HR policies and practices sustaining rather than challenging organisational norms. The organisation may want to increase diversity so that it is representative of the total workforce population, it is representative of the wider public audience, it increases creativity and innovation by bringing new experiences and voices to the table, and it can help change the culture and, ultimately, performance of the organisation.

ALIGNING THE TALENT MANAGEMENT APPROACH WITH THE OD STRATEGY

The key to any successful talent management initiative is being very clear about what it is you are trying to achieve. Blass (2007) outlines a number of strategic approaches to talent management, each impacting on the operationalisation of HRM and HRD. The six strategic perspectives identified are:

- *the HR planning perspective* – This is similar to succession planning in that the talent management programme is aiming to ensure that the organisation has the right people in the right place at the right time to ensure continuity in organisational performance. It can combine an inclusive and exclusive approach
- *the process perspective* – This can look very similar to the HR planning approach in practice, but the aim is to ensure that the organisation has the right process in place to ensure sustainability and development in the organisation. It is therefore focused on how the process occurs rather than on the outcome of the process *per se*, and has to be either exclusive or inclusive in its approach
- *the developmental perspective* – Here the aim is to ensure that those regarded as the future talent high potentials are developed at an accelerated route through the organisation in an effort to secure them as the future leaders of the organisation. This tends to be an exclusive approach
- *the competitive perspective* – Here the aim is keep your top talent away from the competition, and it tends to be seen most in the service industries that are highly dependent on individual account managers, such as consulting, PR and advertising. This is a highly exclusive approach and is driven by what others are doing rather than what the organisation wants to do
- *the cultural perspective* – This is where talent management has become so embedded in the organisation's development that it is seen as part of everyday activity and is seamlessly integrated into HRM and HRD practice. It tends to be a more inclusive approach, although it can occur in exclusive organisations, but it is not a starting point strategy for an organisation but rather a strategic aim for organisations in the long term
- *the change management perspective* – This is where talent management is being used to deliberately bring about change in the organisation, introducing mavericks into the organisation and aiming to shift the culture and working practices that persist in the organisation. It is an exclusive approach to talent management and is not intended to be sustainable in the longer term.

The impact of each of these strategic perspectives on HRM practice is outlined in Table 13.1.

ROLES AND RESPONSIBILITIES IN TALENT MANAGEMENT

There are a number of key players in the talent management system, all of whom can make or break the activity. Senior managers have to lead and support the work of both HRM/HRD and line managers in operationalising the system, and this support has to be visible. It can include making themselves available for career conversations with HiPos, mentoring people who are two or three levels below them, and continually reinforcing the talent culture the organisation is trying to develop when they deliver cross-organisation communications. For talent management to become embedded in developing New OE it must become part of the organisation's culture (again, see Chapter 4).

The role of HRM

Although talent management can shape the entirety of an HRM function and HR specialists may be the key players in setting up an organisation's talent management system, the role of HRM in the implementation of talent management is often one of support (Maxwell

Table 13.1 Differences in the operationalisation of HRM according to talent management perspective

Perspective	Core belief	Recruitment & selection	Retention	Reward	Succession planning	Development approach
Process	Include all processes to optimise people	Competence-based consistent approach	Good on processes such as WLB and intrinsic factors that make people feel they belong	Calculated according to performance review and some element of potential	Routine review process based on performance review cycle	PDPs and development reviews as part of performance management. Maybe some individual interventions
Cultural	Belief that talent is needed for success	Look for raw talent. Allow introductions from in-house	Allow people the freedom to demonstrate their talent, and to succeed and fail	Flexible package according to individual needs	Develop in-house if possible – if not, look outside	Individuals negotiate their own development paths. Coaching and mentoring are standard
Competitive	Keep talent away from the competition	Pay the best so you attract the best. Poach the best from the competition	Good people like to work with good people. Aim to be an employer of choice.	Offer more than the competition. If people leave, it will not be for a better reward package	Geared towards retention – letting people know what their target jobs are	Both planned and opportunist approaches adopted. Mentors are used to build loyalty
Developmental	Accelerate the development of high potentials	Ideally, only recruit at entry point and then develop	Clear development paths and schemes to lock high potentials into career paths	Increments based on development as well as performance	Identified groups will be being developed for each level of the organisation	Both planned and opportunist
HR planning	Right people in the right jobs at the right time	Target areas of shortfall across the company. Numbers and quotas approach	Turnover expected, monitored and accounted for in plans	Clear salary scales and structures	Detailed in-house mappings for individuals	Planned in cycles according to business needs
Change management	Use talent management to instigate change in the organisation	Seek out mavericks and change agents to join the organisation	Projects and assignments keep change agents, but turnover of mainstay staff can occur	Some results bonus on top of standard scales and structures	Can be a bit opportunist initially until change is embedded	Change agents develop others who align with them and become the next generation of talent

Source: Blass, Brockoff and Oliveira (2009)

and MacLean, 2008). Having put in place the performance management process and monitoring processes to ensure that equality of opportunity is being afforded to employees, the role of HRM generally becomes one of supporting line managers and offering guidance and support to both line managers and the individuals they are identifying as talent. It is vital that the HR team offer a consistent message throughout the organisation and support the line managers in promoting diversity. If this role is not performed well, the system may become fragmented and individuals will feel they are not being treated fairly, leading to an increase in staff turnover and a drop in talent retention rates (Frank and Taylor, 2004).

There is also a key role for HRM to play in monitoring and recording the outcomes and activities occurring within the talent management process – otherwise, much of the potential return on investment may be wasted (Tansley *et al*, 2006). Technology – in particular, ICT – can be used both as a means of capturing activity that is taking place and also as a means of facilitating activity itself (see Chapter 8). Opportunities can be posted on electronic noticeboards to ensure that they can be seen by the whole workforce, chat rooms and social networking can be used as means of sharing experiences in projects or job roles, and sophisticated database packages can help record individuals' development and experiences so that they can be highlighted as potential applicants for future opportunities when the need for their particular skills mix arises.

THE MALMAISON HOTEL GROUP

CASE STUDY

One mechanism for assessing, developing and tracking talent is an online tool called the Talent Toolbox. It was first developed and implemented in 2008 for management staff, and proved so useful that it has since been extended to all staff.

Talent Toolbox has various uses including a six-monthly online appraisal, a career review process, a personal development plan, a training needs analysis report and a succession planning element that gives the company data on its whole workforce and helps gauge staff engagement. The Talent Toolbox has also enabled Malmaison to construct a fairly simple 'talent bank' which helps identify high-performing high-potential managers. Completed by line managers, it shows the aggregate average performance ranking of the company's 500 managers as well as their potential (low, medium or high) and the anticipated risk of their leaving. This process has helped the company discover 'hidden' talent.

The role of HRD

The role of HRD depends very much on which strategic approach the organisation chooses to follow, both with regard to talent management and more generally (see Chapter 3) and, indeed, on the strategic approach of HRD itself (Pilbeam and Corbridge, 2010). HRD may be focusing on developing accelerated routes which ensure that everyone has a similar experience but at differing paces, or it may be about developing personalised development opportunities for those identified as 'talent'. Overall, there should be an OD focus to ensure the long-term sustainability of the organisation and the promotion of diversity. If this role is not performed well, it is highly likely that individuals will not be being developed to meet the organisation's needs and a skills gap will arise. It is also likely that the individuals themselves will feel under-utilised and seek employment elsewhere.

The role of the line manager

The line manager is arguably *the* key player in talent management in the organisation – he or she can potentially make or break the process. It is your line manager who makes you feel valued in the workplace, who can offer you opportunities for development, exciting projects and group roles, or who can stifle you, leave you feeling unappreciated and seeking an alternative future to the one mapped out for you in the organisation (Frank and Taylor,

2004). Fortune-500 companies lose their female executives at twice the rate of men, and the changes their employers could have made to keep them were inclusion, flexible environment, feedback and career planning. In short, the women felt under-utilised, and their line managers were the key people responsible (Dickinson Shepard and Betof, 2005).

There is an additional role to the ones mentioned above for HRM and HRD professionals in preparing line managers to be talent managers. Most line managers, at some point, manage people who are more talented than themselves, and it takes an experienced, confident manager to be able to realise the benefit of this and manage them well. Line managers may view their talented employees as threats (Moss Kanter, 1989) but in reality, the opposite can be true, for the ability to develop people for the greater good of the organisation is a very positive reflection on a manager's contribution to the development of the organisation.

REFLECTIVE ACTIVITIES

Line managers can be the most facilitative or destructive players in talent management.

- To what extent do you agree with this assertion?
- What organisational structures and processes can help promote individual employee agency in talent management?

CONCLUSION

In essence, talent management is an HR and OD approach which is aimed at the development of a particular, but frequently varying and diverse, group of 'talented' employees. For the principles of equality and benefit of organisations, talent should not be a permanent title for employees. Instead, talent management should be inclusive of all employees, with all of their diversity characteristics. If an organisation adopts an exclusive, narrow approach to talent management, its practice will very likely limit diversity, ensure that there is little equality of opportunity, and promote a future senior management team that mirrors that of the current executive. This may place organisations at competitive disadvantage in a lack of openness to new ways of thinking and performing because an exclusive approach to talent management is likely to perpetuate the established type of thinking and standard of performance. Having a formal talent management policy with an inclusive approach is an important signal of organisational intent and, consequently, an important foundation for OD activity. This is not to say that conceptualising and operationalising inclusive talent management is without challenges.

As human beings we naturally tend towards people who are similar to us. In a group of unfamiliar people we are more likely to talk to someone of the same gender, ethnicity or age as us than we would to someone from outside this comfort zone. We have something in common with them. In many organisations, this instinct is reflected in limited diversity among employees. Resisting the similarity instinct and, instead, increasing diversity is nonetheless paramount if talent management is to succeed in producing future managers and leaders who can sustain organisations in an increasingly global environment. Many agents have a role to play in conceptualising and operationalising inclusive talent management: HRM and HRD specialists, line managers, individual employees and, possibly, talent managers (as in the case of the BBC). It with these agencies working in concert, working through issues such as transparency and criticism, that talent management is most likely to be effective. At a strategic level, inclusive talent management can contribute to New OE in a range of ways from succession planning to being a driver for bringing about organisational change.

In sum, talent management has much to contribute to the development of a New OE mindset because it is the interface between HRM, OD, line management and employee activity on which is focused the future success of the organisation. It can also play a pivotal role in ensuring that diversity is embraced within an organisation. The CIPD's OD toolkit offers support for organisations seeking and striving to be more inclusive in their talent management and diversity. The following elements of that toolkit may be particularly instructive in addressing some of the inherent challenges: influencing organisational culture, the roles of OD practitioners, helping others to achieve change, exploring reality, and creating insight.

EXPLORE FURTHER

April, K. and Shockley, M. (2006) *Diversity: New realities in a changing world*. Basingstoke: Palgrave Macmillan. An interesting book that looks at diversity issues from a global, holistic perspective and what this means for the reality of organisational life.

Berger, A. and Berger, D. R. (2011) *The Talent Management Handbook: Creating organisational excellence by identifying, developing and promoting your best people*, 2nd edition. London/New York: McGraw-Hill Professional. A collection of case studies and practical guidance to talent management issues in organisations and how they are being addressed. Written from a US perspective.

Blass, E. (2009) *Talent Management: Cases and commentary*. Basingstoke: Palgrave Macmillan. This book outlines the cases studies that were undertaken for the Ashridge/CMI research project in 2007 and discusses their significance with regard to operationalising talent management.

Greene, A.-M. and Kirkton G. (2009) *Diversity Management in the UK: Organisational and stakeholder experiences*. London: Routledge. This evidence-based and wide-ranging textbook offers comprehensive, contemporary insights into diversity in the UK.

HBR (2008) *Harvard Business Review on Talent Management*. Boston, MA: Harvard Business Press. A collected reprint of articles published on talent management within the *HBR*: a very readable book which covers a number of angles including women and diversity.

REFERENCES

Blass, E. (2007) *Talent Management: Maximising talent for business performance*. London: Chartered Management Institute.

Blass, E. (ed.) (2009) *Talent Management: Cases and commentary*. Basingstoke: Palgrave Macmillan.

Blass, E., Brockoff, S. and Oliveira, F. (2009) 'A map of the territory between HRM and talent management', in Blass, E. (ed.) *Talent Management: Cases and commentary*. Basingstoke: Palgrave Macmillan.

Branham, L. (2005) 'Planning to become an employer of choice', *Journal of Organizational Excellence*, Vol.24, No.3: 57–68.

Cappelli, P. (2000) 'A market-driven approach to retaining talent', *Harvard Business Journal*, Vol.78, No.1: 103–11.

Cappelli, P. (2008) 'Talent management for the twenty-first century', *Harvard Business Review*, March, Vol.86, No.3: 74.

Chambers, E., Foulton, M., Handfield-Jones, H., Hankin, S. and Michaels III, E. (1998) 'The war for talent', *McKinsey Quarterly*, Vol.3: 44–57.

Cooke, F. L. (2011) 'Talent management in China', in Scullion, H. and Collings, D. G (eds) *Global Talent Management*. Abingdon, UK: Routledge.

Coyne, K. (2008) 'Enduring ideas: the GE–McKinsey nine-box matrix', *McKinsey Quarterly*, September, No.4: 142.

Dickinson Shepard, M. and Betof, N. G. (2005) 'Building a reservoir of women superkeepers', in Berger, D. R. and Berger, L. A. (eds) *The Handbook of Talent Management*. New York: McGraw-Hill.

Frank, F. D. and Taylor, C. D. (2004) 'Talent management: trends that will shape the future', *Human Resource Planning*, Vol.27: 33–41.

Friedman, L. (2006) 'Are you losing potential new hires at hello?', *Training & Development*, Vol.60, No.11: 25–7.

Harrington, S. (2010) 'Discrimination by degrees (university qualifications)', *Human Resources*, September: 20–3.

Lewis, R. E. and Heckman, R. J. (2006) 'Talent management: a critical review', *Human Resource Management Review*, Vol.16: 139–54.

McKenna, E. and Beech, N. (2008) *Human Resource Management: A concise analysis*, 2nd edition. London: FT/Prentice Hall.

Maxwell, G. and MacLean, S. (2008) 'Talent management in hospitality and tourism in Scotland: operational implications and strategic actions', *International Journal of Contemporary Hospitality Management*, Vol.20, No.7: 820–30.

Mellahi, K. and Collings, G. (2010) 'The barriers to effective global talent management: the example of corporate elites in MNEs', *Journal of World Business*, Vol.45: 143–9.

Morton, L., Ashton, C. and Bellis, R. (2005) *Differentiating Talent Management: Integrating talent management to drive business performance*. London: CRF Publishing.

Moss Kanter, R. (1989) 'Power failure in management circuits', in Levinson, H. (ed.) *Designing and Managing Careers*. Boston, MA: Harvard Business Review Press.

Ng, E. S. W. and Burke, R. J. (2005) 'Person–organisation fit and the war for talent: does diversity management make a difference?', *International Journal of Human Resource Management*, Vol.16, No.7: 1195–1210.

Pilbeam, S. and Corbridge, M. (2010) *People Resourcing and Talent Planning: HRM in practice*, 4th edition. London: FT/Prentice Hall.

Smart, S., Hutchings, M., Maylor, U., Mendick, H. and Menter I. (2009) 'Processes of middle class reproduction in graduate employment schemes', *Journal of Education and Work*, Vol.22, No.1: 35–53.

Tansley, C., Harris, L., Stewart, J. and Turner, P. (2006) *Talent Management: Understanding the dimensions*. Change Agenda. London: CIPD.

Tucker, E., Kao, T. and Verma, N. (2005) 'Next-generation talent management: insights on how workforce trends are changing the face of talent management', *Business Credit*, Vol.107, No.7: 20–8.

CHAPTER 14

Employer Branding and Organisational Effectiveness

Helen Francis and Martin Reddington

CHAPTER OVERVIEW

As HRM begins to assume a greater role in Organisational Effectiveness, there has been growing debate about the need for researchers to provide a more satisfactory means of accommodating workers' interests in the modelling of the employment relationship. This chapter builds upon these arguments, blending them with a critical review of the upsurge of interest in employer branding and employee engagement. In doing so, it draws upon our own research and consultancy practice to illustrate the application of a 'conversational approach' to EVP with explicit links drawn to the model of New OE that frames the book.

LEARNING OBJECTIVES

By the end of this chapter the reader should be able to:

- appreciate the importance of discourse in the functioning of organisations and the employment relationship
- understand the concepts of and the emergent links between social exchange theory, employer branding and engagement
- critically appraise the role of paradox and ambiguity in HRM and Organisational Effectiveness
- examine a more dynamic model of employer branding and its links with New OE.

INTRODUCTION

Amidst the drumbeat of business model change is growing recognition of the need for a shift in mindsets among HR professionals about how we treat 'context', and about the role of language in shaping this. For instance, the CIPD's recent report on *Next-Generation HR* emphasises the need for 'insight-led' HR leaders who are more alert to what is going on outside and inside the organisation, and be able to harness these insights in ways that improve business performance and employee engagement (CIPD, 2011).

In what follows, we draw upon the critical realist lens outlined in Chapter 1 in order to explore the *active* or *performance* role of language in framing employment structures and activities. This is a matter often overlooked in management research and consultancy practice, which relies on a vocabulary of change framed by conventional mindsets and approaches (Butcher and Atkinson, 2001). These tend to adopt a highly mechanistic view of strategic management, treated as something confined to senior management teams. However, as Sparrow and colleagues point out, strategy is 'not rational and never has been' and inevitably involves people at *all* levels of the organisational hierarchy (Sparrow *et al*, 2010).

Critical discourse analysis (CDA) is a relatively new method of enquiry within management studies, which usefully draws attention to the emergent properties of strategy-making, how new vocabularies and 'storylines' crop up in organisational settings, and how they are appropriated and 'recontextualised' by participants (Thomas, 2003). There are many different interpretations of organisational discourse. For our purposes, we use the term to denote a distinctive vocabulary which constitutes a way of thinking, talking and behaving within the organisation, and which is intimately connected to broader social, economic and political contexts within which the organisation is operating.

From this perspective, discourse is not just about language but also about the actual practices and behaviours that go with it. The first learning objective within this chapter is to develop the reader's understanding about the links between language and action, recognising that language is not neutral – it actively frames how we think, and what we say and do. On this basis it can be argued that a change in social systems requires a change in the mix and *ordering* of prevailing discourses at play (Fairclough, 1995).

REFLECTIVE ACTIVITIES

Recruitment consultant:

'Most HR professionals will now have "value added" stamped on their foreheads, because they are being asked always to think in terms of the business objectives and how what they do supports the business objectives and the business plan' (Francis and Keegan, 2006: 239).

Business partner:

'It's a strange word but I don't think there's anybody got permission to be an employee champion in our sort of set-up, really ... The unions see it as their role for the employees to come to them to tell them about their problems – not HR' (Keegan and Francis, 2010: 13).

- To what extent do you agree with the assertion that HR practitioners are mostly concerned with business issues?

- Look back at Chapter 2 and consider the key contextual factors that shape HR discourses in modern-day organisations.

The quotations in the reflective activity above draw our attention to the power of language in shaping our thinking and practice, reflected here in the narrow framing of HR work around business issues and the casting aside of talk about working *with* or *for* employees. They resonate with an unfortunate tendency to use phrases like 'tea and sympathy' to describe employee-facing roles in HR, linked with the suggestion that strategic business partnership is the 'future' – any attempt to reclaim a space for talking about employee well-being is tantamount to dragging the profession back into the dark ages of 'welfare work' (Beckett, 2005; Francis and Keegan, 2006: 239).

From a critical standpoint, this is a storyline that misses the point, because *both* are essential to the future of HR work and sustainable performance, as argued in Chapter 1.

Nevertheless, much of the prescriptive HR and management literatures present a static view of language, failing to recognise its performative role, which is explained below.

LANGUAGE AND PERFORMANCE

We recognise that for new concepts and ideas about language and action to 'take', they must be perceived to be of value in terms of what 'works' within the context in which it is being introduced (Thomas, 2003). Much of the academic work on organisational discourse is couched in a vocabulary that is not easily translated into practical tools for managers and employees. However, we are seeing useful applications of discourse theory entering the world of practice, reflected in the uptake of new OD interventions noted in Chapter 3, which adopt a constructionist outlook to effect change and enhance performance (eg appreciative inquiry and storytelling techniques).

Ford and Ford usefully draw upon the metaphor of organisational change as 'conversations for change' to provide practical tools for managers about how to use language effectively in planned change efforts. They introduce the notions of *conversational responsibility* and *conversation management* to raise the pivotal role of line managers in shaping conversational patterns of language-use within the organisation (Ford and Ford, 1995, 2008). This is described in terms of engineering a 'shift' in conversations across and through four types – initiative conversations, conversations for understanding, conversations for performance, and conversations for closure.

- *Initiative conversations* signal the beginnings of change, by introducing new ideas, directions or possible courses of action. They include the use by change leaders of assertions, proposals, suggestions, and so on, to foster a 'readiness for change' by focusing attention on the 'what', 'when', 'why' and 'value' of change to the individual and the organisation, thereby creating an interest and legitimacy for change.
- *Conversations for understanding* allow more open discussion of opposing views and surfacing of tensions through conversations that increase in the number of 'voices' involved, and the generation of new ideas and possibilities. These take place alongside movement to reduce ambiguity and uncertainty and generate shared understandings about change in terms of value to the individual and organisation.
- *Conversations for performance* focus on generating action and intended results, recognising that this is a contested domain. They include the reaching of pragmatic 'workable arrangements' that are mutually satisfactory for all parties concerned, such as the setting of accountabilities, targets, plans, time-lines at the level of the organisation, team and individual.
- *Conversations for closure* focus on critical reflection of events. They are used to signal the completion of a current initiative and the facilitation of movement on to new projects, comprising an honest review of the successes and failures encountered on the way, and an acknowledgement of new futures and possibilities that did not exist prior to the start-up of the change initiative.

Ford and Ford explain that processes by which organisational members generate a common language for change are recognised as always being in a process of negotiation and/or conflict. One of the values and purposes of effective 'conversations for change' should be to reveal processes that lead to the dominance of particular ways of talking and action which result in systematic exclusion and disempowerment of others. Conversations for performance may therefore be suspended at any time to allow the dialogue to return to earlier conversations – to allow for further explanations, checking of 'political voice', and conversations for understanding.

CONVERSATION MANAGEMENT: SENSITIVITY TO CONTEXT

Ford and Ford (1995, 2008) make the point that successful change requires change managers to alter their conversational patterns, using the four different types of conversation at different times. Little is said, however, about different *levels* of conversational 'arenas' in which these kinds of conversations take place. Francis and Sinclair (2003) present a framework for analysing this dynamic within organisations, articulated in terms of three levels of management activity, referred to in terms of strategic, managerial and operational conversations. As we draw upon Francis and Sinclair's framework in our modelling of EVP we prefer to use the term 'change leader' rather than 'change manager', to support the view that people at all levels of the organisational hierarchy can consciously shape conversations for change, taking a leadership role as and when required (consistent with the notion of distributive leadership noted in Chapter 1).

We argue that efforts to diffuse more collaborative and empowering management practices requires these change leaders to be more sensitive to the power effects of language within organisational settings and beyond. Writing from a critical HRM perspective, Delbridge and Keenoy (2010) outline what such sensitivity should entail among academics writing in this field:

- sensitivity to the wider socio-political context in which (discursively mediated) management practices are enacted
- challenging the unreflective adoption of managerial language/practice used in mainstream research – and the need for analysts to challenge the taken-for-granted beliefs and nostrums that frame this
- a concern to articulate a range of voices 'which are barely heard within the mainstream' (page 804).

Linked with these arguments, critical scholars point to dominance of the unitary HRM discourse within HRM-Performance (HRM-P) research, which has progressively obscured the inherent sources of tension and conflict in employment management noted in earlier chapters (see also Keegan and Boselie, 2006; Keenoy, 2009). Scholars writing from a critical HRM (CHRM) position have argued that although HRM-P practices may provide enhancements in involvement, discretion and engagement, these may come to employees at the expense of stress, work intensification and job strain (Delbridge, 2007; Legge, 2001; Maslach *et al*, 2001). They point to the controlling effects of the language of commitment, engagement, and so on, and the extent to which these pose a threat to employees materially and emotionally. In this case, HRM may represent more insidious forms of ideological control and identity appropriation, rather than offering any real substantive change in the employment relationship (Geary and Dobbins, 2001).

From this position, the 'manipulation of meaning' by employers can appear less as a concern for mutuality between employers and employees and 'more like straightforward corporate takeover of psychological space' (Overell, 2008: 14; Townley, 1998). Moreover, increasing attention to emotions at work and the management of these can arguably lead to a more, rather than less, instrumental orientation of employees (Fineman, 2000; Landen, 2002).

While we recognise the need to be mindful of the potentially manipulative/harmful effects of HRM noted above, we take the view of Keenoy and others, that employees are not simply passive receptacles for management ideas or corporate 'mono-cultures' (Keenoy, 2009; Francis, 2002, 2007; Grant and Shields, 2002). On reconceptualising employees as more active players in constructing their work and organisation, the lens of New OE emphasises the power of words and language for changing mindsets about the exercise of agency and ways in which people exercise choices, even within a 'constrained employment context' (Bolton and Houlihan, 2009: 6).

Understanding of agency within the field of HRM is relatively weak, and both CHRM and HRM-P research streams have been criticised for sharing a common view of the worker as essentially 'objects' that are being exploited to the benefit of the organisation, thereby slipping into some kind of structural determinism (Fleetwood and Hesketh, 2010).

THE EMPLOYMENT VALUE PROPOSITION: THE FULCRUM OF CONSTRUCTIVE TENSION

Following from the arguments presented above, there are increasing calls for researchers to move beyond the either/or orientation and create a more 'balanced agenda' to HR research (Francis and Keegan, 2006). Writing within the mainstream literature, for instance, Paauwe (2009) calls for a more balanced approach to performance-focused research, in ways that pay greater attention to the concerns and well-being of employees.

At the same time, critical scholars point to the increase in 'intellectual space' being given to CHRM within the mainstream as promising, and call for analysts to proactively reframe the HRM agenda in ways that enable constructive engagement of competing approaches and perspectives. This requires the development of alternative interpretations and vocabularies that seek to connect different perspectives rather than synthesising or displacing one with another (Delbridge and Ezzamel, 2005; cited by Delbridge, 2011).

This chapter builds upon these sentiments by drawing upon the notion of constructive tension developed by Evans, Pucik and Barsoux (2002) and social exchange theory which places reciprocity and mutuality at the heart of the employee–organisation relationship. On raising questions about the highly unitarist underpinnings of current research in HRM and performance, we then draw connections between emergent theories of social exchange, employer branding and engagement.

Central to our arguments is the need for HR/OD professionals and change leaders to adopt a mindset which treats the active surfacing of paradoxical tensions as an opportunity to enhance social exchange, employee engagement and performance. Our third learning objective, therefore, looks at the role of paradox and ambiguity in HRM and organisational effectiveness, focusing on their implications in the social construction of employment value propositions (EVPs).

There is a dearth of research around these issues, and our fourth learning objective invites readers to examine a model of employer branding developed by ourselves, presented as a means of promoting fresh debate and further research in this field.

A key point we wish to make is that an over-reliance on statistical modelling of HRM-P has meant a lack of empirical work and practical understanding about the social exchange processes involved in shaping EVPs (Francis and Reddington, 2010). Exchange relationships are more complex than the resources exchanged (Shore *et al*, 2009) and our process-oriented model of EVP moves beyond an examination of 'antecedents' and 'outcomes' in the exchange to one which also gives attention to the dynamic evolving nature of *relationships* and *employment structures* underpinning the employment deal. Depicted in Figure 14.1, this treats the construction of EVPs as a dynamic mix of social exchange processes, shaped by personal, job and organisational characteristics.

Figure 14.1 EVP framework

Underpinned by New OE mindset and behaviours, our framework of EVP characterises the employment deal in the form of social and economic exchange relationships (psychological contract, perceived organisational support), intimately linked to employee engagement as presented in Table 14.1. It will be used as an organising framework for the chapter.

Table 14.1 A model of EVP – key features and links to New OE

EVP lens	New OE lens
Language and action: priming conversations for change Recognition is given to the active role of language in framing the processes by which value propositions are constructed and realised. This draws upon the metaphor of organisational change as a network of conversations, and the notion of conversational responsibility, to promote a concern for context, dialogue and reflective use of the language of change.	Language and action
Authenticity and mutuality: enhancing social exchange A concern with building dynamic forms of social exchange that enhance employee/team agency in shaping the deal, and facilitate the creation of workable arrangements of mutual benefit to the stakeholders involved. Perceived organisational support and psychosocial contract fulfilment are important factors that shape the quality of social exchange.	Authenticity and mutuality
Paradox and ambiguity: surfacing tensions and harnessing constructive tension Emphasis is given to working productively with paradox and ambiguity in the co-construction of workable arrangements. The active surfacing of tensions is treated as an opportunity to enhance conversations for change and to build constructive tension into the strategic planning and ongoing construction of EVPs.	Paradox and ambiguity
Leadership and management: building judgemental competence and conversational responsibility Emphasis is placed upon a person-centred language of authentic and shared leadership, and the building of 'judgemental competence' in ways that generate high levels of trust and feelings of mutual purpose and gains between the parties involved in the exchange.	Leadership and management

SOCIAL EXCHANGE WITHIN ORGANISATIONS

Social exchange theory has arguably become one of the most influential frameworks for understanding exchange behaviour within organisations, and has been used to explain a number of different interactions. Two major contemporary theories include psychological contract theory (PCT) and perceived organisational support theory (POS) (Shore *et al*, 2009), and more recently, employee engagement (Saks, 2006). Although there are different perspectives on social exchange, there is consensus that it involves a series of social and economic interactions that generate obligations to reciprocate, engendering 'feelings of personal obligations, gratitude and trust' (Blau, 1964: 20). Analysts mostly draw on a statistical lens in their examination of these interactions, and as a result they treat social and economic exchange as a duality (eg Song *et al*, 2009). Using the lens of New OE, our approach to EVP adopts a both/and perspective, recognising that all exchange processes have an element of social and economic features, albeit that the emphasis will vary, and in this chapter we mostly focus on the quality of the social exchange.

There is an extensive literature in this field, and in what follows we provide a brief overview of current thinking, showing key connections between the literature on social exchange and the emergent conceptualisations of employer branding and employee engagement.

Social exchange has been differentiated from an economic exchange along the dimensions of resources exchanged, type and strength of obligations, reciprocity, and the quality of the relationship developed over time (Shore *et al*, 2009: 290; see also Conway and Briner, 2009). The section below illustrates these differentiating features, focusing on PCT and OST. According to PCT and OST theories, employees tend to personify the organisation by assigning it human like characteristics with an ability to express feelings for an individual employee such as appreciation, and with whom the employee can form various types of exchange relationships (Chiaburu *et al*, 2011; Rhoades and Eisenberger, 2002). For personification to occur, people attribute organisational policies and practices to various organisational agents or representatives, and a key question arises – who is party to the relationship?

The employee's line manager or HR manager who sends out messages regarding expectations and obligations has been cited as an important 'agent' or proxy for the organisation (see Marks, 2001). HR practices also play an important role in signalling and creating particular employment offerings and images of employee–organisation relationships (Martin and Dyke, 2010; Martin, Gollan and Grigg, 2011).

People differ in their perceptions of the value of such offerings, but the central idea behind the modelling of HRM-Performance, social exchange and employer branding is that it is possible to 'summarise the totality of a common or shared employment experience' (Edwards, 2010: 7). This takes the form of a formally espoused mix of functional, social and economic benefits, used to frame performance expectations among workers, and to foster psychological bonds with the organisation (Guest and Conway, 2002).

Most research rooted in PCT and OST theories draws upon *content models* concerned with what has been exchanged, how much, and the outcomes derived from it, such as employee commitment and performance, and perceptions of psychological 'breach' (Conway and Briner, 2005, 2009). A brief overview of work in this field is noted below.

TWO MAJOR SOCIAL EXCHANGE THEORIES

Psychological contract theory

The psychological contract has been defined by Guest and Conway (2002) as the perceptions of both parties to the employment relationship – organisational and individual – of the reciprocal promises and obligations implied in that relationship. They explain that psychological contracts are clearly expectations, although ones originating from the individual's *belief* in a promise, stated or implied, that he or she has been offered, in exchange for his or her contributions to the organisation.

Most empirical research that draws upon PCT has focused on contract content in terms of 'inducements' from employers (eg pay, training and development, etc) in exchange for 'contributions' from employees – such as effort and ability (see Cullinane and Dundon, 2006).

Attention has been given to the perceived 'state' of the psychological contract – an individual's global impression of whether or not 'promises' are kept, how fair they are perceived to be, and trust in whether they are likely to be delivered in the future (Guest, 2004: 6). The failure of an organisation to meet its promises has been described in terms of perceived 'breach' and 'violation', when breach develops into feelings of injustice or betrayal (Morrison and Robinson, 1997).

Analysis typically draws upon Rousseau's transactional/relational classification, which treats the exchange process as essentially economic or social (Rousseau, 1995), although in practice any given employment relationship contains a mix of these elements in varying degrees (O'Donohue and Wickham, 2008).

A *transactional exchange* emphasises the economic and more tangible aspects of the exchange, such as working longer hours and accepting new job roles, in exchange for more pay and job-related training (Herriot and Pemberton, 1997).

A *relational exchange* emphasises less tangible socio-emotional aspects of the exchange, by which employees come to identify with their organisation and in doing so are expected to demonstrate 'organisational citizenship behaviours' (OCBs) in exchange for job security, financial rewards, and training and development. OCBs include going outside the requirements of the job, or 'going the extra mile', whether in customer service, in ensuring quality, in helping others (Dyer and Reeves, 1995) or in speaking well of the organisation (employee advocacy).

A relational psychological contract is consistent with the idealised employment relationship denoted by 'progressive' commitment-based HR practices linked to a more positive 'state' of psychological contract and improved employee/business performance (Guest and Conway, 2002).

Thompson and Bunderson (2003) introduce the notion of *ideologically infused psychological contracts*, reflecting the growing expectation that employers offer opportunities that enable individuals to contribute to a valued cause.

Organisational support theory (OCT)

Like the inducements-contribution model underpinning PCT, OST is based on the premise that when employees believe that the organisation values their contributions and well-being, they feel obliged to reciprocate. Perceived organisational support (POS) is closely associated with the meeting of socio-emotional needs and an organisation's readiness to reward increased efforts made on its behalf (Eisenberger et al, 1986; Eder and Eisenberger, 2008: 56). Research has mostly focused upon the content of the resources exchanged. Three key aspects of work experience shown to shape POS resonate with antecedents shaping the state of the psychological contract (Aselage and Eisenberger, 2003):

- organisational rewards and working conditions – eg developmental experiences, job autonomy, and visibility to and recognition from upper-level management
- perceived supervisor support – the extent to which supervisors care about the employees and value their contributions
- fairness of formal organisational policies and procedure, linked to notions of procedural justice.

While research into the psychological contract and perceived organisational support are both rooted in social exchange theory, they have nevertheless developed in relative isolation from each other. Both strands of work emphasise the quality of social exchange and procedural justice, although OST placcs more emphasis upon the *delivery* of support rather the types of 'promises' exchanged and the extent to which they have been met (Tekleab et al, 2005: 148; see Chen et al, 2009 and Aselage and Eisenberger, 2003, for a fuller discussion).

Elements of both types of exchange relationships are evident in the ServCo case study presented below. It points to the pivotal role of HR professionals as organisational 'agents' in striking a 'deal' with managers during a period of organisational change, and processes of social exchange shaping various components of the employment deal.

The meaning attached to these components appears to be of more importance than the content or make-up of the deal *per se*, consistent with process models of social exchange (Shore et al, 2009). Training in emotional intelligence was interpreted by one respondent as an indication of increased self-worth by 'the organisation', thereby shaping her perceptions of the value of the deal. Consistent with OST, the case also illustrates how managers attributed to the organisation human-like qualities (eg as 'someone who cares'), and how actions by trainers and coaches are treated as actions by the organisation itself.

LEADERSHIP DEVELOPMENT WITH SERVCO

In ServCo the employment deal operated largely in transactional terms and the case illustrates how the company instigated a culture change programme that promised a move away from a task-oriented management culture to one which encouraged 'leadership' and 'emotional loyalty'. This involved a range of management development activities including a four-day emotional intelligence programme for managers, aimed at enhancing 'leadership skills'. The programme focused on improving participants' self-management of emotions and an enhanced understanding of/ ability to manage the emotions of others. The perceived distinctiveness of the leadership programme appeared to act as a strong signalling device to participants about a move towards a more relational employment deal, illustrated in the accounts of two managers:

In the past people didn't do anything that focused on you as an individual – it was just you, and what they could do to enhance your management skills ... was very much on technical things or on behaviours that would just make you run your store better. Nothing ever focused on your personal need and what was important to you personally. And that I think made me feel 'Mmmm, mmmm: they do recognise me and know I'm here and care about me a little bit as an individual. They care about me!'

It is about you and your own personal feelings ... It was unlike any other ServCo

course I'd been on ... You were talking about feelings, and things like that ... (pause) ... It was structured in a way that it wasn't just about the business.

The enactment of a more relational leadership style was not without difficulty within a strong compliance culture that required managers to strictly follow HR procedures. Noticeably, significant resources were spent upon new structures for coaching managers in translating what they had learned into feasible strategies for 'building employee engagement and boosting store performance'. All participants received coaching from Group-level HR managers in setting up personal development plans in support of these, and this provided an important means for making sense of competing people- and task-oriented management priorities. One coach talked about the 'idealistic nature' of the training programme and the need to reshape managers' expectations in a way that was 'more realistic'. This involved surfacing tensions between the need to follow standard procedures geared to achieve 'consistency in customer service' and also to display emotionally sensitive leadership behaviours promoted by the HRD programme. For this person, her role of coach was to help managers 'understand the parameters within which they [managers] were working'.

Source: adapted from Francis and D'Annunzio-Green (2007); D'Annunzio-Green and Francis (2005)

Shore and colleagues (Shore *et al*, 2009) argue that more ought to be understood about how trust and balance in social exchange evolve, outside the 'norm of reciprocity' that is typically used to explain perceived organisational support, psychological contract breach/fulfilment and employee contributions (Shore *et al*, 2009: 294). More nuanced models are required that take account of individual differences, plus other cultural norms, that are beyond the reciprocation motive (see Chapters 5 and 16 for discussion about the importance of culture and personality traits in shaping employee attitudes and behaviours).

This point is illustrated by recent case study research undertaken by the Work Foundation (Wong *et al*, 2010) concerned with exploring psychological contracting processes from an employee perspective. For instance, a case example is given of how the employment deal among officers within a UK police force was shaped by strong social ties between co-workers who were treated as members of a second family, and this dynamic provided a better theoretical explanation than conventional assumptions of reciprocity and exchange underpinning theories of PCT. The authors conclude that the perceived value of working within an organisation may be more strongly linked with brand values and ideologies than with the more functional economic and social aspects of the deal typically expressed in psychological contract research (see also Cunningham and Kempling, 2010).

An implicit assumption underpinning social exchange theory is that the resources exchanged are valued by the recipient – ie that inducements offered by the employer are valued by employees and that employee contributions are valued by the employer. This is not necessarily the case, and more has yet to be understood about what resources are perceived as valuable, and about mutuality of purpose and gains (see Chapter 1). In our modelling of EVP we have drawn upon Lepak and colleagues' conceptualisation of value (Lepak *et al*, 2007) in a recent case study analysis in respect of how line managers within a services organisation perceived the value of the 'deal' between HR and line managers associated with the introduction of an e-HR implementation programme (Francis and Reddington, 2011).

Our research indicates that people differ in what they experience and in their perceptions of value when working within a particular organisation, which challenges the central idea behind the modelling of HRM-Performance, social exchange and employer branding; that it is possible to 'summarise the totality of a common or shared employment experience' (Edwards, 2010: 7).

Although personification of the organisation usefully allows analysts to assess how people relate to the organisation, Watson warns us of the risk of falling into a unitary language that oversimplifies the actual reality of organisational life, glossing over differing perceptions and values held by organisational members (Watson, 2002: 224). An understanding of the coalitional nature of organisations is therefore important, as noted in the discussion about subcultures and ethics in Chapters 5 and 12, and in Purcell's case example of an attempt to forge the organisation into a community (see Chapter 6).

Purcell notes that a community implies a sense of 'we' as well as 'me', and it is important therefore that HR/OD and line practitioners appreciate the necessity of managing employees as a collective, not just as individuals. At an analytical level, this also requires researchers to look for frameworks that allow for multiple levels of analysis regarding the employee–organisation relationship – at the level of the individual, team and organisation (see Paauwe, 2009). This is a central issue emerging in discussion about the academic–practitioner divide in employee engagement research, for practitioners are shown to be more concerned about aggregating data to inform practice at macro-level, whereas academics focus more towards the micro-level, around defining the psychological concept of engagement (Wefald and Downey, 2009).

BRAND PERSONALITY AND THE VALUE OF WHAT IS EXCHANGED

We have noted that the conceptual language around 'value' within the context of social exchange remains under-explored by academics, reflecting a concern expressed by practitioners of the need for more practical management research that is 'evidence-based' (Rynes, Giluk and Brown, 2007: 987).

Employer branding has been described as an attempt by employers to better define the psychological contract in terms of the value employees derive from their employment in an organisation, linking this to organisational level of analysis, and a corporate personality or identity that both employees and customers will identify with (Barrow and Mosley, 2005; Martin and Hetrick, 2006; Rosethorn, 2009).

Brand personality has become an accepted means to identify associations made with the brand, and research in this area usefully draws links between organisational identity, organisational identification and organisational personality characteristics (Edwards, 2010).

Evidence indicates that expression of a brand image in terms of a 'brand personality' usefully provides a meaning structure by which people can relate to the organisation and make sense of the employment relationship (Lievans, 2007; Davies, 2008). The language associated with this metaphor builds upon what is called the 'Big Five' model as a reference structure for describing human personality: 1) *extroversion*, a preference for social interaction and for activity; 2) *agreeableness*, an orientation towards compassion and caring about others, and away from antagonism; 3) *conscientiousness*, the preference for goal-oriented activity (ie the degree of organisation); 4) *emotional stability*, the ability to cope effectively with negative emotions; and 5) *openness to experience*, a tolerance for new ideas and ways of doing things, particularly experientially (Caprara *et al*, 2001: 380).

Google traits

Below is how Google presents itself to potential recruits, drawing clear links between the employment experience and a corporate brand likened to 'being a good friend', translated into promises about fulfilling work and a supportive workplace (adapted from *Top 10 Reasons to Work at Google*, http://www.google.co.uk/jobs/reasons.html).

Lend a helping hand.
Google has become an essential part of everyday life – *like a good friend – connecting people* with the information they need to live great lives.

Life is beautiful.
Being a part of something that matters and working on products in which you can believe is remarkably fulfilling.

Good company everywhere you look.
… No matter what their backgrounds, Googlers make for interesting *cube mates*.

Work and play are not mutually exclusive.
Here at Google it is not just possible but 'mandatory' to *have fun and work* at the same time.

The paradoxical nature of employment practice illustrated here in the emphasis placed on 'fun *and* work' is poorly conceptualised within the employer branding literature, with practices being criticised for relying upon overly simplistic 'employer of choice' propositions (Martin and Dyke, 2010). This has led to growing concerns expressed by academics about the potential for so-called 'brandwashing' or culture controls that shape employees' sense of self (Cushen, 2009; Martin and Hetrick, 2006: 27).

Like models of PCT and POS, the language of employer branding relies heavily upon a unitarist stance that treats employees as essentially *consumers* buying into their employer's vision and corporate goals and brand or the cultural and symbolic cues which organisations attempt to signal, rather than *producers* of HR practices or corporate brand.

In the next section we explore recent trends within the HRM literature on engagement and employee involvement which have the potential to allow for greater employee agency in the exchange process, thereby conferring greater potential for the creation of 'workable arrangements' (Watson, 2002: 85) of mutual benefit to the stakeholders involved.

MUTUAL PURPOSE AND GAINS: PATHWAYS TO HIGH INVOLVEMENT AND ENGAGEMENT

We have suggested that idealised templates for HRM and performance ought to be reframed to take better account of contextual factors and social exchange processes underpinning the employment relationship. Boxall and Macky (2009) in their examination of the literature on high-performance work systems (HPWS) explain that any 'HR system' encompasses two broad types of practices: *work* practices, to do with the way work is organised – eg self-managing teams; and *employment* practices, to do with the recruitment and deployment of workers in tune with the job, and organisational requirements. The authors then draw on the companion terminology of high-involvement work systems (see below), stemming from Lawler's (1986) focus on high-involvement work practices, and Walton's (1985) focus on high-commitment employment practices. They argue that talking of involvement and commitment is a logical focus in today's competitive climate, where 'smarter working' is of vital importance to policy-makers.

However, they eschew the context-free lists of 'best practice' HRM noted in the PCT and HRM-P literatures, which assume a universalist bundle of practices that somehow result in mutual gains between employer and employee, and call for researchers to focus on identifying the *processes or pathways* that lead to sustainable individual, team and organisational performance.

Vandenberg and colleagues' (1999) model of high-involvement work processes is modified to examine both work involvement and work intensification as underpinning processes, and it is acknowledged (page 17) that:

> There remain serious questions around the interaction between involvement and intensification. It would be extremely unwise for anyone to argue that any particular practice, such as teamwork, automatically enhances employee autonomy and leads on to positive levels of trust, satisfaction and commitment.

Boxall and Macky observe that a review of the evidence indicates that a move to higher involvement can result in increased work intensification for employees (eg Delbridge, 2007). It also indicates that there are possibilities for 'win/win' outcomes for employee and employer in certain contexts. These are 'not without careful management of inherent tensions for both parties' (Boxall and Macky, 2009: 17).

Components of best practice/high-commitment HRM

'Best practice' or 'high-commitment' HRM has a strong ideological component – the identification of the employee with the goals and values of the firm, so inducing commitment. Emphasis is typically placed upon developing an open and trusting employment relationship, with bundles of HR practices geared towards increasing worker autonomy and resourcefulness, grounded in the idea that employees can (and are willing to) become self-managing and self-reliant in ways that act in the firm's interests (Landen, 2002). These types of HR practices have been typified by Marchington and Wilkinson (2005), based on the work of Pfeffer (1998), as follows:

- extensive training, learning and development – a focus on skills development, training and longer-term employee development and organisational learning
- employment security and an internal labour market – an emphasis on effective manpower planning and the avoidance of job reductions, attention to career management
- employee involvement, information-sharing and worker voice – eg through briefing groups, quality circles or joint consultative committees – and the opportunity to express grievances openly and independently
- self-managed teams/teamworking – an emphasis on working 'beyond contract' and a search for continuous improvement
- high compensation contingent on performance – often linked to individual, team and organisational performance
- a reduction of status differentials/harmonisation, underpinned by the harmonisation of pay and conditions of employment between different employee groups.

THE ENGAGED, SELF-RELIANT WORKER

This notion of high involvement and the self-reliant worker is closely associated with increasing interest in positive psychology and engagement (Schaufeli and Bakker, 2003) and the development of 'emotional capital', in which employees are required to effectively manage their feelings and displays of emotion at work (Fineman, 2000). Research into the evolutionary role of positive emotions has increased significantly in recent years, with an explosion of interest in psychological engagement with work and the organisation, heavily marketed by consultancy firms (see also Chapter 16).

There is a marked difference in focus between academic and practitioner research in this regard. The practitioner literature has focused on proprietary measures of engagement developed by consultancy firms such as Gallup, MORI and Best Companies. Engagement tends to be defined as a behavioural outcome aggregated at the level of the organisation and associated with an employee's attachment, loyalty and commitment to the organisation (Robertson-Smith and Marwick, 2009), and there is considerable confusion over whether it is an attitude, a behaviour or an outcome. This has led to scepticism among some analysts who are not convinced that engagement has met a sufficient standard as a distinct and useful construct, compounded by the fact that consultancy measurement tools tend not to be subject to external reviews (MacLeod and Clarke, 2009; Wefald and Downey, 2009).

Notwithstanding these concerns, there is a growing body of academic literature on engagement, but this focuses on very different definitions and measures. Although there is also an interest in outcomes such as advocacy and discretionary effort, attention has mostly centred on micro-level issues, carefully measuring the *psychological state* of engagement, labelled as 'job engagement' (Macey and Schneider, 2008; Saks, 2006: 603).

Shuck (2011) provides an integrative literature review on engagement and identifies four emerging streams across the practitioner and academic realms noted above. He notes that Kahn (1990) is credited with the first application and use of engagement theory at the workplace. Kahn defines personal engagement in terms of a positive affective motivational state, in which an employee is physically, emotionally and cognitively involved in the work, thereby fully involving the sense of 'self'. From this perspective, organisations play an important role in meaning-making and emotional development, specifically in the enabling of 'meaningful work', heightened in an age when there is increasing orientation towards self-expression and self-realisation (Overell, 2009).

Kahn proposed that engaged individuals are prepared to invest significant personal resources to their work, given the right conditions, notably the extent to which they experience a sense of 'return' provided by their employer in the form of organisational support and other factors that meet their individual needs and expectations. Emphasis is placed on personal agency, and how well individual values and ideology align with organisational values (Rich *et al*, 2010). Whereas the practitioner literature also draws links between various psychological bonds connecting the individual and the organisation, employees are viewed in a more passive role and employee engagement treated as a response that can somehow be 'driven' by the organisation, rather than as something that is largely under the control of employees (Wong *et al*, 2010).

Engagement as an act of reciprocity

The treatment of engagement as an element of the social exchange process is central to our modelling of EVP. This is consistent with recent conceptualisation of engagement by Saks (2006), who provides a multi-level analytical approach which treats engagement in work as an act of reciprocity rather than a state of being. He observes that although both Kahn's (1990) and Maslach *et al*'s (2001) models on engagement indicate some key psychological conditions necessary for engagement, they do not fully explain *why* individuals respond to these conditions with varying degrees of engagement (Saks, 2006: 633; emphasis added).

Based on survey evidence, he argues that employees will *choose* to engage themselves to varying degrees (ie cognitively, emotionally and physically) and in response to the resources that they receive from their organisation. In other words the 'condition' of engagement forms part of the social exchange that takes place within the organisation.

Making this point, Balain and Sparrow (2009: 39) argue that sometimes engagement only 'works' when it creates a collective capability, such as in team behaviours and emotions, and that analysts need to understand more about what performance 'beliefs' or 'recipes' look like at a collective level – eg a shared trust in the team's ability.

Self-efficacy has been recognised as an important factor in explaining motivation, work-related effectiveness, burnout and engagement (Luthans and Peterson, 2002; Maslach *et al*, 2001; Saks, 2006). The construct refers to people's beliefs about their personal capabilities (and confidence) to perform a defined task, including perceptions about the ability to *mobilise* resources available to them that are needed to perform that task (Bandura, 1994; Luthans and Peterson, 2002).

Our EVP lens draws upon both personal efficacy and the more recent notion of 'collective efficacy', rooted in social-cognitive theory defined by Bandura (2000: 75) as 'people's shared beliefs in their collective power to produce desired results'. It is perceived not simply as the sum of the efficacy beliefs of individual members but as an emergent group-level property.

Language as a resource in social exchange

Although increasing attention is being given to social interaction and teamwork in the modelling of engagement, there is a noticeable dearth of research into the role of language as a resource in social exchange processes. (More recent modelling of job engagement by the Kingston School, however, points to the benefits of teamwork and social interaction with colleagues. The construct is defined as having three core facets: intellectual engagement, affective engagement and social engagement. The latter is described – Alfes *et al*, 2010: 5 – as 'actively taking opportunities to discuss work-related improvements with others at work'.)

In Chapter 15, Carole Parkes observes the importance of language in creating values and norms in the workplace. Her study of MBA students indicates how language can be used as a resource in developing confidence and capability among managers in raising issues that they had previously thought about but did not know how to construct (see also Gentile, 2010).

More has yet to be understood about how planned change efforts can explicitly draw upon language use as a resource to motivate action and social exchange. Discourse theory has been used to shed some light on such dynamics (see Francis, 2007) and offers an important lens for more critical scrutiny of tensions inherent in social exchange, including unreflective use of embedded metaphors such as an over-reliance on the machine metaphor in describing organisation design and development (Chapter 1).

CONSTRUCTIVE TENSION, LEADERSHIP AND MANAGEMENT

The emphasis of New OE on authentic mutuality paints a picture of 'leadership' very different from classical models of OD, leadership and HRM – one in which different people take the lead depending upon organisational circumstances. As noted in Chapter 1, this approach requires a shift in the balance of power, creating challenges at many levels to the prevailing command-and-control cultures, reflected in Allan Ramdhony's case study of the rise and fall of critical action learning sets (Chapter 9). Examining the political dynamics involved, Ramdhony talks of the need for individuals (in this case HRD specialists) to 'stretch their reflective and problem-solving skills, and increase their political influence to effectively manage these tensions' (page 273).

Similarly, we argue that the notion of authentic mutuality places more responsibility upon the efficacy of individuals and teams to become actively involved in shaping the 'employment deal'. This involves reflecting upon what they need to learn and be able to do differently to reach workable arrangements that are of benefit to themselves, their team and the organisation. We noted in our introduction that an over-reliance on statistical modelling of perceptions of the deal and of employee engagement has meant that there is a dearth of research and practical understanding about the processes involved. This includes the tensions between social and technological structures that enable individuals to use their judgement and initiative vis-à-vis more centralised controls and mechanistic decision-making technologies (Bhidé, 2010).

Judging when to 'break the rules' and being able to legitimise the reasons for doing so is a key feature of 'judgemental competency', a term drawn from the work of Evans (1999) that we have adapted to describe the leadership capabilities needed to manage competing challenges arising from the everyday tensions associated with organisational development and people management. Language use is a critical component in this process of legitimation, and it is important therefore that change leaders are 'conversationally responsible' (Ford, 1999); that they are willing to take ownership of the way they speak and listen, and the practical and ethical consequences of this. As Watson observes, although informal aspects of organisational life have been well documented, managers nevertheless generally talk about the organisation of work as largely a technical and rational exercise, but knowing that things do not in reality get done that way (Watson, 2002: 75).

More also has yet to be understood about the socially negotiated interactions among co-workers and line managers in shaping the deal, and the power relations shaping these. In the USA there is evidence of the growing development of 'i-deals' (idiosyncratic deals) at the workplace, by which managers have the freedom to negotiate customised work arrangements with individuals (Rousseau, 2005). These differ to some extent from those received by co-workers, such as customised duties and individual career opportunities, and are perceived to be beneficial to worker and employer (Rousseau and Kim, 2006; Rousseau et al, 2006, 2009).

Research within the UK suggests that employees are unlikely to proactively negotiate such customised arrangements but that they nevertheless see line managers as critical to the delivery of the deal, acting as employees' 'voice' in the organisation, and in negotiating the deal on their behalf (Wong et al, 2009). Our framework of EVP is explicitly geared to enhance personal and collective self-efficacy in shaping the deal, and our methodology is outlined in the next section.

EVP METHODOLOGY

Our methodology recognises the importance of providing practical tools of action for our readership, while remaining faithful to the richness and complexity of New OE as noted in our depiction of the EVP framework (Fig. 14.1) reproduced below, and explained further in this section.

OE is being treated as open-ended and self-organising *and* as being made up of more structured, planned interventions. This is reflected in our use of dialogic (eg conversational-

style) and traditional (eg survey feedback) OD techniques, primarily used as a means of facilitation/enablement rather than the providing of 'expert advice'. The approach is informed by Marshak and Busche's notion of 'dialogic OD', which places emphasis upon the surfacing of underlying contradictions and tensions, before agreeing on strategies for attaining that vision (Busche and Marshak, 2011: 352).

The *EVP architecture* is a term we use to describe the design and 'realisation' of EVP both in terms of content and process issues. Treated as a form of social exchange, the notion of 'architecture' draws upon a building metaphor to frame a technologically enhanced approach to change used to imply collaboration with all stakeholders in the design and implementation of value propositions.

These value propositions are described as 'position statements' which, taken collectively, become the *espoused EVP*. They embody the unique and differentiating brand promise a business formally makes to its employees and potential candidates, and a broad set of reciprocal obligations and expectations placed on them.

Position statements are structured to capture economic, emotional and social aspects of the employment deal and include high-level overarching statements aligned to organisational ambitions and value statements, and a nested array of localised deals flowing from them. These rest on the proactive surfacing of tensions and the opening up of conversations for understanding and performance about what 'works' and what is feasible both in the short and the longer term.

The construction of an *EVP portal* and associated use of social media technologies is an important feature, used for capturing qualitative and quantitative data in priming conversations for change. Simple visualisations of EVP depicted in the form of an 'inducements-contributions' model, and 'espoused' and 'experienced' value propositions are used during the initial engagement with clients. One example is depicted in Figure 14.2, which depicts a 'line of sight' between the adopted HR strategies of an organisation, the creation of an EVP architecture, and organisational outcomes, expressed in the form of *EVP equity*. This simplifies what in practice is a dynamic and complex process, but nevertheless provides a useful discursive device for raising the strategic importance of EVPs in the building of processual pathways for enhanced employee engagement and performance (see Reddington and Francis, 2011).

The notion of EVP equity is closely associated with the language of social exchange and New OE concept of authentic mutuality. It depicts the relative satisfaction and perceived 'value' of the EVP expressed at individual, team and organisational levels of analysis.

Figure 14.2 A processual approach to EV

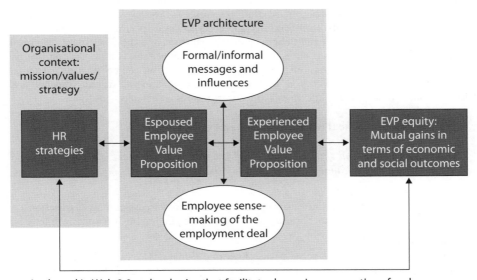

Anchored in Web 2.0 technologies that facilitate dynamic conversations for change

Source: adapted from Reddington and Francis (2011)

PRIMING CONVERSATIONS FOR CHANGE: MUTUAL PURPOSE AND GAINS

Enabling conditions

Our approach to EVP emphasises the need for creating 'enabling conditions' in raising consciousness and dialogue about alternative mindsets, values and structural tensions underpinning people's experience of the employment deal. This involves working with change leaders to set the foundations for people from diverse interests groups to work productively with paradox and ambiguity, and to foster collaboration and a common language for change in the co-constructing of EVP design – eg shared meaning about the realisation of position statements for 'innovation' and 'compliance'.

Priming conversations

Our next case study example, on ConsultCo, illustrates what we describe as our first phase in 'priming conversations' for change, beginning with an initial assessment of the employment relationship 'known' to participants via an EVP survey instrument that has an EVP personality dimension. This does not rely on detailed statistical analysis but is used to stimulate dialogue and co-construction of the 'deal', consistent with 'initiative conversations' (see the section *Language and performance* early in this chapter) aimed at challenging the status quo and fostering a perceived 'readiness for change'. It includes presentation of a basic 'radar plot' derived from aggregations of values representing personality traits, combined with a presentation of statistical correlations between various EVP elements, and our interpretations of free text responses (about what is most 'valued' about the deal, stories about 'workable arrangements' and 'key tensions' in carrying out job roles).

Creating draft value propositions

Survey feedback via an EVP portal, combined with facilitative discussion and practical workshops, assist in the creation of draft (espoused) 'position statements' based on the notion of inducements–contributions noted earlier, and 'personality profiles', which stimulate dialogue and agreement about which social exchange (EVP) elements are most likely to influence employee engagement and performance outcomes. An illustrative position statement drawn from our consultancy practice is provided below. This particular example is what we describe as a 'high-level position statement' around learning and innovation, and describes inducements and contributions associated with this.

Sample position statement on learning and innovation

We want to foster and support a culture of learning that will make our people more dynamic and able to capitalise upon opportunities for innovation.

Why is this important?
Our ability to learn and innovate is critical to the future success of our organisation, enabling us to respond quickly and flexibly to a fast-changing business environment.

How do we do it?
Through the creation of a high-trust learning climate that values diversity and learning opportunities for all, and fosters a willingness and capability for change and innovation.

This will be supported by innovative leadership and working practices that provide pathways for enhanced collaboration, learning, personal development and knowledge-sharing at all levels of the business.

Everyone will be expected to respond to the opportunities provided, taking more responsibility for their own learning and development in ways that add tangible benefits to themselves and to the organisation.

How will we know we have succeeded?
We would expect to see evidence of enhanced engagement and performance at all levels within the organisation. This would be captured by measures of POS,

engagement and performance, and more qualitative data showing personal accounts of people's work experience, including stories of enhanced confidence and mastery in carrying out their roles, and in moving the organisation forward.

PARADOX, AMBIGUITY AND JUDGEMENTAL COMPETENCE

Our approach to EVP places emphasis upon distributed leadership and the building of judgemental competence among both managers *and* employees, through the kind of survey feedback, facilitative discussion and practical workshops noted above. A key responsibility placed on ourselves as researcher-based consultants is to be heedful of the political dynamics around the bringing together of multiple stakeholders and the maintenance of a safe and bounded space for interactions to take place (Busche and Marshak, 2011). This is illustrated in our ConsultCo case example, in which tensions around compliance-enterprise and business-driven/employee-driven activities were given a level of exposure that had not been possible to surface with the company's previous survey architecture.

A key tenet of our approach is the focus given to the ongoing renegotiation of position statements by people involved in these conversations for change, in order to achieve pragmatic 'workable arrangements' that are mutually satisfactory for all parties concerned, depicted in our model as 'Me and my job', 'My team' and 'My organisation'. Individuals and teams who can demonstrate efficacy in working with tensions as a means of improving performance outcomes of mutual benefit to the individual and the organisation can be seen as judgementally competent – a vital part of the leadership capability dimension of New OE.

CONSULTCO

CASE STUDY

ConsultCo is a leading global provider of professional services. This case study is based on an EVP 'audit' of a UK-located division that provides its clients with a range of HR and OD interventions. The case demonstrates the application of our conversational approach to EVP, working with the senior team and staff of the division, to examine perceptions of the current employment deal (the 'experienced EVP') with the aim of revealing insights (both strengths and tensions) that affect sustainable high performance and employee well-being.

The senior partner of the division was the principal sponsor of the EVP audit. The brief was to discover the aspects of the employment deal perceived to be most valued and aligned with high people performance and engagement. Linked with this was an aim to explicitly surface tensions that had most impact on an employee's work experience and perceptions of the deal.

ConsultCo had previously conducted regular internally managed staff opinion surveys, which had provided useful insights into some positive and some less attractive features of the working environment that might be linked to high performance. However, the exercise tended to be characterised as a normative one, detailed statistical comparisons being used to indicate the relative improvement or otherwise of things such as performance management, reward and recognition, knowledge management and diversity. Opportunities for respondents to provide descriptive feedback were limited to a small number of free text questions, and selected examples were used to reinforce the statistical analysis. Furthermore, there were no reliable, consistently applied processes in place for members of the division to discuss the survey results with their line managers, nor to shape broader decision-making about organisational strategy, work and employment practices.

The internal sponsor recognised that their approach to employee voice via a standard opinion survey lacked authenticity – it was too one-dimensional and failed to provide sufficient depth of insight into the social dynamics of the division. On this basis, the senior partner invited us to deploy our EVP audit methodology in order to bring the social dynamics into sharper relief.

ConsultCo regarded as highly important the need for employees to be able to demonstrate reliability, self-confidence and mastery in the delivery of services to their clients, while under consistently high pressure to manage complexity, quality and a high work volume. Accordingly, it was important to understand the factors impacting on this capability.

Taking full account of this, phase 1 of our EVP audit was a web-based survey comprising a range of items representative of the contextual elements of our EVP architecture and which explicitly encouraged the surfacing of tensions and personal accounts of working practices through free-text responses.

From a statistical standpoint, the survey results revealed that overall response patterns to the survey questions were very similar between members and non-members of the leadership team. The division displayed high levels of work engagement, and we were able to draw significant correlations between certain tensions and the wider perception of the ConsultCo employer brand. The division's EVP personality profile showed it to be perceived as highly 'competent' and 'prestigious', with an 'agreeable disposition'. 'Formality' was quite pronounced, indicating that it was nonetheless not always straightforward to get things done.

The free-text survey responses were very rich and revealed a wealth of insights expressed through personal accounts that we clustered into three themes: time pressures and quality of work; support, self-worth and personal development; and leadership and management capability.

The blending of these data in the form of a report was used to prime conversations, initially with the leadership team and subsequently the whole team – phase 2 of our methodology.

Both sessions were conducted in a workshop-style fashion. Groups or 'families'

were created, each assigned a ConsultCo partner, to proactively work through key themes and associated tensions, and to think through potential workable solutions.

We found that describing the division in terms of personality traits provided a useful platform for talking about tensions in a non-threatening way, and helped participants swap ideas and suggestions about new ways of talking about the deal. For example, one issue centred on people being more confident at speaking up about their needs around work–life balance issues, such as 'coming in late on a Monday to be able to go to a Pilates class following a back injury'. Related to this there was some considerable discussion about how and when saying 'no' should be regarded as acceptable, and appeared to be linked to anxiety about 'hidden' impact on later performance reviews.

Our final report to the client included a critical discourse analysis of key themes emerging at the workshop, used to encourage reflection on the language framing conversations among participants. This included an illustrative mapping of the kind of words, expressions and practices cited as good examples of the deal in terms of mutual gains between employer and employee.

Based on the analysis, ConsultCo developed an action plan along three areas: personal development, culture and behaviours, and work–life balance. They defined a preferred future state in each of these areas and identified the actions required to achieve it involving the whole team. To date, good progress has been made on several of these actions, and EVP remains one of the core agenda items for all of their leadership team meetings and quarterly updates with the team.

Questions

1 How does this approach to capturing employee opinions differ from conventional approaches?

2 What are the implications for insight-led approaches to change management?

CASE STUDY COMMENTARY

A well-designed EVP provides a 'meaning structure' that allows individuals and collectives from different disciplines, backgrounds and levels of decision-making to develop a mutuality of purpose and expectations around the employment deal. This meaning structure is not static and change leaders need to build capabilities in effectively working across the 'conversational landscape' of EVP.

The idea of explicitly surfacing tensions and placing emphasis on social exchange, mutual purpose and gains, represented a major departure from the adopted in-house convention at ConsultCo. Accordingly, we were able to provide a persuasive case to justify its fitness for purpose, based on the academic arguments set out in this chapter and evidence from other client assignments, and the whole process received acclaim.

We were also cognisant of the concern expressed by Wefald and Downey (2009) that industry 'instruments' used to provide a measure of engagement are not normally subject to external reviews. In our case, we address this through publication of our work, and we remain open to critical review.

CONCLUSION

In the last decade we have witnessed an upsurge of interest in work and employment strategies which can promote sustainable employee engagement and performance. In this context, employers are seeking more sophisticated means by which to link their people strategy and the company brand to achieve differentiation in the labour market. Developments in employer branding and employee engagement are largely practitioner-led, but increasingly being informed by academic theory that takes more account of the dynamic social and psychological processes underpinning the employment relationship. Linked with this is growing recognition of the need for more process-oriented research into underlying relationships in terms of balance, nature and reciprocity, and how they are associated with relationship quality (Shore *et al*, 2009: 293).

Future research into exchange processes could usefully draw upon a critical discourse lens to shed light on the role of language in shaping structures and processes underpinning the employment relationship, and mechanisms that enhance the scope for employee and collective agency, which remains under-researched. We have noted the dominance of the 'resource' metaphor framing the literature on HR and change management, by which people are essentially treated as a commodity to be used/developed/practised on (Grant and Shields, 2002; Inkson, 2008). As a result, the notion of mutuality or the *two-way* nature of engagement in terms of reciprocity and exchange between individual and employer is underplayed in mainstream HR research and in the world of practice. Our framework of EVP allows us to explore these dynamics which are not readily available through statistical analysis, allowing a more critical reflective stance on everyday language that we tend to take for granted and not scrutinise.

EXPLORE FURTHER

Fleetwood, S. and Hesketh, A. J. (2010) *Explaining the Performance of Human Resource Management*. Cambridge: Cambridge University Press. This book introduces the reader to a critical realist perspective on HRM, and explores how such a stance adds value to our understanding of the work of HR executives and professionals.

Furnham, A., and Petrova, E. (2010) *Body Language In Business: Decoding the signals*. Basingstoke: Palgrave Macmillan. This book provides practical tips and advice about how to become more astute at reading and displaying the right body language.

Grant, D., Hardy, C., Oswick, C. and Putnam, L. (eds) (2004) *The Sage Handbook of Organizational Discourse*. London: Sage. This handbook provides an important overview of the methodologies and perspectives used in research on organisational discourse.

Guest, D., Isaksson, K. and De Witte, H. (2010) 'Introduction', in Guest, D., Isaksson, K. and De Witte, H. (eds) *Employment Contracts: Psychological contracts and employee well-being, an international study*. Oxford: Oxford University Press. This book focuses upon the relationship between temporary employment contracts and employee well-being, within the analytical framework of the psychological contract. It explores a range of potential influences on work-related well-being, including workload, job insecurity, employability and organisational support.

Rosethorn, H. (2009) *The Employer Brand: Keeping faith with the deal*. Aldershot: Gower. This text provides a practitioner perspective on employer branding which includes an array of practitioner insights and case examples.

Sparrow, P., Hird, M., Hesketh, A. and Cooper, C. (2010) *Leading HR*. Basingstoke: Palgrave Macmillan. This book captures the challenges facing HR directors, rooted in twin imperatives to lead their teams towards successful performance and also to monitor and assess the most effective leadership techniques and practices.

The Work Foundation website, http://www.theworkfoundation.com/research/publications.aspx, provides a series of reports on the future of HR, and the employment deal.

REFERENCES

Alfes, K., Truss, C., Soane, E. C., Rees, C. and Gatenby, M. (2010) *Creating an Engaged Workforce*. Research Report. London: Chartered Institute of Personnel and Development.

Aselage, J. and Eisenberger, R. (2003) 'Perceived organisational support and psychological contracts: a theoretical integration', *Journal of Organisational Behaviour*, Vol.29: 491–509.

Balain, S. and Sparrow, P. (2009) 'Engaged to perform: a new perspective on employee engagement'. White Paper 09/04, Lancaster University Management School.

Bandura, A. (1994) 'Self-efficacy', in Ramachaudran, V. S. (ed.) *Encyclopaedia of Human Behaviour*, Vol.4: 71–81. New York: Academic Press. (Reprinted in H. Friedman (ed.) (1998) *Encyclopaedia of Mental Health*. San Diego: Academic Press. Available online at: http://www.des.emory.edu/mfp/BanEncy.html.

Bandura, A. (2000) 'The exercise of human agency through collective efficacy', *Current Directions in Psychological Science*, Vol.9: 75. Edinburgh Napier University. Available online at: cdp.sagepub.com [accessed 7 December 2010].

Barrow, S. and Mosley, R. (2005) *The Employer Brand®: Bringing the best of brand management to people at work*. London: Wiley.

Beckett, H. (2005) 'Perfect partners', *People Management*, 16 April: 16–23.

Bhidé, A. (2010) 'The Big Idea: the judgement deficit', *Harvard Business Review*, September.

Blau, P. (1964) *Exchange and Power in Social Life*. New York: Wiley.

Bolton, S. C. and Houlihan, M. (2009) 'Beyond the control–resistance debate: a fresh look at experiences of work in the new economy', *Qualitative Research in Accounting and Management*, Vol.6, No.1/2: 5–13.

Boxall, P. and Macky, K. (2009) 'Research and theory on high-performance work systems: progressing the high-involvement stream', *Human Resource Management Journal*, Vol.19: 3–23.

Bushe, G. R. and Marshak, R. J. (2011) 'Revisioning organization development', *Journal of Applied Behavioural Science*, Vol.45, No.3: 348–68.

Butcher, D. and Atkinson, S. (2001) 'Stealth, secrecy and subversion: the language of change', *Journal of Organizational Change Management*, Vol.14, No.6: 1–11.

Caprara, G., Barbaranelli, C. and Guido, G. (2001) 'Brand personality: how to make the metaphor fit?', *Journal of Economic Psychology*, Vol.22: 377–95.

Chen, Z., Eisenberger, R., Johnson, K. M., Sucharski, I. L. and Aselage, J. (2009) 'Perceived organizational support and extra-role performance: which leads to which?', *Journal of Social Psychology*, Vol.149: 119–24.

Chiaburu, D. S., Diaz, I. and Pitts, V. E. (2011) 'Social and economic exchanges with the organization: do leader behaviors matter?', *Leadership and Organization Development Journal*, Vol.32, No.5: 442–61.

CIPD Report (2011) *Next Generation HR*, London: Chartered Institute of Personnel and Development. Available at http://www.cipd.co.uk/research/_next-gen-hr

Conway, N. and Briner, R. B. (2005) *Understanding Psychological Contracts at Work: A critical evaluation of theory and research*. Oxford: Oxford University Press.

Conway, N. and Briner, R. B. (2009) 'Fifty years of psychological contract research: what do we know and what are the main challenges?', *International Review of Industrial and Organizational Psychology*, Vol.21: 71–131.

Cropanzano, R. and Mitchell, M. S. (2005) 'Social exchange theory: an interdisciplinary review', *Journal of Management*, Vol.31: 874–900.

Cullinane, N. and Dundon, T. (2006) 'The psychological contract: a critical review', *International Journal of Management Reviews*, Vol.8, No.2: 113–29.

Cunningham, J. B. and Kempling, J. S. (2010) 'Implementing change in public sector organizations', *Management Decision*, Vol.47, No.2: 330–44.

Cushen, J. (2009) 'Branding employees', *Qualitative Research in Accounting Management*, Vol.6, No.1/2: 102–14.

D'Annunzio-Green, N. and Francis, H. (2005) 'Human resource development and the psychological contract: great expectations or false hopes', *Human Resource Development International*, Vol.8, No.3: 327–44.

Dart, D. and Turner, T. (2006) 'New working arrangements: changing the nature of the employment relationship?', *International Journal of Human Resource Management*, Vol.17, No.3: 523–38.

Davies, G. (2008) 'Employer branding and its influence on managers', *European Journal of Marketing*, Vol.42, No.5/6: 667–81.

Delbridge, R. (2007) 'HRM and contemporary manufacturing', in Boxall, P. F., Purcell, J. and Wright, P. (eds) *The Oxford Handbook of Human Resource Management*. Oxford: Oxford University Press.

Delbridge, R. (2011) 'The critical future of HRM', in Blyton, P., Heery, E. and Turnbull, P. (eds) *Reassessing Employment Relations*. London: Sage.

Delbridge, R. and Ezzamel, M. (2005) 'The strength of difference: contemporary conceptions of control', *Organization*, Vol.12, No.5: 603–18.

Delbridge, R. and Keenoy, T. (2010) 'Beyond managerialism', *International Journal of Human Resource Management*, Vol.21, No.4–6: 799–817.

Dyer, L. and Reeves, T. (1995) 'Human resource strategies and firm performance: what do we do know and where do we need to go?', *International Journal of Human Resource Management*, Vol.6, No.3: 656–70.

Eder, P. and Eisenberger, R. (2008) 'Perceived organizational support: reducing the negative influence of co-worker withdrawal behavior', *Journal of Management*, Vol.34: 55–68.

Edwards, M. R. (2010) 'An integrative review of employer branding and OB theory', *Personnel Review*, Vol.39, No.1: 5–23.

Ehnert, I. (2008) *Sustainable Human Resource Management: A conceptual and exploratory analysis from a paradox perspective*. Heidelberg: Physica-Verlag.

Eisenberger, R., Huntington, R., Hutchison, S. and Sowa, D. (1986) 'Perceived organizational support', *Journal of Applied Psychology*, Vol.71: 500–7.

Evans, P. A. (1999) 'A duality perspective', *Organization*, Vol.6, No.2: 325–38.

Evans, P., Pucik, V. and Barsoux, J. (2002) *The Global Challenge, Frameworks for international human resource management*. New York: McGraw-Hill/Irwin.

Fairclough, N. (1995) *Critical Discourse Analysis: Papers in the critical study of language*. Harlow: Longman.

Fineman, S. (2000) 'Emotional arenas revisited', in Fineman, S. (ed.) *Emotion in Organisations*. London: Sage.

Fleetwood, S. and Hesketh, A. J. (2010) *Explaining the Performance of Human Resource Management*. Cambridge: Cambridge University Press.

Ford, J. (1999) 'Organizational change as shifting conversations', *Journal of Organizational Change Management*, Vol.12, No.6: 1–14. Available online at: http:/www.emerald-library.com/brev/12312fb1.htm.

Ford, J. and Ford, L. (1995) 'The role of conversations in producing intentional change in organizations', *Academy of Management Review*, Vol.20, No.3: 541–71.

Ford, J. and Ford, L. (2008) 'Conversational profiles: a tool for altering the conversational patterns of change managers', *Journal of Applied Behavioral Science*, Vol.44, No.4: 445–67. Available online at: http://jab.sagepub.com/content/44/4/ 445.refs.

Francis, H. (2002) 'The power of "talk" in HRM-based change', *Personnel Review*, Vol.31, No.4: 432–48.

Francis, H. (2007) 'Discursive struggle and the ambiguous world of HRD', *Advances in Developing Human Resources*, Vol.9, No.1: 83–96.

Francis, H. and D'Annunzio-Green, N. (2007) 'The impact of emotion management training on the "shifting sands" of the psychological contract', in Hill, R. and Stewart, J. (ed.) *Management Development: Perspectives from research and practice*. Routledge Studies in Human Resource Development. London: Routledge.

Francis, H. and Keegan, A. (2006) 'The changing face of HR: in search of balance', *Human Resource Management Journal*, Vol.16, No.3: 231–49.

Francis, H. and Reddington, M. (2010) 'Redirecting and reconnecting theory: employer branding and the employment "deal"', Paper for the BSA Work, Employment and Society Conference.

Francis, H. and Reddington, M. (2011) 'HR transformation and technology: why language matters', Paper for the 7th Biannual International Conference of the Dutch HRM network, University of Groningen, the Netherlands.

Francis, H. and Sinclair, J. (2003) 'A processual analysis of HRM-based change', *Organization*, Vol.10, No.4: 685–706.

Garber, C. and Tekleab, A. G. (2009) 'Perceived organizational support: a review and recommendations'. Available online at: http://www.midwestacademy.org/proceedings/2010/ Papers/Garber_OB3. pdf.

Geary, J. and Dobbins, A. (2001) 'Teamwork: a new dynamic in the pursuit of management control', *Human Resource Management Journal*, Vol.11, No.1: 3–21.

Gentile, M. (2010) *Giving Voice to Values: How to speak your mind when you know what's right*. London: Yale University Press.

Grant, D. and Shields, J. (2002) 'In search of the subject: researching employee reactions to human resource management', *Journal of Industrial Relations*, Vol.44, No.3: 313–34.

Guest, D. (2004) 'Flexible employment contracts, the psychological contract and employee outcomes: an analysis and review of the evidence', *International Journal of Management Reviews*, Vol.5/6, No.1: 1–19.

Guest, D. and Conway, N. (2002) 'Communicating the psychological contract: an employer perspective', *Human Resource Management Journal*, Vol.12, No.2: 22–38.

Herriot, P. and Pemberton, C. (1997) 'Facilitating new deals', *Human Resource Management Journal*, Vol.7, No.1: 45–56.

Inkson, K. (2008) 'Are humans resources?', *Career Development International*, Vol.13, No.3: 270–9.

Kahn, W. A. (1990) 'Psychological conditions of personal engagement and disengagement at work', *Academy of Management Journal*, Vol.33, No.4: 692–724.

Keegan, A. and Boselie, P. (2006) 'The lack of impact of dissensus inspired analysis on developments in the field of human resource management', *Journal of Management Studies*, Vol.43, No.7: 1492–1511.

Keegan, A. and Francis, H. (2006) 'Facing facts', *People Management*, February: 9–10.

Keegan, A. and Francis, H. (2010) 'Practitioner talk: the changing textscape of HRM and emergence of HR business partnership', *International Journal of Human Resource Management*, Vol.21, No.4–6: 873–98.

Keenoy, T. (2009) 'Human resource management', in Alvesson, M., Bridgman, T. and Willmott, H. (eds) *The Oxford Handbook of Critical Management Studies*. Oxford: Oxford University Press.

Landen, M. (2002) 'Emotion management: dabbling in mystery – white witchcraft or black art?', *Human Resource Development International*, Vol.5, No.4: 507–21.

Lawler, E. (1986) *High-Involvement Management*. San Francisco: Jossey-Bass.

Legge, K. (2001) 'Silver bullet or spent round? Assessing the meaning of the high-commitment management/performance relationship', in Storey, J. (ed.) *Human Resource Management: A critical text*, 2nd edition. London: Thomson Learning.

Lepak, D., Smith, K. and Taylor, M. (2007) 'Value creation and value capture: a multi-level perspective', *Academy of Management Review*, Vol.32, No.1: 180–94.

Lievans, F. (2007) 'Employer branding in the Belgian army: the importance of instrumental and symbolic beliefs for potential applicants, actual applicants and military employees', *Human Resource Management*, Vol.46, No.1, Spring: 51–69.

Luthans, F. and Peterson, S. (2002) 'Employee engagement and manager self-efficacy: implications for managerial effectiveness and development', *Journal of Management Development*, Vol.21, No.5: 376–87.

Macey, W. H. and Schneider, B. (2008) 'The meaning of employee engagement', *Industrial and Organisational Psychology*, Vol.1: 3–30.

MacLeod, D. and Clarke, N. (2009) *Engaging for Success: Enhancing performance through engagement*. A Report to Government.

Marchington, M. and Wilkinson, A. (2005) *Human Resource Management at Work*, 3rd edition. London: Chartered Institute of Personnel and Development.

Marks, A. (2001) 'Developing a multiple-foci conceptualisation of the psychological contract', *Employee Relations*, Vol.23, No.5: 454–67.

Marshak, R. (2002) 'Changing the language of change: how new contexts and concepts are challenging the ways we think and talk about organizational change', Paper for the 5th International Conference on Organisational Discourse, July, Kings College, London.

Martin, G. and Dyke, S. (2010) 'Employer branding and corporate reputation management: a signalling model and case illustration', in Collings, D. and Scullion, H. (eds) *Global Talent Management*. London: Routledge.

Martin, G. and Hetrick, S. (2006) *Corporate Reputations, Branding and Managing People: A strategic approach to HR*. Oxford: Butterworth-Heinemann.

Martin, G., Gollan, P. J. and Grigg, K. (2011) 'Is there a bigger and better future for employer branding? Facing up to innovation, corporate reputations and wicked problems in SHRM', *International Journal of Human Resource Management*, ISSN 0958-5192 (in press).

Maslach, C., Schaufeli, W. B. and Leiter, M. P. (2001) 'Job burnout', *Annual Review of Psychology*, Vol.52: 397–422.

Morrison, E. W. and Robinson, S. L. (1997) 'When employees feel betrayed: a model of how psychological contract violation develops', *Academy of Management Review*, Vol.22, No.1: 226–57.

O'Donohue, W. and Wickham, M. D. (2008) 'Managing the psychological contract in competitive labour-market conditions', *Journal of Global Business Issues*, Vol.2, No.2: 23–32.

Overell, S. (2008) *Inwardness: The rise of meaningful work*. Provocation Series, Vol.4, No.2. London: The Work Foundation.

Paauwe, J. (2009) 'HRM and performance: achievements, methodological issues and prospects', *Journal of Management Studies*, Vol.46: 129–42.

Pate, J. (2005) 'The changing contours of the psychological contract: unpacking context and circumstances of breach', *Journal of European Industrial Training*, Vol.30, No.1: 32–47.

Pate, J., Martin, G. and McGoldrick, J. (2003) 'The impact of the psychological contract on employee attitudes and behaviour', *Employee Relations*, Vol.25, No.6: 557–73.

Pfeffer, J. (1998) *The Human Equation; Building profits by putting people first*. Boston, MA: Harvard Business School Press.

Reddington, M. and Francis H. (2011) 'The deployment of Web 2.0 in re-architecting EVP to enhance the employer brand', in Martin, G. and Cooper, C. (eds) *Corporate Reputation: Managing threats and opportunities*. Aldershot: Gower.

Rhoades, L. and Eisenberger, R. (2002) 'Perceived organizational support: a review of the literature', *Journal of Applied Psychology*, Vol. 87, No.4: 698–714.

Rich, B., Lepine, J. and Crawford, E. R. (2010) 'Job engagement: antecedents and effects on job performance', *Academy of Management Journal*, Vol.53, No.3: 617–35.

Robertson-Smith, G. and Marwick, C. (2009) *Employee Engagement: A review of current thinking*. Brighton: Institute of Employment Studies.

Rosethorn, H. (2009) *The Employer Brand: Keeping faith with the deal*. Aldershot: Gower.

Rousseau, D. M. (1995) *Psychological Contracts in Organizations: Understanding written and unwritten agreements*. Thousand Oaks, CA: Sage.

Rousseau, D. M. (2005) *I-deals: Idiosyncratic deals employees bargain for themselves*. New York: M. E. Sharpe.

Rousseau, D. M. and Kim, T. G. (2006) 'When workers bargain for themselves: idiosyncratic deals and the nature of the employment relationship; Paper presented at British Academy of Management, Belfast.

Rousseau, D. M., Ho, V. T. and Greenberg, J. (2006) 'I-deals: idiosyncratic terms in employment relationships', *Academy of Management Review*, Vol.31: 977–94.

Rousseau, D. M., Hornung, S. and Kim, T. G. (2009) 'Idiosyncratic deals: testing propositions on timing, content, and the employment relationship', *Journal of Vocational Behavior*, Vol.7, No.3: 338–48.

Rynes, S. L., Giluk, T. L. and Brown, K. G. (2007) 'The very separate worlds of academic and practitioner periodicals in human resource management: implications for evidence-based management', *Academy of Management Journal*, Vol.50: 987–1008.

Saks, A. M. (2006) 'Antecedents and consequences of employee engagement', *Journal of Managerial Psychology*, Vol.21, No.7: 600–19.

Schaufeli, W. and Bakker, A. (2003) 'Utrecht work engagement scale, preliminary manual version 1'. Available online at: http://www.schaufeli.com/downloads/tests/Test%20 manual%20UWES.pdf [accessed 10 February 2011].

Shore, L. M., Coyle-Shapiro, J. A-M., Chen, X-P. and Tetrick, L. E. (2009) 'Social exchange in work settings: content, mixed and process models', *Management and Organization Review*, Vol.5, No.3: 289–302.

Shuck, M. B. (2011) 'Four emerging perspectives of employee engagement: an integrative literature review', *Human Resource Development Review*. Available online at: http://hrd.sagepub.com/content/early/2011/06/11/1534484311410840 [accessed 15 June 2011].

Song, L. J., Tsui, A. S. and Law, K. S. (2009) 'Unpacking employee responses to organizational exchange mechanisms: the role of social and economic exchange perception', *Journal of Management*, Vol.35, No. 1: 56–93.

Sparrow, P., Hird, M., Hesketh, A. and Cooper, C. (2010) *Leading HR*. Basingstoke: Palgrave Macmillan.

Tekleab, A. G., Takeuchi, R. and Taylor, M. S. (2005) 'Extending the chain of relationships among organizational justice, social exchange, and employee reactions: the role of contract violations', *Academy of Management Journal*, Vol.48, No. 1, 146–57.

Thomas, P. (2003) 'The recontextualization of management: a discourse-based approach to analysing the development of management thinking', *Journal of Management Studies*, Vol.40, June: 775–801.

Thompson, J. A. and Bunderson, J. S. (2003) 'Violations of principle: ideological currency in the psychological contract', *Academy of Management Review*, Vol.28: 571–86.

Townley, B. (1998) 'Beyond good and evil: depth and division in the management of human resources', in McKinlay, A. and Starkey, K. (eds) *Foucault, Management and Organization Theory: From Panopticon to technologies of self*. London: Sage.

Vandenberg, R. J., Richardson, H. A. and Eastman, L. J. (1999) 'The impact of high involvement work processes on organizational effectiveness: a second-order latent variable approach', *Group and Organization Management*, Vol.24, No.3: 300–39.

Walton, R. E. (1985) 'From control to commitment in the workplace', *Harvard Business Review*, Vol.63: 77–84.

Watson, T. (2002) *Organising and Managing Work*. Harlow: Pearson Education.

Wefald, A. and Downey, R. (2009) 'Job engagement in organizations: fad, fashion or folderol?', *Journal of Organizational Behavior*, Vol.31, No.1: 141–5.

Wong, W., Albert, A., Huggett, M. and Sullivan, J. (2009) *Quality People Management for Quality Outcomes: The future of HR. Review of evidence on people management*. Report. London: The Work Foundation.

Wong, W., Blazey, L., Sullivan, J., Zheltoukhova, K., Albert, A. and Reid, B. (2010) *Understanding the Deal: Placing the employee at the heart of the employment relationship*. Report. London: The Work Foundation.

CHAPTER 15

The OD Role of HRM in Ethics, Corporate Social Responsibility and Sustainability

Carole Parkes

CHAPTER OVERVIEW

Organisations face many challenges in the globalised, interconnected twenty-first century – none more so than the societal expectations of behaving responsibly with regard to people (including employees, customers and communities), profits (in how they are created as well as distributed) and the planet (in reducing, reusing and recycling their resources). This chapter discusses ethics, corporate social responsibility (CSR) and sustainability in the context of business organisation, and their links with emergent theories and practices in organisational development (OD) and human resource management (HRM). It draws upon case study examples to illustrate how change towards 'responsible management' may be facilitated, exploring the contribution of emerging (Organisational Effectiveness) strategies in achieving this.

LEARNING OBJECTIVES

By the end of this chapter the reader should be able to:

- appreciate the nature and importance of ethics, corporate social responsibility (CSR) and sustainability in the context of organisations today
- describe the role that values and organisational culture play in addressing issues relating to ethics, CSR and sustainability
- recognise the importance of ethical leadership
- consider the OD role of HRM in facilitating change in this area
- explore the emergence of New OE (Organisational Effectiveness) strategies in the context of ethics, CSR and sustainability.

INTRODUCTION

This chapter explores the relationship, in theory and practice, between the OD role of HRM on the one hand and the growing importance of business ethics, corporate social responsibility (CSR) and sustainability on the other. It calls for the HRM profession to provide inspirational leadership in working with all stakeholders (including employees) in the area of organisational development and change management to address issues of ethics, CSR and sustainability. The blending of academic and practitioner insights in this chapter is important because one of the key challenges in this area is in implementation. Many organisations struggle to embed these issues into their culture and processes. This can lead to a superficial approach that at best may appear disingenuous, and at worst (for the organisation) exposes them to damaging reputational risk.

WHY ETHICS, CSR AND SUSTAINABILITY? AND WHY NOW?

The pressure for those who prosper financially to behave ethically and be socially 'responsible' has deep historical, cultural and religious roots that are intertwined with the HR profession (Bremner, 1994; Asongu, 2007). Early industrialists who accepted their ethical and social responsibilities delivered this through progressive HR policies that recognised the importance of employee well-being in building successful businesses. In recent times, the succession of ethical scandals and global events have increased expectations for visible evidence of business organisations' ethical, social responsibility and environmental credentials. In addition, technology, and its ability to provide constant access to information (see Chapter 8), ensures that organisations cannot hide from the real risks (especially reputational risks) of ignoring these issues.

At the outset, it is important to clarify what is meant by ethics, CSR and sustainability because of different interpretations used by academics, business practitioners and others. The difficulty this presents is that each constituent group is 'motivated by its own reasoning; each speaks its own language; and each believes that it is the most important' (Scott, 2011: 4). The terms used have been selected because they cover the range of activities to be discussed. Other associated terms include 'citizenship' and 'philanthropy' (mainly US), and 'governance' (regulatory), which will also be explored briefly in the chapter.

ETHICS

One dictionary definition of 'ethics' (*American Heritage Dictionary*, 2004) refers to the 'study of the general nature of morals and of specific moral choices: moral philosophy; and the rules or standards governing the conduct of the members of a profession'. The theme of rules and standards will be returned to in relation to business and management and, specifically, HRM as a profession.

Whether something is moral or not goes beyond this minimalist approach, and decisions taken in business are often justified theoretically and practically using arguments that stem from ethical theory. For example, decisions in business are often justified using consequentialist arguments, that 'the end justifies the means' – that end usually being higher profits. This is also true for the HR profession, for which proving its credentials in terms of profitability has almost become its *raison d'être*. In a review of HRM and performance measures, Boselie *et al* (2005) found that financial measures represented half of all articles (104) included in their analysis, profit being the most common, followed by various measures for sales.

Singer's (2011) review of relating theory to practical decision-making identified two strands of academic thought in connection with ethical theory. The first is from the philosophical tradition, which seeks to prescribe behaviour through 'reflective deliberations'. The second is from the psychological perspective and seeks to describe 'typical' moral behaviour. The former provides a normative approach of setting norms and standards (expectations of what *ought* to happen), and the latter is more descriptive in looking at the ethical views held by individuals and how this affects their behaviour (explanations of what happens in practice). In most organisations, the reality is somewhere between the two approaches. Ethical dilemmas are often difficult and challenging, involving questions that may not be black and white but have many shades of grey, serving to underline the complex, paradoxical and ambiguous nature of organisational life.

CSR

Definitions of corporate social responsibility refer to the connection between the economic, social and environmental responsibilities of business organisations and how values and judgements are critical in making ethical decisions. For example: 'Business decision-making linked to ethical values, compliance with legal requirements, and respect for people, communities, and the environment around the world' (Business for Social Responsibility, 2006; www.bsr.org).

Recent global events and the growth in consumer and public expectations have placed greater pressure on organisations to act responsibly and set out visible evidence of their ethical and social responsibilities (Burchell and Cook, 2006). This shift provides opportunities for all social actors to prove that there is more to ethics and CSR than merely corporate rhetoric.

Carroll's (1999) concept of social responsibility encapsulates four major factors that shape key areas of responsibility for business. The four types of responsibility are philanthropic, ethical, legal and economic. The economic drivers are important for organisations, but the danger of relying only on the 'business case' is that ethics and CSR become 'optional' (any ethical or moral case then being disposable). There can be similar problems with the legal drivers for ethics and CSR. Although adhering to the law is not optional, such a regulatory approach is minimalist. In most cases the law provides a backstop for many of the more obvious abuses, and just complying with the law is not the same as behaving ethically or acting responsibly. In addition, many organisations have seen their 'social responsibilities' as predominantly charitable giving or related activities, and in doing so have really missed the point. Although this activity is laudable and may address the philanthropic responsibilities of Carroll' s model, it still treats ethics and CSR in economic terms as an 'externality'. Thus organisations may have a disconnect between promoting a CSR policy in the community and behaving responsibly as an employer. In short, ethics and CSR should be about how a business makes its money and runs the organisation, rather than just about what it does with any excess profits. An authentic approach to CSR requires real engagement with all stakeholders, particularly employees, to shape the approach and language used both within and outside the organisation. If ethics and CSR are to be successful, the strategies and policies must be internally driven – which contrasts greatly with the popular use of ethics and CSR as a public relations or marketing gimmick.

SUSTAINABILITY

The final definition to explore is that of sustainability. As with CSR, many definitions of sustainability refer to what Elkington (1997) describes as the triple bottom line of economic, social and environmental responsibilities. However, sustainability is most often associated with the environmental domain and implies continuity and more long-term perspectives. This is encapsulated by the Brundtland Commission Report, which describes (UN, 1987: 43) sustainability as: 'Meeting the needs of the present without compromising the ability of future generations to meet their own needs.'

In business and management research, issues of the environment and sustainability have often been subsumed within the ethics and corporate social responsibility (CSR) literature (Porritt, 2007; Ketola, 2008). In the public domain, it is the scientific arguments, mainly about climate change, that have predominated (Goldacre, 2008), and the nature of these debates may encourage the impression that climate change and – more broadly –

sustainability do not dramatically impact upon individual lives, so doing something about it at home or at work can be seen as optional. In essence, climate change and global warming are symptoms of our unsustainability, and whatever the arguments about these issues, the real question is whether our current lifestyles and business models are sustainable.

Although popular discourses in the environmental sustainability debate refer to 'saving' the planet (as an altruistic act), research from environmental science and, in particular, Gaia theorists, demonstrates that nature is more powerful than human society, and that what is at risk from ecological and social degradation is not the planet but humankind and its way of life (Lovelock, 2000). According to the *Living Planet* Report (World Wildlife Fund, 2010), if we (in the UK) continue to use up the Earth's natural resources at the current rate, we will need the equivalent of three planets by 2050. (In the USA, the estimate is six.) It therefore makes sense for all actors in human society (whether they are businesses, governments or individuals) to learn to work with nature rather than against it if they are to benefit in the long term (Capra, 2004). Although political leaders need to act with courage and commitment to reach global agreements, the real success will be the extent to which *all* organisations and the general public engage with the issues and commit to changing the way they conduct their business activities and live their lives. In short, what makes it possible for individuals to make the connection between the information they have, what they need to do in practice and their behaviour? Who else, other than HR within organisations, has a remit for employee engagement and thus has the potential to make a difference? It is in this regard that OD approaches and processes can facilitate change.

IN SUMMARY

What we need to consider is whether or not the existing business paradigms we use and train our future business leaders to adopt make sense. The conventional discourse of organisational strategy, policy and practice mainly focuses on the 'who?', 'what?' and 'where?' But we need to look more at the 'why?' If we look more closely at 'why?', this leads to the implications for strategy and the 'who?', 'what?', 'where?' of the implementation plans, KPIs and activities. Aligning societal purpose with values and strategy requires looking not just at profit for profit's sake but profit with purpose. Nick Main, Global Sustainability Leader of Deloittes (2011: 2), argues that we should try to 'imagine a world where business is celebrated for its contribution to society' (rather than the continual stream of corporate scandals), and suggests that

> business should be based on the broad foundation of the ethical good: the delivery of benefits (products and services) that improve the human existence in the context of a resources-constrained world.

REFLECTIVE ACTIVITY

Think about organisations you are familiar with and list those that have a positive reputation in relation to ethics, CSR and/or sustainability. Then list those that may be perceived in a more negative way. Consider the differences in approach by organisations on the two lists and how this may impact on the individual organisations.

BRINGING ABOUT CHANGE

So how and why do organisations bring about change? There are organisations that see ethics, CSR and sustainability as vital to the way that they do business because it is simply 'the right thing to do' (Cadbury, 2006). For others, raised public expectations, competitor pressures and increased levels of scrutiny (with the associated reputational risk) suggest that ignoring these issues is no longer possible. In addition, there is growing evidence that the career choices of graduates and thus recruitment for employers are influenced by the sustainable development and CSR agenda of employers (HEA, 2007). Thus the recruitment and, perhaps more importantly, the retention of talented employees can be affected by the extent to which organisations are able to demonstrate their credentials in this important area (Turban and Greening, 1997) – see also Chapter 13 on inclusive talent management.

For organisations to embrace ethics, CSR and sustainability, the strategies and policies that underpin them must be part of the value system of the organisation and be embedded in all core activities, including those for which HR are responsible. However, to bring about change, it is not simply a case of using mechanistic instruments such as changing structures or issuing edicts. This chapter explores some of the critical aspects that can influence the success (or otherwise) of changing towards a more ethical, responsible and sustainable organisation. These include paying attention to issues of culture, values and leadership, as well as the OD role of HRM. The notion of what constitutes organisational effectiveness is also brought into question. In taking a triple bottom line perspective (that embraces multiple stakeholders), there is an opportunity to widen the rather narrow economic interpretation of what 'strategic HRM' means. Rather than assuming that 'strategic' equates to showing purely the financial consequences of HRM policies and practices, the legitimate concerns of constituents other than investors can be recognised (McWilliams et al, 2006).

Chapter 1 sets out the lens of a New OE (Organisational Effectiveness) that provides four key components of a New OE mindset. These are language and action, authenticity and mutuality, paradox and ambiguity, and leadership and management. Many of the key features of ethics, CSR and sustainability and how they link to New OE are listed in Table 15.1 and further discussed below.

Table 15.1 Ethics, CSR and sustainability – key features and links to New OE

Key features of ethics, CSR and sustainability	New OE lens
Understanding terms Using the 'right' vocabulary Changing the discourse, going beyond PR rhetoric 'Walking the talk'	Language and action
Stakeholder collaboration and engagement Enacting espoused values Approaches that are genuinely embedded, rather than 'bolt-on'	Authenticity and mutuality
'Competing tensions', including • long- versus short-term pressures and perspectives • organisational and individual values • conflicts of stakeholder interests: power and politics • risk and reputation • questioning 'business as usual' • ethical dilemmas and decision-making	Paradox and ambiguity
Authentic leadership Issues of credibility Leadership communication and passing on skills for future leaders	Leadership and management

LANGUAGE AND ACTION

In the introduction to this chapter, the need to define terms and understand the vocabulary used is explained because of the different language and interpretations used in this area. As a consequence, the terms 'ethics', 'responsibility' (or 'CSR') and 'sustainability' are used throughout this chapter to indicate the breadth of the topic. If only one term was used, there is a danger that it could be interpreted in a restricted way as only referring to (for example) ethical issues or the environment. The use of particular vocabulary is important because language creates norms and values that can become self-fulfilling prophecies. Self-interest and market economics has become the dominant discourse in organisations where performance is measured predominantly in financial terms.

As Eccles and Nohria (1992: 29) contend, 'The way people talk about the world has everything to do with the way the world is ultimately understood and acted in.' Ferraro *et al* (2005) argue that the language and assumptions of economics have adversely influenced human behaviour specifically, creating more self-interested behaviour and also leading to the widespread acceptance of trust-eroding market mechanisms. The assumptions and language that underlies this become self-fulfilling prophecies in that they are taken for granted and normatively valued, and therefore create conditions which make them come true.

In a 2011 study of MBA students' reflections of their studies of ethics, responsibility and sustainability, many reported that one of the most important outcomes was 'providing them with the vocabulary' or 'the confidence' to raise issues and concerns that they had previously thought about but did not know how to construct their arguments around. This issue of 'voice' is an important theme. Others mention 'realising that others have similar thoughts', or that their studies provided 'legitimacy' for their own views (Parkes and Blewitt, 2011: 14).

Values are critical to the integration of ethics, responsibility and sustainability, and the links with language are outlined below. Values are also discussed in more detail later in this chapter.

Values and language use

- Values are the vocabulary of socially approved goals used to motivate action, and to express and justify the solutions chosen.
- Values are also drivers of behaviour, including workplace behaviour (Schwartz, 1999). Chapter 1 refers to managers and leaders being 'conversationally responsible', and to 'conversations for change' (see also the section on leadership and management below).
- Values are therefore particularly important in changing the discourse and bringing about change towards more ethical, responsible and sustainable organisations.
- Values also need to be consistent with actions, involving clear links between talking and acting – what is commonly referred to as 'walking the talk' or 'living the values'.
- In practice, this means being genuine about strategies, policies and practices in this area that go beyond PR rhetoric.

The last bullet point about genuineness now leads us to consider the next New OE lens.

AUTHENTICITY AND MUTUALITY

A stakeholder approach to managing organisations is consistent with the premise of New OE of the need for a rebalancing of interests to achieve greater mutuality, and the cornerstone of definitions of CSR and sustainability. This approach has its roots in the seventeenth and eighteenth centuries with Hobbes and Rousseau's ideas of social contracts, and, as Freeman (1984: 31) points out, is concerned with 'any group or individual who may be affected by its activities' and/or 'without whose support the organisation may cease to exist'. This also speaks to the need to engage with 'different' actors and voices.

However, for many actors the question of access is a prohibiting factor to genuine engagement. As Banerjee (2008: 72) points out, 'Stakeholder theory of the firm represents a form of stakeholder colonialism that serves to regulate the behaviour of stakeholders.' This is because it is always couched in terms that advantage the corporation and diminishes the role of the state, civil society and other stakeholders. Yet in practice, it is important to recognise that the stakeholder model involves complex processes of interaction and negotiation undergone by different actors.

Burchell and Cook (2006) use critical discourse analysis (CDA) to examine the evolution of CSR and highlight the broader, more interactive and critical elements of CSR discourse. They draw on Chouliaraki and Fairclough's (1999) work on discourse to develop a picture of CSR that involves multiple actors and is less about businesses 'managing' stakeholders and more about the very challenging process of 'stakeholder management' through engagement and dialogue between internal and (very significantly) external stakeholders. They argue that the future direction of CSR may be strongly influenced by the ability of different actors to access and influence this dialogue.

The UK Government showed its support for multiple stakeholders through the CSR Academy (set up by the Department of Trade and Industry). Its report states (CSR Academy, 2006: 1) that this approach requires

> a recognition that brand names depend not only on quality, price and uniqueness but on how, cumulatively, companies interact with their workforce, community and environment. In Corporate Responsibility we need to judge results not just by the input but also by its outcomes: the difference we make to the world in which we live.

A further example of this is the work of Mary Gentile (2009), who argues that leaders and managers need to adopt a collaborative approach to developing organisational values. They should recognise that individuals are not devoid of values (just waiting for them to be handed down) but already have their own and, given an opportunity, would like to use their agency to act on them.

Genuine engagement is part of an authentic approach to ethics, responsibility and sustainability, as is the need to embed these issues within the organisation. As Laszlo and Zhexembayeva (2011) contend, it is not sufficient to achieve symbolic wins at the margins of the organisation. Ethics, responsibility and sustainability need to be part of the organisation's DNA, integrated into all systems and processes, and not used as a bolt-on ('scapegoat') department within Marketing, Communications or PR.

REFLECTIVE ACTIVITIES

Draw a Mind map of all the stakeholders (internal and external) for an organisation you are familiar with. Then consider the nature of the dialogue and engagement with each of the stakeholders.

● To what extent is this authentic?

● How could the dialogue and engagement be improved?

PARADOX AND AMBIGUITY

Paradox and ambiguity represent a fundamental aspect of issues relating to ethics, CSR and sustainability. This is because they require an acknowledgement of different perspectives and an understanding of the social, political, environmental and economic context. In addition, as individuals, we face ethical dilemmas (or conflicts in moral imperatives) in our everyday lives, and these can take on greater significance when placed in an organisational context.

There are also competing tensions in what Evans, Pucik and Barsoux (2002) describe as competing tensions of organisational effectiveness (detailed in Chapter 1). Some of these are discussed below.

Tensions can often surface when the focus is on short-term profits in the form of returns to shareholders and crisis management that affect employee policies. Porter and Kramer (2006) argue that companies should operate in the ways that secure long-term behaviour that is not socially detrimental or environmentally wasteful, and should engage in constructive dialogue with regulators, local citizens, employees and other stakeholders. In November 2006 Siemens nearly went out of business because they forgot the words of their founder, 'I won't sell the future for short-term profit' (Werner Siemens, 1848).

Tensions and the potential loss of employee engagement occur when the values of the organisation are at odds with individual values. In a survey of top MBA students in the USA (Aspen Institute, 2008) most students reported that they felt themselves likely to encounter conflict between their personal values and what they were asked to do in business (see also the sections on values below).

The desire to be competitive can result in organisations' losing sight of the valuable input of key stakeholders. Shell recognised the need to take a more collaborative approach after its decision to 'dump' its Brent Spa oil platform in the North Sea created a major crisis for the company because of protests across the globe (Cadbury, 2006).

Organisations have to take risks to be innovative but need to be aware of the reputational damage that can result from a lack of consideration of their ethical, social and environmental responsibilities. Indeed, one of the key competencies for organisations and individuals recognising their ethical, social and sustainability responsibilities is in 'questioning business as usual' (CSR Academy, 2006). This means being open to new ideas and challenging others to adopt new ways of thinking.

In operating with such tensions, the key issue goes back to the question of organisational values and ethics. Are they integrated into all systems and processes within the organisation? Do they naturally form part of the decision-making process? (See the RICOH case study below.)

LEADERSHIP AND MANAGEMENT

Effective leadership and management is key to organisations' embracing a positive approach to ethics, CSR and sustainability. Recent research points to the centrality of top management leadership to a green organisational culture (Govindarajulu and Daily, 2004), and to leadership strategies throughout the organisation as critical to creating ethical organisational climates (Grojean et al, 2004). Earlier in this chapter the notion of reimagining the purpose of organisations was discussed. In light of this, it is important to consider what kind of leadership is necessary to facilitate it.

Within leadership studies there are a range of theories to consider, including trait theories that examine the qualities or characteristics of leaders; behavioural theories that explore the actions of leaders and in particular the way in which they behave towards their 'followers'; contingency theories that look to the situations leaders operate in; and finally theories that distinguish between transactional (based on mutually beneficial forms of exchange) and transformational strategies (looking beyond immediate personal concerns to longer-term and collective achievements (Nahavandi, 2009).

Although there is merit in the variety of approaches, recent research has concentrated on transformational leadership because the increasing complexity of organisations and the high levels of uncertainty experienced by leaders, their staff (and the whole organisation) require more sophisticated approaches. Most of the research in this area looks at issues relating to team leadership acting as a catalyst for change or as a strategic visionary. This is important because, as stated earlier, leadership and management are important at all levels and in all areas of the organisation.

Within transformational approaches researchers have also proposed 'charismatic', 'servant' and 'spiritual' leadership styles, but one development that chimes with growing global concerns following the myriad ethical crises has been the emergence of studies in authentic leadership (Avolio and Gardner, 2005).

An interesting approach to authentic leadership, consistent with the approach to ethics, responsibility and sustainability draws on hermeneutic philosophy – ie the study of the theory and practice of interpretation, the shared meaning of language (Dilthey, 1996). It suggests that authenticity is best achieved through a narrative process in which others play a constitutive role in establishing the core values (Sparrowe, 2005). This calls for a more consensual approach to dialogic leadership – one that requires gaining consent from the workforce rather than just taking control.

According to Bill George (2003: 5), we need (managers) who are able to display authentic leadership behaviours (throughout the organisation), people of the highest integrity, committed to building enduring organisations. We need leaders who have a deep sense of purpose and are true to their core values. We need leaders who have the courage to build their companies to meet the needs of all their stakeholders and who recognise the importance of their service to society. ... In practice this means that they demonstrate a passion for their purpose, practise their values consistently and lead with their hearts as well as their heads. They establish long-term meaningful relationships and have the self-discipline to get results. In other words, they know who they are.

Leadership and management communication also depends on the ability to project a positive image, or more specifically, a positive ethos, inside an organisation and outside, and one of the primary requirements to inspire confidence and induce others to listen is credibility. This links to the notion of managers and their teams being 'conversationally responsible' (discussed earlier in this chapter and in Chapter 1 in relation to the power of language). In their research on leadership, Kouzes and Posner (1993) found that credibility is the primary reason people follow someone. This has been an important aspect of leadership from earliest times. Ramage and Bean (1998) note that Aristotle identified three types of persuasive appeals: *logos*, *pathos* and *ethos*. *Logos* is an appeal based upon the logic of an argument; *pathos* is based on the use of emotions; whereas *ethos* is an appeal based on the perceived character of the sender of the message.

Thus with regard to the leadership approach of individual managers, the questions this leads to are: is the person trustworthy, confident, believable, knowledgeable and someone of integrity? Or as Banerjee (2008: 68) in quoting Karl Marx, quips: 'The secrets of success in business are honesty and transparency. If you can fake that, you've got it made.'

REFLECTIVE ACTIVITIES

Microsoft include in their requirements for what they describe as 'tomorrow's leaders':

- the capacity for collaboration
- being globally astute
- having social empathy
- being guided by and passing on values.

What do you think are the implications for HRM strategies, policies and practices in order to achieve such requirements?

CSR LEADERSHIP IN SMES

Corporate social responsibility is seen mainly as the preserve of the corporate giant, or so it has long been assumed. The PR machines of large corporations highlight charitable donations and campaigns and/or community projects that can sometimes seem to be out of the reach of many small and medium-sized organisations (SMEs). However, as the role of SMEs becomes increasingly important, it is just as important to recognise the contributions these organisations and their managers can make and the implications for their stakeholders. There are four million SMEs in the UK economy, providing 90% of private sector employment (Spence and Painter-Morland, 2010).

The case studies below examine the increasingly significant role of SMEs in a global market, and look at how, despite their lesser resources, they can, through ethical leadership and effective organisational design and development processes, make a bigger impact in terms of corporate social responsibility. Interestingly, both companies have waiting-lists of people wanting to join.

CASE STUDY

CLEONE FOODS

Cleone Foods is a privately owned company manufacturing 'Island Delight' Jamaican patties and slices in inner-city Birmingham. Wade Lyn is the founder and managing director, and much of his approach to business is based on his desire to 'do the right thing' which permeates the business and is influenced by his experience of growing up in Jamaica.

The approach to leadership and management and the commitment to responsible business has resulted in changes and improvements inside the company and has also inspired other organisations to take action. Initiatives include carbon reductions, such as packaging and production efficiencies, resulting in reduced waste and electricity usage; extensive staff training programmes and inclusive policies, which cover literacy and self-development opportunities; and

management practices that encourage involvement and access to managers at all times. Cleone Foods collaborates with A. F. Blakemore (see the case study below) on the Factory to Plate project, giving local school children a better understanding of the food industry. Wade also chairs the 12/8 Group – a unique peer-to-peer business group of Afro-Caribbean businesses committed to supporting start-up entrepreneurs – and is a member of the West Midlands Ethnic Minority Business Forum, where he leads on business and enterprise.

Question

Think about the approach to leadership and management in the above case study. What does it tell us about embedding ethics, responsibility and sustainability, particularly in relation to values and employee engagement?

CASE STUDY

ACME WHISTLES

Acme Whistles started production (as Hudsons) in the 1870s in an inner-city factory in Birmingham's jewellery quarter and made its presence felt all around the globe, making the whistles for the *Titanic*, the Acme Thunderer (still used in football grounds and railway stations around the world) and the Acme Metropolitan (used by police forces in Europe, America and the Far East). The current CEO, Simon Topman, takes his social responsibilities very seriously. He says, 'Who is better

placed to reach out into the community it lives in symbiosis with, and understand that community? One of the problems is that employers underestimate the potential of an area like this.' Topman is chair of a regeneration project that encourages Birmingham employers to follow his example by recruiting from the B19 postcode (an area that came to national attention with the shooting of two young black women one New Year's Day, and plagued by drug-related crime where poverty is endemic). The key to delivery, he maintains, is getting more local people into full-time employment. 'Seventy per cent of all 16- to 24-year-olds have never worked. I was brought up around here, and you never lose that special attachment to your home patch. At our factory, the workforce is a third Asian, a third African-Caribbean and a third white, and that combination works very well for us. There's no reason why it can't be translated more widely.' Topman used another of his roles (on the board of a local theatre) in an innovative intervention to encourage more tolerance and understanding between the different groups in the company. He shut down production early on Friday afternoons and invited theatre professionals to work with employees to write and perform a play about their community. It was successfully

performed to a wide cross-section of local people.

Topman works on a range of local business and community projects and encourages others (including his workforce) to do the same. As he says of his work in local schools, 'We cannot afford to have a team of employees spending a week building a garden (as a large company had recently done) but we can be there year-round helping with the school governance, providing management advice and supporting literacy schemes.'

Question

Consider the approach to stakeholder engagement in the above case study. What does this tell us about the leadership and management in this company?

The key role of values has been briefly discussed in this chapter but it is important to explore the issue of values (both individual and organisational) in more detail, and in particular in relation to organisational culture and the role that ethical codes, strategies, policies and practices play in this.

VALUES AND EMPLOYEE ENGAGEMENT

Values are defined as a small number of core ideas or cognitions present in every group or society about desirable end states (Rokeach, 1973). They are also drivers of behaviour, including workplace behaviour (Schwartz, 1999). Values are a fundamental characteristic that both employees and organisations share, operate at multiple levels (societal, organisational and personal), and play an important role in shaping the organisation's culture with regard to ethics. Schwartz (1994) provides four useful perspectives on the origin and usefulness of values and how they are aligned with behaviour. First, values are cognitive structures that support the interests of some elements of the social environment. Second, values motivate behaviour by providing direction and emotional intensity to action. Third, values are standards to judge and justify action. Finally, values are acquired both through socialisation activities and an individual's unique experiences.

Value statements have become a popular tool in organisational communication, used as 'shorthand' for how the organisation does business and, importantly, how it believes it is perceived by its stakeholders. Yet in many cases organisational values are decided upon and communicated in a 'top-down' manner that individual employees (and other stakeholders) may find difficult to relate to. The notion that values can be easily imposed or changed may therefore be unrealistic, especially where there is a conflict of values. Look, for example, at the difficulties faced by someone who values honesty and integrity but who works in an environment where 'profit maximisation, whatever it takes' is the priority. The same applies for someone who values the environment but who works in an organisation that does not see it as important. The result of placing people in situations at odds with their personal values is unlikely to be positive for either the employee or the organisation. Not only could employees' well-being be at risk but also they are likely to be less devoted to the organisation and possibly less productive.

RESEARCH ON VALUES

Debate about the importance of values, the quest for value congruence and the building of psychological bonds with the organisation, are key themes underpinning emergent literature on employee engagement and commitment. The commitment studies of Meyer and Allen (1991) suggest that commitment comprises three distinct components: affective, the emotional attachment a person feels for the organisation; normative, the feelings of obligation a person has to remain with an organisation; and continuance commitment, the accumulated investments that would be lost if they were to leave the organisation (Meyer *et al*, 1993: 539). Affective commitment in particular is associated with higher productivity, more positive work attitudes and a greater likelihood of engaging in organisational citizenship (Allen and Meyer, 1996). Such organisational citizenship corresponds with individual behaviour that is discretionary, not directly or explicitly recognised by the formal reward system, and in the aggregate promotes the efficient and effective functioning of the organisation (Organ *et al*, 2006: 8).

The positive feelings which affectively committed individuals have towards their organisation are thus accompanied by other beneficial effects for the organisation (see also Chapter 16). Research on employee engagement, defined as 'being positively present during the performance of work by willingly contributing intellectual effort, experiencing positive emotions and meaningful connections to others' (CIPD, 2010: 5), also provides significant insights into employee identification with the organisation. Other important studies in this area include those related to the psychological contract, and the work of Rousseau, Conway and others in exploring the nature of the employee–employer relationship.

Of particular importance here is the research from the Work Foundation (Wong *et al*, 2010). This research explores the link between individual and organisational beliefs and values. Chapter 14 discusses Martin and Hetrick's (2006) description of 'values-based psychological contracts' (employees who commit to an organisation in exchange for a cause or mission) together with branding and the employee value proposition (EVP) – a form of employer brand promise. This is gaining currency in HR theory and practice and, as discussed earlier in this chapter, can differentiate employers of choice. However, the issue from an ethics, responsibility and sustainability point of view is the extent to which it is authentic. The concerns about 'brandwashing' (similar to the problems of 'green washing' in the environmental domain) therefore require to be considered.

The attachment of employees is, however, not a recent revelation, as Edward Cadbury – son of a pioneer of CSR, George Cadbury – states (Cadbury, 1912: xvii):

> The supreme principle has been the belief that business efficiency and the welfare of the employee are but different sides of the same problem. Character is an economic asset; and business efficiency depends not merely on the physical condition of employees, but on their general attitude and feeling towards the employer.

PRACTICAL APPLICATION

As previously discussed, values are the vocabulary of socially approved goals used to motivate action, and to express and justify the solutions chosen. The more closely aligned personal and organisational values are, the more likely individual members are to be motivated towards the goals of the organisation (Howard-Grenville *et al*, 2003). It may not be easy to change values but it is possible to reactivate them. It is also possible to look at social norms and reset them. In developing values, organisations should recognise the values of their stakeholders, and although it would be impossible to reflect all their values (some of which may in any case be in conflict), the core values should draw together key fundamental principles that are important to all and be evident in all aspects of the organisation's activities. (It is often possible to find issues that resonate.) The RICOH case study organisation below uses the model of 'People, Planet, Profit' to guide its approach. Examples of practical approaches used to achieve this include:

- consulting key constituents on the development of value statements through focus groups
- using fairly short, simple statements that can be clearly understood
- developing more in-depth explanations of what these statements mean for all aspects of the business (see the case study example)
- ensuring that it is clear to all in the organisation how the values inform and guide strategy, policy and practice
- using review processes to continue to engage and involve all stakeholders.

CASE STUDY

RICOH UK

RICOH has won numerous awards over many years and has been consistently included in lists of 'the world's most ethical and sustainable companies'.

Everything we do at RICOH is measured against three values: harmonising with the environment, simplifying life and work, and supporting knowledge management. Taken together, and applied with belief, passion and innovative thinking, our values help people move their ideas forward, towards better-value products and solutions, and into a more enjoyable life in a sustainable, better-protected environment.

We are committed to our values in addressing not only the present but also the long term, in improving the environment for future generations.

Question

Wouldn't it be useful to you to take a look at how these values are developed in greater depth across the range of the company's activities? Visit http://www.ricoh.co.uk/about-ricoh/ricoh-overview/our-values/index.aspx.

ETHICAL CODES, POLICIES AND PRACTICES

Standards can be provided in policies and codes, but norms are established through factors influencing the broader organisational culture and subcultures, including managerial language and behaviours. McDonald and Nijhof (1999) point out the complexity of setting standards in an organisational context where there are conditions that influence the way they are interpreted at different levels. These include the social, political, economic, work and personal environment. At the individual level, there are personality and socialisation factors (including individual cognitive moral development and locus of control). At the organisational level, norms, values, decision-making processes and access to resources can influence adherence to such standards. Just publishing a 'code of ethics' or producing CSR and sustainability statements is therefore not sufficient – the principles must be interwoven into everything a business does. In the case of codes of ethics, Ferrell *et al* (2008) argue that they need to be part of an effective ethics programme which is a process of continuous activities that are designed, implemented, and enforced to prevent and detect misconduct. However, this requires the recognition that its code of ethics – just like CSR and sustainability – are part of the value system of the organisation and embedded into CSR discourses and core systems, including those for which HR are responsible. It also requires

HR professionals to see it as part of their responsibility in sensitively engaging with all areas of the organisation to facilitate the development of a culture that is consistent with shared values (both espoused and enacted).

CULTURE

Chapter 5 provides an overview of different perspectives of culture and how they relate to organisational change/development and New OE. An organisation's culture is a critical part of the context of organisational life that embodies the main assumptions, values, symbols and activities within an organisation. Thus the idea that culture may be a driver for appropriate or inappropriate behaviour in organisations is an observation that should come as no surprise, nor that it can reflect what the employees and top management think about sustainability issues (Harris and Crane, 2002). Indeed, organisational culture is considered a key determinant and indicator of the success or failure of positive ethical organisations (Verbos et al, 2007) and environmental management programmes at companies (Brío, Fernández and Junquera, 2007).

Culture (and its associated communications) is often cited as a key area for HR involvement. Legge's 1995 work highlights the management of culture as a central activity – indeed, a distinguishing feature – in normative HR models. Such models convey the organisation's core values through an integrated and internally consistent set of HR policies (Legge, 1995: 75), thereby enacting a 'strong' culture. The epistemological stance taken with respect to organisational culture (eg Smircich, 1983; Meek, 1988; Meyerson and Martin, 1987), and specifically with culture management, raises questions and challenges as to the likely ability of organisations consciously and intentionally to develop or manage culture. One of the enduring problems with the traditional literature on culture has been to assume that organisations are homogeneous. Simply taking a positivist structural-functional view of culture as a core variable that the organisation has and can manipulate to its own ends suggests courses of action which may serve to provide support for ethical behaviour, but overlooks the more phenomenological perspective of culture as systems of shared cognitions and meanings. (Phenomenology is the study of perceptual experience in its purely subjective aspect – Webster, 2010.) This is anomalous because common definitions of culture are in essence phenomenological.

The challenge to the development of a responsible, ethical culture is that the change required is not necessarily one of macro structural change but often a more subtle change of values. Burnes' (2009) framework is one that is responsive to a turbulent environment but is likely to result in a relatively slow transformation because it focuses particularly on behaviours and attitudes and not just on structures and systems. In this way it is consistent with a New OE lens (see Chapter 1) and resonates with the 'critical realist' perspective in which the world is multi-layered involving different structures, mechanism and powers. It is transformational and consists of multiple agents – human and non-human (Fleetwood and Hesketh, 2010).

In such a context the dominant approaches to change are by necessity participative and experiential. They rely on education and modelling of appropriate behaviours in order to bring about learning and acceptance rather than simply writing a new set of procedures or introducing a new 'corporate compliance' department.

Such change is, however, more difficult to bring about than might at first appear. In that it is related predominantly to the 'hearts and minds' of employees, rather than financial or technical structures and systems, it appears to be vested solidly in the HR role.

But merely 'getting people to change their minds' has been the overwhelming challenge to culture change initiatives from the 1980s onwards. For one thing, employees vary in their underlying morality, as Kohlberg's (1981) model of moral development illustrates. This echoes the points made with regard to values. Developing core themes around which individuals can realistically gather is thus likely to gain more support. For example, there are basic tenets on which most of the world's main religions agree. These include treating people the way you wish to be treated yourself and protecting the earth and the environment (Zohar and Marshall, 2004).

In an organisational context, communication is often seen as a key conduit for conveying culture because – as discussed earlier in this chapter and in Chapter 5 – language is a powerful medium for conveying norms and meaning. This is both for formal and informal communication as Rhodes *et al*'s (2010) analysis of narrative and ethics in a downsizing situation demonstrates.

REFLECTIVE ACTIVITY

Using Charles Handy's simple definition of culture – 'The way we do things round here' – take an organisation you know well and list of all the aspects of that organisation that you believe typify its culture. This may include stories, behaviours, symbols, policies and practices. Consider the extent to which this is consistent with the espoused values of the organisation.

THE ROLE OF HRM IN ETHICS, CSR AND SUSTAINABILITY

As stated earlier, the HR profession is deeply linked to ethical and responsible business practices. In common with other professions, HR today is a product of its history but also of pressures, values and institutional arrangements. As Ulrich (1997) remarked, it was born out of concern for human welfare, and HR practices that were underpinned by ethical and social values. Its early days were shaped by predominantly Quaker traditions of social action to promote social justice, and from this developed the welfare role within organisations (Child, 1964). The emphasis was on a more pluralist view of the organisation (long before the stakeholder perspective became popular). This broadly continued through the social and economic changes of the subsequent decades until the 1980s, when UK Government policies and the steady decline of trade unionism saw HR professionals take a more unitarist view (Kochan, 2007). As part of this – as noted in Chapter 2 – the profession sought to gain legitimacy through establishing its role in contributing to the bottom line and distancing itself from the more 'human' aspects of the role, and in particular, employees. As Boselie *et al* (2005) points out, this is quite problematical because financial indicators are influenced by a whole range of factors (both internal and external) which have nothing to do with employees and their related skills or human capital. In addition, as a result of becoming 'perfect agents' of top management in enforcing business strategy, it has been argued that HR lost sight of its roots and, importantly, its essential role in adding value through the human side of the enterprise and supporting employees (Kochan, 2004; 2007).

This is an interesting position because although business as a whole is moving more to accepting its ethical, social and environmental responsibilities, and CSR is shifting to be a core objective for organisations around the world (Matten and Moon, 2008), HR seems firmly wedded to its allegiance to profitability and distancing itself from any connection with welfare (Pinnington *et al*, 2007). Despite this, the HR profession appears to have escaped criticism in the economic and financial meltdowns that have dominated headlines in recent years, CEOs and CFOs being the main 'villains'. Yet in many of the high-profile cases involving corporate difficulties because of unethical practices, the role of cut-throat cultures of targets, policies and practices encouraging or condoning misbehaviour is often highlighted. This may be in the design of performance management and reward systems (including bankers' bonuses) or in the policies of recruitment and training that fail to establish clear ethical norms and expectations (Gladwell, 2002).

Within organisations, the normative myopia of competitiveness and profit has often suppressed awareness of social and ethical issues, and this is replicated at all levels and across professions (Swanson, 1999; Swanson and Orlitzky, 2006). As Parkes and Davis (2012) suggest, HR is no exception to this and cannot be excused from such omissions, especially when there has long been a clear ethical component of the HR role. Sears (2010) points out that there are expectations that HR should have a 'stewardship' role and actively ensure effective governance and ethical practice.

Within professional activity there appears to be at best a lack of visibility in ethical stewardship and at worst a case of 'bystander apathy effect' – a well-defined phenomenon in social psychology (Garcia *et al*, 2002). Although the dominant unitarist view in HR discourse is seductive, it presents an oversimplistic reality of the socio-economic and political environment. This is because there are plural interests in society and thus in organisations that make conflicts inevitable. Many prescriptions of good HR practice are based on the assumption that managerial prerogative will prevail, and that there would be either no ethical issues or if there were, they could be resolved by 'good management'. However, conceptions of business performance and organisational effectiveness – in theory and practice – cannot be restricted to a narrow profit-dominated bottom line (Boxall and Purcell, 2003). Similarly, there are criticisms of the predominant business partnering model. Francis and Keegan (2006), drawing on the work of Ulrich (1997), note that the 'business partner' and 'employee champion' roles are somewhat opposed and hard to reconcile. Peccei and Guest's (2002) major study of partnerships raises doubts about whether this model can work across the range of organisations.

HR AND THE PROFESSIONAL BODIES

Professional bodies and organisations in HR (where they exist) clearly set out an ethical component of the role. In Wiley's (2000) analysis of ethical codes for HR professionals it is clear that there are expectations by which the professional will be judged, that there are preferred character traits to control how the profession is practised by individuals, and that the codes are designed to support and encourage the professional to act in the public interest.

The USA-based Society for Human Resource Management (SHRM) presents a code of ethics to its members that requires individuals 'to set the standard and be an example for others and to earn individual respect and increase our credibility with those we serve'. SHRM also refer to 'serving all stakeholders in the most morally responsible manner and leading individual organisations to conduct business in a responsible manner as well as exhibiting individual leadership as a role model for maintaining the highest standards of ethical conduct' (www.shrm.org).

In the UK the CIPD has articulated ethical requirements within its professional codes since its early days in the 1970s when resignation by members who encountered ethical dilemmas was specifically listed as a possible response. It also requires members to exercise integrity, honesty and diligence, and to behave appropriately and act within the law. Yet in later years, as the Institute embraced the shift to more managerialist strategies, the visibility of wider concerns – particularly in the professional educational standards – diminished. The CIPD's inclusion in its current standards of two new requirements for members is therefore particularly interesting. The first is described as the 'courage to challenge', defined as when individuals 'show courage and confidence to speak up, challenge others even when confronted with resistance or unfamiliar circumstances'. For example, to ensure that employees who have concerns are supported and protected as individuals, HR professionals are to raise ethical and responsibility issues. The second is the requirement to be a 'role model', defined as a person who 'consistently leads by example; acts with integrity, impartiality and independence; applies sound personal judgement in all interactions (CIPD, 2009). This fits with the EVP model discussed in Chapter 14, where emphasis is placed on distributed leadership and the building of judgemental competence among both managers and employees.

The existence of the codes and standards is important, but the questions remain about whether HR professionals can fulfil such expectations. It is therefore important to explore some of the factors that may affect HR professionals' ability to execute their responsibilities in this area – and that may explain their lack of presence in preventing some of the major economic and ethical scandals.

One of key issues that affect the HR profession's ability/willingness to undertake a proactive stance is the problem of the perception of HR. The HR profession is often accused of being obsessed with its credibility, and the strategy of compliance within a dominant financial culture achieves little security for the function (Armstrong, 1989; Legge, 1995). Yet as Kochan (2004: 134) observed, most HR professionals have

> lost any semblance of credibility as a steward of the social contract because most HR professionals have lost their ability to seriously challenge or offer an independent perspective on the policies and practices of the firm.

Where there has been a debate about the ethics of HR it has tended to be either at the macro level – ie is all HR unethical? – or, more commonly, at the micro level, about an individual practice (Winstanley and Woodall, 2000). The micro-level analysis of specific practices or 'bundles of practices' can be of limited value and detract from the bigger picture. Similarly, macro-level analysis based on theory can have theoretical and practical problems (Greenwood, 2002). This highlights the need to distinguish between the ethics of HR and ethical behaviour through HR. In addition, if there is to be a leadership role for HR (as suggested by Kolodinsky, 2006, and Burke, 1999), the notion of ethical frameworks for HR professionals that seek to provide standards and guidelines for enacting the role needs to be clarified.

HR's role in this can be seen as twofold. Firstly, it must ensure that HR strategies, policies and practices are ethical and that the culture of the organisation is consistent with this. Secondly, the HR profession must promote ethical behaviour through each individual professional's own conduct within the organisation. The inclusion in the revised standards of the CIPD of these two distinct requirements for HR professionals that relate to this role (the 'courage to challenge' and being a 'role model') is therefore encouraging.

The desire to see effectiveness in terms of the bottom line also affects HR managers' views of the 'green agenda' (Jackson and Seo, 2010). According to a survey conducted by the Chartered Institute of Personnel and Development, many HR managers criticise 'green HRM' as wishy-washy, not proved and a form of extremism, and some believe that HR managers should avoid 'jumping on political bandwagons [such as environmental management] that do not support the profitability of our organisations' at a time when the field of HRM is 'striving to be taken seriously by business' (CIPD, 2007: 3–4). Yet the integration of strategic HRM and environmental sustainability offers an opportunity to break away from the narrow economic interpretation of what 'strategic HRM' means (Jackson and Seo, 2010).

Similarly, HR's role in CSR has the potential to redefine its interpretation of organisational effectiveness and redirect its strategic focus.

As the CIPD's *Corporate Social Responsibility Factsheet* (June 2006: 1) declares:

> CSR is an opportunity for HR to demonstrate a strategic focus and act as a business partner. CSR needs to be embedded in an organisation's culture to make a change to actions and attitudes, and the support of the top team is critical to success. HR already works at communicating and implementing ideas, policies, and cultural and behavioural change across organisations. Its role in influencing attitudes and links with line managers and the top team mean it is ideally placed to do the same with CSR. HR is also responsible for the key systems and processes underpinning effective delivery.

Through HR, CSR can be given credibility and aligned with how businesses run. CSR could be integrated into processes such as the employer brand, recruitment, appraisal, retention, motivation, reward, internal communications, diversity, coaching and training.

The way a company treats its employees contributes directly to it being seen as willing to accept its wider responsibilities. Building credibility and trusting their employer are being increasingly seen as important by employees when they choose who they want to work for.

One initiative that has been developed to provide a way forward in integrating ethics, CSR and sustainability at all levels in the organisation is the CSR Competency Framework. This was a joint initiative between the CIPD and the UK's Department of Trade and Industry's CSR Academy, which aimed to develop a template to help managers understand CSR and integrate it into their organisations. The CSR Competency Framework identifies six characteristics underpinning effective CSR work:

- *Understanding society* – understanding the role of each player in society, including government, business, trade unions, non-governmental organisations and civil society
- *Building capacity* – external partnerships and creating strategic networks and alliances
- *Questioning 'business as usual'* – openness to new ideas, challenging others to adopt new ways of thinking and questioning 'business as usual' attitudes
- *Maintaining stakeholder relations* – identifying stakeholders, building relations externally and internally, engaging in consultation and balancing demands
- *Adopting a strategic view* – taking a strategic view of the business environment
- *Harnessing diversity* – respecting diversity and adjusting the approach to different situations.

The Framework also sets out five levels of attainment for each characteristic, depending on the depth of knowledge required and the management function. These range from basic awareness to understanding, application, integration and leadership. Further information and practical examples of the use of the Framework can be found at the CSR Academy website: www.csracademy@bitc.org.uk.

HR AND ITS ROLE IN OD / NEW OE

As we have seen from the outset of this book, HR in research and practice is regarded as being concerned with employee engagement, organisational values, culture, changing attitudes and behaviour. It is also responsible for the processes, policies and practices that are critical to implement such changes. Organisation development and change management are posited as the panacea to provide the processes to bring about culture change that reaches into all areas of the organisation. From an HR point of view this includes requirements in recruitment, the training it gives employees, and the expectations placed upon them through performance management and reward systems. Similarly, establishing codes of practice for what is considered ethical behaviour, communicating them and providing appropriate training and reinforcement mechanisms is often perceived as a starting point to provide drivers for moral behaviour. However, the reality is often far more complex. To achieve real change, the sophisticated interaction between many different organisational and contextual factors has to be considered, including the challenge of engaging individuals and groups with the needs of others and with broader ethical principles. This complexity may be better explored from the separate but related perspectives of individual choice in a social context, and the influence of that context on individual choice.

THE FUTURE OF OD

Historically, organisation development's fundamentally humanist and democratic outlook, based in behavioural sciences, has set out to enhance individual development and organisational performance through changing behaviour (Porras and Robertson, 1992). Yet this model has been criticised because the original studies did not take account of the cultural context and because the mechanistic nature of its implementation can be counter-productive. The traditional OD approach has been seen as fundamentally one of problem-solving and as self-reflexive. As a way of enabling organisational learning it seeks to enable the organisation to better adapt and cope with its own challenges as it defines them through empowerment, openness and collaboration. However, as noted in Chapters 1 and 2, conventional OD can be described as doctrinaire and unitarist in its approach. Surfacing the values which an organisation seeks to adopt, and encouraging discussion of what that would mean, in relation to the range of stakeholders and potential outcomes, requires open discussion and critical awareness. This presupposes senior commitment to such approaches to ethical action. Without such commitment, any further discussion is meaningless and unlikely to result in a consistent climate for good ethical behaviour. Modelling of ethical behaviour throughout the organisation is also therefore crucial.

In order to achieve this it is important to point out the importance of promoting leadership beyond the top management level and in all areas including HR. Kolodinsky (2006) discusses the importance of 'HR wisdom' – a unique perspective that must be part of the organisational discourse on values, ethics and responsibility. However, for this to manifest, HR professionals must take on a leadership role – not just with HR issues but also in influencing the organisation to understand the impact each worker's choices can have on all organisational stakeholders. This is an imperative for any leadership role, and HR – as the people-focused profession in the organisation – have an imperative for the explicit (structural) and implicit (processes) aspects of ethics and responsibility within the organisation (Burke, 1999).

CASE STUDY

A. F. BLAKEMORE & SON LTD

Company: A. F. Blakemore & Son Ltd

Founded: 1917

Ownership: Third generation of Blakemore family

Sector: Food and drink wholesaler, distributor and convenience retailer

Head Office: West Midlands

Locations: Welsh coast to East Anglia and Tyne-Tees to central London

Employees: 5,500

Values: The Blakemore Way – launched in 2008 to define the long-standing culture of A. F. Blakemore built upon positive and friendly relations with staff, customers and the communities it serves

Purpose: To grow a family business in ways that are profitable and sustainable for the benefit of our staff, customers and community

The Way We Do Business:

- Maximise staff potential and their contribution to the company's success

- Give great service to all our customers and add value to trade partners

- Make a significant, positive contribution to the community

- Attain excellence in everything we do

- Behave with honesty and integrity in all our relationships.

Integrating The Blakemore Way:

- Communications:
  - Every employee has taken part in a briefing session outlining The Blakemore Way
  - The Blakemore Way now forms a key part of the recruitment and induction process
  - The Blakemore Way is heavily

publicised through handbooks, magazines and noticeboards

- Growing you – The Blakemore Way:
  - A new behaviourally based performance management programme built upon values outlined in The Blakemore Way is currently being rolled out across the company

- Consultation:
  - Staff surveys are now built around key elements of The Blakemore Way to gauge and measure staff perceptions
  - Values meetings are held across the workforce to discuss developments of The Blakemore Way and to generate employee feedback
  - 'Excellence meetings' have been launched to allow staff to embed quality across processes and systems.

- Corporate responsibility (CR):
  - CR is used as a key vehicle for delivery of The Blakemore Way

- The CR policy has been built around key areas of The Blakemore Way with objectives and targets set by divisional boards for workplace, marketplace, community and environment to monitor and measure progress
- The concept of employee-volunteering is playing an increasingly important part of Blakemore culture
- The Blakemore Foundation is a charitable fund representing 1% of pre-tax profits.

Source: http://www.bitc.org.uk/resources/case_studies/afe_2778.html [accessed 18 July 2011]

Questions

1 In what ways does this business embed ethics, CSR and sustainability in its business model?

2 How could this business model be employed within an organisation you are familiar with?

CASE STUDY COMMENTARY

Blakemore are active members of Business in the Community (www.bitc.org.uk). The approach to embedding ethics/CSR into organisation makes sense on a number of levels. As a family business it runs the risk of its approach being seen as related to individual family members, which could threaten the long-term sustainability of the company. By embedding its values and principles into the core activity, systems and processes of the organisation, it becomes part of the culture and 'the way they do things around here'.

One of Blakemore's key successes is its Education Matters Programme (for which it was awarded a Business in the Community Big Tick Education Award in 2011). The company has operated an employee-volunteering programme with a strong emphasis on education since 2005. In 2008 A. F. Blakemore developed a more structured approach to employee volunteering through the launch of The Blakemore Way, with a key emphasis on the role the company has in 'making a significant positive contribution to the community'. Through this strategy a consistent and centrally co-ordinated community programme was rolled out, helping to unify the seven divisions that have their own board of directors and individual cultures. 'We see Community Project Team Leadership as primarily a development tool with the added bonus of being involved in a great experience' – Melanie Walker, Learning & Development Manager, A. F. Blakemore.

Despite the differences of the business units, many sit within areas of deprivation, and education was selected as a unifying theme, common to all. The vast majority of A. F. Blakemore employees live and work in the same community and many schools that the company supports are ones that employees, or their families, have attended. The company regards support for schools as a key ingredient towards becoming an employer of choice and helping to develop a motivated workforce for the future.

While employee engagement and volunteering has been part of the A. F. Blakemore culture since 2005, it was only introduced to the company's 215 Tates SPAR stores in 2010. Tates training manager, Kerry Hunt, notes the impact that the education programme has had on them: 'Our programme brings disparate stores together to work on joint community activities, which not only boosts team spirit but allows us to share ideas from one store to the next.'

A. F. Blakemore deliver a wide range of programmes across their sites but focus upon four key campaigns, which include practical regeneration activity, literacy, employability training and study tours. In 2011 4,820 employee hours have been dedicated to the programme, with 53 schools and over 10,000 young people benefiting from 191 different projects.

Business impact – There is a positive correlation between employee turnover and the launch of A. F. Blakemore's education programme. In 2007/8 employee turnover was 49% compared to 31% in 2010/11. For those who volunteer, this reduces to 4.9%. Employee satisfaction score from colleague survey responses to 'I am proud to work for this company' and 'This company is run on strong values and principles' = 79%. Education Matters has helped the company win two food service contracts and retain a further three.

Social impact – School partner satisfaction score to the evaluation statement 'This event has made a significant positive contribution to our school' = 93%. Reading ages of the 31 pupils who have participated in the literacy programme have increased by an average of 12.3 months.

CONCLUSION

The key question for the OD role of HR in ethics, CSR and sustainability is: will HR managers step up to this role? Will they take on the shift in worldviews that allow them to recognise the legitimate concerns of the wider community and redefine their strategic role to benefit a broader range of constituents? The issues of ethics, CSR and environmental sustainability (and the challenges and opportunities they present) have been generating increased concern among business executives, governments, consumers and management scholars. Yet HRM scholars and practitioners alike have been relatively slow to engage in the ongoing discussions and debates (Jackson and Seo, 2010).

The UN Global Compact has been working with businesses across the world for the last 10 years to legitimate ethical social and environmental responsibilities in the business context. Recently, the UN Global Compact in collaboration with several educational organisations has developed the Principles for Responsible Management Education (PRME), encouraging scholars and managers to work jointly on developing new knowledge to promote ethical, social and environmental responsibility (PRME, 2010).

These areas do present significant challenges, particularly in embedding ethics, CSR and sustainability, so that it becomes 'the way the organisation does business'. These challenges include using OD strategies to pursue social and sustainable value rather than just shareholder value, infusing the core business activity with these concepts rather than just scoring symbolic wins at the margin, making the ethics, responsibility and sustainability part of everyone's job, not just a peripheral activity of a 'scapegoat' department, and ensuring that responsibility is clear for managing across products or service life-cycle value-chains rather than just the company's own activities (Laszlo and Zhexembayeva, 2011). The opportunities for HRM to make a difference come from a consideration of key strategies that seek to address the above challenges. These may include the influence of social, economic, market and other external forces as they relate to HRM. Workforce development needs are created by increasing demand for employees with related skills. Specific HRM philosophies, policies and/or practices that support or inhibit change around these issues include those related to performance management; training, development, and learning; compensation and rewards; organisational culture; and stakeholder engagement. In line with the aims of this textbook, these strategies and interventions for enhancing Organisation Effectiveness must be sensitive to the paradoxical tensions that are an inevitable and defining feature of organisations (Ehnert, 2008).

Note: Some of the ideas discussed in this chapter are further developed in Parkes, C. L. and Davis, A. (2012) 'HR, ethics and social responsibility – the "courage to challenge" or a case of the "bystander effect"?', *International Journal of Human Resource Management* (forthcoming).

EXPLORE FURTHER

Burchell, J. (2008) *The Corporate Social Responsibility Reader*. London: Routledge. This book provides a range of articles about CSR from many different perspectives, authors and companies. It takes readers into areas that they might not ordinarily pursue.

Crane, A. and Matten, D. (2010) *Business Ethics: Managing citizenship and sustainability in the age of globalization*. Oxford: Oxford University Press. A good textbook that provides a mixture of academic and practitioner approaches and covers a wide range of topics in ethics, CSR and sustainability.

Deckop, J. R. (2005) *Human Resource Management Ethics: A volume on ethics in practice*. Greenwich, CT: Information Age Publishing. A US text that goes beyond a 'functional' approach to many areas of HRM, including issues relating to the profession.

Laszlo, C. and Zhexembayeva, N. (2011) *Embedded Sustainability: The next big competitive advantage*. Palo Alto, CA: Stanford University Press. This book explains why sustainability must be embedded within organisations rather than 'bolt-on' approaches, and provides practical examples of how it can be done.

REFERENCES

Allen, N. J. and Meyer, J. P. (1996) 'Affective, continuance, and normative commitment to the organization: an examination of construct validity', *Journal of Vocational Behavior*, Vol.49: 252–6.

American Heritage® Dictionary of the English Language (2007), 4th edition. Boston, MA: Houghton Mifflin. Available online at: http://dictionary.reference.com/browse/Ethics [accessed 27 March 2007].

Armstrong, M. (1989) *A Handbook of Human Resource Management*. London: Kogan Page.

Asongu, J. J. (2007) 'The history of corporate social responsibility', *Journal of Business and Public Policy*, Vol.1, No.2, Spring: 1–18.

Aspen Institute, the (2008) *Where will they Lead? MBA student attitudes about business and society*. Report. New York: Aspen Institute, New York. Available online at: http://www.aspencbe.org/documents/ExecutiveSummaryMBAStudentAttitudesReport2008 [accessed 29 November 2010].

Avolio, B. J. and Gardner, W. (2005) 'Authentic leadership development: getting to the root of positive forms of leadership', *Leadership Quarterly*, Vol.16, Issue 3: 315–38.

Banerjee S. B. (2008) 'Corporate social responsibility: the good, the bad and the ugly', *Critical Sociology*, Vol.34, No.1: 51–79.

Boselie, P., Dietz, G. and Boon, C. (2005) 'Commonalities and contradictions in research on human resource management and performance', *Human Resource Management Journal*, Vol.15, Issue 3: 67–94.

Boxall, P. and Purcell, J. (2003) *Strategy and Human Resource Management*. Basingstoke: Palgrave Macmillan.

Bremner, R. (1994) *Giving: Philanthropy and charity in history*. New Jersey: Transaction.

Brío, J. A., Fernández, E. and Junquera, B. (2007) 'Management and employee involvement in achieving an environmental action-based competitive advantage: an empirical study', *International Journal of Human Resource Management*, Vol.18, No.4: 491–522.

Burchell, J. and Cook, J. (2006) 'Confronting the "corporate citizen": shaping the discourse of corporate social responsibility', *International Journal of Sociology and Social Policy*, Vol.26, No.3/4: 121.

Burke, F. (1999) 'Ethical decision-making: global concerns, frameworks, and approaches', *Public Personnel Management*, Vol.8, No.4: 530–7.

Burnes, B. (2009) *Managing Change*, 5th edition. London: FT/Prentice Hall.

Business for Social Responsibility, 2006. Available online at: www.bsr.org.

Cadbury, A. (2006) 'Corporate social responsibility, contemporary critiques', *21st Century Society*, Vol.1, No.1: 5–21.

Cadbury, E. (1912) *Experiments in Industrial Organisation*. London: Longmans, Green & Co.

Capra, F. (2004) *The Hidden Connections: A science for sustainable living*. New York: Anchor Books.

Carroll, A. B. (1999) 'Corporate social responsibility: evolution of a definitional construct', *Business and Society*, Vol.38, No.3: 268–95.

Child, J. (1964) 'Quaker employers and industrial relations', *Sociological Review*, Vol.12, No.2: 293–315.

Chouliaraki, L. and Fairclough, N. (1999) *Discourse in Late Modernity: Rethinking critical discourse analysis*. Edinburgh: Edinburgh University Press.

CIPD (2006) *CSR Factsheet*. London: Chartered Institute of Personnel and Development. Available online at: http://www.cipd.co.uk/hr-resources/factsheets/ corporate-social-responsibility [accessed 21 March 2009].

CIPD (2007) 'Is greening the workplace on your agenda?' Discussion web page at: www.cipd.co.uk/communities/discussions.htm?command=view&id=35986&boardi.

CIPD (2009) *HR Professional Map*. Available online at: http://www.cipd.co.uk/cipd-hr-profession/hr-profession-map/ [accessed 23 May 2011].

CIPD (2010) *Creating an Engaged Workforce*. Research Report. London: Chartered Institute of Personnel and Development.

CSR Academy (2006) 'The CSR Competency Framework'. Norwich: Stationery Office. Available at: csracademy@bitc.org.uk or www.bitc.org.uk/ document.rm?id=5102 [accessed 10 July 2011].

Dilthey, W. (1996) *Hermeneutics and the Study of History*. Princeton, NJ: Princeton University Press.

Eccles, R. G. and Nohria. N. (1992) *Beyond the Hype*. Cambridge, MA: Harvard Business School Press.

Ehnert, I. (2008) *Sustainable Human Resource Management: A conceptual and exploratory analysis from a paradox perspective*. Heidelberg: Physica-Verlag.

Elkington, J. (1997) *Cannibals with Forks. The triple bottom line of 21st century business*. Oxford: Capstone.

Evans, P., Pucik, V. and Barsoux, J. (2002) *The Global Challenge: Frameworks for international human resource management*. New York: McGraw-Hill/Irwin.

Ferraro, F., Pfeffer, J. and Sutton, R. I. (2005) 'Economics, language and assumptions: how theories can become self-fulfilling', *Academy of Management Review*, Vol.30, No.1: 8–24.

Ferrell, O. C., Fraedrich, J. and Ferrell, L. (2008) *Business Ethics: Ethical decision making and cases*. Boston, MA: Houghton Mifflin.

Fleetwood, S. and Hesketh, A. J. (2010) *Explaining the Performance of Human Resource Management*. Cambridge: Cambridge University Press.

Francis, H. and Keegan, A. (2006) 'The changing face of HRM: in search of balance', *Human Resource Management Journal*, Vol.16, No.3: 231–49.

Freeman, E. (1984) *Strategic Management: A stakeholder approach*. London: Pitman.

Garcia, S., Weaver, K., Moskowitz, G. and Darley, J. (2002) 'Crowded minds: the implicit bystander effect', *Journal of Personality and Social Psychology*, Vol.83, No.4: 843–53.

Gentile, M. (2009) 'Business schools: a failing grade on ethics', Viewpoint, *Bloomberg BusinessWeek*, 5 February. Available online at: http://www.businessweek.com/bschools/content/feb2009/bs2009025_129477.htm [accessed 24 January 2011].

George, W. (2003) *Authentic Leadership: Rediscovering the secrets to creating lasting value*. San Francisco: Jossey-Bass.

Gladwell, M. (2002) 'The greed cycle', *New Yorker*, Vol.78, 23 September: 64–77.

Goldacre, B. (2008) *Bad Science*. London: Fourth Estate.

Govindarajulu, N. and Daily, B. F. (2004) 'Motivating employees for environmental improvement', *Industrial Management and Data Systems*, Vol.104, No.4: 364–72.

Greenwood, M. R. (2002) 'Ethics and HRM: a review and conceptual analysis', *Journal of Business Ethics*, Vol.36, No.3: 261–78.

Grojean, M. W., Resick, C. J., Dickson, M. W. and Smith, D. B. (2004) 'Leaders, values and organizational climate: examining leadership strategies for establishing an organizational climate regarding ethics', *Journal of Business Ethics*, Vol.55, No.3: 223–41.

Harris, L. C. and Crane, A. (2002) 'The greening of organizational culture: management views on the depth, degree and diffusion of change', *Journal of Organizational Change Management*, Vol.15, No.3: 214–34.

HEA (2007) *Employable Graduates for Responsible Employers*. York: Higher Education Academy. Available online at: http://www.heacademy.ac.uk/ourwork/ teachingandlearning/alldisplay?type=projects&newid=esd/esd_employable_graduates&site=york [accessed 7 January 2011].

Howard-Grenville, J. A., Hoffman, A. J. and Wirtenberg, J. (2003) 'The importance of cultural framing to the success of social initiatives in business', *Academy of Management Executive*, Vol.17, No.2: 70–86.

Jackson, S. E. and Seo, J. (2010) 'The greening of strategic HRM scholarship', *Organizational Management Journal*, Vol.7: 278–90.

Ketola, T. (2008) 'A holistic corporate responsibility model: integrating values, discourse and action', *Journal of Business Ethics*, Vol.80, No.3: 419–35.

Kochan, T. (2004) 'Restoring trust in the human resource management profession', *Asia Pacific Journal of Human Resources*, Vol.42, No.2: 132–46.

Kochan, T. (2007) 'Social legitimacy of the human resource management profession: a US perspective', in Boxall, P., Purcell, J. and Wright, P. (eds) *Oxford Handbook of Human Resource Management*. Oxford: Oxford University Press.

Kohlberg, L. (1981) *Essays on Moral Development*, Vol.1: *The Philosophy of Moral Development*. San Francisco: Harper & Row.

Kolodinsky, R. W. (2006) 'Wisdom, ethics and human resources management', in Deckop, J. R. (ed.) *Human Resource Management Ethics*. Charlotte, NC: Information Age Publishing.

Kouzes, J. M. and Posner, B. Z. (1993) *Credibility: How leaders gain and lose it, why people demand it*. San Francisco: Jossey-Bass.

Laszlo, C. and Zhexembayeva, N. (2011) *Embedded Sustainability, The next big competitive advantage*. Palo Alto, CA: Stanford University Press.

Legge, K. (1995) *Human Resource Management: Rhetorics and realities*. Basingstoke: Palgrave Macmillan.

Lovelock, J. (2000) *Gaia: A new look at life on Earth*. Oxford: Oxford University Press.

McDonald, G. and Nijhof, A. (1999) 'Beyond codes of ethics: an integrated framework for stimulating morally responsible behaviour in organisations', *Leadership and Organization Development Journal*, Vol.20, No.3: 133–46.

McWilliams, A., Siegel, D. and Wright, P. (2006) 'Corporate social responsibility: strategic implications', *Journal of Management Studies*, Vol.43, No.1: 1–18.

Main, N. (2011) 'Reflections on current thinking on business sustainability', Paper for EFMD PRME Summit, Brussels, June.

Martin, G. and Hetrick, S. (2006) *Corporate Reputations, Branding and Managing People: A strategic approach to HR*. Oxford: Butterworth-Heinemann.

Matten, D. and Moon, J. (2008) 'Implicit and explicit CSR: a conceptual framework for a comparative understanding of corporate social responsibility', *Academy of Management Review*, Vol.3, No.2: 404–24.

Meek, V. L. (1988) 'Organizational culture: origins and weaknesses', *Organization Studies*, Vol.9, No.4: 453–73.

Meyer, J. P. and Allen, N. J. (1991) 'A three-component conceptualization of organizational commitment', *Human Resource Management Review*, Vol.1, Issue 1: 61–89.

Meyer, J. P., Allen, N. J. and Smith, C. A. (1993) 'Commitment to organizations and occupations: extension and test of a three-component conceptualization', *Journal of Applied Psychology*, Vol.78, No.4: 538–51.

Meyerson, D. and Martin, J. (1987) 'Culture change: an integration of three different views', *Journal of Management Studies*, Vol.24: 623–47.

Nahavandi, A. (2009) *The Art and Science of Leadership*, 6th edition. Upper Saddle River, NJ: Pearson/Prentice Hall.

Organ, D. W., Podsakoff, P. M. and MacKenzie, S. B. (2006) *Organizational Citizenship Behavior: Its nature, antecedents, and consequences*. Thousand Oaks, CA: Sage.

Parkes, C. L. and Blewitt, J. (2011) ' "Ignorance was bliss; now I'm not ignorant and that is far more difficult" – transdisciplinary learning and reflexivity in responsible management education', *Journal of Global Responsibility*, Special Issue: Vol.2, No.2: 206–21.

Parkes, C. L. and Davis, A. (2012) 'HR, ethics and social responsibility – the "courage to challenge" or a case of the "bystander effect"?', *International Journal of Human Resource Management* (forthcoming).

Peccei, R. and Guest, D. (2002) *Trust, Exchange and Virtuous Circles of Cooperation: A theoretical and empirical analysis of partnership at work management centre*. Research Papers No 11. London: King's College.

Pinnington, A., Macklin, R. and Campbell, T. (2007) *Human Resource Management Ethics and Employment*. Oxford: Oxford University Press.

Porras, J. and Robertson, P. (1992) 'Organisation development', in Dunnette, M. and Hough, L. (eds) *Handbook of Industrial and Organisational Psychology*. Washington, DC: Consulting Psychologists Press.

Porritt, J. (2007) *Capitalism: As if the world matters*, revised edition. London: Earthscan.

Porter, M. E. and Kramer, M. R. (2006) 'Strategy and society: the link between competitive advantage and corporate social responsibility', *Harvard Business Review*, December: 78–92.

PRME (2010) 'The six principles for responsible management education'. Available online at: http://www.unprme.org/the-6-principles/index.php [accessed 4 July 2010].

Ramage, J. D. and Bean, J. C. (1998) *Writing Arguments*, 4th edition. Needham Heights, MA: Allyn & Bacon.

Rhodes, C., Pullen, A. and Clegg, S. R. (2010) ' "If I should fall from grace...": stories of change and organizational ethics', *Journal of Business Ethics*, Vol.91: 535–51.

Rokeach, M. (1973) *The Nature of Human Values*. New York: Free Press.

Schwartz, S. H. (1994) 'Are there universals in the content and structure of values?', *Journal of Social Issues*, Vol.50: 19–45.

Schwartz, S. H. (1999) 'A theory of cultural values and some implications for work', *Applied Psychology: An International Review*, Vol.48, No.1: 23–47.

Scott, J. T. (2011) 'New standards for long-term business survival: sustainable business performance'. Available online at: www.sustainbusper.com [accessed 14 July 2011].

Sears, L. (2010) *Next Generation HR: time for a change – towards a next generation for HR*. London: CIPD.

Siemens archives: Werner von Siemens (1816–1892). Available online at: http://www.siemens.com/history/en/personalities/founder_generation.htm [accessed 9 June 2011].

Singer, P. (2011) *Practical Ethics*. Cambridge: Cambridge University Press.

Smircich, L. (1983) 'Concepts of culture and organizational analysis', *Administrative Science Quarterly*, Vol.28, No.3: 339–58.

Sparrowe, R. T. (2005) 'Authentic leadership and the narrative self', *Leadership Quarterly*, Vol.16, Issue 3, June: 419–39.

Spence, L. and Painter-Morland, M. (eds) (2010) *Ethics in Small and Medium-Sized Enterprises: A global commentary*. International Society of Business, Economics and Ethics. Dordrecht: Springer.

Swanson, D. L. (1999) 'Toward an integrative theory of business and society: a research strategy for corporate social performance', *Academy of Management Review*, Vol.24, No.3: 506–21.

Swanson, D. L. and Orlitzky, M. (2006) 'Executive preference for compensation structure and normative myopia', in Kolb, R. W. (ed.) *The Ethics of Executive Compensation*. Malden, MA: Blackwell.

Turban, D. B. and Greening, D. W. (1997) 'Corporate social performance and organizational attractiveness to prospective employees', *Academy of Management Journal*, Vol.40: 658–72.

Ulrich, D. (1997) *Human Resource Champions: The next agenda for adding value and delivering results*. Boston, MA: Harvard Business School Press.

UN (1987) *Our Common Future: Report of the World Commission on Environment and Development* [the Bruntland Report]. Oxford: Oxford University Press.

Verbos, A. K., Gerard, J. A., Forshey, P. R., Harding, C. S. and Miller, J. S. (2007) 'The positive ethical organization: enacting a living code of ethics and ethical organizational identity', *Journal of Business Ethics*, Vol.76: 17–33.

Webster's *New World College Dictionary* (2010) Cleveland, OH: Wiley.

Wiley, C. (2000) 'Ethical standards for human resource management professionals: a comparative analysis of five major codes', *Journal of Business Ethics*, Vol.25, No.2: 93–114.

Winstanley, D. and Woodall, J. (2000) 'The ethical dimension of HRM', *Human Resource Management Journal*, Vol.10, No.2: 5–20.

Wong, W., Blazey, L., Sullivan, J., Zheltoukhova, K., Albert, A. and Reid, B. (2010) *Understanding the Deal: Placing the employee at the heart of the employment relationship*. Report. London: The Work Foundation.

World Wildlife Fund (2010) *Living Planet* Report. Available online at: http://wwf.panda.org/about_our_earth/all_publications/living_planet_report/ [accessed 23 June 2011].

Zohar, D. and Marshall I. (2004) *Spiritual Capital: Wealth we can live by*. San Francisco: Berrett-Koehler.

CHAPTER 16

Emotion at Work

Chiara Amati and Chris Donegan

CHAPTER OVERVIEW

Interest in emotion at work has been with us since the early days of HR. Organisational interest has focused predominantly on influencing and manipulating feelings in order to deliver higher levels of performance; much of the academic literature has focused on establishing links between individual emotion or mood and single elements of the organisational environment. This chapter attempts a synthesis of the range of approaches to emotion at work and emphasises the more complex interplay between individual and organisational context that lies at the heart of how we feel at work. Consideration of this dynamic whole is argued to be critical to understand affective experience at work and how this impacts on performance and the emotional well-being of the workforce.

LEARNING OBJECTIVES

By the end of this chapter the reader should be able to:

- critically evaluate the traditional 'happy-productive worker' model of emotion at work, its legacy and its limitations
- profit from an overview of current directions in academic emotion research and emotion-related practices in organisations
- appreciate a more dynamic model of affective experience, emphasising the interplay between the individual and the organisational context
- reflect upon the links with New OE.

INTRODUCTION

Organisations are places of emotion and objects of emotion. To navigate organisations is to navigate the complexities of the emotional webs within them. Emotions are not incidental to, or disruptive of, work or organisational life – they are an essential part of the human experience of work.

This chapter provides an initial insight into the complex nature of individual affective experience at work, placing employees and their emotions and moods at the centre of a dynamic, changing interplay between individual and context. It emphasises both the individual elements of emotional experience, such as the duration or intensity of personal feeling (eg the difference between emotion and mood), and contextual elements, such as the impact of culture on how the emotion is experienced, talked about and shown to others (eg the difference between feeling and emotion display) – see Table 16.1 (eg Weiss, 2002; Fineman, 2003).

Table 16.1 Elements of affective experience

	Theoretical concepts	Example in organisations
AFFECTIVE EXPERIENCE (AFFECT) – Generic term used to refer to all aspects of feeling, emotion-based experience, including both moods and emotions.	MOOD – Diffuse, longer-lasting type of affective experience; not immediately linked to any specific event or situation.	I generally like my work, and that Tuesday I had arrived at work feeling positive as usual.
	EMOTION – More transient type of affective experience, intense but infrequent; typically linked to a specific event, occurrence or moment.	Then, half-way through the morning, my manager just walked in and told me, in front of everyone, that he felt I'd made a mistake in my figures for the monthly report and I needed to recheck my data. To be honest, my initial reactions was total anger.
	FEELING and DISPLAY – Contrasting more personal element of affective experience with what is seen by others.	I was so angry! I felt it was unprofessional as well as unjust [feeling]. But I didn't say it and just tried to smile [external display of emotion].
	MOOD – A return to the initial mood.	It affected me for most of the day, although my good mood returned later in the afternoon after I'd had a chance to vent my anger a bit with a colleague.

The chapter aims to connect academic and practitioner thinking on emotion at work, by blending short case studies with theoretical models, evidence and expert commentaries. Throughout the links to both classical and new, emerging models of OD will be stressed (see Chapter 1), and there are opportunities for reflection to improve OE practice.

CLASSICAL MODELS OF EMOTION AT WORK

Researchers, managers and allied professionals have been interested in individual affective experience (emotion and mood) for nearly 100 years. This section reviews how this body of understanding has shaped the way emotion at work has come to be currently understood.

THE HAPPY-PRODUCTIVE WORKER AND EMOTION AS 'WIN/WIN'

The emergence of the interest in affect at work is typically traced to studies conducted in the 1930s and the birth of the Human Relations movement. Several influential studies from this period investigated emotion at work in all its complexity, exploring how emotions and moods varied from moment to moment and from day to day – how they were shaped by work itself, by broader social work groups, by the individual's home environment and also by their personality and attitudes (see Weiss and Brief, 2001, for a historical review). This early work was hugely influential; it established the individual and his or her feelings about work as important and legitimate topics for both scientific study and management or HR action.

Over time, the broad remit of these initial studies became narrowed to the specific exploration of the link between the individual worker's feelings about work and his or her performance (Weiss and Brief, 2001). Studies of emotion at work started to revolve around exploring, or proving, what is commonly referred to as the 'happy-productive worker hypothesis'. In simple terms, this is the proposition that people who are happy at work perform better. Generally, it is understood as meaning that feeling happy about work causes improved performance.

There are two important, appealing and intuitive elements to this hypothesis. The first, the 'happy' element, is the assumption that individuals will hold generic, relatively stable, 'positive' or 'negative' feelings about their work. The second, the 'productive' element, is that this affective state has a direct, positive effect on employee behaviour. Together they suggest a 'win/win' scenario in which what is good for the worker – ie feeling happy or 'positive' – is also good for the organisation – ie performing better.

The following quote from the performance review of a small subsidiary of an IT services company shows this well. The introduction to its six-monthly performance appraisal documentation opens with this statement:

> We believe that a happy employee will not only perform more effectively but will increase our ability to retain their skills in the company.

The 'happy-productive' worker hypothesis and its key elements characterised thinking on emotion at work for most of the twentieth century. Its legacy can also be seen across many areas of contemporary organisational study and practice, such as interest in high-performance working practices (HPWPs) (see also Chapter 14). Popular contemporary conceptualisations of, or ways of thinking about, emotion at work follow along similar lines of argument. For example, employee engagement is often defined as being a generic 'positive' emotional state, which is desirable due to its 'win/win' ability to be good for the individual and good for the organisation (eg Bakker *et al*, 2011a, 2011b; see also Chapter 14).

EMERGING QUESTIONS AND NEW DIRECTIONS

Research into the happy-productive worker hypothesis was primarily carried out in studies of job satisfaction. Job satisfaction research combined consideration of emotion or affect (ie how individuals feel about work) with theories of attitudes (ie what they think about work), motivation and performance (ie what people do at work and why). For example, Maslow's hierarchy of needs theory of motivation is reflected in Herzberg's distinction between 'hygiene' and 'motivator' job satisfaction factors, and in Hackman and Oldham's job characteristics theory (Hackman and Oldham, 1980).

By the 1990s a very large number of studies on job satisfaction and performance had been conducted, alongside several meta-analyses to combine and better understand these results. The overall picture was not, however, exactly as expected. A relationship between job satisfaction and performance was fairly consistently found, and people who reported higher job satisfaction also reported, or were reported to have, better performance. But this relationship was weaker than anticipated and is not straightforward to interpret (see the review by Judge *et al*, 2001). Evidence that job satisfaction actually causes improved performance was not that strong; other possible explanations of the relationship with performance exist; and there was evidence that reverse causal effect might be more likely – ie that it is good performance which causes satisfaction. Further factors were also thought to be in play, such as personality or aspects of well-being (eg Wright, Cropanzano and Bonett, 2007). This could be interpreted as showing that happier people tend to report higher job satisfaction and are also generally better performers. Evaluation of the impact of related work interventions has also been mixed – for example, the effectiveness of high-performance working practices, although often assumed by the HR community, is not supported as strongly and consistently by evidence (eg Wall and Wood, 2005).

Job satisfaction research as a whole began to be criticised on a number of fronts. Its tendency to confuse consideration of affective and cognitive components of experience at work was highlighted (eg Fisher, 2000); its focus on assessing the link between generic satisfaction and generic performance was also questioned (eg Brief and Weiss, 2002).

The 'win/win' interpretation of the happy-productive worker hypothesis also began to be challenged: the implied alignment between the organisation's and the individual's interests when it came to emotion was actually harder to achieve in practice. This often resulted in mechanistic attempts at influencing the emotions of employees solely in order to achieve performance benefits. HPWPs, for example, have been criticised as resulting in changes such as work intensification that are detrimental to the employee (eg Sparham and Sung, 2007). The assumption of mutual interest can also be argued to overshadow the extent to which emotion is actively controlled and managed at work to serve the organisation's interest (eg Landen, 2002).

Interest in job satisfaction within the academic community has gradually waned over the last decade, but interest in emotion has increased exponentially. Much of the more recent research aims to distance itself from the earlier models, and has accordingly been described as an 'affective revolution' as old paradigms have been abandoned in favour of new, richer models, ideas and methodologies (Barsade, Brief and Spataro, 2003). The focus on broadly defined 'positive' or 'negative' affective states has been argued to need replacing with an exploration of specific, distinct emotions, distinguishing also between emotion experienced at a specific moment in time and general mood. The need to move beyond an interest in generic performance towards more detailed examination of people's contributions at work is also argued (eg Briner and Kiefer, 2009; Gooty *et al*, 2009). As a result, research is now starting to show more complex interactions between affect and performance: for example, a positive mood tends to influence helping behaviours, co-operation and creativity, whereas specific negative emotions, such as anger or anxiety, have specific and distinct effects on judgements and behaviours (see reviews in Brief and Weiss, 2002; Elfenbein, 2007; Ashkanasy and Humphrey, 2011). Finally, there is a need to disentangle interest in affective experience from the managerial agenda of increasing performance (eg Briner and Kiefer, 2009).

SUMMARY AND COMMENTARY

The simplistic and overly mechanistic understanding of emotion at work offered by the happy-productive worker hypothesis has permeated research communities and organisations for most of the last century. Recently, it has been challenged on a number of fronts, as the expert commentary below outlines. Many of these challenges parallel the limitations argued for the classical model of OD over new, emerging models (see Chapter 1), and a more complex message is now starting to be emphasised – a message that a regenerated (New) OE must consider, as the next section outlines.

Rob Briner is Professor of Organisational Psychology at University of Bath School of Management. His research focuses on the reciprocal links between work and various aspects of well-being such as moods and emotions. He has published widely in both psychology and management journals, is regularly invited to contribute to practitioner and policy debates, and is involved with a number of evidence-based management initiatives. This is his expert commentary on the happy-productive worker hypothesis:

> The idea that happy workers perform better than less happy workers has much appeal. It seems to make sense and reflects everyday experience. However, this apparently straightforward and intuitive idea quickly starts to lose its appeal when we subject it to even a little scrutiny. So why, in spite of well-documented problems, does this idea remain popular?

First, there is something simple and comforting about 'win/win' interventions that claim to increase performance by increasing worker satisfaction. It suggests that organisations can get higher levels of productivity while at the same time making their staff more satisfied. What's not to like? It also helps focus attention away from the far less comforting idea that what most work organisations are actually doing is exploiting workers for their own ends. Second, as mentioned, it does have intuitive appeal. If you want someone to help you with something, are you going to ask the happy person or the grumpy person? Experience suggests that asking the happy person is more likely to get us the help we need, so it follows that happier workers are more likely to be productive workers. At least – it seems to follow.

So what's useful about this idea? Its main and perhaps only value is as a starting point in helping us to understand possible links between how workers feel, how they behave, and how this may affect performance. But it's only a start. It is far too general and vague to be of much value and should not be taken that seriously. Where links do exist between how workers feel and how they perform, they are likely to be specific and to depend on the job. In other words, particular feelings or emotions are likely to be related to relatively specific forms of behaviour, and whether or not such behaviours link to performance will depend on the type of job and organisation.

A further limitation of the happy-productive worker idea is that it suggests that, generally speaking, positive feelings are good for performance, negative feelings detrimental to it. But this is simply not the case (eg Elfenbein, 2007). For example: feeling worried or anxious can help focus our attention on what's important, whereas feeling excited or positive can make us over-optimistic and misjudge the likely success of some action. Again, it all depends on a number of factors including the person, the type of performance behaviour and the job. In general, a mix of positive and negative feelings is vital for performance of all kinds (George, 2011).

Last, it's important to think about the links between feelings and performance as a process, not as a simple 'x causes y'-type relationship. Feelings and behaviour affect each other over time as a process. How we feel affects how we behave. How we behave affects how we feel. And so on. If we want to better understand feelings and performance, we need also to start thinking in terms of a reciprocal process rather than of simple cause-and-effect.

REFLECTIVE ACTIVITIES

Consider an organisation you are familiar with, its policies and its practices. Reflect on the following:

● How would you describe the general approach to emotion at work in this organisation? For example, what are the main emotions that are talked about and given importance? What is the balance between measuring these and taking improvement action?

● What are the underlying assumptions behind this approach? What does the approach say about how the organisation understands employee emotion? For example, does it share features of the mechanistic, simplistic, performance-driven 'win/win' assumption?

In your reflection, consider also Allan Ramdhony's reflections on Critical HRD (Chapter 9).

INDIVIDUAL EMOTIONAL EXPERIENCE

The previous section argued that there has been a recent shift in the frameworks adopted for appreciating the complexity of affective experience at work. This section outlines how this is influencing current understanding of the individual aspects of emotional experience at work.

DEFINING AFFECTIVE EXPERIENCE AT WORK

A new approach to affective experience is argued to need, at its core, a stronger theoretical basis. In the first instance, the temporal/intensity dimension to experience must be acknowledged – the difference between experiencing a diffuse mood and a more intense, short-lived emotion (see Table 16.1). In addition, the broad generic categorisations of 'positive' and 'negative' emotions must be replaced with sensitivity to how specific emotions and moods differ from each other – ie how anger might be different from sadness (eg Briner and Kiefer, 2009; Gooty et al, 2009). This endeavour is typically referred to as efforts to describe the structure of affect or affective experience.

Research in this area has been extensive, and a consensus is gradually building around a theoretical framework that considers emotions and moods to be variations on two dimensions: hedonic tone (pleasantness/unpleasantness) and affect intensity (activation). (For reviews of this body of evidence, see Weiss, 2002; Cropanzano et al, 2003; Seo, Barrett and Jin, 2008.) This model suggests that all emotions, and moods, can be understood in terms of how pleasant they are to experience and the degree of activation they entail. The emotions are typically represented as falling into a broadly circular pattern, and this model is therefore referred to as the 'circumplex' model of affect (eg Russell, 1980). As shown in Figure 16.1, this would suggest that feeling 'happy' and feeling 'sad' differ in the degree of *pleasantness* of the sensation, whereas feeling 'happy' and feeling 'serene' differ in respect of the degree of *activation* that they produce.

Applying this theoretical model to affective experience introduces greater sophistication in talking and thinking about emotion and mood at work. The language it suggests is both more descriptively and more theoretically meaningful; the terms themselves suggest more information about the experience and allow clearer distinctions to be made between

Figure 16.1 The structure of affect

Source: adapted from Cropanzano *et al* (2003)

different affective states. For example, talking of anger and anxiety rather than just 'negative' feelings both provides more information about the experience and highlights how these emotions differ. The language adopted also appears more value-neutral because it differentiates between experiences on the basis of their content rather than on any 'positive' or 'negative' impact they might have.

Adopting this model, and associated language, also highlights the assumptions implicit in current language used to describe emotions in organisations. A broad categorisation of emotions into 'positive' and 'negative' implies a simplistic, linear and unitary relationship between the emotion felt and its impact on behaviour (eg George, 2011), and it allows a discussion of emotion only in terms of its usefulness to the organisation (eg Fineman, 2000). For instance, anger is typically described as a 'negative' emotion because it can result in behaviours that have a negative impact on the organisation, such as sabotage. However, in a situation where an individual has experienced discrimination at work, the emotion might be entirely appropriate and useful, or 'positive', in that it signals that the current situation is wrong and highlights the need for corrective action.

It is useful also to reflect on how contemporary, popular conceptualisations of emotion, such as stress and engagement, are aligned to this endeavour. Within the UK, organisations are encouraged to adopt the regulator, the Health and Safety Executive's definition of work-related stress – see Table 16.2. This seems to steer the reader away from consideration of 'stress' as a specific emotion that might be linked to the model of affect above, towards a more generic process-focused conception: feeling stressed, the definition appears to imply, can mean experiencing a range of emotions. This resonates with contemporary calls to consider stress a broad area of experience, with key affective components, rather than a specific emotion or mood (eg Daniels, 2011).

A discussion of engagement presents different problems. There are problems in its definition – specifically, that the academic/research and the practitioner/organisation communities appear to adopt different definitions of engagement (eg Macey and Schneider, 2008; Wefald and Downey, 2009). Allowing for some degree of continuing debate, there

Table 16.2 Definitions of 'stress' and 'engagement'

State	Definition	Source
Stress	'The adverse reaction people have to excessive pressures or other types of demand placed on them at work.'	UK Health and Safety publications and website [accessed March 2011]
Engagement	'Positive, fulfilling work-related state of mind that is characterised by vigour, dedication and absorption.'	Schaufeli et al (2002); Bakker et al (2011a, 2011b). Typically used in academic research[1]
	'An employee's drive to use all their ingenuity and resources for the benefit of the company.'	Best Companies (UK engagement consultants)[2]
	'Engagement is a force that drives business outcomes.'	Gallup Corporation (US engagement consultants)[3]

[1] There is also considerable research into the impact of non-work events on emotions experienced at work. This literature is not considered in this chapter where the focus is primarily on work itself. For a general review, see Weiss and Brief (2001).

[2] Best Companies website http://www.bestcompanies.co.uk//AboutWIT.aspx [accessed 16 May 2011].

[3] Gallup website http://www.gallup.com/consulting/52/employee-engagement.aspx [accessed 16 May 2011].

is a growing consensus within academic communities over a discussion of engagement in terms of the model of affect as a high-activation pleasant state (eg Bakker, Albrecht and Leiter, 2011a, 2011b). However, within the practitioner domains, the organisation's agenda appears to dominate to the extent that the concept itself is defined primarily in relation to its organisational impact; attention to the emotional experience of the individual is more or less completely lost.

COMPLEX CAUSES AND INFLUENCES

Since the early research into emotional experience at work, there has been a desire to understand how work can impact on emotion. Within organisations, this has been associated with the tradition of designing jobs, or job features, often with the explicit agenda of inducing specific emotional or cognitive-emotional states (like job satisfaction or engagement) that are assumed to assist performance. The research effort has been enormous and it has generated a general consensus of the features of a 'good job' – ie job features that are good for the individual and, arguably, good for the organisation, because they result in improved performance (see Weiss and Brief, 2001, for a review). This body of evidence has accumulated in parallel with research into 'bad jobs' – ie those jobs, or features of jobs, that can cause 'negative' emotions, such as stress (see for example the Health and Safety Executive website).

A comparison of the two reveals several areas of overlap, and an overall picture of a 'good job' emerges, as charted on Table 16.3. Key concepts include employee empowerment, in terms of both ensuring discretion in individual jobs and participation in organisational decision-making; job resources, providing reasonable job demands and appropriate resources; and supportive relationships between colleagues, team members, managers, leaders and followers. Similar concepts to these are present *in reverse* in the literature concerning work-related stress.

The consensus of features of a 'good job' can be misconstrued as a return to theorising about simplistic cause-and-effect relationships between generic job characteristics, generic emotions or moods and generic performance. The picture in practice is considerably more complex and more dynamic.

Firstly, job characteristics cannot be assumed to exist in isolation from each other, nor to have simple, linear, unitary effects on individuals. Features of the job, for example, can work in combination with each other in eliciting emotional responses: stress is typically associated with situations of high demands coupled with low control (eg Karasek, 1979). In a similar vein, job resources are particularly salient in driving engagement in situations of increased demands (eg Bakker *et al*, 2011a). They may also have a more complex effect on individuals – specific features might not just elicit one emotional response but might bring about multiple ambivalent responses (eg George, 2011).

It has also been argued that traditional conceptions of job characteristics should be expanded to include attention to 'enacted job characteristics', or 'the events that reflect jobs as they happen' (Daniels, 2006: 278). This parallels calls for shifting attention from focusing on job characteristics to considering actual work events as causes of emotion: emotions, it is argued, are experienced in reaction to specific situations that happen at work (eg Weiss and Cropanzano, 1996). Understanding emotion at work becomes understanding sometimes complex reactions to situations, events, interactions or important feature of the environment (eg Elfenbein, 2007).

This shift in attention also highlights the importance of specific interactions in shaping individuals' emotional experience at work. Among the possible interactions, those with managers and leaders have attracted considerable attention, and there is a growing literature on leader behaviour and its effect on emotions in followers, whether generally (eg Dasborough, 2006; Humphrey *et al*, 2008) or more specifically in terms of engagement (eg Bakker *et al*, 2011a, 2011b) and stress (eg Yarker *et al*, 2007). There is also interest in

Table 16.3 Sources of stress, job satisfaction or engagement at work

	Hackman and Oldham (1980)	Bakker *et al* (2011a)	CIPD	Best Companies	HSE
	Antecedents of job satisfaction	Model of job engagement	Engagement measurement tool	High-level engagement factors[1]	Risk factors for stress
Meaningful work	✓	✓	✓		
Challenging but reasonable goals or demands			✓	✓	✓
Variety in skill use	✓	✓	✓	✓	
Opportunities for empowerment and involvement	✓	✓	✓		✓
Access to feedback on performance	✓	✓	✓	✓	
Opportunities for learning and development	✓	✓	✓	✓	✓
Access to sufficient resources			✓		✓
Supportive relationships with colleagues/team		✓	✓	✓	✓
Features of managers/ leaders and their behaviour			✓	✓	✓
Pay and benefits received			✓	✓	
Other features of the organisation		✓	✓	✓	
Characteristics of the individual		✓			

[1] Best Companies website http://www.bestcompanies.co.uk//Methodology.aspx [accessed 16 May 2011].

the affective impact of teams and work groups as demonstrated in the influential work of Tuckman (1965, 1977) and, more recently, interest in how groups share and influence each other's emotions (see Brief and Weiss, 2002; Ashkanasy and Humphrey, 2011, for reviews)

THE ACTIVE INDIVIDUAL

In the discussion above, the individual risks appearing to be relatively passive, reacting in predictable, universal ways to stimuli in his or her environment, whether specific events or job characteristics. This has been argued to underplay and therefore undermine the active role the individual has in shaping all aspects of experience at work.

In the first instance, the notion of the active individual is clearly present in recent research into 'enacted job characteristics' that focuses attention on the actions that individuals take to enact, influence and therefore shape their job (Daniels, 2006, 2011). If the job becomes what and how the individual does it, rather than how the organisation or management have dictated it, it becomes problematic to discuss any universal relationships between job characteristic and individual affective reactions.

There is also considerable variability in the way individuals interpret and react to similar external events. This is discussed as the importance of individual appraisal or interpretation within emotional experience (eg Weiss and Cropanzano, 1996; Elfenbein, 2007). Emotional reaction ensues not because of the trigger event itself, it is argued, but according to individuals' appraisal or interpretation of this event in terms of meaning for themselves and their goals, as Table 16.4 suggests. Far from being able to assume a universal, predictable pattern of reactions to events, a more person-centred approach must be taken. Individuals differ in their reactions, so no single 'correct' emotional reaction or interpretation of events can be either assumed or imposed – rather, there are multiple, equally valid, individual perspectives on the same event that have to be acknowledged and understood (see also Chapter 1).

Table 16.4 An example of the role of appraisal

Background	I am new to the job but know most of the people already as I have worked in the organisation for a few years. I generally arrive at work in a good mood.	I am new to the job and the organisation; I am still getting to know the team. I am still uncertain whether this is the job for me.
Trigger event	I receive an email from my boss with a last-minute request.	
Possible appraisal	I immediately think this is a great opportunity to show how quickly and accurately I can respond. I will have to postpone some other work, but it is worth it, and others can help here. I know I have done similar things to this before and feel confident that I can do it.	This is a test of my ability to respond at short notice. I have lots of other work on that will be delayed as a result and am not sure who could help. I know that I have a tendency to worry – and now I am not sure I will be able to do this to the right standard.
Emotion experienced (feeling)	I feel enthusiastic about doing this and proud of the confidence shown in me.	I feel anxious, nervous and a little angry at having been given so little time to complete this task.
Behavioural reaction	I start working on this straight away, complete it quickly, and have time to check it before sending it off.	I find myself delaying starting, worrying, and end up doing it quickly, making mistakes.

The approach ties in with discussion of the influence of disposition or personality on affect. Personality has been acknowledged to influence both the range of emotions individuals experience and the intensity with which these are said to be experienced. This influence is thought to be greater for generic mood than for specific emotions (see Brief and Weiss, 2002; Elfenbein, 2007, for reviews).

The importance of the individual is also present in theories of stress and engagement – for example, in theories which suggest that stress is linked to a discrepancy between what the individual expects or wants from the organisation and what he or she receives (eg Edwards, 1996). The importance of personality and other individual characteristics, for instance, is also acknowledged in the importance given to 'personal resources', such as psychological capital, in theories of drivers of engagement (eg Bakker *et al*, 2011a, 2011b).

SUMMARY AND COMMENTARY

Understanding emotion at work means moving away from simplistic models to adopt a more sophisticated, dynamic, process-driven perspective. It means moving away from a discussion of generic 'positive' or 'negative' states to a focus on specific and distinct emotions at work. It also means moving away from a rigid, mechanistic modelling of cause-and-effect relationships and the idea of stable job characteristics resulting in simple, unitary reactions to an appreciation of the impact of dynamic, complex patterns of events, interactions, behaviours and their impact on emotional realities experienced by individuals. This requires integrating an understanding of the role of employee agency, of the active individual and their shaping of all aspects of the individual affective experience at work. As the expert commentary below captures neatly, a more dynamic picture emerges.

Kevin Daniels is Professor of Organisational Psychology in the Centre for Organisational Resilience at Loughborough University and is Fellow of the British Psychological Society. His current research interests are focused on emotion, stress, well-being, safety and innovation at work. He is particularly interested in the fluid nature of job design and its relationships to effective problem-solving and coping. This, then, is his expert commentary on understanding emotion at work:

If you compare the predictive power of traditional job characteristics theories against personality, the biggest predictor of emotional well-being at work is personality. And typically, this is how research in this area has been done – collect data on job characteristics and on personality and examine their relationships with well-being and various indicators of stress.

However, this logically simple approach, although frequently accompanied by sophisticated methods in recent research, masks the complexity of what really happens. Different people appraise things differently, because people often have different goals at work – one person might react to a bad performance review with anxiety because they were hoping for promotion, whereas another person might not care too much if he or she is looking for another job. One key determinant of how a person appraises an event is whether that person believes the event has implications for their personal goals. When goals are threatened, disrupted or not met, negative emotions like anxiety, anger and sadness might arise. When goals are progressing well or attained, positive emotions might arise. Also, it seems possible that repeated exposure to events that influence goal progress can lead to learning emotional responses by association. For example, if your manager always gives you bad performance reviews, no matter how well you think you've done, you might feel anxious about going into your next review.

Another key factor that explains why people differ in their emotional responses to work is that people react to events that influence their goals or well-being in different ways. For example, some people might respond to problems at work by avoiding thinking about them and trying to do something else, whereas other people might try to do something about the problem. These reactions to emotion-inducing events mean that people shape or craft their work environment over the short term in order to cope.

This is a point of connection with the job characteristics literature. For example, job control and support from colleagues seem to be key features of work – or job resources that help people cope with problems and demands at work. People can reschedule activities (a form of job control) to take a break or talk to work colleagues (support) to distract themselves temporarily from what they may find distressing or frustrating. Or people can reschedule activities or alter how they do their work (job control) to spend more time in finding a solution to a problem or to try out solutions to a problem. Similarly, people can ask advice (support) for what to do about a problem.

Because people react to problems, it means we may have to shift the way we think about how job characteristics are related to affective well-being. In many models of job design, job characteristics are perceived as permanent or semi-permanent features of jobs set by managers and/or organisational processes. Acknowledging that workers are active in interpreting their work (appraisal) and active in regulating their affective responses to work by changing things about their work or seeking support (coping) means that we ought to view job characteristics and job design as dynamic and emergent properties of organisational systems and individual action.

GUIDED REFLECTIONS ON PRACTICE: EMOTIONAL INTELLIGENCE

Talk of emotion at work is often accompanied by talk of emotional skills or, frequently, 'emotional intelligence' (EI or EQ). Although there are several models of emotional intelligence and continued debates about their relative merits (eg Clarke, 2006), central to most models is their argument for the importance of individuals' ability to read, understand, influence and make use of their own feelings and emotions. This argument has been made specifically with respect to leadership effectiveness and capability (eg George, 2000) – as the Masterfoods case study suggests.

 ## EMOTIONAL INTELLIGENCE AT MASTERFOODS

CASE STUDY

Masterfoods Ireland is the Irish division of Mars Inc., the global leader in confectionery, food, pet food, ice cream and other products. Masterfoods was interested finding out what emotional intelligence factors differentiate 'star performers' within its workforce and therefore formed a partnership with Mike Fiszer, Director of Leadership Development at the Edinburgh Institute, Edinburgh Napier University, to investigate.

Masterfoods staff were invited to take part in a confidential, voluntary, personalised programme of EQ assessment and development. The assessment results were collated and discriminant analysis used to identify those factors which make a difference to performance. Masterfoods was therefore able to identify the emotional competencies, across a range of functions, required for the delivery of excellence. This analysis showed that the main differentiating characteristics were mainly intrapersonal competencies,

such as emotional self-awareness. As important was the finding that the factors that differentiated a below-average and an average performer were different from what separated average and star performers.

'The project had benefits for both the individuals and the company,' says Mike. For individuals who participated in the EQ assessment process, it led to voluntary personal development programmes. For Masterfoods, it identified the competencies the company should seek when developing and recruiting staff. Louise Carton, P&O Country Head, Masterfoods Ireland said: 'From our associates' point of view, this activity was not only interesting but insightful and supportive of their development. From the business perspective, it gave us some new ideas to broaden, motivate and further engage our associates.'

Source: Mike Fizser, Edinburgh Institute, Edinburgh Napier University

However, evidence from academic studies to the effect that emotional intelligence contributes to leadership effectiveness is mixed. The last decade has been punctuated by point-counterpoint articles between 'EI supporters' and 'EI sceptics' to unpick the evidence and argue their respective cases (eg Ashkanasy and Daus, 2005; Antonakis *et al*, 2009). Although the argument for the importance of social or emotional skills in managers and leaders is accepted by both parties, there is continued debate about whether these skills are linked to emotional intelligence, as it is typically defined, or are just features of personality or intelligence. Some would conclude that the importance of emotional intelligence has been grossly overrated (Briner and Kiefer, 2009); others that sufficient evidence for its effectiveness has not yet been gathered.

The appeal of an emotional ability in leader effectiveness also tends to gloss over long-standing debates about the nature of emotional intelligence and practices surrounding it. As the previous section has argued, emotional experience is complex, dynamic, inconsistent and difficult to predict. Talking of the skills needed to navigate these experiences as 'emotional intelligence' only makes this process appear neat, logical and manageable and therefore more appealing to organisations (eg Fineman, 2000; Landen, 2004). Some also note that, in practice, emotional intelligence interventions actually help to establish and maintain emotional rules within organisations – they are therefore part of the organisation's effort to influence and control individuals' emotional experience rather than value-free attempts at its development (see the next section; Landen, 2002; Fineman, 2000).

All of these tensions are present in the case study. On the one hand, it illustrates the possible benefit of seeking a more contextualised understanding of the relationship between emotional intelligence and performance, allowing the company to move towards a more considered and contextually rooted understanding of success in its particular setting. However, any possible tensions between an individual's own development and the organisation's agenda are downplayed – the assumption is that these are the same, and that becoming emotionally intelligent will serve both the organisation and the individual. But in this case study, as in most similar interventions, it is the interests of the organisation that have typically driven the assessment and its consequences, notably the areas in which individuals are then expected to develop.

THE CONTEXT OF EMOTIONAL EXPERIENCE

The previous section discussed how individual affective experience is shaped by the dynamic interplay between individuals and events around them. The role of individual appraisal was described as a process through which the individual makes personal sense of emotion-triggering events that happen around them. This should not be interpreted as implying that meaning is solely personally or individually constructed; this section argues that organisational culture must also be considered an example of how context influences individual emotional experience.

EMOTIONAL CULTURES

Culture acts to shape perception and interpretation of what happens around individuals as well as within them, by shaping thinking and feeling (Geertz, 1993; see also Chapter 5). The deepest or core elements of a culture are its most powerful, in part due to the fact that they are often 'invisible', implicit and taken for granted by those within it. Unspoken shared assumptions about issues such as status, authority and the nature of working relationships are established very rapidly and provide a social control mechanism that affects individuals' actions, thinking and emotion (Schein, 2004; see also Chapter 5). This perception of culture as a controlling mechanism is also present in Johnson's (1992) notion of the 'cultural web'. Here, contributory behavioural elements create a reinforcing web of congruent behaviours, driven by the underlying 'paradigm' or pattern of values, beliefs and assumptions that are taken for granted and remain largely hidden and unchallenged in an organisation.

This process also happens in relation to emotions. Organisations, either implicitly, such as through shaping the company's culture, or explicitly, such as during training or development programmes, transmit expectations to individuals about what is considered appropriate in feeling or emotion. This can often be perceived cascading from corporate value statements in which the values explicitly indicate the emotional responses required. All these efforts serve to communicate and ingrain what emotional responses are considered appropriate and valuable within organisations. However, in the light of culture's emergent properties, the actual impact is not straightforward – as the public sector case study below shows.

CASE STUDY

EMOTIONAL CULTURE IN A PUBLIC SECTOR BODY

Eighteen months after the start-up of a small but high-profile public sector body, things were not going as well as expected. The chief executive officer had become increasingly concerned that in spite of the clear remit established for the organisation, decision-making appeared slow, staff seemed confused about who was responsible for what, and things didn't feel right. At the very start the organisation had set out its value statement, in which the following were explicit expectations:

- Show you care
- Faith
- Hope
- Love
- Equality of human dignity and respect
- Rooted in real life.

However, this appeared to be far from what many of the staff were reporting as being their experience. Staff spoke about the 'bipolar' culture in the office, which was confusing and unsettling, and they reported that it created a good deal of resentment and low morale.

In spite of having an intuition about the issues, the CEO wanted more evidence to assess what was going on and to take the most effective course of action. A diagnostic workshop was arranged solely for staff, without the senior team, using the cultural web to identify what kind of culture was emerging across the organisation.

This revealed that two competing cultures had developed around two powerful individuals in the senior team, one closer to the desired culture and another emergent culture that was almost its complete opposite. The underlying 'paradigms' were identified from the analysis of the two culture webs that emerged from the diagnostic exercise.

Culture A	Culture B
<ul><li>Individualism</li><li>Professionalism</li><li>Enthusiasm and commitment</li><li>Minimal structure and planning</li><li>High-energy</li><li>Driven</li><li>Fun</li></ul>	<ul><li>Things need to be controlled from the top</li><li>Low-trust</li><li>Hierarchical</li><li>Bureaucratic</li><li>Risk-averse</li><li>Minimising conflict</li></ul>

The two distinct cultural manifestations were recognised as being the result of the leadership styles of the two senior managers, and each had a distinct impact on the emotional climate of the organisation. Culture A was perceived as more fun to work in and generated a more relaxed and open climate; Culture B generated a more restrained, uncomfortable emotional climate in which staff were more fearful of the consequences of mistakes and putting a foot wrong. Displaying enthusiasm for Culture A could be seen as a sign of motivation and engagement; for Culture B, this would be a sign of lack of professionalism and of superficiality.

In spite of a clear value statement, the nature of the organisational culture that had developed subtly altered the experienced emotion within the organisation. Thus in spite of the organisation's declared intentions, the impact of leadership behaviour at senior level could have a powerful influence on the culture, and as a result, on individuals' emotional experience in the organisation.

EMOTIONAL RULES AND LABOUR

The influence of organisational culture over how emotions are shown or displayed is typically discussed as 'emotion display rules'. These are defined as socially derived beliefs about whether and how to display a felt emotion within a specific context, and are argued to be subtle, changing and complex, with different rules applying to different emotions across situations (eg Diefendorff and Greguras, 2009).

The result of taking on and adhering to emotional display rules is in essence a difference between what is felt and what is expressed. This process is achieved by the use of a series of strategies, from expressing the felt emotion openly to neutralising or masking it (Diefendorff and Greguras, 2009). The individual thus feels an emotion and then takes cues from the organisation on whether and how to express it. As an example, in Hochschild's seminal work *The Managed Heart*, airline stewardesses described how the airline would prescribe the expression of certain emotions in interactions with customers, regardless of the customers' behaviour or the stewardesses' own feelings. Even when a customer was rude, the stewardess was expected to mask her frustration or anger and just display happiness or contentment.

In organisations, therefore, individuals learn what they are expected to display and typically choose to comply. In some cases their efforts will extend to solely displaying the correct emotion; in others they will extend to attempts to change the way they actually feel, to be more in line with what is expected. This has also been described in terms of 'surface' and 'deep' acting, the former associated with feigned display and the latter associated with concerted efforts to change the feeling itself (eg Hochschild, 1983). It essentially refers to the process of allowing the organisation to manage individual personal feelings, allowing the organisation to shape what is felt. This process then becomes part of the employee's work, part of what the organisation expects, rewards and trades; as such, it is defined as 'emotional labour' to clearly identify it as a form of employee labour. The intrusive nature of this process has led some to argue that the inevitable result is psychological strain on the individual (Hochschild, 1983).

SUMMARY AND COMMENTARY

In this section, the impact of organisational culture has been discussed as an example of the influence of the broader social context on emotion at work. This would suggest that the individual's emotional experience is a complex interplay between individual feelings and personal meaning-making and social influences, such as cultural emotional rules and expectations, both managed and emergent, of the group or the organisation. The context provided by organisation culture exerts a complex and powerful influence which, because it is so often covert, is often left unquestioned.

As the expert commentary below points out, seeking to understand individual emotional experience at work as starting and ending solely with the individual is underestimating the power and influence of culture and organisational context. This goes beyond making certain events more or less likely to happen, to influencing the way in which certain events and their emotional consequences are understood by the organisation. Regenerating OE (as New OE) will mean understanding how and why culture shapes emotions – for example, not only understanding why a reorganisation causes anger, but also reflecting on why change management interventions aim to control or reduce anger because it is understood by the organisation to be 'negative' and inappropriate.

Stephen Fineman is Professor Emeritus at the School of Management, University of Bath. He has had a distinguished research and teaching career and is the author of many journal articles, textbooks and specialist books in the area of organisational behaviour and emotion. He is credited with introducing emotion into organisation studies with his 1993 book, *Emotion in Organisations* (a new edition of which was published in 2000). This is his expert commentary on the individual and emotional experience at work:

The cultural and organisational context of emotion cannot be overstated – especially how power is deployed. It is all too easy to 'blame' an individual for their feelings, and how they should control, or deal with, them. Stress is an excellent example, in that many organisations readily hive off their stressed staff onto stress management programmes. This locates the problem as something inside the individual to be fixed (a rare outcome), avoiding the more difficult question of 'What might be wrong with our organisation?'

Feeling happy, oppressed, anxious, angry, resentful, committed or disaffected says as much, if not more, about the political and structural context of the organisation as about the personality make-up of the individual. An organisation that is retrenching, demanding more-for-less from its staff, and imposing very tight targets on its workers, foments anxiety and fear. If staff feel penalised or demonised for events that are out of their direct control, it is a recipe for disaffection and burnout, especially if they are customer-facing and are 'required' to appear bright and cheerful (emotional labour). In other words, it is instructive to turn our attention to the managerial and organisational context that drives the 'events' that trigger different individual emotions. Why are the events there? Who or what is sustaining them? How might they be changed?

Social work is a case in point – a practice now heavily circumscribed by resource stringencies, standardised methods, many boxes to tick, imposed targets, and a shift away from casework to 'care management', routinising dealings with clients. Moreover, the public emotional ethos, or 'emotionology', toward social work is at best circumspect, at worst highly critical. An emotion audit of social work departments makes for sober reading – high levels of absenteeism and stress-related illness; front-line workers feeling victimised by both management and clients. Many social workers are frustrated and angry at the lack of appreciation for their work and the relentless load they are asked to take on. One could offer counselling to help them cope better with their predicament, but this would do little to address the organisational sources of their emotional difficulties: political double-binds, role conflicts, surveillance regimes, and a culture of managerialism – not care.

'HEALTH CONNECTS US ALL' – ASTRAZENECA

The complexity of the organisational context for individual emotions, together with the impact of culture and its tendency to produce unintended consequences if not properly understood, contains an important message on how to deliver improved organisational performance while ensuring employee emotional and general well-being.

Work currently in progress in the global pharmaceutical company AstraZeneca is recognising that you cannot just switch people off emotionally and physically but that you need to tackle issues on a number of interconnected fronts.

AstraZeneca's approach spans a number of areas that involve individual and team training in personal well-being along with the principles of energy management. They have also adopted some of the concepts as set out in 'The making of a corporate athlete' by Loehr and Schwartz (2001), who have underpinned their work on the theory that links mind and body within what is known as the 'high-performance pyramid'. Based on work with top athletes, it has physical well-being as its foundation; above that rests emotional health; then comes mental acuity; and at the top sits a sense of purpose. Behavioural rituals that promote the rhythmic expenditure and recovery of energy link the levels. For example, vigorous physical exercise can produce a sense of emotional well-being.

In employing a range of ideas AstraZeneca have recognised that their development of employee well-being should not be an initiative but should be closely linked to the organisational strategy and interwoven into the ways things are done across the organisation – by implication therefore the 'rituals' of well-being become part of the culture. Their premise is that health and well-being are business-critical and have both qualitative and quantifiable impacts on business operations.

To achieve this they have therefore focused on 'developing a global framework that will provide the context and guidance for behavioural change as efforts are shifted from addressing short-term financial tactics to considering health holistically and the interconnections among physical health, psychological health and social health'.

In practice the approach has a number of interlinked strands:

- individual training in personal well-being and energy management

- 'global principles to support work–life balance' in areas such as global travel, working differently and flexible working

- work and job design that supports the principles

- leadership development – ways of working and leading – that encourages the role-modelling of principles of a healthy work and lifestyle and creates the right climate for maintaining optimal health that creates value for both AstraZeneca and its employees

- 'pick-up services' in HR and medical support that provide the more typical performance improvement and personal recovery services – eg employee counselling and advice on healthy lifestyle and life management.

Currently, this is in its infancy, but in principle the whole approach of AstraZeneca has recognised that employee well-being (including emotional well-being) is not just a 'nice to have' option in organisational life and practices but is at the core of what an organisation should be all about.

The authors wish to express their gratitude to AstraZeneca for the permitted use of this material.

Questions

1 With reference to the work of Schein (2004) and Johnson (1992), what is the basis for the AstraZeneca approach to employee emotional and physical well-being?

2 AstraZeneca explicitly links psychological well-being and emotion at work with concepts such as 'energy management', 'elite athletes' and 'performance'. What does this say about the way the organisation understands emotion at work?

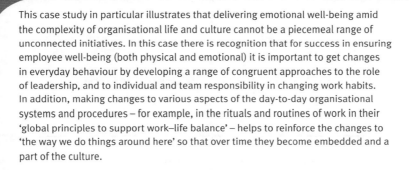

CASE STUDY COMMENTARY

This case study in particular illustrates that delivering emotional well-being amid the complexity of organisational life and culture cannot be a piecemeal range of unconnected initiatives. In this case there is recognition that for success in ensuring employee well-being (both physical and emotional) it is important to get changes in everyday behaviour by developing a range of congruent approaches to the role of leadership, and to individual and team responsibility in changing work habits. In addition, making changes to various aspects of the day-to-day organisational systems and procedures – for example, in the rituals and routines of work in their 'global principles to support work–life balance' – helps to reinforce the changes to 'the way we do things around here' so that over time they become embedded and a part of the culture.

CONCLUSION

This section brings together some of the issues discussed in previous sections and unpacks the link with New OE.

IMAGES OF THE EMOTIONAL WORKER

Throughout this chapter, various images of the emotional worker have been surfacing. The legacy of the happy-productive worker hypothesis, it has been argued, is to consider the individual at work as a passive reactor to organisational action, in its assumptions of a linear, somewhat mechanistic cause-and-effect relationship between organisational 'pulls' and employee satisfaction or emotion. This is coupled with a possibly naive assumption of the emotional 'win/win' scenario, leading to the suggestion that worker emotions can, and should, be influenced and manipulated for the organisation's ends. It allows a categorisation of human feeling into 'positive' and 'negative' based on whether they serve the organisation's purpose.

As we progressed through the chapter, other images emerged. When reviewing literature on individual affective experience, the individual worker emerged as a more active agent in shaping his or her experience. Feelings at work become linked to experienced events and the individual's interpretation of them, reactions and emotions displayed shaped in part by personality but also by the broader social context. As the model shown in Figure 16.2 suggests, emotion becomes an experience that involves private and public spheres, and a greater degree of dynamism and skill on the part of the individual is also suggested in seeking to understand his or her own emotions within a specific cultural context.

What this chapter is therefore suggesting is an image of an active, dynamic worker who navigates between individual, personal domains of feeling and public, collective domains of emotion and emotion display. As Figure 16.2 suggests, this means a constant, dynamic, shifting interplay between different elements of emotional experience, subjective and objective, personal (individual) and social.

Figure 16.2 An integrated model of emotion at work

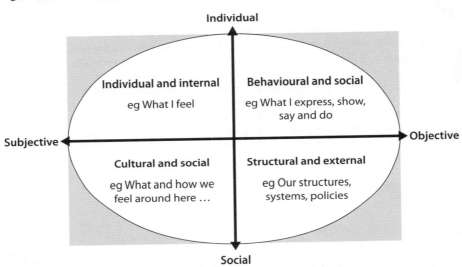

Source: adapted from Küpers and Weibler (2008); reproduced by permission

NEW OE AND EMOTION

Throughout this chapter, reflections on current practice and considerations for regenerating (New) OE have been highlighted. It is useful in this section to summarise some of the main themes.

Firstly, there is a generally recognised need to move beyond overly simplistic conceptions of the relationship between the individual and his or her work and to embrace the concepts of agency and mutuality in emotional experience. Practice driven by assumptions of simple cause-and-effect relationships between management action and employee emotion is unlikely to succeed. The more active, dynamic role of the individual in shaping his or her own emotions has to be recognised as well as the more subtle power of culture to influence the way individuals make sense of their own emotional experience at work.

Part of this effort will mean a greater sensitivity to the tensions between the organisational and personal, individual spheres of emotion. The traditional happy-productive worker hypothesis, with its often-unchallenged 'win/win' scenario, has to make way for an appreciation of the ambiguities and tensions present in efforts to shape and control emotions at work. Much research and practice in this field has been driven by organisational agendas – the OE practitioner must recognise and navigate these complex tensions involved in trying to influence how people feel at and about work.

With this in mind, a final note of reflection should be on the consistent finding that individuals feel better when they are treated respectfully, enabled to form supportive relationships, given meaningful and reasonable demands and control over their working life, involved in decisions that affect them, and provided with opportunities to use their skills and develop. In many ways, therefore, considering emotions in organisations just means adopting greater consideration for the individuals within them.

EXPLORE FURTHER

Ashkanasy, N. M. and Humphrey, R. H. (2011) 'Current emotion research in organizational behavior', *Emotion Review*, Vol.3, No.2: 214–24. An up-to-date review of key aspects of academic research into emotion at work from two established scholars in the field.

Bakker, A. B., Albrecht, A. L. and Leiter, M. P. (2011) 'Key questions regarding work engagement', *European Journal of Work and Organizational Psychology*, Vol.20, No.1: 4–28. This article, alongside all the commentaries and the rejoinder, presents a complete and informed overview of the current research into work engagement, including its drivers, its relationship to leadership and well-being.

Briner, R. and Kiefer, T. (2009) 'Whither psychological research into emotion at work? Feeling for the future', *International Journal of Work Organisation and Emotion*, Vol.3, No.2: 161–73. An insightful and critical overview of research into emotion at work, setting a clear agenda for future research, which is also important for practice.

Daniels, K. (2011) 'Stress and well-being are still issues and something still needs to be done, Or why agency and interpretation are important for policy and practice', in Hodgkinson, G. P. and Ford, J. K. (eds) *International Review of Industrial and Organizational Psychology*, Vol. 25. Chichester: Wiley. Important and necessary review of the current state of play regarding stress and well-being.

Fineman, S. (ed.) (2008) *The Emotional Organization: Passions and power*. Oxford: Blackwell. Essential reading for those interested in the complex, socially bound nature of individual emotional experience.

The cultural web is a way of expressing various aspects of the organisational culture in a visible and analytical way. It is a practical vehicle for exploring culture and identifying the behavioural changes required within an organisation to support the delivery of its strategy. It can form a framework for engaging people in discussing and developing their own cultural web, which provides an insight into what is taken for granted, and facilitates a shared understanding, making the influence of the culture visible. See Johnson, G. *et al* (2008).

www.hse.gov.uk/stress The Health and Safety Executive's website is a useful resource for research, statistics and toolkits for work-related stress. It also provides access to the Management Standards for work-related stress.

www.cipd.co.uk The CIPD website contains informative factsheets on engagement and stress as well as access to related commissioned research and toolkits for HR and OD practitioners.

REFERENCES

Antonakis, J., Ashkanasy, N. M. and Dasborough, M. (2009) 'Does leadership need emotional intelligence?', *Leadership Quarterly*, Vol.20, No.2: 247.

Ashkanasy, N. M. and Daus, C. (2005) 'The rumours of the death of emotional intelligence in organizational behavior are vastly exaggerated', *Journal of Organizational Behavior*, Vol.26, No.4: 441–52.

Ashkanasy, N. M. and Humphrey, R. H. (2011) 'Current emotion research in organizational behavior', *Emotion Review*, Vol.3, No.2: 214–24.

Bakker, A. B., Albrecht, A. L. and Leiter, M. P. (2011a) 'Key questions regarding work engagement', *European Journal of Work and Organizational Psychology*, Vol.20, No.1: 4–28.

Bakker, A. B., Albrecht, S. and Leiter, M. P. (2011b). 'Work engagement: Further reflections on the state of play'. *European Journal of Work and Organizational Psychology*, Vol.20, No.1: 74–88.

Barsade, S. G., Brief, A. P. and Spataro, S. E. (2003) 'The affective revolution in organizational behavior: the emergence of a paradigm', in Greenberg, J. (ed.) *Organizational Behavior: The state of the science*, 2nd edition. Mahwah, NJ: Lawrence Erlbaum Associates.

Brief, A. P. and Weiss, H. M. (2002) 'Organizational behavior: affect in the workplace', *Annual Review of Psychology*, Vol.53: 279–307.

Briner, R. and Kiefer, T. (eds) (2005) 'Psychological research into the experience of emotion at work: definitely older, but are we any wiser?', in *Research on Emotion in Organisations: The effects of affect in organizational settings*, Vol.1. Oxford: Elsevier.

Briner, R. and Kiefer, T. (2009) 'Whither psychological research into emotion at work? Feeling for the future', *International Journal of Work Organisation and Emotion*, Vol.3, No.2: 161–73.

Clarke, N. (2006) 'Emotional intelligence training: a case of caveat emptor', *Human Resource Development Review*, Vol.5, No.4: 422–41.

Cropanzano, R., Weiss, H., Hale, J. M. S. and Reb, J. (2003) 'The structure of affect: reconsidering the relationship between negative and positive affectivity', *Journal of Management*, Vol.29, No.6: 831–57.

Daniels, K. J. (2006) 'Rethinking job characteristics in work stress research', *Human Relations*, Vol.59, No.3: 267–90.

Daniels, K. (2011) 'Stress and well-being are still issues and something still needs to be done, Or: why agency and interpretation are important for policy and practice', in Hodgkinson, G. P. and Ford, J. K. (eds) *International Review of Industrial and Organizational Psychology*, Vol. 25. Chichester: Wiley.

Dasborough, M. (2006) 'Cognitive asymmetry and employee emotional reactions to leadership behaviors', *Leadership Quarterly*, Vol.17, No.2: 163–78.

Dasborough, M., Sinclair, M., Russell-Bennett, R. and Tombs, A. (2008) 'Measuring emotion: methodological issues and alternatives', in Ashkanasy, N. and Cooper, C. L. (eds) *Research Companion to Emotion in Organizations*, New Horizons in Management Series. Cheltenham: Edward Elgar Publishing.

Diefendorff, J. and Greguras, G. (2009) 'Contextualizing emotional display rules: examining the roles of targets and discrete emotions in shaping display rule perceptions', *Journal of Management*, Vol.35, No.4: 880.

Diefendorff, J., Morehart, J. and Gabriel, A. (2010) 'The influence of power and solidarity on emotional display rules at work', *Motivation and Emotion*, Vol.34: 120–34.

Diefendorff, J., Richard, E., Erin, R. M. and Croyle, M. H. (2006) 'Are emotional display rules formal job requirements? Examination of employee and supervisor perceptions', *Journal of Occupational and Organisational Psychology*, Vol.79, No.2: 273–98.

Edwards, J. R. (1996) 'An examination of competing versions of the person–environment fit approach to stress', *Academy of Management Journal*, Vol.39, No.2: 292–339.

Elfenbein, H. (2007) 'Emotion in organizations: a review and theoretical integration', *Academy of Management Annuals*, Vol.1: 315–86.

Fineman, S. (2000) 'Commodifying the emotionally intelligent', in Fineman, S. (ed.) *Emotion in Organisations*. London: Sage.

Fineman, S. (2003) *Understanding Emotions at Work*. London: Sage.

Fisher, C. (2000) 'Mood and emotions while working: the missing pieces of job satisfaction', *Journal of Organizational Behavior*, Vol.21, No.2: 185–202.

Geertz, C. (1993) *The Interpretation of Cultures*. New York: Basic Books.

George, J. (2000) 'Emotions and leadership: the role of emotional intelligence', *Human Relations*, Vol.53, No.8: 1027.

George, J. M. (2011) 'Dual tuning: a minimum condition for understanding affect in organisations?', *Organizational Psychology Review*, Vol.1, No.2: 147–64.

Gooty, J., Gavin, M. and Ashkanasy, N. M. (2009) 'Emotions research in OB: the challenges that lie ahead', *Journal of Organizational Behavior*, Vol.30, No.6: 833.

Gray, E. and Watson, D. (2001) 'Emotion, mood and temperament: similarities, differences and a synthesis', in Payne, R. and Cooper, C. L. (eds) *Emotions at Work*. Chichester: John Wiley & Sons.

Hackman, J. R. and Oldham, G. R. (1980) *Work Redesign*. Reading, MA: Addison-Wesley.

Hochschild, A. R. (1983) *The Managed Heart: Commercialization of human feeling*. Berkeley/Los Angeles/London: University of California Press.

Humphrey, R., Kellett, J., Sleeth R. G. and Hartman, N. S. (2008) 'Research trends in emotions and leadership', in Ashkanasy, N. and Cooper, C. L. (eds) *Research Companion to Emotion in Organizations*, New Horizons in Management Series. Cheltenham: Edward Elgar Publishing.

Johnson, G. (1992) 'Managing strategic change – strategy, culture and action', *Long-Range Planning*, Vol.25,No.1: 28–36.

Johnson, G., Scholes, K. and Whittington, R. (2008) *Exploring Corporate Strategy: Text & Cases*, 8th edition. Upper Saddle River, NJ: FT Prentice Hall.

Judge, T. A., Thoresen, C. J., Bono, J. E. and Patton, G. K. (2001) 'The job satisfaction–job performance relationship: a qualitative and quantitative review', *Psychological Bulletin*, Vol.127, No.3: 376–407.

Karasek, R. A. (1979) 'Job demands, job decision latitude and mental strain: implications for job redesign', *Administrative Science Quarterly*, Vol.24: 285–308.

Küpers, W. and Weibler, J. (2008) 'Emotions in organisations: an integral perspective', *International Journal of Work Organisation and Emotion*, Vol.2, No.3: 256–87.

Landen, M. (2002) 'Emotion management: dabbling in mystery – white witchcraft or black art?', *Human Resource Development International*, Vol.5, No.4: 507–21.

Lazarus, R. and Cohen-Charash, Y. (2001) 'Discrete emotions in organizational life', in Payne, R. and Cooper, C. L. (eds) *Emotions at Work*. Chichester: John Wiley & Sons.

Lewin, K. (1948) *Resolving Social Conflicts: Selected papers on group dynamics*. New York: Harper & Row.

Loehr, J. and Schwartz, T. (2001) 'The making of a corporate athlete', *Harvard Business Review*, January.

Macey, W. H. and Schneider, B. (2008) 'The meaning of employee engagement', *Industrial and Organizational Psychology: Perspectives on Science and Practice*, Vol.1: 3–30.

Margerison, C. and McCann, D. (2000) *Team Management: Practical new approaches*. Kemble, Glos.: Management Books 2000 Ltd.

Russell, J. (1980) 'A circumplex model of affect', *Journal of Personality and Social Psychology*, Vol.39, No.6: 1161–78.

Schaufeli, W. B., Salanova, M., Gonzalez-Romá, V. and Bakker, A. B. (2002) 'The measurement of engagement and burnout: A two sample confirmatory factor analytic approach.' *Journal of Happiness Studies*, Vol.3: 71–92.

Schein, E. H. (2004) *Organisation Culture and Leadership*. San Francisco: Jossey-Bass.

Seo, M., Barrett, L. F. and Jin, S. (2008) 'The structure of affect: history, theory, and implications for emotion research in organizations', in Ashkanasy, N. and Cooper, C. L. (eds) *Research Companion to Emotion in Organizations* (New Horizons in Management Series). Cheltenham, Glos./Northampton, MA: Edward Elgar Publishing.

Sparham, E. and Sung, J. (2007) *High-performance Work Practices: Work intensification or 'win/win'?*, Centre for Labour Market Studies, Working Paper 50.

Stansfeld, S., Woodley-Jones, D., Rasul, F., Head, J., Clarke, S. and Mackay, C. (2004) *Work-Related Stress and Related Disorders*. London: HSE.

Tuckman B. W. (1965) 'Developmental sequence in small groups', *Psychological Bulletin*, Vol.63, No.6: 384–99.

Tuckman, B. W. and Jensen, M. A. (1977) 'Developmental sequence in small groups revisited', *Group and Organisational Studies*, Vol.2, No.4: 419–27.

Wall, T. and Wood, S. (2005) 'The romance of human resource management and business performance, and the case for big science', *Human Relations*, Vol.58, No.4: 429–62.

Wefald, A. and Downey, R. (2009) 'Job engagement in organizations: fad, fashion or folderol?', *Journal of Organizational Behavior*, Vol.31, No.1: 141–5.

Weiss, H. (2002) 'Conceptual and empirical foundations for the study of affect at work', in Lord, R., Klimoski, R. and Kanfer, R. (eds) *Emotions in the Workplace: Understanding the structure and role of emotions in organizational behavior*. San Francisco: Jossey-Bass.

Weiss, H. and Brief, A. (2001) 'Affect at work: a historical perspective', in Payne, R. and Cooper, C. L. (eds) *Emotions at Work*. Chichester: John Wiley & Sons.

Weiss, H. and Cropanzano, R. (1996) 'Affective events theory: a theoretical discussion of the structure, causes and consequences of affective experiences at work', *Research in Organizational Behaviour*, Vol.18: 1–74.

Wright, T. A., Cropanzano, R. and Bonett, D. G. (2007) 'The moderating role of employee positive well-being on the relation between job satisfaction and job performance', *Journal of Occupational Health Psychology*, Vol.12, No.2: 93–104.

Yarker, J., Donaldson-Feilder, E., Lewis, R. and Flaxman, P. (2007) *Management Competencies for Preventing and Reducing Stress at Work*. London: HSE.

CHAPTER 17

New OE: Future Prospects and Possibilities

Helen Francis, Martin Reddington and Linda Holbeche

THE KEY ELEMENTS OF NEW OE

In Chapter 1, we introduced the reader to the notion of 'New OE' as a lens that seeks to challenge and demystify innovations in HRM/OD consulting practice, and explore fresh approaches to Organisational Effectiveness.

We did not provide a working definition of 'effectiveness' other than to say that our aim was to build a language of Organisational Effectiveness that takes better account of the increasing complexity of organisations and their environments, and that can be applied in ways that lead to sustainable organisational performance. In our attempts to distil the essence of our approach to OE we have come to the conclusion that this is regenerative and transformative, and argue that new definitions of what organisational 'success' looks like are called for. In contrast to many other models of OE which focus just on outcomes, our approach represents both a means and an end, and we argue that the 'people' specialists in organisations, whether HR or OD practitioners, or line managers and executives, are central to its delivery.

In presenting a new framework for OE, we believe it is inappropriate to produce detailed prescriptions of 'good practice', especially since we consider this to be a journey of development rather than a terminus. On the other hand, we recognise the importance of making clear what we believe to be the substance of the direction of travel. We therefore crystallise New OE's key elements in terms of

- its purpose
- its essence
- its process

and

- its ends.

ITS PURPOSE

In terms of its purpose, New OE is transformative and emancipatory. It challenges conventional paradigms of what 'good' people/'human resource' management is about. In our view this should not be about aligning people with organisations by rendering them passive subjects of organisational requirements while simultaneously treating them as expendable resources, but instead should involve employees' being able to act as proactive agents. This will require a much more active and democratic partnership with employees, in which each party demands more from the other and in which the benefits and risks of the employment relationship are more genuinely shared.

ITS ESSENCE

At its core, New OE reflects a powerful ethic of mutuality. It demands authentic and meaningful forms of participation, without which the skilled application of approaches described in this book could be perceived as mere manipulation and where employees would be right to be sceptical. Such a democratic form of partnership may represent a serious challenge to existing leadership and management practices and power bases, including those of HR. Yet to some extent such challenges to entrenched power bases are likely to grow, as seen for instance in the part played by social media on the global stage in 'letting the genie out of the bottle'.

Willingly responding to demands for better business and people management practice, and embracing new approaches, might therefore be conceived of as facilitating *evolution*. Not embracing such thinking, we believe, may lead to *revolution*.

ITS PROCESS

In its process, New OE is eclectic since it involves practitioners' embracing humanist and business values, working across and beyond disciplinary boundaries, being strategic and systemic in orientation, and being able to challenge their own and others' mindsets to embrace new ways of thinking, doing and being. It means moving away from an overly mechanistic view of organisational functioning, design and development, to one that looks more critically at the social processes at play, including the language–practice dynamic and related power dynamics associated with it.

ITS ENDS

In its ends, New OE is (re)generative since it has the potential to produce more from less *and* also create new, more sustainable practice and outcomes. It embraces both the goals of organisational development – ie to build healthy and effective organisations characterised by learning, innovation, improvement and self-renewal – and those of HR – ie to build sustainable high performance through people.

We have argued that embracing these elements of New OE requires a shift in mindset about organisational behaviour and change, and that HR has a key role in stimulating this shift. Here we do not seek to promote a singular set of criteria but to draw attention to the design choices and options for enhancing Organisational Effectiveness based on the view that sustainable organisational change should essentially be constructed or negotiated *with* rather than *for* organisational members, thereby reflecting the plurality of stakeholder interests.

Our collection of chapters provides a range of theories, perspectives and examples of what this may mean in practice, and the enabling and constraining role of context in this regard. This has not been an easy task because some terminology, drawn from more academic readings on HRM/OD, is quite different from that used in the business world and mainstream texts within the field. It has also required moving beyond the either/or orientation that characterises much debate about OD and HR practice, such as the employee-versus-business and performance-versus-learning dualisms examined in Chapters 14 and 12 respectively.

Dual viewpoints are inherently problematic because they prevent us at a conceptual level from recognising the 'promise of synthesis', the 'both/and' stance that integrates apparent opposites (Kuchinke, 1998: 377). They are also unhelpful to policy-makers and managers seeking to achieve workable arrangements arising out of the inherent contradictions and tensions within the workplace. In our collection of case material, we have provided examples of the nature of these tensions, such as the creative tension that diversity and difference brings while introducing a culture change programme or moving towards a more inclusive approach to talent management (Chapters 4 and 13).

The economic and political turbulence of recent years has made more visible the paradox and ambiguity inherent in policy development, and tensions arising from them, exemplified in Ramdhony's account of issues associated with embedding new approaches to learning and development within a healthcare organisation (Chapter 9). Pressure on policy-makers and managers to do 'more with less' is now a key theme shaping strategies for change at government, organisational and micro-levels of decision-making, reflected in our Google search for the term, which raised 222,000,000 results in 0.15 second.

A key theme evident in the 'more for less' debate is the premise articulated in a recent CBI report on restoring public finances: 'It is possible to deliver quality services while saving money if there is reform and innovation' (CBI Report, 2009: 5; see also Anthony, 2009). Yet promoting innovation in an environment of strict financial restraints and redundancies is not without its difficulties. A recent CMI report indicated that a vast majority of managers considered innovation to be very important to their organisation in the current economic climate, but there is widespread concern that spending cuts can lead to risk-aversion and heightened emphasis on compliance at the expense of innovation, particularly in the public sector (CMI Report, 2009). The importance of being able to achieve a 'both/and' instead of an 'either/or' set of outcomes has rarely been more evident.

A number of these tensions are set out below, in response to a question within our CIPD/ NHS survey (Chapter 1 refers): 'What is the biggest tension you face in your role?' These reflect the importance of the language–practice dynamic, especially the tendency to shy away from the surfacing of tensions that is consistent with the highly unitary framing of much HR policy development, and the perennial tensions in meeting people-focused and business-focused contingencies.

The gap between what is said and what is done. We say that we want to promote excellence, yet we shy away from performance management. We say that our people are our most valuable asset, yet we don't invest in them. We say that we want people to innovate, yet our first instinct is to criticise any new ideas rather than nurture them. We say we want our first-line leaders to lead the organisation, yet we constantly measure them against top-down compliance.

Encouraging employees to change and develop services at a time when they are worried about the security of their own jobs/organisations.

A culture best described as 'Hurry up and implement – but make sure it is perfect.' Every change project seems to be presented with the challenge of 'Do it more quickly', which is fair enough, but it is also the easiest challenge to make, since you don't need to understand anything about the project in order to make it. As a workplace we've done a lot of work on 'future vision', and people have more or less bought in to this, but there is pressure to make the future happen very quickly without perhaps taking all the steps between now and then.

Maintaining employee commitment and engagement during a period of transformational change.

These and other tensions have been addressed in one form or another in this book. Developing a strategic capability in recognising and working through tensions requires a major shift in the prevailing language of change, which at present reflects embedded assumptions and concepts that tend to suppress the surfacing of tensions (Carr, 2000). A key theme underlying discussion across various chapters relates to the unitary assumptions underpinning conventional models of OD and HRM, and how preferred ways of designing and implementing change strategies tend to reduce ambiguity to a minimum. These are generally framed by an unquestioned and dominant view of systems thinking which treats the organisation as a 'big open-system machine' – something that is designed and 'driven' by managers, and which needs to be 're-engineered' from time to time (Watson, 2002: 41).

We take the view that although the treatment of organisations as 'whole systems' usefully encourages us to look at how various structures and social processes relate to each other and to the 'whole' (Chapters 2, 3, 4 and 5), we also need new metaphors and imagery to better understand and address continuous whole-system change (Marshak and Grant, 2008a, 2008b). These should not be simply treated as replacements of more conventional metaphors. As we noted in Chapter 1, the aim is to build capability in working with competing metaphors in creative ways, in order to challenge mindsets (Butcher and Atkinson, 2001), and be better equipped at dealing with increasingly complex environments, or 'wicked problems'. Wicked problems are characterised by uncertainty and ambiguity about the nature of the problem and how improvements might be made, characterised (Edmonstone, 2011: 47) as:

> complex, rather than complicated, sitting outside single hierarchies and across systems. They may be novel or recalcitrant – even so intransigent that we have learned to live with them. There are different and valid perspectives [arising from different contexts, cultures, histories, aspirations and allegiances ...] Wicked problems are messy, complex, dynamic and interdependent 'tangles' which have no obvious right answers. They are issues where resolving the difficulties may depend on the viewpoint of those concerned and where the issue being addressed may well be embedded in another issue. Securing the right answer is less important than securing collective consent among stakeholders.

Tackling the inherent challenges and 'wicked problems' inherent within the employment relationship requires HR and OD professionals to release their existing 'world views' and acquire new mindsets about transformational change and the role of employees in shaping it. In the 'thought piece' below, Withers and Withers explore how cognitive biases impact on decision-making and point to an emerging need for HR and OD professionals to develop and deploy new capabilities to address the human dimension of risk.

THE PEOPLE DIMENSION OF RISK: A THOUGHT PIECE

Anna Withers is a director of Mightywaters Consulting Limited. She worked for 12 years in investment banking in investment analyst, fund management and trading roles before retraining as a psychologist and coach. She holds Bachelor and Masters degrees from the LSE, and postgraduate diplomas in psychology and qualifications in psychodynamic counselling from the University of Oxford. Mark Withers is the author of Chapter 4 in this book, and biographical notes about him are to be found in the Authors' Biographies section at the front of the book. This, then, is the 'thought piece' – the equivalent of the 'expert commentaries' that were a feature of Chapter 16 – in which Anna and Mark Withers describe the new mindsets that will be required in the very near future.

As business leaders grapple with the complex and uncertain environment in which their businesses operate, the focus on risk assessment and management has sharpened. This spotlight on risk, defined as 'the effect of uncertainty on objectives' (ISO 31000, 2009: 4), has grown as a combination of stricter governance requirements and the collapse in financial markets has challenged orthodox, and largely mechanistic, approaches to risk management – eg risk audits, stress testing, business continuity management and mathematical modelling.

What has emerged from the wreckage of corporate disasters in recent years is that the risk management community is increasingly aware that conventional risk management methods are woefully inadequate. Importantly, there is now recognition that most organisational crises, disasters, scandals are directly or indirectly the result of people factors (CEO and or board/ executive team behaviour, poor people managers, rogue traders, human error, etc). There is also a realisation that a better understanding of the people dimension of risk management is crucial if issues of risk are to be addressed more effectively. The Institute of Risk Management recently stated that 'People risk is a major component – some would say the major component – of risk management, irrespective of organisational type and industry sector' (Lambert and Cooper, 2010). How to deal with people risk is a largely unresolved question, and it is in this area that HR and OD professionals can make a huge contribution.

Although there are many ways in which HR and OD professionals can step into the space of people risk management, we believe the most significant contribution people professionals can make is in drawing on new insights into decision-making.

In Chapter 1, Francis *et al* highlighted Pfeffer's understanding of the role of HR as being vital to the development of New OE (Pfeffer, 2005: 125). Pfeffer argues that the ability to identify and help others discover their mindsets and mental models, *and* the capability to change these when appropriate, are 'among the most critical capabilities an HR professional can have or aquire'. Many of the contributions in this book have been dedicated to helping HR professionals acquire these crucial capabilities. In our view, developing these capabilities is fundamental to addressing people risk, and we can achieve this through drawing upon the insights into the human mindset gained through modern neuroscience and cognitive psychology.

Over the last decade, advances in neuroscience and cognitive and experimental psychology have shown clearly that we receive input from areas in our brain that are outside conscious awareness. This leads us to make decisions that are often biased or to assume judgemental competence. Instances of faulty decision-making in a business context are plentiful (the collapse of the Robert Maxwell empire, Swiss Air, Barings, the BP Gulf of Mexico disaster, the recent financial meltdown … and the list could go on for a long while). Because most of these decisions were made by people who believed they were making competent judgements, we need to understand better the process of decision-making and how we persuade ourselves about what is relevant information and good judgement.

From the perspective of cognitive psychology, all errors due to human factors (other than intentional neglect, sabotage, drug abuse or illness) are now understood to fall into the four categories (Finkelstein *et al*, 2008: xiii):

- inappropriate attachment
- inappropriate self-interest
- misleading experience
- misleading prejudgements.

According to evolutionary psychologists those four categories can be directly traced back to survival strategies learned when we lived in a hunter-gatherer society, rather than developed for the twenty-first century. So *inappropriate attachments* refers to the way we find security in relationships and our decision-making can be unconsciously skewed towards people and things which signify strong emotional bonds; *inappropriate self-interest* is what psychologists refer to as the self-serving bias, namely the unconscious tendency to skew one's decision towards perceived personal gain; *misleading experience* and *misleading prejudgements* are cognitive shortcuts (also known as heuristics) that allow people to make judgements quickly and efficiently. These mental rule-of-thumb strategies shorten the process of decision-making. Quick decision-making can be extremely important in environments where physical dangers are present – eg in the land of the prowling lion – but are less suited to complex environments. Yet we use heuristics a lot, and we therefore want to explore this area a little further.

The most common heuristics include *anchoring* (the premature selection of an option long before all information is evaluated), the *bandwagon effect* (the tendency to do/believe things because many other people do), *confirmation bias* (when, once an option is selected, decision-makers seek to confirm an answer rather than hold open the possibility that they are wrong), and *irrational escalation* (when decision-makers stick to their chosen path even after having been presented with evidence that their original decision was wrong). These are only a few of the heuristics we use to shortcut decision-making. Enquiry into decision-making and the use of heuristics in situations of high uncertainty and ambiguity is still a relatively new area for research. Yet, although based on limited research, experimental cognitive psychologists have already identified over 100 heuristics used regularly by people when making decisions.

Even the most sophisticated decision-makers and the brightest minds are not immune from becoming trapped in a mental cave of their own making. A primary example of this was uncovered by the inquiry into NASA's *Challenger* disaster in 1986, which attributed the disaster to a combination of the *bandwagon effect* and *irrational escalation* on the part of key decision-makers.

In the light of this research, the importance of Pfeffer's call to HR and OD professionals to help others gain insights into how they think, decide and make ethical choices should now be apparent. It is therefore critical that HR and OD professionals have an understanding of the most common biases in human decision-making, that they are able to identify them in themselves and in others, and that through the application of this thinking, risk-management cultures are developed which focus more on counteracting biases in decision-making rather than depending solely on organisational mechanisms. Helping others to see risk from a people perspective, as well as to see people from a risk perspective, could well become one of the most important strategic offerings from the HR department of the future. This will require HR and others to be open to competing perspectives about what makes for 'good' decision-making from business and ethical standpoints (see Chapter 15) and to be mindful of how prevailing discourse tends to reinforce existing ways of thinking and doing – and consequentially narrowing the possibility that new ways of thinking might emerge.

REFLECTIVE ACTIVITIES

Becoming aware of how we make decisions is at the heart of addressing more effectively the people dimension of risk. The great American scientific and political leader Benjamin Franklin developed a process for decision-making which became known as 'Franklin's Rule' (which he likened to moral algebra) and which we know more commonly as 'pros and cons'. It is grounded in rational thinking, and you may want to reflect on how you and your organisation use such rational approaches in the way you run your organisation and the extent to which this approach is tainted with cognitive biases.

You may also want to reflect on Franklin's Gambit – which suggests that in the real world Franklin's Rule is more likely to be used as a way of rationalising decisions that have already been made. You may further want to reflect on a social constructionist perspective that explains how interaction between people in groups creates a reality, which is expressed at its deepest level through culture and is manifested in the language we use, the images we create and the stories we tell. The created reality is therefore dynamic, providing the context for our decision-making. You may want to think about what are considered to be 'truths' about your organisational environment and reflect on whether these are actual or perceived truths.

● To obtain greater self-awareness and appreciation of the cognitive biases outlined in the thought piece 'The people dimension of risk', select a recent episode of *The Apprentice* or *The Restaurant Inspector* (or any other similar TV programme in which significant decisions are made) and look out for evidence of inappropriate attachment, inappropriate self-interest and misleading experience. Look out too for evidence that the decision-maker is using different types of heuristics to guide decisions, which include misleading prejudgements, limitation of options and/or overconfidence in the decision taken among others.

You may also want to challenge your own cognitive biases through the following analogy:

- If your career were a train journey/car journey, what are the most significant landmarks you have seen or visited to date?
- In what ways are these landmarks similar to what you see ahead of you?
- How are these landmarks different from those ahead of you?

WHERE DOES OD SIT?

Although we have focused throughout this book on 'mindset', and less on structure, we argue that structure is nevertheless an important element influencing the nature of collaboration between HR and OD professionals and shaping executive expectations of the nature of functional delivery.

The question of who 'owns' the OD function is typically treated as an 'either/or' issue. Whereas in theory the choice should depend to a large extent on the size of the organisation, the capabilities of the individuals, their relative power and the politics of decision-making, the general structural tendency is for OD to be part of a corporate centre (in the USA in particular), reporting directly to the CEO (Bunker and Alban, 2006). To explore what UK-based HR and OD professionals thought about where OD should sit within organisational structures, we carried out a small survey.

The survey was conducted between November 2010 and January 2011. The first tranche of data was compiled from respondents in the public and private sector who attended a masterclass run by the editors at the 2010 CIPD National Conference. The second tranche of data was captured from respondents in NHS England. These results were combined with the public sector results from the first tranche of data to produce an overall public sector response.

The findings raise some interesting structural issues. Drawing on our survey, Table 17.1 maps the positioning of the two functions against Burke's (2004) typology outlined in Chapter 1. Accepting the caveat of a relatively small sample size, our initial research findings suggest that structure might be important here, because for a quarter of our respondents the preferred option is for OD to be a sub-set of HR.

Indeed, our findings also suggest that structure may play an important role in the level of collaboration between disciplines and engagement with New OE. Table 17.2 shows the

Table 17.1 Survey response rates mapped against different organisational models

Internal OD model	Main characteristics	Survey item	Response rate (n = 106)
Traditional	OD is housed within HR	OD is regarded as a sub-function of HR	25%
Independent	OD operates as a free-standing unit	HR and OD are distinct from one another	14%
Integrated	OD is an integrated aspect of HR	OD is integrated into all aspects of HR	14%
Strategic	OD is a corporate function reporting to the CEO	OD is regarded as a corporate function	13%

The percentages shown represent the proportion of respondents that answered strongly agree/ agree.

Table 17.2 Analysis of internal OD model and adoption of New OE practices (n = 106)

Survey item	Internal OD model				
	Traditional	Independent	Integrated	Strategic	P value
Building sustainable high-performance organisations	54.20%	42.90%	78.60%	38.50%	0.020
Building organisations which are externally sensitive	25.00%	28.60%	50.00%	30.80%	0.017
Building organisations which are internally agile	20.80%	35.70%	64.30%	61.50%	0.013
Creating work climates which balance risk and innovation	33.30%	50.00%	50.00%	46.20%	0.032
My organisation strongly believes in allowing employees to actively shape strategies for change	33.30%	28.60%	50.00%	30.80%	0.011
My organisation strongly believes in allowing employees to actively shape procedures for implementing change	33.30%	42.90%	78.60%	38.50%	0.012
The level of collaboration between HR and OD is very high when undertaking major change initiatives in my organisation	66.70%	21.40%	71.40%	53.80%	0.026

Statements where significant differences in the proportion of strongly agree/agree with HR and OD integration are shown. If a significant difference is found, the percentage of strongly agree/agree for each subgroup is shown together with the P value.

HR/OD structure categories from Table 17.1 mapped against a number of survey items that depict aspects of New OE and the associated statistical analysis to illuminate significant relationships between them.

These results suggest that the respondents from organisations that have an integrated model of HR and OD displayed higher levels of agreement with the approach to New OE when compared with the other model types. The results appear to support our argument that an integrated melding of HR and OD is most likely overall to lead to better collaboration between HR and OD and the adoption of bundles of practices associated with New OE, whereas a traditional OD model makes this least likely overall.

We recognise that more research must be undertaken concerning how this dynamic 'works' as a practical means of strengthening the two disciplines and creating the kind of mindset envisaged by New OE. Our results suggest that there is some potential in embracing new sciences rooted in constructionist *and* realist perspectives (eg Fleetwood and Hesketh, 2010) in order to obtain a better understanding of the interdependency between organisational structures and agency within the field of OD and HR. If HR and OD professionals are to play their part in producing platforms for sustainable performance outcomes, they must work together to take a lead in balancing the needs of employees with those of the business – the requirements of the short term with those of the longer term.

Linked with this, New OE recognises the potential value of adopting social media technologies in both the design and implementation of programmes concerned with sustainable mutual gains between employer and employee. We have noted in Chapters 8 and 14 that the harnessing of technology presents new opportunities (and inevitable problems and issues) in bringing about change through more 'bottom-up' and 'dialogic' modes of inquiry. An additional fruitful line of enquiry would be an investigation of the role of new technologies in shaping structural reformulations between HR and OD, not least because both have been criticised for a lack of interest and engagement in the potential of new technology as a means for rejuvenating the disciplines and challenging the status quo (Burke, 2004; Martin and Reddington, 2009).

Further evidence to support this view can also be found in Table 17.3, which shows the results of our survey in relation to specific questions about the adoption of social media technologies. The results illustrate the generally low level of interest in using these technologies and suggest that HR and OD practitioners should re-evaluate their potential in regenerating OE (see Chapter 8 for more insights into the adoption of social media technologies).

Table 17.3 Levels of agreement to the adoption of social media technologies (n = 106)

Statement	Sector		
	Private %	**Public %**	**P value**
Applying social media technologies – eg Facebook, Twitter – to enhance employee communications	35.00	11.7	0.005
Extensive use is made of social media technologies when designing strategies for change	25.00	8.6	0.027
Extensive use is made of social media technologies when implementing strategies for change	30.00	13.8	0.050
My organisation is willing to experiment with social media technologies	57.50	31.0	0.009

Statements where significant differences in the proportion of strongly agree/agree with sector are shown. If a significant difference is found, the percentage of strongly agree/agree for each subgroup is shown together with the P value.

Regenerating OE does not necessarily involve significant financial investment and complex change programmes, as illustrated in the case study example below, which is based on recent interviews held with a senior HR respondent within the organisation. This indicates that inexpensive, demonstrable commitment to authentic engagement with staff in shaping future strategies can deliver significant benefits, current evidence showing a relationship between better-engaged teams and higher employee performance ratings and lower levels of staff sickness and absenteeism.

ESSEXWORKS

Essex County Council (ECC) – one of the largest (10,000+ employees excluding schools) local authorities – has a clearly defined 'EssexWorks' vision: to deliver the best quality of life in Britain, improve Essex and the lives of its residents, and save at least £300 million in the process. Engaging its employees is considered paramount to this vision, made all the more challenging within the context of severe budget restrictions and what many might perceive as an assault on the employment deal for public sector workers.

Described as working with a 'shoestring budget', the small Employee Engagement in-house team is responsible for developing and putting ECC's employee engagement strategy into practice. Created in April 2009, it has maintained a focus on building relationships and creating opportunities for what are described as 'real conversations' between employees at all levels, which ensures that feedback is listened to and acted upon.

A slogan was created – *Our voice: talk, listen, connect, engage* – which is underpinned by an ongoing and proactive communications campaign entitled 'You said, We did'. This is shaped and sustained through a wide range of communication channels and engagement interventions including an employee engagement intranet site, 'Carlsberg', themed focus groups ('If Carlsberg did leaders/communication at Essex, it would probably be the best in the world – what would it look/feel like?') and the chief executive's blog.

An Our Voice Forum, a group of 'engagement ambassadors' from all service areas and chaired by a senior leader, focuses on sharing best practice and taking the initiative themselves to make a difference – eg a 'Plain English' campaign.

We believe that the assimilation of insights and techniques offered in this book will stimulate interest in New OE. We argue that this formulation of New OE represents a contribution to theory and practice since it provides a basis both for more confident and effective practice and also for further research.

For example, more research is needed in the role of line managers in bringing about New OE, as John Castledine and Douglas W. S. Renwick point out. These authors suggest that although some research studies on involving line managers in HRM do acknowledge some limitations in it, they also appear to be quite positive about it too in general terms (eg Hutchinson and Purcell, 2003; Huy, 2002; Purcell *et al*, 2003; Purcell and Hutchinson, 2007; Jackson and Schuler, 2000). However, a fair (and higher) number of the other works reviewed (above) in this chapter also seem to suggest that the limitations associated with using line managers in HRM are more serious, because they appear to be both endemic and systemic in organisations globally. To move this research base forward we therefore need to know more on whether line managers are capable, committed and consistent in HRM or not, meaning that we need more studies to be completed to build clearer pictures, especially comparative and international ones, and those that give us insights into what is happening on these items in SMEs. Of particular importance is the need to seek the views of all the key actors in HRM: line managers, HR managers and employees – the use of multiple perspectives can give us greater validity and reliability overall when drawing conclusions.

Additionally, we need to know more on how line managers cope with conflicting job demands, both operational and HRM (Lynch, 2003), how they are recruited, inducted, trained, appraised and rewarded in the HR elements of their work, and what leadership roles senior line managers display in developing staff at work (Whittaker and Marchington, 2003). Similarly, more research is needed on how line managers can develop different management styles of tutor, coach or mentor (Gibb, 2003). Indeed, where the use of line managers in HRM in some studies is seen to be positive, we may want to ascertain more data on the capabilities and priorities of managers (Mesner-Andolsek and Stebe, 2005: 327), and where it is negative, more data from employees on the role of their managers in motivating or inspiring employees to produce high performance (ie do line managers contribute to it, or do employees deliver high performance because they ignore their manager?).

Finally, as we have maintained throughout the book, the development and application of this thinking represents work in progress – a metaphorical journey rather than a terminus. We argue that the impetus for this journey is a combination of external 'triggers' and our philosophical and ethical dissatisfaction with the status quo. We recognise that advances in technology, the dynamic nature of changes in the business environment and the workplace will continue to shape that journey, whether we like it or not.

Although much of today's 'good practice' may continue to be relevant in the future, we suspect that changing employee expectations and the increasingly complex nature of employee relations will cause unitarist management practice to be thrown into question. In such circumstances, organisational managements seeking to attract and retain their 'talent' could be seen to be acting in enlightened self-interest by proactively including employee voice in the shaping of a more mutual employment relationship.

We argue that new ways of thinking, and of leading, developing and changing organisations, will be needed to equip people and their organisations to survive and thrive in these challenging times. We think that HR has a potentially key role to play in developing these new capabilities.

As final 'food for thought', we also wish to make the point that as our work on this book progressed, we became aware of the potential capability for a new field of study and enquiry to emerge from the crystallised elements of New OE. The notion of 'New' OE has been used to mark a departure from current usage of the terms organisation/organisational effectiveness, in order to challenge the prevailing, separately constituted fields of Human Resource Management and Organisation Development, by encompassing the 'means and ends' of those fields in a complete, holistic, organisation-wide fashion. Notwithstanding this potential, above all, we believe that in today's dynamically changing environmental context New OE offers an enlightened way forward for people, organisations and the communities they serve.

REFERENCES

Anthony, S. (2009) *Doing More With Less*. Available online at: http://www.forbes.com/2009/02/26/oracle-salesforce-netsuites-leadership-clayton-christensen_cutting_costs.html.

Bunker, B. and Alban, A. (2006) *The Handbook of Large Group Methods*. San Francisco: Jossey-Bass.

Burke, W. W. (2004) 'Internal organization development practitioners: where do they belong?', *Applied Journal of Behavioral Science*, Vol.40, No.4: 423–31.

Butcher, D. and Atkinson, S. (2001) 'Stealth, secrecy and subversion: the language of change', *Journal of Organizational Change Management*, Vol.14, No.6: 1–11.

Carr, A. (2000) 'Critical theory and the management of change in organizations', *Journal of Organizational Change Management*, Vol.13, No.3: 208–20.

CBI Report (2009) *Doing More with Less: A credible strategy for restoring the public finances*. Available online at: http://www.cbi.org.uk/pdf/20091001-cbi-doing-more-with-less.pdf.

CMI Report (2009) *Innovation for Recovery: Enhancing innovative working practices*. London: Chartered Management Institute.

Edmonstone, J. (2011) 'Action Learning and OD', in *Action Learning In Practice*, edited by Mike Pedler, 4th edition, Sage, London

Finkelstein, S., Whitehead, J. and Campbell, A. (2008) *Think Again: Why Good Leaders*

Make Bad Decisions and How to Make it Not Happen to You. Boston: Harvard Business Press.

Fleetwood S. and Hesketh A. J. (2010) *Explaining the Performance of Human Resource Management*. Cambridge: Cambridge University Press:

Garrow, V. (2009) *OD: Past, present and future*. IES Working Paper. London: Institute of Employment Studies.

Gibb, S. (2003) 'Line manager involvement in learning and development: Small beer or big deal?' *Employee Relations*, Vol.25, No.3: 281–93.

Hutchinson, S. and Purcell, J. (2007) *Learning and the Line: The role of line managers in training, learning and development*. Survey Report. London: Chartered Institute of Personnel and Development.

Huy, Q. N. (2002) 'Emotional balancing or organizational continuity and radical change: the contribution of middle managers', *Administrative Science Quarterly*, Vol.47, No.1, March: 31–69.

ISO 31000 (2009) *Risk management – Principles and Guidelines*, Standards Report. Geneva; The International Organization for Standardization, available online at http://www.iso.org/iso/catalogue_detail?csnumber=43170.

Jackson, S. E. and Schuler, R. S. (2000) *Managing Human Resources: A partnership perspective*, London: International Thomson Publishing.

Kuchinke, K. P. (1998) 'Moving beyond the dualism of performance versus learning: a responses to Barrie and Pace', *Human Resource Development Quarterly*, Vol.9, No.4: 377–83.

Lambert, A. and Cooper, D. (2010) *Managing the People Dimension of Risk*. Corporate Research Forum, August.

Lynch, S. (2003) 'Devolution and the management of human resources: evidence from the retail industry', Paper presented to the Professional Standards Conference, Chartered Institute of Personnel and Development, University of Keele.

Martin, G. and Reddington, M. (2009) 'Reconceptualising absorptive capacity to explain the e-enablement of the HR function (e-HR) in organizations', *Employee Relations*, Vol.31, No.5: 515–37.

Marshak, R. and Grant, D. (2008a) 'Organizational discourse and new organization development practices', *British Journal of Management*, Vol.19: 7–19.

Marshak, R. and Grant, D. (2008b) 'Transforming talk: the interplay of discourse, power and change', *Organizational Development Journal*, Vol.23, No.3: 33–40.

Mesner-Andolsek, D. A. and Stebe, J. (2005) 'Devolution or (de)centralisation of HRM function in European organizations', *The International Journal of Human Resource Management*, Vol.16, No.3, March: 311–29.

Pfeffer, J. (2005) 'Changing mental models: HR's most important task', *Human Resource Management*, Vol.44, No.2: 123–8.

Purcell, J. and Hutchinson, S. (2007) 'Front-line managers as agents in the HRM–performance causal chain: theory, analysis and evidence', *Human Resource Management Journal*, Vol.17, No.1: 3-20.

Purcell, J., Kinnie, N., Hutchinson, S., Rayton, B. and Swart, J. (2003) *Understanding the People and Performance Link: Unlocking the black box*. London: Chartered Institute of Personnel and Development.

Watson, T. (2002) *Organising and Managing Work*. Harlow: Pearson Education.

Whittaker, S. and Marchington, M. (2003) 'Devolving HR responsibility to the line: threat, opportunity or partnership?', *Employee Relations*, Vol.25, No.3: 245–61.

Index